Managing Football: An International Perspective

Managing Football: An International Perspective

Sean Hamil and Simon Chadwick

AMSTERDAM · BOSTON · HEIDELBERG · LONDON · NEW YORK · OXFORD
PARIS · SAN DIEGO · SAN FRANCISCO · SINGAPORE ·SYDNEY · TOKYO
Butterworth-Heinemann is an imprint of Elsevier

Butterworth-Heinemann is an imprint of Elsevier
Linacre House, Jordan Hill, Oxford OX2 8DP, UK
30 Corporate Drive, Suite 400, Burlington, MA 01803, USA

First edition 2010

British Library Cataloguing in Publication Data
A catalogue record for this book is available from the British Library

Library of Congress Cataloging-in-Publication Data
A catalog record for this book is available from the Library of Congress

ISBN: 978-1-85617-544-9

For information on all Butterworth-Heinemann publications visit
our website at books.elsevier.com

Printed and bound in Great Britain
10   10 9 8 7 6 5 4 3 2 1

Working together to grow
libraries in developing countries

www.elsevier.com | www.bookaid.org | www.sabre.org

ELSEVIER   BOOK AID
International   Sabre Foundation

Contents

Part 4   Managing Football in Established Markets

Acknowledgements

Sean and Simon wish to thank all the contributors to the book for their hard work and diligence in completing their chapters. In addition, they reserve special thanks for Francesca Ford who commissioned the book and has since left Elsevier, and for Eleanor Blow and Holly Bathie at Elsevier who subsequently took up Fran's mantle and helped us bring the book to final publication. They would also like to thank Hannah Libya Russel, production project manager for the book at Elsevier, for her excellent work throughout.

Biographies

Dave Arthur

Dave is a senior lecturer in the Department of Exercise Science and Sport Management at Southern Cross University, where he coordinates the Masters of International Sport Management degree. He has contributed chapters to many books, a range of articles in leading sport journals, and is a member of the editorial board of *Sport Management Review*. In addition to academia, he has consulted to leading sporting organisations, including the National Rugby League, South Sydney Rugby League Club, and the Australian Sports Commission. His abiding sporting passion, however, is rugby union. As a practicing journalist he was accredited for the 2003 Rugby World Cup, and in 2006, he was privileged to be the Pacific Islanders' media manager for their three Test series versus Wales, Scotland, and Ireland.

Ángel Barajas

Angel is an associate professor of finance at the Faculty of Business Administration and Tourism, University of Vigo, and researcher of the Spanish Economic Observatory for Sport. His main research topic is football finances. He is the author of *El valor económico del fútbol* and *Las finanzas detrás del balón*.

John Beech

John is head of Sport and Tourism Applied Research and codirector of CIBS (Centre for the International Business of Sport) at Coventry University Business School, United Kingdom. His current research interests are in insolvency in English football clubs and postcommercialisation in sports businesses. John is coeditor of *The Marketing of Sport*, *The Business of Sport Management*, and *The Business of Tourism Management* (all published by FT Prentice Hall).

Urmilla Bob

Urmilla is an associate professor in the discipline of geography, School of Environmental Sciences at the University of KwaZulu-Natal, South Africa. She has published in several journals and contributed chapters to many books on sports events—recently focusing on the 2010 FIFA Soccer World Cup. She also supervises postgraduate students who are undertaking research on 2010 and sports events in general. Some of the issues being researched include residents' perceptions, socioeconomic impacts, the greening of sport events, and legacy impacts.

André Bühler

After studying management, marketing and business psychology at Nürtingen University (Germany), André obtained a PhD in the field of sports marketing at the University of Plymouth in 2006. He then returned to Germany and became a research & scholarship consultant and lecturer in management & marketing at the Heidelberg International Business Academy. André currently works for the world-wide leading sports research consultancy IFM where he holds the position of Head of Market Research. He has published a number of papers and co-authored various books on sports management and sports marketing.

Simon Chadwick (Coeditor)

Simon is a professor of sport business strategy and marketing and a director of CIBS (Centre for the International Business of Sport) at Coventry University Business School, United Kingdom. He has researched and published extensively in the area of sport marketing and commercial strategy in sport, and is coeditor of *The Marketing of Sport*, *The Business of Sport Management*, and *The Business of Tourism Management* (all published by FT Prentice Hall), and *International Cases in the Business of Sport* (published by Butterworth Heinemann).

Sergio Cherubini

Sergio is full professor of marketing and director of the Sport Management Unit at Roma Tor Vergata University, Italy. He is author of many books and articles in the areas of marketing, strategy, and organization, with particular interest in sport management, including *Marketing Sportivo,* published by Franco Angeli Editore, Milano.

Scarlett Cornelissen

Scarlett is an associate professor in the Department of Political Science at Stellenbosch University, South Africa. She is the author of a book on South Africa's place in the global tourism system (2005, Ashgate) and the coeditor of three other books, one on African international relations (2006, University of Cape Town Press) and two on comparative perspectives on globalisation (2007, Palgrave). She serves on the editorial board of *Leisure Studies* and is Africa editor of this journal.

Artur Costabiei

Artur is currently a communications manager for LM2, a marketing agency representing Winter sport athletes and organisations in Alto Adige, Italy. Prior to joining LM2, he was an account manager with *Global Sportnet*. He has a masters of arts in sports management from the University of Florence, Italy.

Liz Crolley

Liz lectures in the business and management of football at the University of Liverpool Football Industry Group. She has published widely on social, economic, cultural, and political aspects of football, but her roots as a linguist attract her particularly to Spain, Italy, and South America. Recent books include *Football, Europe and the Press* (coauthor, 2006), *Fútbol, Futebol, Soccer: Football in the Americas* (coeditor, 2007), and *Football and European Identity* (coauthor, 2002).

Michel Desbordes

Michel is a professor at the University of Paris Sud 11, France. He is also a professor at the ISC School of Management (Paris, France). He has published 16 books (United Kingdom, Spain, France, Russia) and 22 academic articles in this field. His last book in English is *Marketing and Football: An International Perspective,* which was published by Elsevier in October 2006.

Trudo Dejonghe

Trudo is professor of economics, international economics, and sports economics at the Lessius University College, Antwerp, and a guest professor of sports economics at the Vrije Universiteit Brussels in Belgium and Copenhagen Business School in Denmark. He has researched and published extensively in the areas of restucturing football leagues and the necessity for new football stadia. He has published Dutch books on sports economics with Arko Sportsmedia Nieuwegein. With Butterworth-Heinemann (2009) he has published a book on sports economics with Paul Downward and Alistair Dawson. Because of his economic and geographical research background he also published a book entitled *Sport in de Wereld* (sport in the global space) with Academia Press Gent.

Harald Dolles

Harald is professor of management and international business at Heilbronn Business School, Germany, and a visiting professor at the Instituto de Empresa Business School, Spain. He researches international cooperative ventures, entrepreneurship, and sports business, all fields in which he has published widely.

Greg Downes

Greg works at Southern Cross University, Lismore, New South Wales, Australia, where he is a sessional unit assessor in sport management in the School of Health and Human Services. Greg has consulted widely in the area of sport management and local government recreational planning, and has had twenty years experience in the field of local government and community planning. He has a bachelor's degree in economics and a masters' degree in international sport management.

Thorsten Dum

Thorsten is a research associate and Ph.D. student at the Department of Management and International Business at Heilbronn Business School. After graduating in sport science from the German Sport University of Cologne, with a specialisation in sport management and sport economics, he has been working as a project manager in the sports business, mainly specialising in planning and implementing sports-related events. His research interest currently focuses on sport sponsorship.

Steve Greenfield

Steve is a senior academic in law at the University of Westminster in London. He has written on many areas of law and film, as well as other areas of popular culture, including music, sport, and leisure. Steve is one of the founding editors of the *Entertainment and Sports Law Journal*. Along with Guy Osborn and Peter Robson, his book *Film and the Law* will be published by Hart Publishing in 2010. Steve is also coeditor of the Routledge book series *Studies in Law, Society and Popular Culture*.

Alexis Hamelin

Alexis is a commercial executive with the Racing Club de Strasbourg football team in France and with the SPORTFIVE consulting firm.

Sean Hamil (Coeditor)

Sean is a lecturer in the Management Department, Birkbeck College, University of London. A graduate of Trinity College Dublin and the London School of Economics, he has published in the areas of corporate social responsibility and the governance and regulation of sport. He has coedited three books on regulation and governance and regulations in the football industry: *The Changing Face of the Football Business: Supporters Direct*, London: Frank Cass (2001); *Football in the Digital Age: Whose Game Is It Anyway?* Edinburgh: Mainstream (2000); and *A Game of Two Halves? The Business of Football*, Edinburgh: Mainstream (1999). He is a cofounder and director of Birkbeck College, University of London's Sport Business Centre. He is an elected director of Supporters Direct, and was responsible for establishing Supporter Direct's activities in Scotland. Supporters Direct is funded by the U.K. government with the aim of promoting and supporting the concept of democratic supporter ownership and representation at football clubs through mutual, not-for-profit structures.

Sjef van Hoof

Sjef is an economic geographer with in an interest in sports research at the NHTV Breda University of Applied Sciences in the Netherlands. He has been editor of the sports section in the *Bosatlas* of the Netherlands.

Maria Hopwood

Maria is a senior lecturer in public relations at Leeds Metropolitan University in the UK. Her research interests are in sports public relations and marketing communications, in which areas she has published a number of book chapters and journal articles. Having a particular interest in the evolution of cricket, her current research is into the public relations impact of Twenty20 cricket.

Pamm Kellett

Pamm is a senior lecturer in sport management in the School of Management & Marketing at Deakin University in Australia. She has published extensively in the area of sport management and is an Editorial Review Board member of *Sport Management Review*.

Chong Kim

Chong is professor of sport industry and management, and director of the SIMC (Sport Industry and Marketing Centre), at Hanyang University, Korea. He has researched extensively in the area of sport industry and marketing. He has also worked as chairman of the Sport Industry Promotion Forum in Korea.

Wim Lagae

Wim is professor of marketing communications at the Lessius University College, Antwerp, in Belgium. He is also a guest lecturer in sports marketing and communications at the faculty of Kinesiology and Rehabilitation Sciences at the Catholic University of Leuven. He is author of *Sports Sponsorship and Marketing Communications: A European Perspective* (Financial Times/Prentice Hall) and has published in the area of sports sponsorship communications.

Jingbo Li

Jingbo is associate professor of physical education at Sun Yet-Sen University, People's Republic of China. He has researched extensively in the areas of physical education and sports training in China. He is the coeditor of *Football* and *Sports and Health* (both published by Sun Yet-Sen University Press), and *Basic Theory in Physical Education* (published by Guangdong Higher Education Press).

Carlos Martí

Carlos is a lecturer at the Centre for Sport Business Management (CSBM) at IESE Business School, University of Navarra, Spain. He received his Ph.D. from *Complutense University*, an MSc. from *Clark University*, and a BAJ. from *University of Navarra*. He has been a consultant with the *Madrid Consulting Group*. He is also a partner and consultant in the *Digital Operators Group* and *Key International Sport* companies.

Heath McDonald

Heath is an associate professor of marketing at Deakin University in Australia. His research interests include sports, arts, and nonprofit marketing, with a specific emphasis on consumer behaviour in subscription markets such as season-ticket holders.

Guy Osborn

Guy is professor of law at the University of Westminster in London and visiting professor at Norwegian University of Science and Technology (NTNU), Trondheim, Norway. Guy is one of the founding editors of the *Entertainment and Sports Law Journal* and has written widely in the area of law and popular culture. Along with Steve Greenfield and Peter Robson, his book *Film and the Law* will be published by Hart Publishing in 2010. Guy is a coeditor of the book series *Studies in Law, Society and Popular Culture* and chair of the Law and Popular Culture Working Group for the Research Committee for the Sociology of Law.

Saurabh Patel

Saurabh is a doctoral student at the Cass Business School, City University, London, England.

Raffaele Poli

A geographer and sociologist by training, Raffaele has worked as a scientific collaborator at the International Centre for Sports Studies at the Université de Neuchâtel since November 2002. Since September 2008, he has been a junior professor assistant at the Institute of Sport Science and Physical Education of the University of Lausanne. He is the cofounder of the Professional Football Players' Observatory and researches issues related to migration, labour markets, globalization, social networks, identity, and geopolitics. He is coeditor of the *Annual Review of the European Football Players' Labour Market*.

Frank Pons

Frank is an associate professor at Université Laval (Canada). He has published in the *Journal of Business Research, Psychology and Marketing*, the *Journal of Services Research*, and the *Sport Marketing Quarterly*. He is on the editorial board of the *International Journal of Sports Marketing and Sponsorship* and was guest editor of several special issues in sport marketing journals.

Adrian Pritchard

Adrian is a lecturer at Coventry University. Since September 2006, he has been based at Guandong University of Foreign Studies, China. His research interests lie in sport and tourism.

André Richelieu

André is an Associate Professor in the Faculty of Business Administration, Université Laval, Canada and a specialist in brand management and sports marketing. His research interests relate to: how professional sports teams can internationalise their brand; how sports teams can improve fans' experience at the sport venue and outside the stadium and increase fans' attachment to the team; and how sports teams and equipment makers can capitalise on the Hip Hop/Urban movement.

Rogelio Roa

Rogelio is the commercial director at DreaMatch Solutions, a sports marketing firm in Mexico. He is the coauthor of the book *La isla del fútbol*, in which he offers a personal view of the English Premier League, developed while he was obtaining his MBA on football industries at the University of Liverpool. He lectures in Sports Marketing at Anahuac University and is a journalist for *www.mediotiempo.com*, the most popular football site in Mexico.

Andrea Santini

Andrea is coordinator of the masters in sports economics and management at the University of Rome Tor Vergata, lecturer in sports management and business communication at the same university, and guest speaker on various courses in marketing and business management. His main research interests are marketing in the entertainment industry, sports facilities planning, and operation and events organisation. He has published various articles and books on these topics.

James Santomier

James is currently a professor at the John F. Welch College of Business and director of the sport management programme at Sacred Heart University, Fairfield, Connecticut, United States. He is also a visiting professor at the University of Bayreuth, Germany, and the University of Florence, Italy. He received his bachelors and masters in physical education from Montclair State University, and a doctorate degree in physical education from the University of Utah. Areas of study include sport management and the psychosocial aspects of physical activity and sport. James has published extensively in the areas of sport management, sociology of sport, and psychosocial aspects of sport. He has presented at international and national conferences and has appeared on numerous radio and television programs.

James Skinner

James is a faculty member at Griffith University, Gold Coast Campus. His research focuses on culture as it relates to organisational change and sporting studies, sport as a vehicle for social change, sport policy and governance, and sport globalisation studies. He has published extensively in these areas and in the use of qualitative research methods and theoretical frameworks for sport management research.

Sten Söderman

Sten is professor of international business at the Stockholm University School of Business and visiting professor at the University of Luxembourg. His research has focused on market strategy development and implementation and is currently concentrated on the international expansion of European firms in Asia and the global entertainment economy.

Leigh Sparks

Leigh is professor of retail studies at the Institute for Retail Studies, University of Stirling, Scotland. He has researched and published extensively on aspects of retailing and distribution and at Stirling teaches sports marketing.

Constantino Stavros

Constantino is a senior academic in the School of Economics, Finance & Marketing at RMIT University in Melbourne, Australia. He has published widely in academic, practitioner, and public outlets, and has taught sport marketing in both Australia and Europe.

Kamilla Swart

Kamilla is a senior lecturer/researcher and director of the Centre for Tourism Research in Africa (CETRA), Cape Peninsula University of Technology. She has researched and published extensively in the areas of sport and event tourism, with a specific focus on the 2010 FIFA Soccer World Cup and event evaluations. Her manuscripts have been published in the *Journal of Sport Tourism, Visions in Leisure and Business, Third World Quarterly*, and *Politikon*, amongst others, and she coauthored the first U.S. text on sport tourism in 2002.

Stefan Szymanski

Stefan is a graduate of the University of Oxford, Hertford College, where he gained a first degree in politics, philosophy, and economics. He began his teaching career at London Business School before moving to Imperial College in 1993. He is professor of economics at Cass Business School, City University London. Stefan is also an economics professor and is widely acknowledged as one of Europe's leading sports economists.

Linda Trenberth

Linda is senior lecturer in management at Birkbeck, University of London. Linda works in a range of areas but in the sport management area has contributed to and coedited the first and only texts in sport management in New Zealand in 1994, 1999, and again in 2006. She also edited a text *Managing the Business of Sport* published in the United Kingdom in 2004, which is about to be revised, and has published in the area of sports marketing. Her other research interests include issues around the management of the employee-employer relationships; HRM and organizational performance; women in management; and work stress, leisure, and health. Linda is a codirector of the Birkbeck Sport Business Centre.

Paul Turner

Paul is a senior lecturer and discipline coordinator for sport management within the School of Management and Marketing at Deakin University in Melbourne, Australia. His scholarly interests are in the areas of sport media (particularly sport broadcasting) and facility and event management.

Ignacio Urrutia

Ignacio is dean of the social science faculty of Nebrija University Madrid, Spain. His interests cover a wide range of business issues including control and sport management. He currently focuses his research on the link between the strategic goals of sports clubs and their implementation. He is a member of the international faculty of IESE Business School's Centre for Sport Business Management (CSBM) and has lectured at Carlos III University and Instituto de Empresa.

Jos Verschueren

Jos is programme director of sports management at Vrije Universiteit Brussel (Brussels Free University). He is also founder of the Sport Management Knowledge Centre at the same university. He has over 15 years of consulting and academic business experience in sports marketing and communication, sports partnership branding, sports business, and management. In 1995, he started Com Together-Sports & Communication (Lennik-Brussels) as a spinoff of his academic activities. He serves a broad range of clients in developing corporate sports partnership strategies (e.g., Siemens), forging cross-brands sports alliances (e.g., Belgian Olympic and Interfederal Committee), and enhancing performance through sports partnership effectiveness (e.g., National Lottery). He holds university degrees from Hogeschool-Universiteit Brussels, Université Libre de Bruxelles, Rijksuniversiteit Groningen in the Netherlands, and Université de Lausanne in Switzerland.

Geoff Walters

Geoff is a lecturer in the Department of Management at Birkbeck, University of London, and a co-director of the Birkbeck Sport Business Centre. A graduate of Lancaster University and the University of Manchester, he completed his Ph.D. at Birkbeck in 2007, examining corporate governance in the football industry. His current research focuses on governance and regulation in sport and corporate social responsibility.

Ruiqi Zhou

Ruiqi is associate professor of English at Guangdong University of Foreign Studies, People's Republic of China. Her main research interest is business English teaching. She is the coeditor of *International Trade Practice* (published by University of International Business and Economics Press), *Business Etiquette in English*, and *A Dictionary of English Synonyms and Antonyms* (both published by Sun Yet-Sen University Press).

Foreword

Football is often referred to as the "global game" and is all-pervasive across most parts of the world. Indeed, countless people play the game, talk about it, and generally organise their leisure time around it. Alongside this, football has progressed from being a ritual and a celebration to become an amateur sport, a professional sport, and now, increasingly, a commercial sport. This means that football in many countries now faces a distinctive set of challenges. In particular, this includes reconciling the history and traditions of the game with the commercial opportunities and problems posed by the twenty-first century.

Managing Football: An International Perspective therefore sets out to examine football in this context. It is recognised that football has a proud, noble heritage as a cultural asset that is worth preserving. However, the underlying premise of the book is that football today faces a future that increasingly requires people involved in, or associated with, the sport to adopt a professional, strategic, and sometimes commercially focused approach to the administration of the institutions that make up what we might describe as the football industry.

As such, the book is not necessarily a celebration of the history and traditions of football or of the increasing commercialisation of it. Rather, it aims to identify and analyse the most important matters facing managers in the football industry in all its facets. It is important to note that this, in part, refers to the people who manage teams of 11 players: the coach, the director of football, and the team manager. Yet, the book focuses much more on management off the field of play. While this inevitably has a link to what happens in football matches, we clearly focus here on issues such as sound business practice, the technological environment in which football clubs operate, the successful marketing of football, and managing football in an international and global context. In essence, therefore, we aim to ensure that readers will have a better understanding of the administration of the football industry, and the institutions within it, after reading this book.

The book is essentially split into two sections: The first deals with the application of mainstream management disciplines to football, as well as consideration of those challenges that are highly specific to, or distinctive in, football. While there are certain aspects of management that all industries and activities share—for instance, managing scarce resources—football faces some key challenges that others do not. These include issues of competition structure, the particular nature of fandom, and the debt levels facing many clubs.

In the second section of the book, the global nature of the sport is acknowledged. It includes chapters that examine contemporary football management issues in countries as diverse as England, Australia, Mexico, and South Africa. Throughout this section of the book, the intention has been to highlight the simultaneous similarities and differences that are evident in a selection of countries in which football is played and watched around the world.

Our ultimate hope is that readers will enjoy this book and find it useful for many reasons. At the very least, because the book is about football, it is anticipated that people will be able to gain an even stronger insight into a sport of which many already have an extensive knowledge. It is nevertheless also anticipated that the book will help contribute to developments in practice and knowledge in the area of the business management of the football industry in all its dimensions and will be of interest not only to students studying sports management but to management practitioners in all areas of the game's administration and related industries.

Sean Hamil and Simon Chadwick
July 2009

PART 1

Managing Football

CHAPTER 1

Introduction and Market Overview

Sean Hamil
Birkbeck Sport Business Centre, Birkbeck College, University of London

Simon Chadwick
Coventry University

Objectives
Upon completion of this chapter the reader should be able to:

- Explain the historic and global development of football.
- Understand issues that serve as the background to football management.
- Identify the distinctive features and characteristics of football.
- Understand the structure of this book and the chapters.

OVERVIEW OF THE CHAPTER

This chapter sets out to achieve a number of objectives, most notably to introduce readers to this book. The chapter begins by providing a brief history of football. Given the global development of the sport, generalising and summarising its history is not an easy task. As such, the history presented is simply one version among many stories, myths, and legends. Significantly, however, it illustrates that the popularity of football is not simply a recent phenomenon and that the sport is deeply socioculturally embedded. When addressing the challenges facing managers in modern football, especially those relating to commercial developments, this is an important point to remember. The chapter then goes on to highlight some of the key features of football, noting the size and nature of the football industry, as well as examining its distinctive characteristics. This is intended to serve as a backdrop against which subsequent chapters in this book should be read. In brief, each of these chapters is then previewed, and the reasons for dividing this book into four sections are explained. The chapter concludes by directing readers to key sources of information; it is hoped that this will help both newcomers to football and those with a long-standing interest in the sport to develop a stronger appreciation of what many people refer to as the "global game."

VIKING HEADS, INDEPENDENT SCHOOLS, AND THE INDUSTRIAL REVOLUTION

Football has variously developed across the world as a ceremony, a celebration, a physical pursuit, a leisure activity, and now, increasingly, a business. As an illustration, consider the case of football in England: some people believe that the sport emerged over centuries, thus giving it an extraordinary depth and context. In its earliest form, myth has it that during the Viking invasions of the late first millennium, victorious battlers among the resident population would cut off the heads of the invaders and kick the decapitated heads around their villages. Thereafter, in medieval times, a ritual emerged that still endures today: Large groups would gather in towns and villages to celebrate Shrove Tuesday,[1] a festival that is repeated across the world to mark the end of winter food stocks and the start of the new planting season. As part of the celebrations, a form of football would be played where a goal would be placed at either end of the town or village, and the objective was simply to score a goal. From these origins, football most notably began to thrive during the nineteenth century in the English independent schools system as a puritanical form of healthy activity for young men. Thereafter, the onset of the industrial revolution led to both an upsurge in the popularity of football as a diversion for the masses away from their harsh industrial lives and to the emergence of the professional game. Throughout the twentieth century, as people's leisure time increased and communication links improved, regular international football began, the game developed, and the popularity of football began to take hold. By the turn of the twenty-first century, in the light of rapid technological and media changes, the impact of regulatory influence

---

[1] The word *shrove* is thought to be derived from the word *schriven*, which means "absolution."

from bodies such as the European Union, the forces of internationalisation and globalisation, and the prevalence of liberal economic- and business-oriented thinking began to pervade across a large number of sports. Beech (2004) has generally characterised such an overall transition as having being comprised of seven phases: foundation, codification, stratification, professionalisation, postprofessionalisation, commercialisation, and post-commercialisation—essentially a journey whereby football evolved from being a simple sporting contest to become a sporting contest situated within a complex set of economic, social, and political structures with huge cultural and financial significance.

For many people across the world, football remains a celebration, a hobby, a leisure pursuit, and a rite of passage; yet, football is increasingly recognized as an industry in itself, an industry that must be managed in a businesslike fashion. There is no doubt that football is universally popular, and it is frequently referred to as the global game, a sport that transcends social, political, economic, and cultural boundaries. Figures reported by the *Federation International de Football Association* (FIFA) appear to confirm this, with the organisation reporting that there are 265 million registered players worldwide, playing for 1.7 million teams in 300,000 official clubs (FIFA, 2007). Although many of these players, teams, and clubs may actually play football simply for pleasure, the top tier of football clubs clearly operate as businesses of a kind, despite their sociocultural significance.

The financial value of football is obvious; Deloitte (2008, page 6) estimated that the total European football market was worth €13.6 million in the 2006/2007 season. It has been estimated (*PR Newswire*, 2008) that Real Madrid's brand value was €1,063 million in 2008.

Football's bigger clubs inevitably attract the attention of the media and public alike, but many other smaller clubs worldwide operate profitably, serve the needs of particular target groups, make a significant contribution to their local economies, or help in the creation and management of community projects. At the same time, financial problems characterise the reality for many football clubs, even at a club like Chelsea (English Premier League Champions in 2004 and 2005), where annual losses were over £75 million in 2006/2007 (Deloitte, 2008, Appendices, page 5). In some countries, massive debt may be less of a problem than general disinterest in the local product with interest in the English Premier League crowding out interest in local teams. Elsewhere, Italy has seen the appeal of football and trust in the game undermined by hooliganism and corruption; in countries like India and Australia, colonial (cricket) and local sports (Australian Rules football—AFL), rather than football, often dominate the sports scene, while the impoverishment, poor infrastructure, and player defections continue to pose problems for football clubs and the football authorities throughout developing countries in Africa. In countries like Argentina and Brazil, despite the passion and fervour of people's support for football, crumbling stadia and serious financial problems represent a major threat to the future development of the game.

In Europe, professional football is fast becoming a major industry characterised by commercialism and the growth of formal, professional marketing practices. The maturity of some European football markets has resulted in leading clubs seeking growth opportunities in other countries, most notably in Asia. At the same time, clubs in many European nations continue to face difficult operating conditions as they struggle to maintain presence and profile in a complex, dynamic environment where the majority of the clubs continue to suffer financial losses.

Outside Europe, the growing popularity of football in Asia continues unabated. Spurred on by their hosting of the 2002 World Cup, football in Japan and South Korea is perceived to be on a growth trajectory, although the product on offer is not at a level of maturity commensurate with the major European leagues. Elsewhere in Asia, the industry essentially consists of two types of countries: countries where the interest in football is strong but is served by overseas clubs and leagues rather than domestic provision and countries where, thus far, receptiveness to football is limited, possibly due to the popularity of other sports or due to economic and social conditions.

In the Americas, the profile of the football industry is a starkly contrasting one. In Central and South America, football is hugely popular, spanning social, economic, and cultural divisions. Nevertheless, the industry is notoriously inefficient, as many clubs operate at a loss and have little regard for formal or professional approaches to marketing. In the United States, this formality and professionalism is present, but football does not enjoy the sociocultural prominence that it does elsewhere in the world, which presents a distinct set of challenges for those involved in managing the sport.

As for the rest of the world, football is very popular in Africa, but the notion of developing managerial focus and competence is one that has yet to effectively establish itself, compounding economic problems and the exodus of players to other countries, particularly to Europe. Yet, the African experience is too complex to generalise, especially as South Africa is set to host the 2010 FIFA World Cup and because North African football enjoys a much higher profile and is much more economically prosperous than football in most sub-Saharan countries. In Oceania, football is largely an immature product; in the former colonies of Northern European countries, there is some interest in football, but this tends to be centred on particular ethnic groups and is often overshadowed by other, often culturally specific, sports.

In light of the prevailing view that football is the global game, as well as the growing recognition that football is an industry in which there is a need to develop managerial competence, this book therefore sets out to examine football management in different geographic areas across the world. The book is not intended to focus on one particular aspect of football management, but rather, it employs subject and country specialists who shed light on the current practice in their areas of expertise. This means that chapter authors focus on subject matter that variously highlights opportunities, threats, reasons for optimism, reasons for pessimism, the major challenges facing those in management positions in the sport and industry of football. But while the main balance of the book consequently lies in the area of off-field management, the importance of building and managing successful teams of players on the field remains at the heart of the text. It is toward the achievement of this aim that all other management practice is focused.

THE NATURE AND DISTINCTIVENESS OF FOOTBALL

Let us begin by asking a very simple question: What is football? To answer this, we must first turn to economists. As Neale (1964) famously noted, the essence of football is the uncertainty of outcome associated with a contest between two teams. It is this uncertainty that draws so many people, groups, and organisations to football. Uncertainty thus helps to create a sense of excitement and expectation. Take the tension or drama away from football and people start to lose interest; promote uncertainty, and it leads people to respond in a variety of different ways. Some will attend games, others will watch football on television, and many will read about games and players in newspapers and magazines for reasons of pure enjoyment, but all of these responses can potentially generate financial revenues. In psychological terms, people will use football as the basis for associating with success (known as BIRGing—Basking In Reflected Glory) and, perversely in some cases, failure (BIRFing—Basking in Reflected Failure). Many people will alternatively see "their" club or "their" sport as being a way they can publicly communicate their affiliations—geographic or otherwise—and others will use football as an expression of their values—social, political, economic, or otherwise.

If uncertainty of outcome constitutes the fundamental basis of football, then preserving the strength of uncertainty arguably becomes the most fundamental challenge facing managers in the sport. To this end maintaining competitive balance is advocated as the central element of promoting uncertainty. One approach to managing uncertainty through competitive balance is via highly regulated models (synonymous with U.S. sport) in which salary caps, draft picks, and franchise location are used as tools to maintain uncertainty. However, such has been the sociocultural development of football across most countries in the world that this approach to regulation is anathema to many involved in football. In all but a small number of countries, football is deeply socioculturally embedded.

This immediately raises a series of issues, most notably that in European football, for example, uncertainty and competitive balance cannot necessarily be managed in the same way as in U.S. sports. Consider the case of the English club Wimbledon FC, which was relocated from south London to Milton Keynes (nearly 100 miles away) at the turn of the twentieth century following serious financial difficulties and was renamed MK Dons in what many would argue was the first attempt in the modern era to create an American-style football franchise. Wimbledon's supporters reacted by forming their own supporter-owned team, AFC Wimbledon, which is currently working its way up the English football pyramid and in the 2008–2009 season was at level 6. Although MK Dons is now building a new fanbase in the Milton Keynes area, this has only followed an initial stage in bankruptcy.

However, although the models of football, or soccer, may differ in various parts of the world (note for example the differences between England's Premier League and U.S. Major League Soccer), the sport has the following key features in common.

Uncertainty of the outcome is at the heart of football. Uncertainty is the core of the football product and is one of the main reasons why so many people are motivated to consume it. As was discussed earlier, uncertainty induces levels of excitement, stress, emotion, and tension that are rarely, if ever, associated with the repeated purchase of any other product. Just how the uncertainty of the outcome and the associated "experience" can be marketed is one of the crucial challenges that football marketers face. Allied to this are the related challenges concerning how marketers should set about marketing the tangible, augmented, and potential features of the football product.

Football is a product-led industry. Most organisations in football are currently product-led. This means the focus and success of management off the field of play are largely determined by what happens on it. This inevitably leads to players and teams dominating what happens in football, with the central role of fans and how to meet their needs neglected with negative commercial consequences.

Fans and other customers help produce the football product. Visit a supermarket, purchase a financial services product, or ask an engineer to install a component for you, and it does not really matter who else is there, if anyone, or what they look like or how they sound. Now contrast this with football: while some might derive immense pleasure from attending a game, even if nobody else is present, the essence of football for the majority of people is the atmosphere and excitement generated by the other people around them. It is good to win a game by a huge margin, but it is even better if you are watching it with friends, family, or other supporters. The marketing of football is therefore unique in the way the presence of other customers is a vital element of the product and of the consumption experience. The individual is therefore of paramount importance in football marketing, simultaneously representing both producer and consumer.

The football product is socioculturally embedded. Football generates a degree of fervour and passion that is unheard of in relation to other products. The sociocultural basis of the sport is such that it presents strongly distinctive challenges that marketers of other products do not face. Among these are the unswerving loyalty that many fans have for their teams and clubs, powerful parental and peer influences on consumption, and the role that geographic identity plays in influencing consumption behaviour. Unlike other products, football is thus often consumed in an irrational rather than a rational economic way. Logic tells us that if a product continually fails to live up to its expectations, people will stop buying it. In football, this logic does not always hold.

Football clubs have limited control over their product. Given that the uncertainty of outcome is at the heart of sport, the principal focus for sport managers therefore becomes how to preserve and develop it. For instance, when the U.S. authorities announced that they wanted to increase the size of the goals for the 1994 World Cup so more goals would be scored (thus making easier to market soccer in the United States), there was a huge outcry in other parts of the world. And, in any case, the rules of the game are dictated by football's traditional governing bodies, at a world level by FIFA. Such external controls therefore limit how much sports marketers can adapt and change the sporting contest. Moreover, in addition to the raft of externally imposed rules that inevitably apply to all organisations, the appeal of football is further regulated by specific criteria that apply to promotion and relegation, player acquisition, and the format of a game or match. If, for example, a team gets relegated from a league to a lower division where the competing clubs are less attractive to television, for example, literally overnight, the nature of the team's marketing is likely to be influenced in a way that other businesses are not routinely exposed to.

Football measures performance in different ways. Managers working in most for-profit organisations are likely to have their performance measured in terms of, for example, increased market share or a growth in sales. Among not-for-profit marketers, measures such as promoting charitable contributions or raising participation may alternatively be important. But in football, the acid test for most organisations is "Did we win the league?", or "utility maximisation." In part, such judgments are bound up in the product orientation of the organisations concerned, although what this does is to effectively relegate traditional measures of marketing success to that of only secondary importance.

Football has a unique relationship with broadcasters and the media. In some respects, one might argue that football does not need to market itself and should just let others do the marketing for it. Indeed, certain football clubs actually take this view; for example, why spend on advertising when television channels, newspapers and websites effectively do your advertising for you? If one opens a daily newspaper, it is likely that you will be faced with a multitude of football stories, factual, salacious, and otherwise. The role and importance of "the media" should not therefore be underestimated because it is instrumental in helping to create the tension and excitement surrounding the football product. Moreover, it has generated a range of additional opportunities for football through, for instance, the promotion of sponsorship deals and endorsement packages. However, one lesson that football marketers do need to learn is that leaving the media to do one's marketing cedes control of how the product is presented and packaged to corporations, some of which may be located thousands of miles away. Taking a more active role both in fostering and managing relations with the media and marketing football beyond this relationship are important tasks that many sport marketers have yet to seriously address.

Football fans are loyal and are unlikely to brand switch or substitute. If one were to ask a fan of Boca Juniors in Argentina, "Would you buy a River Plate replica shirt or apply for a River Plate credit card?," the answer will predictably be "No." What does this tell us about football marketing and the challenges that marketers face? Clearly, marketing products associated with one club or team probably means the product will be viewed as undesirable by rival fans. This implies that many organisations in football are likely to have strongly constrained and geographically defined market places. For some, this is likely to restrict their development. For others, it may mean the marketing effort has to, for example, adopt an international focus or use a brand name and image completely different from those of the parent. With the possible exception of consumers who have strong nationalist motives for buying products ("We only buy from producers in our home country"), this again sets football and football marketing apart from the marketing of other products.

The chapters in this book address a number of important themes and discuss numerous organizations. In advance of the book's other chapters, Table 1.1 provides an indication of the scope of football as an industry. While the table is not necessarily exhaustive, it helps to provide an indication of the

Table 1.1	The Extent of Football—An Example Using Manchester United
Directly Related	**Indirectly Related**

Directly Related	Indirectly Related
■ Fans, spectators, and customers—in other words, the people who buy their tickets at the gate on the day of a game.	■ Places and destinations, such as the Old Trafford museum.
■ Individual players, such as Cristiano Ronaldo.	■ Local economic and social development, such as the profitability of pubs, bars, and cafes that are close to Old Trafford.
■ Teams and clubs, such as Manchester United.	■ Magazines and newspapers, such as *Four-Four-Two* and *World Soccer*.
■ Owners, such as the Glazer family.	■ Betting and gambling services, such as Betfred.
■ Stadium owners, such as, in this case, the Glazer family.	■ Sportswear manufacturers, suppliers, and merchandisers, such as Nike.
■ Leagues, such as the FA Premier League.	
■ Competitions, such as the FA Cup.	
■ Events, such as a Manchester United tour to South Africa.	
■ Commercial partners, such as AIG.	
■ Television and media coverage, such as BSkyB and Setanta.	
■ Governing bodies, such as the English Football Association (FA).	

breadth and diversity of organisations that could be considered as being part of football. Readers will note that the table is split into two parts: "Directly Related" refers to the activities of people and the organisations that are directly related to what happens on the field of play—that is, matches themselves. Marketers might call this the "core product." The "Indirectly Related'" part of the table refers to the activities of people and the organisations that are related to what happens off the field of play but in a direct sense. In other words, they can function independently of games that take place on the field of play.

THE ORGANISATION OF THIS BOOK

This book is split into four sections. The first section (Chapters 2–13) considers football from the perspective of functional management areas—that is, specialist activities in which football managers may already be involved or in which they may be required to get involved at some stage in the future. Therefore, these chapters deal specifically with managing people, customers, the media, technology, facilities, commercial partners, legal and regulatory institutions, and the very competitions and leagues that enable football to be played. The underlying premise of this section is that it will help readers to understand the process and practice of management, while serving as a guide to the art of effectively managing in football.

Each of the subsequent three sections of the book acknowledges that while football is essentially the same game all over the world, the structure, organisation, and management of the game in each country are often different. This may be due to the sociocultural development of the game, but it may also reflect, for example, the way domestic law regulates football or the way it is broadcasted on television, radio, and the Internet. The perfect scenario for the editors of this book would have been to have chapters covering as many football nations as possible. However, for reasons of economy and convenience, a small number of countries have been selected as indicative for analysis. It is anticipated that readers will find that the chapters in this book will motivate them to learn more about football in countries that are not included here.

The second section of this book examines football in England (Chapter 14), Spain (Chapter 15), Italy (Chapter 16), France (Chapter 17), and Germany (Chapter 18). Each of the countries covered in this section exhibit similar characteristics: football is deeply socioculturally embedded; the market for football is a mature one in which people have strong and historic affiliations with teams; attendance at games is well established, and there is a market for off-field products; revenue generated from television contracts is strong and there is further potential for growth from developments in new media; sponsorship and other commercial arrangements have been in place for a significant period of time; legislation and regulatory measures are in place that address issues specific to the football industry; and, to an extent, the football played in these countries attracts the attention of fans, customers, investors, and other relevant parties from outside their domestic boundaries.

The third section concentrates on four key territories that are classified in this book as being emerging markets: Australia (Chapter 19), North America (Chapter 20), China (Chapter 21), and South Africa (Chapter 22). Football in these countries may not be as strong, popular, or well established as the football in those in the second section, as in some cases, no real football heritage exists—North America and Australia being prime examples of this. In countries like South Africa, football is very popular, but the commercial strength of their respective domestic leagues is less notable than in the "Big-5" discussed in the second section. As for China, organisational problems have long hindered the growth of the country's domestic league. Yet, all are now emerging as football nations, in sporting and commercial terms. North America and Australia have recently established professional leagues that are attracting players from across the globe, major commercial partners, and increasing numbers of spectators. South Africa will be playing host to the 2010 FIFA World Cup. China has meanwhile become a major strategic target for many clubs, especially those from Europe, due to its economic prosperity and its people's strong interest in football.

The fourth section explores issues of management in what we call "established markets": the Netherlands and Belgium (Chapter 23), Mexico (Chapter 24), and South Korea (Chapter 25). The countries appearing in this final section can all be characterised as mature football nations in much the same way as those in the second section, although the football in each of these countries is less well established in commercial and managerial terms. The Netherlands and Belgium not only share geographic and cultural characteristics but are also similar in the way their domestic leagues are struggling to prosper. Bereft of on-field success in European competitions and losing players to higher-profile overseas leagues, Dutch/Belgian football does not enjoy the kudos that football does elsewhere in Europe. Mexican football is a little different in that commercially, financially and managerially it is much stronger than football in many other Latin American countries. Yet football in Mexico does not attract the attention that countries like Argentina to the south do, or even the United States to the north. As for South Korea, football is immensely popular, a fact reinforced by the successful hosting by the country (alongside Japan) of the 2002 FIFA World Cup. Football in South Korea is also managerially and commercially well established, but faces a major threat from European clubs that appear to be more popular than the domestic game. Indeed, some European clubs routinely visit the country to play games against one another.

CONCLUSIONS

Football has developed rapidly over the last century and a half, having progressed from an often informal, social activity to a sport that now ranges from children kicking around a football in the streets for fun to major international, multiproduct businesses that capture the world's attention. The aim of this book is not necessarily to present a case for the return to yesteryear amateurism or to advocate that the global advance of corporate football is the most appropriate model for football clubs to adopt. Rather, the book is an acknowledgment that football has an important place in the world that consequently exposes the sport to a multitude of new pressures and challenges. As such, this book sets out to define the position that football finds itself in today and to establish how football in its many forms can be managed in a more effective way. For some people in football, this will probably mean how they can take advantage of commercial opportunities to ensure they achieve a commercial return. But the book's agenda is far broader than this: ensuring that club owners are fit and proper people to own the clubs they are involved in, trying to ensure that the debts incurred by many clubs do not become a threat to a club's continued existence, and the need to manage the often disparate expectations of multicultural teams are examples of some of the other equally important management challenges facing football that are covered in the book. The editors, and all those who have contributed chapters to this book, are, above all, fans and football enthusiasts. But they also bring specialist professional competence and a strong insight into the sport. This means that the book ensures that football is examined in a sympathetic but no less realistic way by the people involved in what we think will be an important contribution to the management of football.

DISCUSSION QUESTIONS

1. To what extent do you think managing in football is the same as or different from managing in other sectors?
2. Is the management of the football industry a rational economic activity?
3. Compare and contrast what you think are the differences between managing a domestic team and a national team. What might be the implications of what you have identified for football managers?
4. Compare and contrast what you think are the key differences, in terms of the challenges faced, between managing a football club's on-field activities—the team—and its off-field activities—commercial activities.
5. Over the next five years, what do you think will be the three biggest challenges facing managers working in football, and how do you think they should respond to these challenges?

GUIDED READING

It is not the intention of this book to necessarily provide a detailed sociocultural or historic view of football. To understand modern football, it is nevertheless important that one appreciates the way in which the sport has developed across the world. Readers should therefore look no further than David Goldblatt's excellent book *The Ball Is Round: A Global History of Football* (2006). Eric Midwinter's book *From Parish to Planet: How Football Came to Rule the World* (2007) is a useful accompanying reading to Goldblatt. Otherwise, a series of books published by the English football magazine *When Saturday Comes* is a very helpful introduction to football in various countries across the world. The series includes *Morbo: The Story of Spanish Football* by Phil Ball (2003); *Tor: The Story of German Football* by Ulrich Hesse-Lichtenberger (2003); and *Soccer in a Football World: The Story of America's Forgotten Game* by David Wangerin (2006). In a similar vein, although more overtly acknowledging the commercial changes that are influencing football, John Samuels' text *The Beautiful Game Is Over: The Globalisation of Football* (2008) is useful background to this book. Michel Desbordes, in *Marketing and Football: An International Perspective* (2006), adopts a similar format to that employed here. Although focused specifically on football marketing, the international nature of its content does serve as a reference point for many of the chapters included later on in this book.

REFERENCES

Ball, P. (2003). *Morbo: The Story of Spanish Football*. London: When Saturday Comes Books.

Beech, J. (2004). Introduction: The Commercialisation of Sport. In J. Beech, & S. Chadwick (Eds.), *The Business of Sport Management*. Harlow: Pearson Education.

Deloitte. (2008). *Annual Review of Football Finance*, Manchester, UK: Deloitte Sport Business Group.

Desbordes, M. (2006). *Marketing and Football: An International Perspective*, Oxford: Butterworth Heinemann.

Fifa.com (31st May, 2007). FIFA Big Count: 270 million people active in football. Retrieved on June 10, 2009, from http://www.fifa.com/mm/document/fifafacts/bcoffsurv/bigcount.statspackage_7024.pdf

Goldblatt, D. (2006). *The Ball Is Round: A Global History of Football*. London: Viking.

Hesse-Lichtenberger, U. (2003). *Tor: The Story of German Football*. London: When Saturday Comes Books.

Midwinter, E. (2007). *From Parish to Planet: How Football Came to Rule the World*. [Studley.] Know the Score Books.

Neale, W. (1964). The peculiar economics of professional sports, *Quarterly Journal of Economics*, 78:1–14.

PR Newswire (20th September, 2008). Real Madrid is Football Club With Highest Brand Value in Europe. Retrieved on June 10, 2009, from http://www. prnewswire.co.uk/cgi/news/release?id=207802

Samuels, J. (2008). *The Beautiful Game Is Over: The Globalisation of Football*. Brighton: Book Guild Publishing.

Wangerin, D. (2006). *Soccer in a Football World: The Story of America's Forgotten Game*, London: When Saturday Comes Books.

RECOMMENDED WEBSITES

BizEd Football, Finance and the Future—Is the Bubble About to Burst?

http://www.bized.co.uk/current/argument/arg7.htm

Deloitte Sport Business Group

http://www.deloitte.com/dtt/section_node/0,1042,sid%253D70402,00.html

ESPN Soccernet

http://soccernet.espn.go.com/index?cc=5739

EU Football Biz

http://www.eufootball.biz/

Football Insider

http://www.pa-sport.com/divisions/en/newsletters/football-insider.html

The Political Economy of Football

http://www.footballeconomy.com/

When Saturday Comes

http://www.wsc.co.uk/

World Soccer

http://www.worldsoccer.com/

CHAPTER 2

Ownership and Governance

Geoff Walters

Birkbeck Sport Business Centre, Birkbeck College, University of London

Sean Hamil

Birkbeck Sport Business Centre, Birkbeck College, University of London

Objectives

Upon completion of this chapter the reader should be able to:

- Understand the historical development of the limited liability structure in English football.
- Identify recent trends in models of ownership at English football clubs.
- Contrast different types of ownership models in European football.
- Appreciate how different types of ownership models impact on governance.

CONTENTS

OVERVIEW OF THE CHAPTER

This chapter provides an account of the different types of football club ownership that have emerged in the English football industry since the formation of the Premier League in 1992. The three types of ownership are the stock market model of ownership, the supporter trust model of ownership, and the foreign investor model of ownership. In all three cases, the football club is legally structured as a limited company, although the type of ownership can impact on football club governance. This chapter also considers other types of legal structure and ownership models found in the other four major European football markets, including the membership model in Spain and Germany, the individual/family-owned model in Italy, and the Public Company for Professional Sport in France. It concludes by discussing how different models of ownership can impact on club governance.

INTRODUCTION

Professional football clubs in England originate from a variety of different forms of institution such as schools, churches, and workplaces. In the first instance, all football clubs were constituted as clubs with a committee elected by club members (Buraimo et al., 2006, page 2). The early regulations of the Football Association did not permit football clubs to employ professional players, although during the 1870s, increased competition to secure the best (semiprofessional) players led to significant increases in player wages (Harvey, 2005, page 220). The decision by the Football Association to allow clubs to become professional in 1885 led to further increases in player wages. Given the reliance on gate receipts to fund wages, the formation of the Football League in 1888 was inevitable, as professionalism increased the need for clubs to participate in a regular schedule of matches out of commercial necessity (Tomlinson, 1991, page 30). The increasing popularity of the Football League in the late 1880s and 1890s required the development of football stadia to accommodate the increase in the numbers of paying spectators. These developments necessitated additional levels of finance. In order to protect committee members from personal liability, football clubs were able to take advantage of the 1856 Joint Stock Companies Act that enabled clubs to convert to private companies owned by shareholders with limited liability status, with Small Heath (Birmingham City) the first to do so in 1888 (Buraimo et al., 2006, page 2). By 1921, 84 out of 86 Football League clubs had converted to private companies with limited liability status (Dobson and Goddard, 2001, page 375).

The private company with limited liability has been the dominant legal structure throughout the course of the twentieth century (Buraimo et al., 2006), and football clubs have commonly been owned by local businessmen prepared to underwrite financial losses. This legal structure is even written into the regulations of the Football League. In order to maintain league status, clubs are required to be constituted as limited companies. For example, in 2008, Dagenham and Redbridge, formerly a members' club, had to convert to a limited company in order to take their place in the Football League (*BBC Sport*, 2008). However, as the football industry entered into a new phase of commercialism in the 1990s, three new types of ownership have emerged. These include the stock market model of ownership and the supporter trust model of ownership, both of which involve the creation of a holding company that owns the majority of shares in the football club, ensuring that the football club continues to be constituted as a limited company. The third type of ownership is the foreign investor model of ownership that has become increasingly prominent since 2004.

THE STOCK MARKET MODEL OF OWNERSHIP

The stock market model of ownership became popular in the mid-1990s, although the first football club to float on the stock market was Tottenham Hotspur in 1983. The introduction of Rule 34 by the Football Association in 1912 restricted the amount payable in dividends to 5 percent of the face value of the shares, prevented directors from being paid for their role at the club, and stated that no owner could wind up a club and profit from the sale of the ground (Conn, 1997, pages 138–139). However, Tottenham Hotspur circumvented this ruling by creating a holding company, with the football club a subsidiary company, and floated the holding company on the London Stock Exchange. The Football Association did not intervene, and the initial share offer raised £3.3 million in capital (Morrow, 1999, page 63). At the time, the City viewed the flotation of Tottenham Hotspur as a unique move; it took a further six years before Millwall became the second football club to float on the London Stock Exchange in 1989, followed by Manchester United in 1991.

The rapid commercialisation of the football industry following the creation of the Premier League in 1992 resulted in the City viewing the industry as one of the brightest sectors of a buoyant stock market in the mid-1990s. This was prompted by the perception that the significant increase in broadcasting rights would enable football clubs to become profitable businesses at a time when the industry was also characterised by improved sponsorship and public image (Morrow, 1999, page 71). During an 18-month period between 1995 and 1996, the share price of Manchester United rose 336 percent, while share prices in Tottenham Hotspur increased by 368 per-cent (Dobson and Goddard, 2001, page 377). Following these successes, other clubs took the decision in the 1990s to convert to Public Limited Company (PLC) status; this decision was vindicated following early share price successes at a number of listed football clubs following flotation. For instance, the initial float price of

55 pence at Chelsea Village in March 1996 had risen to 118 pence by August 1997, while shares in Preston North End were available at 540 pence in August 1997 following an initial offer price of 400 pence in October 1995. Over a four-year period between January 1993 and January 1997, shares in the football sector rose 774 percent and outperformed the overall stock market by a factor of ten (Morrow, 1999, page 91).

By 2000, there were 22 English clubs listed on the London Stock Exchange (LSE), the Alternative Investment Market (AIM), and the OFEX (now the PLUS market). A total of £167 million had been raised through stock market flotation of football clubs (Morrow, 1999, page 67), which was used for a number of purposes, including to redevelop stadia strengthen playing squads; develop commercial operations; improve youth training programmes; improve training facilities; reduce borrowing; provide additional working capital; and improve liquidity to existing shareholders. However, enthusiasm for investing in football clubs was short-lived. Even by late 1997, the majority of listed clubs recorded share prices substantially lower than their initial public offering. One reason for this was the low level of share trading in comparison to other industry sectors. This was due to both a lack of institutional demand and the nature of supporter share-holding (Morrow, 1999, pages 98–103). Upon flotation, many supporters took the opportunity to purchase shares in their football club. This purchase was, more often than not, an emotional purchase based on personal attachment to the club. Supporters were therefore not willing to sell their shares, ensuring that the secondary market for shares in football clubs was highly illiquid (Morrow, 2003, page 133).

Since 2000, a total of 14 football clubs have delisted. Table 2.1 details the 22 English clubs that have held stock market listings, illustrating when they listed and delisted. It also compares the October 2008 share price of the eight remaining listed football clubs with their initial float price. It illustrates that since their respective float dates, Arsenal and Watford are the only football clubs to have experienced a rise in share price. In the other six cases, the share price fell substantially, with Millwall experiencing a fall from 20 pence per share to 0.03 pence. Falling share prices were also symptomatic of the clubs that delisted. For example, Sunderland Football Club originally floated in December 1996, with an initial share price of 585 pence. The flotation raised £10.7 million for the club, which assisted the development of the Stadium of Light. However, Sunderland delisted in 2004 with shares priced at 31.4 pence.

There are three main reasons why the 14 football clubs have chosen to delist. First, although stock market flotation enabled football clubs to generate initial outside investment, investor returns in the form of

Table 2.1	PLC Football Clubs in England listed on the Stock Exchange			
Club	**Market**	**Float Date**	**Float Price**	**October 2008**
Arsenal	PLUS	November 1995	700 (£)	7750 (£)
Aston Villa	LSE	May 1997	1100.00	Delisted: 2006
Birmingham City	AIM	March 1997	50.00	27.00
Bradford City	OFEX	November 1998	55.00	Delisted: 2002
Bolton Wanderers	AIM	April 1997	52.00	Delisted: 2003
Charlton Athletic	AIM	March 1997	80.00	Delisted: 2006
Chelsea	AIM	March 1996	55.00	Delisted: 2003
QPR	AIM	October 1996	72.00	Delisted: 2001
Leeds United	LSE	August 1996	19.00	Delisted: 2004
Leicester City	LSE	October 1997	93.00	Delisted: 2003
Manchester City	OFEX	October 1995	68.00	Delisted: 2007
Manchester United	LSE	June 1991	385.00	Delisted: 2005
Millwall	AIM	October 1995	20.00	0.03
Newcastle United	LSE	April 1997	135.00	Delisted: 2007
Nottingham Forest	AIM	October 1997	70.00	Delisted: 2002
Preston NE	AIM	October 1995	400.00	117.50
Sheffield United	AIM	January 1997	60.00	9.75
Southampton	LSE	January 1997	150.00	28.00
Sunderland	LSE	December 1996	585.00	Delisted: 2004
Tottenham Hotspurs	LSE	October 1993	100.00	85.00
West Bromwich Albion	AIM	January 1997	280 (£)	Delisted: 2005
Watford	AIM	August 2001	1.00	13.50

Note: (Price in pence unless otherwise stated)

Sources: www.footballeconomy.com; www.ofex.com; www.londonstockexchange.com

dividends and capital gains through share price increases were poor. Manchester United was the only club on the stock market to generate annual profits and shareholder returns. Therefore, there is little opportunity for football clubs to continue to raise investment through the stock market, as City institutions no longer see football clubs as viable investment opportunities. Second, the objective of a football club is to promote football as a sporting activity and as a business. In European sport, and football in particular, the sporting objective has long been established and understood. For instance, the seminal work of Sloane (1971) declared that the objective of a football club was to maximise utility, which included multiple goals such as playing success, average attendance, and league health, while at the same time remaining financially solvent. Therefore, the fundamental principles of profit-maximisation and providing a return for investors that govern the stock market model do not dovetail neatly in the context of a football club. As such, some commentators argue that the stock market model has been found to be unsuitable for the football industry given that a football club has multiple objectives rather than a single overarching purpose and a more inclusive stakeholder ownership structure that addresses the economic and social aspects of football clubs is considered more appropriate (Morrow, 2000). Third, there have been recent changes in ownership at many of the listed clubs as foreign investors have become more prominent in English football. A change in ownership is usually accompanied by the football club reverting back to private company status and leaving the stock market as the club is no longer owned by a range of shareholders and it reduces the administrative obligation required to maintain a stock market listing.

THE SUPPORTER TRUST MODEL OF OWNERSHIP

The supporter trust model of ownership has grown in strength since 2000 when the Labour government backed the establishment of an organisation called Supporters Direct, whose remit was to promote the trust concept. The first trust was established in 1992 at Northampton Town, where the trust formed part of a consortium that saved the club from financial collapse. A supporter trust is an independent, not-for-profit, democratic, cooperatively owned organisation that seeks to influence the governance of a football club through improved supporter representation and also to develop stronger links among a club, a community, and a supporter base. There are currently almost 150 supporter trusts in England, Wales, and Scotland. Almost all supporter trusts are constituted as an Industrial and Provident Society, which is a mutual, not-for-profit organisation without share capital and is often used by cooperatives, social enterprises, and mutual investment companies. It remains democratic through the "one member, one vote" status, with additional features, including the explicit commitment to community benefit and the use of profits to improve services or facilities. The first eight years of the trust movement have seen considerable achievements made. Financially, supporters' trusts have invested over £10 million into the game, which has benefited numerous clubs that would have become financially obsolete were it not for the work and assistance of their trust.

Two ways that trusts can increase their influence is through the ownership of shares and board representation. There are now 100 trusts that maintain a shareholding at clubs and 45 supporter-directors (Brown, 2008). The most notable successes include the two clubs in the Football League that are now owned by the supporters trust: Brentford and Exeter City. In order to comply with Football League regulations, the football club remains a private company with limited liability, and the supporters trust, as an Industrial and Provident Society, owns the majority of shares in the football club. For example, the Brentford Supporters' Trust, Bees United, completed the acquisition of a 60 percent majority shareholding in Brentford Football Club in January 2006 after successfully negotiating a financial package of £5.5 million in order to refinance the debts of the club. Outwith the Football League, supporters trusts own ten other clubs.

However, while the supporters trust movement can claim notable successes in the lower reaches of the Football League, in particular the two supporter-owned clubs, there have been questions raised by some observers as to whether this model can be successfully applied in the Premier League. For instance, Brown (2007, page 617) states that the supporters trust model has "totally failed to demonstrate how it can work in a company of the size of Manchester United, where major corporate finance is needed to create a meaningful stake." Likewise, Martin (2007) argues that the conversion to a fully mutual structure is only really feasible at the smallest and cheapest clubs. However, proponents of the supporters' trust model argue that the concept is still in its infancy and has yet to be fully tested at a larger club. In fact, there are currently a number of trusts at Premiership clubs, notably the Manchester United Supporters Trust (MUST). Similarly, ShareLiverpoolFC was set up in 2007 as the supporter-driven vehicle for taking ownership of Liverpool Football Club (see Case Study 2.1). As Premiership clubs entered a period of financial belt-tightening in autumn 2008 and many clubs were being put up for sale, such as Portsmouth, Newcastle United, and West Ham United, but attracting little private investor interest, the possibility of a supporter trust takeover of a Premiership club, particularly one in financial difficulties, has begun to appear more feasible.

THE FOREIGN INVESTOR MODEL OF OWNERSHIP

The foreign investor model of ownership has been a prominent trend within the Premier League in England over the last five years. Of the 20 clubs in the Premier League in 2007, 8 were now owned by foreign investors (Table 2.2).

CASE STUDY 2.1: ShareLiverpoolFC

In March 2007, the ownership of Liverpool Football Club passed into the hands of two American investors, Tom Hicks and George Gillett. This had followed a three-year period in which the previous owner, David Moores, had courted a number of potential buyers, including property developer Steve Morgan, U.S. billionaire Robert Kraft, and the Dubai Investment Corporation, as Moores felt that he did not have sufficient funds to invest further in the club. The new owners had experience in operating sports franchises in the United States and Canada. Tom Hicks owns the Texas Rangers in Major League Baseball and Dallas Stars in the National Hockey League, while George Gillett owns the Montreal Canadians Ice Hockey Franchise. However, the ownership of Liverpool Football Club has proved controversial. Tom Hicks and George Gillett are the co-owners of Kop Investment Limited, a holding company that they created in 2007 that owns Liverpool Football Club. Through this company, £185 million was borrowed to buy the football club and a further £165 million has been loaned taking the total debt at Kop Investment Limited to approximately £350 million which requires an estimated annual interest cost of £30 million (Conn, 2008a). This debt has to be restructured by July 2009, and given the current credit crunch and economic downturn, there are concerns about the ability to restructure the debt.

The concern surrounding the ownership of Liverpool Football Club led to the creation of ShareLiverpoolFC (SLFC). The objective of SLFC is for the supporter members of the organisation to become the ultimate democratic owners of the football club. In the event that the current owners have difficulties in refinancing the debt of the club, the aim of SLFC is to be in a position to be able to take ownership of the club and run it as a member-owned organisation. SLFC is legally constituted as an Industrial and Provident Society with a one share, one vote structure. The shares cost £5,000 each and are non-tradable. Although this will be out of reach for many supporters, there is the option to enter into a group membership where one individual is nominated as the holder of the share on behalf of the group members. By October 2008, almost 40,000 supporters had expressed interest in this scheme. Ownership of a share in SLFC will entitle members to a number of rights such as the right to put themselves forward for membership of the Fans Parliament or for the board of SLFC and the right to vote in elections. The Fans Parliament will be a body of 100 supporters that meet with the SLFC Board and liaise with the board of the football club on issues of importance. The SLFC board will have between 8 and 12 members who have the responsibility to select and oversee the board members of the football club. The football club board will be responsible for the business and commercial functions of the club. The proposed ownership structure for Liverpool Football Club under SLFC is shown in the figure.

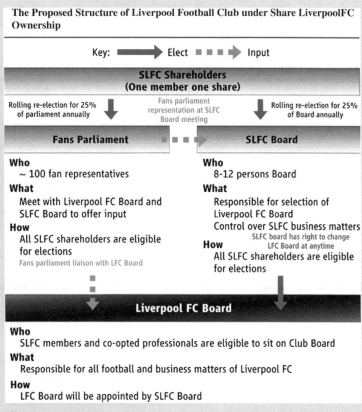

The Proposed Structure of Liverpool Football Club under Share LiverpoolFC Ownership

Key: ➡ Elect ▪▪▪➡ Input

SLFC Shareholders
(One member one share)

Rolling re-election for 25% of parliament annually ⬇ Fans parliament representation at SLFC Board meeting Rolling re-election for 25% of Board annually ⬇

Fans Parliament ▪▪▪➡ **SLFC Board**

Who
~ 100 fan representatives
What
Meet with Liverpool FC Board and SLFC Board to offer input
How
All SLFC shareholders are eligible for elections
Fans parliament liaison with LFC Board

Who
8-12 persons Board
What
Responsible for selection of Liverpool FC Board
Control over SLFC business matters
SLFC board has right to change LFC Board at anytime
How
All SLFC shareholders are eligible for elections

Liverpool FC Board

Who
SLFC members and co-opted professionals are eligible to sit on Club Board
What
Responsible for all football and business matters of Liverpool FC
How
LFC Board will be appointed by SLFC Board

Source: www.shareliverpool.com

Questions

1. Are the ownership plans of ShareLiverpoolFC realistic?

2. What could be potential barriers to the success of the ShareLiverpoolFC model?

There are three clear reasons to explain the rise in foreign investment. First, as the football industry has become more commercialised, the costs required to operate a club in the Premier League, taking into account the significant rise in player wages, have increased substantially. Many owners have been unable to provide the required levels of investment in order to compete and have sold their majority stake in the club to wealthy foreign investors. This was the case at Liverpool, where David Moores sold his 51.6 percent stake in the club, as he was unable to provide the finance needed to

| Table 2.2 | Foreign Ownership in the Premier League | | | |

Club	Deal Date	Owner	Country	Initial Deal Value (in £ million)
Fulham	May 1997	Mohammed Al-Fayed	Egypt	30
Chelsea	July 2003	Roman Abramovich	Russia	135
Manchester United	May 2005	Malcolm Glazer	USA	725
Portsmouth	January 2006	Alexandre Gaydamak	France	68
Aston Villa	August 2006	Randy Lerner	USA	75
West Ham United	November 2006	Bjogolfur Gudmundsson	Iceland	108
Liverpool	March 2007	Tom Hicks and George Gillett	USA	219
Manchester City	September 2008	Abu Dhabi United Group	UAE	82

Source: Deloitte, 2007, p. 60; 2009, p. 62

relocate from Anfield to a new stadium. Secondly, the ownership of a club in the Premier League can be an attractive proposition for foreign investors, notably as a "trophy" asset, conferring global notoriety and fame on owners simply by virtue of owning a participant in the Premier League competition. The Premier League is the most popular league in the world, and there is an element of prestige in owning one of the member clubs. Third, the high value of the most recent domestic, overseas, and highlights broadcasting rights of approximately £2.7 billion between 2007 and 2010 (Hamil, 2008) and the opportunities for global expansion to maximise the brand potential in emerging markets such as Asia are attractive to foreign investors. For instance, a document entitled *A New Model for Partnership in Football* revealed that the Abu Dhabi United Group, the owners of Manchester City, plan to develop a range of partnerships with companies from a diverse range of industries, including food, financial services, fashion, car manufacturing, and communications (Taylor, 2008).

There have been a number of concerns raised about the rise in foreign ownership. In October 2008, FIFA president Sepp Blatter called on UEFA and the European Union to implement tighter regulation regarding ownership, expressing concern that clubs were too easily bought by individuals with no association to the local area. Likewise, UEFA president

Michel Platini has discussed his concern that foreign ownership could result in a loss of local identity. There has also been an issue with one particular type of foreign investment model. While certain investors such as Roman Abramovich at Chelsea act as a benefactor by underwriting all debts and sustaining high annual losses, certain takeovers have been leveraged on debt.

The Manchester United takeover by Malcolm Glazer and his family in 2005 is a case in point. Prior to the takeover, Manchester United was the richest football club in the world with high annual turnover, relatively high levels of profit, and no debt. Following the takeover in 2008, the total debt of the club stood at £667 million, incurring an annual interest payment of £82 million (Conn, 2008a). This has led to an increase in season ticket prices over the past three years in addition to a mandatory obligation that season ticket holders purchase tickets for all cup competitions. It is also critical that Manchester United qualify for the Champions League every season. Failure to do so would potentially threaten the future of the football club.

The recent changes in ownership that have been leveraged on high levels of debt have led to calls for a more stringent "fit and proper" person test in the United Kingdom for new club owners. The Football League was the first of the football authorities to introduce the test in 2004 followed by the Premier League and the Football Association, which administers the test for clubs in the Football Conference and the three feeder leagues: the Southern League, the Isthmian League, and the Northern League. The three versions of the test are similar and currently forbid an individual from owning or being a director at a football club if they are subject to a number of criteria such as having an unspent conviction relating to fraud or dishonesty or are disqualified from acting as a director of a U.K.-registered company. However, it can be argued that the current test does not protect a club from a highly leveraged takeover deal that appears not to be in the short, medium or long-term interest of a football club. Furthermore, in its present state, the "fit and proper" person test does not apply to individuals that are subject to criminal investigation or that are in the process of prosecution. The takeover of Manchester City by Thaksin Shinawatra, the former prime minister of Thailand is a key example (see Case Study 2.2).

CASE STUDY 2.2: The Ownership of Manchester City

In July 2007, Thaksin Shinawatra, former prime minister of Thailand, completed the takeover of Manchester City football club. The deal involved the £21.6 million purchase of the shares in the football club, the repayment of £17.5 million in loans to two of the major shareholders, and the promise of major investment in the club (Conn, 2008b). However, in August 2008, he sold the club to the Abu Dhabi United Group. The period in which he presided over the ownership of Manchester City is an example of a recent takeover that has ultimately proved controversial. It has also led the Premier League to set up a working party to consider the possible ways in which the "fit and proper" person test can be strengthened in the future.

At the time of the takeover in July 2007, Thaksin Shinawatra was living in exile in London, having been removed from power in a military coup amid allegations of corruption and human rights violations. During the negotiations to take over Manchester City, he was charged with corruption, and £800 million worth of assets that he held in Thai banks were frozen. However, he refused to return to Thailand while the military government was in place. The question as to whether Thaksin Shinawatra was an appropriate person to own a football club in the United Kingdom was seemingly not an issue for the board at Manchester City after they recommended the takeover to shareholders in the football club. Moreover, the "fit and proper" person test applied by the Premier League to owners and shareholders with more than 30 percent shareholding was subject to increased levels of scrutiny. The fact that he had not been convicted of a criminal offence, was not disqualified from acting as a director of a U.K.-registered company, or subject to a bankruptcy order, meant that he passed the "fit and proper" person test. Richard Scudamore, chief executive of the Premier League defended the test, arguing that it was more stringent than company law and that the league could not prevent an individual that faced criminal charges from an unelected military government from owning a football club (Winter, 2008):

We have to establish the status of his return to England and where that leaves him as regards to the legal process in Thailand. Our rules are clear.

Somebody has to be convicted of something before they fall under the remit of the "fit and proper" person act. Until such a time as he is convicted, he falls within the rules. But we have always said that the test is meaningful and has to be applied. We need to make sure that if he is guilty of anything we will deal with it.

While Manchester City's performance on the pitch was successful finishing in ninth position, toward the end of the 2007–2008 season, it became apparent that the promise of new funding for Manchester City had not materialised. For instance, during the course of the season, John Wardle, the former chairman, had loaned the club £2 million on three occasions to cover cash flow, while in July 2008 the club had to borrow £25 million from Standard Bank (Conn, 2008b). Amidst the financial turmoil, Thaksin Shinawatra faced increasing pressure from the democratically elected PPP party to return home to Thailand to face the charges of corruption. However, after the Beijing Olympics, he fled to the United Kingdom and was reported to have applied for political asylum (Conn, 2008c). Realising that his ownership could have adverse implications on the reputation of Manchester City, in August 2008 he agreed to sell the football club to the Abu Dhabi United Group and in the process made a profit of £20 million (Conn, 2008c). Since the sale in October 2008, the Thai courts sentenced Thaksin Shinawatra to two years imprisonment and issued a warrant for his arrest, while in November 2008 he was refused permission to enter the United Kindom (Conn, 2008d).

Questions

1. Does the "fit and proper" person test applied by the Premier League provide adequate and appropriate regulation on club ownership?

2. Should the directors on the board at Manchester City have rejected the offer made by Thaksin Shinawatra given the allegations of corruption and human rights violations?

OWNERSHIP IN EUROPEAN FOOTBALL

The ownership of football clubs is an equally important issue across Europe. While football clubs in England are constituted as limited companies, there are different legal structures and type of ownership model that exist within European football. This section looks briefly at types of ownership model found in the four major European football markets, including the membership model in Spain and Germany, the individual/family-owned model in Italy, and the Public Company for Professional Sport model in France.

Spain

The majority of the 42 professional clubs in Spain are constituted as *Sociedades Anónimas Deportiva* (SAD). A SAD is a joint-stock sporting company with limited liability, similar to the English model where the percentage of shares held in the football club determines the voting rights. The SAD model was introduced to the Spanish football industry in 1990 following a period of financial crisis brought on by the lack of central regulation, increasing commercial pressures, rising costs, poor financial performance and high levels of debt (Ascari and Gagnepain, 2006; Castillo, 2007). The legislative changes introduced by the Spanish government through Sport Law 10/1990—*ley del deporte*—contributed €192 million to cancel club debts (Ascari and Gagnepain, 2006, page 79) and brought an end to the membership model of ownership at all Spanish clubs except for FC Barcelona, Real Madrid, Athletic Bilbao, and Osasuna, who were allowed to retain the membership model of ownership as they had recorded a positive balance in their accounts during the 1985–1986 season. These clubs are governed democratically on the one member, one vote basis. At Barcelona, over 160,000 *socios* pay an annual membership fee that entitles them to vote for the club president every four years and to elect members to the board to oversee the administration of the club. They are also eligible for election to the assembly of delegates, a 3,000-member body that has responsibility to vote on issues of club governance.

Italy

The ownership of most of the most successful Italian football clubs is under the control of wealthy individual owners, families or corporations, mirroring ownership structures in the Italian corporate environment (Morrow, 2003, page 117). For example, the Moratti family are the direct owners of Inter Milan; the Agnelli family control Juventus through their holding company, Istituto Finanziario Industriale (IFI); and the majority shareholder in AC Milan, Fininvest, is owned by Italian Prime Minister Silvio Berlusconi

(Morrow, 2003). Three clubs—Juventus, Lazio and Roma—are listed on the Italian stock market, although only a minority percentage of shares are listed, enabling the family or corporations to maintain control and thus demonstrating little separation between ownership and control (Morrow, 2003). Almost all Italian football clubs are loss-making, so the only motive for ownership would be that of holding a "trophy" asset.

Germany

German football clubs were traditionally constituted as non-for-profit member associations. Since 1998, German clubs have been permitted to incorporate the professional football club as a subsidiary of the member association. This subsidiary company is constituted as a limited company or even a public limited company. By 2007, 17 of the 36 clubs in the Bundesliga had adopted this model (Dietl and Franck, 2007, page 665) on the grounds that it permitted a more professional and efficient hierarchical structure (Wilkesmann and Blutner, 2002). A number of clubs even chose to float on the German stock market, although share depreciation has been an issue. For example, the initial float price at Borussia Dortmund of €11 in October 2000 fell to €1.85 by January 2005 (Dietl and Franck, 2007, page 666).

Although German football clubs can list on the stock market, the ultimate ownership and decision-making power remains under the control of the member association. The German Football Association (*Deutsche Fußball-Bund*) rules state that the member association retains 50 per cent plus one vote of the incorporated football club, ensuring that the majority ownership of German football clubs cannot be granted to any one individual (Dietl and Franck, 2007, page 665). The football club remains under the control of the member association with members having the responsibility to elect the chief executive and members of the management board of the football club. This structure has limited foreign investment in German football clubs, although it is under pressure as more clubs want to change the ruling to allow foreign investment in the belief that this might make German clubs more competitive in European competition. Two-thirds of the members of the German Football Association and the Bundesliga are required to vote to accept the removal of this legislation. However, in October 2008, it was voted to keep the ruling in place, with the president of the Bundesliga arguing that it helps to maintain stability and protects the competition (*www.eufootball.biz*, 2008).

France

Football clubs in France were historically bound by the 1901 freedom of association law, which required the clubs to be constituted as non-profit-making organisations, thus limiting outside investment opportunities (King, 2003). However, financial problems in French football in the 1970s and 1980s led to constitutional change that enabled private investment but still forbade directors from receiving remuneration (Dobson and Goddard, 2001). This was altered in 1999 with the introduction of the *Société anonyme sportive professionelle* (Public Company for Professional Sport), which permitted football clubs to convert to limited companies and also to make profits and pay directors (Bolotny, 2006). Despite the introduction of the Public Company for Professional Sport, French clubs were initially not permitted to list on the stock exchange. However, intervention from the European Commission, which perceived this restriction to be a breach of the EC Treaty on the free movement of capital, resulted in legislation passed in 2006 to allow French clubs to list. Since then, only Lyon and Olympique Marseillle have floated and the majority of clubs in France remain under the ownership of a single individual and shares are not commonly available.

CONCLUSIONS

The three models of ownership that have become prominent in English football since 1992—the stock market model of ownership, the supporter trust model of ownership and the foreign ownership model—impact on club governance in different ways. With the stock market model of ownership there is an increase in transparency as football clubs have to publicly report on how they apply best practice guidelines on corporate governance as seen in the Combined Code (Financial Reporting Council, 2003). It can also be argued that the stock market model enables supporters, through minority share ownership, to have an increased voice in club governance through the right to attend annual general meetings and vote, in addition to receiving a copy of the annual report. However, although the Combined Code provides a framework of best practice, it does not guarantee a football club financial success. For example, the majority of football clubs listed on the stock exchange consistently failed to generate profit and delivered poor investor returns with decreasing share prices; a reflection on the difficulties in balancing investor interests with sporting performance. Furthermore, if supporters represent a minority shareholder group, the extent to which they are able to have an effective level of influence on club governance can be questioned. An additional criticism of the stock market model is the vulnerability of clubs to takeover. The Manchester United case is a good example of this. As a stock market–listed club, they were open to takeover and despite supporter protestations, the Glazer family was able to buy the club leveraged on high levels of debt.

The supporter trust model of ownership has clear implications for the governance of a football club. Through the cooperatively owned structure that promotes member democracy through the one-member, one vote status, trust members are able to have greater involvement in the governance of their club. This model also offers protection from outside investors and enables a club to become strongly rooted within its communities through an increased emphasis on an inclusive stakeholder approach. For example, at trust owned clubs there have been mechanisms implemented to integrate the needs of different stakeholders within the governance structures at each club and improve their stakeholder accountability to ensure that the club is more accountable to supporters and the community. A key aim is to also ensure that the club is run on a sustainable financial basis. However, operating on a financially sustainable basis has the potential to put a supporter trust owned club at a sporting disadvantage where other clubs owned by individuals are prepared to underwrite financial losses to achieve success on the pitch.

While the supporter trust model of ownership offers a football club a more sustainable long-term future rooted in the local communities, there is concern that the rise in foreign ownership in the Premier League might lead to a loss of local identity. Moreover, the move to a private company following a buyout leads to less accountability and transparency, two key issues in club governance. While it has been clear that some owners have been prepared to underwrite debts and annual financial losses, enabling an improved sporting performance, some clubs such as Manchester United and Liverpool are leveraged on high levels of debt requiring significant annual interest payments. This is a key issue if they fail to qualify for the Champions League or if broadcasting revenues decline. The need to repay interest on the debt has also resulted in increased ticket prices, which can lead to a further alienation of the core supporter base. With the rise in foreign ownership, there is also concern that the Premier League will in the future move toward the American sports model with a closed league system in order to maximise commercial revenues.

What is clear is that there are advantages and disadvantages to each type of ownership model. However, while the ownership of football clubs is clearly an important issue in the football industry, and different ownership models can impact on club governance, what is equally important is appropriate regulation from the football authorities to protect the integrity of the game and to encourage prudent financial management, accountability and transparency.

DISCUSSION QUESTIONS

1. What are the benefits and disadvantages of the different models of ownership in the English football industry?

2. Is one particular model of ownership more appropriate for a football club?

3. Can a member-owned model such as a supporter trust be successful on the pitch?

GUIDED READING

There is relatively little literature on the ownership and governance in the football industry within mainstream corporate governance texts. However, there are a number of football-specific texts that include sections that discuss the issue of ownership and governance including Banks (2002); Morrow (1999, 2003); Dobson and Goddard (2001); Szymanski and Kuypers (1999); and Hamil et al. (1999, 2000, 2001). The annual *State of the Game* reports from the Football Governance Research Centre (FGRC) at Birkbeck (2001–2006) are recommended to understand standards of club-level corporate governance in the football industry. The work of the sports journalist David Conn (1997) is also invaluable to help understanding of the issue of ownership and governance. Specialist academic journals that feature articles on ownership and governance in football include the *Journal of Sports Economics*, *European Sport Management Quarterly*, and *Soccer and Society*.

REFERENCES

Ascari, G., & Gagnepain, P. (2006). Spanish Football. *Journal of Sports Economics*, 7(1), 76–89.

Banks, S. (2002). *Going Down: Football in Crisis*. Edinburgh: Mainstream Publishing.

BBC Sport. (20th March, 2007). Daggers becomes a limited company. Retrieved on June 10, 2009, from http://news.bbc.co.uk/sport1/hi/football/teams/d/dagenham_and_redbridge/6471449.stm

Bolotny, F. (2006). Football in France. In W. Andreff, & S. Szymanski (Eds.), *Handbook on the Economics of Sport*. London: Edward Elgar Publishing Ltd.

Brown, A. (2007). 'Not for Sale'? The Destruction and Reformation of Football Communities in the Glazer Takeover of Manchester United. *Soccer and Society*, 8(4), 614–635.

Brown, A. (December, 2008). Direct action. *When Saturday Comes*.

Buraimo, B., Simmons, R., & Szymanski, S. (2006). English Football. *Journal of Sports Economics, 7*(1), 29–46.

Castillo, J. C. (2007). The concept of loyalty and the challenge of internationalisation in postmodern Spanish football. *International Journal of Iberian Studies, 20*(1), 23–40.

Conn, D. (1997). *The Football business: Fair game in the '90s?* Edinburgh: Mainstream.

Conn, D. (22nd October, 2008a). The credit crunch: club by club breakdown. *The Guardian*. Retrieved on June 10, 2009, from http://www.guardian.co.uk/football/2008/oct/22/premierleague

Conn, D. (27th August, 2008b). City face up to uncertain future as Thaksin awaits verdict. *The Guardian*. Retrieved on June 10, 2009, from http://www.guardian.co.uk/football/2008/aug/27/manchestercity.premierleague

Conn, D. (8th October, 2008c). Thaksin doubled his money in City sale, claim sources. *The Guardian*. Retrieved on June 10, 2009, from http://www.guardian.co.uk/football/2008/oct/08/manchestercity.premierleague

Conn, D. (12th November, 2008d). Hammers and City takesovers went wrong, says deal-maker. *The Guardian*. Retrieved on June 10, 2009, from http://www.guardian.co.uk/football/2008/nov/12/premierleague-westhamunited

Deloitte (2009). *Annual Review of Football Finance*. Manchester: Deloitte.

Deloitte (2007). *Annual Review of Football Finance*. Manchester: Deloitte.

Dietl, H., & Franck, E. (2007). Governance Failure and Financial Crisis in German Football. *Journal of Sports Economics, 8*(6), 662–669.

Dobson, S., & Goddard, J. (2001). *The Economics of Football*. Cambridge: Cambridge University Press.

EUfootballbiz.com (21st October, 2008). DFL reaffirms Ownership limitations. Retrieved on June 10, 2009, from http://www.eufootball.biz/Clubs/6254-DFL-reaffirms-foreign-ownership-limitations.html

FGRC. (2001–2006). *The State of the Game: the Corporate Governance of Professional Football*, Research Paper series, FGRC. Birkbeck: University of London.

Financial Reporting Council. (2003). *The Combined Code on Corporate Governance*. London: Financial Reporting Council.

Hamil, S. (2008). Manchester United; the commercial development of a global brand. In S. Chadwick, & D. Arthur, *International Cases in the Business of Sport*, Oxford: Butterworth-Heinemann.

Hamil, S., Michie, J., Oughton, C., & Warby, S. (Eds.), (2001). *The Changing face of the Football Business*. London: Frank Cass.

Hamil, S., Michie, J., Oughton, C. Warby, S (Eds.), (2000). Football in the Digital Age: Whose Game Is It Anyway? Edinburgh: Mainstream.

Hamil, S., Michie, J., & Oughton, C. (Eds.), (1999). *The Business of Football: A Game of Two Halves*. Edinburgh: Mainstream.

Harvey, A. (2005). *Football: The First Hundred Years*. London: Routledge.

King, A. (2003). *The European Ritual: Football in the New Europe*. Aldershot: Ashgate.

Martin, P. (2007). Football, Community and Cooperation: A Critical Analysis of Supporter Trusts in England. *Soccer and Society*, 8(4), 636–653.

Morrow, S. (2003). *The People's Game?: Football, Finance and Society*. Hampshire. Palgrave Macmillan.

Morrow, S. (2000). Football clubs on the Stock Exchange: An inappropriate match? *The Irish Accounting Review*, 7(2), 61–90.

Morrow, S. (1999). *The New Business of Football: Accountability and Finance in Football*. Hampshire: MacMillan Business.

Shareliverpool.com. Retrieved on June 10, 2009, from http://www.shareliverpoolfc.com/index.php/work

Sloane, P. (1971). The Economics of Professional Football: The Football Club as a Utility Maximiser. *Scottish Journal of Political Economy*, June: 121–146

Szymanski, S., & Kuypers, T. (1999). *Winners and Losers: The Business Strategy of Football*. London: Penguin Books.

Taylor, D. (8th September, 2008). New City owners plan to be 'the Virgin of Asia'. *The Guardian*. Retrieved on June 10, 2009, from http://www.guardian.co.uk/football/2008/sep/08/manchestercity.premierleague

Tomlinson, A. (1991). The rivalry of the Football League and the Football Association. In J. Williams, & S. Wagg (Eds.), *British football and Social Change: Getting into Europe*. Leicester: Leicester University Press.

Winter, H. (12th August, 2008). Soap Opera involving Thaksin Shinawatra and Manchester City damaging our game: Normally people on the run in England go to Thailand. *The Daily Telegraph*, Retrieved on June 10, 2009, from http://www.telegraph.co.uk/sport/football/leagues/premierleague/mancity/2542658/Soap-opera-involving-Thaksin-Shinwatra-and-Manchester-City-damaging-our-game—Footbal.html

Wilkesmann, U., & Blutner, D. (2002). The organizational restructuring of German Football Clubs. *Soccer and Society*, 3(2), 19–37.

RECOMMENDED WEBSITES

Eufootball.biz website
www.eufootball.biz
Football economy website
www.footballeconomy.com
The main London stock exchange
www.londonstockexchange.com
The Manchester United Supporters Trust (MUST)
www.joinmust.org

The OFEX/Plus stock markets
www.ofex.com
ShareLiverpoolFC
www.shareliverpool.com
Supporters Direct
www.supporters-direct.org

CHAPTER 3

New Media Challenges in the Twenty-First Century

James Santomier
Sacred Heart University

Artur Costabiei
University of Florence

Objectives

Upon completion of this chapter the reader should be able to:

- Understand the synergistic relationship between football content distribution and new media technologies.
- Understand the nature and dynamics of new media technologies and their relevance for football entertainment.
- Understand and identify the most important parameters for developing, implementing, and managing new media projects.
- Identify and discuss important new media challenges and issues facing football enterprise managers.

CONTENTS

OVERVIEW OF THE CHAPTER

As competition for consumer "attention" intensifies, the challenge for football enterprises worldwide is to gain a competitive advantage. Competition for attention, therefore, has become a major tenet for integrating new media within football enterprises. Although the integration of new media technologies offers enhanced access and opportunity for consumers, broadcasters, and sports league/club/event managers, it also has changed the methods used to produce, distribute, and consume sport content. The synergetic relationship between sport and new media is facilitated by the increasing complexity of the global sport industry, the increased demand for sport content by global media companies, and the rapid convergence of consumer needs worldwide. Football managers should be prepared to identify new media resources that are relevant to their enterprise and the benefits and potential opportunities offered by these new technologies. For football managers, emphasis should be placed on understanding conceptual and practical dimensions of developing a comprehensive approach to managing the implementation of new media. This chapter addresses the relationship between football content and new media technologies and discusses the central challenges and issues related to new media integration.

INTRODUCTION

Football is one of the most popular forms of sport content and, regardless of the distribution platform, drives consumer usage and market penetration. Football content is an asset that, if managed properly, should increase in value, generate significant revenue, and attract new consumers, sponsors, and partnerships. The integration of new media has contributed to increasing the value of football content because it offers a broad range of new channels of distribution as well as unique and dynamic ways of connecting with football consumers.

As a direct result of the integration of new media technologies, many football enterprises are now maintaining their broadcast rights, leveraging their digital content, enhancing their brands, and generating significant broadcast revenue. The disintermediation (Real, 1998) of media rights for football content and media fragmentation worldwide has facilitated its distribution across multiple digital platforms. New media has evolved into a dynamic and commercially viable component of football entertainment, and football enterprise managers are establishing or reevaluating organisational objectives and making operational and financial decisions in an increasingly competitive and technologically complex business environment. Therefore, it is important to understand the unique dimensions, issues, and challenges associated with developing, implementing, and managing new media within the football enterprise.

NEW MEDIA

New media is the result of the convergence of telecommunications, computing, and traditional media, and it generally refers to a digital media production that is both interactive and digitally distributed. New media technologies include websites, live and on demand streaming of audio and video content on the Internet and mobile devices, chat rooms, blogs, e-mail, social networking (also referred to as social media), digital advertising, DVD and CD-ROM media, virtual reality environments, Internet telephony, digital cameras, and mobile technologies. The most relevant new media technologies for sport include broadband access to the Internet, high-definition TV (HDTV), interactive TV (iTV), and 3G/4G (third- and fourth-generation mobile communications) wireless technologies.

Broadband

New media technologies are driven primarily by high-speed always on "broadband" delivery and Internet access via cable modems and/or digital subscriber lines (DSL). Broadband access provides a "two-way" capability, which enables consumers to both receive (download) and transmit (upload) data at high speeds. The rollout of wireless fidelity (WiFi) networks has provided millions of "placeshifting" consumers wanting football content anytime and anywhere with wireless connectivity to the Internet and instant access to their favourite teams.

Manchester United, the world's most valuable football franchise and the most popular football franchise online, attracted 2.2 million unique visitors to its website during March 2007. Interestingly, approximately 60 percent, or 1.3 million of Manchester United's 2.2 million monthly visitors, reside outside the United Kingdom. The other most popular football franchise websites in that month were Liverpool (1.5 million global unique visitors), Arsenal (1.4 million), Real Madrid (1.1 million), Barcelona (1.05 million), Chelsea (1.0 million), and A.C. Milan (0.8 million) (*PRNewswire*, 2007).

Due to the rapid penetration of broadband, which is predicted to be in 400 million homes by 2009, football enterprises have increased their global fan base and revenue significantly. For example, FL Interactive, the online business unit of the Football League, provided record financial distributions of more than £3 million to franchises for the 2007–2008 season. The distribution represented a 50 percent increase over the previous year and was the result of a significant redesign of franchise websites, which provide access to 4.5 million consumers. FL Interactive manages and develops Internet and mobile rights for 65 Football League franchises, 6 Premier League franchises, and 8 franchises from the Football Conference (Glendinning, 2008).

Broadband services create additional revenue streams for football enterprises because they are another "distribution channel." Revenue generated from consumers using broadband services to access football content, such as matches, football-related games, or highlight clips, has become a significant revenue stream for broadcasters and rights holders. In addition to subscription services via cable/DSL, satellite, and mobile technology companies, revenues are derived from advertising, sponsorship, e-commerce, content syndication, Pay-Per-View, and gaming, including Fantasy Sports.

High-Definition TV

High-definition TV (HDTV) is perhaps the most significant quality innovation in sport broadcasting. HD presents an opportunity for broadcasters to gain a competitive advantage by maintaining technology leadership and for pay-TV broadcasters, in particular, to attract new subscribers by enhancing their premium offerings. HD provides at least a four times better picture quality than conventional TV, and HD production quickly has emerged as the global industry standard via two common formats, 1080i and 720p. HDTV has twice as many scanning lines as the conventional standard-definition TV and offers tremendous realism and immediacy.

Sports have consistently played an important role in helping to attract consumers to new technologies, and HDTV is especially suited for broadcasting football. It addresses the need of consumers for enhanced picture quality and sound, and watching football via HDTV is a new and often exhilarating experience for many consumers. Images can also be produced in HD quality for Internet streaming and VOD, as well as mobile networks.

Interactive TV

Interactive TV (iTV) delivers digital interactive services that are integrated with traditional TV. These services are broadcast alongside the video feed and are instantly accessible, which allows distributors and advertisers to mass-customise their digital communications. NDS is a company that creates the security and enabling technologies, as well as the interactive applications that allow operators to generate revenues by delivering digital content to TVs, set-top boxes (STBs), digital video recorders (DVRs), PCs, mobile phones, portable media players (PMPs), removable media, and other devices. A leader in sport iTV, NDS created a complex and interactive application specifically for the 2002 FIFA World Cup that allowed consumers to engage in interactive activities such as voting for their favourite team, choosing multiple camera angles, accessing match statistics, and viewing match highlights.

Mobile Technologies

Mobile technologies include a number of wireless devices, including mobile handsets, personal digital assistants (PDAs), and Wireless Fidelity (WiFi) hotspots, which have enabled laptop computers to become part of the mobile universe. Mobile sport content has proven revenue streams because of a large consumer base that subscribes to sport related services. For football rights holders, mobile technologies provide new opportunities to enhance the relationship with consumers, and for mobile operators it is an essential part of their content offering, which is used to drive mobile subscriber upgrades.

Mobile technologies represent an effective way for football brands to reach new consumers and provide value-added components to dedicated consumers. The almost universal availability of mobile phones and significant market penetration worldwide provide football brands with an opportunity to reach a large and often specifically targeted audience. In addition to SMS (short messaging services) and MMS (multimedia messaging services), network operators, in cooperation with their broadcast partners, are able to offer unique football branded ring tones, wallpapers, interactive games, ticketing, voting, and competitions as a dimension of football sponsorship activation.

In 2007, the English Premier League received approximately US$150 million (£74 million/€109 million) over three years from the sale of its mobile and Internet clips. The largest percentage of the fees was from domestic agreements for mobile rights with British Sky Broadcasting for £30 million (€44 million/US$61 million) and for Internet rights with Virgin Media for £25 million. International rights sales for the mobile and Internet clip rights will generate approximately US$40 million over the same period (Pickles, 2007). It is estimated that from 2006 through 2011, mobile sport, leisure, and information content and services are expected to generate cumulative revenue of approximately US$42 billion, of which 40 percent will come from Europe, 33 percent from Asia Pacific, and 18 percent from North America (Pickles, 2007). Since mobile technologies are a significant component of the distribution of football content, it is important for managers to understand the personalisation, search, and content possibilities in a wireless environment.

Other specific new media technologies currently impacting the production and consumption of sport include the following (Bernstein, 2005):

1. Recent innovations in digital asset management, which involve the placement of digital video footage into a network for storage and editing. When that media is recorded with statistics and encoded with time stamps and other data, it can be accessed instantly.

2. Optical tracking systems, which are methods of tracking a moving object, such as a ball, with a camera.

3. Portable people meters, which are devices that pick up an audio tag (silent to humans but detectable by the device) embedded in advertising on various measured radio and television stations. The system is designed to monitor out-of-home viewing and listening.

4. Sports ticker, which is a device that keeps consumers linked to their favourite teams' data stream.

5. Online video gaming.

6. Satellite radio.

NEW MEDIA INTEGRATION IN FOOTBALL—THE CASE OF FIFA

At the International Football Club Summit that was held in South Africa in November 2008, one of the workshops was entitled "21st-Century Foot ball—Broadcasting Platforms, Media Rights & Web 2.0." Participants included FIFA, UEFA, the French Football League (LFP), and Host Broadcast Services (HBS). The panel, which addressed the issue of media rights segmentation and its impact on revenue, included FIFA's Head of New Media, who informed the football industry regarding FIFA's new media strategy of embracing Web 2.0 as a means to improve interaction with consumers.

FIFA has made a significant commitment to new media, and until the 2008 Beijing Olympics, the 2006 FIFA World Cup was the most advanced global sport event relative to the integration of digital broadcast production and distribution technologies. FIFA, with its media partner Host Broadcasting Service (HBS), provided more content, more delivery capacity through more systems and devices, and a larger variety of digital platforms than any previous sport event. HBS produced a "New Media Content Package" that consisted of an extensive range of new media–specific material and services. The content reflected the demands of new media licensees and allowed them to deliver football content directly to their customer base, whether online or via mobile networks, while limiting unilateral end-to-end production costs.

HBS provided the primary broadcast feed in 16/9 HDTV digital format for all 64 games, which required the deployment of 25 widescreen HDTV cameras, hi-motion cameras (which take 300 frames a second), stump cameras (small cameras placed in devices used for the action), and super-slow-motion cameras. The HDTV feed from all venues was delivered directly to the new media unit at the International Broadcasting Centre (IBC) in Munich, where a dedicated new media package was produced so licensees were not required to edit it extensively. Innovations such as "pan-and-scan" technology, which was originally developed to reduce movies to the smaller-format TV screen, were used to allow editors to zoom in and capture key action, such as a specific goal, producing a picture that was much more dramatic and relevant for the smaller mobile screens.

In addition to broadcasting all 2006 FIFA World Cup games in HDTV, other important new media innovations included the involvement of consumers in user-generated content (UGC), which included photo and video sharing as part of the social media experience, and the availability of World Cup content via mobile phones, which was most popular in Italy, the tournament winners.

The 2006 FIFA World Cup website became the most successful single sport event website in history with 4.2 billion page views (Fifa.com, 2006). Regarding the website, FIFA president Sepp Blatter stated the following:

> We are offering a one-stop destination for all information on and around the FIFA World Cup in nine languages. The unparalleled coverage produced by 50 FIFA editors coming from 20 different countries and the wealth and depth of content on FIFAworldcup.com have been recognised by football lovers around the world as the best place to follow the event online.

The website was jointly produced, marketed, and hosted by FIFA and the U.S.-based technology company Yahoo! Inc., which provided more opportunities for sponsorships. Yahoo! experimented with corporate sponsorships for each of its separate features. Sportswear maker Adidas AG sponsored a goal counter, Emirates Airline sponsored a game time chart, Global Gillette sponsored the online voting for the Best Young Player Award, and McDonald's Corporation sponsored the website's fantasy soccer game.

The 2006 FIFA World Cup provided new elements of User Generated Content (UGC) for football consumers and broadcasters, which included the following:

■ New ways of experiencing football events.
■ Participation and involvement through self-production of videos and pictures, blogs, forums, games, file sharing, and message boards.
■ The ability of football enterprises to test what consumers want, what advertisers will buy, and how to filter the right UGC into their websites.
■ The ability of the football enterprise to keep its content germane to the consumer.

CASE STUDY 3.1: The 2006 FIFA World Cup

The following case discusses developments in the run-up to the 2006 FIFA World Cup.

Yahoo!, which managed the international soccer federation's website, decked the site with interactive features: blogs, chats, and contests along with three- to five-minute video highlights following each of the tournament's 64 games. Although it and other U.S. sites were not broadcasting the games live online, fans were able to post their own photos and videos on FIFAworldcup.com, which also offered Match-Cast—a kind of animated telecast of the game that graphically displayed players on the field, ball location, timeouts, and live scores. Jorge Consuegra, general manager of Yahoo!'s FIFA partnership, said the following in an e-mailed interview.

Who argues more than sports fans? We've tried to give them a great mechanism to give their opinions on the Web with the most cutting-edge technology—in as many languages as possible. Creating a global community around the biggest sporting event in the world—that's the biggest step for this site. The marketing itself can play a role in bringing people back to the site. It's all about giving fans something to do once the game is over. We have to be that bridge for fans that carries them from game to game.

Source: Washingtonpost.com (June 10th, 2006).

Question

1. Why is User Generated Content (UGC) so important to include as part of a multi-platform new media strategy?

NEW MEDIA INTEGRATION IN FOOTBALL—THE CASE OF UEFA

In March 2008, the UEFA Media Committee was established to address all media issues relating to UEFA and football. The establishment of the committee may have been directly related to the issues UEFA was addressing with the European Newspaper Publishers' Association (ENPA) regarding "the proposed restrictions on the use of online photography and the amount of access given to non-rights-holders beyond the match stadiums" (*Sports City*, 2008a). Ultimately the ENPA was given more freedom to publish digital photos, and UEFA lifted all restrictions in reporting from nonmatch venues.

The committee's primary role is to advise UEFA "on determining the organisational requirements for media work at UEFA events, on collaborating with organisations covering UEFA events, and on public relations work" (UEFA, 2008). In addition, the committee monitors issues related to accreditation at UEFA events, fosters cooperation with international media organisations, and surveys developments in the media sector and makes proposals for addressing new challenges. UEFA also has created its own new media service company: UEFA Media Technologies SA (UMT). According to CEO Alexandre Fourtoy (2007), it is responsible for the production of all

UEFA's content, including online, mobile, and host broadcasting operations. In addition, UMT's mission is "to explore and exploit all opportunities in the new media world and assist the football family in their technology developments."

The Euro 2008 Championship website, *www.euro2008.com*, which was launched in February 2008, recorded over 1 billion page views by June 24, 2008 (*SportBusiness News*, 2008c). Over 42 million visitors from over 200 countries accessed text, multimedia, and video coverage of the EURO matches in June 2008, and up to 4.3 million visitors accessed the website on a single day of the tournament. The 2008 website traffic represented an increase of 250 percent compared to Euro2004.com. The website, which was available in seven European languages and three Asian languages, was launched one hundred days prior to the start of the competition, and initially the key feature of the website was the ability to view on demand (VOD) 130 historical matches of the tournament. Once the 2008 competition began, the website featured live video streaming of the 16 competing teams, as well as video, audio, text, and photo content and a forum for user participation, which allowed consumers to leave comments and opinions on blogs and photo blogs as part of the "Fanzone" section.

All of the Euro 2008 content was distributed from a central location, which provided video, audio, text, and photo content needs. In addition, the website offered three different types of video coverage: live match simulcast in collaboration with UEFA broadcast partners, video on-demand offering individual matches, and highlights and free videos produced as "vodcasts." UEFA also offered a video service, which was available at *http://video.uefa. com*. For €19.99, consumers could purchase a Euro 2008 Pass that included all of the 31 matches in the tournament as well as reruns and highlights (*SportBusiness News*, 2008b).

In addition, KIT, a global provider of Internet protocol TV (IPTV) technology and SNTV (a joint venture between IMG and the Associated Press), one of the world's leading sport news agencies, produced and packaged coverage of Euro2008. The package delivered to subscribers included ten daily clips of events online or on their mobile handsets, including pre- and postmatch reactions and interviews with players, tournament organizers, and spectators.

Regarding the sales of media content rights going forward, UEFA has made major changes in the rights sales format for the 2009–2012 cycle of the UEFA Champions League, UEFA Super Cup, and the UEFA Cup. The process will be managed by TEAM marketing AG, which is the exclusive marketing partner of UEFA for these competitions. The rights package consists of 205 games over 15 match weeks each season. The most interesting of the changes is that media content rights will be granted on a platform-neutral basis. Essentially, what this means is that the bidders who are successful for live match rights will also benefit from exclusivity across all media platforms, including TV, Internet, and mobile during the live match. According to *Sports City (2008*c), "By implementing a platform neutral rights structure, UEFA has recognised the convergence of transmission techniques while further promoting the use of Internet and mobile technologies to deliver content."

NEW MEDIA CHALLENGES

Marketing

Probably the most significant opportunity for football enterprises presented by new media is its ability to develop deeper relationships with consumers. The opportunity to increase the distribution of football content, generate new audiences, connect with highly identified consumers, and create dynamic communities is extremely valuable and in the long-term will result in significant financial value. Interactivity, niche information, and person-alisation are core elements of almost all new media initiatives, and as new media technologies evolve, they will provide increased distribution of specific football content. In addition, customer relations management (CRM) software tools provide marketers with consumers' identities, addresses, purchasing habits, and other personal information.

The key to integrating new media successfully into the football enterprise ultimately depends on the ability of specific football content to aggregate a sufficient number of consumers over multiple platforms. The ability to aggregate, identify, and track large numbers of consumers enables the football enterprise to satisfy their specific needs through mass tailoring on an individual basis. Therefore, the challenge for football brands is to successfully integrate social media and niche marketing as well as extend their global reach. Football managers should understand the dynamics and strategies of social media and viral marketing. For example, online communication allowed the entire world to share in the sudden increase of interest regarding David Beckham's new position with U.S.-based Major League Soccer (MLS). Although football enterprises should leverage the Internet for branding, marketing campaigns should be part of an integrated strategy that is benchmarked using diverse metrics and multiple-media platforms, including TV and print. The key value proposition of new media is that it allows consumers to drill deeper into visual and textual information, resulting in increased revenue.

User-Generated Content

User-Generated Content (UGC) describes a variety of new sources of online information that is created, initiated, and circulated by consumers who are intent on educating one another about products, brands, services, personalities, and issues. UGC refers to any number of online or social media vehicles, including but not limited to consumer-to-consumer e-mail, postings on public Internet discussion boards and forums, consumer ratings of websites or forums, blogs (short for weblogs, or digital diaries), moblogs (sites where users post digital images/photos/movies), and social networking and individual websites.

The growth of UGC, however, may pose challenges and opportunities primarily, in part, because some UGC content may be potentially negative for football brands or players. From a content distribution perspective, football enterprises should develop an appropriate strategy for managing and integrating appropriately selected UGC with traditional football content. Generally, content such as videos, blogs, photos, and so forth is developed and posted by users. However, some football content may be made available to consumers so they can create their own services. In some instances, users may collect football content from a variety of digital feeds and create their own services—a video, blog, and so on. In this case, the football enterprise is in the position of determining what specific football content will be made available to users for self-production.

The Eurosport group, for example, launched an innovative Facebook application that was available in five language versions: English, French, German, Spanish, and Italian. Arnaud Maillard (*SportBusiness News*, 2008a), Eurosport's Internet Director, said the following:

> We are excited to increase our presence on the world's largest social networking portal. The Eurosport online team focuses on exchange and interactiveness between the Eurosport platform and sports fans all over the world. We are constantly working on revamping our online offer, offering our users cutting-edge online products within the world of sports.

Digital Rights

Media fragmentation has resulted in significant issues within the broadcast industry, and the numerous ways that content can now be viewed seriously impacts its value. Broadcast enterprises worldwide are confronted with the need to protect their digital assets, and for football, as well as other sports enterprises, the central intellectual property issue is how to monetise digital rights, develop a brand, and at the same time remain open to some degree to important grassroots, consumer-driven, interactive efforts such as blogging, video posting, and UGC (Fisher, 2008). This goal is becoming more daunting by the day, as video sharing sites proliferate on the Internet. According to Haynes (2007, page 48), "In the age of Beckham and Rooney, Ronaldo and Zidane, the attempt to commercially control both images and information around football has never been so great."

The Digital Millennium Copyright Act provides safe harbour to those websites that take down copyright-infringing content on request from the copyright owner. However, policing websites takes an enormous amount of time and effort. In 2007, the English Premier League sued Google Inc.'s YouTube for copyright infringement. The lawsuit charged that YouTube "deliberately encourages massive copyright infringement on its website to generate public attention and boost traffic. This has resulted in the loss of valuable content" (Kahn and Auchard, 2007). Lawyers for Google contended that the plaintiff misunderstood the Digital Millennium Copyright Act. A football enterprise's broadcast rights are its most important asset, and organisations are taking important steps to guard them. One example of this is the increasing worldwide demand for digital rights management software, which is expected to reach US$3.6 billion by the end of 2008.

Managing New Media

Although new media offers many opportunities, developing and integrating new media into the football enterprise presents a number of challenges, including the following:

1. Identifying the objectives and opportunities for integrating new media.
2. Determining what specific new media technologies are appropriate.
3. Developing (or finding) relevant new media management skills.
4. Creating new financial resources to maintain existing levels of media expenditure and funding.
5. Developing necessary production skills within the enterprise to capture and store digital content and use it effectively and efficiently.
6. Sourcing the technology skills that will enable all the previous challenges to be met.

The following brief summary, which is adapted from Briggs (2003), should provide football managers with a basis from which to develop, implement,

CASE STUDY 3.2: English Premier League to Sue YouTube

The following review from the Mashable.com website (2007) illustrates a key battle line over the use of content in new media.

"We reported previously that the English Premier League, the football/soccer body in England, was riled about YouTube's use of unauthorized clips. Now it's going to the courts: The Premier League, along with sheet music publisher Bourne Co., has filed a class action suit against YouTube, adding more legal woes to the $1 billion suit brought by Viacom.

Soccer is big business: the Premier League took £2.7 billion (US$5.4 billion) for the TV, radio, and Internet rights to live games and highlights over the next three years. It's the most lucrative football league in the world, with games shown in 204 countries worldwide. The action has been filed in a New York federal court.

What's more, the Premier League is drumming up support from others, essentially declaring all-out war on Google and YouTube. They've set up YouTubeClassAction.com, which argues the League's, side of the case and invites others to join the class action.

Long story short: old businesses making a lot of money from established business models come under threat and sue. But in truth, it's really just putting the brakes on: there's a massive demand to watch all these games and highlights online (preferably for free), and eventually deals will be worked out somehow. We hate these cases reflexively because of their anti-innovation: YouTube has figured out a way to give consumers what they want, and the Premier League's business model hasn't caught up."

Source: http://mashable.com/2007/05/04/english-premier-league-sues-youtube/

Questions

1. Why are a football enterprise digital rights so important, and why is the English Premier League so concerned about a few clips showing on YouTube?

2. Go to *www.youtube.com,* and search for football videos. What specific football teams have agreements with YouTube to place content on the website?

and manage new media projects. A number of characteristics are shared by successful new media projects:

1. They are relatively simple conceptually.
2. Revenue is considered during the development phase of the project.
3. Revenue is maximised by a repeatable format, which means that subsequent versions of the format should appeal to audiences over time.
4. Formats include "viral" elements and possibly a format that allows consumers to contribute material or opinions, or to vote on specific football topics.
5. Consideration is given to the strengths and weaknesses of specific new media platforms, knowing that success is more likely if a multiplatform approach is selected.
6. There is a cultural fit with the target audience and with prevailing and emerging trends and attitudes.

In addition to the preceding elements, managers may want to use the following steps to ensure that the project is developed and implemented appropriately.

Assembling a core team to assist in the development. Select appropriate personnel with the conceptual understanding and practical skills needed to develop new media multiplatform projects.

Brainstorming specifically about content and technology opportunities in order to take the concept beyond the initial idea. Provide an opportunity for the development team to identify and discuss alternative strategies and technologies that might be appropriate for the project. With any new media project, it is necessary to encourage key personnel to "think outside of the box."

Market testing on a representative audience or focus group. It is always good marketing practice to present the initial new media project or a prototype to a group of potential consumers/users so they can provide the development team with feedback regarding user interface issues, accessibility, content, and so on.

Financing, budgeting, and revenue. It is necessary to develop a realistic understanding of the initial start-up costs of a new media project, establish appropriate budget guidelines, and understand the nature and source of the revenue streams that will eventually be generated by the project. It may require considerable investment in time and money before anticipated revenue streams are realized.

Legal and rights issues. In the initial stages of development, it is necessary to identify the most important legal parameters under which the development team will be working. Specific legal requirements related to broadcast or e-commerce, or corporate policies related to the establishment of the new media project, including the nature and extent of the content that will be distributed through the project, should be identified and addressed well in advance. In addition, if appropriate, it should be very clear that the distribution of the specific football content is within the negotiated rights agreement.

Technology planning. This involves identifying the specific technology hardware and software required by the development team in order to successfully execute the project. This may include digital cameras, T-1 digital trunk lines, servers, e-commerce platforms, and so on. The development team generally will make a determination about which hardware and software requirements will be outsourced.

Prototyping. A new media prototype may be a new computer concept.

Constructing and testing a beta version. The new media development team is responsible for developing and delivering a new project. Once a project has been constructed and scrutinized from different perspectives (financial, marketing, legal, etc.), it may be deemed "consumer ready." At this stage the project is presented to a very select group of consumers who have been charged with providing feedback to the development team. Once the feedback is received and any additional modifications are required, the project is approved and ready to "go live."

Quality control. This is a process that continues throughout the new media project's life cycle. Depending on the nature of the project, it may require data management, website updating, addressing technical issues that may arise, and generally ensuring that consumers are receiving the specified football content when and where they demand it.

Delivery and marketing. This issue addresses the need to ensure that the delivery of the specified football content is as intended and that appropriate marketing management processes are in place to be sure that consumers are aware of the dynamics involving multiplatform delivery. It may also include elements of sponsorship activation, CRM, and advertising.

Ongoing management/maintenance. Because of their nature, all new media projects require significant attention and effective management. The fast-moving digital space requires managers to address multiple issues, including the maintenance of new technologies, including e-commerce platforms.

CONCLUSIONS

Developing and implementing a multiplatform new media project is a significant undertaking that requires many different and unique skills on the part of the manager. Dynamic strategic planning is needed for developing and integrating mission-critical new media into the systems and operations of football enterprises. Most important, business managers of football clubs must realise that although new media is complex, with intelligent and rational strategic planning and e-business implementation, it allows for maximum adaptation to environmental changes.

DISCUSSION QUESTIONS

1. The development and integration of new media into a football enterprise can be a daunting experience for football managers, even at the professional level. What kind of new media projects might be appropriate for a lower division or even a local football club?

2. What are the purposes and objectives of integrating new media into the football enterprise? Would these be the same at all levels of competition? What would the differences be, if any?

GUIDED READING

Although new media has become an important dimension of the sport industry worldwide, there is a paucity of literature available that addresses this issue directly. Much of the information that is available can be found in online newsletters such as *Online Media Daily* and *Marketing Daily*, both of which are Media Post publications (*http://mediapost.com*). *Sport & Technology.com* was an excellent resource for new media information; however, it is no longer available. There are articles covering a variety of dimensions of new media in *SportBusiness International* and via its online platform at *http://www. sportbusiness.com,* and *Sports Business Journal* and via its online platform at *http://www.sportsbusinessjournal.com.* A recent issue of the *European Sport Management Quarterly* (Vol. 7, No. 4) included an excellent article by Paul Turner, which addressed "The Impact of Technology on the Supply of Sport Broadcasting". *The Journal of Broadcasting and Electronic Media* does not address sports specifically, but the information available is often appropriate for sports industry professionals. *The Journal of New Media and Culture* (*http://www.ibiblio.org/nmediac/#*) is an excellent online journal that addresses numerous issues related to the emergence of new media.

REFERENCES

Bernstein, A. (8th August, 2005). Ten Technologies That Are Changing the Way People Consume Sports. *SportsBusiness Journal*, p. 15. Retrieved on August 10, 2005, from *http://www.sportsbusinessjournal.com*.

Briggs, J. (16th June, 2003). Managing New Media Projects: From Conceptual Development to Commercial Exploitation. *OTHER Media*. Retrieved on August 15, 2005, from *http://othermedia.com*

Fifa.com (9th July, 2006). A record breaking kick-off for FIFA worldcup.com. *Fifa.com*. Retrieved on June 2, 2009 from *http://www.fifa.com/worldcup/ archive/germany2006/media/newsid=17358.html*

Fisher, E. (4th February, 2008). Guarding Online Content. *Sports Business Journal*. Retrieved on February 4, 2008, from *http://www.sportsbusinessjournal.com*

Fourtoy, A. (2007). Q & A: Alexandre Fourtoy, CEO UEFA Media Technologies. *Sport And Technology*, October. Retrieved on November 15, 2007, from *http://www.sportandtechnology.com*

Glendinning, M. (2008). £3m Payout to Football League Clubs. *Sportbusiness.com*. Retrieved on October 22, 2008, from *http://www.sportbusiness.com/news*

Haynes, R. (2007). Footballers' Image Rights in the New Media Age. *European Sport Management Quarterly, Vol. 7*(No.4), 361–374.

Kahn, M. & E. Auchard. (2007). Premier League Soccer Sues YouTube Over Copyright. *Reuters*. Retrieved on May 4, 2007, from *http://www.reuters.com*

Mashable.com (4th May, 2007). English Premier League to sue YouTube. *Mashable.com*. Retrieved on July 24, 2009, from *http://mashable.com/2007/05/04/english-premier-league-sues-youtube/*.

Pickles, J. (2007). Ad Growth Drives New-Media. *TV Sports Markets, Vol. 11* (No. 16), 1–2.

PRNewswire. (2008a). KIT Digital Brings Euro2008 and Summer Olympics to Broadband and Mobile Providers Around the World. *PRNewswire*. Retrieved on June 16, 2008, from *http://www.prnewswire.com*.

PRNewswire. (2008b). The Official UEFA EURO 2008(TM) Website—Euro2008.com. *PRNewswire*. Retrieved on April 17, 2008, from *http://biz.yahoo.com/prnews*

PRNewswire. (2007). Top European Football Clubs Have Global Fan Base. *PRNewswire*. Retrieved on May 16, 2007, from *http://www.prnewswire.com*

Real, M. (1998). MediaSport: Technology and the Commodification of Post-modern Sport. In L. Wenner (Ed.), *MediaSport*. London: Routledge.

SportBusiness News. (6th June, 2008a). Eurosport Launches on Facebook. Retrieved on June 6, 2008, from *http://www.sportbusiness.com/news*.

SportBusiness News. (3rd June, 2008b). UEFA Launches Online Video Service for EURO 2008. Retrieved on June 3, 2008, from *http://www.sportbusiness.com/news*.

SportBusiness News. (24th June, 2008c). 1 Billion Page Views Sets a New Record for Euro2008.com. Retrieved on June 24, 2008, from *http://www.sportbusiness.com/new*.

Sports City. (2008a). FIFA and UEFA to Take Part in Media Focused Workshop At Soccerex 2008. Retrieved on October 10, 2008, from *http://www.sports-city.org/news*.

Sports City. (2008b). UEFA Agree to Relax Euro 2008 Media Restrictions. Retrieved on April 30, 2008, from *http://www.sports-city.org/news*.

Sports City. (2008c). UEFA Launches Media Content Rights Sales. Retrieved on January 17, 2008, from *http://www.sports-city.org/news*.

Turner, P. (2007). The Impact of Technology on the Supply of Sport Broadcasting. *European Sport Management Quarterly, Vol. 7*(No. 4), 333–360.

UEFA. (2008). Media Studies on Agenda. Retrieved on March 3, 2008, from *http://www.uefa.com*.

Washingtonpost.com (June 10th, 2006). With World Cup, A New Media Game. Retrieved on June 2, 2009 from *http://www.washingtonpost.com/wp-dyn/content/article/2006/06/09/AR2006060901643.html*

RECOMMENDED WEBSITES

Arsenal
http://www.arsenal.com/
English Premier League
http://www.premierleague.com
ESPN Soccernet
http://soccernet.espn.go.com/
Euro 2008
http://en.euro2008.uefa.com/
FIFA
www.fifa.com
GOL TV
http://www.goltv.tv/en_index.php
Manchester United
http://www.manutd.com/
Soccer Blog.com
http://www.soccerblog.com/
World Cup 2006 Streaming Media
http://www.streamingmedia.com/r/printerfriendly.asp?id=9334
Yahoo! Sports MLS
http://sports.yahoo.com/mls

CHAPTER 4

Public Relations and the Media

Maria Hopwood
Leeds Metropolitan University

"Public relations may be more important in sport organisations than in almost any other field."
—Stoldt et al. (2006, page v)

Objectives

Upon completion of this chapter the reader should be able to:

- Define and identify the scope and nature of public relations.
- Define and identify the scope of media relations.
- Appreciate the role of both public relations and the media in contemporary football.
- Understand the dynamics of the relationship between public relations and the media.
- Appreciate the need for a strategic approach to football media relations.
- Understand the role of the football media manager.

CONTENTS

OVERVIEW OF THE CHAPTER

Public relations continues to be one of the least understood and appreciated communications tools available to contemporary sports managers and professionals. There are many reasons for this, but the main one is that strategic communications management within sports and football—as in other areas of business—is rarely given the serious investment and attention it requires. The role of the media in football is increasingly pervasive, frequently intrusive, and sometimes controversial. Appreciating the necessity of creating and developing mutually beneficial media relationships with a whole range of publics, of whom the media is one, however, is a critical requirement for today's football administrators. Realising that this can only fully be achieved through an understanding of public relations may come as something of a surprise.

This chapter introduces some basic theoretical concepts of public relations that are integral to the management of football and applies these within a media relations context. In an attempt to address the misunderstandings surrounding the discipline, the chapter begins with a discussion of what public relations is and what it is not. Contemporary definitions of both public relations and sports public relations are given in order to illustrate the extent and remit of the practice. Basic theoretical elements of public relations are introduced together with a discussion on the models of public relations practice, which shows why the media must be regarded as both a public in its own right and a gatekeeper and "framer" of its own messages. Jefkins's (1994) model of The Public Relations Transfer Process is introduced as a means of explaining and clarifying the overall aims and objectives of public relations.

The second part of the chapter focuses on media relations and the role of the media within the sport and football context. A definition of media relations is given together with a strategic plan for dealing with the media. The chapter concludes with a case study that gives the reader valuable insight into the role of the contemporary football media manager.

INTRODUCTION

Sports public relations involves many aspects and approaches. From persuading a diverse range of publics and managing the voracious and demanding media to community relations and training for interviews and media appearances, public relations professionals play an increasingly significant part in communicating the messages of the sport entity—whether that be a local gym or a Premier League football club—to its key constituents. According to Pedersen et al. (2007, page 267), "The importance of public relations to the sport entity should not be overlooked, especially when trying to influence public opinion." Influencing public opinion is the core business of public relations in the world of football, as it is public opinion which provides the all-important licence to operate for the football organisation.

Regardless of whether it finds itself among the elite of international teams or as a fledgling squad in its first season of the local junior football league, without the vital support of a whole range of publics—from long-suffering parents to deadline-tied journalists to billionaire investors—the football club simply will not survive. As Pedersen et al. (2007) quite rightly point out, sports public relations is of huge significance to sport entities, as creating and establishing effective public relations strategies will ensure that sports organisations communicate in a most favourable manner with key constituents, both internally and externally. For all of these reasons, an understanding of public relations is vital to success in today's football business because, as Schoenfeld (2005) observes, more than ever before, sport public relations professionals are being used to support the sport entity's overall objectives by crafting and reinforcing the organisation's brand image.

Sport globalisation and expansion have also placed much greater emphasis on sport public relations. Contemporary football is an "industry without borders" (Pedersen, 2007, page 264), which demands that clubs carefully manage global perceptions of their organisations. This requires paying close attention to all of the various cultures and demographics that combine to create the football public. This globalisation and expansion has, of course, largely been made possible by the mass media and the Internet and other new media such as podcasting and mobile technology that all provide instantaneous links with and easier access for the sport consumer. As Pedersen et al. (2007) correctly point out, this greater access emphasises the need to effectively manage public perception because new technologies are instrumental in shaping public opinion.

WHAT IS PUBLIC RELATIONS?

Public relations is arguably the least understood of all the tools available to contemporary business and sports. For all sorts of reasons (but mainly to do with ignorance and lack of understanding), public relations is also the marketing communications discipline that attracts the greatest criticism and negative opinion. However, because of its unique characteristics, public relations, when it is implemented by practitioners who understand its benefits, has a great deal to offer football organisations. Public relations is the most misunderstood and maligned element of the contemporary marketing communications mix. Frequently associated with the negative concepts of "spin" and subterfuge, the true value and potential of public relations remains overlooked and underused, and this is particularly evident within the context of sports. When public relations is mentioned and referred to, it is largely within the narrow confines of publicity and media relations, which means that the true potential of professionally conducted public relations is completely overlooked.

From a football public relations perspective, word of mouth communications and media interest are critical to attracting a range of "publics," including the sponsors and supporters on whom the sport's livelihood and survival depends. However, true professional public relations involves a great deal more than merely publicity, media relations, and event management. As Jahansoozi (2006) observes, many models and theories of public relations involve the concept of communicating with groups, group dynamics and behaviour, and building relationships with specific groups or publics, a bias resulting from an emphasis on the media relations function. What has been sidelined is the central concept of the individual and interpersonal communication (persuasive communication) and interpersonal relationships that is emphasised in the relational perspective of public relations, a concept that is gaining ground in public relations academia and one that is of great relevance to football public relations.

If embraced and practiced professionally, public relations can arguably become the purest form of relationship management, particularly in the sporting and football context. Public relations is a field that is more often characterised by what it does rather than what it is (Ledingham and Bruning, 2000). The overall aim of public relations is to create goodwill and good feelings about the organisation and its products. This can be done partly through the establishment of a sound "corporate" reputation and partly by getting people to think positively about the organisation's activities. Changing the way people think and feel about an organisation—including a football club—can be a long, drawn-out process, but when knowledge of public relations exists within the organisation and when public relations is a recognised and well-managed element of the overall communications function, public relations can lead to very real and measurable benefits. For a sports organisation such as a football club, public relations can, if handled professionally, become its most cost-effective communications mechanism. This recognition of public relations is particularly pertinent to minor, non-, and junior league clubs, where budgets are frequently low and expenditure on communications and promotion is often neglected or sacrificed. To put it another way, public relations is all about making sure that the sports organisation does the right things at the right times and ensuring, when necessary, that those publics that need to, know what it is doing.

Public relations in the sporting arena has an increasingly broad remit that goes well beyond the purely commercial activities with which sports marketing is usually associated. More than anything else, public relations has the unique ability to build relationships, establish credibility, and create understanding between the organisation and all its many publics, all of which are vital commodities to any sports enterprise. Too often public relations is mistakenly seen as being the responsibility only of the public relations department or consultancy, but the reality is that everyone in the organisation has a vital role to play in public relations. This is perhaps especially the case for the football organisation, in which many employees carry an important public relations responsibility through their inherent visibility and public interest both on the field of play and in their personal lives. As we are aware, increasing numbers of today's professional footballers are achieving celebrity status, frequently for reasons that appear to have very little to do with their prowess on the football pitch. For example, though the memory of some of David Beckham's less comfortable moments in the media spotlight may have faded, it is clear that a better understanding of public relations on his part at the time of such incidents could have deflected, or at least allayed, some of the negative media coverage he has attracted during his career. Because football is of such interest and means so much to so many millions all over the world, it is essential that everyone involved in the game at all levels has an understanding of public relations. If we think of public relations as being everything we say, everything we do, and everything anyone says or thinks about us, then we can begin to appreciate its importance.

A useful perspective to start with an analysis of public relations is that it is the management of corporate image through the proactive and professional management of relationships with the organisation's publics and from that point, we can move on to considering some practical definitions and applications of public relations within the context of sport. The U.K. Chartered Institute of Public Relations (CIPR) offers this definition of public relations on its website (*http://www.Cipr.co.uk*):

> *Public relations is about reputation—the result of what you do, what you say, and what others say about you. Public relations is the discipline which looks after reputation, with the aim of earning understanding and support and influencing opinion and behaviour. It is the planned and sustained effort to establish and maintain goodwill and mutual understanding between an organisation and its publics.*

This, together with other definitions found within the public relations literature, focuses on the unique qualities and potential of professional public relations, illustrating again that the reach of the discipline extends far beyond that of publicity and media relations.

To take this definition further and to apply it firmly to the football context, it is worthwhile defining *sports public relations.* Stoldt et al. (2006, page 2) offer the following definition:

> ... *A managerial communication-based function designed to identify a sport organisation's key publics, evaluate its relationships with those publics, and foster desirable relationships between the sport organisation and those publics.*

The different elements of this definition require closer analysis and consideration. The first key point is that sports public relations is a *management function,* which means that it is as vital to the effectiveness of the organisation as all the other managerial activities, such as marketing and human resource management. A greater appreciation of public relations shows that it actually overlaps with both of these other core disciplines in many ways, which is a clear statement that public relations can only be effective when it is integrated with the other management functions within the football club.

The second feature of this definition is that public relations is all about communication. All relationships are, after all, reliant on truthful, open, honest, and transparent two-way communication, and the potential lifelong relationships enjoyed by many football clubs require total investment in communication. Sports public relations is not exclusively comprised of communications activities, but everything in sports public relations has to be grounded in excellent two-way communication strategies. This is where sports public relations differs from sports marketing. Where sports marketing is consumer focused and not exclusively interested in creating a dialogue, sports public relations seeks to create a dialogue with everyone who has an interest in sports, so creating feedback opportunities is an essential component of sports public relations.

The third point to highlight is that public relations must be a *systematic practice* if it is to be fully effective. This means that public relations is something that needs to be embedded within the organisation; it cannot be done as an afterthought or in a last-minute panic. Systematic public relations is *strategic.* It involves thorough research and analysis, the setting of achievable and measurable objectives, and constant monitoring and evaluation.

The Public Relations Transfer Process

In order to assist the football organisation in gaining a better understanding of basic public relations and its objectives and outcomes, it is worthwhile to examine some key public relations theoretical principles. A good place to start is by looking at the concept of the Public Relations Transfer Process model (Figure 4.1), which was developed by Jefkins (1994) and demonstrates that professionally handled public relations has the power to convert a negative situation to positive achievement. This process occurs through creating relationships and dialogue between the organisation and its publics. It requires a complete knowledge of all the public groups, and it requires truth, openness, honesty, and clarity in all communications between the organisation and its publics. Time after time, emotions, attitudes, and behaviours such as those listed in the Negative Situation box are converted, through the implementation of specific and well-thought-out public relations techniques, to those listed in the Positive Achievement box. As emotions, attitudes, and behaviours are essential components of contemporary sport, it is clear that the Public Relations Transfer Process has great relevance to sport management in all its forms. From the football organisation's perspective, the process is of particular relevance to the monitoring and development of relationships with all fans and supporters and other football-related publics. Glasgow Rangers Football Club is an example of a football organisation that should have implemented the Public Relations Transfer process as a key element of its public relations strategy following the riots in Manchester that followed the defeat of Rangers by Zenit St. Petersburg in the UEFA Cup Final in May 2008. Though UEFA exonerated the club of any blame for its fans' behaviour and though the chairman, David Murray, and the CEO, Martin Bain, both issued media statements, postings on the Scottish Football fans forum website Pie and Bovril (*http://www.pieandbovril.com/*) showed the

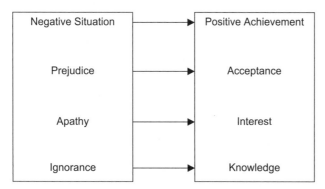

FIGURE 4.1 *The Public Relations Transfer Process*
*When the negative situation is converted into positive achievement, through knowledge and communication, the result is the primary objective of public relations: **understanding**.*
Source: Jefkins (1994)

depth of feeling felt by that most important stakeholder group: the football fan. Comments such as the following illustrate the importance to football organisations of staying in touch with the mood and feelings of their key publics.

> *Not a single outright condemnation. One statement of "disappointment"—and a very vague one at that—tempered by another allusion to the big TV being a harbinger of violence akin to the "Two Minutes' Hate" screen in 1984. I can fully understand Rangers wanting to accentuate the positive, and I have sympathy with their view that it was only a minority involved, but this is nonetheless an absolutely awful statement, and one that I hope they reconsider.*

Through more effective application of the Public Relations Transfer Process, Rangers FC should have considered gaining the support of its own most important internal public—the supporters—before issuing media statements with which they were clearly unhappy. The unfortunate fact remains that Rangers FC (and, sadly, British professional football generally) has a continuing poor image in terms of fan behaviour, one that many Rangers supporters, it would seem at least, would like to actively change.

FOUR MODELS OF PUBLIC RELATIONS FOR FOOTBALL

The "dominant paradigm" in contemporary public relations theory is grounded in the work of American theorist James Grunig (1992) whose key contributions to the public relations theoretical literature began to emerge as relatively recently as the mid-1980s. Since that time, public relations theory has continued to evolve. Public relations theory is based on the principle of establishing, nurturing, and maintaining relationships with a range of publics. In order to achieve effective and mutually beneficial relationships with these publics, Grunig and others have identified four key models of public relations that continue to be the most widely accepted and practiced worldwide and that can be adapted to meet the needs of sports organisations such as football clubs and their publics. These models are the press agentry–publicity model, the public information model, the two-way asymmetrical model, and the two-way symmetrical model. Each of these models has specific characteristics that we will now examine in more detail.

The *press agentry–publicity model* is probably the one that is used most often in sport public relations, as its primary focus is on getting positive and favourable coverage from the media. According to Pedersen et al. (2007), sport attracts more media coverage than any other industry, so sport orga-nisations have become quite proficient at keeping the media supplied with information such as statistics and injury reports. The global obsession with football means that the game is dependent on the media for communicating with its publics, but it is critically important to realise that "the media" is a public in its own right as well as a gatekeeper for communications. For this reason, the football organisation/media relationships of necessity have to be handled differently from other relationships. This will be looked at more closely later.

The *public information model* is also commonly used in sports public relations and is especially prevalent in the United States, where the specialist roles of the Sport Information Director (SID) and the Media Relations Director (MRD) are a feature of all college and professional sports organisations. Staff in these positions do nothing but disseminate accurate and timely information to the media by being constantly available and highly trained in media and communications skills. A key feature of this model is the focus on distributing unbiased and accurate information regarding the sport organisation. Though this is just one narrow aspect of public relations practice, it is evident that for football organisations, it is imperative that a trained professional in media relations is always avail-able. Neil Favager is Media and Communications Manager for Gold Coast United Football Club, which is one of the ten professional football clubs in the Australian "A" league. In his opinion (personal interview), football media relations involves working in "a surreal world. . . complete escapism; you insulate yourself from the outside world" where the media person has to be available 24/7 to meet the insatiable needs of a football hungry public.

Both of these models are regarded as one-way communication models, which means that the dominant partner in the communication relationship is the organisation and that feedback is not integral to the communication's success or otherwise. However, this perspective needs to be tempered with caution as it can be argued that all communications have feedback associated with them, and this can be implicit or explicit. For example, Martin Bain of Rangers FC's statement following the previously mentioned riots in Manchester—which is an example of the public information model—has been interpreted variously as either a thoughtful, measured response to the outrage or an anodyne attempt to shift blame from the club elsewhere. Perception and interpretation are examples of feedback. Even if they might not be directly received by the organisation, they are powerful influences on image and reputation, which confirms the point that feedback is present in all communication.

The *two-way asymmetrical* and *two-way symmetrical* models, on the other hand, emphasise that feedback is integral to the establishment of effective and favourable relationships. The two-way asymmetrical model's main aim is to persuade the organisation's key publics by shaping messages in such a way that the public will respond in a way that the organisation intends. This model works best when there is minimal conflict in the relationship. The football club may carry out research among its publics to ascertain the level of satisfaction with various aspects of the football product, and rather than use these findings to make changes, the club might modify the way in which it sends its communications or alter the communication in some way to achieve a desired result. For example, if supporters are visiting the club website or getting their regular information fixes via SMS in preference to receiving printed information updates, then the club could consider reducing its production of printed communications.

According to many public relations theorists, the ideal model of public relations is the two-way symmetrical model, which recognises that communication is a two-way process and that feedback is an essential component of all public relations practice. This model is based on research and advises conflict resolution through the principle of mutual understanding between the organisation and its publics. This model is widely used in football in areas such as player contract negotiations, sponsor relationship management, season ticket price increases, and negotiating with parents on car sharing to junior league away matches. Websites are an excellent example of a two-way symmetrical model in action, and a particularly good example is the "Football Unites, Racism Divides" website (see the Recommended Websites section at the end of this chapter), where interested publics' views are sought on a whole range of issues concerning football, including the development of women's football. Football organisations at all levels are becoming much more aware of the importance of brand image and other elements of differentiation as a means of fighting off competition from other sources. Public relations has an important role to play here, and by actively seeking feedback, football organisations can gain much better understanding of the needs and desires of their key publics. It is no accident, for example, that Middlesbrough Football Club, which has a strong community presence and social responsibility ethic and is consistently held up as an example of excellence in community relations, regularly works with public relations undergraduate students from the local university to better understand the benefits of public relations to football.

MEDIA RELATIONS IN FOOTBALL

Martin O'Neill OBE (Macesport UK), manager of Aston Villa Football Club, said:

> *Sport and the media have become ever more closely linked in recent years. That's why it is so important that the relationships between the sport, [and] all sections of an ever-increasing media . . . are managed effectively and efficiently.*

According to Stoldt et al. (2006), media relations is the most common form of public relations in sport, which is not surprising considering the relatively high number of people employed in sports media relations jobs worldwide and the amount of coverage the mass media devotes to sport. Referring to "King Football," Nicholson (2007, page 47) points out the following:

> *Almost wherever it is played, football in its various forms is a leader in the sport media nexus. Globally, football is played in more than 200 countries and in many countries is the most popular spectator sport for live and mediated audiences.*

Within the football context, media relations is concerned with developing and maintaining desirable and favourable relationships with members of the mass media. As an integral element within promotional communication, the media is the perfect way of promoting a business and gaining exposure. Though most business organisations will have a clearly defined strategy for maximising media coverage, those employees engaged could be detrimental to long-term relationship management. Those involved in football public relations, therefore, need to be mindful of L'Etang's (2008, page 119) warning that "there is often, too, an overdependence on media within PR strategies and campaigns and a lack of imagination in relation to other media, or to networking and interpersonal communication."

Based on research gathered from a range of sports media sources, these are some useful strategies for developing positive relationships with the media.

- *The media should be treated as a direct link to the club's consumers.* If they so choose, contemporary football consumers can have constant, instantaneous access to media sources, so for this reason, positive relations with the media must be cultivated. As Pedersen et al. (2007, page 268) point out, "The mass media shape public opinion, and oftentimes the media's perception of the sport-focused organisation will be the public's perception as well."
- *The media must be provided with much-needed "scoops."* Because football clubs, whether professional or amateur, are firmly rooted in their

community, the local media will play a huge role in shaping public opinion and perception at a local level. At the national and international level, the same thing happens but in a much more public forum. It is essential, therefore, that the media are "kept onside," treated with respect and given the information they need when they need it. As Nichols et al. (2002, page 63) observe, the mass media possess the power to "shape the content of the message generated by a news release, a postgame interview, or another form of indirect public relations".

■ *It is important to create and maintain an honest and open relationship with the media and to encourage a level of trust between the two parties.* As Neil Favager highlights in the case study that follows, this is a critical element of football public relations. Members of the media totally depend on trustworthy contacts within the club, so it is absolutely essential that anyone involved with football media relations works hard at fostering favourable working relationships with all elements of the media. This relationship is also critical to the brand and image shaping of the football club. Fostering a positive and mutually beneficial relationship with the media is an undoubted necessity, but it can also be challenging, and if the relationship is not properly maintained, it can quickly become adversarial. It is undoubtedly the case that the nature of the football club/media relationship enhances the likelihood or otherwise of media coverage. The findings gathered from recent research conducted by Pedersen et al. (2007) among media relations directors working in a range of professional American sports organisations make interesting reading:

■ Sixty-six percent of the research sample felt that the way in which they handle the media directly affects the *type* of coverage—positive or negative—received by their sport organisation.

■ Sixty percent believed that fostering positive relationships with members of the media increases the *quantity* of media exposure for their sport organisation.

■ Approximately 74 percent indicated that cultivating positive media relationships increases the *quality* of media coverage for their sport organisation.

Though these findings relate specifically to the American sports media experience, it is a fact that, as Hall et al. (2007, page 41) observe, "The power of selection in coverage and interpretation of events rests with sports journalists and the media organisations." Anyone working in public relations in football must be constantly aware of the synergy between public relations and media relations and ensure that a strategic approach to developing these all-important mutually beneficial relationships is followed at all times.

CONCLUSION

Public relations within the context of sport generally is currently experiencing a surge in academic and professional research interest. In summer 2008, the highly regarded academic journal *Public Relations Review* produced its first ever Special Issue on Public Relations and Sport (L'Etang & Hopwood, 2008). Showcasing work from authors around the globe and dealing with a wide range of sports public relations issues, publications such as this point to the necessity for a greater understanding of the role of public relations in sport. In the case of football, whose share of the global media will only continue to grow, football public relations specialists are finding that their expertise and advice is becoming highly sought after. In 2005, Paul Mace of Macesport set up the first independent sports public relations consultancy in order to fill a huge void in sports communication that he had observed during his time as Leicester City Football Club's Communication Director. During his time in that role, he had become acutely aware of the power of public relations and how huge potential in relationship management was being lost because people in the sport did not understand or value public relations. Paul's extensive experience of media relations, together with his innate understanding that "you can't succeed in this game without knowing about public relations" (personal interview), has seen him and his company go from strength to strength as the specialist field of sport public relations has finally begun to develop.

For anyone interested in pursuing a career in football public relations and media relations, this chapter has made it clear that acquiring an understanding of professional public relations is essential. As well as having a love and understanding of football, it is vital to gain as much knowledge and appreciation as possible about the discipline of contemporary public relations and to really get to know how the media operates. Neil Favager's insight into the day to day life of the football media manager should therefore prove to be invaluable.

In his book *Marketing and Football*, Michel Desbordes (2007, page 10) says, "Football is played all over the world, and universal marketing tools are necessary in order for it to be profitable." This is undoubtedly true, but as Shilbury et al. (2003, page 267) state, "It is important for the sport marketer to know how the sporting organisation's publics perceive the organisation and its product range." In other words, without public relations, full profitability in both financial and relational terms will be impossible to achieve. As the author observes elsewhere, for those sport organisations that come to understand public relations' benefits and are willing to invest time and engage in creating proactive public relations strategies, competitive advantage and long-term mutually beneficial relationships between the organisation and its publics can be the reality, not merely the dream (Hopwood, 2005). With this belief very much in mind, this chapter introduced a range of concepts and ideas that will hopefully encourage greater understanding of and stimulate a more professional approach to football communication.

CASE STUDY 4.1: Neil Favager, Media and Communications Manager, Gold Coast United FC

Since emigrating from England, Neil has worked in football administration in Australia for 11 years and has witnessed and been involved with the great changes that have taken place in the game in recent years. Like so many others in the game, Neil went into football administration when an injury curtailed his playing career at semiprofessional level. His love of the game made it impossible for him to consider a career outside football, so he forged a pathway in football media management in both the United Kingdom and Australia, which resulted in him eventually being sought out for the position of Media and Communications Manager with Gold Coast United Football Club, which will be making its "A" League debut in the 2009–2010 Australian football season.

In his opinion, Australian football sunk to its lowest ebb in 2002, the year in which the national team failed to qualify for the World Cup. Australian football's governing body at that time was the National Soccer League, which eventually disintegrated and was replaced by the Football Federation Australia (hereafter the FFA), an organisation that, according to Neil, "changed the world of football in Australia." In 2005 the "A" League was formed with Hyundai as its major sponsor and that, together with Fox Sports, has been critical to the success of the FFA.

So Neil has been involved with the Australian football media since the beginning. With no formal media or journalistic training, Neil admits that he has honed his craft through learning on the job and through having a natural affinity with both the game of football and the craft of writing and understanding the media psyche. His early lessons in football media were learned during the time he produced and published a local football magazine called *Extra Time*. This magazine was at the time the first of its kind, and it very quickly gained a circulation of 3,000 in the Brisbane area and became a source of information for local newspaper, radio, and television journalists. Mutually beneficial relationships between Neil and the journalists began to flourish as his football contacts and stories became important material and sources for the media and he developed a reputation as a reliable, trustworthy, and informative source. He came to realise the necessity of learning about the idiosyncrasies of the different media. He learned that every journalist has his or her own character and "modus operandi" and that it was critical to understand the individual journalists and their editorial direction: "I used to keep notes about all the media people I met. I got to know what they eat, whether or not they swore, things like that. You have to be able to communicate at every different level and to get to trust one another. They need to have the confidence that you understand the pressures they are under; you have to be sensitive and sympathetic at all times. There is a hierarchy of relationships, but I have to be mindful of everyone, and I am very helpful to the younger journalists. I'm a great believer in giving opportunities to young people."

A key feature of football media relationships according to Neil is "doing little deals and winning little battles." He says that during the season he does three or four deals per day, which necessitates understanding the editorial direction processes that exist in the media: "You have to learn and understand what the editor of the media outlet wants, and this can be a lengthy process. You have to understand the physical process and appreciate the commercial principles which underlie today's media reporting and operations."

From his years of media management experience, Neil has learned a great deal about what makes media relationships work, and here are some useful tips and advice for anyone involved in football media operations:

- Throughout the season, be tuned in to what's happening nonstop, 24/7. *Never* not return a call from someone in the media.

- Always be available; you always have to know what's going on and have an answer to a question.

- Let journalists know that we're all in this together. Blocking information is not part of the job; reassure journalists and media people of that.

- If there's a story, it will get out. You can't defend the indefensible, but there are times when a little sensationalism goes a long way.

- You are fulfilling a customer service role—the journalist is your client. You need them as much as they need you. Journalists become cynical if you don't help them, but it makes their job easier if you provide them with the information they want when they want it.

- The public relations element of working with the media is very much concerned with the shaping and influencing of public opinion through the media.

- Creating and shaping media relationships is a way of exerting control. Be honest and upfront, and open up everything to the media through such techniques as the daily press conference.

- Learning to interpret nonverbal communication cues is very important when dealing with the media. Be mindful of and learn about persuasion and suggestion techniques that become invaluable for allowing the placement of questions in media briefings and press conferences. Learning how best to use other body language techniques, such as touch, can really help in relationship building.

What comes across extremely clearly from talking to Neil is his passion for both football and his work. Perhaps more than anything else, it is precisely that combination that is necessary to create the vital alchemy in football public and media relations.

Questions

1. Contact any sports organisation of your choice and interview their public relations/media relations person to find out what his or her job entails. Is this the kind of career path you would like to follow?

2. If you were in Neil Favager's job, what do you think your biggest challenges would be?

DISCUSSION QUESTIONS

1. How would you define sports public relations, and how do you think it contributes to contemporary sports business?

2. What is media relations, and how does this differ to public relations?

3. After reading this chapter, do you have a deeper understanding of what underpins sports public relations and sports media relations?

GUIDED READING

Media Relations in Sport by Hall et al. (2007) is a useful text for anyone interested in learning more about public relations and the media within the context of sport. The book deals with everything from an examination of the working relationships between journalists and sport organisations to ethics. It also provides extensive practical guidelines on everything from writing news releases to organising media events. *Sport Public Relations: Managing Organisational Communication* by Stoldt et al. (2006) is the first text that deals exclusively with the subject of sport public relations. It is an American text, so its focus is predominantly that of media relations and publicity, and it refers exclusively to U.S. sports. It does, however, provide a useful and readable insight into this subject area. *Strategic Sport Communication* by Pedersen et al. (2007) is another recent American text. This is a particularly useful text, as it covers a wide range of sport communication techniques and presents a model of sports communication that is helpful in gaining an understanding of how strategic sports communication works. *Sport and the Media: Managing the Nexus* by Nicholson (2007) provides a good combination of analysis of the sports media industry and the necessary sports management skills required for successful sports media management. A key strength of this text is its international coverage and focus. Both *The Marketing of Sport* (2007) and *The Business of Sport Management* (2004) edited by John Beech and Simon Chadwick are both extremely useful and readable texts with contributions on a range of sport business and marketing issues from a diverse and international authorship. Essential reading for anyone interested in the subject of sport. *International Cases in the Business of Sport* (2008) edited by Simon Chadwick and Dave Arthur contains an up-to-date collection of international case studies on a range of sport management issues.

Marketing and Football: An International Perspective (2007) edited by Michel Desbordes gives a fascinating insight into a variety of off-field issues affecting contemporary football around the world.

REFERENCES

Beech, J., & Chadwick, S. (2004). *The Business of Sport Management*. Harlow: Pearson Education Limited.

Beech, J., & Chadwick, S. (2007). *The Marketing of Sport*. Harlow: Pearson Education Limited.

Chadwick, S., & Arthur, D. (2008). *International Cases in the Business of Sport*. Oxford: Butterworth-Heinemann.

Chartered Institute of Public Relations (CIPR). Careers & Education. Retrieved on the June 11, 2009, from www.cipr.co.uk - http://www.cipr.co.uk/education/index_home.asp

Cutlip, S. M., Center, A. H., & Broom, G. M. (2006). *Effective Public Relations* (9th Edition). New Jersey: Prentice-Hall, Inc, Upper Saddle River.

Desbordes, M. (Ed.). (2007). *Marketing & Football: An International Perspective.* Oxford: Butterworth-Heinemann.

Grunig, J. (Ed.). (1992). *Excellence in Public Relations and Communication Management.* Hillsdale, New Jersey: Lawrence Erlbaum Associates.

Hall, A., Nichols, W., Moynahan, P., & Taylor, J. (2007). *Media Relations in Sport* (2nd Edition.). Morgantown, West Virginia: Fitness Information Technology.

Hopwood, M. K. (2003). *Public Relations Practice in English County Cricket: A Case Study of Yorkshire County Cricket Club and Durham County Cricket Club. Unpublished thesis.* Scotland: University of Stirling.

Hopwood, M. K. (2005). Applying the Public Relations Function to the Business of Sport. *International Journal of Sports Marketing and Sponsorship, 6(3).*

Hopwood, M. K. (2007). Sport Public Relations. In J. Beech, & S. Chadwick (Eds.), *The Marketing of Sport.* Harlow: Pearson Education Limited.

Jahansoozi, J. (2006). Relationships, Transparency, and Evaluation: The Implications for Public Relations. In J. L'Etang, & M. Pieczka (Eds.), *Public Relations: Critical Debates and Contemporary Practice.* Mahwah, NJ: Lawrence Erlbaum Associates.

Jefkins, F. (1994). *Public Relations Techniques* (2nd Edition.). Oxford: Butterworth Heinemann.

Ledingham, J. A., & Bruning, S. D. (2000). *Public Relations as Relationship Management: A Relational Approach to the Study and Practice of Public Relations.* Mahwah, NJ: Lawrence Erlbaum Associates.

L'Etang, J. & Hopwood, M. (Eds.) (June 2008) *Public Relations Review.* Special Issue: Public Relations and Sport. Volume 34, Issue 2, Pages 87–206.

L'Etang, J. (2008). *Public Relations: Concepts, Practice and Critique.* London: SAGE Publications Ltd.

Macesport UK. www.macesport.co.uk. Retrieved on July 25, 2009, from http://macesport.co.uk

Nichols, W., Moynahan, P., Hall, A., & Taylor, J. (2002). *Media Relations in Sport.* Morgantown, West Virginia: Fitness Information Technology.

Nicholson, M. (2007). *Sport and the Media: Managing the Nexus.* Oxford: Butterworth-Heinemann.

Pedersen, P. M., Miloch, K. S., & Laucella, P. C. (2007). *Strategic Sport Communication.* Champaign, Illinois: Human Kinetics.

Pieandbovril.com. Retrieved on May 15, 2008, from http://www.pieandbovril.com/forum/index.php?s=82e20f95f5024d41ee7d4ea3690def5f&showtopic=83690.

Schoenfeld, B. (2005). PR Playbook: Forget Game Notes: Today's Communication Managers Called On to Shape Teams' Images. *SportBusiness Journal, 8*(18), 35–37.

Shilbury, D., Quick, S., & Westerbeek, H. (2003). *Strategic Sport Marketing* (2nd Edition.). Crows Nest NSW, Australia: Allen and Unwin.

Smith, A., & Westerbeek, H. (2004). *The Sport Business Future.* Basingstoke: Palgrave Macmillan.

Stoldt, G. C., Dittmore, S. W., & Branvold, S. E. (2006). *Sport Public Relations: Managing Organizational Communication.* Champaign, Illinois: Human Kinetics.

Westerbeek, H., & Smith, A. (2003). *Sport Business in the Global Marketplace.* Basingstoke: Palgrave Macmillan.

RECOMMENDED WEBSITES

Football Unites, Racism Divides
http://www.furd.org/default.asp?intPageID=1
Macesport Independent Sports Public Relations Agency
http://www.macesport.co.uk/
Sport Business International
http://www.sportbusiness.com/
The Chartered Institute of Public Relations
http://www.cipr.co.uk
The Football Association
http://www.thefa.com
The Football Federation of Australia (FFA)
http://www.footballaustralia.com.au/
The Public Relations Society of America
http://www.prsa.org/

CHAPTER 5

Law and Regulation

Steve Greenfield
University of Westminster

Guy Osborn
University of Westminster

Objectives

Upon completion of this chapter the reader should be able to:

- Explain instances of the role played by both the criminal and civil law in sports.
- Understand some of the problems of regulation in sports.
- Appreciate the many ways in which sport and law may interact.
- Consider different approaches to future sport regulation.
- Articulate the advantages and disadvantages of applying the law to different problems and issues within sports.

CONTENTS

OVERVIEW OF THE CHAPTER

This chapter provides a brief guide and orientation as to how sport is regulated. It shows that although the law maintains an important presence, often directly intervening or threatening intervention, sport in many situations also attempts to regulate itself. While this chapter focuses on issues particularly pertinent to the situation in England and Wales, the general ethos and approach are applicable throughout other jurisdictions. As such, the case studies are vehicles to explore issues, dealing with themes that can be applied in other areas. First, the chapter outlines some of the theoretical debates about law's role in sport. Second, we examine professional boxing as an example to demonstrate the various ways in which law has encroached upon the ability of the sport to govern itself. Third, we consider how the law has been at the centre of the changes that have occurred within the top strata of professional football: in particular here legislation has been used to alter the physical configuration of the grounds through the imposition of all seater stadia, whilst fans have been subjected to a barrage of restrictions through specific statutory intervention. Football also provides a good example of direct government involvement and attempts to provide a vehicle for regulation through an independent football regulator. Finally, the chapter outlines some of the likely future issues, trends, and directions in the area.

INTRODUCTION

The debate as to the role of law within sport has been condensed into the aphorism "When should the law cross the touchline?" Put simply, this is concerned with whether what happens on the "field of play" should be left to the governing body of the sport or whether criminal and civil law should be applicable. At its most obvious, this occurs when a player is badly injured through a violent incident on the field. The offending player may be sanctioned by his club and/or banned by the governing body; for example, in October 2008, Neil Best, the Northampton flank forward, was banned from rugby for 18 weeks for a gouging offence. Any ban would be subject to an appeal process and could also be challenged in court. In July 2008, Dwain Chambers unsuccessfully sought to have the British Olympic Association's lifetime ban, imposed for a drugs offence, overturned in the High Court so he could participate in the Beijing Olympics.

An injured player may seek compensation for the injuries against the other player and his employer, the football club. In August 2008, Ben Collett, a young Manchester United player, was awarded £4.3 million in damages by the High Court in his case against Middlesbrough FC and one of their players after a tackle broke his leg in two places and he was forced to quit the game. This award was the highest ever in sport for injuries and reflects the enormous earning power that professional footballers at the highest level have, as well as the potential of youngsters.

Academically, the debate about the role of law is perhaps best illustrated by the "dialogue" between Grayson (1996) and Gardiner et al. (2006). Anderson (2005, page 26) provides a very useful overview of approaches to criminal law on the sports field across a number of jurisdictions, arguing that "overall, an established pattern is identifiable in the attitude of the major common law jurisdictions towards violence in sport: so long as the internal disciplinary mechanisms of the sport in question are satisfactorily drawn, the authorities and the criminal courts are reluctant to intervene."

Foster (2006) has argued that law has become increasingly invasive and that very few, if any, spheres of social life are immune from the law. This can be seen by the encroachment of the law into various aspects of sport. A whole host of commercial issues covering intellectual property and broadcasting rights have developed because of the value of such rights. In 2001, Arsenal FC brought a case against a street trader selling unofficial merchandise. After an intervention from the European Court of Justice, the club succeeded in its claim for trademark infringement. Broadcasting rights are a similarly controversial area that has again seen European influence as to whether rights can be bundled together and limited or excluded from terrestrial television. In addition, there is a separate debate that has been played out at European level concerning the way in which European law should interact with sports. For example, the *Independent European Sport Review* (Arnaut, 2006, page 29) reported the following:

> *Sport has a specific nature that sets it apart from any other field of business activity and the Nice Declaration attempts to describe what some of these unique features are. Among other aspects, the Nice Declaration recognises that sport has important social, educational, and cultural functions and that these must be taken into account when European Community law is applied.*

This debate was at the heart of the different approaches to cases brought before the European Court, such as *Bosman,* and subsequent cases, such as *Kolpak.* The latter was a judgment of the European Court of Justice involving a Slovakian handball player that permitted a massive influx of "overseas players" (largely from South Africa) into English County Cricket. Traditionally non-EU players had been strictly limited to one or two per county. One game in the 2008 Cricket County Championship between Leicestershire and Northamptonshire contained 11 Kolpak players. A similar situation has developed in French rugby with the movement of South African players who have become eligible under the ruling. The response of the England and Wales Cricket Board has been to introduce new visa requirements to attempt to limit the influx of players. In these European cases, the primary issue is whether sport is sufficiently unique to warrant it being treated differently from other areas of commercial life. If it were considered to have a unique cultural or social value or contribution to national identity, then the law relating to the free movement of workers could be modified to preserve that dimension.

Within sport and law, discourse around the concept of *juridification* has become increasingly important. Foster introduces a useful typology to describe the nuances of this. Arguing that the term has been used quite narrowly by some in the past, he argues that juridification describes a process by which law, while not necessarily actually having to "invade" a particular area, has an impact in that because of it, social spheres become more legal in the way they constitute themselves and the way they operate (Foster, 2006). Therefore, at the same time that we have seen an increased attempt to colonise by the law, the role of governing bodies in terms of regulating themselves has become more pronounced. Foster takes the concept further and adopts a more sophisticated approach. For example, in terms of limits placed on the autonomy of a sporting body by the law "colonising," we may see instead a process of "domestication," where sport adopts specific approaches because of the law in a more indirect fashion. In addition, it is interesting to note that in many sports the rules of the game are in fact called "laws"; this could be seen as part of the social field (sport) constituting itself in a legal image. According to Foster (2006, page 159):

> The rules of major sports are codes. Lawyers often originally drafted them, and they named them the laws of cricket or whatever. They have the characteristics of formal legal rules; they appear precise, clear and unambiguous.

The two concepts that (1) the law has become increasingly more involved in sports and (2) that governing bodies have become more legalistic, are explored using case studies of professional boxing and football. In the former, the key aspect is the participants, while in football, we consider how the law has been used to deal with fan behaviour.

CASE STUDY 5.1: Professional Boxing

A central issue for professional boxing has been the challenges made to its very existence on health and safety grounds. The British Medical Association (BMA, 2007) has consistently argued that it should be outlawed:

> The BMA's opposition to boxing is based on medical evidence that reveals the risk not only of acute injury but also of chronic brain damage which is sustained cumulatively in those who survive a career in boxing. It may take many years before boxers and ex-boxers find out they are suffering from brain damage. The BMA believes that there is sufficient evidence for the risks of brain injury associated with boxing for the Secretary of State at the Department for Culture,

Media and Sport to call for an independent inquiry into these risks.

There have, partly as a response to this, also been periodic calls in Parliament arguing for its abolition (Gunn and Ormerod, 2000). In a legal sense, boxing has created a number of problems; in particular, it has proved difficult to work out boxing's relationship with the criminal law (Parpworth, 1994). It seems difficult to academically justify how an activity that would be unlawful outside of the boxing ring is legally acceptable within it. Indeed, as far back as 1882, the court outlawed prize fighting but permitted sparring. Today, professional boxing seems closer to the idea of prize fighting than sparring. In the Attorney General's Reference (No. 6 of 1980), Lord Lane noted the following:

> *It is not in the public interest that people should try to cause or should cause each other bodily harm for no good reason. Minor struggles are another matter. So, in our judgment, it is immaterial whether the act occurs in private or in public; it is an assault if actual bodily harm is intended and/or caused. This means that most fights will be unlawful regardless of consent. Nothing which we have said is intended to cast doubt on the accepted legality of properly conducted games and sports, lawful chastisement or correction, reasonable surgical interference, dangerous exhibitions, etc. These apparent exceptions can be justified as involving the exercise of a legal right, in the case of chastisement or correction, or as needed in the public interest, in the other cases. ([1981] 2 All ER 1057 at 1059)*

What is clear from this pronouncement is that it is because contact sports are properly conducted that they are immune from the criminal law even if the intention of the participants is to inflict grievous bodily harm on one another. Given that boxing's existence has been threatened, the boxing authorities have sought to maintain a strong system of internal regulation. The Broughton Rules, the London Prize Ring Rules, and the Queensbury Rules were all enacted to protect against the perceived threat of outside intervention, illustrating a trend toward recognising a need for greater control (Sugden, 1996). These rules were seen as civilising the sport, or at least making it safer. This process has continued, with safety issues at the fore, and the response of boxing to this has been to increase the safety standards and safeguards that exist, much in the same way that Queensbury had advocated the adoption of the glove and fixed duration of rounds. This has manifested itself in higher medical standards in terms of licensing individual boxers and the contests themselves, something that also progressed after the decision in *Watson v. BBBC*. Watson brought a claim for negligence against British boxing's governing body, the British Boxing Board of Control (BBBC), following the injuries he suffered and the medical care provided at his 1991 fight against Chris Eubank. He won his case but wasn't fully compensated because of the BBBC's financial position. Licensing is a crucial safeguard developed by the BBBC to ensure that participants are capable and fit enough to box and that the bouts themselves are balanced, as far as possible, to make sure there is not a mismatch that may be more likely to lead to a serious injury (Greenfield and Osborn, 1998).

However, these licensing procedures have themselves been subject to challenge, illustrating the more limited notion of juridification outlined by Foster, where areas of law begin to colonise a social field. These challenges cover a number of areas, including a claim on the basis of natural justice for the failure to issue a licence (*McInnes v. Onslow-Fane*). There was also a successful claim by a woman boxer, Jane Couch (known as the Fleetwood Assassin), under the sex discrimination legislation (*Couch v. BBBC*) at an Industrial Tribunal. Following the *Couch* decision, a further ten successful applications were made even though professional women's boxing has not yet developed commercially.

The other area that has seen litigation is the standard form Boxer-Manager contract that is issued and required by the BBBC. In two separate cases—*Warren v. Mendy* and *Watson v. Praeger*—the enforceability of the contract was challenged. At the heart of the disputes were two essential questions:

1. Did the terms of the contract and the operation of those terms lead to an unreasonable restraint of trade on the boxer?

2. Did the potential conflict of interest when a manager promotes his or her own boxer mean that the contract was unenforceable?

The first point ties in to the issue of restraint of trade more generally and the ways in which restrictive clauses in contracts of a long duration may deprive a person of their ability to ply their trade and therefore be struck out by the courts (Greenfield and Osborn, 1998). The second point raised a number of interesting questions, including the extent to which subsequent contractual terms would be altered by the court's ruling. The fundamental problem with the agreement was the potential for a conflict of interest if the manager also acted as a promoter for the boxer. The promoter is responsible for setting up the fight, providing the purse on offer, organising the venue, and exploiting television rights. The promoter's profit is dependent on maximising income and reducing costs, so the size of the purse that is on offer is a crucial element. Clearly the function of the boxer's manager is to vigorously negotiate on the boxer's behalf with the promoter. This creates a clear conflict of interest, as Chief Justice Scott in the Second *Watson* case observed:

In a case where the manager is also a promoter, I do not regard the agreements as either ordinary or commonplace. There is an obvious conflict of interest affecting a manager who contracts for his boxer to fight in a promotion in which he, the manager, has a financial interest. ... A boxer may, for the whole duration of his contract, find himself fighting only on his manager's promotions. For the whole duration of the contract he may find himself unable to take any contest otherwise than on terms unilaterally fixed by the manager/promoter. In all these contests, the financial interests of the manager in the capacity of promoter will be in

conflict with the duty of the manager to obtain for the boxer the most advantageous financial terms possible. ([1991] 3 All ER 487 at 506-7)

The whole issue of the duality of licensing and the potential conflict has been of concern to the boxing authorities since the 1950s, when dual licensing was first prohibited. The position fluctuated as policies were altered when interested parties exerted pressure on these policies. The issue was raised previously in the court proceedings of *Warren v. Mendy*:

It may be that there are many cases in which it works to the boxer's advantage. But the emergence of one where it may well have worked to his disadvantage is something which we would respectfully think ought to cause the board concern. They may well wish to consider whether the regulations ought to be revised in such a way that the relationship can, if it is thought to be desirable, continue to exist, but only with stringent safeguards to protect the boxer. (Nourse LJ [1989] 3 All ER 103 at 117)

The BBBC was unable to modify the structural difficulties because of its own system of governance that gave promoters a voice in the decision-making process. Furthermore, the Office of Fair Trading (OFT) intervened, arguing that preventing managers from promoting could amount to a restrictive practice (Greenfield and Osborn, 1998). Thus, there has not been any resolution of a significant contractual issue despite the concerns raised by the Court of Appeal. The current manager/boxer agreement expressly recognises the potential for a conflict of interest that was highlighted in these cases. Section 6 of the contract sets out the procedure to be followed where the manager also acts as the promoter or has a financial association with the promoter. The manager must advise the boxer, using a standard form, of the clash of interests and must ensure that the terms are not disadvantageous. However, the structural problem has not been resolved, as the potential clash remains despite attempts to provide a "paper" solution.

CASE STUDY 5.2: Football and Regulation

Football provides a rich and interesting case study to consider law's intervention, though it should be noted at the outset that many of the fundamental issues only apply at the higher levels of the game. Football at an amateur level, or even professionally lower down the pyramid, is relatively untouched by the vast array of legislation that has been implemented since 1985. Some of these developments are charted in Greenfield and Osborn (2001), showing that although regulation was initially framed around issues of public order, it has developed to embrace areas such as contractual issues and, more recently, commercial ones.

Here we focus on one particular aspect of regulation: the way fans are controlled and restricted and specifically the requirement for the clubs to develop all-seater stadia. Football has a long history of disasters and inquiries. The events of the fire at Valley Parade that resulted in 56 deaths; the Heysel stadium disaster that saw 39 Juventus fans crushed to death; and the death of a fan at a Birmingham versus Leeds match led to the two *Popplewell Reports*. However, it was the Hillsborough tragedy where 96 fans lost their lives that became the final catalyst for intervention.

These safety failings were combined with more than a decade of disorder and hooliganism both at home and abroad. Such disorder was a political embarrassment to a law and order government, and, in legal terms, the upshot of these events has been an increased legal regulatory framework around the act of attending a football game. The following is a list of the key statutes that have been passed by Parliament since 1985 that apply solely or mainly to football:

- Sporting Events (Control of Alcohol, etc.) Act 1985.
- Football Spectators Act 1989 (FSA1989).
- Football (Offences) Act 1991 (FOA 1991).
- Football Offences and Disorder Act 1999 (FODA 1999).
- Football Disorder Act 2000 (FDA 2000).
- Football (Disorder) (Amendment) Act 2002 (FDA 2002).

In addition, football is singled out in other pieces of legislation such as the Criminal Justice and Public Order Act 1994 s166 (as amended) that focused on ticket touting within football (see Greenfield et al., 2008). The various pieces of legislation deal with racist chanting, throwing missiles, and encroaching onto the pitch (FOA, 1991); the reconfiguring of exclusion orders such as Domestic and International Banning Orders and amendments to the racist chanting and ticket touting provisions (FODA, 1999); and provisions strengthening or extending the banning order provisions (FDA, 2000; FDA, 2002).

The first piece of legislation noted above demonstrates the nature of the government's impulsive reaction. Little evidence was produced to demonstrate the link between alcohol consumption at games and disorder, yet the statute banned consumption at matches. This in turn created two distinct problems. First, clubs were now denied a vital source of revenue at a time before the influx of broadcasting revenues that was needed to be spent repairing and improving old grounds. Second, it was likely that fans would not abandon drinking before games altogether but arrive at the game later, contributing to a gate rush nearer the time of kickoff. The legislation was subsequently amended within a year to permit limited alcohol consumption. The owner of English Premier League club Newcastle United fell foul of the amendment in the 2008 season, though he escaped with a police caution.

The second piece of football-specific legislation, the FSA 1989, is particularly interesting, as it had a dual function, looking both at the licensing of, and safety in, the stadia (including the creation of the Football Licensing Authority), and the regulation of supporters (including the creation of exclusion and restriction orders and the recommendation of a Football Membership Scheme). The initial move toward all-seater stadia in England and Wales came in the wake of the *Taylor Report*, when Lord Justice Taylor (1990, para 6.1) argued, "There is no panacea which will achieve total safety and cure all problems of behaviour and crowd control. But I am satisfied that seating does more to achieve those objectives than any other single measure." The football legislation just noted did not explicitly provide that football must have all-seater stadia but rather it created a Football Licensing Authority (FLA), and the FLA subsequently made seating a condition of the licence that is required to stage matches. Pressure groups such as the Football Supporters Federation

(FSF) have made strong arguments for the reconsideration of safe standing at football (FSF, 2007), and indeed other reports (FLA 2001) have shown its success in other jurisdictions. Interestingly, there is a separate thread of regulatory practice running through this, particularly in the form of fan self-regulation, although the government has taken little heed of this (*Greenfield and Osborn*, 2001, page 169):

> *If there has been a degree of self-regulation of crowd behaviour—and there are signs of a growing articulate fan movement through pressure groups and fanzines—this has been ignored by successive governments who have consistently turned to legislation.*

In Germany, for example, it was found that fans themselves regulated behaviour within the standing areas, partly for fear that this privilege would be taken away.

We have demonstrated a number of instances detailing how the law and other regulatory frameworks operate and some of the tensions and difficulties that exist. The question of how, and whether, sports should be regulated and controlled can be summed up in the debate around the football regulator. One of the early acts of the incoming Labour Government in 1997 was the creation of the Football Task Force. This was partly based on the Labour Party's *Charter for Football,* published the previous year, which stated the following (*Brown*, 1999, page 57):

> *It is important for it to set out the basis for the formation of the Football Task Force. It was, in many ways, a response to a perceived crisis in English football at a time (1995–1996) when the game seemed plagued by bungs, bribes, misbehaviour, and bad leadership.*

It included representatives from a number of groups including the Football Association, the Professional Footballers Association, the FA Premier League, the Football Supporters Association, and the Commission for Racial Equality, among others, and it received submissions from many other groups. It produced four reports, including the "split" final report. When the final report of the Football Task Force was published, there was a disagreement on how football ought to be regulated (*Davison*, 1999):

> *Differences were such that each side of the government-appointed body produced separate versions of the report, covering some of the most contentious issues in football including commercialisation, ticket prices, and club merchandising. But the key disagreement was over how the booming industry should be regulated.*

While the majority wanted a permanent, independent, football audit commission, the clubs proposed a more toothless independent scrutiny panel with less power. Here we see one of the key problems writ large: the industry wants to regulate itself and fears outside intervention, while at the same time using all the regulatory powers at its disposal to challenge activities such as fans posting video clips on YouTube or otherwise interfering with its product.

CONCLUSIONS

The interaction between sport and the law is complex and far reaching. Across a whole host of sports and subjects, legal resolution is sought to provide an answer to problems that governing bodies and participants are unwilling to address and solve. Many contemporary disputes arise around money, and this is most obvious in those sports where there is revenue to be fought over. In cricket, the rise to power of India as a dominant player in the marketing and ownership of various forms of the game has led to splits and acrimony and the banning of players who have participated in the "wrong" league. Similarly, the Stanford Game in cricket, reputedly the largest team prize available for any sport based on a single game, in this case a 20 over a side match between the Stanford All Stars and an England XI (with its $20 million winner-takes-all prize money)—only went ahead after sponsorship litigation that caused considerable anxiety among many commentators. New modes of games designed for a global television audience may well threaten existing structures and disrupt "tradition." Such games bring with them a host of commercial issues to resolve, not least regarding the contractual arrangements for the players.

However, contemporaneously we can see signs that disputes may draw attention to the notion that sport has much more than commercial values and that it plays an important role in our national, social, and cultural life. If this argument is accepted, the next stage is to argue for different legal treatment and some respite from the free-market anti-competition requirements. There may be claims for a more equal distribution of income in football and a requirement that clubs do not operate at a loss. Quotas may be imposed on player nationality or country of development basis to preserve a national base. We may see legislation expanded to preserve the right to see more international and national sporting events on free-to-air broadcasts and the principle of "crown jewels" events extended to anti-ticket-touting provisions. What remains clear is that the law crossed the touchline many years ago and will continue to encroach upon the autonomy of sports.

DISCUSSION QUESTIONS

1. Should sportsmen and sportswomen face criminal action for events that occur on the field of play? What alternatives might there be to suing a player for a career-ending injury?
2. What trends can you identify in terms of how sport has been regulated historically?
3. How is the fan regulated at sporting stadiums?

GUIDED READING

Sport and the Law is a reasonably new discipline, and perhaps the best place to start is some of the textbooks in the area, such as Gardiner et al. (2006) and the late Edward Grayson's book (1996). In addition, the work of Foster

(2006) provides an important theoretical underpinning that all serious students should be cognisant of. Weatherill (2008) provides an important insight into a number of areas relating to the impact of EU law and approaches to regulation in sport, with particular reference to the European White Paper on Sport and "better regulation." The football case study in particular is well provided for by websites, as detailed following. See, for example, the Independent Football Commission (now the Independent Football Ombudsman), and the Safe Standing campaign.

The area is also pretty well served by journals, which include the following:

- *Entertainment and Sports Law Journal.*
- *International Journal of Sport and the Law.*
- *Marquette Journal of Sport and Law.*
- *Soccer and Society.*

REFERENCES

Anderson, J. (2005). Policing the Sports Field: The Role of Criminal Law. *International Sports Law Review* 25.

Arnaut, J. (2006, October). *Independent European Sport Review: Final Version.* UK President of the EU. Retrieved on June 1, 2009, from *www.independentsportsreview.com*.

BMA. (2007). Boxing: the BMA's Position. Retrieved on October 28, 2008, from *http://www.bma.org.uk/health_promotion_ethics/sports_exercise/BoxingPU.jsp*.

Brown, A. (1999). Thinking the Unthinkable or Playing the Game? In S. Hamil, J. Michie, & C. Oughton (Eds.), *A Game of Two Halves? The Business of Football.* Edinburgh: Mainstream. Chapter 3.

Davison, J. (1999). Football Taskforce Produces Report of Two Halves after Split on Future. *The Independent Online.* Retrieved on October 26, 2008, from *http://www.independent.co.uk/news/football-taskforce-produces-report-of-two-halves-after-split-on-future-1134190.html*.

FLA. (2001). FLA (Football Licensing Authority). *Report on the "Kombi" Seating—Volksparkstadion Hamburg, February 23–24.* FLA.

Foster, K. (2006). The Juridification of Sport. In Greenfield and Osborn, (Eds.), (2006). Readings in Law & Popular Culture. London: Routledge.

FSF. (2007). The Case for Safe Standing at Major Football Stadia in England and Wales. Retrieved on October 26, 2008, from *http://www.fsf.org.uk/media/uploaded/safe-standing-report-web.pdf*.

Gardiner, S., James, M., O'Leary, J., & Welch, R. (2006). *Sports Law.* London: Cavendish Press.

Grayson, E. (1996). *Sport and the Law.* London: Butterworths.

Greenfield, S., Osborn, G., & Roberts, S. (2008). Contradictions Within the Criminalisation of Ticket Touting: What Should Be the Role of the Law? *Web Journal of Curent Legal Issues (JCLI)* 3.

Greenfield, S., & Osborn, G. (Eds.), (2006). *Readings in Law and Popular Culture.* London: Routledge.

Greenfield, S., & Osborn, G. (Eds.), (2001). *Regulating Football. Commodification, Consumption and the Law.* London: Pluto Press.

Greenfield, S., & Osborn, G. (Eds.), (2000). *Law and Sport in Contemporary Society.* London: Frank Cass.

Greenfield, S., & Osborn, G. (1998). *Contract and Control in the Entertainment Industry. Dancing on the Edge of Heaven.* Dartmouth, Ashgate.

Gunn, M., & D. Ormerod. (2000). Despite the Law: Prize-fighting and Professional Boxing. In Greenfield and Osborn (2000). *Law and Sport in Contemporary Society.* London: Frank Cass.

Parpworth, N. (1994). Boxing and Prize Fighting: The Indistinguishable Distinguished. *Sport and the Law Journal, Vol. 2*(Issue 1), 5.

Sugden, J. (1996). *Boxing and Society.* Manchester: Manchester University Press.

The Taylor Report (1990). *The Hillsborough Stadium Disaster: Final Report.* HMSO, London, Cm 962.

Weatherill, S. (2008). The White Paper on Sport as an Exercise in "Better Regulation." *International Journal of Sport and the Law.*, 1/2, 3.

LEGAL CASES

Attorney General's Reference (No 6 of 1980) [1981] 2 All ER 1057

Couch v. British Board of Boxing Control (1997) unreported, IT No. 2304231/97

Deutscher Handballbund eV v. Kolpak (Case C-438/00) (Kolpak)

Eastham v. Newcastle United Football Club [1964] Ch 413

McInnes v. Onslow-Fane and Another [1978] 1 WLR 1520

Union Royale Belge des Societes de Football Association ASBL v. Bosman, Royal Club Liegois SA v. Bosman and Others, Union des Associations Europeens de Football v. Bosman (Case C-415/93) [1996] All ER (EC) 97 (Bosman)

Warren v. Mendy and Another [1989] 3 All ER 103

Watson v. Prager and Another [1993] EMLR 275

Watson v. BBBC. (1999) 2 (6) Sports Law Bulletin 3

RECOMMENDED WEBSITES

European White Paper on Sport 11.7.2007, COM (2007) 391 final
http://ec.europa.eu/sport/white-paper/index_en.htm#
Football Licensing Authority
http://www.flaweb.org.uk/
Independent Football Commission
http://www.theifc.co.uk
Independent Football Ombudsman
http://www.theifo.co.uk/
Safe Standing Campaign
http://www.safestanding.com/

CHAPTER 6

International and Global Development

Sten Söderman
School of Business, Stockholm University

Harald Dolles
Heilbronn Business School

Thorsten Dum
Heilbronn Business School

Objectives

Upon completion of this chapter the reader should be able to:

- Understand the distinctive features of the football business and its international dimensions.
- Identify and define the stakeholders in football business.
- Identify international trends.
- Identity further trends based on a conceptual framework.
- Develop own international strategies for the business of football.

OVERVIEW OF THE CHAPTER

This chapter examines the unique challenges in the management of football and introduces the "network of value captures" framework. The framework helps to analyse specific activities through which football can create value and competitive advantage. The chapter then outlines six "minicases" that will be linked to the framework. These cases depict the increasing internationalisation of football and its particular interest for research in the field of international business.

INTRODUCTION

Why is European football of increasing importance to ongoing research in international business and business administration? The answer is because it is a huge and fast-growing business, operating worldwide, but still in need of a more systemised knowledge. If this is a bold statement, it is backed by many arguments: Football is highly popular (this in itself should generate interest in research); it has rabid fans (whose sociology is well researched); it involves high uncertainty and it is an activity where ethnic, gender, social, and economic backgrounds are irrelevant to its practice (but still of great interest to spectators). The skillful team or the talented football player is visibly obvious, something that is intuitively perceived by all spectators. The game has become famous because it is generally linked to our childhood, and its professional teams are on top of pyramid-like organisations of several leagues, with amateur players at all levels, from silver-aged teams to kids' teams. And football today is an international business, as players are transferred frequently around the globe, international professional leagues are created, and the European Cup finals or the FIFA World Cup finals are top media events (see Dauncey and Hare, 1999; Horne and Manzenreiter, 2002a; Beech and Chadwick, 2004; Dolles and Söderman, 2008a).

In recent years, the world of football has been referred to more and more as an industry in its own right. Its characteristics have been getting closer to those of services or the entertainment business, as people worldwide may choose whether to go to the cinema, an amusement park, or the stadium to watch a match. The ranking of football as a business activity has risen in the economies of those countries where football is promoted as a national sport. In many of these countries, it represents today a large percentage of a nation's GDP (gross domestic product), because football events also drive a considerable number of other sectors, such as media and different services like catering and transportation. The globalisation of the football industry has provoked a concentration of resources in the hands of a few big European and South American clubs, which have had the ability and, most of all, the economic resources to face enlarged competition from foreign clubs and other businesses in the entertainment industry.

There is a multibillion-euro business in professional football that is hardly recognised in scientific articles, as recently illustrated by Nilsson (2005). And this is becoming a truly international business, as the same few rules on the visible pitch enable skillful players regardless of their ethnic and social background to play in those teams that create big media interest. The problems and challenges in the field of football are the same everywhere on the globe, such as amateurism versus professionalism, young players going to big clubs, league teams versus national teams, branding and sponsorship growing as a source of revenue, and media creating uncertain expectations for better incomes. Football has successfully outmanoeuvred many other team sports, such as ice hockey, basketball, or handball, and has been accepted as the number one sport with regard to media attention and audience reception worldwide (Horne and Manzenreiter, 2002b; Dolles and Söderman, 2008b). It should by now be obvious that football is a global business, rapidly expanding and developing on a worldwide scale.

THE MANAGEMENT CHALLENGES OF FOOTBALL

The complexity, the specifics, and the changing nature of the football business and its environment strain conventional approaches to theory building in management sciences and hypothesis testing. Early sport management research offered no theory for examining the professional football club and its business environment. To advance both knowledge and practice, we preferred a framework approach to theory building rather than developing a model of the football business. A model abstracts the complexity of the football business to isolate a few key variables whose interactions are examined in depth. The normative significance of the model then depends on the fit between its assumptions and reality. Porter (1991, page 97) concludes, "No one model embodies or even approaches embodying all the variables of interest, and hence the applicability of any model's findings is almost inevitably restricted to a small subgroup of firms or industries whose characteristics fit the model's assumptions."

Instead of developing a model, our approach was to build a framework. A framework is particularly valuable, as it encompasses many variables and seeks to capture much of the complexity. According to Porter (1991, page 98), "Frameworks identify the relevant variables and the questions which the user must answer in order to develop conclusions tailored to a particular industry and company. In this sense they can be seen as almost expert systems." The approach to theory embodied in the framework is contained in our choice of included variables, the way we organised the network of value captures, the proposed interrelations among the value captures, and the way alternative patterns of value captures and club management choices might affect outcomes. In addition, it is a common view that a network describes a number of entities that are connected. The concept of interorganisational networks was initially developed in sociology (Park, 1996). In this study, however, we have adapted an empirical-based network theory with inspiration from the field of industrial marketing that concerns the real-life interorganisational settings (see Alter and Hage, 1993; Ritter and Gemünden, 2003).

Our chosen methodology is based on existing theoretical, but to a big extent also empirical, literature on stories of success or failure of professional football clubs. To confirm our findings, we requested comments from football club managers, football associations' officials, and sport management experts during about 20 interviews and a research seminar at Stockholm University, School of Business. Some comments were very general in nature or related to fundamental concerns about the cases and theories we used or the assumptions that were formulated. Other comments were more specific and very detailed in nature. We responded to the more general, broad-based comments, concerns, and issues in order to develop a general framework that can be applied by the management of a football club.

What becomes obvious during the interviews is that the management challenges of professional clubs seem to increase endlessly. Most business concepts assume that the firm develops, produces, and sells a product to a consumer or a buyer based on a mutually agreed price. The service society requires a tangible product combined with a certain set of services to be successful (Normann, 2001). This service stage has become so rooted and so prevalent that in many instances it is becoming commoditised. In order to differentiate themselves, many companies are moving beyond services into "experiences" or "entertainments" (Levitt, 1983; Wolf, 1999; Pine and Gilmore, 1999).

Our framework of value captures in professional football has three key dimensions (Figure 6.1): the product and its features, the customers, and the business process and strategic vision (see Dolles and Söderman, 2008c, for a comprehensive explanation of the framework). Having combined the six "offerings" with the five groups of "customers," 30 relations appear. Each of these constitutes a value capturing and an equivalent value creation. **1.F** meets **2.A** when the "merchandise product" is coproduced or sold to the "fan base." Then the "players" (**1.E**) are of interest to the "sponsors" (**2.D**) or the "media" (**2.C**). Thus, a mixture of such relations does constitute the bulk of the football industry, observing that not all lines are equally important. By adding the strategy dimension to our framework of value captures, we

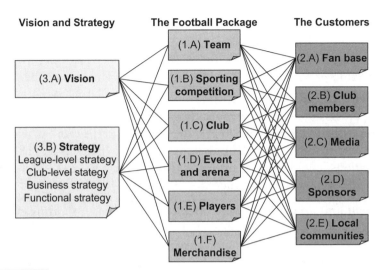

FIGURE 6.1   *The network of value captures in professional football (Dolles and Söderman, 2008c).*

introduce the vision and imagination of the future of the game, which influences the football package. The multiple dimensions of the football package are central to the level of strategy aggregation. The network level of strategy (**3.B**) is, for example, closely connected to the league's procedures of promotion and relegation (**1.B**), the costs of scheduling games for the club (**1.C**), requirements to develop their arenas (**1.D**), or a regulated labour market for player movements (**1.E**).

The problem in defining the product in the football business is partly the result of every individual having his or her own experience and expectation of the game or events around the match—a "something else" associated with the football experience. It is not one single product, service, or entertainment that a football club offers. We can consider the following possible "offerings": (**1.A**) Team, (**1.B**) Sporting competition, (**1.C**) Club, (**1.D**) Event and arena, (**1.E**) Players, and (**1.F**) Merchandise.

1.A: *Team—top-performance team.* Football is a team sport. But 11 skilled players do not necessarily make a winning team. A team with superior physical ability alone cannot beat an opponent that has good technique and a carefully planned strategy.

1.B: *Sporting competitions—league structures.* Football as a team sport also requires coordination among the contesting teams, because the game involves at least two distinct teams that must agree on the rules of the game. Leagues need to be organised by the club's national governing body, depending on the division their teams play in. In order to manage competition efficiently, rules also need to be developed for determining a champion.

1.C: *Club—administration.* Hosting a winning team has a dual meaning for professional sports organisations. Not only must the players on the sporting team be able to give their utmost to the cause of winning, but the financial and administrative structure (marketing, public relations, etc.) behind it must also work closely to ensure that its business goals will be achieved.

1.D: *Event and arena—the football match and arena.* A sporting event (football match) is intangible, short-lived, unpredictable, and subjective in nature. It is produced and consumed by the spectators in the arena at the same time, mostly with a strong emotional commitment from the fans. In recent years those football games have been transformed into media events for the benefits of millions of spectators, few of whom were in attendance at the live event. Such mediatised events affect even the stadium or arena they are attached to. Arenas of most of the top clubs represent the state of the art in sports-leisure multiplex architecture.

1.E: *Players—stars, top players as assets.* Players and their development are of prime concern to football managers. Football clubs send out their scouts to discover young players in the region or worldwide and to sign contracts with them, as some of them might later find their way to a professional team.

1.F: *Merchandise.* Football merchandise means goods held for resale but not manufactured by the football club, such as flags and banners, scarves and caps, training gear, jerseys and fleeces, footballs, videos and DVDs, blankets and pillows, watches, lamps, tables, clocks, and signs.

Why do supporters choose one team over another? Cost is certainly not the only argument for fans in the football business, but rather, fun, excitement, skilled players, and regional embeddedness might all be good reasons for supporting a team. Consequently, the variety of offerings creates a broader customer approach in football, addressing (**2.A**) the spectators and supporters, (**2.B**) the club members, (**2.C**) the media, (**2.D**) the sponsors, and (**2.E**) local communities.

2.A: *Fan base—spectators and supporters.* When it comes to "sales" in the football business, the main attention is created by the supporters with regard to ticket sales and merchandising. Fan motivation and behaviour vary, depending on the type of fan. By introducing the international dimension, we distinguish two different types of fans: "Local fans" exhibit their behaviour because of identification with a geographic area in which they were either born, living, or staying in the home region of the club. "International fans" live abroad and do not get many opportunities to see the team play live. Their attendance is mainly virtual via the radio, television, or Internet.

2.B: *Club Members—membership.* Football by nature is fun; it involves exercise and is competitive. For this reason, the football club facilitates opportunities for its active members to engage in exercise and to play football in a team. Others may join the football club as passive members to support their favourite team.

2.C: *Media.* The media is the main sales channel. The importance of football for the media business can be seen in the increasing amounts of money paid for broadcast rights, as well as the growth in the number of sports-oriented radio talk shows and TV networks.

2.D: *Sponsors—sponsorships.* Football is a natural area for sponsorship, as it carries very strong images, has a mass-international audience, and appeals to all classes. Depending on the level of sponsorship, the benefits for the sponsors might include but are not limited to product category exclusivity; naming rights; the sponsor's logo on jerseys, uniforms, and websites; perimeter advertising (boards and/or banners) in the arena; VIP tickets; advertisements in the club's official magazine; cross-promotion, and so on. Sponsorship deals are promoted either by the club or an intermediary agency specialising in sponsorship activities.

2.E: *Local Communities—public authorities, local sport governing bodies.* Football is firmly rooted in the local setting and plays a vital part of the cultural and social makeup of local communities, and as a result, community funds or pooled resources sometimes are used as a last resort to keep those clubs in business. In this sense football clubs remain largely untouchable by economic forces that determine the fate of other companies.

The highest and broadest level business objective is the *vision of the club* (**3.A**). This is a statement of broad aspiration, as it deals with where the club hopes to be in the future. This is not about winning the next game but is the attempt by the club management to define where it expects the club to be at a later time: to win the championship, to stay in the league, to make profit, or to go international. With the exception of merchandising, the football business lacks the option of producing and storing inventory for future sale, as the main characteristic of football is its ambiguity and the uncertainty of the outcome of a game. In order to reach the goals attached to the vision where the club should be in the future, what kind of *strategies* should be applied? (**3.B**) Strategies can be made for different activities within the club, where the lowest level of aggregation is one specific task, while the highest level of aggregation encompasses all activities within the club. A logical extension of this distinction is the league-level strategy.

NECESSARY ELEMENTS FOR THE DEVELOPMENT OF FOOTBALL AT AN INTERNATIONAL LEVEL

The following six minicase-studies demonstrate how strategies are applied to develop football at the international level.

Minicase 1: Meeting the requirements of a dispersed fan base

Without a local fan base (**2.A**) and local revenues, a team (**1.A**) cannot expect to survive and prosper beyond its market of origin. Devotion is to be loyal, to repeat a purchase. There are clubs for the owners of a Porsche, of a Louis Vuitton bag, or of other luxury goods (Tapp and Clowes, 2002). A devoted fan never switches a football club, but a Porsche owner may very well switch to another sportscar producer. Genuine football fans might burn their flags due to disappointment at the performance on the pitch but will never sympathise with the rival team.

Attracted by the huge potential market and their growing fan base in Asia, Europe's top football clubs, like Manchester United, Real Madrid, FC Barcelona, and FC Bayern Munich, are occasionally visiting Asia. As part of their profile-building drive in the Asian market, German Bundesliga Club FC Bayern Munich did a nine-day promotional tour to Indonesia and India in May 2008 playing friendlies. In the first of two matches, a Munich lineup featuring only a handful of established stars and some up-and-coming youngsters won over the Indonesian national team in Jakarta, attracting more than 70,000 spectators. After the official foundation of Indonesia's first

FC Bayern Munich fan club, the party then travelled to India, playing a friendly at Kolkata's (formerly known as Calcutta) oldest club. An astonishing 120,000 fans packed the Salt Lake stadium to watch Bayern's victory over their home team, Mohun Bagan AC.

Besides the football matches, Bayern Munich was engaged in local social projects such as visiting the Kolkata Police Youth Tournament. Prior to the delegation's takeoff back to Munich, Bayern's general manager, Uli Hoeness (FC.bayern.com, 2008), declared that "it wasn't just about winning two matches; we've made a host of new friends for Bayern Munich and for German football."

Questions

1. What is the appropriate strategy for football clubs to gain competitive advantage in order to make a profit out of their Asia tours?

2. What role do top stars play when they play friendlies abroad?

3. Why do football clubs engage, even abroad, in local social projects?

Minicase 2: Creating New Markets

In creating new markets overseas, nothing seems to be impossible in the football business. Take the English second division Stockport County FC as an example. In Chinese cities like Shenyang and Wuhan, the tiny 125-year-old Stockport club (Forbes.com), 2008 is considered "the hottest thing going." Stockport was the first international professional football team to play in Urumqi, Xinjiang province. "People travel for four days to watch us in China," says Steve Bellis, the club's international marketing manager.

Stockport County's success in China shows both shrewd marketing activities and a willingness to seek out new revenue sources. To intensify its activities in China, in 2003 Stockport County FC (**1.C**) purchased 50 percent of a club in China that is now called "Stockport Tiger Star" in Shenyang, Liaoning Province, targeting several customer groups (**2.A, 2.B, 2.C, 2.D**) (Independent.com, 2003; UEFA.com, 2004).

Already in 2004, 30 percent of Stockport County FC's total revenues were coming from this investment. The home arena of Stockport takes only 6,500 spectators, while the Chinese sister club takes 24,000. Young players from Shenyang travel to England to play for the club's youth and reserve sides, and vice versa. "One lad came over to play for the Stockport youth team and has gone on to make China's Olympic squad," said Bellis. There also is an educational element to the relationship: 50 youngsters from Shenyang have already been accepted at a college in Stockport.

Manchester United, Real Madrid, and their activities in Asia can be said to have opened the market for Stockport, enabling a small local business to be progressively expanded. However, while large football clubs have concentrated their marketing efforts on Beijing and Shanghai, Stockport's managers have spent the last six years quietly building regional links in China. It is a business challenge to be a good club in a small country, with a limited customer base, only just surviving as a kind of "secondary professional" or an "amateur club." Globalisation and IT provide new opportunities for these clubs to capture other (business) positions in the large football hierarchy and to use different competitive strategies for market development.

Questions

1. What is the special challenge for football clubs to create new markets across national borders?

2. What are additional sources of value creation of an international collaboration?

Minicase 3: Crossing Entangled Revenues

The revenue streams in the football business are changing in character. The richer clubs monitor decreasing ticket revenues and increasing dependence on sponsors and media. A strict cost-revenue analysis is possible only in ticketing. Media revenues (mainly from TV) become a residual and can seldom be calculated in advance. The media business (**2.C**) transfers the money when the season is over, and qualification for the various UEFA pan-European tournaments (**1.B**) will create extra revenues. According to UEFA's allocation formula (Uefa.com, 2008), qualified teams for the Champions League receive €2 million as a start premium, €400.000 for each first-round match, and a remarkably high performance fee. Thus, depending on their success within the competition, top teams can achieve more than €20 million in income per year.

However, there are only a few top teams that almost always qualify, such as Juventus of Turin, AC Milan, Real Madrid, FC Bayern Munich, or Manchester United. Since the insolvency of the KirchGruppe, which had purchased the exclusive rights to live transmission of the German first and second Bundesliga, less money has been transferred around Europe for TV rights (see Fowler and Curwen, 2002, for a detailed description of the collapse). More and more clubs (e.g., Manchester United, Chelsea FC,

Juventus of Turin, AC Milan, Internazionale Milan, and FC Barcelona) have their own TV channels, something that might eliminate these risks. They offer chances for worldwide distribution, but the possibilities to outperform the major channels in the home country are limited.

Questions

1. What are the difficulties and spillover effects that football managers have to take into consideration before they develop future international concepts for generating revenue?

Minicase 4: Partnering Should Be Untangled and Debundled

Football is perceived differently by different groups; it is a masquerade where perception is the product. Manchester United, Chelsea FC, and the other top clubs are dressed differently depending on whether or not it is a home match (**3.B**). If they play in Asia, Manchester United has two tiers of alliance: their major sponsors and then their secondary sponsors (**2.D**) (Manutd.com, 2008). In 2008 the major alliances were the American Insurance Group (AIG) and the leisure apparel giant Nike. These two sponsors were visible on the Manchester United kit that the team plays in every game, so the exposure for the two major sponsors was a lot greater than that of the secondary sponsors. The secondary sponsors of Manchester United go to great lengths to grab the attention of their wide audience, since their fans come in all shapes and sizes. The secondary sponsors included companies such as Budweiser, AirAsia, BetFred and Audi, which represent an assortment of industries including beer, tourism, gambling, and automobiles.

In October 2004, the Premier League's Arsenal unveiled a £100 million sponsorship deal with Emirates airlines shortly after the club's rival Chelsea had chosen not to extend its contract with the Middle East airline (Gibson, 2004). Until 2021 Emirates sponsors the Arsenal shirt and have had Arsenal's new ground named after the company (Mortimer, 2004). In order to concentrate on securing a brand that better fitted with its global ambitions, Chelsea's then management was looking for a new partner. At that time, that move looked like a case of the west London club getting its public relations retaliation in first, having been informed by the airline of its intention to sign a major deal with its rivals.

Questions

1. Why is there a need for stakeholder-analysis and sponsor evaluation?

Minicase 5: Developing the Arena

Due to the increasing event character (**1.D**) of football matches, higher demand for comfort of spectators, and at least the need to generate more turnover, some football clubs (**1.C**) as well as the public authorities (**2.E**) were forced to act. After new development, reconstruction, or modernisation, present-day football arenas are not only sporting venues. They also include restaurants, merchandise shops, VIP and hospitality areas, conference centres, administrative offices, and sometimes even museums. Mobile playing fields (e.g., Veltins-Arena, FC Schalke 04, Germany) as well as closable stadium roofs (e.g., Wembley national stadium, England) represent an inherent part of the modern football arena. In addition, small and large events such as football matches or concerts take place on a regular basis, mega-sporting events such as the FIFA World Cup including qualifying matches take place occasionally. Multifunctional stadiums nowadays, however, require high-capacity use, which, for example, inevitably leads to increasing demand for energy and high infrastructure costs. As far as the budgeting of a stadium is concerned, the management needs to develop viable concepts for subsequent use (Feddersen and Maennig, 2003).

For example, the German "Kölner Sportstätten GmbH," an outsourced subsidiary of the City of Cologne, is taking care of maintenance, leasing, and promotion of Cologne's sporting venues, including the RheinEnergieStadion (formerly known as the Müngersdorfer Stadion, named after the sponsor Rhein Energie, Cologne's local electricity provider) (Koelnersportstaetten.de, 2008). The arena, in which German Bundesliga club 1 FC Köln plays its home games, was reconstructed for the 2006 FIFA World Cup from 2001 to 2004. After completion, the arena has about 50,000 seats, 1 restaurant, 51 VIP areas, 1 two-story business lounge, 1 press-conference center, 1 FC Köln administrative office, and 1 museum. In order to foster sustainable development for subsequent use, the Kölner Sportstätten GmbH has recently conducted some minor and major activities. The list of events includes but is not limited to live concerts (e.g., German superstar Herbert Grönemeyer, Rolling Stones, etc.), "floodlight" and night-guided tours, sightseeing tours every Saturday, and "Colonia Noctes" (a partylike event series within the business lounge). Not surprisingly, in the years 2004–2006, total turnover of the Kölner Sportstätten GmbH increased from € 6.5 to € 12.7 million.

Questions

1. What are the advantages and disadvantages of developing the arena?

Minicase 6: Forcing Corporate Environmental and Social Responsibility

Internationalisation has deep social, political, and environmental consequences. Within this context, corporate social responsibility has been defined as "the obligations of firms to society or more specifically to those affected by corporate policies and practices" (Smith, 2003, page 3) **(3.B)**. Recent studies prove that the spectators' travel, food and drink consumption, and waste, have the most significant environmental impact (Collins et al., 2007). With its commitment to the United Nations Agenda 21 environmental sustainability initiative the International Olympic Committee (IOC) has addressed this. Since 1994 environmental protection programmes are an obligatory part for applicant cities. It was the German Organising committee for the 2006 FIFA World Cup that was catching up on ecological matters in the football business. "Green Goal," (Oeko.de, 2008) which was founded on the voluntary involvement of the Organising Committee as well as participating cities, arenas, and World Cup partners, was the first environmental World Cup concept with ambitious objectives. The programme comprised measures for the economic use of water, reduction of waste, increase in energy efficiency, sustainable transport, and climate neutrality, and was a huge success, as it aroused great interest and wide approval.

The implementation of international and national projects such as "Sustainable Management of Sports Facilities" (SMS, Europe-wide conjoint project) or "Qualification in Sustainable Sport Facility Management" (QuaSpo, Germany) depict the challenges facing sustainability in sport facility management. According to SMS's mission statement (Leonardo-sms.eu, 2008), the main objectives of the project are "support of a European exchange in regard to the initial education and training of managers and technicians on the topic of sustainable management of sport facilities and development of respective programmes for education and training throughout Europe."

Questions

1. How can corporate policies in the football business be designed to contribute to global environment protection?

CONCLUSIONS

In this chapter we applied a framework for analysing football management that varies from those of any other business. By identifying six value offerings and five customer categories, we can construct up to 30 value captures in professional football reflecting the complexity of the football business and its international dimensions. These captures are in a real world preceded by the management's strategy intent, and it requires strategies on different levels of aggregation. This framework recognises the product and its features, the various customer groups, and the vision of the future of the club central to different levels of strategy aggregation.

Subsequent to defining our framework, we provided six minicases of emerging international trends in the football business linked with the value captures of the framework. Knowing how those value captures are interlinked is of significant practical relevance and importance. As suggested in sports management research, the sporting success of a football club might increase its revenue potential, but the extent to which this potential is fulfilled depends on the strategy, sound club and product management, and good working relations with all customer groups, nationally and internationally. Our major goal is to offer challenges and to create intuition for trends in the international development of the football business. In this sense, our network of value captures aims to link context, practices and institutions of a specific industry and respond to the calls for building theoretical models that capture the international dimension of sports (Maguire, 2005; Smith and Westerbeek, 2004).

GUIDED READING

Global Strategic Management by Philippe Lasserre (2007) embraces traditional strategic management teaching but extends it to an international scale. It offers insight into the impact of globalisation on business organisations and how managers could and should react. The text combines to great effect a strategic and managerial approach to global issues, blending theory, and practical examples.

International Business: The Challenges of Globalization by John J. Wild, Kenneth L. Wild, and Jerry C. Y. Han (2007) engages students to learn by highlighting that culture is an inescapable element of all international business activities. Culture is presented early and integrated within the text through culture-rich, chapter-opening company profiles, and lively examples of cultural differences in business. Employing culture in this way fosters enthusiasm among students and makes concepts relevant to their world. Wild, Wild, and Han present the fundamental changes that occur in the globalisation of both markets and production, the drivers behind globalisation, and recent attempts to measure how "global" different nations are.

S. Tamer Cavusgil, Gary Knight, and John R. Riesenberger's *International Business: Strategy, Management and the New Realities* (2008) systematically addresses recent changes in the cross-border flow of products, services, capital, ideas, and people. It also covers the changing nature of the international business landscape, not just the Triad regions (Europe, North America, and Japan), and introduces the challenges for a variety of businesses—not only multinational enterprises—engaged in international activities.

REFERENCES

Aaker, D. A. (1996). *Building Strong Brands*. New York: The Free Press.

Alter, C., & Hage, J. (1993). *Organizations Working Together*. Newbury Park, CA: Sage.

Beech, J., & Chadwick, S. (Eds.), (2004). *The Business of Sport Management*. Harlow: Financial Times/Prentice Hall.

Cavusgil, S. T., Knight, G., & Riesenberger, J. R. (2008). *International Business: Strategy, Management and the New Realities*. Upper Saddle River, NJ: Pearson Prentice Hall.

Collins, A., Flynn, A., Munday, M., & Roberts, A. (2007). Assessing the Environmental Consequences of Major Sporting Events: The 2003/04 FA Cup Final, *Urban Studies*, Vol. 44, No. 3, pp. 457–476.

Dauncey, H., & Hare, G. (1999). *France and the 1998 World Cup*. London: Frank Cass.

Dolles, H., & S. Söderman. (2008a). Mega-Sporting Events in Asia: Impacts on Society, Business & Management-An Introduction, *Asian Business & Management*, Vol. 7, No. 2 (special issue), pp. 1–16.

Dolles, H., & S. Söderman. (2008b). The Internationalisation of Sports and Sports-Related Industries, *International Journal of Sports Marketing and Sponsorship*, Vol. 10, No. 1 (special issue), pp. 7–8.

Dolles, H., & S. Söderman. (2008c). The Network of Value Captures: Creating Competitive Advantage in Football Management, *Wirtschaftspolitische Blätter Österreich* [Austrian Economic Policy Papers], Vol. 55, No.1, pp. 39–58.

fcbayern.t-home.de (6th June, 2008). Successful Asian Tour. Retrieved on June 10, 2009, from http://www.fcbayern.t-home.de/en/news/news/2008/16431.php?fcb_sid=553edce70e5f7b43a13410f87c80c592

Feddersen, A., & Maennig, W. (2003). *Nachhaltigkeit von Sportstätten*. Wissenschaftliche Berichte und Materialien des Bundesinstitut für Sportwissenschaft. In M.-P.Büch., W.Maennig., & H.-J. Schulke. (Eds.), *Sustainability in Economics—Consequences for the Construction of Sports Venues*, Vol. 12, No. 3, pp. 11–22.

forbes.com (4th December, 2008). Madness of Crowds. Retrieved on June 10, 2009, from http://www.forbes.com/forbes/2004/0412/120.html,%20accessed%2023. 07.2008.

Fowler, T., & Curwen, P. (2002). Can European Media Empires Survive? The Rise and Fall of the House of Kirch. *The Journal of Policy, Regulation and Strategy for Telecommunications*, Vol. 4, No. 4, pp. 17–24.

Gibson, O. (5th October, 2004). Arsenal-Emirates deal worth £100m. *The Guardian*. Retrieved on July 25, 2009, from http://www.guardian.co.uk/media/ 2004/oct/05/business.marketingandpr.

Horne, J., & W. Manzenreiter. (Eds.) (2002a). *Japan, Korea and the 2002 World Cup*. London: Routledge.

Horne, J., & W. Manzenreiter. (2002b). The World Cup and Television Football. In J. Horne and W. Manzenreiter (Eds.), *Japan, Korea and the 2002 World Cup*. London: Routledge.

Independent.com (13th December, 2003). Stockport Profit from China. Retrieved on June 10, 2009 from http://www.independent.co.uk/sport/football/football- league/stockport-profit-from-china-link-576490.html

Koelnersportstaetten.de/. Retrieved on May 28, 2008, from http://www.stadion- koeln.de/kss/downloads/kss_daten_und_fakten.pdf

Lassere, P. (2007). Global Strategic Management, 2nd Edition. Houndmills, Basingstoke: Palgrave Macmillan.

Leonardo-sms.eu. Retrieved on May 28, 2008, from http://www.leonardo-sms.eu/ project_en.htm

Levitt, T. (1983). *The Marketing Imagination*. New York: The Free Press.

Maguire, J. (2005). *Power and Global Sport: Zones of Prestige, Emulation and Resistance*. London: Routledge.

Manutd.com. (1st July, 2007). Reds launch new home kit. *Manutd.com*. Retrieved on July 25, 2008, from http://www.manutd.com/default.sps? pagegid=%7B48C41513%2DA376%2D4D1F%2D981D%2D660FC5BB193E% 7D&newsid=439738.

Mortimer, R. (2004). Chelsea shrugs off its blues: Chelsea is embarking on a new era of wealth and success. *Brand Strategy. Strategic Thinking for Today's Marketing Professionals, No. 187*. Retrieved on May 18, 2009, from http:// findarticles.com/p/articles/mi_go2028/is_200411/ai_n9674672/.

Nilsson, D. (2005). *Published Articles in the Field of Football*. Master's Thesis: Stockholm University School of Business.

Normann, R. (2001). *Reframing Business: When the Map Changes the Land- scape*. New York: John Wiley & Sons.

Oeko.de. Retrieved on May 20, 2008, from http://www.oeko.de/oekodoc/292/ 2006-011-en.pdf

Park, S. H. (1996). Managing an Inter-Organizational Network: A Framework of the Institutional Mechanism for Network Control. *Organizational Studies*, Vol. 17, No. 5, pp. 795–824.

Pine, J. B., & Gilmore, J. H. (1999). *The Experience Economy—Work Is Theatre and Every Business Is a Stage*. Boston: Harvard Business School Press.

Porter, M. E. (1991). Towards a Dynamic Theory of Strategy. *Strategic Management Journal*, Vol. 12, Special Issue Winter, pp. 95–117.

Ritter, T., & Gemünden, H. G. (2003). Interorganizational Relationships and Networks: An Overview. *Journal of Business Research*, Vol. 56, No. 9, pp. 691–697.

Smith, C. (2003). Corporate Social Responsibility: Whether or How? *California Management Review*, Vol. 45, No. 4, pp. 1–25.

Smith, A., & Westerbeek, H. (2004). *The Sport Business Future*. Houndmills, Basingstoke: Palgrave Macmillan.

Tapp, A., & Clowes, J. (2002). From Carefree Causals to Professional Wanderers: Segmentation Possibilities for Football Supporters. *European Journal of Marketing*, Vol. 36, No. 11/12, pp. 1248–1269.

Uefa.com (19th March, 2004). China Beckons for Stockport. Retrieved on June 10, 2009, from http://www.uefa.com/magazine/news/Kind=128/newsId=154210.html

UEFA.com (2008). *Financial Report 2007/2008*. UEFA.com. Retrieved on July 25, 2008, from http://www.uefa.com/multimediafiles/download/officialdocument/uefa/others/81/53/06/815306_download.pdf

Wild, J. J., Wild, K. L., & Han, J. C. Y. (2007). *International Business: The Challenges of Globalisation*. Upper Saddle River, NJ: Pearson/Prentice Hall.

Wolf, M. J. (1999). *The Entertainment Economy. How Mega Media Forces Are Transforming Our Lives*. New York: Random House.

RECOMMENDED WEBSITES

Bundesliga website
http://www.bundesliga.de
FIFA's website
http://www.fifa.com
IEG sponsorship website
http://www.sponsorship.com
Sustainablemanagement of sports facilities website
http://www.leonardo-sms.eu
The United Nations Environment Programme
http://www.unep.org/sport_env/
UEFA's webiste
http://www.uefa.com

CHAPTER 7

Sports Marketing and Sponsorship

James Skinner
Griffith University

Objectives

Upon completion of this chapter the reader should be able to:

- Define and identify the nature of sponsorships, naming rights, and merchandising.

- Identify the benefits that corporate sponsorship may bring to football.

- Consider the legal and ethical implications of corporate sponsorship and what control these sponsors can and do exercise over football teams and individuals.

- Identify ambush marketing techniques and what measures can and should be undertaken by corporate sponsors to protect their investment.

CONTENTS

OVERVIEW OF THE CHAPTER

This chapter discusses the changing nature of the political economy of sport, and football in particular, in the last quarter of the twentieth century and the beginning of the twenty-first century. Focusing on the United Kingdom for a national perspective and on the *Fédération Internationale de Football Association* (FIFA) for the international perspective (FIFA is the governing body of world football), this chapter identifies the nature of the market for sponsorships and endorsements, the fan base of national and international soccer, and the Horst Dassler–led FIFA assault on the traditional promotion of world football and the establishment of corporate partnerships that generate millions of dollars of revenue both for corporate identities and football associations.

INTRODUCTION

To begin with, the concept of *sports marketing* is defined as the process in which corporations and companies use popular mainstream and alternative sports, and the athletes prominent within those sports, to connect with consumers. Sport marketing and the utilisation of sports stars in advertising, promotional activities, and sponsorship deals are not phenomena unique to the latter part of the twentieth century. For example, in the nineteenth century, the uniquely recognisable visage of English Cricket captain W. G. Grace endorsed a range of domestic products. It is the difference in the scale of commercial involvement that uniquely defines the contemporary political economy of sport. Tomlinson (2005) believes that the rapidly growing international economy and expanding global communications infrastructure in the last quarter of the twentieth century were crucial to both the reimaging of many sports and therefore the remaking of the political economy of world sports. The rising profile and popularity of some international football players and teams led multinational companies, among them sports equipment and clothing retailers, to view sport and sports stars as irresistible vehicles for the marketing of their products. Corporate sponsorship began to target whole sports, not just individuals, with some corporations seeing a financial advantage in establishing exclusive rights for years at a time rather than just one-off events.

The attraction of sports for corporate sponsorship is the potential for massive profits, enhanced in the last quarter of the twentieth century by the global communication revolution and the increasing popularity, partly by virtue of global accessibility, of such mega-events as football's World Cup and European Championships, globally spectated sporting competitions such as the Champions League and numerous national league competitions. Aiding the corporate world's foray into sport sponsorship was the long-established institutional infrastructure of organisations such as the *Fédération Internationale de Football Association* (FIFA) and the recognition by its former President Joao Havelange of the unexploited and potentially unlimited market potential at their fingertips.

Fan Demand for Football

The massive profits generated from football are only possible because of the huge, continuing fan demand for the sport. Borland and Macdonald (2003) identify "fan interest" as the essential element that drives demand for the game or sporting contest. Fans demonstrate their interest in the game or sporting contest in a variety of ways, including watching or listening to the game, buying merchandise associated with the contest, or simply following the contest in the local newspaper. Traditionally, fans have an identification or association with a particular team, typically founded on a geographic or emotional connection.

Fans are consumers; they are the demand-side of the market for professional sporting competitions. They are the market for team merchandise, souvenirs, and the other products of team sponsors. They buy the newspapers that report on the matches and the subscription TV channels that provide exclusive live coverage. They are also the consumers who buy the tickets and fill the stadia and thus become part of the product itself, as part of the spectacle of the live event that is sold to other consumers.

Sports marketers try to isolate the particular characteristics of football fans—often referred to as "segmenting the market"—in order to establish specific promotional activities that target different groups from within the fan base. On any given weekend, professional football attracts millions of spectators/consumers. These spectators/consumers may engage with football for a variety of reasons. By segmenting the marketplace, sports marketers can more judiciously allocate market resources to promoting specific products, which should result in greater returns on the investment for the corporate sponsor. The challenge facing the football business manager is to develop appropriate market segmentation strategies that will allow consumer product companies to match their products to the most appropriate groups of football fans.

On the basis of projected fan demand for sporting events, TV and radio broadcasters sell advertising space and time to targeted advertisers and/or sell on a subscription or pay-per-view basis to targeted organizations and individuals. Multinational corporations also engage in marketing campaigns to gain recognition for or enhance the brand name and reputation of their products through advertising via media or at sporting events (Borland & Macdonald, 2003), based on the interest or demand in a particular sport or event. This process is aimed at developing brand loyalty with consumers. Brand loyalty occurs when a consumer's preference is for a particular brand because of the perception that the brand offers the right image, quality, and price. This perception then becomes the basis for a new buying habit, where the consumer will continue to purchase this brand as opposed to its competitors. Sponsorship and naming rights are also important marketing tools that corporations use to link their product or services to major sporting events and facilities utilised by fans.

Sponsorship and Naming Rights

Sponsorship is an important marketing tool utilised by corporations by which they obtain a commercial advantage by gaining rights or association with a particular individual, team, or event. It can be seen as a reciprocal arrangement, where those being sponsored may receive funding (for ongoing team costs such as development costs), resources (such as the team kit), or services (training facilities, support services, etc.), and the sponsoring corporation receives the financial benefit from their strong visual imprint on the team or individual. Corporate organisations are then able to sell merchandise with an "identity" associated with teams, events, and/or athletes. Stadium and venue owners also seek to establish financial relationships with large corporations whereby those corporations will purchase naming rights and develop entertainment packages to sell seats at their stadia and to sell marketing opportunities to advertisers/sponsors at those games via boundary advertising, onfield entertainment, and direct marketing (Borland & Macdonald, 2003).

Naming rights are those rights granted to an individual or corporate identity to name a building, facility, or event in exchange for some financial consideration. Traditionally, naming rights have long been associated with institutions such as universities, hospitals, even schools, where the financial contribution secures the right to have the donor's name ascribed to the facility. Stadium naming rights have taken this financial relationship literally into the sporting arena. In the United States, stadium naming rights have been a corporate sponsorship tool since the 1950s. In the following years, the practice has extended to other countries, including Australia and the United Kingdom. In the United Kingdom, Emirates Airlines contributed £100 million for the naming rights of Arsenal FC's new stadium, which opened in 2006. The stadium project itself had an estimated cost of approximately £400 million. The 15-year deal with Emirates is representative of a number of similar deals with major corporate sponsors and sporting stadia worldwide (*BBC*, 2004).

Fans have not always openly embraced the intrusion of corporate sponsorship into football. Tomlinson (2005) describes how some commentators expressed disquiet at the English Football Association's decision to allow its member clubs to engage in shirt sponsorship deals as late as the 1980s. By 1992, all the teams in the inaugural English Premier League had secured lucrative sponsorship deals, with a variety of different sponsors promoting products as diverse as food, electronic equipment, alcohol, and communications. By 2002, almost half the sponsors were telecommunication companies, a divergence that recognised the massive potential of the worldwide telecommunication revolution and the increasing digital dependence of the up and coming fan base.

While football supporters will generally favour the additional funding and service support to their club that corporate sponsorship can provide, the overcommercialisation of football is often seen as purely profit driven, with the long-term good of the club and the players relegated to the far end of the sponsor's list of motives. Budd (2001, page 3) describes how "British Sky Broadcasting (BSkyB)'s bid for Manchester United provoked an anti-Murdoch campaign by the Independent Manchester United Supporters' Association, forcing a referral to the Monopolies and Mergers Commission." Rupert Murdoch, chairman of Newscorp International (which owned 40 percent of BSkyB), was accused by Manchester United supporters of being more interested in the commercial television interests that would be derived from the deal rather than a love of the sport and a commitment to the future development and success of the team itself.

There is a perceived class dimension to corporate sponsorship, particularly in the United Kingdom, due to the working class origins of many teams and the generational fan base that has maintained club loyalty in both good times and bad. Their loyalty has often led to a strong reaction against overt commercialisation of their club. Giulianotti (1999, page 105) describes how television and merchandising companies have "successfully targeted a new, young, middle-class audience whose club affiliations are the most plastic of all." He further goes on to discuss the different class allegiances and affiliations to football teams, where the working and lower middle classes are more closely tied to "local" cultural practices and identities and are more likely to support the community football team. Middle and upper classes tend to be more "cosmopolitan" in their cultural commitments and allegiances, and tend to follow the "big" or more successful football teams, changing their support for teams and even sports easily. As Giulianotti (1999, page 105) notes, this is a warning that football sponsors should heed as the "new, cosmopolitan fan may abandon the game as quickly as he or she arrived in it."

On a global scale, however, there seems little danger of the fan base, and thus the profit base, for corporate sponsorship disappearing overnight. FIFA's own publicity machine (FIFA.com, 2009a) states that the "FIFA World Cup is the most popular event worldwide that stands out amid a fast-changing media landscape [and] there is a growing respect for the contribution made by sponsors, and that the event embodies a powerful, emotive brand with prized assets that touch all demographics" (FIFA.com, 2009b). A bold claim, but perhaps borne out by FIFA's own statistics from the 2006 World Cup:

- A total of 3,359,439 spectators at 64 games in 12 stadiums, with over 15 million applications for tickets on offer to the public.
- The World Cup was broadcast to 214 countries on 376 channels, for a cumulative TV audience of 26.29 billion.

- FIFAworldcup.com became the most successful sports event website, with 4.2 billion page views from June 9 to July 9-more than double the traffic recorded during the 2002 event.

FIFA AND THE GROWTH OF WORLD FOOTBALL

FIFA has overseen the phenomenal growth of world football and the increasing profile of the World Cup. Tomlinson (2005, page 39) describes how the world governing body of the game has established partnerships that have changed the financial base of the game and established the FIFA World Cup as a "major global spectacle and … a marketing opportunity for the world's most powerful corporate investors." Founded in 1904, FIFA is one of the world's oldest and largest nongovernmental organisations (NGOs) and has since expanded to include 208 member associations. British president Sir Stanley Rous was replaced in 1974 after 13 years by Brazilian Joao Havelange. Havelange gained the presidency with the support of African and Asian allies, to whom his campaign commitments necessitated some radical rethinking of FIFA's role in the marketing of its product in order to fulfill those campaign commitments. FIFA soon became a much more commercial institution at this time. With an eye to the global markets that increased participation in the World Cup could provide, Havelange increased the number of participant nations from 16 to 24 in 1982, and then to 32 at the 1998 World Cup (Tomlinson, 2005).

It was in FIFA's partnership with Horst Dassler and Adidas that the global marketplace for football rapidly expanded, and a new age of corporate sponsorship emerged. Havelange had quickly recognised the potential to FIFA of a fuller relationship with Dassler, and Dassler became a key figure in the commercialisation of the World Cup (Smit, 2006, Tomlinson, 2005). Horst Dassler had great financial foresight and saw that with the increasing professionalism of international sports federations and the huge influx of TV money already generating vast profits, there was an opportunity for someone to work within the football system itself to take advantage of what Tomlinson (2005, page 42) calls "the new commercial logic of world sports." At this point, the new nexus of sponsorship and world football began to take shape, with marketing and sponsorship deals, television and media coverage deals, and the associated promotion of teams and players all becoming critical aspects for the growth of world football.

Tomlinson (2005) outlines the seminal deal in Dassler's association with FIFA as one negotiated with Coca-Cola by Patrick Nally and then goes on to summarise its profound consequences. Patrick Nally had been involved in the early growth of sport sponsorship in Britain. His marketing initiatives had included establishing sponsorship deals with brewery companies, Benson & Hedges (cigarettes), Kraft (food), and Esso (petroleum), just to name a few. The deal with Coca-Cola established a development programme, taking administrators, coaches, medicine trainers, and the like into various countries around the world, and led to the creation of a World Youth Championship.

Havelange had acted decisively; he saw the need for efficient liaisons with partners as important as a major sponsor—and such liaisons would best come from within his own organisation by virtue of his association with Horst Dassler and Patrick Nally. The outcome of the negotiations with Coca-Cola was that for the first time the company would sponsor one sport worldwide. The result was, as Tomlinson (2005, page 44) says, "an enormous FIFA programme, giving Havelange the ability to honour his election mandate: to develop Africa and Asia, create a World Youth Cup, and bring more Third World countries into the World Cup."

Getting a big corporate name such as Coca-Cola into the football programme gave the right credibility and image to world football, and these negotiations became the blueprint for everyone who wanted to try to bring money into international football via large corporate sponsorship. This was a multimillion-dollar investment package that concentrated initially on the World Youth Cup and a development strategy aimed at emerging football nations. This led to the emergence of African and Asian teams that could then compete at an international level against European and South American nations (Tomlinson, 2005). This demonstrated the positive benefits that sponsorship could bring to football.

Nally and Dassler set about establishing "sponsoring clients' exclusivity in all aspects of merchandising and franchising" (Tomlinson, 2005, page 45), setting a standard in corporate sponsorship deals that would to some extent guarantee the elimination of competition and give those sponsors some measure of reassurance that the large sums of money required for this level of corporate sponsorship were worthwhile and sensible business investments. The formation of International Sport and Leisure (ISL) in 1982 established Dassler as the undisputed master of world sports marketing, and their association with both FIFA and the International Olympic Committee (IOC) gave ISL a virtual monopoly over the promotion of major world sporting events. Within months of its establishment, ISL had secured merchandising and advertising rights with FIFA, UEFA (*Union des associations européennes de football*) – European football's governing body, and the IOC on behalf of such clients as Coca-Cola, Cinzano, and Bata (Tomlinson, 2005).

The global sponsorship of football has been based around a wide variety of popular consumables, including fast food, fast cars, and electronic and photographic equipment, and the marketing of these items worldwide in association with international football has been extremely effective. FIFA confirmed after Dassler's death that the sponsorship rights for the 1994 and 1998 World Cup Finals would remain with ISL (Tomlinson, 2005), although the dramatic collapse of ISL in 2001 signalled the end of one of the most profitable and influential partnerships in sporting history.

The fallout from ISL's split and dramatic collapse in 2001 continues today. Bond (2008) indicates that the 2008 fraud case investigating alleged bribes paid by ISL to sports officials to secure marketing deals threatens to damage FIFA's reputation, despite FIFA having initiated the court action after discovering that ISL had withheld £50 million of their money just prior to the company's collapse. Despite the demise of the FIFA/ISL partnership, there is no doubt it was the financial success of the partnership that changed the face of commercial sponsorship of football. In 1994, Joao Havelange had boasted that football generated $225 billion annually, and he later stated that his successor would inherit contracts worth $4 billion (Galeano, 1997). By 1997, the European football industry was estimated to be worth $10 billion (Giulianotti, 1999).

FIFA closed the 2003–2006 financial period with a best-ever overall result of CHF 816 million. FIFA's equity of CHF 752 million (£369,816,277) on December 31, 2006, represented the highest figure in the governing body's 103-year history (FIFA.com, 2009c). With this corporate sponsorship success, problems started to emerge that had the potential to threaten the financial success of FIFA. Rival corporations, recognising the great potential football offered for increased sales, brand recognition, and the development of a positive corporate image through a public association between the brand and football, started to engage in ambush marketing techniques.

AMBUSH MARKETING

Ambush marketing first appeared after the potential huge financial windfall from sponsorship and other associated rights became apparent. In ambush marketing, an entity or organisation that is not actually a financial sponsor attempts to give the impression that it is in fact a sponsor, thereby gaining a financial advantage by the perceived association with the individual, team, or event. During the 2002 World Cup, an Argentinian court found

PepsiCo guilty of engaging in ambush marketing after Pepsi used some major football players in commercials with the intention of leading consumers to believe that Pepsi was an official sponsor of the 2002 FIFA World Cup (Meikle, 2002). It was in fact Pepsi's major competitor, Coca-Cola, that was the official sponsor.

As sponsorship costs increase, and the financial rewards from major sponsorship deals also increase, organisers of major sporting events have a duty to protect the rights of their major sponsors and therefore need to take steps to prevent or mitigate the effects of ambush marketing techniques. The *FIFA 2002 World Cup Spectator Guide* advised patrons to "not bring commercially branded material (company names, logos, etc.) into the stadium, such as flags, banners, hats, balloons, scarves. Please be aware that stadium security will be removing all such items at the stadium entrances" (cited in Tomlinson, 2005, page 59).

In June 2008, it was reported that UEFA, the governing body of European soccer, had angered fans by implementing what some perceived as excessive sanctions to protect its sponsors from ambush marketing techniques (Gallu, 2008). During the 2008 European Soccer Championships, some fans said UEFA had "put profits ahead of their interests" and planned to turn them away from stadia and "fan zones" if they wore clothing bearing the logos of companies that were not official sponsors of the championships. UEFA denied that it would target individuals, saying only that groups organised by "ambush marketers" would be the focus of its attention during the competitions in Switzerland and Austria.

CASE STUDY 7.1: Ambush Marketing—FIFA versus PepsiCo

It is no surprise that protective measures to stop ambush marketing techniques are necessary when official sponsors have committed millions of dollars to be involved with mega-events such as the FIFA World Cup. For example, prompted by 2010 World Cup organisers, South African legislators amended two of its laws to essentially make ambush marketing illegal. These amendments to the Trade Practices Act prohibit the publication or display of false or misleading statements that imply that an official association exists with any sponsored event. The new laws were designed to prevent nonsanctioned advertisements from appearing within one kilometre of the World Cup final draw, venues, or stadia, in addition to a 100-metre restriction around FIFA Fan Parks. Furthermore, such advertisements will not be permitted to appear on main public roads within 2 kilometres of the final. These tough new laws clearly demonstrate how much official sponsors of the 2010 World Cup need to be protected from ambush marketers.

This level of protection is a result of an ongoing campaign by FIFA to stop ambush marketers infringing on the rights of official sponsors. For example, in 2002 FIFA World Cup organisers accused Nike and Pepsi of ambush marketing tactics against two of their official sponsors: Adidas and Coca-Cola. Both Nike and Pepsi produced television campaigns featuring soccer stars such as Ronaldo, Luis Figo, and

Roberto Carlos, which FIFA believed inferred an official connection between Pepsi, Nike, and the 2002 World Cup.

Given that Nike and Pepsi are the direct major competitors of Adidas and Coca-Cola, which were among 15 of FIFA's official sponsors of the 2002 World Cup, the financial investments of Adidas and Coca-Cola needed to be protected through decisive action. Adidas and Coca-Cola were reportedly paying between US$20 and $25 million each to be official sponsors of the 2002 World Cup.

While admitting that the Nike and Pepsi campaigns were clever and would make legal action difficult, FIFA felt compelled to take legal action against Pepsi to maintain their credibility and protect their long-term relationships with their corporate sponsors.

In June 2002, an Argentinean court ordered PepsiCo to immediately stop broadcasting its advertisements. FIFA had complained that the advert was unfair competition because it suggested that there was an association between Pepsi and the World Cup. The court agreed, finding that the advertisement would cause confusion among consumers, as it suggested that a sponsorship relationship existed between PepsiCo and the FIFA World Cup. The advertisement in question used the phrase "Tokyo 2002," as well as the images of famous footballers—all in conjunction with the logo of PepsiCo. Had FIFA not taken action against Pepsi, the value of its exclusive relationships with its corporate sponsors would have been severely compromised.

Source: Bhattacharjee et al, 2006; McCarthy, 2002; Vassallo et al, 2005.

U.K. CLUBS AND TV RIGHTS

Football had developed into such a strong cultural staple of late-nineteenth-century English life that some club directors recognised the financial potential of their sport, converting the status of their clubs to limited companies (Birley, 1995), giving them more control over future development. The 1960s saw the start of football's political economy undergoing a rapid modernisation. As Giulianotti (1999, page 88) notes, star players and clubs have become an intrinsic part of contemporary popular culture. It was becoming apparent that there were financial advantages to take into consideration in relation to a range of marketing strategies such as trackside advertising, TV commercials, sponsorships, and the merchandising of club paraphernalia.

Football clubs were understandably worried about the impact of televised football on attendance at matches. At this time, TV fees for matches were very low. However, by the late 1970s, Giulianotti (1999) asserts that club directors had become reassured that regular, controlled TV actually helped to increase the popularity of the game by making it more accessible, which would potentially increase match attendance.

The 1970s saw the beginning of television's growing financially profitable relationship with the football associations in the United Kingdom, and eventually in Europe and worldwide. Following early deals with the British Broadcasting Commission (BBC) in 1978 worth £9.8 million, in 1992 the English Premiership League struck a five-year deal with the BBC for £22.5 million for the regular match highlights. At this time, British Sky Broadcasting (BSkyB) paid £191.5 million to screen 60 live matches, and the English Premiership League was expected to earn an additional £90 million from sponsorship and television rights from overseas (Giulianotti, 1999, page 92). This massive increase in returns to the Premier League clubs over a relatively short period of time was both an indicator of, and catalyst for, the continued relationship between football and the corporate sponsor.

Technological breakthroughs in satellite broadcasting were vital to the next stage of development in the relationship between football and the telecommunications industries. Pay-per-view TV (PPV) was the next generation of televised football viewing, allowing subscribers to pay for single sports events. Viewers could have the option of paying to see a single club match or world events such as the World Cup. There was also the additional potential of clubs, pubs, and other facilities purchasing PPV for important matches in order to attract patrons to their premises. Giulianotti (1999, page 93) recognises the importance of the huge potential market share of the national and transnational dimensions of PPV, with even an "audience share of only 2 percent guaranteeing highly profitable returns in countries such as the United Kingdom, France, Italy, Germany, and Spain".

The spectacular financial turn in the relationship between football associations and corporate sponsors can be seen reflected in the commodification of football's cultural heritage. While some fans may feel alienated by the increasing commercialisation of the club that they and their family have supported for generations, there is no escape from their own part in this commodification process. Even searching for a link with the presponsorship roots of their club by purchasing, for example, a "classic" football shirt or viewing classic matches on video or DVD, the fan is still contributing to the current commercialised status of his or her favourite team. As Giulianotti (1999) asserts, football's economic relationships are extremely complex, and fans are contributing either directly or indirectly to this commodication process. Paying for satellite TV contributes funds to the clubs being shown, and the purchase of merchandise puts money not only into the hands of the club but into the hands of the sponsors, Nike, Adidas, Umbro, and so on, which then allows these sponsors to look for bigger and better merchandising and sponsorship deals.

CASE STUDY 7.2: Sponsorship and Ethics—Nike and the Brazilian National Team

One case that highlights the financial power that corporate sponsorship wields over both individual players and national team interests is that of Brazilian Ronaldo Luis Nazario de Lima (better known simply as Ronaldo) and corporate sports giant Nike.

Nike first signed Ronaldo to an individual contract in 1996, in a deal reportedly worth a minimum of £10 million over ten years, and as much as £120 million over his lifetime. While this private deal with Nike put Ronaldo in conflict with the sponsors (Kappa) of his then team, Barcelona, it was still disputed details of the deal that Nike struck with the Brazilian Football Confederation (CBF) and the fallout from that deal following Brazil's defeat at the 1998 World Cup that highlight the tensions and conflicts of interest between brand-led sponsorship and national interest and the ethical dilemmas that can arise (Giulianotti, 1999, page 89).

In 1996, CBF signed a £100 million contract with Nike—at the time the largest ever deal involving a national side—with Nike supplying the sports kit and becoming co-sponsor of the Brazilian national team. In 1998, a global controversy erupted after favourites, Brazil, lost spectacularly to France 3–0 in the World Cup Final, and reports surfaced that "Ronaldo had been forced to play the full 90 minutes of the game only hours after being hospitalised and given sedative medication following a seizure" (Giulianotti, 1999, page 90). In Brazil, Nike became a scapegoat for the Brazilian loss in the eyes of the general public, while continuing to profit from its sponsorship of the national side.

In 1999, a visibly unfit Ronaldo again focused attention on Nike's control of the Brazilian national team when he played in a special centenary match between the Brazilian national team and Barcelona. That same year, leaked details of the Nike deal with Brazil highlighted a clause in the contract that stipulated Nike's right to organise five international games a year with at least eight first team regulars, including Ronaldo. There was also some speculation from other Brazilian team members that the deal also specified that Ronaldo must play the full ninety minutes in every international (Giulianotti, 1999, page 90).

A Brazilian Congressional Commission into the Nike deal with the Brazilian national team did not incriminate Nike. Ronaldo himself was called to testify before the Commission, and, as he has done publicly on other occasions, he denied that he was forced to play in the World Cup game against medical advice. He stated that he played because he was fit to do so and not because he was pressured into doing so, a stance taken also by the team coach and Nike, which denied it had any influence on team lineups. The investigation moved to focus on the CBF, which was attacked for selling out the national sport. Subcommissions ended up investigating the trafficking of underage players to Europe, false passports, and disorganisation in the state football federations. At the end of the Commission, it presented evidence to prosecute 33 people for corruption, including Brazilian Football Federation (CBF) president Ricardo Teixeira on 13 counts of fraud (Bellos, 2001).

Alex Bellos, in his commentary on the scandal for the *Guardian* newspaper, reported that in spite of the controversy, Nike was accused of nothing, and it continued to sponsor the Brazilian national team. Head of the Brazilian Congressional Commission into the Nike deal with the CBF, Aldo Rebelo, summed up the feelings of a multitude of football fans when he said, "The CBF sold the national team to Nike. It should have sold the spectacle, not the product" (Bellos, 2001). Moreover, former Brazilian international star Tostao commented that "in my time it was the army generals running Brazil who tried to pick the team. …Today, it is the sponsors, the businessmen, the media moguls" (Budd, 2001, page 9).

CONCLUSIONS

As the changing political economy of football demonstrates, selling football is much more than just selling the game, and it will become a greater challenge for football managers in the future. Cars, soft drinks, alcohol, fast food—almost any consumable can be linked to sporting stars and sporting events. An event on the world stage the size of the World Cup can earn sponsors billions of dollars from consumer spending. While sporting purists may mourn the over-commercialisation of their sport and the changing face of the teams they support, their support contributes, albeit unknowingly and perhaps unwillingly, to the increasing intrusion of corporate entities into every facet of football at almost every level of the game. To date, corporate entities have reaped all of the benefits and so far have had to face little of the fallout from any perceived negative aspects of their involvement in the sport, as the case of Ronaldo and Nike demonstrates. The challenge for the football administrations of the future is to find the right balance between the commercialization of the game and its financial benefits, against catering to the needs and expectations of the general football supporter.

Sponsorship, merchandising, and stadium naming rights do provide clubs, national teams, and governing bodies such as FIFA a revenue base from which to build the sport. Servicing the increasingly spiralling costs of player wages, providing development programmes across the globe and armchair viewing access to the sport via global communications technologies, some would argue, would not be possible if not for corporate sponsorship and the association of big business and its vast financial resources with the game. Future challenges for the football business manager may be to determine how much control of the game must be relinquished in the quest for further corporate revenues.

DISCUSSION QUESTIONS

1. Explain why corporations would want to be involved in the sponsorship of football.
2. Identify the benefits that corporate sponsorship may bring to football.
3. What ethical concerns are raised by the relationship between Nike and CBF?
4. Discuss the consequences that an increase in ambush marketing could have for FIFA and its corporate sponsors?

GUIDED READING

The following texts provide a thorough overview of the sports marketing and sponsorship environment in the global football industry.

Chadwick, S., & Holt, M. (2008). Building global sports brands: An analysis of key success factors in marketing the UEFA Champions League. *Marketing Review.*

Desbordes, M. (Ed.). (2006). *Marketing and Football: An International Approach.* Oxford: Butterworth-Heinemann.

Giulianotti, R. (1999). *Football: A Sociology of the Global Game.* Cambridge: Polity Press.

Shilbury, D., Quick, S., & Westerbeek, H. (2003). *Strategic Sport Marketing.* St Leonards, NSW: Allen & Unwin.

Tomlinson, A. (2005). The Making of the Global Sports Economy: ISL, Adidas and the Rise of the Corporate Player in World Sport. In M. L. Silk, D. L. Andrews, & C. L. Cole (Eds.), *Sport and Corporate Nationalisms.* Oxford: Berg.

REFERENCES

BBC Sport (5th October, 2004). Arsenal name a new ground. *BBC Sport.* Retrieved on June 12, 2009, from http://news.bbc.co.uk/sport1/hi/football/teams/a/arsenal/3715678.stm

Bellos, A. (9th July, 2001). How Nike Bought Brazil. *The Guardian.* Retrieved on June 6, 2008, from *http://www.guardian.co.uk/media/2001/jul/09/marketingandpr.worldcupfootball2002.*

Bhattacharjee, S. & Rao, G. (2006). Tackling Ambush Marketing: The Need for Regulation and Analysing the Present Legislative and Contractual Efforts. *Sport in Society, 9*(1), 128–149.

Birley, D. (1995). *Land of Sport and Glory: Sport and British Society, 1887–1910.* Manchester: Manchester University Press.

Bond, D. (13th March, 2008). The £66m "Bribe" Shadow Hanging over FIFA. *The Telegraph.* Retrieved on June 6, 2008, from *http://www.telegraph.co.uk/sport/main.jhtml?xml=/sport/2008/03/13/sfnbon113.xml.*

Borland, J., & Macdonald, R. (2003). Demand for Sport. *Oxford Review of Economic Policy, 19*(4), 478–502.

Budd, A. (2001). Capitalism, Sport and Resistance: Reflections. *Culture, Sport & Society, 4*(1), 1–18.

FIFA.com (2009a). Research. *FIFA.com.* Retrieved on July 25, 2009, from http://www.fifa.com/aboutfifa/marketing/factsfigures/research.html.

FIFA.com (2009b). TV Data. *FIFA.com.* Retrieved on July 25, 2009, from http://www.fifa.com/aboutfifa/marketing/factsfigures/tvdata.html.

FIFA.com (2009c). Financial Report. *FIFA.com*. Retrieved on July 25, 2009, from http://www.fifa.com/aboutfifa/marketing/factsfigures/financialreport.html.

Galeano, E. (1997). *Football: In Sun and Shadow*. London: Fourth Estate.

Gallu, J. (12th June, 2008). Swiss Cry Foul as UEFA Targets Fans to Fight "Ambush Marketing." Retrieved on June 10, 2008, from *http://www.bloomberg.com.au/apps/news?pid=20601109&sid=aAgM1tkB5we0&refer=exclusive*.

Giulianotti, R. (1999). *Football: A Sociology of the Global Game*. Cambridge: Polity Press.

McCarthy, M. (2002). Marketers freely capitalize on soccer fever. *USA Today*. Retrieved on June 12, 2008, from http://www.usatoday.com/sports/soccer/cup2002/2002-05-28-usat-marketing.htm.

Meikle, E. (2002). Lawless Branding: Recent Developments in Trademark Law. *Brandchannel.com*. Retrieved on July 25, 2009, from http://www.brandchannel.com/features_effect.asp?pf_id=103. Retrieved June 10, 2008.

Smit, B. (2006). *Pitch Invasion: adidas, puma, and the making of modern sport*. London: Penguin-Allen Lane.

Tomlinson, A. (2005). The Making of the Global Sports Economy: ISL, Adidas and the Rise of the Corporate Player in World Sport. In M. L. Silk, D. L. Andrews, & C. L. Cole (Eds.), *Sport and Corporate Nationalisms*. Oxford: Berg.

Vassallo, E., Blemaster, K., & Werner, P. (2005). An International Look at Ambush Marketing. *The Trademark Reporter*, *95*(6), 1338–1356.

RECOMMENDED WEBSITES

euFootball.BIZ

www.eufootball.biz/

FIFA website

www.fifa.com

The Football Association website

www.thefa.com

Sport Business International-magazine website

www.sportbusiness.com

CHAPTER 8

Finance in the Football Industry

John Beech

Centre for the International Business of Sport, Coventry University

Objectives

Upon completion of this chapter the reader should be able to:

- Identify the key contributing factors that must be considered when conducting financial planning and drawing up financial strategy for a football club.
- Understand the difficulties associated with controlling revenues and costs that are unique to the football industry.
- Appreciate how financial planning and strategy must be integrated into a club's overall planning and strategy.
- Research and assess the strengths and weaknesses of the financial planning and strategy of individual clubs.

CONTENTS

OVERVIEW OF THE CHAPTER

Having outlined the potentially conflicting demands of performance on the pitch and financial success, this chapter reviews the worrying state of contemporary football finances. The major elements of both revenues and costs are discussed, and their stability or instability are highlighted. Next, the buying and selling of players is discussed. Finally indebtedness is reviewed, and the implications of going into administration are discussed.

INTRODUCTION

In October 2008, Daniel Levy, the chairman of Tottenham Hotspur, wrote an open letter to the club's fans. It included the following passage:

> There is also an inaccurate perception that our Club is run entirely for profit and that football is secondary. Success on the pitch is the sole determinant of the future of the Club and its financial stability, so it would be entirely counterproductive to have anything other than football as our first and foremost priority, and it is ridiculous to suggest otherwise. At a time when football clubs are criticised for losing money and for their debt levels, I am surprised that we should be criticised for running our Club on a sound commercial basis and for making a profit. Thank goodness we do make a profit because it has significantly supported the progress we have made over the last seven years and has helped to make us one of Europe's most secure Clubs. I make no apologies for the fact that we reinvest the Club's positive cash flow in both players and infrastructure (Levy, 2008).

What is interesting from the *business* perspective is that it constitutes a denial that the club, or rather the company (for that is what Tottenham and all other senior football "clubs" are),[1] is run entirely for profit. In fact, Tottenham is not only a company but one whose shares are traded openly on the Stock Exchange (their share price can be checked at *http://www.growthcompany.co.uk/company/TTNM/tottenham-hotspur.thtml*). In a conventional business, one might expect the *only* motivation for running the business to be to make a profit.

If, as Levy argues, the strategic aim of a football club when planning its finances is to make a profit that can be reinvested in the club, the question arises as to whether this actually happens in practice. Table 8.1 makes it very clear that this is not, in fact, what actually happens. The aggregated loss for the 92 English league clubs over five seasons is £1,014,000,000, although it should be pointed out that Chelsea accounted for almost a quarter of this in the two seasons 2004–2005 and 2005–2006 alone. Even allowing for this, the picture is of an industry sector that is in financial disarray and that is dysfunctional.

---

[1] To avoid the tedious repetition of single quotation marks as in the usage 'club', it will be assumed that the reader will mentally insert these single quotation marks and recall that the use of the word *club* actually means *company*. This distinction is an important one in the understanding of the finances of the game.

Table 8.1	Pretax Aggregated Profit/Loss of English Clubs				
	2001–2002	2002–2003	2003–2004	2004–2005	2005–2006
Premier League	–£137m	–£153m	–£128m	–£78m	–£69m
Championship	–£36m	–£126m	–£47m	–£65m	–£47m
League 1	–£28m	–£34m	–£16m	–£13m	–£17m
League 2	–£3m	–£5m	–£4m	–£4m	–£4m
Total	–£204m	–£318m	–£195m	–£160m	–£137m

Developed from Deloitte (2001–2007).

When a club can either no longer maintain a positive cash flow or no longer see how it can service its debts in the longer term, it will seek the protection of the courts to avoid its debtors seeking a winding-up order. In Britain this is known as "going into Administration"; in the United States, it is known as "filing for Chapter 11 bankruptcy." Whatever the legal code under which such action is taken, it is seen as an act of desperation, if only because a court nominee, the Administrator in the United Kingdom, is appointed to run the club, and the directors thus cede their control. Going into Administration has become a far from rare occurrence in English football. The pattern of these occurrences over time is shown in Figure 8.1.

The peak of the number of the cases in 2002 is often attributed to the collapse of ITV Digital, the then rights holder for broadcasting Football

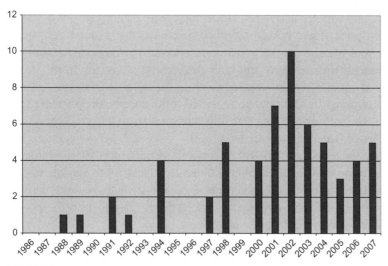

FIGURE 8.1 *Occurrences of insolvency among English football clubs by season start.*
Source: Beech et al. (2008a)

League matches. This is simplistic as an explanation, however, as the number of clubs going into Administration was already on the rise, and further investigation of the particular cases suggests that the loss in broadcasting rights was generally markedly lower than the overall figure for debts. The collapse may well have been the "straw that broke the camel's back" for some clubs, but they were already in financial trouble. The worrying current upward trend suggests that the "credit crunch" will see high numbers of clubs falling into insolvency.

How, then, is it that such high numbers of clubs fail to achieve the business model that Levy set out? To consider why profit is such a rare occurrence, we need to consider the two elements that combine to determine profit or loss: revenues and costs. Let us first consider revenues—the "plus" factor in the profitability equation, which a club would seek to maximise. The issues surrounding buying and selling players is considered in the following section. Revenue streams for football clubs fall under three main headings: matchday receipts, broadcasting rights, and commercial receipts.

MATCHDAY RECEIPTS

The money a club takes in on the day of the match was traditionally its major source of revenue, and, at the lowest level of league, still will be. It consists of money paid in advance by season ticket holders, ticket money from home fans, ticket money from away fans (these will be shared with the opposing team), and monies derived through hospitality packages.

The price of season tickets will be affected by intrinsic factors, such as the success of the club in the previous season, and by extrinsic factors, such as the state of the economy and fans' propensity to pay "up front" quite large sums of money. A club can increase its financial stability by selling more season tickets. Its ability to do so will be influenced by the price of the season ticket, the number of seats it allocates to season ticket holders, and the number of seats it has available to sell.

Broadly, the sale of one-off tickets will be influenced by the same factors, but with the additional variable of how much capacity to allocate to the away fans. The ability to change the number of seats available to away fans may be inhibited by security considerations. Typically it will only be possible to increase the number in quite large steps.

Most Premier League clubs are already playing to capacity crowds most weeks and so are only able to maximise their profit from the sale of tickets by pushing prices up to the limit at which fans will start declining to buy tickets. At a club where there is normally spare capacity, the club has much greater opportunity to experiment with ticket prices, either with the simple change in price or with more complex package deals such as family tickets.

Table 8.2 shows the wide variation in ticket prices across three tiers of English football and the top tiers in three other European countries. Although the samples for each league are small, its results are indicative. English fans may baulk to discover how much more they pay to watch football than do their European counterparts—even at the level of League 2, the fourth tier, tickets cost the same as for Spanish Primera A (widely known as La Liga), and *more* than for Serie A (Italy), the Bundesliga (Germany), and Ligue 1 (France).

Table 8.2 Ticket Prices (February 2007)

England—Championship		Germany Bundesliga1	
Barnsley	£20	Stuttgart	€ 25
Hull	£23	Bayern Munich	€ 12
Leeds	£30	Hertha Berlin	€ 21
Sheffield Wednesday	£23	*Average*	*£13*
Average	*£24*		
		French Premier Ligue	
England—League 1		Lyon	€ 20
Bradford	£20	Monaco	€ 10
Chesterfield	£17	Nantes	€ 12
Huddersfield	£18	Lens	€ 12
Rotherham	£20	Lille	€ 10
Doncaster	£18	*Average*	*£8.80*
Scunthorpe	£17		
Average	*£19*	**Spanish Premiera**	
		Real Madrid	€ 25
England—League 2		Valencia € 30	€ 20
Boston	£13	Espanyol	€ 25
Grimsby	£17	Celta Vigo	€ 20
Lincoln	£17	*Average*	*£16*
Mansfield	£16		
Average	*£16*		
Italy Serie A			
Inter Milan	€ 20		
Fiorentina	€ 20		
Atalanta	€ 15		
Empoli	€ 15		
Sampdoria	€ 23		
Average	*£12*		

Source: *Inside Out (2007).*

In the longer term, a club may seek to increase matchday receipts by increasing the number of seats in the stadium. Again, this can only be done in large incremental steps and must be considered in the light of the cost of extending the stadium at its current site, or the much more expensive option of relocating to a new stadium.

To provide corporate hospitality suites and packages, a stadium requires suitable premises, which again needs to be seen in the light of the investment required. Two examples of how things can go wrong in balancing these various elements are discussed in Case Study 8.1.

CASE STUDY 8.1: Darlington and Newcastle United Tackle Their Capacity Problems

In 2000, the chairman of Darlington, George Reynolds, declared that he wanted to model the club setup on Manchester United. Ignoring both the different sizes of the catchment areas and the on-pitch performance of the two clubs (Darlington had been playing in the Conference (Tier 5) as recently as 1989–1990 and were then playing at what had been their habitual level, Tier 4—today's League 2), Reynolds pressed ahead with ambitious plans to bring Premier League football to Darlington. In 2003, a brand-new 25,000-seater stadium was opened and named after Reynolds. The first game was played against Kidderminster Harriers in front of a crowd of 11,600; the stadium was thus less than half full for its first match. Reynolds had not invested in the team to any significant scale, and the new stadium was inappropriately large for a club in League 2. Spectator numbers averaged over a year have infrequently been above 5,000.

The stadium had cost £25 million, and Reynolds had hoped to earn extra revenues through using it for other purposes, such as car boot sales, but had become locked in a legal battle over permission for alternative uses with Darlington Borough Council. Unable to meet the repayments on loans obtained to fund the building of the new stadium, and facing pressure as the Inland Revenue was seeking a winding-up order, in December 2003, Reynolds was forced to place the club under Administration. In May 2004, a new owner, who was in fact one of the club's main creditors, took over, and in September of that year, the club came out of Administration. A typical attendance in the 2007/2008 season was in the order of 3,500 spectators.

At nearby Newcastle United, the challenge of maximising matchday revenues in an old and regularly full stadium was being faced. In 1996, the then chairman, Sir John Hall, had announced plans for a new 55,000-seater stadium—a rather more realistic proposition for a club that had not been outside the top flight since promotion to the Premier League in 1993 and has one of the staunchest fan bases of any English club. However, in 1999, when new owners announced a £75 million plan to increase seating at St James's by 16,000, it invoked a furious response from fans. Approximately 4,000 season tickets holders were told that (1) they could only continue having a place in the ground if they "relocated" to the new hospitality facilities being built where their existing seats were and (2) paid an increase of 300 percent on the price of their season tickets. Many believed that their seats had been guaranteed for ten years when they bought £500 bonds from the club. Six of these season ticket holders, acting on behalf of another 2,134, sought legal redress. In March 2000, the judge ruled against them, indicating that small print in the terms of the bond allowed the club to move them. The club's costs for the hearing were estimated to be between £155,000 and £200,000, while fans faced a legal bill of £80,000, the shortfall of what they had covered by insurance to meet their actual costs of £198,000. However, the fans were given leave to appeal on the grounds that the club had misrepresented its original bond offer. The case was heard in June 2000, and again the fans lost. In the context of its own financial difficulties, in November 2000, the club decided to waive the costs due from the fans.

As a financial strategy, Newcastle United must have felt their plans had a strong rationale. As an exercise in public relations, the whole sorry episode had been a disaster, and one of the claimants announced that she had no intention of ever returning to St James's.

Source: Various.

Questions

1. What are the implications of a club regularly playing in a stadium that is nowhere near full?

2. How would you assess what happened at Newcastle United?

BROADCASTING RIGHTS

While the advent of large revenues from broadcasting rights has become a major feature of postcommercialised football, they have brought with them serious problems for clubs with regard to financial planning. Table 8.3 gives some indication of the scale of escalation in the price of broadcasting rights in the major European football countries and shows how the English fan in particular is thus having to pay for football on television.

Two features of Table 8.3 should be noted. First, the data make clear that a particular contract for broadcasting rights has historically lasted for three or four years. During that period, a club has a clear idea of what its annual income from these rights will be. Second, as the contract comes up for renewal, there will be considerable uncertainty about the new price. Experience suggests firmly that the value of the contract increases each time it is replaced with the subsequent contract, but it would be dangerous to assume

Table 8.3 Major Football Broadcasting Rights Contracts

Country	Previous	Current
England	2001–2004 Domestic BSkyB/ITV £450m (apx. €725m)	2007–2009 Domestic and International BSkyB/ Setanta £1,706m (apx. €2,500m)
France	2001–2004 Canal Plus/TPS €125m	2005–2008 Canal Plus €600m per season
Germany	2000–2004 Kirch Group 750m DM (apx. €385m)	2006–2008 Unity Media €420m

that this trend will continue unabated. The distribution of the revenues from broadcasting rights for the Premier League is given in Exhibit 8.1.

For a club that is not in danger of relegation, which would result in a drop in the fees received, broadcasting rights thus offer a reasonable basis for financial planning—at least in the short term. For the very top clubs, the prospect of further broadcasting rights from appearances in, for example, the UEFA Champions League, are a tempting but uncertain prospect as Leeds United learned to their considerable cost. First, the club must qualify for the competition, and, second the final phase is on a knock-out cup basis.

COMMERCIAL RIGHTS

These fall into three main revenue streams: sponsorship, merchandising, and ancillary services.

Sponsorship

Table 8.4 shows some of the key details of shirt sponsorship with the clubs in the English Premier League for season 2008–2009. Some significant features with implications for financial planning and strategy can be identified:

- Although there are still examples of the traditional sponsor—a local company—major international companies have achieved a significant presence. While the traditional sponsor was spending their money as part

Table 8.4 Details of Shirt Sponsorship in the Premier League, 2008–2009

Club	2008–2009 Season Shirt Sponsor	Sponsor's Base	Sponsor's Industry Sector	Length of Current Contract (Years)	Reported Annual Value	Club Finish 2007–2008 Season	Shirt Supplier
Arsenal	Emirates	UAE	Airline	8	Bundled with stadium sponsorship	3rd	Nike
Aston Villa	Acorns	Local U.K.	Charity	1	Free	6th	Nike
Blackburn Rovers	Crown Paints	Local U.K.	Paint manufacturer	3	Performance related; up to £5m for the 3 years	7th	Umbro
Bolton Wanderers	Reebok	Germany (ex Local U.K.)	Trainers and sports clothing	7	£1.2m	16th	Reebok
Chelsea	Samsung	Korea	Electronics manufacturer	5	£10m	2nd	Adidas
Everton	Chang Beer	Thailand	Brewery	3	£2.7m	5th	Umbro
Fulham	LG	Korea	Mobile phones	2	£3m	17th	Nike
Hull City	Karoo	Local UK	Internet Service Provider	2	£800k	Promoted from Championship	Umbro
Liverpool	Carlsberg	Denmark	Brewery	3	£7.5m	4th	Adidas
Manchester City	Thomas Cook	Germany (ex U.K.)	Tour operator	1	£1m	9th	Le Coq Sportif
Manchester United	AIG	U.S.	US insurance company	4	£14.1m	1st	Nike
Middlesbrough	Garmin	U.S.	Sat-Nav manufacturers	1	£1m	8th	Errea
Newcastle United	Northern Rock	U.K.	Mortgage lender	5	£5m	12th	Adidas

(Continued)

Table 8.4   Details of Shirt Sponsorship in the Premier League, 2008–2009 *(continued)*

Club	2008–2009 Season Shirt Sponsor	Sponsor's Base	Sponsor's Industry Sector	Length of Current Contract (Years)	Reported Annual Value	Club Finish 2007–2008 Season	Shirt Supplier
Portsmouth	Oki	Japan	Info-telecomms & printers manufacturer	3	£1.5m	8th	Canterbury
Stoke City	Britannia	Local U.K.	Building society		£1m	Promoted from Championship	Le Coq Sportif
Sunderland	Boylesports	Ireland	Online betting	4	£3m	15th	Umbro
Tottenham Hotspur	Mansion	Gibraltar	Online casino	4	£8.5m	11th	Puma
West Bromwich Albion[1]						Promoted from Championship	Umbro
West Ham United	XL Leisure Group[2]	U.K.	Tour operators	3	£2.5m	10th	Umbro
Wigan Athletic	JJB Sports	Local U.K.	Sports retailer		£1m per season	14th	Champion

[1]Details of shirt sponsor not known at time of writing.
[2]The sponsorship contract was cancelled on September 12, 2008, as a result of the collapse of XL, and XL logos were removed from the shirts.
Source: Various.

of a "feel good" effect, the major international organisations are more likely to be looking for exposure through the medium of television, and certainly not with a view to the local market. Martin Sullivan, the then chief executive officer of AIG (shirt sponsors of Manchester United), when questioned by a shareholder as to why an American insurance company was spending so much on sponsoring an English "soccer" club, replied, "I am not buying the U.K. [*sic*]. I am buying Asia" (quoted in Smith, 2007). Qualifying for the UEFA Cup or the Champions League thus has a second positive financial implication: the more a club's television exposure, the more it can expect to earn through shirt sponsorship.

■ Sponsors fall into groups of particular industry sectors reflecting whether they are aiming their promotion directly at fans to increase sales or simply seeking a broader presence or exposure in specific marketplaces. The former group of producers and service providers includes those of lifestyle products and services, such as mobile phones and gambling websites, while the latter includes those such as insurance and mortgages.

■ Some sponsors are more concerned with sponsoring *a* team rather than developing a long-term relationship with only one club. Crown Paints, the current sponsors of Blackburn Rovers, have in the past been sponsors of Liverpool, and, more recently, Emirates switched from sponsoring Chelsea to sponsoring Arsenal.

■ The length of contract signed between club and sponsor varies, although it must be kept in mind that in some cases, the current contract is an extension of one or more previous contracts. The longest continuous arrangement in Table 8.4 is that between Liverpool and Carlsberg, which has existed through extension continuously since 1992.

■ The revenue a club can command depends almost entirely on its previous season's performance on the pitch. The Big 4 clubs who appear in the Champions League are able to command figures in the order of £10 million per year, whereas newly promoted clubs can only expect to earn a tenth of this. Chadwick (*SportBusiness International*, 2008) has estimated that winning the Champions League is worth more than £85 million in terms of broadcasting rights, enhanced sponsorship deals, and higher valuations of players and growth in ticket sales. Additionally, approximately £30 million is earned during the campaign to reach the finals.

■ The sale of the rights to *manufacture* shirts has little to do with the shirts the players wear; the attraction to the supplier is in part the exposure of its logo, but it is mainly to do with acquiring the lucrative contract to produce the replica kits. In a few cases, the shirt manufacturer becomes both the shirt sponsor *and* the kit manufacturer—for example, Carbrini at Oldham, Bournemouth, and Luton.

Some care must be taken in the choice of sponsor. In recent seasons a number of sponsorship deals have been jeopardised or even cancelled through the financial difficulties of the sponsor. These include Bradford City (Bradford and Bingley), Oldham Athletic (twice—Horners Group and then Hillstone Developments), Manchester United (AIG), Newcastle United (Northern Rock), and West Ham (XL Leisure Group).

Besides shirt sponsorships, clubs offer a wide range of other sponsorship deals to boost revenues. Where the club is the owner of its stadium, naming rights offer a significant revenue opportunity. The greatest opportunity for a club is at the opening of a new stadium; examples of this are at Arsenal (the Emirates), Stoke (the Britannia), Coventry (the Ricoh), and Leicester (the Walkers). Selling the naming rights for an existing stadium commands a lower price because the original noncommercial name will be difficult to override. Bradford City, for example, have done this, their stadium having been named at times the Pulse, the Bradford & Bingley, the Intersonic, and, currently, the Coral Windows. In all its manifestations it has tended to retain its original noncommercial name, Valley Parade, among fans and the general public. The practice of selling stadium naming rights is far from universal, but it is widespread in clubs at Germany, Japan, and Sweden. At the next level down, individual stands within the stadium are offered for commercial naming.

Within the stadium are the familiar advertising hoardings that provide yet another revenue stream. Lower down the tiers, clubs strongly promote a whole range of lower cost sponsorship possibilities. These can include sponsorship of the matchday, the programme, the ball, individual players, and the mascot.

Merchandising

A visit to the online shop of virtually any football club reveals the wide range of branded merchandise that is offered for sale to the club's fans. The most significant of these, primarily because of its retail price, is the replica kit. Most clubs offer at least three variants of the shirt: home and away variants and a third alternative in contrasting colours. A typical price for a shirt in the top four tiers of English football is £40. To maximise revenues, clubs introduce new versions each season.

As Table 8.5 shows, at the top level, English clubs lead in the revenues they earn from merchandising, Italian clubs do not earn particularly much, and Dutch fans are willing to spend significantly on shirts, although the Dutch clubs have fewer fans.

Table 8.5	Merchandising Revenues and Spending-2007/2008		
League	Total Revenues (€m)	Revenue per Club (€m)	Average Annual Fan Spending (€)
English Premier League	171	8.6	65.40
Spanish Primera División	145	7.3	44.90
German Bundesliga	127	7.1	35.40
French Ligue 1	86	4.3	42.60
Italian Serie A	64	3.2	22.30
Dutch Eredivisie	22	1.2	46.50

Source: *Rohlmann and Zastrow (2008).*

As with matchday tickets, English fans are paying significantly more than their European counterparts. Whatever fans may feel about the rights and wrongs of this in the "people's game," the higher levels of revenues generated should result in richer clubs able to finance better football. The revenues from merchandising are important enough for clubs to protect themselves legally against unofficial merchandising. For example, both Arsenal and Tottenham have taken legal action to stop the sale of unofficial material (Williams, 2003).

Ancillary Services

Ancillary services that can generate revenue streams for a club include both those that are matchday related, such as the variety of hospitality packages now widely offered, and those that are not matchday related, such as non-matchday use of the stadium for events such as pop concerts.

Although clubs that have a new stadium are much better positioned to offer high-value (and thus high revenue) hospitality packages, traditional stadia were not built with bespoke hospitality facilities, although clubs have been quick to adapt existing facilities to attract corporate custom. In the case of Newcastle United (see Case Study 8.1), the importance of hospitality revenues to the club is evident from the fact that in order to provide new hospitality facilities at the revamped St James's Park, the club was prepared to fight some of its long-standing season ticket holders in court because of their unwillingness to give up their seats so new hospitality facilities could be built.

Similarly, clubs with a new stadium are better positioned to offer nonfootball facilities and services on nonmatchdays. The traditional stadium only generated revenues on matchdays—one day every other week for only three-quarters of the year, an approach to yield management that does not make sense to accountants. The modern stadium will incorporate conference and hotel facilities, shops, and restaurants to create revenues all week and all year.

COSTS

The biggest costs a club faces are its players. For example, the salary paid to a very top football player is approaching £200,000 per week. Table 8.6 shows the annual salaries of the ten highest-earning players in March 2007. Of course, only the clubs that appear regularly in the Champions League could afford to pay salaries on this scale. Table 8.7 gives a broader perspective of top-tier salary bills.

Table 8.6	Highest-Earning Players — MARCH 2007	
Player	**Club**	**Annual Salary**
Ronaldinho	Barcelona	£16.0m
David Beckham	Real Madrid	£15.8m
Ronaldo	AC Milan	£12.7m
Wayne Rooney	Manchester United	£9.3m
Michael Ballack	Chelsea	£9.1m
Thierry Henry	Arsenal	£8.6m
Zinedine Zidane	Real Madrid	£8.5m
Fabio Cannavaro	Real Madrid	£7.9m
John Terry	Chelsea	£7.7m
Steven Gerrard	Liverpool	£7.7m

Source: Forbes.com, 2007.

The general trend is clearly one of increasing costs—one that clubs would wish to control. The seemingly irresistible temptation is, of course, to pay more to get better players, but this continual escalation is unsustainable in the long term. The collective approach of a league-wide wage cap—setting a maximum wage that a club can pay any player—has long been unlawful, as it is a restraint on a player's potential to earn that has been imposed by what is, in effect, a cartel. An alternative approach is for individual clubs to apply a "salary cost management scheme." With this approach, a club is constrained in how much it can spend in salaries as a percentage of its revenues. It is an approach strongly endorsed by Michel Platini, president of UEFA, who would like to see a limit of 60 percent of revenues being paid as salaries, but one that, to date, finds limited backing from the richer clubs (Harris, 2009). In 2008/2009 in England, it was only a requirement for clubs in League 2 and the Blue Square Premier League (Tier 5).

Table 8.7	Premier League Salary Costs				
Club	Wage Rank 2006–2007	League position 2006–2007	Total wages 2006–2007 £m	Total wages 2005–2006 £m	% Increase
Chelsea	1	2	132.8	114.0	17
Manchester United	2	1	92.3	85.4	8
Arsenal	3	4	89.7	83.0	8
Liverpool	4	3	77.6	68.9	13
Newcastle United	5	13	62.5	52.2	20
Average			48.5	42.7	13
West Ham United	6	15	44.2	31.2	41
Tottenham Hotspur	7	5	43.8	40.7	8
Aston Villa	8	11	43.2	38.3	13
Everton	9	6	38.4	37.0	4
Middlesbrough	10	12	38.3	n/a	n/a
Portsmouth	11	9	36.9	24.8	49
Blackburn Rovers	12	10	36.7	33.4	10
Manchester City	13	14	36.4	34.3	6
Fulham	14	16	35.2	30.1	17
Charlton Athletic	15	19	34.3	34.2	0
Bolton Wanderers	16	7	30.7	28.5	8
Reading	17	8	29.8	14.2	109
Wigan Athletic	18	17	27.5	20.6	34
Sheffield United	19	18	22.4	15.2	48
Watford	20	20	17.6	10.0	76

Notes: Italicised clubs not in Premier League in season 2008–2009. Table does not include Middlesbrough's wage costs for 2005–2006, as the accounts represent a six-month period ending December 31, 2005.
Source: *BBC News (2008c) from Deloitte data.*

Another approach is to offer contracts that are based on general performance-related pay. In a specific respect, this has been used for many years—for example, the payment of bonuses as part of the rewards package for on-the-pitch success in a Cup competition. The latest approach, however, is to measure performance in terms of relegation (and promotion) so players are paid less if their team is relegated to a lower division where many of the revenues will be reduced. In spite of the obvious advantage to a club in terms of financial planning, the annual survey of football club finance directors by UK accountancy and business services firm PKF (2008, pages 12–13) indicated that in 2008 performance-related pay remained a small proportion of most English and Scottish clubs total wage bill. Though it was becoming increasingly more important, particularly at English Premier League clubs.

With the exception of the buying and selling of players, all the major revenues and costs have now been reviewed. Table 8.8 provides an insight into the strengths of the top-tier leagues in England, Italy, Germany, Spain, and France, and the relative importance of the broadcasting stream; it also shows how revenues compare with the major cost: player salaries.

Total revenues have risen quite consistently across all of these leagues over the last ten years, although there is evidence that in the two English leagues and in France, revenues are beginning to plateau. The financial scale of the English game is clear: the current revenues of the Championship are bigger than the revenues of Serie A in 1996, of the Bundesliga in 1997, of Spain's Primera Liga in 1996, and the French Ligue 1 in 1999.

Michel Platini, president of European football's governing body UEFA, has stated that a benchmark of 60 percent should be the upper limit for the ratio of salaries to club revenues (Harris, 2009). By this measure it can be seen that the Premier League (that is, the aggregated total for all clubs) seems to have wages under control; in Italy, wages have been brought back to sustainable levels from a worrying peak in 2002; in Germany, salaries have always been held at sustainable levels; in Spain and France, clubs are nearing the benchmark, albeit from the wrong side; in the English Championship however, salaries remain worryingly high, having peaked in 2001 at the totally unsustainable figure of 101.5 percent—in other words, the clubs were actually paying out more in player salaries than they were earning through all revenue streams!

The full impact of the credit crunch and recession on revenues remains to be seen and will depend on the extent to which fan spending is discretionary or, to put it another way, whether they consider the money they spend on football a luxury or a necessity. Clubs who are concerned that this will further dent their profitability have already started to introduce cost-cutting measures. Favourite targets include youth academies, women's teams, and scouting staff.

The PKF (2008, page 6) survey of football club finance directors provides clear indications of the priorities of these directors and Table 8.9 shows their responses when asked to rate the importance of the various income streams to the financial performance of their club over the 2008–2009 period.

The PKF Football Industry Group noted that the 'big five' revenue streams remained the most important: ticket sales, sponsorship, TV/radio deals, merchandising and conferencing/catering. The finance directors also reported that while revenue from tickets continued to grow, the rate of growth weakened for the second year running, suggesting that there was some cause for concern regarding the impact of the credit crunch.

Table 8.8 Big Five European League Revenue Ratios Post-Bosman (€ million)

Big Five League/Season End	2005	2004	2003	2002	2001	2000	1999	1998	1997	1996
Total Revenue										
English Premier League	1987	1976	1857	1688	1397	1151	998	867	692	516
Italian Serie A	1336	1153	1162	1127	1151	1059	714	650	551	452
German Bundesliga	1236	1058	1108	1043	880	681	577	513	444	373
Spanish Primera Liga	1029	953	847	776	676	722	612	569	524	328
French Ligue 1	696	655	689	643	644	607	393	323	293	277
English Football League 1	456	428	380	444	306	276	240	277	195	155
Broadcast Revenue										
English Premier League	862[a]	884	810	709[a]	537	357	290	225[a]	145	62
Italian Serie A	739[b]	632	642	595	619	596[b]	248	241	199[a]	104
German Bundesliga	321	291	365[a]	414	399[a]	212	168	143[a]	111	84
Spanish Primera Liga	409	391[b]	256	251	243	251	237	241	222[b]	73
French Ligue 1	344[c]	306	357	333	326	343[a]	164	137	95	89
Total Payroll										
English Premier League	1171	1209	1134	1052	838	712	582	454	325	243
Italian Serie A	830	845	884	1010	868	660	512	417	317	256
German Bundesliga	549	547	556	553	447	382	317	278	223	187
Spanish Primera Liga	658	608	607	559	491	390	342	303	230	175
French Ligue 1	437	450	467	441	414	324	273	222	178	161
English Football League 1	325	310	340	320	310	258	191	209	130	
Broadcast Percent of Revenue										
English Premier League	43.4	44.7	43.6	42.0	38.4	31.0	29.1	26.0	21.0	12.0
Italian Serie A	55.3	54.8	55.2	52.8	53.8	56.3	34.7	37.1	36.1	23.0
German Bundesliga	26.0	27.5	32.9	39.7	45.3	31.1	29.1	27.9	25.0	22.5
Spanish Primera Liga	39.7	41.0	30.2	32.3	35.9	34.8	38.7	42.4	42.4	22.3
French Ligue 1	49.4	46.7	51.8	51.8	50.6	56.5	44.7	42.4	32.4	32.1

(Continued)

Table 8.8   Big Five European League Revenue Ratios Post-Bosman (€ million) *(continued)*

Big Five League/Season End	2005	2004	2003	2002	2001	2000	1999	1998	1997	1996
Payroll Percent ***of Revenue***										
English Premier League	58.9	61.2	61.1	62.4	60.0	61.9	58.3	52.4	47.1	49.8
Italian Serie A	62.1	73.3	76.1	89.6	75.4	62.3	71.7	64.2	57.5	58.6
German Bundesliga	44.4	51.7	50.2	53.0	50.8	56.1	54.9	54.2	50.2	50.1
Spanish La Liga	63.9	63.8	71.7	72.0	72.6	54.0	55.9	53.3	43.9	53.4
French Ligue 1	62.8	68.7	67.8	68.6	64.3	53.4	69.5	68.7	60.8	58.1
English Football League 1	71.2	72.5	89.4	72.1	101.5	93.5	79.5	75.3	66.4	—

[a]*New pooled TV contract.*

[b]*New individual TV contract.*

[c]*Ligue 1 first year of 50/30/20 equity/merit/facility sharing; TV previous split 83/10/7.*

Notes: Other 2004–2005 Revenues: Dutch Eredivisie: €321 million, broadcast ratio 14%, wage ratio 61%; Scottish Premier League: €257 million, broadcast ratio 17%, wage ratio 57%; Portuguese Super-Liga: €193 million, broadcast ratio 24%, wage ratio 72% and Belgian Jupiler League: €126 million, broadcast ratio 12%; UEFA Champions League 2005: total revenue €598 million, broadcasting €472 million with about 72% (€439 million) to 32-team Champions League, the rest to European Football.

Exchange rate, July 1, 2004: €1 = £0.671 = $1.206.

Original sources: Deloitte Sports Group, Annual Football Finance Report; EPL, Ligue de Football Professionnel; Liga Calcio, Bundesliga, La Liga.

Source: *Vrooman (2007, page 328).*

Table 8.9	Perceived Importance of Revenue Streams 2008–2011						
	All	**EPL**	**EFLC**	**FL1**	**FL2**	**SPL**	**SFD**
Ticket sales (including corporate boxes)	7.2	6.7	7.3	5.8	7.8	8.0	7.0
Sponsorship	6.6	6.0	6.4	6.3	7.1	6.8	7.5
TV and radio deals	6.2	7.2	6.1	6.3	5.1	7.5	5.0
Merchandising	5.5	5.7	5.3	5.5	5.4	5.5	5.0
Conferences and catering	5.2	5.3	5.1	5.8	5.7	4.0	
Alternative use for stadium on nonmatch days	4.2	3.6	4.3	5.5	4.4	2.5	8.0
New media	4.1	3.8	4.3	5.3	4.9	3.3	1.0
Ground naming rights	3.6	2.8	4.8	4.0	4.0	2.0	2.0
Casinos	1.4	1.5	2.1	3.0	0.6	0.8	1.0

Note: 1 = least important; 9 = most important.

Note 2: English Premier League (EPL), English Football League Championship (EFLC), Football League One (FLI), Football League Two (FL2), Scottish Premier League (SPL), Scottish First Division (SFD).

Source: PKF Football Industry Group (2008, page 6).

BUYING AND SELLING PLAYERS

Although English clubs dominate the finances of European football, a different picture emerges with the transfer of players. Table 8.10 shows the 20 biggest transfer deals throughout the world up to 2008.

Italian and Spanish clubs emerge as the biggest spenders at this highest level of the market, willingly entering into international transfers, while English clubs do not engage to the same extent in international transfers and tend to be less prepared to pay the highest prices.

Top prices peaked around 2001, but in spite of general concerns about the credit crunch, the richest clubs again started to pay very high prices for top players in 2007 and 2008. An analysis of the top 50 transfers reveals a slightly different picture (Table 8.11). Italian and Spanish clubs account for 70 percent of the appearances in the list, but although 6 Italian clubs (out of a total of 15 clubs in total) account for 40 percent, only Barcelona, Real Madrid, Chelsea, and Manchester United make more than two appearances. Fifty percent of the transfers are international; only 6 (5 involving English players) of the 14 transfers to English clubs were domestic. It would seem that the top English clubs, with the arguable exceptions of Chelsea and Manchester United, are more reluctant to spend really significant money for players compared with their continental competitors in the Champions League.

Table 8.10	World's Top 20 Transfers by Transfer Fee — up to 2008			
Player's Name	**From Club**	**To Club**	**Fee**	**Year**
Zinedine Zidane	Juventus (Ita)	Real Madrid (Spa)	£45.62m	2001
Luis Figo	Barcelona (Spa)	Real Madrid (Spa)	£37m	2000
Hernan Crespo	Parma (Ita)	Lazio (Ita)	£35.5m	2000
Robinho	Real Madrid (Spa)	Manchester City (Eng)	£33.87m	2008
Gianluigi Buffon	Parma (Ita)	Juventus (Ita)	£32.6m	2001
Christian Vieri	Lazio (Ita)	Inter Milan (Ita)	£32m	1999
Dimitar Berbatov	Tottenham Hotspur (Eng)	Manchester United (Eng)	£30.75m	2008
Andriy Shevchenko	AC Milan (Ita)	Chelsea (Eng)	£30m	2006
Rio Ferdinand	Leeds United (Eng)	Manchester United (Eng)	£29.1m	2002
Gaizka Mendieta	Valencia (Spa)	Lazio (Ita)	£29m	2001
Ronaldo	Inter Milan (Ita)	Real Madrid (Spa)	£28.49m	2002
Juan Veron	Lazio (Ita)	Manchester United (Eng)	£28.1m	2001
Rui Costa	Fiorentina [old] (Ita)	AC Milan (Ita)	£28m	2001
Pavel Nedved	Lazio (Ita)	Juventus (Ita)	£25.5m	2001
Daniel Alves	Sevilla (Spa)	Barcelona (Spa)	£25.33m	2008
Arjen Robben	Chelsea (Eng)	Real Madrid (Spa)	£24.46m	2007
Michael Essien	Lyon (Fra)	Chelsea (Eng)	£24.43m	2005
Didier Drogba	Marseille (Fra)	Chelsea (Eng)	£24m	2004
Nicolas Anelka	Arsenal (Eng)	Real Madrid (Spa)	£23.5m	1999

Source: *FootballTransfers.co.uk (2008)*.

When a club decides to buy a player, it needs to consider the total cost it will face. For example, let us say a player is priced at £15 million in the transfer market, and the club agrees to pay him £100,000 per week on a three-year contract. The salary to be paid during the three years is greater than the transfer fee. There may also be agents' fees to be covered, bonuses

Table 8.11	Analysis by Club and Nationality of Purchasing Club in World's Top 50 Transfers		
Italy	**Spain**	**England**	**France**
AC Milan 2	Barcelona 4	Chelsea 5	Paris-SG 1
AS Roma 2	Real Betis 1	Leeds United 1	**Total 1**
Inter Milan 3	Real Madrid 10	Liverpool 1	
Juventus 5	**Total 15**	Manchester City 2	
Lazio 6		Manchester United 5	
Parma 2		**Total 14**	
Total 20			

Source: *Developed from FootballTransfers.co.uk (2008)*.

relating to appearances for the club, and special appearances in such tournaments as the Champions League. The total commitment may thus be more in the order of £33 to £35 million.

As transfer fees have risen to such high levels, two features of the payment arrangement have emerged. First, payment may be staggered over an agreed period of time. Second, it is now not uncommon to include a clause relating to the number of appearances for the purchasing club. This results in the dysfunctional outcome that a manager may be under pressure to not play a player in order to avoid triggering an extra payment to the player's previous club.

In 2002, FIFA introduced the transfer window system—that is, players can only be transferred during two periods (or "windows") per year—one during the summer between seasons and the other in January. While this gives clubs a certain stability in constraining "want away" players, it creates problems for those clubs who might, for example, need to sell a player because of spiralling costs. Whatever its advantages as a system are, it has come under criticism from many managers. From the director of finance's perspective, it is a mixed blessing: on the one hand it brings periods of stability when the window is closed, but it creates major problems when a club wants the flexibility to sell a player or players—for example, when it is trading at a loss. As a result of the system, there has been an increase in the number of loan deals, which can take place at any time of the year, with increasingly complex contractual arrangements. For example, the perceived benefit in a loan is not only the receiving club's, but often the loaning club's, who may want a younger player to gain first team experience in a lower tier.

BENEFACTION, INVESTMENT, AND INDEBTEDNESS

As we saw early in the chapter (see Table 8.1), the summation of the various flows of cash, both as revenues and costs, generally results in a club losing money at a worrying and unsustainable rate. It should be noted that although this is a clear trend, it is not *invariably* the case. Walsall, for example, a club in the third tier of English football, in 2008 announced an annual profit for the third year running (*BBC News*, 2008d). The tight financial management that had produced this rare case of consistent profit was not popular with Walsall fans, however, who thought that the chairman lacked ambition for the club (*BBC News*, 2008a).

If the majority of clubs consistently fail to break even, let alone make a profit, how do they sustain this seemingly unsustainable situation? There are three (overlapping) approaches to solving this conundrum: benefaction, investment, and borrowing. All are variants of what is, at least technically, indebtedness. Lord Triesman, chairman of the Football Association, has expressed grave concerns over the indebtedness of English football clubs, estimating a figure of £3 billion in total (Munro et al., 2008). The major part of this figure is attributable to the "Big Four" clubs: Manchester United (£754m), Chelsea (£716m), Liverpool (£368m), and Arsenal (£352m). Richard Scudamore, chief executive of the Premier League, was swift in his defence of this situation, arguing that not only were such debt levels manageable but also that the debts of the "Big Four" should be classified as "soft debt," meaning a debt that does not result in pressure for repayment.

There are, however, clear examples of how seemingly soft debt can turn into hard debt, or can become a point of leverage against the club. The most extreme example is that of Gretna and its benefactor Brooks Mileson who, having bankrolled the promotion of a minnow to a place in the Scottish Premier League, suddenly and unexpectedly withdrew his support because of ill health, resulting in the liquidation of the club. More typical examples are the cases where an owner or a director takes ownership of the club's stadium in return for writing off debt. Case Study 8.2 shows how this action played a part in Rotherham United being forced to leave Rotherham in order to survive as a club.

Table 8.12 illustrates further data from the PKF football finance director survey and shows the extent to which loans being guaranteed by a director or shareholder has become common practice, especially in the Premier League and in Football League 1. PKF noted that among Premier League clubs, there had been a rise from 54 percent in the previous year to the level of 89 percent in 2008.

Benefaction

The role of benefactor in a club is a long-standing one. Going back to the late nineteenth century and the foundation of football clubs, it was

Table 8.12	Response to "Has the debt funding at your club been guaranteed by a director or shareholder?"						
	All %	**EPL**	**EFLC**	**FL1**	**FL2**	**SPL**	**SFD**
Yes	54	89	33	75	44	25	50
No	41	11	67	25	33	75	50

Note 1: English Premier League (EPL), English Football League Championship (EFLC), Football League One (FLI), Football League Two (FL2), Scottish Premier League (SPL), Scottish First Division (SFD).

common for a local benefactor to pump-prime a club financially. The motivation for this was either a feel-good factor for the benefactor or was connected to the business of the benefactor; the team represented the factory of the owner, and playing or watching football deterred workers from spending their leisure time in ways that clashed with Victorian values. Often it was difficult to separate out these two elements of motivation.

In the modern game, many of these more traditional kinds of benefactors still exist, providing funds for what in effect is their "trophy club." Some examples include Eddie Davies (Bolton Wanderers), Steve Gibson (Middlesbrough), and Dave Whelan (Wigan). To this list should be added examples of a more modern variant: Roman Abramovitch (Chelsea) and Milan Mandaric (Portsmouth and Leicester City). As just noted, benefaction provides major benefits for a club, but it can carry implicit dangers in the long term.

Investment

Investment is the hard-nosed business equivalent of benefaction, only without benefaction's "social good" overtones. Recent examples include the takeover of Liverpool by George Gillett and Tom Hicks in February 2007, a takeover that has proved problematic in terms of the estimates of funding required to achieve success, and the takeover of Manchester City by the Abu Dhabi United Group for Investment and Development (ADUG) in September 2008.

Albeit surprisingly, football is beginning to attract serious interest from the investment sector, a good example being the activities of Ray Ranson's group Sisu Capital, which specialises in the attempted rescue of clubs that are ailing financially. Sisu have taken over Coventry City and have also been reportedly at various times discussed the possibility of taking over Bournemouth, Derby County and Manchester City.

The takeover of clubs by organisations which see the clubs as vehicles for investment is potentially problematic in that the aim of the investor is to make a profit (treating the club as just a business), and this may bring them into conflict with the supporters of the club, who are the ultimate source of revenues. In the case of Liverpool, the reaction of fans to the management of Gillett and Hicks has provoked an attempt by fans to raise the capital to take over the club themselves by forming ShareLiverpoolFC a proto investment company for supporters.

Borrowing

Borrowing takes two forms: direct and indirect. Direct borrowing is in the form of either using an overdraft facility with the club's bank or taking out a loan with the bank. In either case, a business case has to be made that the debt can be serviced. The stability of cash flows, at least within a season, and, if relegation can be avoided, for the period of the current broadcasting rights contract, gives football clubs an apparent advantage over other businesses in presenting the business case. However, borrowing may be prompted by the urge to buy players in order to avoid relegation, which may not be successful. In the case of Bradford City, chairman Geoffrey Richmond has referred to his "six weeks of financial madness" (*Guardian*, 2002) in buying players in an ill-fated attempt to stave off relegation from the Premier League, compounded by the collapse of the ITV Digital broadcasting company which broadcast matches in the three English divisions below the Premiership.

Indirect borrowing occurs when a business does not pay suppliers and debtors when their debts are due. Increasingly, clubs are following this practice, with Her Majesty's Revenue and Customs (HMRC, the now-unified government agency that collects all taxes, including PAYE tax deductions, UK Value Added Tax, National Insurance contributions, etc.) often being on the *non*receiving end. Andrew Fitton, head of the consortium that owns Swindon Town, has been quoted as saying "HMRC was effectively the bank of football" (quoted by *BBC News*, 2008b). The relationship between clubs and HMRC is complex, but it is estimated that more than £28 million of football club debt has been written off in deals negotiated while clubs are in Administration (Grant, 2008).

ADMINISTRATION

When a club in the UK, or indeed any business, faces the fact that its cash flow has become irreconcilably negative or it will be unable to service its debts in the long term, it can seek the protection of the courts from its creditors by going into Administration. The court-appointed Administrator takes control of the business and is charged with trying to rescue the football club. A number of outcomes are possible, ranging from the liquidation of the business to the handing back to the existing owners. If liquidation is avoided, the next step in the process is for the Administrator to negotiate a Company Voluntary Arrangement (CVA) between the owners and the creditors whereby a structured repayment plan is agreed, often involving a reduction of the debt, with debtors only receiving an agreed number of pence in the pound. The Football League now requires that a club exit Administration into a CVA; failing to do so will incur a 25-playing point deduction.

Research at the Centre for the International Business of Sport at Coventry University (Beech et al. 2008a; Beech et al., 2008b) has identified that a route out of Administration that is particularly frequent with football clubs involves a change of ownership. In spite of the intended effect of deterring clubs from going into Administration, the ongoing research has identified 61 clubs in the English leagues that have suffered this fate on 76 occasions—in other words, some clubs have been into Administration on more than one occasion. At the start of the 2008–2009 season, 41 percent of the clubs in the top four tiers had been in Administration at some point in their history.

If there is a typical route into Administration for a club, research suggests that it is the following (Beech et al., 2008a):

■ A trend of poor performance on the pitch leads to relegation and reduced revenues.

■ Costs are not cut back (in particular players' wages) and are wrongly prioritised.

■ If the club owns its stadium, as the most valuable asset this becomes an issue. If the club does not own its stadium, it raises different issues; borrowing becomes extremely difficult, but creditors may hold off, as there is no major asset to strip.

■ Management faces a dilemma of whether to spend in the hope of improved performance on the pitch and thus promotion with its attendant financial gains or whether to release its better players in order to reduce costs.

Based on a survey of clubs that have gone into Administration, this research also suggests that there are "inappropriate" levels of debt for a club. In other words, above a certain level of debt, a club can be identified as vulnerable to its creditors, and its creditors may become nervous and seek a winding-up order. These are the average levels for the clubs in the five tiers of English football below the Premiership:

Tier 2	£10m
Tier 3	£3m
Tier 4	£1m
Tier 5	£1m
Tier 6	£1m

Table 8.13	Self-Assessment of Club's Current (2008) Financial Position						
	All %	EPL	EFLC	FL1	FL2	SPL	SFD
Very healthy	24	22	22	0	22	75	0
Could be better, but not bad	62	67	44	75	78	25	100
In need of attention	11	11	22	25	0	0	0
A cause for grave concern/on verge of Administration	3	0	11	0	0	0	0

Source: *PKF Football Industry Group (2008, page 11).*

Being in Administration is a low point for a club, but there are ways to bounce back. In 2008/2009 there were three clubs in the Premier League who had previously emerged from Administration. Hull City went into Administration in 2002 when they were in Tier 4, Middlesbrough were saved from liquidation in 1985 by local benefactor Steve Gibson when they were in Tier 3, and Portsmouth were bought from the Administrator by benefactor Milan Mandaric in 1999 when they were in Tier 2. Who, then, was under threat of going into Administration in 2008? Table 8.13 shows the responses of finance directors to the question "How would you rate your club's current financial position?" With the exception of the Scottish Premier League, there was little unbridled optimism. The must vulnerable clubs, by their own assessment, were those in the Championship, with a third of them expressing at least some cause for concern.

CASE STUDY 8.2: The Sorry Story of Rotherham United

Rotherham United can trace their origins back to 1870, and they have played in the third tier of English football for most of their existence although in the 2008/2009 season they were in the fourth. Although Rotherham has a population of approximately 250,000, the club is surrounded by the two Sheffield clubs (Wednesday and United) some six miles away, Doncaster Rovers (12 miles) and Barnsley (13 miles), all four of whom are currently in the Championship, two tiers above Rotherham United.

In the 1980s and 1990s, Rotherham United moved several times among the second, third, and fourth tiers, making financial planning very problematic. In 1987 they had been rescued from Administration by Ken Booth, a local businessman who had inherited his father's highly successful metal recycling business.

In 2002, for the first time in many years, the club recorded a profit, and there was talk of redeveloping one of the stands, with £2 million of funding already in place. Turnover was almost three times that of the previous year, but the salary bill was rising as Rotherham fought to remain in what is now the Championship, reaching £3.3 million, an increase of £1.38 million from the previous year. The ITV Digital broadcasting company had collapsed, and the £2.5 million expected from that source would not be available in the coming year. A deficit of £1 million was projected.

By early 2003, concern was being expressed regarding funding for the stand redevelopment. In August a key player was sold for £850,000, and in November, following the announcement of an annual loss of £730,000, Rotherham United chief executive Phil Henson made it quite clear there was no danger of the club going into Administration. He said, "The chairman, Ken Booth, is fully committed to the club for the immediate future, and his company will continue to underwrite the overdraft as they have done since 1987, so nothing has changed. Rotherham United have no debts."

The following month, Rotherham United Supporters Trust called upon local businesspeople to invest in the club in the light of the pending retirement of Ken Booth. In December 2003, an annual loss of £1.3 million was reported, and Ken Booth confirmed that he was looking to sell the club as his sons had "other hobbies."

After protracted negotiations, the sale of the club to former director Neil Freeman fell through in June 2004. In October another attempted takeover by local company Earth Mortgages, a main sponsor of the club, also fell through. In December a group of local businesspeople who were supporters of the club finally managed to buy the club, and Ken Booth, by then in his eighties, was made Life President. The club's debts were cleared, but Ken Booth was to retain ownership of Millmoor, the club's stadium, and the club's training ground in exchange for the £3 million he was owed by the club. New investment amounted to £100,000 and the club would continue to play at Millmoor under a sale-and-lease-back arrangement. Operating at breakeven was envisaged for the start of the 2005–2006 season.

However, the attempt to break even proved a real challenge. New problems since the takeover included a response of only £12,000 to a share rights issue, a reduction in season tickets sales, and declining gate receipts. In February 2006, the new board reported that the club was losing £140,000 a month. Chairman Peter Ruchniewicz admitted that the club's financial position had entered a critical phase. The following month, another group of local businessmen, headed by Dennis Coleman, took over the club. An unpaid PAYE tax bill of over £500,000 was bringing intense pressure from the tax authorities and three experienced players were released. In desperate circumstances, a CVA with the creditors was negotiated, but this incurred a ten-point penalty for the start of the following season.

The new board sought further investment in vain, and in March 2008, the club again went into Administration. As a consequence of taking the club into Administration for a second time, Dennis Coleman became the first person to be banned from being a director of a football club through the "fit and proper persons" test. In addition to continuing problems with paying HMRC, the club was struggling to meet rental payments on Millmoor.

The next month the Booth family threatened legal action if the package of privileges negotiated under the earlier agreement were not honoured in any future agreement, which made any sale of the club difficult. Nonetheless, in May Tony Stewart acquired the club and announced that Rotherham United would be leaving Millmoor to play at the Don Valley stadium in nearby Sheffield. In the short term they would be training at Doncaster Rovers' training facilities. These moves created problems of their own: in July, the Football League announced that Rotherham United would forfeit a bond of £750,000 if they did not move back to the town of Rotherham in the next four years (the local council stepped in and guaranteed £500,000 of the bond in August).

Rotherham began the 2008–2009 season with a deduction of 17 points. Bournemouth also faced a 17-point deduction, and Luton Town had a total of 30 points deducted. There are two relegation slots in League 2, so at least one of the three clubs stands a chance of avoiding relegation and a continuing downward financial spiral.

Source: Various

Questions

1. Whom would you blame, if anyone, for Rotherham's financial distress?

2. Do you think Dennis Coleman should have been barred by the "fit and proper persons" test? Give your reasons.

CONCLUSIONS

Football *is* different as a business, as indeed are all professional sports—a fact that is becoming recognised by the European Union, with its promotion of the concept of the "specificity" of sport, although arguably "uniqueness" would be a more appropriate term. Although the outcomes of the European Commission's White Paper on Sport (Commission of the European Communities, 2007) in which specificity is emphasised may have broad implications for football, such as in employment and competition law, a case can be made that financial regulation of professional sport deserves unique consideration.

Football clubs have less direct control over their revenues and costs than other businesses. Except for the clubs at the level of the Champions League, who compete over merchandising in the Far East, the main area of competition is in the recruitment of players. They can compete in the transfer market, or they can "grow their own" in their Youth Academies (provided they haven't shut them in a cost-cutting exercise).

To be healthy financially, a club should do the following:

- Maintain a steady position in the centre of the table of a league that is appropriate for their potential fan base, avoiding relegation, and, to some extent, promotion.
- Develop a committed local fan base.
- Develop a long-term relationship with a sponsor that is itself financially stable.
- Avoid the longer-term uncertainty of benefactor dependency.
- Own its own stadium, one that has been built new since the Taylor report and that has appropriate facilities for matchday hospitality and nonmatchday activities that generate revenue streams.
- Have performance-related contracts with its players.
- Maintain a squad that reflects its current league position in terms of performance and wages.
- Employ a manager who is successful on the pitch and appreciative of financial constraints.

Too few clubs are in the enviable position of matching all these needs.

DISCUSSION QUESTIONS

1. To what extent is it possible to maintain a balance between the playing needs and the financial resources of a football club?

2. Do you consider entering Administration to be a valid business tactic?

3. Should clubs in, for example, the Blue Square Premier League of the Football Conference consider reverting to semiprofessional or even amateur squads?

4. Is the "bubble finally going to burst" in the postcommercialised era of English football because it is financially unsustainable?

5. Do you think that for each club there is a "natural" tier that is determined by the size of their fanbase to play in?

6. What are the financial implications and broader implications of cost-saving by reducing or eliminating (1) youth academies, (2) women's teams, and (3) scouting staff? Consider both the short-term and long-term implications.

GUIDED READING

Two annual reports are essential reading for the student of football finance: the PKF Football Industry Group *Annual Survey of Football Club Finance Directors* (available free online from *http://www.pkf.co.uk/pkf/publications/football_survey&goto=4*) and the Deloitte *Annual Review of Football Finance* (highlights are downloadable at no cost from *http://www.deloitte.com/dtt/article/0,2297,sid%253D2855%2526cid%253D56148,00.html*). The former provides considerable insight into current planning and strategy, and the latter is a useful source of financial data. Financial data on many clubs is available through the FAME database, which most universities subscribe to through their e-libraries. Most broadsheets provide some financial news of football clubs, but coverage tends to be restricted to the Premier League. Walters and Hamil (2008) provides a good overview of the state of English football from a financial perspective.

REFERENCES

BBC News. (10th October, 2008a). Bonsor angered by ambition claims. *BBC.* Retrieved on November 22, 2008, from *http://news.bbc.co.uk/sport1/hi/football/teams/w/walsall/7664177.stm*.

BBC News. (2008b). Football clubs face tax scrutiny. *BBC.* Retrieved on November 22, 2008, from *http://news.bbc.co.uk/1/hi/business/7721251.stm*.

BBC News. (28th May, 2008c). Football finances in detail. *BBC.* Retrieved on November 14, 2008, from *http://news.bbc.co.uk/1/hi/business/7424134.stm*.

BBC News. (17th October, 2008d). Walsall in third straight profit. *BBC*. Retrieved on November 22, 2008, from *http://news.bbc.co.uk/sport1/hi/football/teams/w/walsall/7675509.stm*.

Beech, J., S. Horsman and J. Magraw. (2008a). *The circumstances in which English football clubs become insolvent*. Centre for the International Business of Sport, Coventry University.

Beech, J., S. Horsman, and J. Magraw. (2008b). The Circumstances which Cause English Football Clubs to Go into Administration. In Proceedings of *Challenges facing Football in the 21st Century*, Berne.

Commission of the European Communities. (2007). *White Paper on Sport*. Brussels: European Commission.

Deloitte (2001–2008). *Annual Review of Football Finance*. Manchester: Deloitte.

FootballTransfers.co.uk. (2008). *World's Highest Transfer Fees*. Retrieved on November 22, 2008, from *http://www.footballtransfers.info/transfers/rectrans.php*.

Forbes.com (2007). In Pictures: Top-Earning Players. *Forbes.com*. Retrieved on July 25, 2009, from http://www.forbes.com/2007/03/28/soccer-valuations-beckham-biz-services-cx_pm_07soccer_0329earners_slide.html.

Grant, P. (11th November, 2008). Football clubs owe tax millions. *BBC*. Retrieved on November 22, 2008, from *http://news.bbc.co.uk/1/hi/uk/7741859.stm*.

Growthcompany.co.uk. Retrieved on June 24, 2009, from *http://www.growthcompany.co.uk/company/TTNM/tottenham-hotspur.thtml*.

Guardian (17th May, 2002). Richmond: My financial madness. *The Guardian*. Retrieved July 7, 2009, from *http://www.guardian.co.uk/football/2002/may/17/clubsincrisis.bradford*.

Harris, N. (19th February, 2009). *Platini warns of 'impending implosion'*, The Independent.

Inside Out. (2007). Do we pay too much for our football? *BBC*. Retrieved on November 17, 2008, from http://www.bbc.co.uk/insideout/yorkslincs/series11/week4_football_ripoff.shtml.

Levy, D. (2008). *Open letter from the Chairman, Daniel Levy*. Tottenham Hotspur FC, London. Retrieved on November 3, 2008, from http://www.tottenhamhotspur.com/news/articles/openletterfromthechairmandaniellevy261008.html.

Munro, J., C. Whyatt, and D. Ornstein. (7th October, 2008). FA chief fears '£3bn' club debts. *BBC*. Retrieved on November 22, 2008, from http://news.bbc.co.uk/sport1/hi/football/7656862.stm.

PKF Football Industry Group. (2008). *Under Pressure: Is it time for the industry to go on the defensive?* London: PKF.

Rohlmann, P., & Zastrow, H. (2008). The European Football Merchandising Report. *Sport + Markt*. Cologne.

Smith, A. (26th April, 2007). England's Goal Rush, *Time*.

SportBusiness International. (21st May, 2008). Champions League winner to claim £85m, says MasterCard. *SportBusiness International.* Retrieved on November 5, 2005, from http://www.sportbusiness.com/news/166841/champions-league-winner-to-claim-85m-says-mastercard.

Vrooman, J. (2007). Theory of the Beautiful Game: The unification of European football. *Scottish Journal of Political Economy, Vol. 54*(No. 3), pp. 314–354.

Walters, G. and S. Hamil. (July, 2008). *All Party Parliamentary Football Group—Inquiry into English Football and its Governance: Memorandum of Written Evidence,* London. Retrieved on November 16, 2008, from http://www.sportbusinesscentre.com/images/APPFG%20Written%20EvidenceFinal20October2008_2_.pdf.

Williams, G. (2003). Arsenal and Spurs Win Kit Trading Cases. Retrieved on November 17, 2008, from http://www.footballeconomy.com/archive/archive_2003_jan_01.htm.

RECOMMENDED WEBSITES

euFootball.biz
http://www.eufootball.biz/Finance
sportbusinessinternational
http://www.sportbusiness.com

CHAPTER 9

Supply Chain Management and Retailing

Leigh Sparks
University of Stirling

CONTENTS

Objectives

Upon completion of this chapter the reader should be able to:

- Understand some of the complexities of supply chain management for football products.
- Define the components of the logistics mix.
- Understand the need to ensure appropriate channel performance from production to consumption.

OVERVIEW OF THE CHAPTER

Football demands the development of effective and efficient supply chains to deliver products and information to a range of customers and consumers. Whether it is the supply of products and services to enable a match to take place, the availability of the new change (or away) strip in the club shop, or the desire to purchase a pair of football boots for personal use, making sure that the "right products are in the right place at the right time" cannot be left to chance. Significant opportunities exist to generate additional sales and brand value by ensuring an effective supply system.

This chapter is about supply chain management and retailing in a football context. It presents the principles of supply chain management and the functions of logistics that need to be understood and implemented.

This focus is extended by consideration of outcomes of supply chain behaviour, both positive and negative, and aspects of retail supply of products to customers and fans.

The retailing of football products takes many forms, but retailers, brand owners, and clubs have increasingly realised the opportunities for them of controlling supply chains and in presenting effective and efficient retail operations to their customers. The merchandise mix, store design, and atmospherics of shops (including where possible online) are increasingly seen as brand enhancing. For football brands, the supply chain is the conduit to the customer and must be managed appropriately.

SUPPLY CHAIN MANAGEMENT

Supply chain management is about making products and services available efficiently and effectively. This availability has at least two aspects. First, products are made available for purchase. Second, they are made physically available for use or consumption. Making products available to a consumer can occur with the simultaneous transfer of sale, ownership, and, thus, use. For example, a fan who buys a replica shirt at a club shop buys, owns, and takes physical possession of the shirt immediately. Alternatively, however, the sale and consumption of a product can occur at separate times. Purchasing season tickets is one example. They are bought at one place and time and consumed at a different place and time. Both aspects, however, require flows of information and then product to enable such transactions to occur. Customers need to know about the products available and to be able to physically "use" or "consume" them. These flows are organised in supply chains or distribution channels—that is, networks of organisations involved in assembling and moving products from points of production to points of consumption.

In football, supply chains can take many forms in carrying out these—on the surface—comparatively simple activities. There are many choices to be made and many potential operations and routes to consider. A range of organisations and approaches may coexist and serve to meet the demand and supply issues that arise. Manufacturers, wholesalers, brokers, and retailers exist in these channels to provide aspects of production, finance, risk, product, and information movement management and control (e.g., inventory, storage, break of bulk, deliveries) and sale, all geared at meeting consumer demands for "football products."

Sparks (2007) provides simplified illustrations of distribution channels for both sports products and services. He focuses on the complexity of even seemingly straightforward channels and on the changes that have occurred in supply chains and distribution channels in recent years. For example, digitalisation and the Internet have opened up new opportunities. Thus, football clubs now offer a range of digital products electronically, such as club TV channels, club web TV channels, telephony and video subscription services, and ticket sales.

Sparks's (2007) illustrations suggest that distribution channels are organised and controlled by those who exhibit degrees of power. Power is often seen in terms of scale, but it exists also importantly in terms of control of content and brand. Ownership of image rights is a prerequisite to the distribution of content, in exactly the same way that ownership of the club logo (trademark) is a prerequisite to "official merchandise." Ownership and power are the keys to value generation and disaggregation (see Lonsdale, 2004, for a consideration of value and football players in a supply network framework).

THE LOGISTICS MIX AND CHANNEL MANAGEMENT

Supply chains are often stated as being about "getting the right products to the right place at the right time." In the case of physical products such as replica shirts or matchday programmes, products have to be physically moved, so issues of stock, handling, and transport come to the fore. In the case of digital products such as mobile services, then information (capture, storing, sending, and where to send it) is at the heart of the distribution channel. In terms of match events at the stadium, there may be particular requirements for equipment movement for participants, broadcast media, caterers, sponsors, and so on. Many elements may have to be brought together at the same place and time.

Managing distribution channels is a complex activity that involves both anticipating and reacting to both known and volatile consumer and other demands. For example, if a football team wins the FA Cup, then celebratory merchandise (e.g., flags, scarves) and shirts need to be produced almost immediately. The financial risk in producing in advance is too great. Some football products are thus very close in production, demand, and supply patterns to "fast fashion" or other "fashion" items with very peaked demand and supply times. The management challenge is thus to get these activities right. Here are some other typical logistical challenges:

■ The production and provision of programmes for a football match require that information is up to date and that demand is accurately assessed.

Programmes have little informational value after the game. While some material can be printed and prepared in advance, team news may need to be inserted quite late, yet the programmes have to be available for sale in a narrow time frame.

■ The launch of a new kit has high publicity and financial value for a club. This provokes in many cases a surge in demand that requires shops and websites both to be in stock and to respond quickly. Similarly, the signing of a new superstar will change demand patterns. The adoption of squad numbers to allow product customisation has enabled clubs to better manage such issues and has expanded the market.

■ Text and video updates to mobile telephones have to be almost instantaneous in order to have value. There is thus pressure on the length of the message, the speed of response to, for example, a goal, and on the accuracy of contacting the subscriber base. Tolerance of failure of these elements will be extremely limited. Control of content, such as a manager's conferences, can drive demand but can need rapid dissemination.

These examples demonstrate that the concern in supply chains is with both product and information flows. In order to make products or events available, product movement and demand management must therefore be managed. This essentially requires the management of the "logistics mix" (Figure 9.1).

Inventory

Inventory (a.k.a. stock) is a necessary but unloved part of the channel activities. Stock generally represents capital that is tied up in unsold product. As such, businesses often try to minimise stockholding. However, stock is

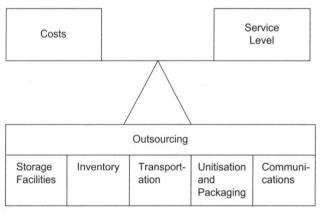

FIGURE 9.1   *The management task in logistics.*

needed in order to meet anticipated demand and to bridge the gap between production and sale, both in terms of distance and time. How much inventory to hold (and where) is thus a vital part of managing channel activities, as is managing the ownership of the stock and thus the risk profile for various intermediaries. A key component of stock management is the principle of postponement, whereby products are held in a neutral rather than a finished state until demand is confirmed—for example, holding football shirts without names and allowing the production of customised shirts to order. Inventory can, however, also be beneficial and valuable, as, for example, where there is a product launch (new kit) or a scarcity of product or under-supply, whether generally or in specific situations (ahead of a Cup Final). Being in stock when needed can add to brand credibility.

Storage Facilities

Stock needs to be stored somewhere. The management of such facilities or locations is important in meeting both anticipated and unanticipated demand. These facilities may be traditional warehouses where product is stored and put away for later recall. Retailers and others may themselves have on-site storage areas at their own facilities, such as in the back room of a club shop or at a football stadium, in order to meet demand fluctuations and heightened matchday purchasing patterns.

Transportation

Most physical products require transportation at some time. Even telephonic products require a network over which to transport the messages or images. Physical products often need to be transported over considerable distances, perhaps very rapidly. As such, organisations need to consider the appropriate mode and scheduling of transport—air, road, sea, train. Club and other websites need to be able to deliver the products purchased in a timely manner.

Unitisation and Packaging

Most products require some form of packaging. This packaging may be part of the selling activity or might be needed for protection and handling during transportation. Generally, packaging will also carry information that can be of use to the consumer (product content, instructions) or to others (e.g., bar codes for retailers or transportation). Products tend to be purchased by consumers in small quantities. Separate handling of each of these small quantities from production to consumption would be inordinately wasteful. Convenient combinations of products are thus assembled into regular sizes (unitisation) so as to aid handling and transportation. Standardisation on generally agreed sizes helps channel efficiency. For example, a pair of football boots comes in a box. This regularly shaped box assists handling. Set numbers of boxes make up cartons, pallet loads, and even container loads for transportation. Regular, consistent, known shapes, sizes, and weights allow better planning and handling and reduce logistics costs.

Communications

Distribution channels are a method of joining production to consumption and thus overcoming space and time barriers. To work effectively, channels require information. As such, the logistics mix is as much about data and information collection, dissemination, and use as it is about product storage and movement. Data are needed to ensure that appropriate actions are taken and that linkages are made. For example, communication networks are needed to use the data captured on consumer demand in retail stores to reorder product from storage or to ensure further production to meet the demand. Without good information flows, the logistics mix will function more inaccurately, adding expense and inefficiency.

Managing this logistics mix represents the core components of the logistics task (see Figure 9.1) and thus supply chain operations, but it raises a number of other issues, not the least questions of outsourcing and cost and service balance. Here are some examples:

■ The focus on cost-effectiveness suggests that there is a balance to be struck between service and cost if the activity is to add value. Thus, while immediate delivery can always be promised, the cost of doing it may be too high. Having all products always available at all shops to meet any possible level of demand would be ruinously expensive and inefficient. The balance between cost and service varies depending on the situation and the risk assessment of the outcomes of over- and understocking.

■ The management task involves the search for trade-offs in the mix, whereby suboptimal behaviour in one or more elements is balanced by optimal behaviour across the mix as a whole—for example, large orders may be placed but with more infrequent deliveries. Stock may be held at suppliers' premises and "called off" when needed but at the price of a small time delay and some extra cost.

■ These points come together in the concept of outsourcing, where it might make sense for some (or all) of the distribution operation, such as transport or warehousing, to be outsourced to logistics specialists to gain from their expertise and other synergies.

RETAILING IN SUPPLY CHAINS

Many football goods supply chains focus on delivery to a retail outlet. Retailing is concerned with the sale of products (normally individual items or in small quantities) to the final consumer. Retailers use their knowledge of changing consumer demands to better serve customers and to reflect tastes, needs, and wants. In football, it is clear that customer demands have changed in a number of ways:

- Products, such as boots, have developed through technology and safety enhancements.
- The gender balance of participants and consumers in football has become less biased toward the male category.
- Football clothing ("kit") has ceased to be a functional need and has in many cases become leisure-related casual wear.
- Style has become as important in some categories of equipment or clothing as function.
- Demand around major football events—for example, Cup Finals, Euro 2008, World Cup 2006—has become larger and more volatile.
- Association and overt identification with football teams and major football events has risen, opening up merchandise possibilities.

If customer demands and needs have altered in these (and other) ways, then it is to be expected that retailers should have responded to these changes by developing their retail operations. The sports retail shop of today looks different from the sports retail stores of yesteryear. It merchandises and sells different products, services, and experiences. For example, the revamped Nike Town in London has leading-edge design, displays, and experiences in its new football-focused area. This change has involved the creation of new businesses, approaches, brands, and methods of operating through which football products are made available:

- There has been an increase in the scale of sports retailing businesses, many of which carry large football related ranges.
- Store design ideas and capabilities have developed.
- Club shops and distribution channels have developed strongly at stadia, on the Internet, and on dedicated broadcast media.
- Internet-based football-related retailing has expanded dramatically, including ticketing sites, You Tube, and eBay.

Given their significance in the structure of the U.K. sports retailing market, Table 9.1 provides a brief description of the largest sports retailers. There

Table 9.1 Leading Sports Goods Retailers in the UK

Company	Description	Financial Details
Sports Direct International (www.sportsdirect.com) (www.sports-direct-international.com)	Sports Direct is the UK's leading sports retailer and the owner of several internationally recognised sports and leisure brands. Sports Direct offers a wide range of competitively priced branded sports and leisure apparel, replica kit, footwear and sports equipment through its retail operations and also operates an international wholesale and licensing business through its brands operations. Sports Direct (set up by Mike Ashley in 1982 and formally called Sports Soccer and then Sports World) has grown to its present position through a combination of organic growth and acquiring other chains. These takeovers include Lillywhites, Gilesports, Hargreaves, Original Shoe Company and Streetwise. Brands owned include Donnay, Dunlop, Karrimor, Slazenger, LA Gear and Kangol. The company was floated on the London Stock Exchange in 2007.	Sales : £1.35bn Pre-tax profit: £151m Stores: 414 in the UK Market Share: 23% UK Retail Ranking: 37 Data for Sports Direct for financial year 2006/7 i.e. end April 2007.
JJB Sports (www.jjbsports.com) (www.jjbcorporate.co.uk)	JJB Sports is a leading UK retailer of sports clothing, footwear, accessories and equipment, trading from high street outlets and increasingly out of town superstores (some jointly with healthclubs). In 1998 JJB Sports acquired the then market leader Sports Division and became the undisputed #1 in the UK. It has lost this position in recent years as sales and profits have fallen and Sports Direct has out-competed it. The principal aim is to supply high quality branded sports and leisure products at competitive or discount prices and to be viewed as "Serious about Sport". Founder Dave Whelan sold his 29% share of the company for £190m in 2007 to Icelandic financial group Exista and Chris Ronnie, a sports retailer who has previously worked at Umbro and Sports Direct. Since the 2007/8 results, the company has embarked on a restructuring, closing 65 shops.	Sales: £812m Pre-tax profit: £10.8m Stores: 409 Market Share: 17% UK Retail Ranking: 46 Data for JJB Sports for financial year 2007/8 i.e. end January 2008.
John David Group (www.jdsports.co.uk)	John David Group is a leading specialist retailer of fashionable branded sports and leisure wear. It has grown mainly by acquisition of First Sport (200 stores) from Blacks in 2002 and Allsports (70 stores) from the administrator in 2005. Fashion chain Bank was bought in 2007. JD Sports is 57% owned by the Pentland Group plc, though Sports Direct also own 12.3%. The Pentland Group bought out the two owners of JD Sports in 2005 for £44.6m. The chain would view itself as being more fashion oriented and upmarket than its two main competitors, though this does bring it into competition with other youth fashion oriented retailers.	Sales: £592m Pre-tax profit: £35m Stores: 432 Market Share: 12% UK Retail Ranking: 66 Data for JD Sports for financial year 2007/8 i.e. end January 2008.

Source: Annual Reports, Mintel (2005, 2006, 2007).

are a number of issues that arise from this table. First, the considerable scale of these businesses is well demonstrated, with substantial sales volumes and number of retail stores. These three retailers are ranked in the 100 largest retailers in the United Kingdom. The largest of these retailers has over £1.35 billion in sales. Second, the sector has been concentrating through natural growth and the strategic acquisitions that companies have made. Strategic acquisitions have been combined with significant store expansion programmes, though more recently these have been combined with closures and repositionings as consumer demand and trading locations develop and/or decline. Third, store formats and locations have been undergoing changes. Fascias have changed as acquisitions have been made, but much of the expansion has been focused on out-of-town superstores or in-town, larger stores. Scale is thus seen at both the organisational and the operational or store level. Out-of-town superstore or retail park development fits with broad consumer and retail trends. Fourth, the sports retailing market has not been in particularly good shape. The profits shown in the table are small, and businesses are not necessarily sustainable at these levels (the number 4 store in the market in 2004—Allsports—became insolvent in 2005 and was closed down by administrators). Market pressures have been seen in the sales and takeovers of major chains and in some of the store closures.

The basic retail idea is a simple one: the retailer acquires products and makes them available for sale to consumers. Retailers thus have to consider issues of shop location, consumer market segmentation and positioning, store design, buying and merchandising, staffing and customer service, as well as operational practicalities such as cash flow, security, product availability, heating and lighting, and so forth. Some of these issues have to be considered by Internet retailers. Retail sales of football products via the Internet have expanded rapidly in recent years, suggesting that they are successfully meeting aspects of consumer demands. Fundamental to this is product availability and quality of distribution.

ISSUES IN SUPPLY CHAINS AND RETAILING FOR FOOTBALL PRODUCTS

As noted earlier, the management task in football supply chains consists of strategically managing distribution channels for products and services. A wide range of issues could be identified in any discussion. Here, two particular cases have been chosen, based on the high profile and importance of the issues and the ways in which they illustrate the broad topics outlined earlier.

Price-Fixing and Replica Shirts

The final price to a consumer for any product is made up of a variety of cost and profit decisions. Inefficiencies in the supply chain will drive costs and thus final prices up. This could lead to adverse consumer reactions. There is thus competitive pressure to ensure supply chain efficiency by members of the supply chain working closely together.

However, there is a darker side to the interrelationships between producers and distributors that can have a different effect on consumers. If suppliers collude with a range of other actors in the channel (e.g., retailers, clubs, associations) and the supply and demand can be artificially regulated or controlled, then price-fixing can be implemented. Thus, a supplier might agree with a number of retailers to distribute a particular item. They all agree on a final price to the consumer and also agree not to discount this price. The agreed price does not represent supply-and-demand realities. It bears no relation to the costs of doing business and reduces competitiveness in the market. Retailers not privy to this agreement will find it hard to obtain supplies from official sources. Retailers who break the agreement may find that their usual sources of supply will no longer supply them.

Such vertical restraints on trade/supply can occur in any distribution channel where manufacturers, retailers, or others have power and are willing to abuse their position and where there is a degree of product distinctiveness. Where the product is licensed or "official," such supply control is clearly more possible, as the product has particular separate characteristics obviating substitutes—for example, if you require an official English football shirt, then a Scottish shirt will not do! Such agreements or collusion are illegal in the United Kingdom (and elsewhere) under the Competition Acts, as they are considered cheating the customer (anticompetitive).

Case study 9.1 examines a recent (but long-running) high-profile instance of price-fixing involving replica football kit. Some of the highest-profile manufacturers, retailers, and football organisations were involved. The competition authorities found that price-fixing did occur. The case illustrates the interactions and interlinkages that occur both vertically and horizontally in supply systems. It also suggests that there is a need to be vigilant over the activities of channel partners in order to protect the consumer.

CASE STUDY 9.1: Did You Pay Too Much For Your Football Shirt?

In August 2003, ten businesses were fined a total of £16.8 million by the Office of Fair Trading (OFT) after an investigation into price-fixing for Umbro replica football shirts. In a major breach of the Competition Act of 1998, the OFT found that the companies fixed the prices for various shirts through a number of agreements. These included the top-selling short-sleeved adult and junior shirt of the England team and for Manchester United. Other agreements involved replica kit for Chelsea, Celtic, and Nottingham Forest. Most of the agreements covered key selling periods, such as the launch of new kits or England's participation in Euro 2000. Supply was constrained to some retailers selling below an agreed price known to the manufacturer, some retailers, clubs, and other organisations. Price information was shared and price levels were maintained through collusion. The overcharging was estimated to be £15 to £20 per shirt. The following fines were levied by the OFT:

JJB Sports	£8.37 million
	(later reduced to £6.3 million)
Umbro	£6.64 million
	(later reduced to £5.3 million)
Manchester United	£1.65 million
	(later reduced to £1.5 million)
Allsports	£1.35 million
	(later increased to £1.42 million)
Football Association	£158,000
Blacks	£197,000
Sports Soccer	£123,000
JD Sports	£73,000
Sports Connection	£20,000
Sportsetail	Fine set at zero by leniency

JJB Sports was extremely annoyed by the decision, calling the OFT a "kangaroo court" and denying any wrongdoing or any involvement in price-fixing. It launched an appeal against the decision and the fine, as did Allsports (no longer trading), whereas Umbro and Manchester United appealed against the level of their fines.

In October 2004, the Competition Appeal Tribunal (CAT) found that JJB Sports had been involved in some price-fixing agreements (England and Manchester United), and the majority of the OFT findings were upheld. JJB continue to press their claim of innocence but lost further appeals before the CAT (May 2005) and the Court of Appeal (October 2006). In February 2007, JJB Sports were refused leave to appeal to the House of Lords, effectively concluding the OFT case.

In an ironic twist, in October 2005 *Which?*, the consumer rights magazine, was granted powers (under the Enterprise Act 2002) by the CAT to represent consumers for damages in the case. Their argument was that whilst OFT fines provide recompense to the government, individual consumers do not get reimbursed for the cost to them of illegal activity. JJB Sports' continuing appeals brought them within the time limit for action. In February 2007, *Which?* brought a case on behalf of people overcharged for the shirts involved in the OFT case. The action was settled out of court in February 2008, with JJB Sports paying all legal costs and reimbursing consumers who could prove their purchase of the shirts involved.

Which? represented 550 fans, who received £20 compensation. Almost 15,000 others took up a free shirt and mug offer from JJB Sports and received £5. Anyone else who could prove they bought one of the shirts involved could get £10. These rights ended in February 2009. JJB Sports still argue they did nothing wrong and have commented, "Whilst JJB recognises the right of *Which?* to bring an action for damages against the company, JJB does not, in settling the action, acknowledge or admit that any consumers suffered loss giving rise to an action for damages as a result of its words, actions, or behaviour."

Question

1. Is price-fixing against the consumer interest or does it reflect business realities?

Sources/Further Information:

Competition Appeals Tribunal (2004-7) *JJB Sports v Office of Fair Trading*. Case 1021/1/1/03. Downloaded from http://www.catribunal.org.uk/archive/casedet.asp?id=65 on 9th June 2008

JJB Sports (2008) JJB Settle *Which?* Court Action. *www.jjbsports.com* downloaded on 9th June 2008.

Office of Fair Trading (2003) *Price Fixing of Replica Football Kit*. Decision CA98/06/2003. Downloaded from

http://www.oft.gov.uk/shared_oft/ca98_public_register/ decisions/replicakits.pdf. on 9th June 2008.

Which? (2008) Football Shirts. *www.which.co.uk/reports_and_campaigns/consumer_ rights/campaigns/Football%20shirts/index.jsp* Downloaded on 9th June 2008.

The New Generation of Football Club Shops

The football club shop has in the past often been the repository for an odd collection of rather sad merchandise that no one really looks after or wants to buy. This, however, has begun to change, particularly in those clubs with a large fan base and a heightened sense of the possibilities for their brand. As clubs have expanded their thinking about product and service sales, the need for modern, well-run retailing facilities and operations has increased. With modern stadia catering to a different set of fans than before, providing an enhanced leisure experience, and with the Internet expanding sales reach, clubs such as Manchester United, Arsenal, and Liverpool have begun to recognise the need for efficient and effective modern retailing.

Thus, product ranges have altered and expanded to meet these new fan segments and their pride in the club. Speed of reaction to events and services on matchday have had to be enhanced. These issues have extended into how the retailing is run; how the merchandise mix is put together, sourced, and delivered; and the quality of the retail outlet and service itself. For some clubs, outsourcing the retail operations can make sense. For example, in 2006 Glasgow Rangers signed a ten-year licensing agreement with JJB Sports for JJB to design, develop, source, and retail all Rangers merchandise through JJB stores, to take over existing Rangers stores where appropriate, and to run the Rangers online retail shop. The price for JJB was £18 million initially plus £3 million per annum guaranteed, with additional payments if turnover targets are met.

Case study 9.2 examines the activities of S'porter Limited at Arsenal and Liverpool football clubs. S'porter is the brainchild of George Davies, the fashion retail expert behind Next (in the 1980s), George at Asda (in the 1990s), and now Per Una at Marks and Spencer. S'porter brings together fashion and football to produce products and shops suitable for modern clubs

CASE STUDY 9.2: S'Porter Limited

In late May 2008, one of the largest official football club shops in Europe opened as part of the new Liverpool One mega shopping, leisure, and residential complex. With more than 10,000 square feet of selling space, the new store has a Heritage Wall along one side, a personalisation zone to offer customised Liverpool football club merchandise, a relaxing chill-out area, a dramatic spiral staircase to the first floor, and a shirt print area where customers can see their shirts being printed. The store and the wide merchandise range has been designed by Liverpool-born, Reds-supporting fashion and retail guru George Davies (Next, George at Asda, Per Una). His design company, S'Porter Limited, established in 1995 specialises in combining fashion with sport.

S'Porter runs three other stores in Liverpool for the club, but it has been most known in recent years for its development of The Armoury store at the Emirates Stadium. When Arsenal moved to the Emirates in 2006, they took the opportunity to upgrade and extend the retail merchandise and club shop offer. The Armoury is supported by two other smaller stores (All Arsenal and Arsenal World of Sport at Finsbury Park tube station). S'Porter took on the role of creating a new range of Arsenal merchandise, helping design the new retail spaces and sourcing the products. The Armoury has been exceptionally successful, taking £150,000 each matchday, reflecting the event-driven nature of the business.

S'Porter makes money from design and sourcing with the club making the retail money. With the rising brand power of football clubs and the growing female and youth interest, the product and merchandise mix has changed markedly in recent years, becoming more lifestyle and fashion oriented. The retail space dramatically reflects the quality and ambition of the club, whether it be Arsenal or Liverpool.

Davies has talked about expansion possibilities, focusing on limited opportunities in the United Kingdom in locations where there is a focused support for certain clubs (e.g., Liverpool in Belfast) but, more significantly, perhaps opportunities in Asia. In stores in China, for example, he envisages a portfolio of English football club brands being carried as the supporters of clubs are widely dispersed rather than being city focused. As yet, development of this form has not occurred. S'Porter however has seen its turnover rise from £5.8 million in 2005 to £22.9 million in 2007 reflecting the Arsenal deal and putting S'Porter on the way to Davies' target of £100 million turnover.

Question

1. In what ways should football club shops reflect the changing nature of football supporters?

Sources/Further Information:

Arsenal Football Club – *www.arsenal.com*

Berwin L (19th October, 2007). Kitting out the Nation. *Retail Week*.

Liverpool Football Club – *www.liverpoolfc.tv*

Weston A (21st May, 2008). Stairway to Heaven for Liverpool FC Shoppers. *Liverpool Daily Post*.

and stadia and to meet modern consumer demands. It is arguably at the forefront of the football retailing revolution.

CONCLUSIONS

"Getting the right product to the right place at the right time" may sound easy, but the reality is, however, rather more complex and difficult. Whether it is the distribution of football scarves or the webcast of football internationals, issues of availability, ownership, possession, and use abound. From the buying of a programme at your local football club to the logistics needed to put the Cup Final together, there are major management issues in matching demand and supply.

Supply chains and logistics management bridge this gap between supply and demand. Distribution channels have to be efficient and effective in order to provide timely product availability. Football channels are under considerable pressure due to the demands from consumers, which are increasingly volatile, and due to the changes in the nature of product supply. Volatility of demand and speed of supply are key issues that require good management of the basic logistics activities. Information and communications technology have thus become ever more important in the management of supply chains in football.

Distribution channels can be complex and nuanced. They can contain a host of intermediaries and choices to be made. The opportunities to get things wrong are endless. Perhaps this helps explain the shadier sides of distribution channels, whether it is ticket touts or price-fixing. What they provide is a "hedge" against error. The complexities are huge, and the gains are considerable, so temptation to cut corners or to collude in unfair practices becomes too great. On the positive side, customers are continually rein- venting demand patterns and do not take kindly to being "ripped off." Distribution channels thus allow consumers to exercise their choices and to reward those who get it right and do it properly. If you can meet merchandise demands in a timely fashion, whether in the shop or online, then loyalty will be reinforced and the brand strengthened. When the club shop shouts quality and efficiency, the club brand is enhanced.

This reinvention emphasises the need for supply chain managers to be aware of the potential for change. Reaction to demand is a key focus, and technology has aided in this in terms of knowledge and time saving. Techno- logical advances are also being felt elsewhere in distribution channels. If there is one key message for the future it is that information capture and use will be every bit as valuable as product movement in distribution. Notwithstanding this, however, many football products still require physical product distribution to match production to consumption. Getting basic logistics management tasks right will remain fundamentally critical to successful football marketing.

DISCUSSION QUESTIONS

1. For a football match of which you have knowledge, list the elements that need to supplied logistically to ensure its occurrence.
2. To what extent is it possible to get the "right products to the right places at the right times" *all* the time?

GUIDED READING

Given the importance of supply chains to the delivery of sports products to consumers and sports events to spectators, there is remarkably little written on the topic of sports logistics and distribution channels, or even sports goods retailing. There is little coverage of the sports sector in mainstream retailing texts. This is even more curious given the sports participation and brand recognition rates of teenagers and student markets. Standard sport marketing text books generally contain a brief chapter on distribution, often combined with sports retailing. The exceptions are the recent books by Beech and Chadwick (2007) and Chadwick and Arthur (2008). Sports marketing journals have little coverage of the subject of distribution. Logistics and supply chain books tend not to cover the sport sector. A web search of major journal databases turns up very few relevant articles. Therefore, if you want to know more about the subject, you will need to do some groundwork yourself.

Given that the coverage of sport supply systems and retailing generally is so poor, it should not be surprising that football-related distribution and retailing are also poorly covered, though there is some material in Desbordes (2007). In terms of supply chain and logistics generally, then an introductory chapter in a retail context is Sparks (2003). A good general logistics text is Christopher and Peck (2003). Application of many of the logistics and supply chain elements discussed in this chapter in the retail field can be found in Fernie and Sparks (2009). An introductory chapter on retailing is Sparks (2008).

Some specialist academic retail journals include:
International Review of Retail, Distribution and Consumer Research.
International Journal of Retail and Distribution Management.
Journal of Retailing.
Journal of Retailing and Consumer Services.

Some specialist logistics and supply chain journals include:
International Journal of Logistics Management.
International Journal of Physical Distribution and Logistics Management.
Journal of Business Logistics.
Supply Chain Management.

For sport:
International Journal of Sport Management and Marketing.
International Journal of Sports Marketing and Sponsorship.
Sport Marketing Quarterly.

REFERENCES

Beech, J., & Chadwick, S. (Eds.), (2007). *The Marketing of Sport*. Harlow: FT Prentice Hall.

Berwin, L. (19th October, 2007). Kitting Out the Nation. *Retail Week*.

Chadwick, S., & Arthur, D. (Eds.), (2008). *International Cases in the Business of Sport*. Oxford: Butterworth-Heinemann.

Christopher, M., & Peck, H. (2003). *Marketing Logistics* (Second Edition). Oxford: Butterworth-Heinemann.

Desbordes, M. (Ed.), (2007). *Marketing and Football: An International Perspective*. Oxford: Butterworth-Heinemann.

Fernie, J., & Sparks, L. (Eds.), (2009). *Logistics and Retail Management* (Third Edition). London: Kogan Page.

Lonsdale, C. (2004). Player Power: Capturing Value in the English Football Supply Network. *Supply Chain Management: An International Journal, 9*(5), 383–391.

Mintel. (2007). *UK Retail Rankings 2007*. London: Mintel.

Mintel. (2006). *Sports Fashion*. London: Mintel.

Mintel. (2005). *Sports Goods Retailing in the UK*. London: Mintel.

Sparks, L. (2008). Retailing. In M. J. Baker, & S. J. Hart (Eds.), *The Marketing Book*. Oxford: Butterworth-Heinemann.

Sparks, L. (2007). Distribution Channels and Sports Logistics. In J. Beech, & S. Chadwick (Eds.), *The Marketing of Sport*. Harlow: FT Prentice Hall.

Sparks, L. (2003). Retail Logistics. In P. Freathy (Ed.), *The Retailing Book*. Harlow: FT Prentice Hall.

Weston, A. (2008). Stairway to Heaven for Liverpool FC Shoppers. *Liverpool Daily Post*. 21st May.

RECOMMENDED WEBSITES

Professional Retailing and Logistics Organisations

British Retail Consortium

http://www.brc.org.uk/

U.K.—Chartered institute of Logistics and Transport

http://www.ciltuk.org.uk

Universities with Strong Retailing (R) and Logistics (L) Interests

Cardiff (L)

http://www.leanenterprise.org.uk/

Cranfield (L)

http://www.som.cranfield.ac.uk/som/groups/iscm

Heriot-Watt (L)

http://www.sml.hw.ac.uk/logistics/

Hull (L)

http://www.hull.ac.uk/logistics

Oxford (R)

http://www.sbs.ox.ac.uk/oxirm/

Stirling—Institute for Retail Studies (R)

http://www.irs.stir.ac.uk

CHAPTER 10

Organising and Human Resource Management

Dr Linda Trenberth

Birkbeck Sport Business Centre, Birkbeck College, University of London

Objectives

Upon completion of this chapter the reader should be able to:

- Explain the concept of human resource management (HRM).
- Evaluate the evidence for the link between HRM and organisational performance.
- Discuss the role of motivating factors in the HRM performance link.
- Identify the key functional areas of HRM.
- Explain the factors of HRM that are important for sports organisations.
- Discuss the importance of developing distinctive human resource practices in sports organisations.

CONTENTS

OVERVIEW OF THE CHAPTER

Human resource management (HRM) has been written about extensively in a range of settings and contexts, including more recently in sport settings and in particular Olympic Sport Organisations (Chelladurai and Madella, 2006). It is not the intention here to replicate unnecessarily what has been done before (see Hoye et al., 2006), and there must be a case made for why the core concepts that make up HRM should be treated any differently in sport organisations than in any other organisation. As Hoye and colleagues point out, the sheer size of some organisations and the difficulties in managing unusual organisations in the sport industry make human resource management a complex issue in practice. This chapter discusses HRM as a key management and organising tool in the context of sport, with particular reference to the football industry. Rather than focusing on the key functions of HRM, such as selection, training, induction, performance, and management, as other texts have done (see Wendell Braithwaite in Beech and Chadwick, 2002; Whitrod Brown and Green, 2001; Wolsey and Whitrod Brown, 2003), this chapter concentrates on the link between HRM and organisational performance (Becker and Huselid, 1998) and its relevance for sport. Ultimately, if managers and boards of directors are not convinced that HRM will enhance outcomes such as organisational and employee performance, they are unlikely to invest in it.

What Is Human Resource Management?

Human resource management (HRM) is the term used to represent that part of an organisation's activities that is concerned with the recruitment, development, and management of its employees (Wall and Wood, 2005). HRM seeks to provide a strategic approach to managing people, developing commitment rather than controlling, with the spotlight firmly on the individual and the positive and full utilisation of human capital in organisations (Guest, 1990). The traditional need for human resource planning and the functions offered by "personnel" departments have being overtaken by a more progressive view of the key role of people within organisations (Wolsey and Whitrod Brown, 2003). Slack (1997) suggested that strategic HRM, underpinned by an HR philosophy, is about matching HRM activities and policy to business strategy and treating the people in the organisation as strategic resources in the achievement of competitive strategy. Sport, which was previously amateur, has moved to become a professionally focused activity. In a sport organisation, the human resource function may range from the simple maintenance of employee records to designing complex personnel training and development systems, negotiating remuneration, and dealing with grievances (Slack, 1997). Essentially, HRM is about managing the human capital in organisations, including sports organisations.

THE HUMAN CAPITAL APPROACH

According to Wendell Braithwaite (2004), human capital in sports organisations can be largely classified into technicians (i.e., amateurs, self-employed professionals, employed professionals); technical specialists (including operatives and support staff); managers (who may be paid administrators or volunteers); and board members. Chelladurai and Madella's (2006) book on human resource management in Olympic sports organisations also identifies athletes and volunteers as critical human resources.

Wall and Wood (2005, page 430) identified a "human capital enhancing" approach to HRM as including such practices as sophisticated selection procedures, appraisal, training, teamwork, communication, empowerment, performance-related pay, and employment security, but how sophisticated are HR practices in sport organisations and how dominant is this human capital enhancing approach in sport organisations? Taylor and McGraw's (2006) research on the adoption of HR practices by state sports organisations in New South Wales in Australia shows that despite pressures to become more strategic in their people management, only a minority of sports organisations have formal HR systems, and that holds true for the United Kingdom as well. Sports organisations represent people-oriented operations (Sawyer and Smith, 1999), where "human resources" should be the single most important managerial consideration (Chelladurai, 1999).

It has been shown that a commitment to HRM can give an organisation a competitive advantage that, in an increasingly consumer-led economy, could be a critical success factor in a highly competitive and volatile industry (Wolsey and Abrams, 2001). Despite the reported evidence for the positive link between HRM and performance, promises with regards to reduced absenteeism, and increased turnover through "high-performance" HRM practices, there is plenty of evidence to show that sport organisations, for the most part, are simply not investing sufficiently in their most costly resource: people.

THE EVIDENCE FOR THE HRM AND PERFORMANCE LINK

In considering the HRM and performance link as a reason for sport organisations to take HRM more seriously, it is important to look at the evidence for such a link. Briner (2007, page 1) states, "From fortune tellers to football managers … all practitioners tend to believe quite strongly that what they do is based on evidence." According to Briner, evidence-based practice is about integrating individual practitioner expertise with the best available external evidence from systematic research in making decisions about how to deal with problems and issues (2007, page 2). Briner feels that if HRM is serious about improving the effectiveness of organisations, then organisations need to find the evidence that HRM works and operates in new ways to make that happen. This fits with Cappelli and Crocker-Hefter's (1996) suggestion that rather than follow the crowd in human resource practices without the evidence that what works for one organisation also works for another, organisations should think about how being different can help them create distinctive human resource practices that will enable them to improve performance and create a competitive edge.

Early attempts to link HRM with organisational performance were based on the idea that improving the way people were managed would lead to enhanced organisational performance without any real justification in theoretical terms (Ulrich, 1997). Enough theoretical research has been carried out now to show that investment in HR practices does indeed result in business outcomes such as improved financial results and improved market value, as well as reduced absenteeism and lower turnover at the individual level. A range of theories have been proposed to explain the link between HRM and outcomes at the level of the organization, but few have attempted to explain the intermediary link between HRM and individual outcomes such as productivity, quality, and innovation. Guest (1997) developed a theoretical model based on theories of motivation, such as expectancy theory, which proposed that high performance at the individual level depends on high motivation plus possession of the necessary skills and abilities and an appropriate understanding of the role. This sets the basis from which to specify the HRM practices that encourage high skills, abilities, and motivation to direct behaviour toward organisational goals.

In essence, the heart of the model is the mediating role of positive employee attitudes and the idea that HRM practices should be designed to result in the HRM outcomes of high employee commitment, quality, and flexibility. Commitment is to both the job and the organisation; quality is the knowledge, skills, and capability of staff; and flexibility is the functional flexibility, rather than the numerical flexibility, of employees. Positive employee attitudes are said to mediate the relationship between HRM and performance; thus, HRM practices should be designed so organisations can motivate employees and improve performance through lower turnover and greater productivity (Truss, 2001). For example, using performance appraisals to assess performance and linking those with incentive pay might achieve these outcomes. However, a focus on the HRM and performance link and the theories underpinning it gives managers a basis from which to develop HRM practices. It is important to base practice on evidence and to take into account the individual context of the sports organisation and its own unique characteristics.

THE STATE OF PLAY IN HRM AND SPORT

HRM has been recognised and adopted to varying degrees of success by organisations in the wider leisure industry. In 1998, it was reported that the leisure industry faced shortages of skilled, motivated staff, who were discouraged by low salaries, poor working conditions, and a perceived lack of career opportunities. Salmon's 2007 paper put forward the case for fairer rewards to improve the industry's image. However, there have been clear attempts to address the changing business climate by incorporating a business-focussed HR approach into the wider leisure sector, including sports organisations, especially at the National Governing Body (NGB) level. For example, in 2006, British Tennis appointed a Head of Human Resources Lawn Tennis Association, 2009 (The NGB for tennis in Britain). The post holder had previously held the same position at Sport England, the government agency charged with developing community sport. The purpose of this key role is to develop and implement the LTA's HR and Learning and Development strategies. Practically this means driving organisational change, managing quality recruitment processes and maximising employee engagement, all indicating a commitment to ensuring HR good practice is a trend set to continue in supporting British Tennis.

One way to tell how seriously an organisation views the HR function is whether it has a director of HR on the board of directors. For example, the English Football Association (FA) has a head of human resources, but in 2008 that role was under the directorship of the director of finance, although under previous management (see Case Study 10.1), the HR director was a member of the executive board. However, despite not having a director of HR on the FA executive board, the head of human resources at the FA commands a six-figure salary package and is required to provide innovative and pragmatic people strategies and solutions with a strategic focus. This example demonstrates that sport organisations at the NGB level are beginning to view the HR function more seriously, although there is clearly more work to be done at the club level (FGRC, 2003 & 2005). As Slack (1997) observed, sport organisations are in a constant state of change. As new people enter the organisation, the structure of the organisation can be rearranged and new programmes developed. In order to thrive and survive, human resources in sports organisations must be managed in association with market paradigms, as it is the human resources who are able to put material resources to use and convert them to products (Chelladurai, 1999).

FOOTBALL AND HRM

A survey conducted among Premier League and Football League clubs as part of a study into corporate governance shows that sport organisations, and football clubs in particular, have a long way to go with regards to the level of HR practices in place at their organisations. As for the training provided and required for directors of clubs in the Premier League and Football League, only 4 percent claimed to provide training when directors were appointed to boards. With regards to induction procedures for new board members, only 4 percent of clubs provided any sort of induction, while in 2005, 29 percent of clubs in the Premier and Football Leagues claimed to have a process in place to evaluate the effectiveness of individual board members, down from 40 percent in 2003 (FGRC, 2005, pages 31–32), and only 15 percent claimed to have appraisal procedures in place for directors (FGRC, 2005, page 32). Twenty-two percent of the clubs surveyed reported they had a remuneration committee, but only 6 percent reported that they published the terms of reference. This research shows there is a lack of investment in what have been termed "high-performance" work practices (Pfeffer, 1994) in football clubs in England. There is a need to embrace HRM practices more fully if, as the research shows, an investment in high-performance work practices enhances organisational and employee performance (Purcell et al., 2003).

Unlike other areas of commerce and industry, few football team managers complete application forms or prepare written career resumes, preferring instead to network with others in the game (Perry, 2000). There are few written job descriptions for the football manager with clear accountabilities, and as Perry suggests, localised and mostly ill-defined expectations and conditions, coupled with the manager's own personality, most often dictate the precise tasks the manager performs. One might venture to suggest that a more rigorous selection policy, induction programme, and better preparation for football managers at all levels might result in fewer turnovers of football managers and more success on the pitch. As Perry (2000) observed, between one in two and one in three clubs can expect to start each new season with a different manager. A critical aspect of the football manager's role is that of maintaining key stakeholder relationships, but without formal training of some sort, it is unlikely that football managers will succeed in maintaining their effectiveness in winning and building confidence.

As Davakos (2006) stated, training should be an integral part of the strategic planning for sport organisations, and that doesn't just mean for participants. Training employees in today's turbulent economic times allows organisations to deliver better-quality products with fewer resources and personnel and has been recognised as having added value to both organisations and employees. One could argue that the disastrous start experienced by Tottenham Hotspur, who were in the relegation zone halfway through the 2008–2009 Premier League season, was down to a lack of appropriate recruitment and selection practices, HR planning, training, and induction. Manager Juande Ramos had been successful with other teams (notably at Seville in Spain's La Liga), but there seemed to be a significant lack of person–environment fit in the appointment of Ramos, as notably demonstrated by the fact that his proficiency in working English was extremely weak. His contract eventually terminated in October 2008 and he was replaced by the experienced English manager Harry Redknapp.

SPORT AND "MANAGEMENT"

As Uriely and Mehrez (2006, page 273) so astutely observed in relation to football in Israel, the problem with applying HRM and business management concepts to sport, particularly professional football, is the ambiguity that exists between the idea of professional management and the notion of football as a business. Head coaches or managers tend to claim authority over "professional decisions such as the acquisition or release of players and in contrast, club owners tend to promote a business oriented approach toward football management, one in which money is emphasised." The lack of clear guidelines regarding such aspects of managerial authority usually results in conflicts with club owners, head coaches, players, and fans. This is best exemplified by the aforementioned case of Tottenham Hotspur (Hytner, 2007), who were languishing at the bottom of the Premier League table midway through the 2008–2009 English football season before the contract of the coach was unceremoniously terminated. Notably there appeared to be a confusion of roles between that of the manager, Juande Ramos, and the director of football, Damien Comolli, the latter supposedly having final authority on all player transfer spending. The case reveals a clear lack of guidelines with respect to managerial authority in football clubs and shows a lack of investment in HRM practices such as selection and training. In professional football, one cannot underestimate the power of the club owners who put up money for the football clubs but one could question the effectiveness of some of the most widely cited high-performance HR practices, such as performance or competency tests, preference for internal candidates, induction programmes, performance appraisals, and performance-related pay before appointing their football "managers."

In an article in the *Daily Telegraph*, Bolchover (2006) claimed, "Where sport is, business will follow." This claim suggests that in sport, including football, there has been a realisation that the team manager is the key to team success. Bolchover stated that unlike previously, when former players were appointed as managers simply because of their history, the sport industry has finally "accepted the power of management," as they now appoint managers who have not been professional players and who have a "rare managerial ability." He cited the fact that the champions of English football in 2004/2005 and 2005/2006 (Chelsea) had a Portuguese coach in 2008 (Jose Mourinho) who had never played professional football. However, despite the Chelsea example, even in football's current environment, the appointment of the manager is still overwhelmingly just as hit and miss as appointing an ex-player in the past. Without appropriate HRM planning, such selections are doomed to fail in the long term, which is why we see managers come and go throughout the football season. It is possible that business can learn from sport, and evidence exists that it has done so. However, given that sport itself is often cited as a model for business, it is amazing how few sports organisations have strategically adopted significant HRM systems. Bolchover's article is essentially about leadership and coaching rather than management, and even with great leaders, what works for one situation or one team does not necessarily work for others, as the Tottenham case demonstrates.

SPORT AS A BUSINESS MODEL

Back in 1984, Keidel looked at baseball, American football, and basketball as models for business and observed that sports are strategic in the area of human resources, which provides a great opportunity for managers to learn from sport. In each of the three sports he looked at, the management of human resources was a central part of an overarching strategy—especially because strategic decisions take place within a sport, league, season, and game framework, and because sports are unequivocally "people-intensive." The net effect is that sport provides a direct window on strategic human resources management. Keidel (1984) suggested that the parallels between team sports and business were striking because of the need to compete externally, the need to cooperate internally, and the need to manage human resources strategically. Allen (cited in Keidel, 1984, page 9) stated, "A football team is a lot like a machine. It is made up of parts. If one doesn't work, one player pulling against you and not doing his job, the whole machine fails."

Gordon (1995) and others have suggested that managers and leaders in organisations would be well served by adopting many of the principles thought to be intrinsic to sport coaching. Carling and Heller (1995) also suggested that the development of elite sport teams is a good model for the leadership of businesses. But while other organisations have learned from sports and adopted the characteristics of sports as an exemplar for running their businesses, sports organisations themselves fail to transfer the qualities that make teams and individuals successful on the field to their business operations and HRM. In discussing the sport industry, Wallace (2003, page 51) noted the following:

> There are very few well-trained or commercial skill sets in the (sport) industry. As training is often seen as an expense in this cost-conscious market, it has been given mere lip service. There is a greater need for training courses to not only focus on classic management skills, but also on specific functions of the industry such as sponsorship, rights negotiation and CRM.... But over the next five years, I believe the industry will benefit from a new peer group of key decision makers who see training as an integral part of a company's continued growth and competitive advantage.

HRM AND THE COMMUNITY

There is pressure for HRM change in community sports organisations that are driven by government policy and funding stipulations (Cuskelly et al. 2006). Government agencies support the management of volunteers in community sports organisations in the United Kingdom through such mechanisms as Sport England's *QUEST UK Quality Scheme for Sport and Leisure*, which, like other programmes in Australia and New Zealand, recommends an HRM system of planning, recruitment, selection, induction, training, and recognition practices in the management of volunteers. The link between improved HRM practices and performance for volunteers is hardly acknowledged, and more research is needed in sports organisations of different types to explore the link that has been shown to exist between HRM and organisational performance in corporate organisations.

Cuskelly and colleagues (2006) showed that extensive use of HRM practice in the management of volunteers was associated with fewer perceived problems in retaining volunteers. Chelladurai and Madella (2006) suggested that HRM practices need to be assessed within particular sport organisational contexts, as the unique characteristics of community sport organisations such as their resource base, culture, history and existing use of HR practices influence HRM practices. Notwithstanding, research conducted in any sport organisational context, be it Olympic sport organisations, community sport organisations, or commercial football organisations, will provide relevant HRM principles that can be applied in any sport organisation.

Sport organisations represent people-oriented operations (Sawyer and Smith, 1999); therefore, "human resources" should be the single most important managerial consideration (Chelladurai 1999). Service delivery, staff recruitment, retention, motivation, and absenteeism have all been identified as problems within the sports industry. There has been enormous commercial expansion in the health and fitness sector, in which the Sport Fitness Recreation Training Organisation (SFRITO) described employees as seeing employers more concerned about profits and business-driven objectives than in employee development and the industry generally (Wolsey and Whitrod Brown, 2004). Research by Dundjerovic and Robinson (2001, page 22) showed that the health and fitness industry continues to exploit the passion people have for working in the industry in terms of pay and working conditions. However, there is always the threat that other creative industries will lure such people away from sport.

In 2003, the *Sunday Times* conducted research by examining 47,000 employees across a range of occupational sectors, evaluating policies, processes, and services that influence work environments to identify what makes excellent companies. Their results indicated the following:

> *The 100 best companies to work for provide a tremendous example but also a great challenge to the rest of the U.K. industry. They are the living proof that highly motivated and happy workforces go hand-in-glove with delighted customers and superior business performance.*

It was the most comprehensive study of its kind undertaken in the United Kindom and indicated that putting staff before profits is a sound business strategy. The *Sunday Times* research suggested adopting a model of HRM that pervades the internal and external environments to create an empathetic and productive organisational culture founded on high levels of employee satisfaction. This places the employee at the heart of the consumer-driven markets of the twenty-first century. However, although this concurs with other longitudinal research, there is a need to adopt a more critical view when attempting to apply such good intentions to sport organisations, as the preceding evidence-based approach demonstrates.

HRM AND CORE COMPETENCIES

Some researchers and writers promote the universalist model of HRM or "best practices" model, which suggests there is a single set of best practices that are readily identifiable and transferable across organisations (Guest, 1997). However, Cappelli and Crocker-Hefter (1996) make the case for unique, differentiating resources—the notion of core competencies. They cite professional sports that are obviously big businesses in their own right as a case in point. The link between people management practices and the way organisations compete is most direct in professional sports, as employees themselves create what the organisation sells—where the "product" is a service provided directly by employees interacting with customers. Their research showed that sports clubs create reputations that contribute to the self-selection of players and fans. To some extent, sport clubs compete for fans the same way that firms compete for customers, and having distinctive styles of play may help build a national/international audience (Cappelli and Crocker-Hefter, 1996). This is clearly the case with professional football teams who develop distinct playing styles and particular management styles that suit some players better than others and appeal to different audiences.

According to Cappelli and Crocker-Hefter (1996), a distinctive and unusual style of play may be useful on the field as well in that it demands unusual responses from the other side that may be difficult to cope with. The point that the authors are advocating is that people management practices are the drivers of efforts to create distinctive competencies and in turn business strategies. As Chelladurai and Madella (2006) state, the human resource is the most critical resource for sport organisations, as it is people who convert other factors into "real" resources. Yet, the recognition of and the importance attached to human resources are much lower than one would expect in sport organisations overall.

CASE STUDY 10.1: Managing Change in the Face of External Pressures

Gordon Gibb, the youngest serving chairman in the football league with Bradford City FC and owner of the Flamingo Land theme park, represented the changing face of football in the United Kingdom in the early twenty-first century. Commenting on the collapse of TV revenues through the demise of ITV Digital in 2002 (Reeder, 2003), he said the following:

> As an industry, those old ways of doing things are just what got us into this mess to begin with.... There is no room for a soft business approach. We need to be positive and dynamic.

According to Wolsey and Whitrod Brown (2004), Adam Crozier adopted this approach when he assumed the position of FA chief executive in January 2000, leaving his former position as head of Saatchi & Saatchi advertising agency. The following are Crozier's key activities between January 2000 and November 2002:

- Moved the FA's headquarters from the historic site of Lancaster Gate to Soho Square in London (Campbell and Morgan, 2002).

- Injected unparalleled commercial awareness into the FA (Campbell and Morgan, 2002).

- Renegotiated a partnership with the BBC to reestablish the role and importance of the FA Cup (Campbell, 2002).

- Increased the speed of decision making by replacing the previously incumbent 91-member board with a 12-member executive board. (Campbell, 2002).

- Presided over a changing age profile in the FA. When he started, the average age was 55; it reduced to 32 (Stevenson, 2002).

- Recruited 70 percent of FA employees from outside the football sector (Wallace, 2003).

- Appointed the director of HR to the executive board and instigated a wide-ranging training and development programme (Wallace, 2003).

Despite these achievements, Crozier resigned in November 2002 amidst claims of an autocratic leadership style, spiralling costs and mistrust from some football club chairmen. However, Crozier had transformed the FA from an old-style organisation with antiquated systems into a modern one.

Three years after the departure of Crozier, the FA appointed Lord Terry Burns to conduct an operational review of the organisation and report on the governance structures and decision-making processes amidst claims that the FA was failing in its role as regulator of the national game. The recommendations in the final report were approved by the FA Council in 2007, and the FA has undergone further restructuring. One of the main developments was the appointment of an independent chair that sits on the FA

main board. However, key issues at the board level remain, including the following:

- The size of the board: The *Higgs Review* (2003) illustrated that the average board size at stock market–listed companies was 7, whereas there are 12 members on the FA board. Is the board too large?

- There are five representatives from the professional game and five from the national game. Is there the potential for a conflict of interest?

- The Premier League has three representatives to the Football League's two. Should the Football League have equal representation?

- The board of the Italian FA contains representatives from players, managers, youth development, technical development, and the professional and amateur leagues. Should the FA board have representation from other stakeholders and less from the professional and national game?

- The head of HR is no longer on the executive board.

The case shows that sport organizations can evolve successfully, albeit but that they have significant organising and HRM challenges ahead.

Source: This case has been adapted from the case reported by Wolsey and Whitrod Brown (2004) and updated to show developments in the FA since 2004.

CONCLUSIONS

Organisational context has been identified as a critical aspect in determining effective HRM practices, and there have been consistent calls for researchers to locate HRM practices in the broader context of organisations like sports organisations. However, little research has taken place in sporting contexts, both in nonprofit and commercial sports organisations. Chelladurai and Madella (2006) show how the special needs and unique characteristics of athletes and volunteers can influence HRM practices. Cappelli and Crocker-Hefter (1996) show that professional sports are big businesses in their own rights and that employee performance matters. By developing distinctive human resource management practices, they can create unique competencies that differentiate products and services that consequently drive competitiveness.

It is widely recognised today that effective human resource management has a significant contribution to make to the success of businesses, including sport businesses, and that an organisation's people are its most important resource. Organisations must ensure that their HRM practices are evidence-based so as to create unique differentiating resources rather than simply adopting (when they do at all) "best practices" or "benchmarking" in the hopes of emulating another organisation's success. Ulrich and Brockbank (2005) exhort HR professionals to be clear about the results they produce for the business and to maintain a clear "line of sight" to the customer. The five functional areas of employee development (training, training needs analysis, evaluation, CPD); employee welfare (health and safety, support services, status considerations); employee relations (grievance/disciplinary procedures, management/union relationships, internal communications, conflict management); reward management (pay, employee benefits, career development); and staffing (recruitment, selection, job analysis, skills audit, HR planning and induction) provide a useful starting point for sport organisations from which better practice can emerge (Wolsey and Abrams, 2001).

DISCUSSION QUESTIONS

1. Why is human resource management important for the effective management of sport organisations?
2. What are the unique characteristics of applying HRM to sport?
3. Should the same human resource management practices be applied to both volunteer and paid staff? Why or why not?
4. Should professional football team managers be subjected to the same recruitment and selection practices as other managers appointed to business organisations? Why or why not?
5. Should the human resource management role within sports organisations be combined with another functional role such as finance? Why or why not?
6. How can sports organisations ensure that what they do is based on evidence?
7. What areas can be suggested for further development in both HRM theory and practice as applied to the sport sector?
8. Why are motivating factors important in the HRM and performance link?

GUIDED READING

The following two article provide an excellent overview of the role of human resource management in sport organisations.

Chelladurai, P., & Madella, A. (2006). *Human Resource Management in Olympic Sport Organizations*. Champaign: Human Kinetics.

Wolsey, C., & Whitrod Brown, H. (2004). Human resource management and the business of Sport. In L. Trenberth (Ed.), *Managing the Business of Sport*. Australia: Thomson Learning.

REFERENCES

Beech, J., & Chadwick, S. (2004). *The Business of Sport Management*. Harlow: Pearson Education.

Becker, B., & Huselid, M. (1998). High performance work systems and firm performance: A synthesis of research and managerial implications. *Research in Personnel and Human Resources Management, 16*, 53–101.

Bolchover, D. (16th January, 2006). Where sport is business will follow. *The Daily Telegraph*. Retrieved on October 28, 2008, from *http://www.telegraph. co.uk/finance/2930190/The-truth-about-work-Where-sport-is-business-will-follow.html*

Briner, R. (2007). *Is HRM evidence-based and does it matter?* Institute for Employment Studies, University of Sussex. Retrieved on June 12, 2009, from *http://www.employment-studies.co.uk/pubs/report.php?id=op6*

Campbell, D. (1st December, 2002). The blue tide. *The Observer Sports Section*. Pages 8–9.

Campbell, D., & Morgan, O. (1st December, 2002). The new goal for former FA Chief. *The Observer*.

Cappelli, P., & Crocker-Hefter, A. (1996). Distinctive human resources are firms core competencies. *Organizational Dynamics, 24*(30), 7–22.

Carling, W., & Heller, R. (1995). *The Way to Win*. London: Little Brown.

Chelladurai, P. (1999). *Human Resource Management in Sport and Recreation*. Champaign, Il: Human Kinetics.

Chelladurai, P., & Madella, A. (2006). *Human Resources Management in Olympic Sport Organizations*. Champaign, IL: Human Kinetics.

Cuskelly, G., Taylor, T., Hoye, R., & Darcy, S. (2006). Volunteer management practices and volunteer retention: A human resource management approach. *Sport Management Review, 9*, 141–163.

Davakos, H. (2006). An integral part of the strategic planning for sport organizations: training employees. *International Journal of Sport Management and Marketing, 1*(4), 390–399.

Dundjerovic, E., & Robinson, L. (2001). Jobs Worth. *Health Club Management*. November p. 22.

FGRC. (2003 & 2005). *State of the Game: The Corporate Governance of Football Clubs*. Birkbeck, University of London: Football Governance Research Centre.

Gordon, C. (1995). Management skills for the new millennia. *Management*. March, pp. 5–7.

Guest, D. (1990). Human resource management and the American Dream. *Journal of Management Studies, 27*(4).

Guest, D. (1997). Human resource management and performance: a review and research agenda. *International Journal of Human Resource Management, 8*(3), 263–276.

Higgs Review (2003). *Review of the Role and Effectiveness of Non-Executive Directors*. London: Department of Trade & Industry.

Hoye, R., Smith, A., Westerbeek, H., Stewart, B., & Nicholson, M. (2006). *Sport Management Principles and Applications*. London: Elsevier.

Hytner, D. (27th October, 2007). Comolli picks Ramos and puts his neck on the line. *The Guardian*. Retrieved on June 12, 2009, from *http://www.guardian. co.uk/football/2007/oct/27/sport.comment4*

Keidel, R. (1984). Baseball, football, and basketball: Models for business. *Organizational Dynamics*. Winter, 5–18.

Lawn Tennis Association (LTA) (2009). Personal Correspondence.

Perry, B. (2000). *Football management as a metaphor for corporate entrepreneurship?* Working Paper Series, WP002/00, Wolverhampton Business School Management Research Centre. University of Wolverhampton.

Pfeffer, J. (1994). Competitive advantage through people. *California Management Review 34*(2), 9–28.

Purcell, J., Kinnie, N., Hutchinson, S., Rayton, B., & Swart, J. (2003). *Understanding thePeople and Performance Link: Unlocking the Black Box*. London: Chartered Institute of Personnel Development.

Reeder, M. (11th January, 2003). Gibb tacking dynasty of dinosaurs. *Yorkshire Post*.

Salmon, J. (2007). Pay, pressures and priorities in the leisure industry. *Review 311*, January, pp. 21–23. Retrieved on June 12, 2009, from *http://www. btinternet.com/~janet.salmon/downloads/Speakerscorner.pdf*

Sawyer, T., & Smith, O. (1999). *The Management of Clubs, Recreation and Sport*. Sagamore.

Slack, T. (1997). *Understanding Sport Organizations*. Champaign, Il: Human Kinetics.

Stevenson, J. (31st October, 2002). Profile: Adam Crozier. *BBC Sport*. Retrieved on June 12, 2009, from *http://news.bbc.co.uk/sport1/hi/football/2376331.stm*

Sunday Times (2nd March, 2003). The 100 Best Companies To Work For. *Sunday Times Supplement*.

Taylor, T., & McGraw, P. (2006). Exploring human resource management practices in nonprofit sport organizations. *Sport Management Review, 9,* 229–251.

Trenberth, L. (2003). *Managing the Business of Sport.* Australia: Thomson Learning.

Truss, C. (ed.), (2001). Complexities and controversies in linking HRM with organizational outcomes. *Journal of Management Studies, 38*(8), 1121–1149.

Ulrich, D. (1997). Measuring human resources: an overview of practice and a prescription for results. *Human Resource Management, 36*(3), 303–320.

Ulrich, D., & Brockbank, W. (2005). *The HR Value Proposition.* Harvard Business School Press.

Uriely, N., & Mehrez, A. (2006). Soccer culture in Israel: a state of anomie. *International Journal of Sport Management and Marketing, 1*(3), 268–278.

Wall, T., & Wood, S. (2005). The romance of human resource management and business Performance and the case for big science. *Human Relations, 58*(4), 429–462.

Wallace, T. (2003). Bringing in the Outsiders. *Sportsbusiness International,* 50–51, March.

Wendell Brathwaite, T. (2004). Human resource management in sport. In J. Beech, & S. Chadwick (Eds.), *The Business of Sport Management* (pp. 93–127). London: FT Prentice Hall.

Whitrod Brown, H., & Green, A. (2001). Human resource management in the leisure Industry. In C. Wolsey, & J. Abrams (Eds.), *Understanding the Leisure and Sport Industry.* Essex: Pearson Education.

Wolsey, C., & Abrams, J. (2001). *Understanding Leisure Organizations.* Longman.

Wolsey, C., & Whitrod Brown, H. (2003). Human resource management and the business of Sport. In L. Trenberth (Ed.), *Managing the Business of Sport.* Australia: Thomson Learning.

RECOMMENDED WEBSITES

Evidence-Based Management website

www.evidence-basedmanagement.com

Sport England

http://www.sportengland.org/index/get_resopurces/resource_downloads/funding_information.htm

Sport and Recreation New Zealand

http://www.sparc.org.nz/research-and-policy.com

CHAPTER 11

Leagues and Competitions

Saurabh Patel
Cass Business School

Stefan Szymanski
Cass Business School

Objectives

Upon completion of this chapter the reader should be able to:

- Understand the relationship between governance, law, and the organisation of football.
- Differentiate between the different league structures in European Football.
- Appreciate the influence that different structures are likely to have on club behaviour and league performance.

OVERVIEW OF THE CHAPTER

This chapter explains briefly the governance structures of professional football in Europe. The organisation of football is broadly similar across all countries, consisting of clubs, leagues, and national and international governing bodies. But in each country the structure of ownership and control has developed in ways that reflect both culture and legal institutions. Most notably, the role of the state in football varies widely, with, at one extreme, the English system where the state plays almost no role, to the other extreme of France, where the state officially licences all professional sports. This chapter analyses five of the main European football leagues—France, Germany, England, Italy, and Spain—looking at who owns and controls the league and how the league is governed. Key issues involve the rights of clubs to run their own financial affairs and especially the rules on financial distress, the rights of ownership in clubs, who determines the policies of the league, and the relationship between the league and national federation.

INTRODUCTION

Whenever there is a crisis in football—and there seems always to be a least one crisis in progress—the public and media call for action. Yet, most critics take little account of the governance system. By *governance system* we mean the rules and regulations of the national associations, the leagues, and the clubs, and the rights and obligations laid down at each level of the game. For example, in October 2008, when the global banking crisis led to corporate bankruptcies and bailouts, the English Football Association (FA) chairman, Lord Triesman, warned that the borrowing of English Premier League clubs might have exposed themselves to similar risks. Many outside observers wondered why Triesman did not step in to regulate debt burdens of FA Premier League (FAPL) clubs, but the fact was, he had no power to do so within the governance structure of football in England. This chapter describes the governance structures of England, France, Germany, Italy, and Spain.

Before considering these, it is worthwhile to briefly describe the relationships between governance in each of these countries and the international federations UEFA and FIFA. FIFA, (2008), was founded in 1904 as an assembly of national football associations, and is football's world governing body. Each member has a single vote in the FIFA Congress, which, among other things, elects the FIFA president who runs the day-to-day business of FIFA. FIFA administers competitions such as the World Cup and promotes the development of football and relationships between regions and national associations. Article 6 of the statutes recognises the International Football Association Board (IFAB) as the body that decides the rules of the game and specifies that its membership consists of four members nominated by FIFA and four members nominated by the four British associations (England, Scotland, Wales, and Northern Ireland). This effectively gives the British a veto over changes in the rules of the game—a state of affairs that does not always please other national associations. However, Article 26 specifies that a change to the FIFA statutes requires support of over 75 percent of FIFA members, and therefore change is unlikely.

UEFA was created in 1954 as an association of European national football associations, and it currently has 53 members (UEFA, 2007). Its stated mission is *"To create the right conditions for the game in Europe to prosper and develop,"* and it aims to achieve this in four ways:

- Promoting football competitions at all levels in Europe.
- Creating closer links with national governing bodies.
- "Optimising" TV revenues.
- Improving its internal governance.

Like FIFA, it has a Congress that elects a president who runs the day-to-day activities. In principle, UEFA is a subordinate body to FIFA, but they are frequently seen as competitors for the support of the important European associations, from whom most of the money in international football is ultimately generated.

THE "BIG 5" EUROPEAN LEAGUES AND COMPETITIONS

Let us now review the organisation of football in England, France, Germany, Italy and Spain.

England

Football in the United Kingdom is unique for many reasons. The first national association was founded in England in 1863, and England is commonly acknowledged to be the founder of "Association football," the proper name of the game (and from which the word *soccer* is thought to derive as an abbreviation). The first "international" game of football was played in 1872 between teams representing the English and Scottish Associations, and by the time the first international game was played between nations outside of the British Isles (the United States versus Canada in 1885), 41 internationals involving England, Scotland, Ireland, and Wales had already taken place. To this day, only the United Kingdom is permitted by world football to maintain more than one national association (indeed, four), a privilege jealously guarded and widely envied.

While the English FA founded the FA Cup in 1872, a group of clubs established the Football League in 1888, acknowledging the jurisdiction of the FA but claiming autonomy in administration. The Football League (Football-league. co.uk) grew rapidly from one division of 12 in 1888 to four divisions of 88 teams in 1923, connected by the institution of promotion and relegation. For over a century, the FA and the League battled over the governance of *professional* football, until in 1991, when the FA sanctioned the Premier League (FAPL) breakaway of the top division. While the FA may have hoped to have more control over the new elite league, the rivalry has remained; meanwhile, the Football League survives as an organisation of three divisions below the FAPL.

Organisationally speaking, the FAPL (*Premierleague.com*) is an independent body affiliated to the FA and that is run as a corporation. It has 20 shareholders, which are the clubs participating in any given season in the FAPL. The FAPL operates a system of relegation and promotion with the Football League, and when a team is relegated from the FAPL, the club gives up its membership and vote to the promoted club. Each club has one vote, and the clubs elect an FAPL chairman, chief executive, and board of directors to oversee the daily operations of the league.

The Football Association has no day-to-day control over the FAPL, but it is a "special shareholder" with certain limited rights, including veto over the appointment of the FAPL chairman and maintaining the system of promotion and relegation. More generally, as governing body of the game in England, the FA sets the framework within which the game is played at all levels, including the FAPL.

The FA (*FA.com*) is a limited company with 2,000 shares, with each share held by a football club or a member association. The membership organisation dates back to the nineteenth century and includes county associations that were once powerful but are now relegated to a much-reduced role; as a result, the professional clubs have often perceived the FA to be out of touch with the needs of the modern game. At the same time, the FA seeks to balance the interest of the amateur and professional games, whose needs are often quite different. While the government has no direct say in the governance of the FA, it exerted considerable pressure over the last decade to restructure the organisation. The highest decision-making unit of the FA is its Board, with a balance of representatives of the amateur and professional game as required by the rules of the Association. The Council, a much larger body, now has a significantly reduced role, while the main business of the FA is carried out by the executive arm under the chief executive and numerous specialist committees.

The roles and responsibilities of the FA are as follows:

- Promoting the development of football in England at all levels.
- Running the national team and the FA Cup, and other competitions.
- Maintaining international football relations.
- Legislating over the rules of the game and the rules that member associations must comply with.
- Organising compliance (e.g., through refereeing).
- Operating disciplinary measures to ensure member clubs comply with the rules of the game.

While the U.K. government does not directly control the FA or professional football, it does influence in a number of ways. First, through the Minister for Sport at the Department for Culture, Media and Sport (DCMS), the government seeks to formulate and implement a policy that serves its objectives in relation to sport (e.g., addressing hooliganism, promoting participation for health reasons, bidding to host the World Cup). Second, the football authorities have to comply with national laws, and as part of the European Union, with EU law. Thus, rules on the transfer of players were significantly altered by the Bosman judgment of the European Court of Justice in 1995.

It should now be apparent that several bodies might reasonably claim the right to control football, and therefore there is much contested territory. Thus, the entry of highly paid foreign players into England is complex and governed by FAPL and FA rules on transfers, which in turn must be compliant with FIFA and UEFA statutes but are also governed by U.K. rules on immigration and subject to the free movement of labour within the EU guaranteed by the Treaty of Rome.

The United Kingdom has also been unusual in permitting an influx of foreign owners into the highest level of the game, with nationals of Egypt, Russia, the UAE, and the United States freely purchasing ownership of FAPL clubs. When Thaksin Shinawatra, deposed prime minister of Thailand and accused of large-scale corruption by the military government that ousted him, bought Manchester City Football Club in 2007, his takeover was approved by the Premier League (*Premierleague.com*, 2007). In 2004, the FA, the FAPL, and the Football League introduced a "fit and proper persons" test for club directors, a more stringent test of competence than the one already required of company directors under English company law, although they make no restriction on foreign investment (Rowe, 2004). However, critics have argued that these regulations lack teeth.

France

While football in England is organised almost entirely independently of the state, football in France is a creature of the state. Even though football was played from the 1870s onward in France, the French Football Association (*Fédération Française de Football*, FFF) was not created until 1919, and a league employing professional players did not start until 1932, eventually evolving into what is now called the *Ligue de Football Professionel* (LFP), organised into two divisions of 20 clubs each. Under French law, all organised sport is the responsibility of the state, which delegates organisations such as the FFF to run sport on their behalf. These activities are governed by statute, and in the case of football, the key law is Loi n 84-610 du 16 juillet 1984, which was amended by subsequent decrees (e.g., Décret no 2002-762 du 2 mai 2002 and Décret no 2007-883 du 14 mai 2007).

As might be expected of a system administered by the state, French football places great emphasis on directing resources to be spread broadly across the country, while limiting the potential of individual clubs to exploit commercial opportunities. This has produced the paradoxical situation that France has produced some of the best football coaches and best players in world football over recent decades and has enjoyed great success at the national level, while domestic clubs have struggled to be competitive. French clubs have limited opportunities to generate income to pay for players. Until recently, clubs could not pay directors or pay dividends, making it difficult to attract commercial managers and wealthy investors. These restrictions have been diminished in recent years, particularly for clubs adopting the legal form of a *société anonyme sportive professionnelle*, and as of 2006, clubs may even float themselves on the stock exchange. However, a recent government report (*Accroître la compétitivité des clubs de football professionnel français*-Besson, 2008) still highlighted the limitations that the regulations place on the commercial freedom of clubs.

A second form of constraint is imposed by *La Direction Nationale du Contrôle de Gestion* (DNCG). The DNCG was created by the French government in 1990 to act as a financial regulator of football clubs and to fight against the increase in corruption cases in the French leagues during the 1980s. The DNCG is run jointly by the FFF and LFP and has far-reaching powers over football clubs' finances. Each club must submit its accounts and budgetary plans annually, and the DNCG has the right to disallow expenditures, including whether clubs can buy players. Failure to comply with DNCG rulings can lead to severe penalties, including relegation.

When interviewed by Michel Desbordes (2006, page 159), DNCG president Francois Ponthieu laid out the obligations clubs have to the DNCG:

Football clubs have to satisfy the specific accounting rules. For example, a club must set out an expenditure and revenue plan from games, transfers, subsidies from communities, sponsorship, and so on. They must also satisfy the usual legal obligations of private companies, particularly those concerning the control of the accounts.

One example of its impact came in 2003 when Paris St Germain had difficulties selling Brazilian star Ronaldinho, as the DCNG had placed sanctions against them buying any players due to their high debt levels (*BBC Sport*, 2003).

French football's governance by the DCNG is widely recognised as the most stringent in European football, and Ligue 1's financial stability is achieved in an environment where football clubs have relatively little control over how they spend or make money, such as the TV rights that are secured by the football league. Coupled with this financial performance is the recognition that French clubs have performed poorly on the European stage in comparison to the other leagues of Europe. Talent retention is difficult as a result, and the bright stars of French football usually move on to the English, Italian, and Spanish leagues. Nonetheless, the French typically view the DNCG as an achievement, having successfully controlled the financial activities of clubs. Thus, the French government has argued during its presidency of the European Union in the second half of 2008 that the French model should be adopted across the whole of Europe. However, somewhat embarrassingly, Ligue 1 has suffered in recent years from a distinct decline in competitive balance manifested by the fact that Olympique Lyon has won seven consecutive titles between 2001/2002 and 2007/2008.

Germany

Germany, despite its great football traditions, was one of the last to set up a national professional league. The Bundesliga was formed in 1963 out of the regional leagues which had been reestablished in 1945. While the German Football Association (DFB, founded 1900) has oversight over all football in Germany, the Bundesliga is controlled by an association of its member clubs. This is called *Die Liga—Fußballverband* (The League Association), formed by the 32 member clubs in Bundesliga 1 and 2 in 2000. The Bundesliga is operated by a subsidiary of the League Association, the *Deutsche Fußball Liga* (DFL), on behalf of the League Association. Most German clubs operate under the Verein legal structure, where members pay subscriptions and are entitled to vote on policy, and only a small number have converted to joint-stock company status (e.g., Dortmund). While this limits the financial flexibility of German clubs (because of limitations on ownership, control and the payment of dividends raising capital is difficult), the Verein system is seen as a crucial part of the German social fabric.

The DFL is the most powerful element of the Bundesliga, managing all the league's business operations independently from the DFB, and bears some similarity to the DNCG, although critics sometimes argue that it is not stringent enough. It controls much revenue through its selection of TV contracts and licensing opportunities, implements financial guidelines on clubs and decides which clubs can join and remain a member of the Bundesliga. The DFL operates independently under a Supervisory Board elected by the League Association, through which clubs can exert influence on the DFL. The DFL's responsibilities fall under the headings of Rights and Licenses, Match Operations, Finances and Licensing, and Marketing and Communication (Bundesliga, 2008).

To be a member of the Bundesliga, the clubs must be awarded a licence by the DFL, and to gain a licence, clubs need to abide by the DFL's rules of governance. Clubs must maintain a level of liquidity to get a licence and are required to submit profit and loss statements to the DFL on an annual basis. Likewise, debt levels must be within strict DFL guidelines and the "50+1" rule prevents foreign ownership, or any single-shareholder ownership over 49 percent. Indeed, in 2008 the DFL confirmed after an extensive debate that it will keep the 50+1 rule in place (*Independent*, 2008).

On the face of it, the German system has been successful, with all Bundesliga clubs reporting a profit, while the percentage of total club revenue expenditure on player salaries is only 39 percent. Moreover, in the Forbes Football Club Rich List 2008 (*Forbes.com*, 2008), 25 percent of the clubs profiled are from the Bundesliga, and no Bundesliga club has had to file for bankruptcy since its formation in 1963. However, the Bundesliga is significantly behind the likes of England's FAPL in terms of generating income, despite a population that is 60 percent larger. As in France, restrictions on player spending due to liquidity constraints have hampered German clubs from attracting the top international players, and ownership restrictions have prevented capital injection through foreign investors. Moreover, some critics argue that the absence of an auditing function for the DFL means that data quality is poor and losses may be hidden. Additionally, there have been power struggles between the DFL and clubs, as demonstrated in the 2003 Bayern Munich TV rights case; when the German broadcaster Kirch went bankrupt the DFB discovered that Bayern has a secret contract in relation to broadcasting rights, contrary to DFL rules. As a result Bayern were obliged to pay a substantial fine (*Soccernet.espn.go.com*, 2008).

Italy

The governing body of Italian Football is the Italian Football Federation (*Federazione Italiana Giuoco Calcio*, FIGC), founded in 1898. League football is controlled by three different organisations: the *Lega Nazionale Professionisti* (commonly known as Lega Calcio) which governs Serie A and B, the top two divisions; the Lega Pro, which governs Serie C; and the *Lega Nazionale Dilettanti*, which governs amateur leagues. Clubs are mostly controlled by wealthy individuals or companies, although some have also floated on the stock exchange (Foot, 2006). In May 2009 plans were announced for an English-style breakaway Italian premier league.

Clubs have faced limited regulation in Italy, which has resulted in a league that has produced some of the most successful clubs in European competition, and it has been a draw for top footballers from all over the world (especially in the 1960s and 1980s). However, it has also meant that clubs have been unusually prone to financial crises and scandal. Poor governance has had a negative impact on Italian Football throughout the league's history, and more recently, the corruption scandals of 2006 have caused a significant shakeup. There have been many instances of creative accounting as in the case of Parmalat, sponsor of Parma, which turned out to be insolvent with a 'hole in the accounts' of around €4bn (*Observer*, 2004). In 2006, Italian football was further damaged by match fixing scandals. As a result of a police investigation and in addition to hefty fines, the FIGC relegated Juventus as well as docked points from AC Milan, Lazio and Fiorentina (*Guardian*, 2007). The fallout continued as the FIGC president and vice president resigned and the FIGC was put in emergency administration (*Sportbusiness.com*, 2009).

In 2009 the league was in a healthier state and, with recent significant wins for the national team (World Cup 2006) and AC Milan (Champions League 2007), performance on the pitch has improved. However, the spectre of poor financial governance remains, with many clubs facing financial uncertainty. Clubs face commercial limitations, especially in relation to stadia which are generally owned by municipalities that place restrictions on ticket prices. The severe financial crisis has been associated with rising levels of violence, similar to England's hooliganism problems in the 1980s.

One of the biggest commercial issues in Italy has been the control of TV rights. In 1999, the Italian government passed a law banning collective selling of broadcast rights, allowing the big three clubs (AC Milan, Juventus, and Internazionale) to retain the lion's share of total TV income. While the clubs agreed to share income separately, by 2003, Serie A's total debt for all clubs was over £600 million. The Italian government has tried to relieve this financial pressure in controversial fashion and in 2004, passed a law that allowed football clubs to amortise player expenditure across 10 years rather than the term of a player's contract, which was in violation of European law. A compromise of allowing the asset to be written off over five years was accepted in 2005 (Morrow, 2006).

Spain

The governing body of Spanish football is the *Real Federación Española de Fútbol* (RFEF), founded in 1913. Spain's Primera Division (known as "La Liga") was created by the RFEF in 1928. Over the years, Spanish football has been beset by a series of financial crises followed by *planes de saneamiento* (healing plans). A crisis in the early 1980s led to the creation of the *Liga National de Fútbol Profesional* (LFP) in 1984, which is an association of the top division clubs (20 teams) and the second division (22 teams). Much of the regulatory framework of Spanish football was laid down in the *Ley del Deporte* of 1990, which was drafted in response to another financial crisis. Essentially, the government wanted all clubs to adopt a new legal structure known as a *Sociedad Anonima Deportiva* (SAD), which is a joint stock company with a sporting purpose. Prior to this, clubs operated as membership clubs with a large number of paying subscribers and were managed by elected officials who were able to borrow money to fund player acquisition but with no personal liability if the debts could not be repaid. The government's aim was to clarify liability, and thereby also introduce some financial restraint. In the end, several clubs were able to avoid converting to SAD status and retain their financial flexibility, most notably Real Madrid, Barcelona and Athletic de Bilbao.

Unlike other leagues, the LFP does not claim that revenue redistribution is a high priority. Notably, clubs negotiate their television rights independently with television organisations and the league is not involved. Spain does have government-run lotteries, such as the "Sportsbook of the State," that help to fund the LFP, which it in turn distributes to its member clubs. The football pools (*quinielas*), which have always been popular in Spain, also distribute money to the clubs via the *Consejo Superior de Deportes* (CSD).

CASE STUDY 11.1: Leeds United Football Club

Leeds United Football Club (AFC) was a success story for the 1990's. Having last won significant silverware over a decade previously, it was now making headlines as its young team, under the stewardship of David O'Leary, performed strongly in the Premiership, finishing third in 2000, and in the Champions League, reaching the semifinal in 2001. Most football fans at the time agreed that Leeds would continue to progress and that this was just the start of something big.

The Leeds United board certainly agreed with this, and the chairman, Peter Ridsdale, was keen to ensure the continued success of Leeds by funding the enhancement of the Leeds squad. The problem was that Leeds did not have the revenue to fund this and its other spending, so the club borrowed heavily and had two significant methods of doing so.

Player purchases, and in particular their high-wage contracts, were purchased on a hire-purchase scheme by getting REFF (Registered European Football Finance), a Guernsey-based investment vehicle, to buy top players and lease them back to Leeds. These players were owned by REFF and its institutional backers, such as Barclays Bank (a spokesman once quipped "that some of them might turn out for our five-a-side team").

Leeds United had been spending significantly on players even before working with REFF and were in need of a cash injection for their expansion plans. In order to realise their plans, they securitised their gate receipts by issuing a bond for £50 million, which was snapped up by investors like M&G, Teachers, and MetLife. At the time, the atmosphere at Leeds was buoyant, and Peter Ridsdale spoke of Leeds United as "living the dream."

The problems started when Leeds didn't qualify for the Champions League for the 2001–2002 season. They had based their interest spend and debt repayment on participating in the Champions League, and when they didn't, there was a growing hole for them to fill as costs began to vastly outstrip revenue. Even without this hole, the spending of Leeds United was by now far greater than its revenues. In 2002, this became visible to the public as Leeds sold one of their star players, Rio Ferdinand, to a key rival, Manchester United.

A downward spiral quickly developed as the manager fell out with the board because of the sale, results continued to worsen, the manager was sacked and relegation became a very real possibility, as well as not qualifying for the Champions League. Revenues became smaller every year and the debt mountain grew as Leeds owed its creditors over £100 million.

Cost cutting became paramount, and star players, such as Lee Bowyer, Robbie Fowler, and Jonathan Woodgate, were sold to reduce the wage bill. Ridsdale was ousted in 2003, and a succession of chairmen—John McKenzie, Trevor Birch, Gerald Krasner—took over the Leeds FC reins and embarked on significant cost cutting exercises. The culture of spending was halted and remarkable stories of misspending were unearthed. While the £240 Ridsdale spent on goldfish for his office has become a symbol of this overspending, the £600,000 a year on company cars and the £70,000 in one year on director's air flights had more significance.

Even selling star players was costly. When the club sold Robbie Fowler to Manchester City in 2003, they continued to pay £500,000 a year of the player's wages; buying clubs knew how badly Leeds needed to sell players. The club's ground, Elland Road, and its training ground, Thorpe Arch, were sold and leased back to the club as the club fought to avoid going into administration and incurring the 10-point penalty deduction.

In the end, the creditors took a significant hit. The bond holders accepted £12.5 million for their £60 million debt, and REFF accepted £2.5 million of the £23 million they had provided, which was more than they would have received if the club had been put into administration. After this entire financial crisis, 2008 was a relatively good year for the club, as Leeds United had now turned a profit though it had fallen in stature and was playing in the third tier of English football.

Sources: BBC News (2004); Bose (2004); Bose (2005); Dukach (2006); Foley (2001); Parkes (2003); Rich (2003 & 2004).

Questions

1. Imagine that a club had tried to adopt the Leeds United strategy in France. How different would the outcome have been?

2. Discuss the extent to which the organisational structures in German, Italian, and Spanish football differ from the English structure and how these differences would have affected the Leeds United strategy.

3. What damage did the Leeds United experience do to the English football economy?

One constraint on spending has been the threat of enforced relegation if clubs were not solvent. However, in 2004, the government introduced a new bankruptcy law (*ley concursal*) that enabled clubs to enter negotiations with creditors to pay off as little as 50 percent of their debt while retaining their company status. There are often strong incentives for regional governments to financially support their local La Liga team. An extreme case of government intervention in the league on behalf of a club in financial stress was when the Madrid city government bought Real Madrid's training ground to fund its purchase of "Los Galacticos"—a stream of top-level international players bought at high market prices in 2000 and 2001.

CONCLUSIONS

Football in Europe started as a purely amateur sport and has evolved successful national professional leagues consisting of clubs that enjoy huge followings and dominate the finances of the sport. Unlike in the United States, where the major leagues have developed as businesses independently,

European leagues have remained wedded to the national associations that govern the entire sport, and have been engaged in a constant power struggle for the control of the rules, control of executive decision making and, ultimately, control of resources. In this chapter, we have sketched the ways in which these conflicts have played out in five major national leagues. Our starting point was that the rules of the game determine how the game will be played. The governance of English football, for example, is so utterly different from the governance of French football because the legal and institutional structure of the two nations dictates what is and is not possible.

In most of Europe, the discussion of regulation has reflected fears about the financial stability of league football. In essence, competition in a league can turn into an arms race in which teams seek to outbid each other for the same pool of talent, leading ultimately to the financial ruin of all. Football has been beset by financial crises in almost every country, and in several cases, severe regulation has been imposed on clubs in order to control excess. Nonetheless, one might reasonably ask why this is necessary. After all, the owners of football clubs may lose all their money if a club goes bankrupt, but the club itself seldom disappears. Indeed, one might argue that it is more interesting for fans to watch competition fuelled by competing billionaires willing to fritter their fortunes on hiring the latest talent, rather than a state directed football in which all are solvent and none can do much to change their situation.

Be that as it may, there is increasing pressure to standardise governance across Europe and to adopt common standards and metrics. It should be clear from this chapter that this would fundamentally alter the way in which the game is played in some, if not all, member states.

GUIDED READING

Clear information on the way in which leagues are organised, owned, and regulated is remarkably hard to come by. Each country is different, and often subtle aspects of national regulation have a large impact on how decisions are made. However, there are some surveys. On the nations discussed here, see also Chapters 49–53 in the *Handbook on the Economics of Sport*, edited by Wladimir Andreff and Stefan Szymanski, 2006 (Cheltenham: Elgar). Volume 7, Issue number 1 (2006) of the *Journal of Sports Economics* was devoted to a discussion of the financial crisis in European football across 11 European nations and also provides some insight into the impact of national regulatory systems. The regulatory debate in Europe takes place against a background in which there is seen to a need to defend the "European model of sport," which is explained in some detail in the 1998 European Commission paper

The European Model of Sport consultation paper of DGX; *http://www. sport-in-europe.com/SIU/HTML/PDFFiles/EuropeanModelofSport.pdf.* For an analysis of the difference between the European and American models, see Hoehn and Szymanski (1999), The Americanization of European Football, *Economic Policy* 28, 205-240. Finally, for a statement of more regulation that should evolve, see J-L Arnaut (2006), The Independent European Sports Review; *http://www.independentfootballreview.com/doc/Full_Report_EN.pdf.*

DISCUSSION QUESTIONS

1. Is there a trade-off between financial stability and the attractiveness of league competition?
2. What form of ownership is appropriate to running a football club? Why?
3. Should rules for the regulation of football clubs be harmonised across Europe?

REFERENCES

Andreff, W., & Szymanski, S. (2005). *Handbook on the Economics of Sport.* Gloucester, UK: Edward Elgar Publishing.

Arnaut, J. (2006). *The Independent European Sports Review.* UK Presidency of the EU 2005. Retrieved on July 8, 2009, from http://www. independentfootballreview.com/doc/Full_Report_EN.pdf.

BBC News (29th January, 2004). Q & A: Leeds United on the brink. *BBC.* Retrieved on July 8, 2009, from http://news.bbc.co.uk/1/hi/business/3417261. stm

BBC Sport (2nd July, 2003). PSG reject Ronaldinho bid. *BBC.* Retrieved on July 8, 2009, from http://news.bbc.co.uk/sport1/hi/football/teams/m/man_utd/ 3017556.stm

Besson, E. (November, 2008). *Accroître la competitivite des clubs de football professionnel francais.* Paris: Premiere Ministre. Retrieved on July 8, 2009, from http://lesrapports.ladocumentationfrancaise.fr/BRP/084000693/0000.pdf

Bose, M. (1st May, 2004). *Leeds Reach the Point of No Return.* Daily Telegraph.

Bose, M. (26th January, 2005). *Bates Figures out Leeds.* Daily Telegraph.

Bundesliga. (2008). *Bundesliga Report.* Bundesliga. Retrieved on July 8, 2009, from http://www.bundesliga.de/media/native/dfl/dfl_bundesliga_report_2008_ eng.pdf

Desbordes, M. (May, 2006). Interview with Francois Ponthieu, President, Direction Nationale du Controle de Gestion, France. *International Journal of Sports Marketing & Sponsorship*, Vol. 7 (No. 3), pages 158–162.

Dukach, S. (2006). Living the dream has created a nightmare. *Brianmooreshead*. Retrieved on July 8, 2009, from http://brianmooreshead.wordpress.com/?s=Dukach

European Commission, DG X (1998). *The European Model of Sport*. Consultation Paper. European Commission. Retrieved on July 8, 2009, from http://www.sport-in-europe.com/SIU/HTML/PDFFiles/EuropeanModelofSport.pdf.

FA.com. Who We Are. The FA. Retrieved on July 8, 2009, from http://www.thefa.com/TheFA/WhoWeAre.aspx

FIFA (May, 2008). *FIFA Statutes*. FIFA. Retrieved on July 8, 2009, from http://www.fifa.com/mm/document/affederation/federation/01/24/fifa_statutes_072008_en.pdf

Foley, S. (9th July, 2001). Leeds FC Plans Gate Receipts Bond for Expansion. *The Independent*.

Foot, J. (2006). *Calcio*. UK: HarperCollins Publishers.

Football-league.co.uk. About Us. *Football League*. Retrieved on July 8, 2009, from http://www.football-league.co.uk/page/AboutUs/0,10794,00.html

Forbes.com (30th March, 2008). Soccer Team Valuations. *Forbes.com*. Retrieved on July 8, 2009, from http://www.forbes.com/lists/2008/34/biz_soccer08_Soccer-Team-Valuations_Rank.html

Guardian. (21st May, 2007). The loophole that allowed Milan to take Athens road. *The Guardian*. Retrieved on July 8, 2009, from http://www.guardian.co.uk/football/2007/may/21/championsleague.newsstory1

Hoehn, Thomas, & Szymanski, S. (1999). The Americanization of European Football. *Economic Policy, 28*, 205–240.

Independent (17th October, 2008). Bundesliga foreign ownership ban continues. *The Independent*. Retrieved on July 8, 2009, from: http://www.independent.co.uk/sport/football/european/bundesliga-foreign-ownership-ban-continues-964737.html

Lago, U., Simmons, R., & Szymanski, S. (2006). *Journal of Sports Economics, Vol 7*(No 1). February.

Morrow, S. (2006). Impression management in football club financial reporting. *International Journal of Sports Finance*, 1(2). Pages 96–108.

Observer (4th January, 2004). Pamalat dream turns sour. *The Observer*. Retrieved on July 8, 2009, from http://www.guardian.co.uk/business/2004/jan/04/corporatefraud.parmalat2

Parkes, I. (29th October, 2003). McKenzie Sees Rosy Future for Troubled Leeds. *Irish Examiner*.

Premierleague.com. About Us. *Premier League*. Retrieved on July 8, 2009, from http://www.premierleague.com/page/Contact

Premierleague.com (31st July, 2007). Premier League defends ownership test. *Premierleague*. Retrieved on July 8, 2009, from http://www.premierleague.com/page/Headlines/0,12306~1082205,00.html

Rich, T. (21st May, 2003). How Leeds splashed out on Goldfish and Jets. *The Independent*.

Rich, T. (23rd March, 2004). Leeds' New Owners will keep club at Elland Road. *The Independent*.

Rowe, D. (4th October, 2004). Premier League reveals tough new governance rules. *The Leisure Report*.

Soccernet.espn.go.com (16th April, 2008). Bayern v DFL explained. *Soccernet.espn.go.com*. Retrieved on July 8, 2009, from http://soccernet.espn.go. com/columns/story?id=264271&root=europe&cc=5739

Sportbusiness.com (16th May, 2009). FIGC put under emergency administration. Sportbusiness.com. Retrieved on July 8, 2009, from http://www.sportbusiness. com/news/159808/figc-put-under-emergency-administration

UEFA (June, 2007). *UEFA Statutes*. UEFA. Retrieved on July 8, 2009, from http:// www.uefa.com/newsfiles/19081.pdf

RECOMMENDED WEBSITES

England
Premier League
http://www.premierleague.com
Historical Statistics:
http://www.staff.city.ac.uk/r.j.gerrard/football/aifrform.html

The FA:
*http://www.thefa.com/NR/rdonlyres/8F1F05B1-15E3-49BF-97F4-
BC8FDA72B687/150136/RulesoftheAssociation08091.pdf*

France
The French Federation of Football
http://www.fff.fr/
Ligue 1
http://www.lfp.fr
Regulations
http://admi.net/jo/loi84–610.html
http://admi.net/jo/20020430/MJSK0270058D.html
www.droit.org/jo/20070515/MJSS0752128D.html
http://lesrapports.ladocumentationfrancaise.fr/BRP/084000693/0000.pdf

Germany
Bundesliga
http://www.bundesliga.de/en/

Italy
The Italian Football Association
http://www.figc.it/index_en.shtml

Serie A

http://www.lega-calcio.it/

Spain

La Liga

http://www.lfp.es/

Real Federación Española de Fútbol

http://www.rfef.es/

International

FIFA

http://www.fifa.com

FIFA Statutes

http://www.fifa.com/mm/document/affederation/federation/01/24/fifa_statutes_072008_en.pdf

UEFA

http://www.uefa.com

UEFA Statutes

http://www.uefa.com/newsfiles/19081.pdf

CHAPTER 12

Agents and Intermediaries

Raffaele Poli

*Institute of Sport Sciences and Physical Education, University of Lausanne &
International Centre for Sports Studies, University of Neuchâtel*

Objectives

Upon completion of this chapter the reader should be able to:

- Understand the multiple roles fulfilled by agents in the football players' labour and transfer markets.

- Identify the main reasons explaining the increasing importance of players' agents in the football industry.

- Recognize the strategies followed by intermediaries to bind supply and demand of labour on a transnational scale.

- Distinguish the different types of agents' companies involved in the players' representation business/networks.

CONTENTS

OVERVIEW OF THE CHAPTER

This chapter focuses on the analysis of players' agents within the football industry. First of all, it analyses the plurality of roles played by these intermediaries and elucidates from an empirical perspective the different ways in which these functions are fulfilled. This part of the chapter is analytically structured around the three principal agent tasks: the negotiation of contracts for players, the scouting of footballers for clubs and the management of the best-known players' image rights. It also introduces FIFA's new legal framework governing the activity of players' agents, which came into force on January 1, 2008 (FIFA, 2008a). The second part of the chapter addresses the issue of the increasing power acquired by players' agents in the last 15 years. It gives a brief statistical overview on the progression of licensed agents and explains why the number of middlemen is on the rise.

Beyond the easing of the requirements necessary to obtain a licence, it is noted that the increase in agent power is due to three main factors: the increased freedom of movement of players resulted from the Bosman ruling of 1995, which has benefited agents to the detriment of clubs; the internationalisation of the football players' labour market, necessitating the development of transnational networks in which intermediaries occupy a central position; and the general growth of clubs' turnover, which is reflected in the increase in fees paid for the signing of players and has boosted the earnings possibilities for middlemen. The last factor drives the strategies elaborated by players' agents companies to maximise their profits, or to acquire a competitive advantage vis-à-vis their rivals. This chapter proposes a typology of the agency industry according to two criteria: their geographical reach and their degree of specialisation in terms of the number of sectors of the entertainment industry with which they deal.

FUNCTIONS AND FUNCTIONING OF PLAYERS' AGENTS IN FOOTBALL

Traditionally, the role of agents in football has been to assist well-known players in the signing of contracts with clubs and in the protection of their rights once a contract is signed. Today, intermediaries have created larger companies through which they offer multiple services. Agents now work very often simultaneously for players and clubs. This possibility is inscribed in the new FIFA players' agents' regulation, which came into force in 2008 (FIFA, 2008a, page 19). This defines the latter as "a natural person who, for a fee, introduces players to clubs with a view to negotiating or renegotiating an employment contract or introduces two clubs to one another with a view to concluding a transfer agreement." Agents combine henceforth the negotiation of contracts for players, the scouting of footballers for clubs, and, for those working with major celebrities, the management of the players' image rights. The following paragraphs describe the empirical functioning of each of these specific tasks.

NEGOTIATION OF CONTRACTS

The first role fulfilled by agents—the negotiation of contracts—is closely linked to the transfer of players from one club to another and the agent may represent a club. In this case, he negotiates on behalf of the buying or selling club the fee to be paid. The agent may also represent the player. In this case, his task is to negotiate the footballer's contract and signing-on fee. Article 19, paragraph 8 of FIFA's players' agents' regulation (FIFA, 2008a) prohibits double representation by stating, "Players' agents shall avoid all conflicts of interest in the course of their activity. A players' agent may only represent the interests of one party per transaction." Nevertheless, the director of First Artist Corporation, Jon Smith (2006), mentioned that in 2005, "there was a deal in which we represented a buying club, an Italian subsidiary represented the selling club and a Spanish subsidiary acted for the player."

According to Holt and colleagues (2006, page 17), the problem of conflicts of interest "arises when the agent is also offered payments by clubs and these offers are not disclosed to the player. In this case the agent has an incentive to place the player with the club that offers the highest combination of agent fee and wage commission to the agent. This may not be the club that offers the player the highest wage or the best non-wage conditions." Most of the time, commission fees received by agents remain undisclosed, although in recent years, some figures have been released. A study carried out by the German professional league has shown, for example, that in the 2003–2004 season, Bundesliga clubs paid €28.1 million to agents. During the same period, Manchester United announced they had paid about £5.5 million to agents for the signing of nine players, including £1.129 million to the Portuguese agency Gestifute (Jorge Mendes, Luiz Correia) for the recruitment of Cristiano Ronaldo. About £1.5 million was also paid by Manchester United to Proactive Sports for the signing of Wayne Rooney (Holt et al., 2006).

While the greatest profits for agents derive from players' transfers, intermediaries also earn their living by levying money from players' salaries. Article 20, paragraph 1 of FIFA regulations (FIFA, 2008a) mentions that this remuneration "is calculated on the basis of the player's annual basic gross income, including any signing-on fee that the players' agent has negotiated for him in the employment contract." The remuneration can be made through "a lump sum payment at the start of the employment contract" or through "annual instalments at the end of each contractual year." If an agent and a player cannot reach an agreement on the amount of the remuneration to be paid, the former "is entitled to payment of compensation amounting to three per cent of the basic income". Generally, the percentage that intermediaries levy from the players' salary is of 5–10 percent, even if abuses, notably for young African footballers, have been recorded (Poli, 2004).

In exchange for the placement of a player in a club, agents may also negotiate a percentage on the future selling of the footballer. The purchase of players' transfer rights by private investors regrouped in public limited companies or investment funds has become a common practice in the last decade, especially in Latin America. After several affairs, notably that of Carlos Tevez (examined in Case Study 12.1), FIFA decided to intervene on this subject. Article 18bis (FIFA, 2008b) of the "Regulations on the Status and Transfer of Players" states that "no club shall enter into a contract which enables any other party to that contract or any third party to acquire the ability to influence in employment and transfer-related matters its independence, its policies or the performance of its teams." Article 29 (FIFA, 2008a) of the "Players' Agents Regulations" asserts that "no compensation payment, including transfer compensation, training compensation or solidarity contribution, that is payable in connection with a player's transfer between clubs, may be paid in full or part, by the debtor (club) to the players'

CASE STUDY 12.1: The Private Ownership of Footballers' Transfer Rights

The rise in fees paid by clubs for the purchase of the best footballers has stimulated private investments in the players' transfer market. Today these investments are common practice in Latin America, but have also been documented in Africa and in Europe. The case of the Argentinean striker Carlos Tevez is particularly interesting in illustrating new trends in the trade of footballers. Born on February 5, 1984, Tevez had played since the age of 16 for Boca Juniors. The Buenos Aires club had specialised over the years in the training of young players, who were subsequently re-sold to richer clubs. In December 2004, Tevez was signed by the São Paulo club of Corinthians Paulista for an estimated fee of around $20 million. The deal was the biggest transfer ever in South American football. Corinthians was then run by Media Sports Investments (MSI), an international investor fund led by the Iranian businessman Kia Joorabchain. In exchange for its support for Corinthians, MSI retained the transfer rights of the club's best players.

In August 2006, Tevez was placed by MSI with West Ham United in the English Premier League on a loan basis. One year later, Tevez was signed by Manchester United. This transfer has been the subject of controversy. Indeed, West Ham officials demanded a fee, while MSI retorted that it was the single proprietor of the player's transfer rights. The Premier League and the Football Association (FA) then asked FIFA to rule on the ownership of Tevez. Finally, MSI consented to pay approximately £2 million to West Ham to allow them to loan Tevez to Manchester United for a period of two years for an estimated fee of £10 million, with an option to buy him for over £20 million. In the meantime, FIFA has introduced articles in the Regulations on the Status and Transfer of Players (FIFA, 2008b) (article 18) and the Regulations in Players' agents (FIFA, 2008b) (article 29) that explicitly forbid private investors to take control over footballers' transfer rights.

Source: Various

agent. ... This includes, but is not limited to, owning any interest in any transfer compensation or future transfer value of a player."

Thanks to their lucrative business, the most powerful agents have purchased clubs in order to benefit from the transfer of players without breaking the rules. This is indeed the case with the Argentinean agent Gustavo Mascardi, who controls the careers of about 150 players and, through the public limited company Gerenciar Sociedad de Fútbol S.A indirectly owns the club of Ferro Carril Oeste. Club officials who are not and have never been licensed agents also benefit from player transfers by taking advantage of strategic positions. As several books (Bower, 2003) and reports (SCPC, 2003; Arnaut, 2006; Stevens, 2006a & b; Julliot, 2007) have shown, backhanded deals are a common practice in European football. The "bungs culture" consists of the payment of agents by clubs for the signing of a player and the return of part of this sum to club officials and managers. From a legal perspective, this practice falls under the offence of misappropriation and abuse of corporate assets (Poli, 2007).

TRANSNATIONAL SCOUTING NETWORKS

Beside contract negotiations and transfer management, the second principal role played by agents is the development of transnational scouting networks. Once a young player is detected, the intermediaries organise short-term trials in the clubs with which they collaborate. For non-EU players, agents are very often responsible for undertaking the necessary procedures to obtain visas, usually a tourist one, which enables players to come to Europe. To facilitate trans-continental transfers, European based agents are used to working together with tipsters living in the players' exporting countries. In exchange for a regular salary or of periodical commissions, these collaborators scout local talent and organise tournaments where their European-based partners are present. These tipsters are also in charge of the first contact with local footballers and their family. In the U.S. sports system, this task tends also to be fulfilled by unofficial middlemen called "runners" or "street agents" (Shropshire and Davis, 2003).

Agents dealing with non-EU footballers mostly organise football trials abroad, which are subject to the signing of an exclusive contract of representation. According to FIFA rules, this cannot be longer than two years. If the player performs well or is not happy with his agent, he has then the possibility to sign specific mandates with other intermediaries, which, for example, are only valid for a transfer to a particular club. This allows the footballer to have more options for possible moves. Indeed, agents work in close collaboration with club officials and managers, who can intervene to facilitate a transfer. Thus, having a well-connected agent becomes essential if the player wishes to be recruited by a specific club. As in other sports such as golf or tennis, agents of the most successful football players have to define commercial strategies to promote the image of their protégés and to sell the associated rights. For big names such as Ronaldinho, Beckham, Ronaldo, Rooney, or Del Piero, these rights are henceforth more lucrative than the salaries paid by clubs. The latter only represented 32 to 37 percent of their total incomes for the 2005/2006 season (Barret and Notarianni, 2006).

The ability to manage the commercial endorsements of players necessitates competences that are especially present in "full-service providers"—agencies such as, among others, IMG, Wasserman Media Group, First Artist, Formation, or Athole Still International. These agencies manage the careers of a multitude of celebrities in the entertainment industry (actors, musicians, singers, TV presenters, sportsmen, etc.). Through mergers, joint ventures, and strategic partnerships, they have evolved into offering a large array of services. These may include "providing advice regarding financial matters such as tax, investment, insurance, and money management; obtaining and negotiating endorsement contracts; medical and physical health and training consultations; legal (including criminal) consultation; post-playing career counselling; counselling players regarding their media image; counselling players on matters pertaining to everyday life" (Shropshire and Davis, 2003, page 27).

THE INCREASING POWER OF INTERMEDIARIES

While players' agents have been in existence for several decades, their importance in the football industry is greater today than in the past. The number of licensed players' agents strongly increased after 2001, when, under pressure from the European Union's Competition Commission, FIFA modified the rules governing the acquisition of an official licence. Before 2001, agents had to pay US$100,000 to be inscribed in the official list. Today, it is sufficient to pass an examination, which is organised twice a year in all national football federations, and to conclude professional liability insurance. As a result, licensed players' agents are now present in 123 countries (Case Study 12.2). After the examination of September 2007, the number of licensed agents was greater than 4,000, compared to only 613 in February 2001 (Poli, 2008). Beyond the easing of the requirements to get a licence, the increase in the number of the players' agents worldwide is linked to three main factors.

From a legal perspective, the Bosman ruling, promulgated in 1995 by the Court of Justice of the European Community, has given players a greater

CASE STUDY 12.2: The Geography of Players' Agents

About a half of all licensed players' agents are registered in Italy, Spain, England, Brazil, Germany, France and Argentina (Table 12.1). The first three countries import players, while the fourth is the one that exports the most worldwide. According to the Brazilian football federation, 1,085 players have been transferred abroad from national clubs in 2007. Only three other countries in the twelve first places of the ranking are net exporters: Argentina, Nigeria, and Serbia.

The over-representation of importing countries in the top positions of the table shows that for agents it is more profitable to be socially and geographically close to buying clubs than to selling ones. This is probably related to the fact that agents are generally paid by clubs and not by players. In Spain, the ratio between licensed players' agents and Primera Liga footballers is 1.16. This ratio is 1.19 in Italy and 1.59 in England. These statistics, which do not take into account the numerous unregistered middlemen, show how intense the competition between agents is.

Most of the countries in top positions of the ranking are net importers of footballers (Italy, Spain, England, Germany, Netherlands, Russia, and Turkey). These countries are all situated in Europe, most of them in the western part. The development of professional football in Russia and Turkey explains the increasing presence of agents in these two countries. Brazil, Argentina, Nigeria, and Serbia are net exporters. France is a special case, as French clubs are host to many African players, while French footballers are very numerous in England, Italy and Spain. France can then be considered as both a "hub" and "launching-pad" country.

Question

1. What are the similarities and the differences among the countries in the ranking according to their role in the international trade of footballers?

Table 12.1	Countries with the Most Licensed Players' Agents (April 2008)	
Country		**Number**
Italy		457
Spain		454
England		325
Brazil		237
Germany		190
France		158
Argentina		143
Nigeria		106
Serbia		102
Netherlands		93
Russia		78
Turkey		77

Source: FIFA.com (2008c)

freedom of movement. A football player whose contract has expired now has the possibility to sign with another club without the payment of a transfer fee. Agents have benefited from this situation in dealing with clubs on behalf of their protégés in exchange for commission fees. Before the Bosman decision, fees were much more likely to end up in the hands of selling clubs. As underlined by Matthew Shank (1999, page 26) concerning the introduction of the free agency system in North American basketball and hockey, "It is not the agents themselves that have provoked their current rise to prominence, but rather the increased bargaining power of their clients."

From an economic point of view, the increase in the number of players' agents is explained by the concomitant augmentation of football clubs' turnover. European clubs, notably those which are part of the "Big Five" leagues, have more than doubled their revenues since the end of the 1980's, due to the spectacular growth of TV rights. As a consequence, the salaries paid to players and the amounts of money invested in the signing of new footballers have strongly increased. According to the French Union of Professional Clubs (UCPF, 2009), the summer of 2007 saw clubs of the best five European leagues spend €2.017 billion in transfer fees, while English Premier League teams paid one-third of this sum. The financial stakes of the football trade are nowadays so great that more and more middlemen want to enter the market. As mentioned previously, the most powerful companies now have a turnover that allows them to take control over players' transfer rights and even over clubs. Therefore, they acquire a key position within the football industry.

From a sociological perspective, the growing number of players' agents is linked to the greater possibilities acquired by clubs to recruit footballers abroad. As underlined by the sports correspondent Vivek Chaudhary (Roderick, 2006, page 125), "With the game becoming more global and international transfers increasing, the number of people involved in the buying and selling of players has also multiplied." The internationalisation of football's transfer and labour markets (Poli and Ravenel, 2008) has also reinforced the strategic position of players' agents in the economy of football. Indeed, these intermediaries favour the job-matching process (Martin, 2006) on a large scale in furnishing reliable information on the availability of talents all over the globe.

The issue of disposing firsthand information is very relevant when the geographical distance between commercial partners is great, such as in the context of globalisation. Due to their knowledge of markets and territories, the middlemen assume the role of "broker" and "bridge" (Granovetter, 1973; Meyer, 2001) and acquire a strategic advantage in the management of player flows. The relational capital accumulated year by year allows them to occupy a central position in the setting up of the 'migratory channels' (Findlay and Li, 1998) in which footballers must be integrated in order to move abroad.

As noted by Roderick (2006, page 104), "In terms of the process of transferring, mediators between two networks that are only weakly connected are often indispensable links in the chain of information regarding available players." The same author (Roderick, page 46) underlines that "no matter how the structure of the industry evolves, the basic manner of doing business—one key point person recruiting a single athlete – does not appear to be evolving. The truth be told, recruitment of athletes still takes place in the old-fashioned way: person-to-person, one-on-one recruitment of clients."

This explains why the networks underlying the internationalisation of football's labour market are still geographically selective. Latin American players tend to go to Spain and Italy, and Brazilians to Portugal; West African footballers from former French colonies are strongly overrepresented in France; German clubs primarily recruit Eastern-Europeans; and England still imports relatively more players from the British Isles, Scandinavia, Australia, and the United States (Maguire and Stead, 1998; McGovern, 2002; Poli and Ravenel, 2005).

A TYPOLOGY OF PLAYERS' AGENTS COMPANIES

This section proposes a typology of the player agents' companies, a "milieu," which is not as homogeneous as it might appear at first glance. This typology is inspired by Coe and colleagues' (2007) classification of transnational staffing agencies. These authors distinguish firms according to their geographical dimension and to the range of professional settings with which they deal. Four categories of company may thus be identified: the global generalist, the regional generalist, the global specialist and the regional specialist. This typology may also be applied to football. The global generalist agencies are active in more continents and cover more than one sector of the entertainment industry. At the opposite end of the table, the regional specialist companies are active in one single country or continent and only in football.

Global Generalist

The firms that can be categorised as global generalist have emerged in the last two decades as a result of consolidations. A first form of consolidation consists of the purchase of companies active in the management of footballers by firms which were not previously involved in this sector. This is notably the strategy employed by the Marquee Group, an American marketing company, which, prior to its purchase by SFX Entertainment in 1998, had acquired two influential English players' agencies previously run by individuals, Jon Holmes and Tony Stephens.

A second form of consolidation consists of the progressive enlargement of the activities' spectrum by companies that were in the past exclusively involved in football, or in sport. This is, for example, the case of the Formation Group, a British company set up in 2004 through the renaming of the football players' agency Proactive Sports Management. The latter was created in 1994 by three agents, Kevin Moran, Jesper Olsen, and the founding director Paul Stretford. Proactive had first purchased other players' representation firms (Tempo Management and International Sports Management Group). It then took control over companies providing a wide array of services (Fox Sports, Kingsbridge Asset Management, Sponsormatic, RC&A Sports Management, Capital Sports Solutions, OJ Kilkenny & Co, Columbia Design & Build) to become a full-service sports marketing agency. Thanks to the purchase in February, 2008, of James Grant Media Group, Formation is now active in the management of personalities across all sectors of the entertainment industry in the United Kingdom and the United States. The sports representation division has offices in these two countries and advises over 100 professional footballers across the globe. The First Artist Corporation (Case Study 12.3) and the Sport & Entertainment Media Group have followed a similar path to the Formation Group in acquiring several agents'

CASE STUDY 12.3: First Artist and the Consolidation of the Players' Representation Business

The First Artist Corporation was created in 1986 by the agent Jon Smith. The London company has progressively expanded its range of influence by absorbing agents' firms in other European countries. In 2001, it bought the Swiss-Italian company FIMO, previously run by Vinicio Fioranelli and Vincenzo Morabito, which was renamed Promosport. In 2005, First Artist acquired Team Sports Management, a company created by the agent Mel Stein. In October of the same year, First Artist entered into a joint venture with the German agency Fair Sports Marketing GmbH. In July 2006, First Artist took control over Proactive Scandinavia (renamed First Artist Scandinavia), the leading football agency in Denmark. This company has offices in Denmark, Norway and Portugal and also operates in Germany, Holland, Sweden, and Belgium. First Artist has also opened subsidiaries outside the Old Continent and has offices in the United States and in Qatar. First Active has also developed "a pan-global network of associated agents throughout Europe, South America, the Far East and Australia." In 2008, the company managed the careers of about 410 professional football players.

The First Artist Corporation has progressively enlarged the scope of its activity since 2004, including the management of actors, actresses, sport and TV presenters and other media personalities. First Artist is also active in the organisation of entertainment and sports related events, and in the marketing and sponsoring domains through its subsidiaries Dewynters, Newman Displays, Sponsorship Consulting, and First Rights. The company has also created an optimal wealth management division through which it offers financial advice. First Artist has become one of the most influential global generalist firms involved in the players' representation business.

Source: *Firstartist.com*

companies and enlarging the scope of their activities to the representation of people from all entertainment sectors.

Global Specialist

A good example of a global specialist firm is Wasserman Media Group (WMG). This California company has progressively expanded its activities into Europe. It has acquired a key position in football through the acquisition of the soccer European division of SFX Sports Group in November, 2006. Four months previously, WMG had already purchased SportsNet, the leading American agency of football players' management, which was established in 2002 through the merger of two influential agencies run by Richard Motzkin and Dan Segal. WMG manages the careers of players such as Andryi Shevchenko, Steven Gerrard, and Michael Owen. The company has also developed a network of recruiters that cover all continents, including Africa.

While WMG focuses exclusively on sport, football is by no means the only discipline covered. The company is also active in baseball, basketball, rugby, golf, motorsports, boxing, skateboarding, snowboarding, BMX, volleyball, and surfing. WMG is also involved in the search for sponsors for sports organisations, the marketing and development of sporting events, the negotiation of television rights, the distribution of sports contents, the management of mergers and acquisitions, and much more. Other global specialist firms do not provide as many services as WMG. This is notably the case with companies of agents which have transnational networks enabling them to be present on several continents, but whose activities are mainly focused on the scouting and transferring of players (these would include Gestifute, Stellar Group, Pastorello & Partners, International Sports Consulting, Zahavi & Glynne Sports Agents, and Rogon Sportmanagement).

Regional Generalist

Athole Still International can be categorised as a regional generalist firm. Indeed, the core of its activity is in the United Kingdom. Established in the late 1980s, it operates from one single office situated in London, England. The agency represents football players and a manager (Sven Göran Eriksson) but also other celebrities such as opera singers, theatre directors, musicians, TV presenters, and so on. Their services range from personal management to promotion, public relations, sponsorship, endorsements and fundraising. Another example of a regional generalist firm is Panathénée Stratégie Management (PSM). This company, whose office is located in Toulouse, France, was founded and is still run by the licensed football players' agent Michel Fareng. PSM provides a broad spectrum of services and represents footballers, rugby players, and cyclists of French teams, but also artists, dancers, and musicians.

Regional Specialist

A large number of licensed players' agents may be considered in the regional specialist category. Although transcontinental signings are on the rise, the ones carried out within national borders still represent the vast majority. Transfers between clubs of the same country represented 64.7 percent of the total number of signings undertaken by clubs of the "Big Five" European leagues at the start of, or during, the 2006–2007 season (Poli and Ravenel, 2007). Except in the English Premier League and the Portuguese Super Liga, teams in most European leagues are still made up by a majority of indigenous national footballers.

Regional specialist agents focus their activities on sport, usually only on football. They generally do their job within national borders, or between neighbouring countries, by taking advantage of their close relationships with club officials. Well-known regional specialists include Miguel Santos (Grupo Santos Idub) in Spain, Thierno Seydi and Pierre Frelot (Mondial Promotion) in France, Willie McKay in France and the UK, Rune Hauge in Scandinavia and the United Kingdom, Max Urscheler (Gold-Kick) in Switzerland, and Christophe and Roger Henrotay in Belgium.

CONCLUSIONS

It is clear that agents' companies do much more than simply represent players. Consolidations in the last two decades have created large agencies whose common ground is the diversification of activities. TV rights management, sponsorship, commercial endorsement, stadium marketing, and the organisation of sport events tend to now accompany players' representation within the same firm. Mergers, joint ventures and strategic collaborations have favoured a trend towards an integrated approach that responds to the multiple needs of people involved in the entertainment industry. The emergence of generalist companies both provokes and reflects the ever-closer association of elite sport and the entertainment world.

However, aside from the most powerful agencies, smaller structures with a much smaller turnover still exist. These are based on the work of a few persons who have patiently built up a relational capital that allows them to manage the switching of more or less experienced players from one club to another. Even if less subject to media attention, the role of such "small" agents in the working of footballers' market should not be neglected. Indeed, a majority of licensed players' agents work on the field within flexible and dynamic networks. They take the risk to bet on young talents by speculating on their eventual upward career paths. By contrast, the most important agencies tend to focus on more seasoned and better known footballers, or on young players whose talent is indisputable. The process of consolidation in the business of players' representation is thus not being accompanied by the disappearance of smaller firms centred on the work of individual agents.

The strong competition between agents, does however, push some to have recourse to illegal or ethically debatable practices. As underlined by several reports, it is necessary to find solutions that can prevent abuses. One of the major problems is the discrepancy between FIFA and national regulations (Siekmann et al., 2007). Other problems of the players' representation business are conflicts of interest, lack of financial transparency, corruption, money laundering, embezzlement, work exploitation, human trafficking, and smuggling. If agents are not the only actor involved in these practices, their responsibility in many cases is also undeniable. Although there have been recent studies carried out related to the players' representation business, much remains to be done. As mentioned by Chadwick (2004), the role of agents and representatives is without any doubt an emerging trend and challenge in sport studies. The vast study on "sport agents in the European Union" launched in October 2008 (European Commission, 2008) by the Directorate General of Education and Culture of the European Commission should provide a better understanding of what is actually at work in this key domain of the sport industry.

GUIDED READING

Meyer (2001) and Findlay and Li (1998) introduce the crucial role played by intermediaries in the migration of highly skilled professionals. From a broader perspective, Granovetter (1973 and 1985) explains the importance of adopting a relational approach to understand the social embeddedness of economic action. Coe and colleagues (2007) present a typology of the global temporary staffing industry, which is also useful to understand ongoing processes within the players' agents' industry.

Holt and colleagues (2006) deal with the issue of players' agents in European football from a regulatory perspective. They propose and discuss 23 recommendations toward a regulatory reform of the agents' business. Shropshire and Davis (2003) present a detailed analysis of sports agents' activities in the United States, mainly through material sourced from the press. Roderick (2006) treats the question of players' agents in the English game from an internal point of view, through data collected from interviews with professional football players. Tom Bower (2003) exposes in investigative journalistic style some hidden aspects of the football players' transfer market.

Siekmann and colleagues (2007) present an impressive list of contributions dealing with the legal aspects of players' agents activities in 41 countries worldwide, while McGovern (2002), Poli and Ravenel (2005 and 2007) indicate that the international spatial integration occurring in football through players' transfers still occurs in a geographically selective way. They indirectly show that agents' work doesn't happen in a "placeless" world, but it is still constrained by social and cultural factors.

REFERENCES

Arnaut, J. L., (2006). *Independent European Sport Review*. Bruxelles: UK Presidency of the EU.

Barret, X., & Notarianni, R. (2006). Les salaires des stars. *France Football, 25,* 6–10, April, no 3133.

Bower, T. (2003). *Broken Dreams. Vanity, Greed and the Souring of British Football*. London: Pocket Books.

Chadwick, S. 2004. The Future for Sport Businesses. In *The Business of Sport Management*, edited by John Beech & Simon Chadwick. Harlow: FT Prentice Hall. 452–473.

Coe, N., Johns, J., & Ward, K. (2007). Mapping the Globalization of the Temporary Staffing Industry. *The Professional Geographer, 59*(4), 503–520.

European Commission (Sport) (14th October, 2008). Public contract no. DGEAC/13/08, to be awarded by open procedure: *Invitation to tender for a study on sport agents in the European Union*. European Commission. Retrieved on April 15, 2008, from http://ec.europa.eu/sport/news/news547_en.htm

FIFA (2008a). *Regulations: Players' Agents*. Zurich: FIFA. Retrieved on July 8, 2009, from http://www.fifa.com/mm/51/55/18/playersagents_en_32511.pdf

FIFA (2008b). *Regulations on the Status and Transfer of Players*. FIFA. Retrieved on July 8, 2009, from http://www.fifa.com/mm/01/06/30/78/statusinhalt_en_122007.pdf

FIFA.com (April, 2008c). *Players Agents List*. FIFA. Retrieved on April 15, 2008, from http://www.fifa.com/aboutfifa/federation/administration/playersagents/list.html.

Findlay, A., & Li, L. (1998). A Migration Channels Approach to Study of Professionals Moving to and from Hong Kong. *International Migration Review, 32*(3), 682–703.

Firstartist.com. About Us. *First Artist.* Retrieved on July 8, 2009, from http://firstartist.com/sports/aboutus.asp

Granovetter, M. (1985). Economic Action and Social Structure: The Problem of Embeddedness. *American Journal of Sociology, 91*(3), 481–510.

Granovetter, M. (1973). The Strength of Weak Ties. *American Journal of Sociology, 78*(6), 1360–1380.

Holt, M., Michie, J., & Oughton, C. (2006). *The role and regulation of agents in football,* London: The Sports Nexus.

Julliot, D. (2007). *Les conditions de transfert des joueurs professionnels de football et le rôle des agents sportifs.* Paris: Assembleé nationale. Commission des affaires culturelles, familiales et sociales (Rapport d'information, 3741).

Maguire, J., & Stead, D. (1998). Border Crossings. Soccer Labour Migration and the European Union. *International Review for the Sociology of Sport, 33*(1), 59–73.

Martin, P. 2006: Regulating private recruiters: the core issues. In Kuptsch, C. (Ed.), *Merchants of Labor,* Genève: ILO, 13–25.

Meyer, J. B. (2001). Network Approach versus Brain Drain: Lessons from the Diaspora. *International Migration, 39*(5), 91–110.

McGovern, P. (2002). Globalization or Internationalization? Foreign Footballers in the English League, 1946–95. *Sociology, 36*(1), 23–42.

Poli, R. (28th April, 2008). Interview with Omar Ongaro (FIFA), Head of Player's Status Department.

Poli, R. (2007). Transferts de footballeurs: la dérive de la marchandisation. *Finance & Bien commun, 26,* 40–47.

Poli, R. (2004). Les footballeurs africains en Suisse: Victimes de discrimination salariale. *TANGRAM, 15,* 79–84.

Poli, R., & Ravenel, L. (2008). *Annual Review of the European Football Players' Labour Market,* Neuchâtel: CIES.

Poli, R., & Ravenel, L. (2005). Les frontières de la libre circulation dans le football européen. Vers une mondialisation des flux de joueurs? *Espace Population Société, 2,* 293–303.

Roderick, M. (2006). *The work of professional football. A labour of love?* London: Routledge.

Service central de prévention de la corruption (SCPC). (2003). Le blanchiment: les implications dans le sport. In *Rapport d'activité pour l'année 2003, édité par SCPC* (pp. 70–91). Paris: SCPC.

Shank, M. D. (1999). *Sports marketing. A Strategic Approach.* New Jersey: Prentice Hall.

Shropshire, K., & Davis, T. (2003). *The Business of Sports Agents.* Philadelphia: University of Pennsylvania Press.

Siekmann, R. C. R., Parrish, R., Branco Martins, R., & Soek, J. W. (2007). *Players' Agents Worldwide.* The Hague: T.M.C. Asser Press.

Smith, D. (2006). Bringing Agents into the Line. *Sport Business International, No 110*, 58, February.

Stevens, J. (2006a). *The Quest Inquiry. Inquiry Process Paper.* London: Quest.

Stevens, J. (2006b). *The Quest Inquiry. Inquiry Recommendations.* London: Quest.

Union des Clubs Professionels de Football (UCPF) (2009). *Plus de 2 Mds € dépensés en transferts.* Retrieved on July 26, 2009, from http://www.ucpf.fr/index.php?lng=fr&a=35112&pid=101002

RECOMMENDED WEBSITES

Further information on the players' representation business and on the European football players' labour market can be found in the following websites:

Athole Still International

www.atholestill.com

FIFA

www.fifa.com

First Artist

www.firstartist.com

Football Association

www.thefa.com

Formation Group

www.formationgroupplc.com/

IMG

www.imgworld.com

Information on the Transfer Market

www.transfermarket.de.

Panathénées Stratégie Management

www.psm-pfm.com

Professional Football Players' Observatory

www.eurofootplayers.org

Soccer Association

www.soccerassociation.com

Wasserman Media Group

www.wmgllc.com

CHAPTER 13

Stadia and Facilities

Paul Turner, Pamm Kellett, Heath McDonald
Deakin University

Constantino Stavros
RMIT University

<table>
<tr><td>

Objectives

Upon completion of this chapter the reader should be able to:

- Provide an outline of the changing nature of the sport facility sector as it applies to football management.
- Identify the markets within the football sector and discuss the implications of managing facilities for football teams.
- Outline the added value associated with facilities as they apply to football.
- Demonstrate the need for and application of managerial skills applied with a strategic vision for football facility operations.
- Discuss the multi versus singular purpose use of facilities.
- Review the importance of flexibility, location and design associated with football stadia.

</td></tr>
</table>

OVERVIEW OF THE CHAPTER

Following an initial "facility boom" during the Greek and Roman periods of civilisation, there was minimal interest in the development of purpose-built stadia to host major events until the latter part of the nineteenth century. The development of internationally standardised football codes led to the building of many stadia across the world that had, in some cases, capacities in excess of 100,000 people. These stadia were built to accommodate the event requirements of the times, but were largely built without seating and offered only the most basic of amenities. Many of these early period stadia are still in the same location in which they were built, but have been recycled and refreshed many times in order to meet the quality standards of the third millennium (Westerbeek et al., 2005). Since the 1980s, heightened professionalism and commercial development of sport has seen a period of continual improvement of facilities and expansion of the importance of sporting events to communities.

Within this period of professionalisation of sport, the requirement for state-of-the-art facilities has become paramount. Anderson (2000) noted that 57 teams in the major U.S. professional sports leagues (NFL, MLB, NBA, and NHL) were playing in facilities that were constructed between 1990 and 2000. Ten teams constructed new facilities in the 1980s, and 15 teams had major renovations or upgrades to their facilities during the 1990s. Thirteen teams had new stadia built for the new millennia, and 15 more were in the process of planning renovations or new building projects. The estimate at the time was that by 2005, 84 percent of all major league teams would be playing in facilities that had been newly constructed or undergone major renovation since 1980. The reality is that as at 2008, approximately 78 percent of teams in the four major leagues in North America were playing in new or substantially renovated facilities (Anderson, 2008).

Within these four major North American sporting leagues, approximately $240 million was spent on new facilities in 1950–1959, $3.7 billion in 1960–1969, $8.85 billion in 1970–1979, $3.3 billion in 1980–1989, $15 billion in 1990–1999, and it is estimated that $20.8 billion will be spent in the period 2000–2010 (Anderson, 2008). Depending on the details of the accounting method employed, approximately 70 percent of the funding for these new facilities has come from public coffers (Siegfred and Zimbalist, 2006).

Other global markets have seen a similar trend with the ongoing development of new and improved facilities for major events and sporting leagues. In the United Kingdom, football stadia were required to become all-seating following the *Taylor Report* into the Hillsborough stadium disaster in 1989 in which 96 Liverpool supporters died at a semi-final of the FA Cup (Taylor, 1990). While initially experiencing some resistance, the resulting positive impact on attendances, particularly to football matches in England, led to a surge in new development through renovation of existing grounds or relocation into brand new facilities. In the English Premier League during 2008, clubs such as Tottenham, Liverpool, and Everton were evaluating moves to new stadia, and at least eight other Premier League clubs were planning substantial redevelopments to their home grounds.

The key issues involved in the development and management of sporting facilities are the focus of this chapter, particularly in relation to the global expansion of football. The way in which renovation or building of new stadia has become critical to success will be examined, broadly from the perspectives of design, occupancy, usage, and ownership. Each of these aspects will be identified and presented with reference to examples and supporting evidence. Case studies that develop these themes will also be presented.

INTRODUCTION

The number of sporting facilities throughout the world has increased significantly, as have the costs of building, managing, and maintaining such facilities. There are now over 450 stadia throughout the world that have seating capacity in excess of 40,000. This requires sporting facilities that are planned and designed in a cost-effective and community-responsive manner. While there are many attributes that are important to consider in facility management, such as risk management, operational management, event identification, resource management, and marketing activities, this chapter takes an approach focusing on the identification of the more strategic aspects surrounding the actual proliferation of facility development. This emphasis on the expansion of facility development is examined by looking at the stadium from the perspective of some key attributes connected with the design, occupancy, usage, and ownership. Each of these aspects is covered in broad terms, with an emphasis on the impact in a football context and supported by globally linked examples of cases.

PROLIFERATION OF SPORTS FACILITY DEVELOPMENT

The proliferation of sports facility development in the last 20 years can be identified through six features that Anderson (2008) broadly describes as the "sports facility boom":

1. *Obsolescence.* Due to the period in which most facilities were built (pre-1970), it is often more cost efficient to replace the facility than to renovate it to meet current standards and expectations.
2. *Edifice.* New facilities are being built to be more than merely a home ground. They are built to present a focal point for community development, with commercial and residential interests being encouraged into the area.

3. *Expanding use*. New facilities are more likely, through the novelty and increased amenities and services, to boost attendance.

4. *Competitive balance*, or "state-of-the-art-facility theory," where new facilities provide teams with increased revenues and which means competitors will have to follow or risk the consequences of becoming a less attractive state of the art entertainment venue for fans.

5. *Increasing cost*. New facilities realise enhanced revenue streams enabling the owners to receive an attractive profit on their investment. While costs may also have increased, the return on investment through many additional revenue opportunities enables greater profits to be made. Facilities are now often larger and boast more lavish amenities to produce more revenue, and they are built in locations to enhance access and attendance. The impact of the corporate customer is one aspect of this enhanced revenue activity, whereby the revenue derived from these corporate activities often outweighs the revenues generated from the average spectator. Whereas in the past teams raised money to fund new stadia by pledging the future revenues from corporate hospitality, this practice is no longer sensible, as these revenue streams have grown substantially.

6. *Exclusive use*. There is a push, particularly in Europe and the United States, for teams to seek new facilities which they will have the right to use for their own events and which also provide them with additional revenues from other events. Many sporting organisations seek to control all revenue streams generated through the sport facility rather than sharing them with other tenants or the facility owner.

The selection process to host the FIFA World Cup highlights the pressure on leagues to update facilities. Potential World Cup hosts now require between 9 and 12 stadia with a minimum of 40,000 seats for the group matches. Semifinals, the opening game, and the final must all be played in minimum 60,000-seat stadia. Other criteria include "clean" advertising space, provision for a minimum of 600 media seats, and up to 30 camera platforms. Sporting infrastructure is clearly critical to these events.

The impact of stadia on the World Cup was most apparent in 2002 when cohosts Korea and Japan engaged in a remarkable construction game of oneupmanship to ultimately produce 20 high-standard stadia for the event between them, the vast majority of which were brand new.

Australia, which is expected to bid against England, China, Russia, a joint Netherlands/Belgium bid, the United States, and Mexico for the 2018 World Cup, has only four stadia that meet the minimum FIFA standards. The bid is being used as leverage in the push for redevelopment of three other stadia, with two completely new venues in Perth and Adelaide also to be built. The construction programme would be unprecedented in Australian sporting history and dwarf the costs associated with the 2000 Olympic Games (Cockerill, 2007). It would, however, give the national football league (known as the A-League) in Australia a strong foundation for the future. The decision to commit to these new stadia is fraught with political considerations however, as public investments in sporting infrastructure are closely scrutinised. Already, other sporting codes such as the Australian Football League (AFL) are demanding that governments not favour the development of one code over the others by supporting public funding of sport-specific stadia.

A key feature of the many aspects related to sport stadia is the impact that sport facility development has had in terms of the seating and amenities design of these facilities; the occupancy issues; the usage conditions; and ownership. While the issues involved in each of these areas are numerous, this chapter provides an overview of the broad questions surrounding each attribute.

CASE STUDY 13.1: The Sportscape of Football Stadia

When a fan walks into a football stadium, it is not uncommon for them to feel a strong stirring of the heart as the playing field and the stands surrounding it come into view. This emotional response is strongly linked to the passion of sport in general, which typically relies on a facility to not only provide the socialisation inherent in major events, but to also capture the atmosphere and excitement of sport. Designers of such facilities must further ensure easy and secure access, provide conveniences modern spectators have become accustomed to and also, increasingly in the case of football, provide a playing surface upon which the ball can travel with certainty in all kinds of weather. This summation of elements, both tangible and intangible, is referred to as the "sportscape," a derivative of the "servicescape" concept, which became established in marketing literature in the early 1990s to represent the surrounds of a service experience.

Bitner (1990, 1992) demonstrated that the physical surroundings of a consumer's interaction with a service provider influence their perceptions of the experience, including their overall satisfaction. This servicescape environment could thus readily be managed or manipulated to influence those that came into contact with it in either a negative or positive way. A few years later, the concept was extended to leisure service settings (Wakefield and Blodgett, 1994), and Wakefield and Sloan (1995) indicated that the desire to attend and stay at sporting events is directly influenced by modern stadium design and services. These influences fell into two areas, those such as perceptions of crowding and a lack of seat comfort which would deter fans from returning and positive aspects such as the size and quality of the scoreboard and ease of stadium access which would enhance the experience and thus lead to greater satisfaction.

Football stadia provide facilities managers with many issues that must be addressed with regard to the sportscape. This includes determining how a stadium can maintain high levels of comfort, including legroom and seat access, yet still provide fans with opportunities to feel the strong group identification that is often considered a motivation for attendance. Coaches often talk about the crowd as an extra player for the home team, adding encouragement, noise, and support that motivate players to perform above expectations. While some facility managers in North America have been accused of adding to crowd noise by using the public address system as an amplification tool, football stadia must cater to highly allegiant fans whose singing and chanting are often considered integral to the event.

The managers of the Letzigrund stadium in Zurich, Swtizerland had to consider the impact of fan involvement and comfort when they upgraded their stadium in preparation for the 2008 European Football Championships. Needing modification to meet a UEFA requirement for an all-seater venue, the stadium was reconfigured immediately after that competition so that it allowed for standing room at one end of the field, as this was considered an important feature for athletics fans that attended the IAAF Golden League Event held at the stadium each year.

Football must also contend with the relatively unique problem of playing pitch dimensions. Unlike many other sports, a football pitch generally has no exact[1] length or width requirement. Instead, maximums and minimums apply, allowing a football team to adjust its field dimensions to suit a particular playing style. It is often considered that more skilful teams prefer larger pitches to exploit their advantages, while less skilful teams can crowd other teams by using the smallest dimensions. A facility manager in football must thus take into consideration tactical requirements of the coaching staff as well as factors such as proximity of the pitch to the stands and the need to meet standards for major competitions in marking out the dimensions.

From a financial sense, research (Wakefield and Blodgett 1996) on sportscapes has indicated that the longer consumers remain inside a facility, the more money they are likely to spend. Modern football stadia are thus designed to not only provide an environment that facilitates the playing and consumption of sport, but also one that allows fans to arrive long before kick off and stay long after the final whistle. This involves the provision of parking, restaurants, shopping centres, museums, nightclubs, banks, conference centres,

and lounges. This ensures that for some consumers, watching a football match is not always the reason for visiting a football stadium. Similarly, many football stadia can become city icons or tourist visitation areas (Camp Nou in Barcelona, for example), opening up opportunities to generate increased revenues.

Finally, from a simple aesthetic perspective, the modern football stadia must also provide a sportscape that can exist with the surrounding streetscape and landscape in a manner that satisfies a variety of stakeholders, including environmental groups, surrounding residents and city planners. One prominent issue in this regard is the physical location of a sports facility. While some cities such as Melbourne, Australia, are blessed with close to the city sporting precincts and others, such as Detroit, Michigan, have used sport stadia to encourage inner-city renewal, many other cities, such as Paris, have been forced to locate large stadia considerable distances from the city centre.

Questions

1. Think of the last sport stadium (preferably football) that you visited. Putting aside the actual event performance and result, what aspects (if any) of the sportscape made you feel like returning and what aspects (if any) made you feel like not returning?

2. The sportscape of a football stadium has changed considerably over the years. Draw up a table with three columns, the first listing the characteristics of the typical football stadium sportscape as you would imagine it in 1950; the second in current time and the third column with what you envisage it being in 2050.

Sources: Bitner (1990), Bitner (1992), Wakefield & Blodgett (1994), Wakefield & Blodgett (1996), Wakefield & Sloan (1995).

---

[1] UEFA in 2006 issued stadium infrastructure regulations that require an "elite" classified stadium, such as one capable of hosting a Champions League final, to meet exact playing dimensions criteria of 105 metres by 68 metres.

DESIGN

While the impact and effect surrounding stadium design cover many planning and management issues such as the research requirements, strategic brief preparation, stakeholder approvals, tender requirements, design brief preparation, pricing, financial management, and construction planning, the emphasis here is to look at one specific component of design that had a profound impact on stadia design, and in particular football in the United Kingdom.

Following the worst tragedy in the history of British football in 1989, the Hillsborough disaster, where 96 Liverpool fans were crushed to death on the terraces at the Leppings Lane End of Hillsborough Stadium during the FA Cup semi-final match between Liverpool and Nottingham Forest, Lord Justice Taylor, a High Court judge, was commissioned by the UK government to investigate the needs of crowd control and safety at sports events (Taylor, 1990). A key feature of the report was to recommend a move to all-seater stadia for football throughout the country. While there was some initial resistance by some fans and clubs, announcements by both UEFA and FIFA at this time also indicated a determination to stage all major games played under their auspices in grounds where all fans would be seated. This approach toward the elimination of terracing was seen by the authorities in England as being an important step towards increasing spectator safety and crowd control (University of Leicester, 2008).

While the fear of losing the "terrace culture" raised concerns about damaging the unique atmosphere that passionate and committed fans craved, the impact on encouraging more families and women to attend matches and thereby reduce the potential for hostility by 'feminising' the atmosphere at matches was being sought. While all seater stadia are now common throughout the football world, they have not fully solved the issues of crowd safety and security, and it is not uncommon throughout a football season to have the media illuminate examples of crowd disturbances at football matches in various parts of the world. While English stadia meet the UEFA requirement of not having fans enclosed behind fencing, many other stadia in different parts of the world continue to physically segregate fans into sections behind fencing or moats, making a trip to football matches particularly unpleasant for families.

Alongside the emphasis on design to incorporate full-seating within the stadium, there has been a focus on the stadium being built to be both fan and corporate friendly. This has meant that the stadium has been built to incorporate luxury suites, preferred seating options, restaurants, auxiliary developments such as microbreweries, hotels and theatres, ATMs, built-in signage lines, electronic scoreboards, on-site parking, and sponsor (corporate) name and administrative office space, among other attributes (Anderson, 2008). Part of the design process has also included an emphasis on "future-proofing" the new facility in order to enable the stadium to be built in sections over time (for example, the McAlpine Stadium in Huddersfield, England, saw development of a new multiuse 25,000-seat covered stadium with conference facilities as a cost-effective and future-proof stadium that complied with the new stadium safety regulations [RHB Partnership, 2008]).

As a result, the role of facilities manager has become much more complex. The International Association of Assembly Managers (*www.iaam. org*) is a group formed to assist and advise managers of all types of facilities. The IAAM conducts research into, and training on, best practice in facilities management such as disabled access, alcohol provision, emergency planning and crowd control.

CASE STUDY 13.2: Melbourne Victory "Out with the Old and in with the New": relocating from one stadium to another

Three home stadia within the first five years of operation is not something most clubs would envy. For the Melbourne Victory, however, rapidly changing venues is a sign of how far football has come in Australia in a very short space of time. The Melbourne Victory was formed in 2005 to compete in Australia's new "A-League," an elite, professional football competition. The A-League was one in a number of attempts over the years to coordinate football in Australia into a national competition. Other attempts had been beset by financial difficulties, intense competition and political infighting and had failed to reach a broad audience. The A-League though, was established with all new teams that did not reflect the traditional ethnic rivalries that plagued past national leagues.

The fresh approach was immediately successful, and capitalised on growing interest in football stemming from Australia's successful qualification for the 2006 World Cup and increased coverage of the English, Spanish and Italian Leagues on pay television. The Victory was initially based at a venue known as Olympic Park, which had been built

for Melbourne's 1956 Olympic Games. Olympic Park is a small venue with a capacity of 18,500 spectators, of which only 11,000 are seated. The football pitch sits within a full-size athletics track, meaning that fans are set back from the pitch.

The inaugural 2005–06 season of the A-League saw seven teams from Australia and one from New Zealand compete. The Melbourne Victory was instantly popular, with over 4,000 fans turning up to pre-season matches and a near-capacity crowd of almost 18,000 attending their first match. Crowds averaged over 14,000 in the first year—well above expectations, particularly given the Victory's poor on-field performances that year.

Such success put pressure on the home venue. Although close to the Central Business District (CBD), and located near the main sporting precinct of Melbourne, the ground was not well suited to the needs of the club or its audience. The ground was shared by a professional rugby club, and the playing surfaced suffered on occasion. Facilities such as toilets, catering and security were outdated, and government desires to build a new stadium meant that further investment in Olympic Park was unlikely. Most problematic was that fans were already being turned away from games when capacity was reached in that first season. Olympic Park simply left the Victory with few options for growth.

Despite limited seating, issues with sun glare and the deteriorating facilities, the ground was liked by fans. In a survey of over 1,100 Melbourne Victory season-ticket holders at the completion of the first season, satisfaction with Olympic Park was rated at 6 out of 10. Fans were dissatisfied with the food and beverage options and the entertainment both pre- and postgame, but they liked the "home ground" atmosphere and the ease of access to the venue (see Table 13.1).

When the 2006–2007 season started, interest in the Victory and their greatly improved team soared. After only one game of the season, the club announced all future matches (bar one that clashed with a Robbie Williams concert) would be transferred to the city's newest venue, The Docklands Stadium (or "Telstra Dome," as it was then called).

In contrast to Olympic Park, Docklands offered a 55,000-capacity audience, all seated under a roof that could be opened and closed as necessary. Facilities included large corporate hospitality areas, modern bars and food halls, big screen scoreboards and excellent disabled access. The stadium is also close to the CBD and well served by parking and public transport. It too, was a mult-purpose venue, although during the A-league season, the Victory was the only sporting team in residence.

The move was very successful on many levels. The Victory increased season-ticket sales by almost 100 percent, the stadium sold out for one regular season game and the final championship match, and average crowds, at almost 28,000, grew to double the A-League average. Crowds of this magnitude were the largest ever seen for this

Table 13.1   Comparing Season Ticket Holder Attitudes to Two Different Home Ground stadiums

	Season 2005–2006 Olympic Park ($n = 1,136$)	Season 2006–2007 Docklands Stadium ($n = 2,450$)	Difference in Mean Scores*
As a place to watch football	6.07	7.62	1.55
The feeling of a "home ground"	7.47	7.79	0.32
The standard of facilities	5.52	8.69	3.17
The ease of getting to the venue	7.23	8.75	1.52
How "family friendly" the venue is	6.90	8.55	1.65
The value for money of food and beverages at venue	3.61	3.15	–0.46
Entertainment (summed pre- and postmatch)	4.45	5.57	1.12
Overall, how satisfied are you with the Club's home ground?	6.09	7.57	1.48

*All differences at statistically significant at the 0.05 level. Scores are on a 0–10 scale, with 0 being "poor" and 10 being "excellent,", except the satisfaction measure where 0 was "highly dissatisfied" and 10 "highly satisfied."

football code in Australia, and rivalled those of peer major leagues around the world.

In other ways, however, the move was difficult. Fans took some time to adjust to the new stadium. Issues arose in relation to entering the ground (which took more time due to complex scanning systems and larger crowds) and new rules on crowd behaviours and seating positions. The clubs "unofficial" supporter groups were used to standing together as one, but this was problematic in an all-seater stadium. Fans who liked their reserved seats at Olympic Park did not always like the new seating arrangements being offered to them. The much larger, oval-shaped stadium did not offer the same intimacy, and its multipurpose nature meant it was hard to generate the same "home ground" feel. Again, a survey of season ticket holders was conducted at the end of the season, and provided an interesting insight into how fans viewed the venue change (see Table 13.1).

The results show clearly that Docklands Stadium was preferred by fans overall, and in all areas except the pricing of food and beverages. The steps taken by Victory management to ease fan transition from one venue to the next were effective. These actions included clearly informing fans of what was happening and why, along with careful reallocation of reserved seating and efforts to work with supporter groups to accommodate their preferred manner of enjoying matches.

Perhaps there is no greater testament to the success of the Victory than the announcement that the government would fund the building of a new, $AUS270 million rectangular stadium to house the club. Original designs limited the capacity to 25,000, but the club was able to successfully have this increased to 31,000 with scope for further development later. The stadium is due for completion in 2010, meaning that the club will once again need to shift fans. With an average crowd in 2008–2009 running at almost 25,000, there is a strong likelihood that the new stadium will be fully ticketed to season ticket holders. Once again, the Victory faces the challenge of moving a satisfied crowd to a new stadium without upsetting the positive habits many fans have established.

Questions

1. What can the Victory do to ease fan transition to the new stadium prior to the 2010–2011 season?

2. What implications does a fully ticketed stadium have for the club's fan-base in the short and the long term?

Source: Hay & McDonald (2007).

OCCUPANCY

By 1910, 66 English Football League clubs had moved into the stadia they still occupied in the early 1990s. Most other clubs had moved in between 1912 and 1955 and prior to the *Taylor Report* only two new football league grounds had been built, at Scunthorpe and Walsall (University of Leicester, 2008). Since 1990, 25 new club football stadia have been built in England and eight clubs in the 2007 English Premier League season played in stadia built since the Premiership began in 1992. At least half of all Premiership clubs have plans for further investment in new stadia or redevelopment of their existing ground. The clubs with new stadia were listed as reaping the benefits of their investments within the first season at a new stadium, as football club turnover (excluding broadcast income) increased on average by 66 percent (Deloitte, 2007).

In excess of £2.2 billion had been spent on new stadia in English football up to the end of the 2005–2006 season. Mark Taylor, senior consultant in the Sport Business Group at Deloitte (2007) has observed, "While the *Taylor Report* provided the initial catalyst for this expenditure, these impressive amounts illustrate the fact that stadium investment can deliver a significant element of a successful club business strategy." A critical component of the extent of this success is that many clubs experienced that the new all-seated venues were in fact too small, with the result being that many of these clubs have sought to rebuild brand new facilities at new sites.

When interpreting overall attendance figures per football club in England, Boon (1999, page 62) found that all English Premier League clubs averaged an occupancy rate of 90 percent, with the top five displaying occupancy rates of 98 percent or higher. The outcome of these improvements saw the Premier League clubs seeking to engage in stadium renovation or new construction. However, those clubs in leagues below the Premier League were actually experiencing difficulties in achieving full occupancy with occupancy rates dropping to 69 percent for Division One, 47 percent for Division Two, and 33 percent for Division Three. Boon concluded the following:

> [There is] a clear need for some lower-division clubs to temper their dream stadium plans with a degree of realism. It may be great to have a 20,000-capacity stadium, but an average attendance of only 4,000 creates a negative atmosphere. A 10,000- or 12,000-capacity stadium can provide a better atmosphere and—paradoxically—increased support.

Boon's comments indicate that having "excess capacity" in stadia is not necessarily desirable for football clubs. Matchday attendance can be positively stimulated by a limited supply of seats in the stadium. The end result might be that a focus on optimum capacity rather than maximum capacity needs to be considered (Westerbeek et al., 2005).

USAGE

Previously, many facilities were designed to be single-purpose with little thought given to multiple usage, social impacts or even effective strategies for management (Arthur, 2004). One result has been an emphasis on critical areas of purpose or usage of the stadium.

One of the key outcomes of the development of football stadia in the United Kingdom in the modern period is that these stadia are now functioning less as sport facilities and increasingly as sites for a range of functions, leisure consumption and business activities. At many grounds, communal areas below the seats were previously unused or only developed for informal activities, but now they have been converted into areas for bars and shops, becoming the "streets of the stadium." Clubs like Leeds United established a veritable "shopping mall" under its East stand, while Liverpool and Manchester United have stadium museums. Most clubs offer a range of conference facilities within their stadium, and community rooms and classrooms are being offered to the local people (University of Leicester, 2008).

New stadia, despite often catering predominantly for one particular sport, now incorporate modern technological and design aspects to allow multiple users when required. These include grass playing fields that can be moved in and out of the stadium as necessary, roofs that open and close in a matter of minutes, seats that can be easily configured into a variety of shapes and directions, and partitioning that can compartmentalise a large sport stadium into numerous microvenues suitable for smaller events.

This concept of usage has been developed into such a form that in Australia most major stadia have been developed into 'major entertainment destinations'. Stadia such as the Melbourne Cricket Ground offer facilities to a variety of sports, including Australian Rules Football, cricket, soccer, rugby league, concerts, daytime cafes, bars and restaurants, and a number of sporting museums, all with the capacity from a few hundred up to maximum attendance approaching 100,000 (Westerbeek et al., 2005).

While this chapter commenced by highlighting some of the crowd issues that led to a major redesign of football stadia, more modern concerns now exist with regard the security of the large numbers of people attending such facilities and of the athletes performing within them. Suggestions by government agencies that sporting events present an attractive target to terrorists has meant that facility managers have had to rethink not only the screening of fans into the stadium, but where such perimeters need to be established and whether the local police have the sufficient resources to undertake such work. This has often meant that sport stadia now feature multiple perimeters and the employment of specialist security staff to assist with the various processes required.

CASE STUDY 13.3: Maintaining Football Grounds when Water Is Scarce

Globally, almost every nation is facing some form of water shortage crisis (World Commission on Water, 2000). The sport and recreation industry, particularly turf-based sports, such as football, are one of the highest consumers of water. Football teams and clubs use water for many purposes in their facilities, such as irrigation of playing fields/pitches, stadium amenities and facilities, kitchens, maintenance and cleaning, and clubhouse amenities. Football is a heavy user of water for the maintenance of playing fields and as such, the impacts of drought and water restrictions have been severe. Australian Rules football has reported an increase in the risk of injury to participants because of the condition of un-watered playing fields (Sport and Recreation Victoria, 2007). Others sports (including rugby league, soccer and rugby union) have been forced to delay or shorten their seasons (Sleeman, 2007) or, worse still, cancel training and organised competition completely (Connolly and Bell, 2007) in the Australian setting.

While the impact of water restrictions has been profound on most football teams, there are some sports that are not heavy water users and the impact of drought and water restrictions has been minimal. The future of those sports that cannot conduct their competitions is in jeopardy as the sport development pathways are obstructed due to lack of water available for facilities. Water, and those who control the supply of it, then defines which sports are able to flourish and sustain sport development pathways. This case explores the management and governance issues that have resulted for Australian Rules football in the City of Greater Geelong (CoGG) located in Victoria, Australia, a region that has been in a long-term water crisis.

The supply and maintenance of sport and recreation facilities in the CoGG (like most municipalities in Australia) is largely the responsibility of the municipal council in partnership with the teams and clubs who use the facilities. The corporation responsible for the supply of water to the municipality is Barwon Water. Although other sport and recreation facilities exist in the CoGG, the municipal council of CoGG owns and maintains (among other facilities) over 120 football ovals, including the stadium used by its professional Australian Football League (AFL) team, the Cats.

The ten highest users of water in the municipality are sport and recreation facilities—which between them use almost one-third of the city's total water consumption (City of Greater Geelong, 2006). The municipal council is under considerable pressure to find ways to continue to provide sport and recreation opportunities for community members—in particular, to provide the community with facilities on which to play amateur competition Australian Rules football which underpins its professional team.

During 2007, the CoGG kept 16 of its 120 sporting ovals open for participation through allocating all of sport and recreation's available water (supplied through an allocation from Barwon Water) to only these fields. This ensured that these 16 fields could be kept in a safe and playable condition. However, CoGG and Barwon Water were required to devise a rating scale to determine which sports (and their sport facilities) were to share the allocated water, and which were not. This rating was based on the sport's perceived social benefit. The sports and facilities that were deemed to provide greater community social benefits were more likely to secure water allocations and therefore the ability to stage their competitions.

In order to ensure the safety of the playing surfaces, the CoGG and Barwon Water also restricted use of the 16 fields to competition only; therefore, participants were forced to train on local beaches and other parkland areas, thus transferring issues of safety and public liability to other locations and facilities in the community. Further scheduling of club competition seasons and individual matches as well as the allocation of "home ground" gate receipts and concessions profits were required to be governed by the CoGG and Barwon Water as the competing sports were unable to agree on a fair and equitable process of dividing profits.

Clearly, the water allocation rating scale, and approach taken in this municipality to the continued delivery of sport and recreation, has provided a workable solution. However, this case also signals that new stakeholders have entered the arena for the management and governance of sport, and new problems have arisen.

Questions

1. If football competitions are unable to be staged at community levels, what are the impacts for sport development?

2. If you were to devise a social benefits rating scale to determine which football codes receive water allocations in your region, what factors would you consider should be part of the scale? How would you measure them?

3. What issues of governance and management arise from this case?

OWNERSHIP

The situation of stadium ownership has an interesting and chequered past. Within the major league sports in North America, approximately 70 percent of the funding for new stadium development has come from public subsidies. Given the status of many professional sports teams in the United States being owned by wealthy private individuals, the public purse is providing a handsome windfall to some of the richest Americans (Siegfried and Zimbalist, 2006).

Much of the thinking behind this public support of facility construction in North America is that cities have for some time had a belief that sports facilities and teams "put a city on the map," enabling increased tourism and business activity to emerge through ongoing interest in the team or via the staging of mega-events within the stadium. To this end, many teams, such as the NFL's Indianapolis Colts (who moved from Baltimore) and St. Louis Rams (who moved from Los Angeles), have relocated to another city through the lure of access to a brand new stadium. A number of Major League Soccer teams now play in cities different from the major cities they are associated with. The Chicago Fire now play in neighbouring Bridgeview, FC Dallas play in Frisco, and the San Jose Earthquakes play in Santa Clara. All of these teams moved to take advantage of purpose-built stadia or are transitioning toward one.

The European football stadia example has some common themes to that of North America, although public ownership, rather than private, is a strong tradition with very few teams owning their own stadium. Only one club in the French Ligue 1 owns its home stadium, and Juventus claim to be the only club in Serie A with plans in place to own their own stadium without local government assistance. Even in the United Kingdom's Premier League, teams are being tempted to move from traditional boroughs if the facilities are better. Bolton F.C. moved from Burnden Park to the new Reebok Stadium, six miles north of Bolton in Lostock to take advantage of improved facilities. Everton is currently considering a move from Liverpool to Kirkby, for which it would need to contribute around £80 million of club money. The attraction of improved stadia is obvious, but these teams risk losing touch with their traditional fan base. Moving stadia can also cause deep divisions among supporter groups, as the formation of the "Keep Everton in our City" group shows (*www.keioc.net*).

The situation in Australian Rules football serves as another example, as the sport was traditionally organised along the lines of most European football competitions. In the past, AFL clubs owned or leased their own football stadia and most home matches were played at their suburban grounds. In the mid-1980s, a step change occurred in Australian football, with the League seeking to develop a more national approach to the game, moving beyond the Melbourne-based competition of the past. Part of the strategy employed by the League at the time was one of facility rationalisation. Clubs were forced to move from their small, outdated, and often unsafe suburban stadia into the few AFL-designated playing facilities throughout the country (Westerbeek et al., 2005).

The result was that most of the clubs entered into ground access and usage agreements with the major football stadia within their home state. This arrangement requires the clubs to enter into a service agreement with the stadium in which they will receive a share of the gate receipts should the minimum attendance figure be achieved. It also presents issues in terms of catering and concession arrangements with existing facility contracts over food distribution needing to be resolved. The situation with existing stadium sponsorship signage needs to also be addressed, as does the accessibility to the full range of corporate facilities. Most stadia in Australia have an existing membership base already in place who have some priority access to the venue, which in certain cases overrides the capacity of the football club to "sell out" the stadium. This creates a situation in which the club and the league are entering into facility agreements in order to ensure that the stadium meets the obligations to the competition, while at the same time presenting itself as a viable commercial operation.

One valuable modern revenue stream that stadium owners can benefit from is naming rights to the facility. Historical football grounds, often linked strongly to the community for many decades, prove difficult to rename despite interest from sponsors. It would be hard, for example, to have Liverpool's home ground known as anything other than "Anfield," Manchester United's ground as "Old Trafford" or Chelsea's as "Stamford Bridge." One could argue that Arsenal's "Highbury" ground was in this category just a few years ago, but with the move (of approximately one kilometre) to a new stadium in 2006, Arsenal were able to negotiate a lucrative sponsorship deal with the Middle Eastern airline Emirates, which included a fifteen year deal for the new facility to be called "Emirates Stadium". This sponsorship is particularly advantageous as the new facility, having no previous name, provides a fresh start with limited opportunity for confusion or for other names to be used.

CONCLUSIONS

This chapter focused on the impact of new facility development from the following perspective:

1. *Design*—with a particular focus on the all seating requirement that emerged especially in English football driven by safety and security

issues. There was also development of state-of-the-art amenities such as restaurants, hotels and bars in a bid to offer different services and attract a corporate clientele.

2. *Occupancy*—where the emphasis is on developing stadia to entice people to visit the complex while also maximising the attendance at competition games and events. One method of achieving this is presenting a stadium with some flexibility in design, through a future proofing arrangement where the facility can be adapted to meet future needs (or capacity can even be reduced when demand is not as great).

3. *Usage*—which reflects the multipurpose opportunities of facilities. While there is a general wastage associated with any facility's day-to-day activities, many modern stadia are being built to offer greater access and amenities. This may relate to offering 24 hour service to a few hundred people through a conference through to additional events and services such as cultural events including concerts, theatre, and plays. While this multipurpose approach is being sought by most newly established stadia, there is an emphasis in the United States and the United Kingdom for club ownership and therefore priority usage to apply. Even though this singular use is somewhat sought by clubs in these countries, they still seek to generate greater usage through offering a range of different services.

4. *Ownership*–A number of ownership models exist, with public ownership, private ownership and a hybrid of the two all being employed to varying extents around the world. Two trends are evident: the costs of stadium development and maintenances are rising and are becoming prohibitive to all but the world's largest clubs. Public funding, meanwhile, is becoming more accessible, as regions and towns strive to attract sporting teams as part of destination tourism or urban renewal programmes. Where stadia are not team owned, securing the rights to revenue streams such as in-ground advertising, naming rights, and food and beverage profits are often vital to club finances.

DISCUSSION QUESTIONS

1. What are the advantages and disadvantages of having a commercial organisation sponsor the naming rights to a stadium?

2. Modern football stadia must do a lot more than host a biweekly match to maximise returns. What activities and services would you recommend be

incorporated into a modern, medium-size stadium located near a major residential precinct?

3. Many modern stadia are now being built away from central community locations. What are the advantages and disadvantages associated with a stadium located on the city fringes as opposed to one located in the centre of a city?

GUIDED READING

Stadia and facilities management is a rapidly changing area but not one that has traditionally been the focus of academic research. All general texts on sport management tend to cover this area, although that discussion is often limited in scope, or is dated. To gain a more detailed understanding of the broad area, books by Farmer and colleagues (1996) and Westerbeek and colleagues (2005) both provide excellent coverage. The academic work on the "Sportscape" concept, cited earlier, is also essential reading for those trying to obtain a customer perspective on the management of sports facilities.

REFERENCES

Anderson, P. (2000). *Sports Facilities Reports.* Volume 1, Number 1. National Sports Law Institute of Marquette University Law School, Milwaukee. Retrieved on November 21, 2008, from http://law.marquette.edu/cgi-bin/site.pl?2130&pageID=489.

Anderson, P. (2008). Professional Sports Facilities: The Costs, the Public, the Benefits and the Law of the Deal. *Econ 296: Seminar in Economics—The Economics of Sports.* National Sports Law Institute: Marquette University Law School. Retrieved on November 21, 2008, from http://law.marquette.edu/s3/site/images/sports/professional-sports-facilities.pdf.

Arthur, D. (2004). Sport Event and Facility Management. In J. Beech, & S. Chadwick (Eds.), *The Business of Sport Management,* pp. 321–349. Harlow: Pearson Education.

Bitner, M. J. (1990). Evaluating service encounters: the effects of physical surroundings and employee responses. *Journal of Marketing, 54*(2), 69–82.

Bitner, M. J. (1992). Servicescapes: the impact of physical surroundings on customers and employees. *Journal of Marketing, 56*(2), 57–71.

Boon, G. (1999). *Deloitte & Touche Annual Review of Football Finance (1997–1998 Season).* Manchester: Deloitte & Touche.

City of Greater Geelong. (2006). *Sustainable Water Use Plan.* In Department of Sustainability and Environment, City of Greater Geelong.

Cockerill, M. (October 31, 2007). World Cup bid gets serious for biggest show on planet. *Sydney Morning Herald*.

Connolly, E., & Bell, A. (4th February, 2007). Drought cancels footy season. *Daily Telegraph*. Retrieved on July 9, 2009, from http://www.news.com.au/dailytelegraph/story/0,22049,21165853-5006010,00.html.

Deloitte (14 August, 2007). *New stadiums boost football club turnover by 66%*. Retrieved on November 22, 2008, from http://www.deloitte.com/dtt/press_release/0,1014,sid%253D2834%2526cid%253D167402,00.html.

Farmer, P. J., Mulrooney, A. L., & Ammon, R. (1996). *Sport facility planning and management*. Morgantown, WV: Fitness Information Technology, Inc.

Hay, R., & McDonald, H. (2007). A Victory for Fans. *Soccer & Society, 8*(2/3), 298–315.

Keep Everton in Our City. *www.keioc.net*. Retrieved on July 9, 2009, from http://www.keioc.net/

RHB Partnership (2008). *Leisure*. Retrieved on November 22, 2008, from http://www.rhbpartnership.co.uk/showcase_detail.php?id=34&catid=4.

Siegfried, J., & Zimbalist, A. (2006). The economic impact of sports facilities, teams and mega-events. *The Australian Economic Review, 39*(4), 420–427.

Sleeman, E. (2007). *Stonnington Winter Sports Season Delayed to Saturday 28 April*. Retrieved on June 15, 2008, from http://www.stonnington.vic.gov.au/resources/documents/3_Apr_2007_Stonnington_Winter_Sports_Season_Delayed_to_Sat_28_April.pdf.

Sport and Recreation Victoria. (2007). *Ground conditions and injury risk–implications for sports grounds assessment practices in Victoria*. Melbourne: Sport and Recreation Victoria.

Inquiry by the Rt Hon Lord Justice Taylor (1990). *The Hillsborough Stadium Disaster: Final Report*. Cm962. HMSO.

University of Leicester (2008). *Fact Sheet 2: Football Stadia after Taylor*. Department of Sociology: Sport Resources. Retrieved on November 22, 2008, from http://www.le.ac.uk/sociology/css/resources/factsheets/fs2.html.

Wakefield, K. L., & Blodgett, J. G. (1996). The effects of the servicescape on customers' behavioural intentions in leisure service settings. *Journal of Services Marketing, 10*(6), 45–61.

Wakefield, K. L., & Blodgett, J. G. (1994). The importance of servicescapes in leisure service settings. *Journal of Services Marketing, 8*(3), 66–76.

Wakefield, K. L., & Sloan, H. J. (1995). The effects of team loyalty and selected stadium factors on spectator attendance. *Journal of Sport Management, 9*(2), 153–172.

Westerbeek, H., Smith, A., Turner, P., Emery, P., Green, C., & Van Leeuwen, L. (2005). *Managing sports facilities and major events*. St Leonards, NSW: Allen & Unwin.

World Commission on Water. (2000). Report of the World Commission on Water. *Water Resources Development, 16*(3), 289–320.

RECOMMENDED WEBSITES

International Association of Assembly Managers website.

www.iaam.org.

The worldstadiums website is an excellent resource that lists more than 10,000 sport stadia (including many pictures) across the world.

http://www.worldstadiums.com.

PART 2

Managing Football
in the Big Five

CHAPTER 14

England

John Beech
Centre for the International Business of Sport, Coventry University

---

Objectives

Upon completion of this chapter the reader should be able to:

- Appreciate the unique nature of management in English football as an outcome of its unique history.
- Identify the key features of the commercialisation of the English game.
- Understand the significance of cash flows in the modern game.
- Explain the uncertainties that currently face English football management and managers.

OVERVIEW OF THE CHAPTER

The chapter begins with an explanation of the historical context of the management in English football and how, in particular, the long period of stability between professionalisation in the 1880s and commercialisation at the end of the twentieth century made the onset of commercialisation an exciting challenge for managers and yet led to some of the obstacles that dog management even today.

The postcommercialised era is explored from both a financial perspective, with the emphasis on financial strategy rather than an accountant's eye for detailed figures, and a human resources perspective, looking at the difficult role of today's manager. The chapter includes two case studies, one featuring early developments in commercialisation and the other following the varied career of a modern manager.

INTRODUCTION

The role of England in the evolution of both football as a game and football as an arena for management has been seminal. In England, the period between professionalisation and commercialisation was unusually long—over one hundred years. For much of this time, there was a policy of isolationism and the game, particularly its management, evolved in a unique way, which in turn shaped the way that commercialisation came to the game. An understanding of the historical perspective is thus essential to the understanding of today's management in the English game.

It must straightaway be declared that the claim that the English invented the game is utterly spurious (see Chapter 21 on Chinese football, page 374). Nonetheless, in England, the game was first codified—first in a disparate set of rules established in universities and schools and then in a common agreed format by the (English) Football Association in 1863. These rules proved contentious to some clubs, and those that favoured a game which allowed handling the ball formed the Rugby Football Union in 1871, resulting in a permanent schism between Association Football and Rugby Football.

At the time of the formation of the Football Association (FA), all clubs were amateur and were mostly prevalent as clubs for upper class players, officials, and supporters. The game quickly spread across a much wider spectrum of society. The pressure to perform on the pitch quickly resulted in shadow payments to players in the form of expenses or of employment opportunities in shadow jobs. This fundamental drift toward a professional game was strongly resisted by English football's founding fathers, but they were unable to prevent the drift as it became endemic throughout many parts of the game. A north-south divide began to appear, with northern clubs keen to adopt a professionalised game. In the early 1880s, the state of the game had become such that players were beginning to admit openly their "not-entirely-amateur" status, and by 1885, the FA had little choice but to allow the payment of players. Football had officially entered the professionalised phase (Beech, 2004) many years ahead of other countries outside the United Kingdom. As we shall see in this chapter, England remained in this professionalised phase for just over a hundred years, enjoying a long period of relative stability that shaped the English game from a management perspective that was different from other countries, where the period between professionalisation and commercialisation (the phase that followed) has been much shorter.

An immediate consequence of professionalisation was that the previous ad hoc arrangement of fixtures was no longer adequate. The wages that had to be paid to players who were employees of a club required a regular flow of funds from the sale of tickets to spectators. To meet this pressing need, William Macgregor, a director of Aston Villa FC, approached the secretaries of Aston Villa, Blackburn Rovers, Bolton Wanderers, Preston North End, and West Bromwich Albion in 1888 with a proposal to form a league of clubs that would play one another on a regular basis, with points awarded according to the result of each match. Thus the Football League (FL) was born, with a strong emphasis on northern clubs and an organisation quite separate from the organisation of the Football Association. The Football League grew quickly, adding a Second Division in 1892 with the absorption of a rival league, the Football Alliance, which had been formed in 1889, again with an emphasis on clubs from the north and the Midlands. Southern clubs, including now major London clubs such as Arsenal and Tottenham Hotspur, were not among the early members, and in fact it was not until 1931 that a London club won the title of champion of League Division 1 (Inglis, 1988).

THE IMPLICATIONS OF PROFESSIONALISATION

Professionalisation of football in England is widely seen as a significant factor in the evolution of the game in terms of the players and their conditions as employees. Certainly this was a significant factor in the regulation of the game by the Football League. In 1890 it imposed transfer restraints on players changing clubs and ten years later it introduced a Maximum Wage Rule for soccer players (a basic rate of £4 per week—roughly equivalent to a salary of £16,200 a year at 2008 value; it had risen to £20 per week by 1961, when it was abolished, the equivalent of a salary of £16,700 at 2008 value). Players could however earn bonuses, a form of payment by results, and benefits in kind (Inglis, 1988).

Professionalisation, and the way it happened in England, had other far-reaching consequences:

- The regulation of the game on the pitch, governed by the FA, and the management practice of clubs, strongly influenced by the Football League, became separate processes.
- The involvement of the Football League led to regulation which was generally pro-club but often anti-player.

■ Governance of football as a business moved away from clubs and to the Football League. Although the clubs obviously were instrumental in the running of the Football League, clubs with minority views on how the League should be run had little choice but to bow to the wishes of the majority.

Arguably the most significant consequence of professionalisation was a change in the way that clubs were managed. In the amateur era, clubs were run by officers elected by members who were also the players; the club secretary held the pivotal role in the day-to-day management of the club, both with respect to its team and to its business affairs. After professionalisation, the notion of "club" became a largely titular construct. Clubs had become businesses with employees—the players—who had no control in club affairs. Indeed, they were socially isolated from the club's owners and a new role emerged to bridge the gap between the club's directors and its players: the "manager." The manager was thus an intermediary between employers and employees, whereas his predecessor, the club secretary, was normally a peer of both the committee members and the players. For the first time, the club had become a private limited company, requiring appropriate management skills and procedures. As stakeholders, the players and the fans (or rather, the playing and nonplaying members of the club) effectively lost their stake in the club.

In spite of these disjunctures in management resulting from professionalisation, the changes led to a period of remarkable stability that was to last almost a century. The FA laid down rules which seriously limited any possibility of an open market in players emerging and ensured that a reasonable level of competitive balance was maintained. These rules made it very difficult for a team to achieve the kind of dominance that the so-called "Big Four" of Manchester United, Chelsea, Arsenal and Liverpool have today. The key restraints were as follows.

Profit-taking

The FA's Rule 34 was designed to ensure that directors of football clubs could not drain profits out of them by restricting the dividend that could be paid to the shareholders. Although the permitted percentage increased slowly over the years (Table 14.1), the Rule remained effective in ensuring that the private limited companies continued to behave more or less as if they were still clubs until the 1980s.

Table 14.1	Changes to FA's Rule 34 on Allowed Dividend Payment
Year	**% of Paid-Up Equity Capital Allowed to Be Paid as Dividend**
1896	5
1920	7.5
1974	10
1983	15

(Samuels, 2008, page 92)

The Retain and Transfer Principles

As a means of preventing rich clubs simply buying the most talented players available, the principles of "retain and transfer" were introduced by the Football League. It worked as follows. Shortly after its foundation in 1888, it introduced a far stricter system of player registration with a club than even the FA had introduced at the onset of professionalism. From the start of the 1893–1894 season, a player was required to be registered with one club only and he was not allowed to play for any other club. The harshness of this system, and its antiplayer aspect, was that a club retained the player's registration even after the player's contract had come to an end. To counterbalance retention of a player's registration was the possibility that a club would transfer the registration of the player to another club and duly be compensated with an agreed transfer fee. One interpretation of this system is that it reduced players from being free agents in a labour market to chattels to be bought and sold by their clubs.

The Wage Cap

As if the retain and transfer system was not enough to restrain a footballer earning what he might see as his optimal wage, the FL introduced a further restraint in 1901, the wage cap, in other words a maximum wage that any club in the Football League was allowed to pay (Table 14.2).

These three restraints had quite remarkable effects:

1. As a backlash to the suppression of the players' rights, an underswell of militancy, albeit rather ineffective, emerged, and the players began to unionise, forming what was to become the Professional Footballers' Association (PFA).

Table 14.2	The Maximum Wage	
Year	Maximum Weekly Wage	2007 Equivalent Annual[1] Salary* (nearest £100)
1901	£4	£16,200
1919	£10	£17,100
1922	£9	£18,300
1947	£12	£17,500
1951	£14	£16,500
1953	£15	£15,700
1957	£17	£15,300
1958	£20	£17,500
1961 (abolition)	£20	£16,700

[1] *Calculated as purchasing power by* Measuring Worth *at* http://www.measuringworth.com/ppoweruk/?redirurl=calculators/ppoweruk/.

2. The already shady practices adopted by some clubs to circumvent the spirit, if not the letter, of the wages cap became normal—performance bonuses, signing-on fees, external sinecure jobs, special accommodation packages, and so on.

3. The restraints nonetheless ushered in a remarkable period of stability for the clubs of the league. With the exception of a small number of clubs who faded quickly in the early days of the league, the expansion of the league to 92 clubs, bringing in clubs from, in particular, London, created a truly national system and little was to change until the 1960s.

Figure 14.1 shows the main revenue flows during this relatively stable professionalised era. The main income to clubs was from the sale of matchday tickets, with the distribution of revenue between home and away teams being subject to the rules of the Football League. The main cost to clubs was players' wages, which also was constrained, through the application of the maximum wage. Clubs therefore had considerable control over their finances, and financial failure was rare. In the postwar years of the professionalised phase, only Accrington Stanley (1962), Gateshead (1973), and Bradford Park Avenue (1974) suffered the ultimate failure of being wound up through insolvency.

The women's game did not enjoy such stability or success, however. Pre–World War I social attitudes were responsible for its lack of development. Women's games are known to have taken place in late Victorian

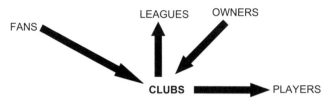

(Widths and lengths of arrows are not indicative of size of revenue flow)

FIGURE 14.1 *Main revenue flows in the professional era.*

times, but in 1902 the FA decided to ban games between the sexes. During the war, however, with men away fighting and women taking their place in factories, they formed teams, notably in munitions factories, and participated in matches to raise funds for charity. Skills were rapidly developed and immediately after the war the women's game thrived. On Boxing Day 1920, in a match between the most famous of the women's teams, Dick, Kerr's Ladies FC (a manufacturer of light railway equipment) beat St. Helens in front of a crowd of 53,000 at Goodison Park. Such crowds did not go down well with the male authorities, and on December 5, 1921, the FA banned women from playing on the grounds of any of its member clubs, effectively stopping the women's game in its tracks. Dick, Kerr's promptly set off on a tour of North America, but, in the face of the ban, the women's game all but disappeared until its revival much later in the twentieth century.

THE LATER PROFESSIONALISED ERA

The Professional Footballers' Association had started to promote a new militancy first under the secretaryship of Jimmie Guthrie (1946–1957) and then under Jimmy Hill (1957–1961). Hill fought in particular for the abolition of the maximum wage, and in 1961 the FA was forced to abolish this iniquitous practice. The football industry was suddenly to be shaken from its long period of stability.

In 1960, following a series of disputes with his club, Newcastle United, George Eastham refused to sign a new contract and requested a transfer. Newcastle declined to release him, thus preventing him from signing for another club. He himself described the contract binding him as a "*slavery contract*" (Spurling, 2004). Eastham briefly left the game, Newcastle then relented, and Eastham resumed his playing career with Arsenal. However, with the backing of the Professional Footballers' Association, Eastham took the matter to court, arguing that his treatment had amounted to "restraint of trade." The key element of the ruling handed down in 1963 was that the long-standing retain-and-transfer system was unreasonable, or at least that the retain element was unreasonable (McArdle, 2000).

The impact of the abolition of the maximum wage was immediate. Johnny Haynes of Fulham rapidly achieved a wage of £100 per week, five times the maximum at abolition, and a steady spiral upward of wages for the elite of the profession had begun, exactly what the clubs had feared.

To pay these higher wages, clubs for the first time began to adopt more aggressive attitudes to raising revenues, and the first buds of commercialisation appeared. Now the norm, shirt sponsorship had been expressly forbidden under FA rules. Jimmy Hill—by 1981, a poacher turned gamekeeper, in the guise of the managing director of Coventry City—attempted to circumvent the rule by displaying the logo of Talbot, the car manufacturer based in Coventry. Such was the antipathy to this move that the club was forced to wear logo-less shirts when playing in a match that was being broadcast! By the 1983–1984 season the ban had been lifted, however, and the sponsored shirt quickly became the norm. At first sponsors tended to be local companies, but with the increasing exposure through broadcasting, major international businesses began to seek this opportunity to gain global exposure for their brand.

CASE STUDY 14.1: Jimmy Hill

Although Jimmy Hill is probably thought of today as an elder statesman of television football punditry, his early career as the secretary of the Professional Footballers' Association has been noted. A radical, he finally managed to break the maximum wage rule and allowed players to enter an era of ever-rising financial success.

Between these two career phases was an equally significant one: his work in football management. Forced to retire from playing through injury, his first managerial appointment was at Coventry City. He joined them when they were playing in the third tier and masterminded their climb to the top tier, where they were to remain for over 30 years.

He was notable as a manager for adopting an innovative and externalised view of what was needed by a football club from a management perspective. His innovations included the following:

- Rebranding the club as the Sky Blues.

- Inviting young fans to a "pop and crisps party" under one of the stands at Highfield Road, then the home of Coventry City, following a Boxing Day match.

- Writing and promoting a club song, launched at the pantomime in Coventry's theatre with players forming the choir.

- Insisting on being called "JH" by the players rather than the traditional "boss" or "gaffer." His argument for doing this is significant in that it shows an awareness of the more conventional techniques of

Human Resource Management that is rare in English football:

I reasoned that you can't expect a team to be treated as office boys from Monday to Friday and then play like senior executives when they are on their own on Saturday. . . . I saw public relations as the most neglected part of football, and my ambition was to encourage our followers, particularly those from our city, to feel part of our club and that our success was their success.

- Hiring entire trains for supporters to go to away matches, selling the tickets to them as a club operation, and branding each train the "Sky Blue Express."

- Introducing a vice president's club, which brought corporate hospitality to Highfield Road, and a social club for supporters.

- Introducing closed-circuit broadcasting of live away games at Highfield Road.

- Developing long-term promotional links with Talbot and their successor, Peugeot.

- Making Highfield Road an all-seater stadium as an antihooliganism measure, at a time when the

English game was beginning to suffer badly from this social phenomenon. When he left Coventry City, this was abandoned due to unpopularity with many fans, only to be reintroduced, of course, in 1990 following the *Taylor Report* recommendations in 1990 (following Lord Chief Justice Taylor's investigation into the Hillsborough stadia disaster of 1989 which saw the death of 96 Liverpool supporters).

Hill even planned to introduce firework celebrations when Coventry scored, but this idea was abandoned on safety grounds.

Source: Hill, 1998

Question

1. At the time, Jimmy Hill's innovations at Coventry City were in stark contrast to the unimaginative status quo found at most other senior English clubs. Should Hill be seen as a bold prophet who foresaw the need for a business to develop custom through sophisticated marketing strategies or as being at the vanguard of the movement that has destroyed the "beautiful game" in England?

Although there was an increasing sense of commercial instinct among English football clubs in the three decades from 1960, as Case Study 14.1 exemplifies, it was in 1991 that major changes ushered in the fully commercialised phase.

THE COMMERCIALISED ERA

By the late 1980s, English football had weathered a number of negative forces. The scourge of football hooliganism had culminated in English clubs being banned from Europe for five years in 1985 immediately following the Heysel stadium Disaster in Brussels in which 37 Juventus supporters died. The major health and safety issue of unsafe stadia brought to the foreground by two disasters in England with major loss of life—the Bradford City fire (May 1985) and the Hillsborough disaster (April 1989)—had been addressed by the *Taylor Report* of 1990.[1] Football had begun to resume its former appeal as a spectator report. At last, there seemed cause for optimism in the industry.

While Rule 34 had constrained profit taking from the private limited companies that almost all clubs had become many years previously, the 1980s saw clubs begin to find ways to circumvent the Rule. Some owners realised that there were not only the cash-raising benefits to becoming a stock exchange–quoted public limited company (as opposed to the almost ubiquitous format of private limited company). In terms of raising cash by floating the company either on the Stock Exchange or, for the smaller club, the Alternative Investment Market (AIM), few clubs showed any significant measure of success, and the price of shares generally failed to maintain the price at flotation. However, the new format enabled clubs to become wholly owned subsidiaries of holding companies, a situation which potentially gave the possibility of removing cash surpluses from clubs.

In stark contrast to the local ownership of the English football clubs in the professionalised era, foreign ownership has increased in the last two decades. By the 2007–2008 season, 9 of the 20 Premier League (PL) clubs had fallen to foreign ownership:

Aston Villa	United States
Chelsea	Russia
Fulham	Egypt
Liverpool	United States
Manchester City	Thailand
Manchester United	United States
Portsmouth	Israel
Sunderland	Ireland
West Ham	Iceland

From a financial perspective, the most significant outcome of commercialisation has been the counterintuitive one: clubs today do not make profits.

---

[1] An indicator of the state of Britain's football stadia at the time is the fact that the first dedicated football stadium in senior football to be opened since the old Wembley Stadium was built in 1923 was as recently as August 1989 (McDiarmid Park, for St. Johnstone in Perth, Scotland). By 2008, eight of the English Premier League clubs had moved to entirely new stadia, with many of their fellow clubs planning to follow suit.

Table 14.3	Pretax Profit/Loss of English Clubs				
	2001–2002	**2002–2003**	**2003–2004**	**2004–2005**	**2005–2006**
Premier League	– £137m	– £153m	– £128m	– £78m	– £69m
Championship	– £36m	– £126m	– £47m	– £65m	– £47m
League 1	– £28m	– £34m	– £16m	– £13m	– £17m
League 2	– £3m	– £5m	– £4m	– £4m	– £4m
Total	– £204m	– £318m	– £195m	– £160m	– £137m

Source: Deloitte, 2003–2007.

As Table 14.3 shows, in a five-year period the 92 clubs in the top four tiers of English football managed to make a loss of £1,014,000—just over a billion pounds. By any standards, this shows an industry sector operating in a severely dysfunctional manner. To understand how this is possible in an era that, through commercialisation, might be expected to be achieving significant profits, it is necessary to review the change in cashflows that commercialisation has brought. These are shown in Figure 14.2.

From a fan's perspective, more money appears to be going into "the game." Not only does the fan now buy matchday tickets but also buys the multifarious versions of club shirts that seem endlessly to be produced, has to pay to watch the matches on television, and may be buying additional goods and services that have been marketed to him or her through various sponsorship arrangements with his or her club.

English football supporters also pay the highest prices to watch Premier League football on television, as reflected in the escalating prices secured by the PL for its broadcasting rights since its inception: £190 million 1992–1997; £670 million 1997–2001; £1.2 billion 2001–2004; £1.024 billion 2004–2007; £1706 billion 2007–2010; £1.782 billion 2010–2013 (Harris, 2009b).

For broadcasters, sports (and football in particular) became a major supplier. As a strategy to gain more control over their supply chain, broadcasters began in the nineties to buy shares in football clubs. In 1999, BSkyB launched a full-blown takeover bid for Manchester United but this was blocked by the Monopoly and Mergers Commission on the grounds that it was anti-competitive with respect to the Premier League broadcasting market (Monopoly and Mergers Commission, 1999).

If any time can be pinpointed as the time at which the commercialised era began in English football, it would be the secession of 22 clubs (shortly thereafter reduced to the present 20) from the Football League in 1992 to form the Premier League, a "new" Tier 1 League, and the concomitant selling

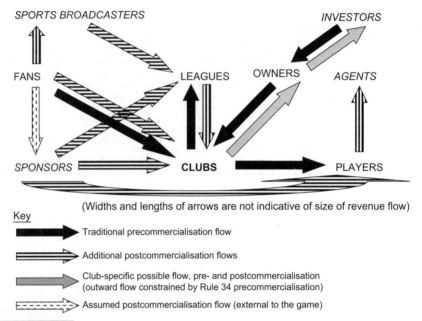

SPORTS BROADCASTERS

INVESTORS

FANS   LEAGUES   OWNERS   AGENTS

SPONSORS   **CLUBS**   PLAYERS

(Widths and lengths of arrows are not indicative of size of revenue flow)

Key

➤ Traditional precommercialisation flow

⇒ Additional postcommercialisation flows

➤ Club-specific possible flow, pre- and postcommercialisation
(outward flow constrained by Rule 34 precommercialisation)

⇢ Assumed postcommercialisation flow (external to the game)

FIGURE 14.2   *Main revenue flows in the commercialised era.*
Note: The pair of arrows from "fans" to "clubs" indicate the separate revenue flows from match tickets and from merchandising. The arrow between "fans" and "sponsors'" is hachured to indicate that the link is an assumed one and that this assumption may in practice be tenuous. It should also be noted that payments made by "sports broadcasters" are shown as being to "leagues." This varies across Europe, and, while this is correct for England, for example, it is not the case in Spain, Italy, and the Netherlands, where clubs have established their right to negotiate their broadcasting rights individually.

of the Premiership broadcasting rights to BSkyB. In 1988 the Football League television rights were sold for £44 million for a four-year period; in 1992 the Premier League rights were sold for £190 million for a five-year period. So significant has the revenue from broadcasting rights become to clubs that both the Premier League and, more recently, the Football League have felt it necessary to introduce parachute payments for clubs who are relegated, as the differential between revenues at different levels is increasingly large.

The growing scale of sponsorship, which draws fans in directly through the purchasing of shirts, has become more and more sophisticated in terms of who the sponsoring firms are. Where the sponsor in the late professionalised era, when shirt sponsorship began, was likely to be a local business, by 2008 it was far more likely to be a global business with little, if any, local association. Table 14.4 shows the shirt sponsors of Premier League clubs since its inception.

Table 14.4	English Premier League Shirt Sponsors (1992 to Date)	
Club	**2007–2008 Season Shirt Sponsor**	**Previous Sponsors (Not Historically Exhaustive)**
Arsenal	Emirates *UAE* (Airline)	2002–2006: O2 *UK* (Mobile network)) 1999–2002: SEGA Dreamcast *USA* (Video games consoles) 1982–1999: JVC *USA* (Consumer electronics)
Aston Villa	32Red *UK* (Online casino)	2005–2006: DWS *Germany* (Financial services) 2002–2005: MG Rover *Local UK* (Car manufacturer) 2000–2002: NTL *UK* (Telecomms cable provider) 1998–2000: LDV *Local UK* (Van manufacturer) 1995–1998: AST *USA* (Computer manufacturer) 1993–1995: Müller *Germany* (Dairy products) 1983–1993: Mita *Japan* (Photocopier manufacturer)
Birmingham City	F&C Investments *UK* (Investment group)	2003–2007: FlyBe *UK* (Airline) 2001–2003: Phones4U *UK* (Mobile phones) 1995–2001: Auto Windscreens *UK* (Windscreen replacements) 1992–1995: Triton Showers *UK* (Shower manufacturers)
Blackburn Rovers	Bet24 *European* (Online bookmaker)	1998–2006: HAS *UK* (Healthcare plans) 1996–1998: CIS *Local UK* (Financial services) 1991–1996: McEwan's Lager *UK* (Brewery)
Bolton Wanderers	Reebok *Germany (ex Local UK)* (Trainers)	1986–1990: Normid Superstore *Local UK* (Foods and furnishings superstore chain) 1983–1986: HB Electronics *USA* (Consumer electronics)
Chelsea	Samsung *Korea* (Electronics manufacturer))	2001–2005: Emirates *UAE* (Airline) 1997–2001: Autoglass *Local UK* (Windscreen replacements) 1995–1997: Coors *USA* (Brewery) 1989–1995: Commodore/Amiga *USA* (personal computers)

(Continued)

Table 14.4	English Premier League Shirt Sponsors (1992 to Date) (*continued*)	
Club	2007–2008 Season Shirt Sponsor	Previous Sponsors (Not Historically Exhaustive)
Derby County	Derbyshire Building Society *Local UK*	2001–2005: Pedigree *UK* (Brewery) 1998–2001: EDS *UK* (Business technology) 1995–1998: Puma *Germany* (Leisurewear) 1991–1995: Auto Windscreens *UK* (Windscreen replacements)
Everton	Chang Beer *Thailand* (Brewery)	2002–2004: Kejian *China* (Mobile phones) 1997–2002: One2One *UK* (Mobile phone service) 1995–1997: Danka *USA* (Copiers and printers) 1985–1995: NEC *Japan* (Conglomerate of manufacturing industries)
Fulham	LG *Korea* (Mobile phones)	2005–2007: Pipex *UK* (Internet service provider) 2003–2005: dabs.com *UK* (Internet shopping) 2002–2003: Betfair.com *Local UK* (Online bookmaker) 2001–2002: Pizza Hut *USA* (Franchised restaurants) 1998–2001: Demon Internet *Local UK* (Internet service provider) 1993–1998: GMB *Local UK* (Trade Union)
Liverpool	Carlsberg *Denmark* (Brewery)	1990–1992: Candy *Italy* (Electrical goods manufacturer) 1984–1990: Crown Paints *Local UK* (Paint manufacturer) 1977–1984: Hitachi *Japan* (Consumer electronics)
Manchester City	Thomas Cook *Germany (ex UK)* (Tour operator)	2002–2004: First Advice *UK* (Mortgage broker) 1999–2002: EIDOS *UK* (Video games) 1987–1999: Brother *USA* (Printers and fax machines)
Manchester United	AIG *USA* (US insurance company)	2000–2006: Vodafone *UK* (Mobile phones) 1982–2000: Sharp *USA* (Electronic goods)

Table 14.4	English Premier League Shirt Sponsors (1992 to Date) (*continued*)	
Club	**2007–2008 Season Shirt Sponsor**	**Previous Sponsors (Not Historically Exhaustive)**
Middlesbrough	Garmin *USA* (Sat-Nav manufacturers)	2004–2007: 888.com *Gibraltar* (Online casino) 2002–2004: Dial-a-Phone *UK* (Mobile phones retailer) 1995–2001: Cellnet/BT Cellnet *UK* (Mobile phone service) 1994–1995: Dickens *Local UK* (DIY retail) 1992–1994: ICI *Local UK* (Chemicals manufacturer)
Newcastle United	Northern Rock *UK* (Mortgage lender)	2000–2003: NTL *USA (ex UK)* (Internet broadband) 1990–2000: Scottish & Newcastle *Local UK* (Brewery)
Portsmouth	Oki *Japan* (Info-telecomms & printers manufacturer)	2002–2005: Ty *USA* (Toys) 2000–2002: Bishops Printers *Local UK* (Printers) 1999–2000: The Pompey Centre *Local UK* (Retail park) 1997–1999: KJC *Local UK* (Mobile phones sales and services) 1995–1997: The News *Local UK* (Newspaper publisher) 1985–1995: Goodmans *Local UK* (Hi-fi electronics goods manufacturers)
Reading	Kyocera *Japan* (Ceramics & electronics)	1999–2005: Westcoast *Local UK* (IT equipment distributor) 1992–1999 Autotrader *International with local UK HQ* (Car sales media)
Sunderland	Boylesports *Ireland* (Online betting)	1999–2007 Reg Vardy *Local UK* (Car sales) 1997–1999: Lambtons *Local UK* (Brewery)
Tottenham Hotspur	Mansion *Gibraltar* (Online casino)	2002–2006: Thomson *UK* (Tour operator) 1999–2002: Holsten *Germany* (Brewery) 1995–1999: Hewlett Packard *USA* (Computers and printers) 1983–1995: Holsten *Germany* (Brewery)

(*Continued*)

Table 14.4	English Premier League Shirt Sponsors (1992 to Date) *(continued)*	
Club	**2007–2008 Season Shirt Sponsor**	**Previous Sponsors (Not Historically Exhaustive)**
West Ham United	XL Leisure Group *UK* (Tour operators)	2003–2007: Jobserve.com *UK* (Internet recruitment) 1998–2003: Dr Martens *UK* (Boots manufacturer) 1993–1997: Dagenham Motors *Local UK* (Car dealer) 1989–1993: BAC Windows *Local UK* (Double glazing manufacturer)
Wigan Athletic	JJB Sports *UK* (Sports retailer)	1984–1994: Heinz *USA* (Food manufacturer) 1982–1983: Bulldog Tools *Local UK* (Gardening tools)

Note: Current sponsorships from club websites. Dates and previous sponsors developed from a variety of web sources including memorabilia sales sites including kitclassics.co.uk.

With considerable increases of money flowing into clubs, there has been a corresponding outflow of cash from clubs, principally in one-off payments to other clubs for the transfer of a player and in the associated wage paid to the player for the duration of the contract (unless the player is sold before the end of his contract). It is here that the major changes in a club's finances have occurred since the earlier restraints of the professionalised era have been lifted.

Dart (2000) gives some idea of the midterm impact these changes—both the abolition of the retain and transfer principle and the abolition of the maximum wage together with the increased commercialisation of the game—had on the labour market and on the finances of football clubs (see Table 14.5).

Table 14.5	Escalating Costs (Developed from Dart, 2000, using *Measuring Worth*[2])					
	1960s	**1990s**	**Factor**	**1960s @ 2007 value**	**1990s @ 2007 value**	**Adjusted Factor**
Top-division game: price to spectator	2/6	£25	200	*£1.74*	*£34.64*	*19.9*
Top-division player: weekly earnings	£20	£20,000	1,000	*£278.79*	*£27,713.04*	*99.4*
Transfer values: (Man Utd 1968 and 1999)	£110,000	£36.5m	330	*£1,375,089*	*£45.6m*	*33.2*

[2] *Calculated as purchasing power by* Measuring Worth *at* http://www.measuringworth.com/ppoweruk/?redirurl=calculators/ppoweruk/

The fact that ticket prices rose in the 30-year period by a factor of almost 200 and players' wages rose in the same period by a factor of almost 1000 should have rung alarm bells, notwithstanding the additional revenue flows from merchandising and broadcasting rights. Both the latter are affected to some extent by performance on the pitch, and are reduced as a result of relegation. Clubs however have been reluctant to try and impose player contracts that allow for the possibility of relegation and a reduced wage as a result. This has made those clubs that are relegated particularly vulnerable to becoming insolvent. Recent research (Beech et al., 2007) has begun to explore the worrying incidence of insolvency among English clubs. In the period 1986–2007 there had been 68 instances (involving 56 clubs; some clubs have become insolvent more than once) of clubs going into administration, the legal process of seeking protection from a company's creditors. Figure 14.3 shows how these incidences have varied since 1986.

While the collapse of ITV Digital, a purchaser of Football League broadcasting rights, in 2002 has had some impact on the number of clubs becoming insolvent, it is clear that there are other major factors involved.

Poor performance on the pitch and relegation impact not only a club's finances; they impact at the level of the key person in the club's organisational structure: the manager. Research by Bridgewater (2006, page 21), covering a period from 1992 to 2005, makes clear just how vulnerable managers are, and how uncertain their world of employment is. She found that while Premier League managers were *relatively* safe in their jobs, those

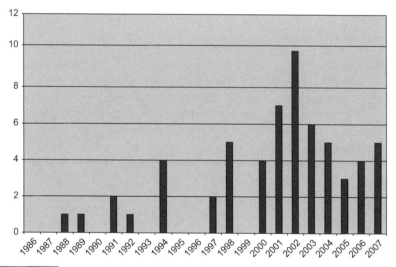

FIGURE 14.3 *Occurrences of insolvency among English football clubs by season start.*
Source: (Beech et al, 2008, page 7)

in the next three tiers, especially Tier 4, were at a higher risk of being sacked. A main conclusion of her study was that "the rate of management change in football shows a high level of instability and change which has a damaging effect on the industry both in terms of cost (legal fees and settlements amount to many millions of £s during this period) and … on the success of clubs." She also found that "the average tenure of managers has declined from an average of 2.72 years to 1.72 years over the period."

Given the significance that transfer fees and wage bills have on the overall financial state of a club, some have introduced the new appointment of Director of Football. The person who is appointed in this role is a member of the Board of Directors and is charged with the responsibility of overseeing transfers and the contractual agreements that go with them. This can be a source of conflict as the two roles of Director of Football and Manager may not be so clearly separated in practice, as Case Study 14.2 illustrates.

CASE STUDY 14.2: Harry Redknapp

Harry Redknapp, born in 1947, began his career as a footballer with the youth team at West Ham United. After seven years at West Ham, where he made 149 first-team appearances, he moved to AFC Bournemouth for four years, followed by spells with Brentford and the Seattle Sounders in the now defunct North American Soccer League.

In 1982 he returned to Bournemouth as Assistant Manager. A year later, Redknapp was promoted to manager with the team struggling in the old Third Division. He showed his potential as a manager by taking Bournemouth into the Second Division in 1987. By 1990 the team had been relegated and Redknapp, reportedly disillusioned by the lack of funds to build his team with, resigned in 1992.

Returning to a club from his playing days once more, Redknapp joined West Ham as assistant manager, and in 1994 again was promoted to manager. His period at West Ham resulted in a very successful youth scheme, developing players such as Michael Carrick, Joe Cole, Jermain Defoe, Rio Ferdinand, and Frank Lampard. West Ham enjoyed a strong spell under his hand, consolidating their position in the Premier League and, in 2000, winning the Inter Toto Cup. However, in 2001, following some injudicious comments about the Chairman made to a fanzine, Redknapp left abruptly.

Within a few months Redknapp was appointed Director of Football at Portsmouth, which was then struggling in the old Division 1 (English football's second tier). Portsmouth's manager, Graham Rix, was sacked by the Chairman, Milan Mandaric, in March 2002, and Redknapp's impact was immediate.

Redknapp began by bringing in older established players such as Paul Merson and, subsequently, Teddy Sherringham, a move that pleased the fans; plus some players from his former club, West Ham, and other talented but not at the time so well-known players such as Yakubu Ayegbeni. He was joined by Jim Smith as Assistant Manager. At the end of the 2002–2003 season Portsmouth won the race for the second flight title and Redknapp won the League Managers' Association Manager of the Year award.

The 2003–2004 season was a difficult one, as it always is for a club moving up to the top flight. Portsmouth faced some serious long-term injury problems, but Redknapp spent money wisely, bringing in both established players such as Eyal Berkovic and also talented younger players such as Lomano Tresor LuaLua. The end of the season saw a good run for the club and they stayed up, finishing thirteenth, one place behind Southampton, Portsmouth's local rivals. The highlight of the season had been the drubbing of Leeds United 6-1.

However, things were not so rosy off the pitch, as tensions were reportedly growing between Mandaric and Redknapp. Mandaric was reported as being unhappy with Jim Smith in the role of assistant manager and that he wanted to bring in a coach in a role more familiar in continental Europe. Redknapp was fiercely loyal to his assistant and no changes took place.

The 2004–2005 season started unspectacularly for Portsmouth on the pitch. Fans had started to assume that off-the-pitch tensions were diminishing, but a series of events were about to unfold which made clear that this was a false assumption.

On November 11, 2004, Mandaric had a meeting with Velimir Zajic, Director of Football with Greek side Panathinaikos. Reportedly, Redknapp said, "I've not seen the manager/director of football link-up work, and we don't know each other. ... You tell me one time in England when a manager and a director of football combination has worked [perhaps forgetting that he joined Portsmouth as Director of Football, a role he held for five months before replacing Rix as Manager]." Mandaric responded, "I don't know why he would be upset, it wouldn't jeopardise his position but make it stronger."

On November 14, 2004, Mandaric was reported to be interviewing for the post of director of football. He said, "I do not think Harry Redknapp will leave; he will have no reason to. When we talk, he will find out we are enhancing the quality of the club. ... We are helping Harry with his job. He will be in control; he will still be responsible for players. The final word will be Harry's; no one is taking that away from him." Redknapp had earlier indicated he would leave if Mandaric did bring a director of football to the club, saying, "I think you know I'm a football manager, and if I'm not in control, I'm not here, am I? The chairman said he is looking to bring someone onto the board who knows about football. I'm a football manager. I've got Jim Smith, who is 60-odd years of age and a football manager. Do you really think we need someone to tell us what to do?" Mandaric, added that a director of football was necessary if the club were to continue to move forward. "Bringing a director of football onto the board who is responsible for football is a great addition."

On November 16, 2004, "peace talks" were reported as having taken place. Although Zajec had been offered the role of executive director and a seat on the Portsmouth Board, Redknapp commented, "My responsibility will be exactly the same, and I've been assured he [Zajec] will not cut across my job in any shape or form. ... The chairman has assured me that I'm completely in charge of my own job. It's fine with me. We need someone to have a look at players abroad we could follow up on, and he will recommend players we can have a look at by scouting abroad. But no players will come in without my approval." Later that day Redknapp was quoted as saying that he had came close to quitting. However, he had been able to add Joe Jordan to his coaching staff of Jim Smith and Kevin Bond.

On November 19, 2004, Redknapp briefed the press, saying, "I have felt unwanted over the last week or so and I would be a liar if I said otherwise. I thought I was being manipulated out. The chairman has promised me my role would not change. ... I buy the players and I pick the team and if someone else comes in and starts trying to get involved in those things there will be some aggravation. You can only believe what people tell you and I do not want to walk away. I love it here."

On November 24, 2004, despite the earlier reports, Redknapp announced his resignation, and Jim Smith, his assistant, was reported as being ready to leave too. Redknapp claimed his decision was nothing to do with the Zajec issue, adding, "It is something I have been thinking about for a while. I made it without any pressure from the chairman or the board. ... I will now spend a short period of time to rest, recharge my batteries before contemplating my future. I would like to place on record my sincere thanks to the chairman and his board for their support, to the players and all the supporters who have been absolutely fantastic to me and the club during my time at Portsmouth FC." Mandaric issued a statement saying, "Harry and I remain great friends. I have tremendous admiration and respect for where he has taken this club—a feat several managers before him could not get near to. ... People will obviously make their own minds up and say that Harry has stepped down for the reasons that have been intensely speculated over in the media. That could not be further from the truth but then the speculations were pretty wide of the mark also. The truth is Harry sees this as a perfect opportunity to bow out."

On November 24, 2004, the Portsmouth players were reported to be "devastated" by the departure of Redknapp and, shortly afterward, Smith.

On November 25, 2004, Portsmouth was reported to be looking for a new manager. Names suggested by the press as being under consideration included Glenn Hoddle and Gordon Strachan, both ex-Southampton managers. The BBC suggested that neither would be popular choices with Portsmouth fans. BBC journalist and Portsmouth fan Neville Dalton posted an article in the *BBC Sport* website (Dalton, 2004) pointing out that fans needed to be aware of the significance of Mandaric in the recent history of the club, while at the same time acknowledging the importance of Redknapp's role in bringing the club up to the Premiership.

On November 27, 2004, the "war of words" entered a new phase. At a press conference, Mandaric pointed out that "Portsmouth spent £3 million on agents' fees during Harry Redknapp's time as manager"; admitted he would be "disappointed if Redknapp made a quick return to football management after saying he wanted a break from the game," adding that "[Redknapp] told me he wanted to spend more time with his wife and their family, and I have to accept he's telling the truth. If he ends up at Wolves or Southampton, I would be very disappointed with him, but right now I believe he needs some rest."

Later that day he distanced himself from this report, saying that Redknapp had not been involved in financial aspects of transfers and had been entirely honest and straightforward.

On November 28, 2004, Jim Smith stated that the appointment of Zajec was "the last straw" for Redknapp. He also accused Mandaric of conducting his business through the media in a reference to the events of the previous day. Nevertheless, he also played down—but carefully did not dismiss totally—speculation linking Redknapp and himself to Southampton, where Steve Wigley, the manager, was struggling to find success on the pitch.

On November 30, 2004, Mandaric called a press conference with Harry Redknapp present. In it he [Mandaric] clarified his position, which was against the scale at which agents take money out of the game, and reiterated that, "Harry was never involved at any time in any transfer and contract negotiations throughout his period at the club. And at no time did I ever imply that there was any wrong doing by Harry Redknapp in these transactions."

By early December, things seemed to have quietened down, and Mandaric repeated his support for Zajec, who had taken over as manager temporarily; the appointment of a new manager was to be expected.

On December 8, Southampton announced that Harry Redknapp was replacing Steve Wigley as Southampton manager. He was joined by Kevin Bond and subsequently Jim Smith, leaving only Joe Jordan still on the coaching staff at Portsmouth. Rupert Lowe, the Southampton chairman, insisted that talks had only begun two days previously.

Redknapp has commented (Dawe, 2007) on this period:

> I had a great time at Portsmouth first time around.
> I walked in and took over a team that had finished
> fourth from bottom in The Championship, and from
> day one we won our first game and never looked
> back. We were fantastic. Then I really made a bad
> decision. Not that Southampton are not a good club,
> it's terrific. But I dived into it a little bit without
> realising the bad feeling between the two clubs.

His spell with Southampton was also one dogged by club politics. Rupert Lowe insisted on bringing in Sir Clive Woodward, who had no football experience but had a distinguished track record as a coach at international level in Rugby Union, as Southampton's Performance Director.

Velimir Zajic took over at Portsmouth as caretaker manager, but in April 2005, he was replaced by Alain Perrin. Perrin's career with Portsmouth was unspectacular and on November 24, 2005 Mandaric sacked him. Portsmouth then approached their rivals Southampton for permission to talk to Redknapp. When this was refused, he resigned from Southampton and on December 7, following much speculation, it was announced that Harry Redknapp was returning to Portsmouth. The following month Alexander Gaydamak became co-owner of Portsmouth with Mandaric, becoming sole owner in July 2006. With fresh capital available to build the team, Redknapp brought renewed success to the team, leaving them firmly in the top half of the Premier League and, for the first time since 1939, the winners of the FA Cup, and hence on the verge of European football for the first time in the club's history.

In October 2008 Redknapp moved to Tottenham Hotspur, taking Portsmouth's first-team coach, Joe Jordan, with him.

The only cloud on Redknapp's horizon is a continuing enquiry into his transfer dealings. Bower (2003), in a book subtitled *Vanity, Greed and the Souring of British Football*, includes a chapter on Redknapp's transfer dealings over a long period, and, at the time of writing, Redknapp was still subject to a police investigation into alleged tax irregularities centring on a small number of specific transfers. All suggestions of any improper dealing or conflict of interest are strenuously denied by Redknapp.

Question

1. A director of football is an appointment at the board level of a football club. Are clashes between a director of football and a club's manager, an employee not on the Board of Directors, inevitable?

Source: various, *BBC.co.uk/sport*

The potential for confusion and conflict between the two post-holders is well illustrated by the appointment of Dennis Wise as director of football at Newcastle United (*BBC Sport*, 2008; see also McKenzie, 2004).

WOMEN'S FOOTBALL

If the men's game offers a picture of a management scenario full of uncertainty and with cause for concern for its future, the picture is as worrying, and arguably more worrying, in the women's game. One of the less well-known outcomes of England's hosting of and success in the 1966 World Cup was a revival of interest in the women's game. This led ultimately to the formation of the Women's FA three years later, and in 1972, the FA, acting under pressure from UEFA, finally lifted its ban on women playing on Football League grounds. It was not until 1992, however, that a partly professional league was established and operated alongside the men's game in that at the senior level men's clubs have parallel women's teams. As a result, the women's game is vulnerable to the problems within the men's game. In 2007 one of the more successful women's teams, Charlton Athletic LFC, was disbanded as part of a cost-cutting exercise following the relegation of the men's team. In defending the decision to close the women's team, Charlton Athletic pointed to the failure to achieve significant sponsorship deals or broadcasting rights contracts in the women's game (Varney, 2007).

CONCLUSIONS

English football has been experiencing instability due to commercialisation, and only in the last decade is the game beginning to try and come to terms with a post-commercialised phase. At the level of the Premier League, the game has adapted to the business needs of being a sector of the entertainment industry, a situation that is not readily accepted by the fans, or, as the clubs should now see them, the customers. The adaptation has not been entirely successful however. While spending the new revenue streams has been all too easy, controlling costs to ensure a profit, however small, has proved extremely difficult.

Those that call for the re-imposition of a maximum wage ignore the fact that such a measure would only be possible if there was a fundamental change to European law, a change that is most unlikely to happen. An alternative approach is the notion of a salaries (note the plural!) cap. Michel Platini (Harris, 2009a), the president of UEFA, has suggested that clubs be limited to spending a fixed percentage of their revenues on salaries, the limit being of the order of 50 to 60 percent. (By way of comparison, this is the sort of percentage that universities—another kind of organisation where the skills and talents of their employees are the organisation's chief asset and source of competitive advantage—spend on the salaries of academics.) The downside of such a proposal is that it would tend to reinforce the divide between rich clubs and poor clubs, thus making it even less likely that an attractive level of competitive balance would reappear in English football. As in other areas of the game, much will depend on governance from outside England, both in the form of European law and UEFA regulations. In particular, much will depend on the outcome of the debate following on from the publication of the European Union's White Paper on Sport with its discussion of the 'specificity' of sport (Commission of the European Communities, 2007). It seems unlikely that it will lead to a change in European Law, which would allow the plan of Sepp Blatter, president of FIFA, to introduce his "6+5 quota" rule (six home nationals plus five foreign players). Nevertheless, the dominance of the multinational teams of the "Big Four"—Arsenal, Chelsea, Liverpool, and Manchester United—remain a serious problem with respect to both the lack of success of the England football team and in the way it negatively affects competitive balance in the Champions' League.

The future for English football can be characterised by high levels of change and uncertainty. This does not necessarily mean that there will be no measure of stability, only that any equilibrium will be dynamic rather than static. Risk assessment will certainly become a necessity in management's decision making process.

DISCUSSION QUESTIONS

1. England was the first nation to embrace commercialisation fully at the highest levels of the football sector of its sport industry. Is this a claim to fame or a claim to infamy?

2. The present cashflows within the sector lead to money passing out of "the game" and into the pockets of players, agents and, at least in theory, club owners. How might this be stopped without invoking "restraint of trade" among players and potential breaches of European competition and employment law?

3. The organisational structure of many English clubs might be argued to be dysfunctional. What organisational structure would best meet the needs of the various stakeholders in the game?

4. Is it right that sports broadcasters should not be allowed to control their supply chains, as in other industries, by buying football clubs?

5. What exemptions to current law should be allowed under a principle of the "specificity'" of sport?

GUIDED READING

Several texts provide an insight into football management in the professionalised era. Particularly recommended are Inglis (1988), Tischler (1981), and Douglas (1973).

Among a host of books on English football since commercialisation, relatively few stretch beyond attacking the fact that clubs are businesses. Significant exceptions, and strongly recommended, are Bower (2003), Hamil et al. (1999), Hamil et al. (2000), and Morrow (1999).

A thorough history of the football manager in England is provided by Carter (2006), covering the whole period from the game's origins to the present day. The Deloitte *Annual Reviews of Football Finance* are a very useful resource for sports management researchers and students. A thorough generic background to the study of management in sport is provided by Beech and Chadwick (2004).

REFERENCES

BBC Sport. www.bbc.co.uk/sport

BBC Sport (1st February, 2008). Wise explains role at Newcastle. *BBC Sport*. Retrieved on July 17, 2009, from http://news.bbc.co.uk/sport1/hi/football/teams/n/newcastle_united/7223479.stm

Beech, J. (2004). Introduction: The Commercialisation of Sport. In: *The Business of Sport Management*. Beech, J. & Chadwick, S. Harlow: Pearson Education.

Beech, J. & Chadwick, S. (2004). *The Business of Sport Management*. Harlow: Pearson.

Beech, J., Horsman, S., & Magraw, J. (2008). *The circumstances in which English football clubs become insolvent*, Working Paper Series No.4. Centre for the International Business of Sport: Coventry University.

Beech, J., Horsman, S., & Magraw, J. (2007). The Football Association's (and the Scottish Football Association's) changed view of financial difficulty. *Proceedings of Challenges facing Football in the 21st Century*. Reykjavik: Play the Game.

Bower, T. (2003). *Broken Dreams: Vanity, Greed and the Souring of British Football*. London: Simon & Schuster.

Bridgewater, S. (2006). *An Analysis of Football Management Trends 1992–2005 in all Four Divisions*. League Managers' Association and Warwick Business School, Coventry.

Carter, N. (2006). *The Football Manager: A History*. Abingdon: Routledge.

Commission of the European Communities. (2007). *White Paper on Sport*. Brussels: European Commission.

Dalton, N. (25th November, 2004). Harry's farwell is not the end. *BBC Sport*. Retrieved on July 17, 2009, from http://news.bbc.co.uk/sport1/hi/football/teams/p/portsmouth/4041561.stm

Dart, T. (2000). Playing in a different League. In *Football in the Digital Age: Whose game is it anyway?*. Hamil, S., Michie, J., Oughton, C. & Warby, S. (Eds.). Edinburgh: Mainstream.

Dawe, J. C. (2007). Saints: A Bad Decision. Retrieved on March 24, 2008, from http://sport.setanta.com/en/Sport/News/Football/2007/10/26/Premier-League-Redknapp-on-Friday-Football-Show-0012357/

Deloitte. (2002–2007). *Annual Review of Football Finance*. Manchester: Deloitte.

Douglas, P. (1973). *The Football Industry*. London: George Allen & Unwin.

Hamil, S., Michie, J., & Oughton, C. (1999). *The Business of Football. A Game of Two Halves?* Edinburgh: Mainstream.

Harris, N. (19th February, 2009a). Platini warns of "impending implosion". *The Independent*. Retrieved on August 3, 2009, from http://www.independent.co.uk/sport/football/news-and-comment/platini-warns-of-impending-implosion-1625713.html

Harris, N. (7th February, 2009b). £1.78bn: Record Premier League TV Deal defies economic slump. *The Independent*. Retrieved on July 17, 2009, from http://www.independent.co.uk/sport/football/premier-league/163178bn-record-premier-league-tv-deal-defies-economic-slump-1569576.html

Hamil, S., Michie, J., Oughton, C., & Warby, S. (2000). *Football in the Digital age: Whose Game Is it Anyway?* Edinburgh: Mainstream.

Hill, J. (1998). *The Jimmy Hill Story*. London: Hodder & Stoughton.

Inglis, S. (1988). *League Football And The Men Who Made It: The Official Centenary History of the Football League 1888–1988*. London: Willow Books.

McArdle, D. (2000). One Hundred Years of Servitude: Contractual Conflict in English Professional Football before Bosman. *Web Journal of Current Legal Issues*. Vol. 2. Retrieved on July 16, 2009, from http://webjcli.ncl.ac.uk/2000/issue2/mcardle2.html

McKenzie, A. (24th November, 2004). The Director of Football Debate. *BBC Sport*. Retrieved on July 17, 2009, from http://news.bbc.co.uk/sport1/hi/football/4015605.stm

Monopoly and Mergers Commission. (1999). *British Sky Broadcasting Group plc and Manchester United plc*. London: Competition Commission.

Morrow, S. (1999). *The New Business of Football: Accountability and finance in football*. Basingstoke: Macmillan Business.

Samuels, J. (2008). *The Beautiful Game is Over*. Brighton: Book Guild Publishing.

Spurling, J. (2004). *Rebels for the Cause: The alternative history of Arsenal Football Club*. Edinburgh: Mainstream.

Tischler, S. (1981). *Footballers and Businessmen*. London: Holmes & Meier.

Inquiry by the Rt Hon Lord Justice Taylor (1990). *The Hillsborough Stadium Disaster: Final Report*. Cm962. HMSO

Varney, P. (26th June, 2007). Door still ajar for threatened women's team. *Charlton Athletic*. Retrieved on July 17, 2009, from http://www.cafc.co.uk/newsview.ink?nid=30951&newstype=l

RECOMMENDED WEBSITES

A useful website for keeping up with developments in English football management is The Political Economy of Football:

http://www.footballeconomy.com/.

BBC Sport

www.bbc.co.uk/sport

The Football Association:

http://www.thefa.com/

The Football League:

http://www.football-league.co.uk/

The League Managers' Association:

http://www.leaguemanagers.com/

The Premier League:

http://www.premierleague.com/

The Professional Footballers' Association:

http://www.givemefootball.com/

To follow developments in fans' engagement with the management of clubs, visit the Supporters Direct website:

http://www.supporters-direct.org/home.asp?country=engwal,

To monitor individual clubs see the Clubs in Crisis website:

http://www.clubsincrisis.com/.

CHAPTER 15

Spain

Carlos Martí
CSBM—IESE Business School, University of Navarra

Ignacio Urrutia
Nebrija University

Ángel Barajas
University of Vigo

Objectives

Upon completion of this chapter the reader should be able to:

- Know the structure of the national-level competitions in Spain.
- Distinguish between the roles of the Spanish Football Federation, the League, and the individual clubs.
- Understand the peculiarities of Spanish football.
- Recognize the key elements of the football business in Spain.
- Gain insights into future trends and perceptions of the sector as viewed by the top management of the most powerful Spanish clubs.

CONTENTS

OVERVIEW OF THE CHAPTER

This chapter provides an overview of professional football in Spain, with particular emphasis on those distinctive aspects that characterize it. First, we present the main data on football in Spain and the competitions in which the Spanish clubs participate at national level. Then we will describe the role of the Professional Football League (*la Liga Nacional de Fútbol Profesional*; "LNFP" or LFP or *La Liga*) and the economic implications of competitions for the clubs. Following that is an overview of the main business activities of the football clubs in Spain. To achieve this, we have decided to show the earnings and expenses of one of the wealthiest clubs (FC Barcelona), one of the middle-ranking clubs (Getafe FC), and one that, despite having played in the UEFA Champions League, was relegated to the second division (Real Club Celta de Vigo). We also detail some peculiarities of football clubs in Spain, concerning the possible ways of exploiting the income potential of their stadia. The chapter concludes with the future challenges faced by Spanish football as seen through the strategic visions of the two leading—in both financial and sporting terms—clubs in Spain: Real Madrid C.F. and F.C. Barcelona.

INTRODUCTION

Football in Spain is a significant economic activity (Ascari & Gagnepain, 2006) and matches are well-attended (Garcia & Rodriquez, 2002). A survey by the LNFP (LNFP 2004; *Noticias*, 2004) estimated that it made a contribution of approximately €4 billion to the economy, representing some 0.9% of GDP; providing direct and indirect employment to nearly 66,000 people. Spain's top division, known as La Liga, had the fourth highest average attendances at league games in Europe in the 2007/2008 season (Deloitte, 2009, page 14), and the third largest collective revenues from TV broadcasting (Deloitte, 2009, page 13), a reflection of the extraordinary popularity of televised Spanish football in Spain.

These are just a few of the numbers that demonstrate the sheer size of football in Spain and give an idea of how much of a social phenomenon it is, going way beyond the match or even the sport. According to statistics in a 2004 survey (Fundes & LFP), 90 percent of Spanish fans believed that football is an "agent for social integration," and 63 percent considered that clubs fulfill a social function of promoting sport among young people. For 69 percent of the fans, football allowed the blending of different social and cultural identities. Furthermore, 73 percent of the fans considered that the clubs represented the towns or cities in which they were located, while almost half considered the players as ambassadors of the values held locally to the area they inhabited.

This chapter focuses on the competitions and the professional football clubs, leaving aside the national squad. It is worth noting here that there is, arguably, a higher priority given to the clubs than to the national team, and this can be explained by a number of reasons: the poor results of the national team in international competitions until its success is winning the EURO

2008 tournament, the local clubs' greater capacity to animate their fans, and the greater potential *competitive continuity* of the local clubs compared to the national team (Llopis, 2006). Let's now examine the official football tournaments in Spain.

TOURNAMENTS IN SPAIN

In Spain, all the official football tournaments at state level come under the authority of the RFEF, the Spanish Football Association. A professional football club may participate in the following official competitions: the League of the First and Second Divisions, the Spanish Cup (The King's Cup), and the "Supercup" (played by the winners of the previous season's League and King's Cup).

The league championship is a recurring competition, every season. The teams that comprise the league play one another twice during the season, once at home and once away. Each team is awarded points for the result and the accumulated total determines each club's position in the competition. The current classification system in the Spanish national league depends on the points obtained; three points for a win, one for a draw, and nothing for a loss.

With the current configuration of 20 teams in the First Division (and 22 in the Second), each team in the First Division plays 38 games; 19 home and 19 away. This means that, in the league championship, each team has a guaranteed gate income of 19 matches for the First Division and 21 for the Second.

To 2007/2008, there had been 77 league championships, but only 9 teams had won the title; 3 of them having done so only once. As may be seen in Table 15.1, the concentration of the League champions is extremely high. The accumulated percentage shown in the table demonstrates that Barcelona and Real Madrid had won 63.6 percent of the championships between them, and if we add Atlético de Madrid then three teams represented 75 percent. Finally, if we add Athletic de Bilbao and Valencia, then these 5 teams represented 93.5 percent of the league victories.

The increasing wealth generated by football could be the cause of the increasing imbalance in the competition. Participation in international competitions explains, at least in part, the large amount of money obtained by just a few clubs. Furthermore, the existence of an elite international competition, such as the UEFA Champions League, automatically creates an imbalance in the national competitions (Gómez et al, 2008).

The second competition in which the professional clubs participate is the Spanish Cup, also known as the King's Cup or, simply, the Cup. This is

Table 15.1	League Champions up to the season 2007–2008	
Team	N° Leagues Won	% Accumulated Leagues
Real Madrid	31	40.3
FC Barcelona	18	63.6
Atlético de Madrid	9	75.3
Athletic de Bilbao	8	85.7
Valencia CF	6	93.5
Real Sociedad	2	96.1
Sevilla FC	1	97.4
Deportivo de la Coruña	1	98.7
Betis	1	100.0

Source: LFP

competed for on an elimination basis. There is a preliminary phase in which lower-ranked teams take part. The final match is played on neutral ground, and there is only one playoff.

The takings from the single-match elimination rounds—after deducting the referees' fees, taxes, and costs of ground and ticket staff —is split 50-50 between the two contending teams. The impact of the money that the professional clubs receive from this competition is minimal. Indeed, it is the other considerations, such as prestige and, above all, a way-in to European competitions, since the winner has the right to participate in the Europa League, that justify the costs incurred by the professional clubs.

Finally, the Supercup pitches the winner of the King's Cup against the champion of the League First Division in a competition of two matches between those two teams, the games falling under the auspices of the RFEF.

THE NATIONAL PROFESSIONAL FOOTBALL LEAGUE (LNFP)

The law governing sport in Spain (España, 1990) allows for other entities besides clubs, called intermediaries, created for the organization of sporting activities. Perhaps the most important of these entities are the Federations; in the case of football, this is the *Real Federación Española de Fútbol*, the Spanish Football Association, whose objective is the management of footballing interests. This law also instituted the so-called Professional Leagues, which monitor and regulate their affiliates in the professional leagues. The Leagues' function exclusively within the ambit of the Association. The objective of the National Professional Football League (LNFP) is the organisation and promotion of official professional competition of national level, as well as the commercial exploitation of the same.

This sports law also created the entities known as the SADs, *Sociedades Anónimas Deportivas*, Sporting Limited Companies, by which the business activities of those sporting clubs participating in competitions are recognized. The clubs constitute the basic business unit in the football industry, but at the same time, the Leagues, through their indispensable role of coordinators and with the cooperation of the clubs, make sporting competitions—the product offering—possible and thus they acquire a higher profile (Bertomeu, 1995).

The SADs tend to be governed by an administrative collective known as *Consejo de Administración*, the Board of Directors. Just as the General Shareholders' Meeting is the highest decision-making body for a company, the Board of Directors is in charge of running the company that is the club. The board functions as a body, but it typically grants powers to specific members to enable a more agile management style. *La Junta Directiva*, the Board of Directors, is the equivalent in clubs that are not SADs. In Spain, there are just four clubs—Real Madrid, Barcelona, Athletic de Bilbao and Osasuna—which have maintained their legal status as sporting clubs and are, therefore, not SADs.

As another prerequisite of being part of the League, the SADs and the other four clubs must comply with certain requirements (Rodríguez, 2007). One of these specifies that the sporting clubs or SADs, in order to participate in the national championship of the professional league, must be in possession of the sporting "right," a certification recognized by the RFEF, as well as meeting certain economic, social and infrastructure requirements established by the LNFP.

THE FOOTBALL BUSINESS IN SPAIN

The business of football in Spain does not differ much from the model developed in other European leagues. However, there are some significant differences in the management of the clubs' principal sources of income, costs and investments. There are also some differences between the models developed by the larger clubs and those of the smaller clubs. Some of the differentiating elements of Spanish football have a legal origin, and others historic. In particular, it is worth explaining, in some detail, the negotiation of television rights, contributions from public institutions, and the ownership and uses of the stadia (the existence of the different SADs and clubs has already been explained, and therefore needs no further treatment here).

It is a key point that Spanish law has recognized that the clubs are the copyright owners of their images and televised matches. The result of this is that each club can individually and independently negotiate the broadcasting rights to each of their home games (Martialay, 1996; Palomar & Descalzo, 2001). This business model is radically different to that usually found in other countries where the league is recognized as the copyright owner of the competition as a whole, and negotiates broadcasting rights on a collective basis on behalf of member clubs, which typically (for example in the English Premier League) means there is a more egalitarian distribution of broadcasting income than in leagues such as in Spain, and Italy, where rights are individually negotiated.

Nevertheless, there is the contradiction in Spain that the least economically-powerful clubs have a greater dependency on the television income than the larger clubs do. Figure 15.1 clearly illustrates the relative importance of television income for a small club such as Getafe compared to a large one such as Barcelona. While it represents some 45 percent for the former, this figure is only 32.8 percent for the latter. That said, when we look at the figures in absolute terms then the income for a club like Barcelona, which also regularly plays in the Champions League, shoots up exponentially. For instance, in the 2004–2005 season, Getafe's income was some €6.8 million, while Barcelona's exceeded €81 million.

From an income point of view, one of the most dramatic changes for a First Division club is to be relegated to the Second Division; the income they can expect is far, far lower than in the First. Celta de Vigo (2005) is an example; they played in the Second Division in the 2004-05 season, and the income generated by television rights amounted to a little over €2 million. Contrast this with the almost €24 million they had received the previous season while playing in the First Division and the UEFA Champions League. As a consequence of the loss of such an important income stream, clubs have to maximize other income sources. The sale of players as a club is relegated is a necessary evil which, as well as representing a lump-sum income for the transfer, can also help to alleviate the salary costs. It is for this reason that Celta de Vigo's sale of television rights only represented 5.7 percent of the total income, while the extraordinary income (principally generated by the sale of players) represented 55.3 percent.

It is common to find clubs receiving public assistance, with public institutions regularly supporting their local clubs; in some cases directly in the form of financial subsidies. Getafe, for example, received more

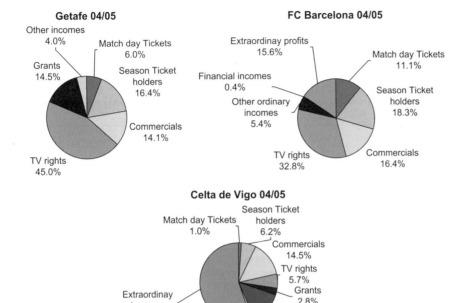

Getafe 04/05
- Other incomes 4.0%
- Match day Tickets 6.0%
- Grants 14.5%
- Season Ticket holders 16.4%
- Commercials 14.1%
- TV rights 45.0%

FC Barcelona 04/05
- Extraordinay profits 15.6%
- Match day Tickets 11.1%
- Financial incomes 0.4%
- Other ordinary incomes 5.4%
- Season Ticket holders 18.3%
- Commercials 16.4%
- TV rights 32.8%

Celta de Vigo 04/05
- Match day Tickets 1.0%
- Season Ticket holders 6.2%
- Commercials 14.5%
- TV rights 5.7%
- Grants 2.8%
- Other ordinary incomes 13.4%
- Financial incomes 1.1%
- Extraordinay incomes 55.3%

FIGURE 15.1 *Income distribution (2004–2005 season).*
Source: Barajas, 2007; Celta de Vigo (2005); FC Barcelona (2005); Getafe CF SAD (2005).

than €2.2 million in the 2004–2005 season, representing 14.5 percent of their income, while Celta de Vigo received almost €1 million in the same period, but in their case it represented only 2.8 percent of their income for the season.

Another differentiating element in Spanish football is the ownership of the stadia (García & Rodríguez, 2003). Many teams play in municipal football grounds and, of course, this is more common among the lower-income clubs. Table 15.2 shows the First Division clubs of the 2007–2008 season, the name and ownership of the stadium in which they play, and the attendance figures. It is worth noting that more than half of them play in municipal stadia, but it is also significant that the clubs with higher average matchday attendance all own their own stadia. In general, this latter phenomenon also coincides with the clubs being the most powerful, from both the financial and sporting points of view.

The fact that the clubs do not have to invest in their sporting installations means, in theory, that they are able to use their funds to invest in players instead. Nevertheless, it also implies that the clubs' ability to exploit their stadium in other ways is limited. For this reason, Espanyol, for instance, is

Table 15.2 Stadia of the First Division Clubs (2007–2008)

Club	Stadium	Capacity	Average Attendance	Owner
Barcelona	Camp Nou	98,772	74,138	Club
Real Madrid	Santiago Bernabéu	80,000	63,808	Club
Atlético de Madrid	Vicente Calderón	54,851	52,000	Club
Valencia	Mestalla	55,000	45,000	Club
Sevilla	Ramón Sánchez Pizjuán	45,500	42,649	Club
Athletic de Bilbao	San Mamés	40,000	33,726	Club
Betis	Manuel Ruiz de Lopera	55,000	33,000	Club
Zaragoza	La Romareda	34,596	31,000	Council
Deportivo	Riazor	34,600	29,716	Council
Espanyol	Olímpico Lluis Companys	56,000	24,300	Council
Levante	Ciutat de Valencia	25,354	18,000	Club
Recreativo de Huelva	Nuevo Colombino	20,694	18,000	Council
Racing de Santander	Campos de Sport del Sardinero	22,251	17,500	Council
Mallorca	Ono Estadi	23,142	16,343	Council
Osasuna	Reyno de Navarra	19,800	15,200	Club
Murcia	Nueva Condomina	31,179	15,000	Council
Villarreal	El Madrigal	21,700	14,500	Council
Valladolid	Municipal José Zorrilla	26,512	13,042	Council
Almeria	Juegos Mediterraneos	22,000	12,000	Council
Getafe	Coliseum Alfonso Pérez	17,000	10,000	Council

Source: LFP

building a new stadium, despite having played for over a decade in the Barcelona council-owned Olímpico Lluis Companys Stadium.

Clubs have long known how to obtain profit from real estate operations. The reclassification of the grounds (in terms of valuation in their financial accounts) where the stadia are located has enabled them to obtain funds to construct new stadia or simply to get their accounts back in the black. This is what Real Madrid did when it famously sold its building rights on the *Ciudad Deportiva*—Sport City—training ground where now can be seen Spain's four tallest office blocks. Atlético de Madrid, Athletic de Bilbao, and Valencia have all carried out similar exercises, and in December 2007, the Tarragona town council presented its project plans to build a new stadium for the local team Gimnàstic de Tarragona. It was a covered venue seating some 18,000 spectators and, with the ground reclassification mentioned earlier, the project will be built on the site of the existing stadium and the profits from this operation will be shared between the club and the town council.

When studying the management of a football club, it is interesting to analyze what the clubs spend their money on, and, in particular, it can prove very useful to observe the spending differences between a large club such as Barcelona, a smaller First Division club such as Getafe, and one from the Second Division such as Celta. Figure 15.2 shows the distribution of expenditure during the 2004–2005 season (Barajas, 2007).

In Figure 15.2, it can easily be seen that in the case of FC Barcelona, the proportion of salary and amortization expenditures (largely tied up in the first-team players) represents almost 70 percent of the total club expenses. In the case of Getafe, this figure decreases considerably due to the club's policy of working with on loan players, although this results in a somewhat higher proportion

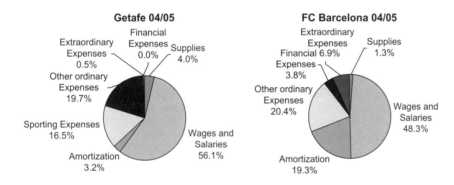

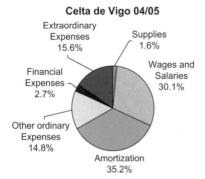

FIGURE 15.2 *Distribution of expenditure (2004–2005 season).*
Source: Barajas, 2007; Celta de Vigo (2005); FC Barcelona (2005); Getafe CF SAD (2005).

of salaries. The case of Celta de Vigo is different, where the burden of the amortizations is higher with a corresponding lower salary burden. The reason may be found in recent history: The club was relegated after having played in the Champions League, for which it bought in some bigger names for the team.

It is also important to underline the fact that the Spanish clubs are not renowned for their profitability or their financial acumen; indeed, from a sample of 29 clubs from the First and Second Divisions in the 2004–2005 season, 48.3 percent of them showed net losses, and the same percentage showed negative net assets (a position that would never be sustainable in any other business sector). Even worse is the revelation that only 20.7 percent reported any operating profit (Barajas, 2008). While it is true that, in theory, Spanish clubs work on a non-profit, break-even, basis (with any excess destined for strengthening the team profile), the problem is that it remains a theory; Spanish clubs almost never meet the objective of breaking even (Boscá et al, 2008).

CASE STUDY 15.1: The Business Models of FC Barcelona and Real Madrid

The rivalry between Madrid and Barcelona, Spain's two principal cities, has occasioned a high level of competitiveness, especially, but not exclusively, in sport, and the effects of this has impacted social identity. Both Real Madrid and Barcelona have based their international success on the "fact" that neither of them has ever given up believing (and claiming) themselves to be the best team in the world. This aspiration and objective has led the top management personnel to become public figures in football, not only in Spain but also in much of Europe.

In November 2007, the authors conducted interviews with José Angel Sánchez and Ferrán Soriano, General Managers of Real Madrid and FC Barcelona respectively (see also Urrutia et al, 2007). The vision of the two team leaders influence the conduct of the rest of the clubs. In addition, the football sector depends, in a large measure, on the money that the large clubs bring in, for example through their purchase of players from other clubs. For this reason we considered their visions to be relevant in explaining the current situation of the sector, its limitations, challenges, and opportunities.

The big clubs currently find themselves in a strong economic position. Nevertheless, it is improbable that their income can continue growing at the same rate as it has up to now, given that the growth in recent years has been nothing short of spectacular. The challenge for the future, therefore, is to explore possibilities of new business lines while, at the same time, developing the sporting capacity of the clubs.

When talking about Barcelona's financial situation, Ferrán Soriano mentioned that one of the challenges for the club is to generate profits every year. The democratic governance structure—one member, one vote—forces them to operate a very transparent business model (so much so that, in 2008, after two years of having not won any titles, the club's president received a motion of censure, something that can only be brought with a petition signed by more than 5000 members).

When legislation was approved in Spain to convert the clubs into SADs, the idea was to make the management team more financially responsible since, with this new formula, they would be risking their own money. It has been said that, previously, the clubs' management never bothered to look at the costs, as they were only focused on obtaining good sporting results. Lamentably, it would appear that the situation has not changed much; under pressure from the fans to produce good sporting results, management is still taking decisions that would not be considered prudent from a solely business perspective.

Another element to bear in mind is that many of the Spanish clubs are "multisection"—in other words, they have various teams that participate in various sports. This represents an additional financial challenge, since clubs find it much more complicated to obtain profit than clubs which are dedicated exclusively to football. For a club like FC Barcelona, it's like starting the football season with a €27 million deficit, since this is what the other sporting activities cost it. Not all clubs have this diversity, but many clubs do, seeing it as part of their corporate social responsibility. Although this increases their social impact, it may have positive effects in terms of marketing impact and generating increased fan loyalty.

The football sector contains many inefficiencies. We examine some of them now.

The regulator is also a competitor. This is the only business sector in which the body making the rules competes (in this case with the clubs) to capture revenue streams. This is the case with FIFA and UEFA, who define the sporting calendar and impose restrictions on the national teams and clubs, while at the same time competing with them for sponsorship and audience through their competitions, notably the Champions League. It is significant to note, for example, that FIFA supports the African Football Federation's (CAF) African Nations Cup, which is held in January, and to which all the world's teams are obliged to lend eligible resources (their players) for free and from which the organizers (the CAF) benefits. FC Barcelona has been particularly vocal in complaining about this issue in recent times.

The distortions caused by the value chain. The industry has grown at a dizzying pace, and the clubs have suffered a few distortions that put the current management structures at risk. These are some of the most important ones:

- In the first place, and in another situation that doesn't exist in any other sector, the *employees* (at least the famous ones) are rich, while the *employers* (the clubs) are comparatively poor, thus increasing the bargaining power of the players and encouraging dramatic wage inflation and hence financial unprofitability.

- *The "new" owners:* among the recent wave of new investors in football clubs in Spain, and indeed across Europe, their investments often follow a personal logic or even a whim with no economic rationale that dramatically affects the rest of the clubs in a knock-on fashion by forcing all clubs to spend beyond their means in order to compete.

- *The reclassification of the grounds* by some councils. This causes the influx of vast sums of money into the market from sources that are external to the logic of the sport, thereby causing an imbalance in financial power amongst clubs.

The mechanism for setting the price of a player should have some logic. Normally, for clubs such as Real Madrid or Barcelona, the price is set by the selling team. There is only room for further negotiation when the selling team is looking for a guaranteed sale or they have some other pressing need to sell. Again, this encourages wage inflation.

In the view of the general manager of Real Madrid, the football industry has changed incredibly, and this has been largely influenced by the changes experienced by the various stakeholders. For example, in the telecommunication sector, the clubs' clients—the television channels—have defined football as the best content provider. For a television channel, Real Madrid is not just a club, and its games are not just sporting events; the club and the games are the content with massive audience potential. Whenever the content distributors decide to modify their rules or their delivery systems, the clubs must follow. The spectacular evolution of the sector is such that the end consumers will soon be able to enjoy a one-to-one service. For example, a fan with a telephone can decide, in real time, what he wants to watch, how he wants to watch it, where he wants to watch it, and when.

Real Madrid sees a value creation opportunity in the improvement of their scouting networks, considering that they must be more focused on their core business. They have noticed many missed opportunities through poor scouting or by losing talented players. This loss is often caused by changes in trainer personnel or scouting teams. They also see the improvement of the player recruitment process as a fundamental need. Considering the vast quantities of money and resources invested by Real Madrid in its players, it is perhaps surprising that they do not focus more on recruitment from within and this would appear to offer major potential to reduce financial costs.

Asia is seen as having high potential for increased revenue growth by both Real Madrid and FC Barcelona. To be able to convert the opportunity into value, the clubs need to implement business models that are sustainable in the long term. By contrast, there is huge interest in Spanish football in Latin America, but it does not represent the same income opportunities for Real Madrid or FC Barcelona (as the region has less developed and lower income mass consumer markets than in the Far East) and, above all, there is a lot of competition with the local teams that already have a long tradition and a loyal following. By contrast the smallest clubs, or those with a smaller international presence, need to establish a more selective overseas image. For example, clubs in Galicia should orient themselves less towards Asia and more towards those countries in central Europe and Central America which have traditionally experienced a large volume of emigration from Galicia, such as Mexico.

At the same time, clubs need to understand their local markets. They need to ask themselves the following questions: Who is my competitor? Could it be other sports? Is it local football or international football? The key is to convert all those who say they are fans of the club into value.

It is difficult to maintain the same performance level when participating in strong national leagues when many teams are trying to combine that with participation in European competitions. Because of this, it is difficult to ensure a series of games, year after year, which can command such a high level of interest for the media and the fans.

CONCLUSIONS

All the official football competitions at national level are overseen by the RFEF (*Real Federación Española de Fútbol*). The Professional Football League, the LNFP, organizes, promotes and commercially exploits the official professional competitions.

One indicator of the competitive imbalance is the number of teams that have been League Champions and how often. In Spain, only nine clubs have won the League, and only three teams (Real Madrid, Barcelona, and Atlético Madrid) have won 75 percent of the time. Furthermore, the last few years have seen an emerging cycle: the clubs which have won La Liga and therefore regularly featured in European competitions have accumulated additional potential wealth and therefore a greater potential capacity to win the league again.

The League's attraction is beyond question: La Liga had the fourth highest average attendances in Europe in 2007/2008, and had the third highest TV revenues, the latter a proxy for TV viewer interest.

It is of paramount importance that Spanish law has recognized that the clubs are the owners of their television rights, meaning that clubs can individually negotiate—unless they choose to group together—the broadcasting rights of home games. There is a contradiction that the least economically-powerful clubs in Spain have a greater dependency on the income from these broadcasts than the bigger clubs.

Many clubs play in municipal stadia. This phenomenon is more usual for poorer clubs. Spanish clubs can be characterized by their search, largely unsuccessful, for profit or financial control. From a sample of 29 clubs from the First and Second Divisions, in the 2004–2005 season, 48.3 percent showed net losses, and the same percentage had negative net assets (Barajas, 2008)—a situation that would be unsustainable in any other sector.

The management of the leading clubs point out that the sector needs to explore developing into other possible revenue streams. The clubs need to manage their structural problems, such as the regulator also being a competitor, or the value chain distortion caused by the influx of large sums of money from outside of the football industry. They see the future in globalization in parallel with better management of their local markets. For this to happen, there needs to be significant evolution of the internal management of the clubs as well as the management of the competitions.

DISCUSSION QUESTIONS

1. Why does it make sense to call football in Spain a "social phenomenon"?

2. What is the competitive balance of the Spanish League? Make a comparison with the other major European Leagues.

3. In the financial results of a First Division club, which is the most significant expense? Are there differences among different clubs?

4. How can the ownership of the stadia affect the clubs' management?

5. Bearing in mind the opinions of the management of Real Madrid and Barcelona, where are the European leagues heading? What might happen to them in the future?

6. What differences can you think of between managing a club as a brand and managing a club as a sporting entity?

GUIDED READING

El valor económico del fútbol: Radiografía financiera del fútbol español (2005), by Ángel Barajas, clearly presents the key elements of the football business: the competition, profits and losses, assets and financing of football clubs. *Real Madrid CF—FC Barcelona: Business Strategy V Sports Strategy,*

2000–2006 (2007) (Kase et al.) by IESE Business School's CSBM (Center for Sport Business Management) is a paper that aims to answer the following questions: what kinds of strategies have Real Madrid CF and FC Barcelona made use of in order to turn their success in one field into success in another, from sports success in one period into economic success in the following? What variables could explain the different outcomes obtained by each sport entity? The article presents a matrix for the analysis, which contrasts sporting entities' economic/business strategies with their sports strategies. *Impacto del Fútbol Profesional en la economía española* (2004), published by the Liga de Fútbol Profesional (LFP), is a report that illustrates the economic impact of football on the Spanish economic system.

REFERENCES

Ascari, G., & Gagnepain, P. (2006). Spanish football, *Journal of Sports Economics*, n. 7, pp. 76–89.

Barajas, A. (27th February, 2008). *The Financial Performance of Middle Ranking Football Clubs in Spain in the Context of Relegation*. Presentation of unpublished research analysis at Birkbeck College, University of London. Retrieved on June 26, 2009, from *http://www.bbk.ac.uk/management/mscmres/sb/seminars/abarajas.shtml*

Barajas, Á. (2007). *Las finanzas detrás del balón: El negocio del fútbol*. Madrid: Ciedossat.

Barajas, Á. (2005). *El valor económico del fútbol*: *Radiografía financiera del fútbol español, EUNSA* Pamplona.

Bertomeu, J. (1993). *Transformación de clubes de fútbol y baloncesto en Sociedades Anónimas Deportivas*. Madrid: Cívitas.

Boscá, J. E., Liern, A., & Sala, R. (2008). The Spanish football crisis. *European Sport Management Quarterly, 8*(2), 165–177.

Celta de Vigo (2005). *Annual Report & Accounts – 2004/2005 Season*. Vigo: Celta de Vigo.

Deloitte, (2009). *Annual Review of Football Finance*. Manchester: Deloitte.

España. Ley 10/1990, de 15 de octubre, del Deporte. *Boletín Oficial del Estado*.

FC Barcelona (2005). *Annual Report & Accounts – 2004/2005 Season*. Barcelona: FC Barcelona.

Fundes, & LFP (2004). *Estudio de opinión sobre los Clubs de Fútbol*. Madrid: Fundes—LFP.

García, J., & Rodríguez, P. (2002). The determinants of football match attendance revisited: empirical evidence from the Spanish football league. *Journal of Sports Economics, 3*(1), 19–38.

García, J., & Rodríguez, P. (2003). From sports clubs to stock companies: The financial structure of football in Spain, 1992-2001. *European Sport Management Quarterly, 3*(4), 235–269.

Getafe CF SAD (2005). *Annual Report & Accounts – 2004/2005 Season*. Madrid: Getafe CF SAD.

Gómez, S., & Opazo, M. (2007). Características estructurales de un club de fútbol profesional de élite. *Center for Sport Business Management-IESE Business School (DI, 705)*, 17.

Gómez, S., Opazo, M., & Martí, C. (2008). Structural Characteristics of Sport Organizations: Main Trends in the Academic Discussion. *Center for Sport Business Management—IESE Business School Working Paper* No. 730.

Kase, K., Gómez, S., Urrutia, I., Martí, C. & Opazo, M. (2006). Real Madrid CF FC Barcelona: Analysis of Business Strategy V Sports Strategy During the Period 2000–2006. Madrid: *Center for Sport Business Management-IESE Business School (OP-06-12)*

Llopis, R. (2006). Football Clubs and National Football Teams: The Ethnoterritorial Dimension of Spanish Football. *Revista Internacional de Sociología, LXIV, 45*, 37–66.

LFP.es. www.lfp.es

LNFP. (2004). *Impacto del Fútbol Profesional en la economía española*. Madrid: Report Liga de Fútbol Profesional.

Martialay, F. (1996). *Implantación del profesionalismo y nacimiento de la Liga*. Madrid: Real Federación Española de Fútbol.

Noticias.info (11th November, 2004). The total impact of the sector of professional football in the Spanish economy. *Noticias Info*. Retrieved on June 26, 2009, from *http://www.noticias.info/archivo/2004/200403/20040312/2004 0312_20205.shtm*

Palomar, A., & Descalzo, A. (2001). *Los derechos de imagen en el ámbito del deporte profesional*. Madrid: Dykinson.

Rodríguez, J. (2007). *Derecho disciplinario del fútbol español*. Barcelona: Editorial Bosch.

Urrutia, I., Kase, K., Martí, C. & Opazo, M. (2007). The proto-image of Real Madrid: implications for marketing and management. *International Journal of Sports Marketing & Sponsorship, 8*.

RECOMMENDED WEBSITES

Center for Sport Business Management, IESE Business School
http://www.iese.edu/CSBM
Fútbol Club Barcelona
http://www.fcbarcelona.com
Real Madrid Club de Fútbol
http://www.realmadrid.com

Spanish Football Association
http://www.rfef.es
Spanish Players Representatives Association
http://www.afe-futbol.com/
Spanish Professional Football League
http://www.lfp.es/
The Rec.Sport.Soccer Statistics Foundation
http://www.rsssf.com

CHAPTER 16

Italy

Sergio Cherubini
University of Rome Tor Vergata

Andrea Santini
University of Rome Tor Vergata

Objectives

Upon completion of this chapter the reader should be able to:

- Know the main characteristics of Italian football management.
- Understand the complexity of the football markets from a marketing approach.
- Understand the importance of the "sport convergence" concept for a football club that intends to be competitive.
- Understand the development of football management in Italy.
- Identify the main opportunities and challenges for Italian football clubs.
- Understand the complexity of the relationship between Italian football and media and the consequences for the stadia attendances.

OVERVIEW OF THE CHAPTER

The complexity of the Italian football management derives from the fact that the club has to be successful in three different markets—people, companies, and public institutions—at the same time and in a synergetic way. This complexity is differently managed according to three identified strategic groups within the Italian football Serie A and it is particularly difficult to decide one development strategy that is suitable for all the twenty clubs. The chapter includes three case studies: the repositioning of Juventus F.C., the relationship between football and the media, and the development of the stadia in Italy.

THE THREE MARKETS OF FOOTBALL MANAGEMENT

Football has undergone an intense development during the last decade. When focusing on professional football, it is evident that its popularity has made this sport an extremely complex phenomenon. Emotional and rational aspects, international and local, individual and group, professional and amateur, high-tech and high-touch, traditional and innovative, private and public, competitive and collaborative, and short term and long term are all present at the same time.

The football club, in fact, operates more and more in markets with different characteristics, logics, and methodologies. In the consumer market, the team has to deal with a large number of people as a target, emotionally involved and loyal to the team. In terms of marketing, this means organizing a wide offer, with differentiated pricing and a distribution close to the client.

The business market has, instead, a smaller dimension and has companies as the target group. The approach to the client needs to be personalised, and the logics must be rational. Furthermore, the value of the customised offer is based on its economic return.

The football club is also playing a social role in territorial marketing, with public institutions as the targets that are providing facilities, locations, and services like security, transportation, and others, included sponsorship. In this case, a relational approach is required, with the team talking with a limited number of public institutions, located in the area where it is based. The main characteristics of the three markets are summarized in Table 16.1.

The three markets include different targets with specific needs. In the consumer market, people can play football or attend a match, as well as buy and use products and services like football apparel, betting, and information.

At the same time, the football match can be delivered in different ways: in the stadium, on television, and via new technologies, such as the Internet or a cell phone. As a consequence, the level of participation is different, from the fan attending every match to the person who lives far from the club.

Companies are approaching football for various reasons. Sponsors are mainly interested in increasing their awareness and/or improving their image by associating their brand with football, while media and publishers use football as their news. The possible target groups of the three markets for a football club are shown in Table 16.2.

Table 16.1	The Main Characteristics of the Three Markets of the Football Organisation		
	Consumer Market (B2C)	**Business Market (B2B)**	**Public Market (B2P)**
Dimension/Size	Large	Small	Minimum/Limited
Logics	Emotional	Rational	Relational
Loyalty	High	Low	Medium
Buyer behaviour	Simple	Complex	Very complex
Segmentation	Highly differentiated	Differentiated	Concentrated
Service/Offer	Wide and involving	Personalised	Institutional
Price	Differentiated	Based on competition	Public support
Distribution	Gravitational	Customised	Local
Relationships	Public	High level	Personalised
Communication	Publicity Direct marketing	Promoter	Personal

These three markets are strictly related, although with different characteristics. If the club is able to attract many supporters, sponsors and public institutions will offer the team money and collaborations in order to have the possibility to communicate and interact with its fans. At the same time, the additional resources available will reinforce the team, activating a virtuous circle where the club uses the resources coming from spectators as well as from sponsors to reinforce the team (Figure 16.1).

Table 16.2	Possible Target Groups of the Three Markets for a Football Club		
Consumer Market	**Business Market**	**Public Market**
People that look for entertainment	Sponsor	State
Fans	Media industry	Region
Supporters	Technical producers	Province
People that like football	Commercial producers	City
People that play football	Publishers	City districts
People that buy information	Real estate developers	Other public institutions
Technical equipment buyer	Entertainment companies	
Football apparel buyer		
Other products (i.e., betting) buyer		

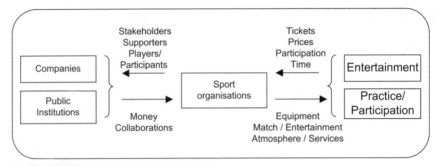

FIGURE 16.1 *The three markets of the football organisation.*
Source: Model developed by Cherubini S., (Cherubini et al, 2003).

These days, the club is surrounded by other organisations, although it remains the heart of the movement. This leads to the creation of a network based on collaboration: "Alone you lose, together we win." As a result, a "sport convergence" (to paraphrase the more familiar multimedia convergence) can be achieved.

The concept of the "sport convergence" is illustrated in Figure 16.2, where commercial partners (before considered simply sponsors), technical partners, new and traditional media, the territory (with its territorial offices and the entire social-economic context), distribution partners and users of football services (seen as pro-sumers, able to contribute to the perceived quality of the service) have interaction with the football organization.

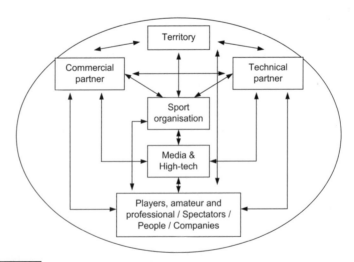

FIGURE 16.2 *The chain of the sport convergence.*
Source: Model developed by Cherubini S., (Cherubini et al, 2003).

A BRIEF HISTORY OF FOOTBALL IN ITALY

Football is the most popular sport in Italy. In terms of practice, the football movement in Italy can count on about 1.2 million athletes registered with the Italian Football Association, more than 14,000 clubs and about 50,000 teams involved in more than 500,000 matches every season. If intended as a spectacle, this sport represents one of the most followed and most requested content (FIGC).

Football was brought to Italy during the 1880s, with Genoa Cricket and Football Club being the first Italian football club to be established in 1896, when the Englishman James Richardson Spensley arrived in Genoa and introduced the football section of the club and became its first manager (Foot, 2007 pages 4–5). The move to a single national league structure occurred in 1929 with initially 18 teams in the top league. The first winners in 1930 were Internazionale.

The Italian Football Federation (Federazione Italiana Giuoco Calcio, FIGC; also known as Federcalcio) is the governing body of football in Italy (www.figc.it). It organises the Italian football league, the Coppa Italia, the Italian national football team, and the Italian women's national football team. It is based in Rome. It was a founding member of both FIFA and UEFA.

The Italian football league system is a series of interconnected leagues for football clubs in Italy (Figure 16.3).

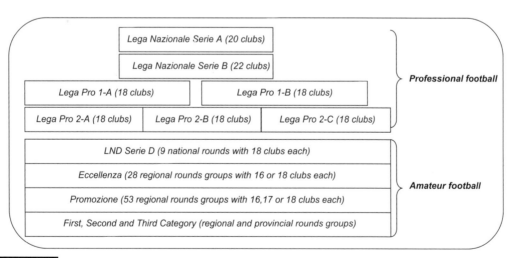

FIGURE 16.3 *The Italian football league system.*
Source: FIGC.

THE CURRENT STATE OF DEVELOPMENT OF FOOTBALL MANAGEMENT IN ITALY

The management of football clubs in Italy has been traditionally focused on technical aspects. Football is the core activity, and all the efforts, starting from the trade in players' contracts, are dedicated to the improvement of the team in order to achieve better results. This situation is, in fact, still present in many clubs, since the organisation of the team directly influences the results on the pitch and since the trading of players still represents the main source of income for many small-medium sized teams. The Bosman ruling of 1995, which gave players freedom of movement without a transfer fee at the end of their contract, has certainly reduced the attractiveness of this activity, making the practice of covering losses with the sales of players harder to realize in the long run.

Nevertheless, the management focus on technical matters relating to team performance has led to successful sports results. The Italian national football team has won the Football World Cup four times (1934, 1938, 1982, and 2006), trailing only Brazil (with five); Italy is the current title holder. Italy's club sides have won 27 major European trophies, making them one of the most successful footballing nations in Europe.

Despite the positive results obtained on the field, the economic and financial situation does not look quite as positive in every area except broadcasting income. When compared with the English Premier League, it is evident that the Italian football movement is becoming less competitive, as shown in Figures 16.4–16.7. In the period 1999–2000 to 2005–2006, the

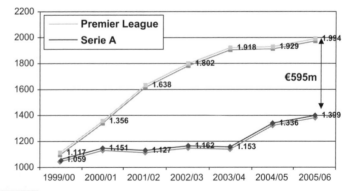

FIGURE 16.4 *Total turnover (€ billion) of the Premier League (England) and of Serie A (Italy) from 1999–2000 to 2005–2006.*
Source: Deloitte, 2007, page 12.

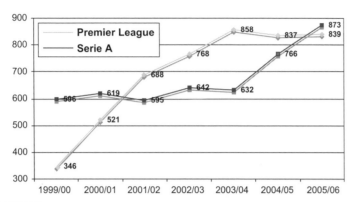

FIGURE 16.5 *Turnover (€ million) from broadcasting of the Premier League (England) and of Serie A (Italy) from 1999–2000 to 2005–2006.*
Source: Deloitte, 2007, Appendices, page 18.

total turnover of the Premier League has grown 78 percent, whilst that of Italian Serie A grew by only 32 percent. However, it is important to emphasize that this negative situation in Italian football is also affected by the negative general economic climate in Italy during this period.

The situation doesn't change when analysing the top teams. The list of the first five European teams in 2007 in terms of turnover doesn't include any Italian teams, as shown in Figure 16.8.

For a complete description of the Italian football movement, it is important to emphasize that the system includes organisations with

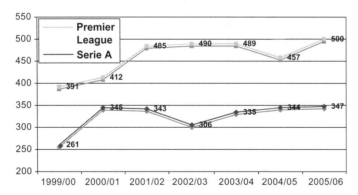

FIGURE 16.6 *Turnover (€ million) from commercial income of the Premier League (England) and of Serie A (Italy) from 1999–2000 to 2005–2006.*
Source: Deloitte, 2007, Appendices, page 18.

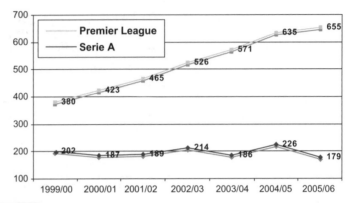

FIGURE 16.7 *Turnover (€ million) from matchday income of Premier League (England) and of Serie A (Italy) from 1999–2000 to 2005–2006.*
Source: Deloitte, 2007, Appendices, page 18.

different characteristics and objectives. Are Juventus FC and Reggiana real direct competitors, although they are playing in the same division?

Based on this consideration, it is possible to classify Serie A clubs into three strategic groups—Back stage, Followers, and Top Three—according to the variables (1) sports success and (2) economic potential, as

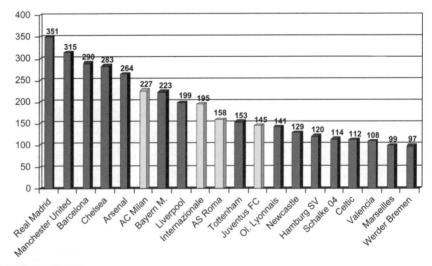

FIGURE 16.8 *Ranking list of European football clubs in terms of turnover (€ million) (2006/2007).*
Source: Deloitte, 2008, Appendices, page 19.

highlighted in Figure 16.9 (Abel, 1980). The clubs in each of these groupings are characterised as having similar characteristics and objectives, which are clearly differentiated from the clubs in the other groupings. Sporting success is clearly linked to economic potential and power. "Back stage" clubs are those fighting relegation. "Followers" are those fighting to qualify for European competition. "Top Three" are those competing to win the Serie A title.

It is possible for teams to move from one category to another one, as in the cases of Udinese and Palermo trying to achieve the "Followers," and Fiorentina and Roma the "Top Three." It goes without saying that this strategic evolution is not easy to achieve, since it requires each club to significantly improve sporting results and to capitalise on this. In some cases, sports results are obtained through unbalanced economic potential, either using too much debt capital or drawing too much on the personal resources of the owner and/or of the parent group. From this perspective, the Juventus FC case study represents a meaningful as well as particular example of a company that achieved a turnaround from Serie B to the top of Serie A in only 20 months.

Given this overview of the current state of development of football management in Italy, it is interesting to analyse in more detail the two main sources of revenue for Italian football clubs: the sales of broadcast rights and matchday commercial exploitation.

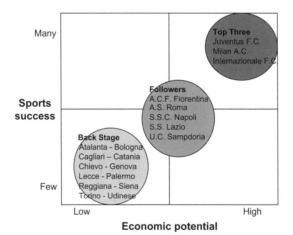

FIGURE 16.9   *Strategic groups in the Italian Serie A, season 2008–2009.*

CASE STUDY 16.1: Juventus FC, a Company Turnaround

The summer of 2006 was certainly a significant moment in the history of the Italian football movement. The scandal of "calciopoli", whereby wholesale match-fixing was uncovered, led to the relegation of Juventus FC to the Serie B for the first time, a penalty of nine points when starting the next season, and the cancellation of its last two Serie A titles. A glorious team, founded in 1897, listed on the stock exchange in 2001, ready to commence the construction of a new stadium is suddenly relegated to Serie B.

The first steps taken by the owner of the club based in Turin were the appointment of a new top management, the recognition of a central role for the board of directors, and the definition of a stronger corporate governance. Furthermore, the mission was modified as follows:

- To be a leading club in Europe and a successful listed company.
- To obtain high and regular sports performance on the field, developing a sustainable business model.
- To lead change in football in Italy and to position Juventus as the benchmark of a modern company, close to fans and respectful of the educational values of sport.
- To manage the company with great professionalism.

The president, Giovanni Cobolli Gigli, and the CEO and general director, Jean-Claude Blanc, were supported by the newly established "Comitato sportivo" (Sports Committee) and "Comitato per il controllo interno" (Committee for the internal control). The former was set up following the reorganisation of the sports division of the club, the relaunch of the youth team, and the redefinition of a code of ethics. The latter contributed to the redefinition of the internal rules and organisational procedures and to the control of their application.

On a sports-technical level, the management first tackled and managed the changes in the technical staff. Various top players, like Cannavaro, Ibrahimovic, Viera, Zambrotta, Thuram, left Juventus to reinforce other competitors like Internazionale FC, Real Madrid and Barcelona, reducing the players' assets on the company balance sheet from €107 million to €53 million. However, the management retained other top players on significant financial terms, like Buffon, Del Piero and Trezeguet, in order to win in Serie B and to lay foundations for the future.

Furthermore, the new management moved the focus from results to appreciation of talent. Together with the renewal of the scouting sector, a professional, integrated football school was established with 17 teams, about 350 players, more than 60 technical staff, and an investment of over €5 million per year. The school profited from the collaboration with the first team's technical staff, sharing the preparation with the Primavera team with the intention of regularly bringing new talent into the first team. The opening of the new training centre in Vinovo (Turin) in July 2006 also allowed the company to have only one place for all the teams.

The scandal and the relegation to the Serie B negatively influenced the economic and financial results of the company, with turnover reducing from €251 million to €186 million during the season 2006–2007 (in Serie B).

The club had to renegotiate the TV and sponsor contracts, with the main sponsor, Tamoil, informing Juventus of its intention of ending the contract after the season 2006–2007. The technical partner, Nike, and the media partner, Sky, instead, confirmed their intention to work with the company. A fundamental contribution came also from the FIAT Group, with the subsidiary company New Holland, becoming main sponsor.

In this sense, a new commercial strategy had been developed, aimed at selecting a limited group of national and international partners to enhance the Juventus brand. This strategy, based on the philosophy "less is more," was intended to increase the visibility of partners' brands and the average value of contact, to create more stable and lasting relations and to transfer more value to partners.

Thanks to its enormous media coverage and the fan base it can count on in Italy, Europe, and throughout the world,

Juventus developed three main initiatives aimed at establishing a closer relationship with the fans:

- Juventus Membership, the first online membership project for fans in Italy, able to attract approximately 30,000 members in just 9 months and consequently to create the biggest "black and white virtual community."

- Juventus Channel, a TV channel on air 24 hours a day, fully dedicated to the Juventus world, providing interaction and information for fans, with 40,000 subscribers in 12 months.

- The "stadium sensation project," aimed at providing a new way of experiencing the matches by creating family entertainment, shows, and events for spectators and initiatives with commercial partners.

The first positive results reached by the new management, with the immediate return to Serie A and to the preliminary round of the UEFA Champions League, were positively welcomed by the investors. In June 2007, a capital increase of €104 million was entirely underwritten, with a consequent reduction in indebtedness and an increase in new investment capacity.

The next fundamental step in this turnaround strategy is the realisation of a new stadium in place of Delle Alpi stadium. The objective is to generate additional revenue to invest in the first and youth team, increasing the matchday income from about €20 million to €35 million per annum. The new 40,000 seat stadium will cost €105 million, and it will be ready for the 2011–2012 season. It is intended to be a state-of-the-art facility, with high-quality services, comfort (including skyboxes and business seats), and significantly enhanced views.

Source: Santini, 2008a.

BROADCASTING RIGHTS

Football and media have a relationship of mutual dependence in Italy. The former represents one of the favourite contents for the latter. According to a survey conducted by Makno-Deloitte in Italy in 2002, the football audience was estimated to be almost 23 million people, while Formula 1 registered 16 million, and cycling 5.9 million.

At the same time, the football movement in Italy is heavily financed by and highly dependent on the broadcasters, as described previously. The revenue from the sale of broadcasting rights represents the most important source of income for clubs.

Football clubs are, then, at the same time (1) clients of the media when organising communication initiatives (like for their season tickets campaign); (2) suppliers of highly appreciated content; and (3) competitors, since they are competing with media for the communication budget of companies. Mediaset and AC Milan and Cairo Communication and Torino are two examples of this close relationship between football and media sponsors.

As is discussed in Case Study 16.2, the industry has undergone an intense development in the last 25 years in Italy. Clubs are nowadays working on the following major objectives:

- The identification of the most appropriate mechanism for the sale of TV broadcasting rights: collective or individual selling.
- The organisation of a revenue distribution system able to avoid a sporting competition that is too unbalanced and consequently less attractive for the various parties involved, from supporters to broadcasters and commercial partners.
- The identification of a football offer (packaging) in line with the new broadcasting landscape able to prevent any cannibalisation between the different broadcasting channels and to manage the competition between the "real stadium" and the "virtual stadium," so that there is no reduction in gate receipts (see, for example, the sale of broadcast rights in the English Premier League restricted to less than one-third of games being shown on TV so as to avoid cannibalisation of match crowds).
- The management of the content delivery, since Italian football organizations have been slow to systematically leverage the potential of new technologies such as digital terrestrial TV, satellite TV, Internet Protocol TV (IPTV), mobile phase TV with UMTS technology and the standard DVB-h (Digital Video Broadcasting handheld).

The development of new broadcasting technologies has allowed new operators to enter the market and determined a new type of competition, known as "intertype competition," where telecom operators are interested in the content football to provide visibility to their platforms. The "product football" represents, in fact, a perfect killer application and a driving force for the development of a specific platform and it is not exclusive for TV broadcasters any more. Consequently, the competition between the different operators has increased, with the football clubs benefiting in terms of larger revenues.

The distribution of the content is also important for the internationalisation of the Italian football movement. The delivery of the content to the fanbase, wherever located around the world, through the club's official website, TV channel, monthly magazine, matchday programme, radio station should be central to the team's commercial strategy. The content production, with the creation of dedicated TV-Web channels (as is the case at AC Milan, AS Roma, FC Internazionale, and Juventus FC) and the reorganisation and commercialisation of their libraries via merchandising products is becoming a key objective for major Italian clubs.

CASE STUDY 16.2: The Evolving History of the Relationship Between Football and the Media in Italy

The relationship between football and media has evolved through various, sometimes contradictory, phases. This history starts at the beginning of the 1980s and it evolves through the years, reflecting the development of modern football, being influenced by new laws and regulations and empowered by new technologies.

Phase 1 (1980–1981 to 1992–1993)

In the 1980s, the Italian Football League (Lega Calcio) was entitled to sell the rights for the broadcast of the highlights of Serie A and Serie B competitions, as described in Table 16.3. RAI was the only broadcaster, with Mediaset commencing broadcasting Italian Cup matches from season 1990–1991. The analogue terrestrial was the only technology used to broadcast the highlights of the matches.

Phase 2 (1993–1994 to 1995–1996)

Season 1993–1994 saw the introduction of Pay-TV in Italy with a new operator, Telepiù, broadcasting a limited number of Serie A and Serie B matches (respectively, 28 and 32 games).

Table 16.3   Phases of the Relationship Between Football and Media in Italy

	Phase 1 1980–1981 to 1992–1993	Phase 2 1993–1994 to 1995–1996	Phase 3 1996–1997 to 1998–1999	Phase 4 1999–2000 to 2001–2002	Phase 5 2002–2003 to 2003–2004
Rights	Free TV for highlights	Free TV for highlights and Pay-TV for limited Serie A and Serie B matches	Free TV for highlights, Pay-TV and pay per view	Free TV for highlights, Pay-TV and pay per view	Free TV for highlights, Pay-TV and pay per view
Broadcasting technology	Analogue-terrestrial	Analogue-terrestrial	Analogue-terrestrial and Digital-satellite	Analogue-terrestrial and Digital-satellite	Analogue-terrestrial and Digital-satellite
Broadcaster	RAI and since 1990 Mediaset	RAI, Mediaset and Telepiù	RAI, Mediaset, Telepiù and Stream	RAI, Mediaset, Telepiù and Stream	RAI, Mediaset, Telepiù and Stream and then SKY
Negotiation	Collective	Collective	Collective	Collective (free-TV) and individual (Pay-TV and pay per view)	Collective (free-TV) and individual (Pay-TV and pay per view)
Revenue distribution system	Equal between Serie A and Serie B	Equal between Serie A and Serie B	Not equal between Serie A and Serie B	Not equal between Serie A and Serie B	Not equal between Serie A and Serie B

Source: *Elaboration based on data provided by Lega Calcio.*

The negotiation for both free-to-air terrestrial TV highlights and Pay-TV was conducted by Lega Calcio, which distributed the revenues equally between the Serie A and B clubs. As a result there was an increase in revenues, from €56 million (season 1992–1993) to €93 million (1993–1994).

Phase 3 (1996–1997 to 1998–1999)

Competition for the acquisition of the rights for the highlights of the Serie A and B appeared for the first time before the season 1996–1997, when the Cecchi Gori Communications company tried—unsuccessfully against RAI—to buy the rights for free-to-air TV.

Furthermore, the introduction of the digital satellite technology allowed the two operators, Telepiù and Stream, to add to their existing offer (the live broadcast of the Sunday evening match) the pay-per-view (live matches) product.

For the first time, revenue from broadcasting rights was higher than gate receipts in the season 1996–1997. The revenue distribution system changed for season 1997–1998, with:

- Revenue from free TV: 58 percent to Serie A and 42 percent to Serie B, and then equally distributed amongst the respective clubs.

- Revenue from Pay TV and pay-per-view: 75 percent to Serie A and 25 percent to Serie B, and then distributed based on the final league ranking list and the number of matches broadcast on TV.

- Revenue from rights sold abroad: 100 percent to Serie A.

Phase 4 (1999–2000 to 2001–2002)

A landmark in the development of the distribution system for the resources generated by broadcasting rights was introduced through Law n.78 in 1999, that recognised the right of each club to sell individually the rights related to Pay TV and pay-per-view screenings of their own matches.

This new arrangement led to a dramatic increase in revenue from broadcasting (as illustrated in Figure 16.10) but increased also the disparity in income between the clubs, with the top teams absorbing most of the revenues as described in Table 16.4 and Figure 16.11.

Phase 5 (2002–2003 to 2003–2004)

In summer 2002, broadcasters initiated a debate concerning the value of TV rights. RAI, for the first time, signed a three-year contract under which for the first time, the value of payments to clubs was related to the TV viewing market share for their games. Telepiù and Stream secured the reorganisation of the playing calendar, with two matches now broadcast on Saturday (at 6 pm and 8:30 pm; previously all matches were typically played on Sunday afternoon).

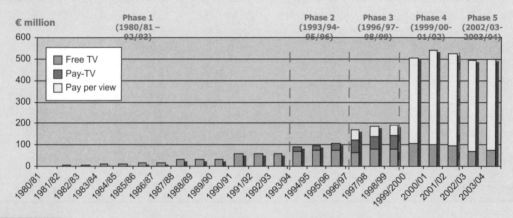

FIGURE 16.10 Evolution of the revenue (€ million) from broadcasting during the phases 1-5. Source: Elaboration based on data provided by Lega Calcio.

Table 16.4	Total Revenue Distribution Among Serie A Clubs			
	1997–1998	**1998–1999**	**1999–2000**	**2000–2001**
Group 1	52.4 percent	54 percent	58.2 percent	60.6 percent
Group 2	26 percent	26.7 percent	24 percent	22.4 percent
Group 3	21.6 percent	19.3 percent	17.8 percent	17 percent

Source: Deloitte, 2006.
Note: Group 1 (1st–5th team per turnover), Group 2 (6th–10th team per turnover), Group 3 (11th–18th team per turnover)

Summer 2003 saw the entrance into the Italian market of News Corporation, through Sky Italia, through the purchase of Telepiù from Vivendi (for €900 million) and the subsequent merger with Stream. The new entity, controlled by the media Tycoon Rupert Murdoch, is obliged to sell the analogue terrestrial and digital signals of Telepiù by the European Union and transmit only via digital satellite.

Phase 6 (2004–2005 to 2008–2009)

Season 2004–2005 saw Mediaset acquiring for the first time the rights to broadcast highlights on free TV and the development of new telecommunication technologies allowed operators to enter the Pay TV market:

■ Via the DTT (Digital Terrestrial Technology), free-to-air TV operators (RAI, Mediaset, La7).

■ Via cable TV, telecom operator (Fastweb).

■ Via UMTS, mobile operators (TIM, Vodafone and Tre).

In 2006, three rulings by the European Commission, relating to the (1) recognition of the possibility to sell broadcasting rights collectively in order to ensure redistribution of revenue to effect greater competitive balance in a league, to the (2) segmentation of the product in various packages and to the (3) setting of a time limit for which exclusivity is applied for ownership of broadcasting rights, is brought into effect in Italy. The law n.106 in 2007 (c.d. Melandri-Gentiloni) recognises that:

■ The broadcasting rights belong to the organiser of the competition, the Lega Calcio, and consequently can be sold collectively.

■ Forty percent of the broadcasting revenue are to be distributed equally to all the clubs, 30 percent based on sporting performance and 30 percent based on the size of their fanbase.

■ Club channels as well as archives belong to the club.

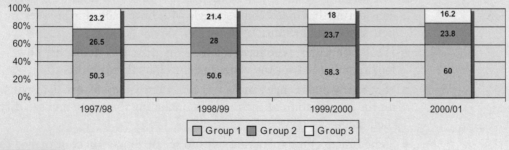

FIGURE 16.11 *Revenue share from broadcasting between Serie A clubs.*
Source: Deloitte, 2006.
Notes: Group 1 (1st–5th team per turnover), Group 2 (6th–10th team per turnover), Group 3 (11th–18th team per turnover)

MATCHDAY EXPLOITATION

Italian league football has witnessed a steady decline in attendances from it's leading position in Europe in the mid-1990s. Serie A, Italy's top-tier division, boasted an average attendance of 29,500 per game in 1996-1997, but has since fallen to fourth place in 2006-2007, reporting a 19,200 average (Deloitte, 2007, page 15).

Furthermore, the predominantly publicly owned Italian facilities have suffered from a lack of investment in the past 20 years. While English clubs have invested over £1.5 billion in their facilities since 1990, the majority of Serie A and Serie B stadia have remained unchanged in the same period. Italy's hosting of the 1990 FIFA World Cup triggered major renovation work at some of these, but the stadium concept has not really evolved since then.

While the great Italian stadia can boast capacities in excess of 75,000, this also means higher maintenance and event production costs. To put this in some perspective, Serie A stadia incurred capacity utilisation in 2003-2004 of 56.1 percent, compared to nearly 95 percent for Premiership stadia.

Italian teams have so far not been particularly successful in managing their stadia and in using them as revenue generators. A new stadium, in fact, represents an important opportunity to further improve the club's match day revenue by attracting more fans to the new facility. The higher level of comfort and amenities offered and factors like curiosity and the image of the building can significantly increase the turnover related to the match. A better facility also enhances the potential for sponsorship and corporate hospitality by providing facilities and services more in line with the expectations of corporate customers (Cherubini et al, 2003; Santini, 2008).

However, the outlook for a change in the Italian stadia situation is positive:

- The stadium is starting to be seen as an important revenue generator, considering that many clubs struggle with huge debts and are seeking out new sources of income.
- Local authorities, who have traditionally managed stadia, are now looking to hand over the venues to the clubs that use them.
- New safety and security measures consider football teams as responsible for the organisation of the matches, including the safety and security of their stadia.
- Some Italian clubs are taking steps to secure long-term control over their ground and to commercially exploit their control.
- Some Italian teams are implementing new pricing strategies in order to compete with the offer of the "virtual stadium offered through the media."

CASE STUDY 16.3: The Development of Stadia in Italy

Despite the failure of the candidature to host the UEFA European Championship in 2012, which would have certainly represented an important opportunity for the renovation of stadia in Italy, the Italian football movement has realised the importance of having functional, safe and comfortable facilities in which to stage the football event.

This renovation process has been led by the major clubs, AC Milan and Internazionale FC with Stadio San Siro, AS Roma and SS Lazio with Stadio Olimpico, and Juventus FC with the replacement of Stadio Delle Alpi.

In July 1, 2000, the Consortium SanSiro2000, an equal shares joint venture between F.C. Internazionale and A.C. Milan, signed a 30-year lease agreement with the City of Milan. The contract stipulated an annual rental payment of about €7 million. The Consortium pays for the daily maintenance, while the costs sustained for the improvement of the facility can be deducted from the rent, for a maximum of €10 million every five years. Revenue coming from the organisation of extra events is taken by the Consortium, while gate receipts from football matches as well as advertising revenue are directly taken by the individual teams.

Recent renovation works have improved the VIP and business area as well as the security of the stadium. A museum for both clubs, attracting about 50,000 visitors a year, and a stadium store were also built.

The agreement signed in 2000, does not fully satisfy the Consortium. The exploitation of the stadium is limited by restrictions and long procedures. Talks with the City have been started in order to obtain the full availability of the stadium and the surrounding area, in line with what has taken place in Turin with Juventus F.C. A development project for the surrounding area has been presented to the City. The project, called "forth ring," includes the creation of a ring of entertainment facilities and services, like restaurants, cafés, and shops, that will circle the San Siro stadium, for a total of 16,000 square metres.

This represents the first phase of a wider project that includes around 265 hectares, where a ground park for sport and leisure should arise. The vision is to link various facilities, like the stadium, the horse race track and parks, through pedestrian walks and bike routes, in order to create a large leisure area. For this reason, an ad hoc development agency, ASanSiro, was set up, with the two football teams being equal shareholders (45 percent each) together with the Foundation ChiamaMilano (10 percent).

The Stadio Olimpico, the home of A.S. Roma and S.S. Lazio, built in 1953 and renovated for the 1990 World Cup, is undergoing renovation works. The Minister of Economics assigned the property of the area to CONI Servizi, the National Olympics Committee (CONI) service company. The area, named Parco del Foro Italico, is a 40-hectare complex featuring, beyond the stadium, incompassing Olympic swimming pools, tennis courts, the offices of CONI and a 1930s running track.

With football representing the main content for the stadium, the long term operation and viability of the project is highly dependent on the participation of the two football teams and therefore the Italian Olympic Committee is trying to obtain a commitment and involvement from the two parties eventually hoping to involve them in a stadium operation company.

The move of Juventus to a new stadium in Turin was temporarily halted by the club's relegation to Serie B for the 2006/2007 season. But it has been reactivated with the completion of construction works anticipated in 2011. Juventus FC has founded, together with a service engineering company, a company called Semana that will take care of the maintenance of the stadium and which plans to develop a business park on land adjacent to Juventus' training ground.

Source: ConiServizi, Consorzio San Siro, Juventus.com, Santini, 2005.

CONCLUSIONS

The prospects for change across Italy are improving. Football is experiencing a period of particular development, moving from a mono- to a multi-business environment. The match remains the heart of the movement, but around it many different activities, with interesting potential, could be developed. Italian football clubs are keen to diversify their revenue streams, aiming at further increasing and stabilising the team profitability.

In this complex environment, Italian football clubs should base their initiatives on their main assets. The most valuable asset of a football club is the supporter base. The football team's value is, in fact, very closely related to its popularity and fan base. Unfortunately Italian football has not been so successful in activating these relationships, converting that enormous latent interest into consumers. The challenge for the clubs is to convert this latent, passive interest into passionate, active consumption.

Technology also plays an important role in the football industry. Football clubs should use it properly in order to maximise broadcasting revenues. New technologies like the Internet and the mobile phone have proved to be powerful tools for activating and developing a relationship with the fan base.

Diversification is possible and viable if the football team has a strong, recognised brand and the new business is somehow correlated. Brands represent the tool through which a football team can develop and keep supporters' loyalty, and they can create the competitive advantage able to increase actual and future cash flows.

Stadia can become important profit generators. The Giglio stadium, the first in Italy owned by a private party, is emblematic. AC Reggiana, owner of the stadium, went bankrupt after selling the development rights of the surrounding area (24,000 sqm) to business developers. A cinema with 12 theatres, a commercial area, and two towers that host a hotel and a cultural centre have now been constructed close to the stadium, where a new Serie C2 team is playing its home matches.

Furthermore, as football brands mature, they must expand into additional markets, in terms of overseas television deals, international sponsorship deals and grassroots programmes designed to help their global branding efforts. Top European football teams are extending their game schedules and licensing efforts into Asia.

Nevertheless, this more complex reality requires a more innovative approach in defining the various business areas. Furthermore, clubs must clearly identify demand needs and critical success factors for each area in order to fully capitalize from their exploitation.

The negative results of the majority of Italian clubs, both at the professional and amateur level, show that it is not easy to turn the extreme popularity of football into positive economic results. The evolution of football clubs from a technically focused organisation into a multibusiness company must be guided by a clear strategy.

The organisational structure should follow and support the strategic decisions taken. Merchandising initiatives, for example, can be either in-house or outsourced to third parties. Both the solutions could be valid, if supported by an appropriate organization and integrated into a more systemic vision.

Strategic decisions are affecting also the selection of the staff, both from a quantitative (size of the company) and qualitative (skills and competences required) point of view.

If the club decides to outsource the development of the merchandising business, it will need people to coordinate the different partners directly involved in the commercial usage of the team's brand, while in the case of direct involvment a dedicated division, with specialised personnel, will be necessary.

Clubs will also have to revise their investment strategies by increasing the money invested in the new business areas and controlling those ones for the technical football area if they want to fully govern, and benefit from, this complex environment.

Football's rules have not changed a lot since its foundation. Playing a ball with the feet has been going on for thousands of years. By contrast the industry, instead, has recently experienced a huge development in a short period of time that modern Italian clubs will have to consider if they want to remain competitive and win on the field.

DISCUSSION QUESTIONS

1. Do you think that there is a good balance between the Italian football reputation and the economic results of the Italian clubs? If yes, why? If not, why not?
2. What is your opinion about the future of Juventus F.C.? Will the club be able to be successful again at the top European level? Do you agree with the new strategy?
3. Considering the failure of the candidature to host the UEFA Euro2012, do you think that the Italian football movement will still be able to fill the stadia gap? Why?

4. What is your opinion about the policy adopted by the Italian football governing bodies concerning the sales of broadcast rights and the related revenue distribution system? Is this system more beneficial to the top clubs or to the average performing clubs?

5. Do you think that the Italian clubs will be able to manage the new challenges presented by the increasingly complex football industry?

6. How can the three markets – consumer, business and public – of the football organization be managed in a genuinely synergetic way?

GUIDED READING

Il marketing sportivo. (2000) by Sergio Cherubini provides a systematic and practical approach to sports marketing for both people (mass marketing) and companies (business marketing) drawing an both Italian and international case material. *Il co-marketing degli impianti sportivi* (2003) edited by Sergio Cherubini, Marco Canigiani and Andrea Santini, intends to promote a new way of operating sports facilities, based on the principles and tools of comarketing, in order to assure the maximum return from the exploitation of public and private sports complexes. The text is integrated with various cases, from the Amsterdam Arena, SanSiro2000, Autodromo di Vallelunga to specific experiences of different Sports Associations. *Media e co-marketing sportivo: Strategie di convergenza nel mercato globale e locale* (2000), edited by Sergio Cherubini and Marco Canigiani, explains that the success of sports activities all around the world is certainly favoured by the mass media that are particularly interested in sports as a content able to generate audience or readership. Therefore, the cooperation between sports organizations and media to reach their own specific marketing objectives is important. The text is integrated with various cases, from Nike and Puma, S.S. Lazio and A.C. Milan, RAI and La Gazzetta dello Sport. *Il Co-Marketing Sportivo: Strategie di cooperazione nel mercato sportivo* (1999) edited by Sergio Cherubini and Marco Canigiani highlights that sports organisations are engaged in a process of continuous improvement and for this it is essential to have the support and cooperation of other organizations (private and public), with particular regard to the media, the companies involved as sponsors both commercial and technical, so as to develop competitive comarketing programmes. The text examines various cases.

Marketing & Football: an international perspective (2007) edited by Michel Desbordes provides an entirely global approach to football marketing. Written by an international team of contributors who are active researchers in the field, it is a seminal text for academics and practitioners researching and working in the football industry. *Sport management* (2006) by Russell Hoye, Aaron Smith, Hans Westerbeek, Bob Stewart, and Matthew Nicholson, provides a comprehensive introduction to the practical application of management principles within sport organisations operating at the community, state, national and professional levels in sport.

REFERENCES

Abel, D. (1980). *Defining the business. The starting point of strategic planning*. Englewood Cliffs, NJ: Prentice Hall.

Cherubini, S. (2000). *Il marketing sportivo*. Milan: FrancoAngeli.

Cherubini, S., & Canigiani, M. (Eds.), (2000). *Media e co-marketing sportivo: Strategie di convergenza nel mercato globale & locale*. Milan: FrancoAngeli.

Cherubini, S., Canigiani, M., & Santini, A. (2003). *Il marketing sportivo: analisi, strategie, strumenti*. Milan: Franco Angeli.

Cherubini, S., & Canigiani, M. (Eds.), (1999). *Il co-marketing sportivo: strategie di cooperazione nel mercato sportivo*. Milan: FrancoAngeli.

ConiServizi. http://impiantisportivi.coni.it/

Consorzio San Siro. http://www.sansiro.net/

Deloitte. (2008). *Annual Review of Football Finance*. Manchester: Deloitte.

Deloitte. (2007). *Annual Review of Football Finance*. Manchester: Deloitte.

Deloitte. (2006). *Rapporto sul calcio italiano: analisi economico-finanziaria sui conti della serie A e B*. Deloitte.

Desbordes, M. (Ed.), (2007). *Marketing & football: an international perspective*. Oxford: Elsevier Ltd.

FIGC. www.figc.it.

Foot, J. (2007). *Calcio: a history of Italian football*. London: Harper Perennial.

Hoye, R., Smith, A., Westerbeek, H., Stewart, B., & Nicholson, M. (2006). *Sport management: principles and applications*. Oxford: Elsevier Ltd.

Juventus.com. http://www.juventus.com/site/eng/index.asp/

Lega Calcio. www.legacalcio.it

Santini, A. (2008a). *Marketing major sport venues*. In Sport Marketing UK: Henry Stewart Talks.

Santini, A. (22nd October, 2008b). *A case-study of corporate turnaround: Juventus FC*. Presentation on the Birkbeck College, University of London, Sports Business Seminar Series. Retrieved on July 10, 2009, from http://www.bbk.ac.uk/management/mscmres/sb/seminars/asantini.shtml.

Santini A. (2005). Where have all the fans gone? *Stadia*. Issue 39.

RECOMMENDED WEBSITES

For details of Juventus FC's economic and financial results and company presentations as well as the results of their commercial strategy see the club website.

www.juventus.com

For more information on elite professional football in Italy see the Lega Calcio's website.

www.lega-calcio.it

The sporteconomy.it website reports the latest news on football as well as other sports economic and financial issues.

www.sporteconomy.it

CHAPTER 17

France

Michel Desbordes
ISC School of Management

Alexis Hamelin
SPORTFIVE

Objectives

Upon completion of this chapter the reader should be able to:

- Understand the cultural and national context in which the management of the football industry in France operates.
- Describe the key market players and stakeholders of the French football market.
- Describe the key elements of the regulatory system for French football, in particular the powerful role of the public authorities.
- Describe the key financial drivers in French football.
- Understand the necessity for the rebuilding of French football's stadia stock.

CONTENTS

OVERVIEW OF THE CHAPTER

In this chapter, we focus on the French Ligue 1 (L1). Managed by the LFP (Ligue de Football Professionnel), it is an interesting marketing case. Since the end of the 1990s, the L1 has considerably increased the value of its TV rights through two successful deals. The last one, signed in 2008, gives the clubs the opportunity to share €668 million (Repition, 2008). At the same time, the financial situation is healthy: clubs make a profit and thanks to the DNCG (Direction Nationale du Contrôle de Gestion, French football's regulatory authority), their budgets are strictly controlled. In spite of all these positive aspects, clubs are now deadlocked because stadia are too old. This implies a lack of revenues generated through ticketing, catering and merchandised products as French spectators do not spend enough on match day. This is a "heritage" of the 1998 World Cup, when most of the budget was dedicated to the construction of the Stade de France in Paris. No other arena was built at this time. Following the German example of the 2006 World Cup, French clubs are looking to catch up by constructing or renovating 18 different stadia. In order to illustrate this project, we will focus on two particular projects: Lyon and Le Mans. The interest of these cases lies in the many differences between these projects: their size, the type of governance and property, and the financing of the investment or the use of naming rights practice.

CONTEXT OF THE LIGUE 1 ORANGE[1]

Football as a Social Phenomenon

Football is the most popular sport in France, as it is in many other countries. According to a survey conducted by TNS Sport in December 2006, 41 percent of the Germans, 48 percent of the British, 45 percent of the Spanish, 61 percent of the Italians and 32 percent of the French consider football as their favourite sport.

Presentation of the Ligue 1 Orange

The Ligue 1 Orange represents the highest level in French football. The French system is very classical in the sense that the League organises professional football, while the federation manages amateur football (see Figure 17.1).

The Ligue 1 Orange is managed by the LFP that deals with, for example, negotiating TV rights. It is an open league with 20 teams that compete for the championship while trying to qualify for a European competition or simply to avoid relegation to Ligue 2 Orange.

As football is the most developed professional sport in France, it is not a surprise we find clubs in every region in France (see Figure 17.2 Map of clubs in the Ligue 1 Orange). There is no regional concentration, as in the Top 14 rugby championship, where 13 of the 14 clubs are located in the southern part of France.

---

[1] The mobile phone company gave its name to French Ligue 1 in 2002. But this naming operation failed in the sense the complete name was almost never used in the media. The company stopped this sponsorship deal in 2008.

FIGURE 17.1 *Notes:*
Ministère de la Jeunesse et des Sports = Ministry for Youth and Sport
Football Professionnel = Professional football
Football Amateur = Amateur football
Equipe de France = French national team
Equipe de France Espoirs = French national under-21 team
Equipe de France Feminine A = French national women's team
Coupe de France = the French Football Association Cup
Coupe de la League = the League Cup
Source: www.fff.fr

At the European level, the Ligue 1 belongs to the Big 5: the Premier League (England); la Liga (Spain); Lega Calcio (Italy); and the Bundesliga (Germany), despite the poor results experienced by Ligue 1 clubs in European competition in the last 15 years (the European Cup won by Olympique de Marseille in 1993, and the European Cup Winners' Cup by Paris St. Germain in 1996).

Media Exposure of the Ligue 1 Orange

On average, nearly 14 million people watch football in France on a weekly basis (Table 17.1 and TV audiences have been stable for the period 2001/2002 – 2006/2007). Since the creation of the Canal + television station in 1984 football has been a strategic central choice. An IPSOS survey in September 2007 showed that 40 percent of Canal+ subscribers were faithful because it broadcast Ligue 1. Though it is perhaps worth noting that the people behind the survey were the managers of the LFP, who obviously had the interest in attracting other potential broadcasters before inviting bids.

FIGURE 17.2 *Map of clubs in the Ligue 1 Orange in 2007/2008.*[2]

The good news for the LFP in 2008 was the arrival of Orange as a broadcaster (€203 million spent for three of the 12 lots available for purchase: Saturday's game, video on demand the week after the game, and the Ligue 1 on mobile phones). Thanks to football, Orange was able to demonstrate its future ambition of becoming a premier global competitor in the world of communication (TV, Internet, mobile phone, etc.). The LFP was also able to sell the TV rights at a higher price than the previous deal (€668 million per season for the 2008–2012 period, compared to €600 million for the 2004–2008 period) (Ligue 1.com; Severac, 2008).

A Healthy Financial Situation

The DNCG (*Direction Nationale du Contrôle de Gestion*—National Board for Management Control—NBMC) is an independent institution whose

---

[2] The twenty teams who started the 2007/2008 League Season were Auxerre, Bordeaux, Le Mans, Lens, Lille, Lorient, Lyon, Marseille, Metz, Nancy, Nice, Paris Saint-Germain, Rennes, Saint-Étienne, Souchaux, Strasbourg, Toulouse, and Valenciennes.

Table 17.1	Average Weekly TV Audience for Football in France in 2006						
Network	Canal +	Canal +	Canal + Sport	Canal +	TF1	France 2	M6
Programme	Live	Live	Live	Jour de Foot (highlights)	Telefoot (highlights)	Stade 2 (highlights)	Sport 6 (highlights)
Day	Saturday	Friday or Sunday	Sunday	Saturday	Sunday	Sunday	Sunday
Time	5:15 PM	8:45 PM	6:00 PM	10:15 PM	10:50 AM	6:00 PM	8:30 PM
Average audience	1,054,685	1,535,172	340,000	1,321,930	2,800,000	3,105,800	3,233,000

Source: *Médiamétrie, 2006.*

mission is to regulate French professional clubs' financial accounts. Its declared aim is to ensure that clubs who begin each championship season will be able to finish it without filing a petition for bankruptcy, which could possibly distort the competition. In 2009, the situation was sufficiently stable that the DNCG's aim consists more in encouraging good practice in business planning than attempting to control club activities. In the case a club's accounts are not in accordance with the DNCG's terms of agreement, they are punished seriously, potentially even facing relegation. (For example, Toulouse was relegated to Ligue 2 in 2001, and subsequently declined further to the third national level for financial reasons.)

This strict financial control is one of the reasons why clubs have balanced budgets: in 2008, the L1 achieved a global net profit of €43.0 million, compared with €28.0 million in the previous season (see Figure 17.4).

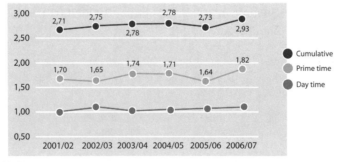

FIGURE 17.3   *Evolution of the average TV audience for Canal+ live matches (millions of TV viewers).*
Source: *Ligue de Football Professional, 2008, page 44.*

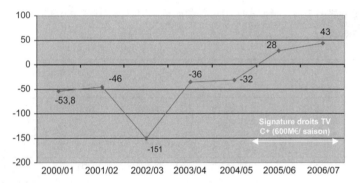

FIGURE 17.4 *Global profit of the 20 clubs in Ligue 1 (€ million).*
Source: Moatti (2008a).

These good results are connected with the TV deal signed between the LFP and Canal+ for the 2005–2008 period. The League garnered a profit from the competition between Canal+ and another provider, TPS, and ultimately, Canal+ paid €600 million per season for the exclusive rights to broadcast Ligue 1. It was a strategic bet and following this period, the two companies merged. This contract was an excellent one for the clubs, because their income increased significantly, but this was also dangerous because they are now "TV dependent." The contract was re-signed successfully in February 2008 with Canal+ and Orange sharing the rights for €668 million per season (*eufootball.biz*, 2008).

Some commentators believe that French football has become dangerously dependent on television income. Alexandre Bazire, marketing director of League 1 Team MUC 72 Le Mans has (interview with author, 25th April, 2008) stated that "when a customer represents 60 percent of a company's turnover, this company is becoming dangerously dependent on a single client." This situation has evolved dangerously: TV rights used to represent only 47% of Ligue 1 income in 2003/2004 but by 2006/2007 this had risen to 58% (see Table 17.2 and Figure 17.5).

Table 17.2 Revenues of L1 Clubs in € million (2006–2007 Season)		
Ticketing	139	14%
Sponsors and advertising	169	18%
Public subsidies	24	2%
TV rights	565	**58%**
Other products (Merchandising)	75	8%
Total	972	100%

Source: *DNCG, 2008, page 16.*

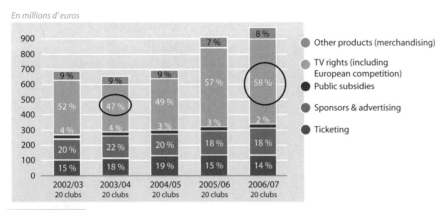

En millions d'euros

Legend:
- Other products (merchandising)
- TV rights (including European competition)
- Public subsidies
- Sponsors & advertising
- Ticketing

	2002/03 20 clubs	2003/04 20 clubs	2004/05 20 clubs	2005/06 20 clubs	2006/07 20 clubs
Other products				7%	8%
TV rights	9%	9%	9%	57%	58%
Public subsidies	52%	47%	49%	3%	2%
Sponsors & advertising	4%	4%	3%	18%	18%
	20%	22%	20%	15%	14%
Ticketing	15%	18%	19%		

FIGURE 17.5   *Revenues of L1 clubs in € million (Season 2006–2007).*
Source: DNCG, 2008, page 22.

More and More Spectators

Since the 1998 World Cup, there has been a significant increase in attendance at Ligue 1 matches. In spite of the 2002 "disaster" (the extremely poor performance of the French national team in the Japan/korea World Cup) and the exodus of the best French players to other European leagues, Ligue 1 is still attractive (see Figure 17.6).

The L1 Compared to the Other European Leagues

France and Italy are the two countries where we can observe a "TV dependency" issue (see Table 17.3).

Television contributed indisputably to the expansion of the professional sport spectacle in the 1990s. However, the French League is currently behind the rest of the Big 5 in terms of total revenues generated and the main explanation is the inferior quality of its stadia (Ponsot & Wenes, 2008).

Table 17.3	Income of Clubs in the Big 5 – 2006/2007 Season				
	England (20 clubs)	**Germany (18 clubs)**	**Spain (20 clubs)**	**Italy (20 clubs)**	**France (20 clubs)**
Ticketing	35%	22%	26%	13%	14%
TV rights	39%	35%	42%	63%	58%
Sponsorship	26%	26%	32%	12%	18%
Other commercial	0%	17%	0%	12%	10%

Note: For England and Spain sponsorship and commercial income is combined
Source: Deloitte, 2008a, page 14.

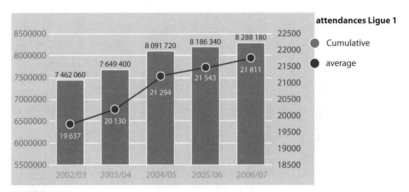

FIGURE 17.6 *Number of spectators in L1 (2002–2007: total and average).*
Source: Ligue de Football Professional, 2008, page 43.

Almost no French club owns its stadium, virtually all are owned by public authorities, and there are no "high-level" facilities.

A TV viewer was worth nearly four times a spectator in the stadium to the average Ligue 1 club in the 2006/2007 season (See Figure 17.7). In the Premier League (England), ticketing generated five times more revenues than in Ligue 1 in 2006/2007. This derives from the supreme seat capacity filling rate (over 90 percent), but also to the high-price policy that clubs tend to employ; for example, 43 percent of the turnover on a match day at

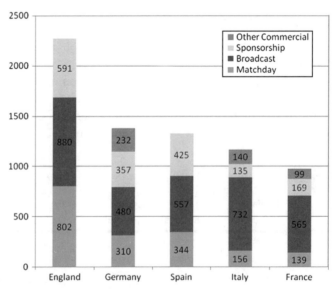

FIGURE 17.7 *Revenue Breakdown for European Leagues 2006/2007 in € million.*
Note: For England & Spain sponsorship and commercial income is combined
Source: Deloitte, 2008a, page 14.

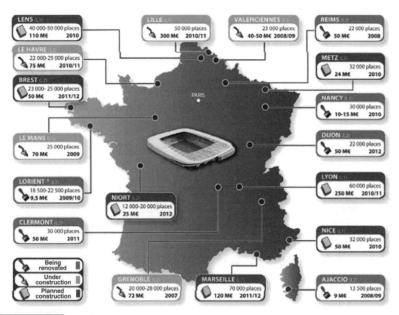

FIGURE 17.8 *Stadia construction projects in France.*
Source: LFP, 2008.

Manchester United comes from 9 percent of the most expensive VIP seats and hospitality suites.

Italy's Serie A also derives comparatively low levels of income from match receipts. This is because of violence at matches, match-fixing scandals and stadia which are old and unadapted to modern football business (Bolotny & Monna, 2007).

In Germany, on the other hand, the 2006 World Cup was an incredible impetus to build modern stadia. Now, the Bundesliga has the highest average match attendances in Europe. Spectators come early to the stadium and consume a lot (they can drink alcohol, which is not the case in France because of the 1991 Evin law to protect young people from the dangers of alcohol consumption). German clubs have also signed the highest number of stadium naming rights deals of any European country, as this marketing practice does not currently exist in France. (However, Le Mans will be the first club to sign such a contract when its new stadium is completed.)

The Spanish la Liga has more balanced revenue streams. It derives significantly more revenue from gate receipts in part thanks to the well developed *socio* fan culture.

The French Ligue 1, even though it is profitable (€43 million profit in 2006/2007 – Ligue de Football Professional, 2008, page 3), is not balanced at all in terms of revenue generated. Ticketing revenue reached €139 million for the entirety of L1, which is almost what English Premier League club Arsenal generated on match days alone (€134.6 million or 51 percent of Arsenal's turnover (in 2006/2007 – Deloitte, 2008b, page 10). TV rights are too important compared to other income streams and this could lead to a dangerous situation for French clubs.

THE SITUATION OF STADIA IN FRANCE

Is Euro 2016 an Opportunity?

France is currently a candidate for the 2016 UEFA Euro national team competition. But 10 years after the World Cup and 22 years after the last Euro tournament organised in France, there is much work to be done to ensure that football infrastructure is up to standard to win the 2016 Euro bid.

Even though France is a potential candidate, there needs to be further consideration of the size of arenas and the need to invest in infrastructure. There are 18 projects in France for new stadia, with an estimated budget of €1.5 billion (Stadiums Commission Report, 2008). In the case of a renovation, it is faster and cheaper, but these stadia tend to deteriorate quite fast (see for example the renovated 1998 World Cup stadia), and it is more complicated to sign a naming rights deal for such stadia, as according to Nicolas Bailly, Director of Stadium Consulting at SPORTFIVE, (interview with author, 22nd April, 2008), "Signing a naming rights deal, for Geoffroy Guichard (Saint-Etienne), or at the Vélodrome (Marseille), it is more complicated, for cultural reasons as supporters are attached to the old names". The following two case studies illustrate the challenges in marketing football stadia in France.

CASE STUDY: Two innovating development models in france

The MMArena

Created in the middle of the 1980s, Le Mans UC 72 is often considered a small club by the media, but it has a strong vision of the future and solid foundations. At the beginning of 2010, a new stadium will take the place of the current Léon Bollée stadium. Known as the "MMArena," it will be the first stadium in France to use naming rights. The insurance company MMA gave its name to the arena for €1 million per season for a 10-year period.[3]

---

[3] MMA was chosen from among 70 companies, according to Alexandre Bazire, Director of Marketing & Development at Le Mans UC 72.

The objective of this new stadium is to be "a place to live" and not only a place that is full every two weeks. The financial model looks something like this: Vinci, the construction company, will build the stadium, pay 50 percent of its cost and initially manage the arena, and local communities will finance the other 50 percent (City, Department, Region). After a commercial deal with Vinci, the club will take over the running of the stadium, which will be unique in France, and will give the club the opportunity to organise exhibitions, conference, and other revenue-generating events. The location of the stadium was integrated to the city, located near the following:

- Antarès arena, which hosts Le Mans Sarthe Basket (MSB) who won the French basketball championship in 2008.
- The "24h du Mans" circuit.
- The Bugatti circuit that hosts the Motorcycle "Grand Prix de France".
- A karting circuit.
- A velodrome.
- The racecourse.

The objective is to integrate the stadium into a "sport centre of attention," connected to the town centre by tramway. It will have year-round economic activity due to hosting football and basketball games, in addition to car races that will take place in May and June. The stadium will host the club's offices and its official capacity will reach 25,000 seats (compared to 18,000 in the old stadium), and up to 40,000 for concerts. The commercial offer will be renewed thanks to new business boxes and new partnerships with other local interests (packages for football, basketball and motor sport). The new complex will also include a three or four-star hotel, a panoramic restaurant, a fitness centre, a kindergarten (to attract women), and a "fun-park" for 12- to 25-year-olds in front of the stadium. Bazire points out, "As in England or in Germany, we really want to attract people earlier to the stadium."

Source: Bassi, 2008.

OL Land Stadium

"If we do not build decent stadia in France, our country will not represent anything in Europe in some years, it is THE priority for now," said Jean-Michel Aulas, Olympique

FIGURE 17.9 *The future MMArena.*
Source: www.MUC72.fr – Retrieved on June 28, 2008.

FIGURE 17.10 *First draft plan of OL Land Stadium.*
Source: www.olweb.fr – Retrieved on July 18, 2008.

Lyonnais president, in an interview in *L'Equipe* in 2008 (Moatti, 2008b).

For now, the existing Gerland stadium works very well: Over 90 percent of tickets were sold in Ligue 1, and 100 percent for the Champions League. With its new stadium, the club hopes to attract 1.5 million spectators per season (against 1 million in Gerland).

This project will be a pioneer for France: if Le Mans is the first naming deal, OL will be the first club to build its stadium with 100 percent private financing. Before launching this project, the OL Group was listed on the stock market ("It is not a football club anymore, but a entertainment spectacle company", according to Marino Faccioli, stadium manager, OL interview with the author, 29th April, 2008) and €96.2 million in capital

FIGURE 17.11 *Aerial view of planned OL Land Stadium.*
Source: OL Group (2007).

was obtained through this mechanism. A 50 hectares complex will be created which will include:

- A 60,000-seater stadium (including 10 percent allocated to business/corporate-seats).
- Offices for the club in a 3,000m² space.
- A museum.
- An official store.
- A training complex with five playing fields.

The other part of the project will be financed by Accor group, which includes:

- One three or four-star hotel and one two-star hotel.
- A sport park (karting, bowling, indoor golf).
- 3,000m² offices to rent.

As in the case of Le Mans, the objective is to create a multi-functional facility with 35 events a year (OL for football, but also the French national teams for rugby and football, and concerts). Additionally, seminars and conferences can be conducted year-round.

With the proximity to a big city, the international airport Lyon-St Exupéry (more than 7 million passengers annually), and its ideal geographic place, this stadium should be able to obtain the maximum five-star UEFA label.

Source: Anonymous, 2008.

The Ideal Stadium?

The "ideal stadium" does not exist (Duluc et al, 2008). But if France wants to reach a balanced business model in its football industry there are some important characteristics to take into account:

- This stadium needs to be brand *new*, because renovations do not allow ambitious projects. Furthermore naming rights deals are easier to sign with a new arena, and therefore it generates more revenues from the exploitation of the stadium.
- Having an *innovative architecture* that sticks in people's minds (for example, the Allianz Arena in Munich that can change its colour). In most cases, clubs should avoid athletics tracks around the outside of the playing pitch (Martin, 2007).
- A *home club* takes a major stake. The Stade de France is one of the most beautiful stadia in Europe, but there is a lack of history, as in the cases of Santiago Bernabeu in Madrid or simply the Parc des Princes in Paris, because it is not the home of a league club. This is also a way to secure the necessary minimum number of events every year.
- Concerning *facilities,* there is no checklist, but most stadia include: *"Classical" facilities,* such as an all-seater stadium, a convenient press zone, a roof, and a heated pitch for winter, some multifunctional facilities, such as a hotel, restaurants, shopping centres, fitness centres, cinemas (Accor group for hotels, Pathé group for cinemas, etc.).

FIGURE 17.12   *Allianz Arena of Munich.*
Source: www.allianz–arena.de

- It is also wise to think about the stadium's environmental impact. FIFA can award a stadium an EMAS label (Eco Management and Audit Scheme). For an example of good practice, Berne Stadium includes 12,000 m2 of solar panels.[4]
- Concerning transport, it is necessary to think about *public transport* during the conception of the stadium. With its Emirates Stadium, Arsenal decided to apply a "no car" policy, instead trying to attract 100 percent of people through the underground railway network, rail lines and buses.

CONCLUSIONS

In 2009 French clubs are deemed not able to compete at the European level because they do not have the financial power of the English Premiership clubs and the leading clubs in Spain and Italy. If this is partially true, it is also obvious that increasing revenue from French stadia is a key element in addressing this problem. According to Jean-Michel Aulas, president of Lyon (Stadiums Commissions Report, 2008), "If TV rights had been sold with the

---

[4] This produces 1,2 MkWh, the equivalent of the annual consumption of 400 families! (Belayge, 2007).

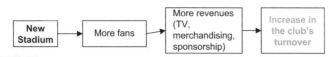

FIGURE 17.13   *New stadium Value Chain.*

stadia Lyon and Lille are going to build, the value would have been negotiated with €300 or €400 million more. [And] By the way, the number of spectators increases with the quality of the facility."

That is how Arsenal joined the Top 5 in Europe thanks to its new stadium. Shifting from Highbury to the Emirates during the summer of 2006 led to a 37 percent increase in turnover (€70,8M) (Stadiums Commission Report, 2008). Nicolas Bailly notes that "Nowadays, almost every Ligue 1 club has a project (renovation or construction)" and if French clubs want to catch up, there is no other alternative.

For example, Grenoble was promoted to Ligue 1 in 2007–2008, after they had finished building a high-tech arena. After the completion (February), the average attendance was 15,000, compared to 5,000 for the previous season and good results on the pitch alone cannot explain this enormous increase. Of course, this is an important decision for managers to make because it implies hundred of million euros, new bank loans, and a ten-year business plan for the future. But, according to Alexandre Bazire (Director of Marketing & Development, Le Mans UC72), the game is worth it: "Offer creates its own demand. Today, stadia are bad. When these stadia will allow new services, we will sell more season-tickets. For example, multiplex cinemas have created a new way of going to the movie. It is a place where you can eat, drink, and … see a movie!"

DISCUSSION QUESTIONS

1. Is the fact that French football is so heavily regulated a help or a hindrance to the competitiveness of French clubs in European football?
2. Is French football too heavily reliant on TV income?
3. Would French clubs benefit from taking ownership of their stadia?

GUIDED READING

Published by Elsevier in 2006, *Marketing and football: an international perspective* (Desbordes, Ed.) is an edited collection which examines "football and marketing" drawing on examples from fifteen different countries including France. *Marketing du sport* (Desbordes et al, 2004) is the first French-speaking book about sport marketing. First published in 1999, it was renewed in 2001 and 2004. It gives an overview of the way sports marketing is considered in France, compared to the "Anglo-Saxon" vision. *Stadia: A Design and Development Guide* (Geraint et al, 2007) is probably the best handbook explaining how architects build stadia from a technical point of view. The annual report of the French Professional Football League (the LFP), (Ligue de Football Professionnel, 2008), is an excellent source of data on French football.

REFERENCES

Anonymous. (28th April, 2008). Le grand Stade de l'OL. *Lyon Mag.* Page 2.

Bassi, O. (23rd April, 2008). Le Mans va concéder son stade au Groupe Vinci. *Les Echos*. Page 5.

Belayge, J. (2007). Nouveaux Stades, la Suisse est à l'heure. *Footpro*. No 36, 4–9.

Bolotny, F., & Monna, O. (September, 2007). Modèle économique des clubs: des stades et vite!. *Footpro*. 60–65.

Deloitte. (2008a). *Annual Review of Football Finance*. Manchester: Deloitte.

Deloitte. (2008b). *Football Money League*. Manchester: Deloitte.

DNCG (February, 2008). *Compte des clubs professionnels - Saison 2006/2007.* DNCG Retrieved on July 15, 2009, from http://www.lfp.fr/telechargement/0708_dncg_tout.pdf

Duluc, V., Dupont, R., & Tarrago, S. (1st March, 2008). Interview de J-M Aulas et Michel Seydoux: On a plus d'audace. *L'Equipe*. Page 2.

euFootballbiz (8th February, 2008). Canal Plus and Orange win LFP TV rights. *euFootballbiz*. Retrieved on July 15, 2009, from http://www.eufootball.biz/Television/5150-0802085-Canal-Plus-Orange-LFP-TV-rights.html

FFF.FR. www.fff.fr

Geraint J., Sheard R., & Vickery B. (2007). *Stadia: A Design and Development Guide*. 4th ed. Amsterdam: Elsevier/Architectural Press.

IPSOS (December, 2007). *Canal+ et le football*. Survey conducted for the Canal+ group. Paris: France.

Lfp.fr. www.lfp.fr

Ligue1.com. http://www.ligue1.com

Ligue de Football Professionnel. (2008). *Situation du football professionnel français, saison 2006–2007*. Paris: LFP Publisher.

Martin, F. (2007). Moderniser les stades, le défi français. *Sport Stratégies*. No 90. Pages 14–19.

Médiamétrie (December, 2006). *Audiences du football français*. Survey conducted for the Canal+ group. Paris: France.

Moatti, E. (12th February, 2008a), 43 millions d'euros de bénéfices. *l'Equipe*. Page 7.

Moatti, E. (8th February, 2008b). Un succès et des questions. *l'Equipe*. Page 9.

OL Group. (2007). *Projet OL Land – document de présentation*. Olympique Lyonnais Publisher.

Ponsot, V., & Wenes, G. (September, 2007). Les nouvelles formes d'exploitation des stades. *Footpro*. Pages 68–69.

Repition, I. (10th April, 2008). Orange défie Canal+ dans la télévision payante. *La Tribune*.

Severac, D. (8th February, 2008). Interview de F. Thiriez: La gourmandise est un vilain défaut. *Aujourd'hui en France*. Page 36.

Stadiums Commission Report (November, 2008). *Survey for the French Ministry of Sport*. Paris: France.

TNS (December, 2006). *Etude sur le football en Europe*. Survey conducted for the LFP (French Football League). Paris: France.

RECOMMENDED WEBSITES

Official website of the French Football Association

www.fff.fr:

Official website of the French Professional Football League

www.lfp.fr:

website of the famous French economic journal *Les Echos* which frequently comments on football industry issues.

www.lesechos.fr:

CHAPTER 18

Germany

André Bühler

Heidelberg International Business Academy

Objectives

Upon completion of this chapter the reader should be able to:

- Recall the historical milestones of German football.

- Describe the key market players and stakeholders of the German football market.

- Explain the structure of German football and the importance of the German national teams.

- Describe the Bundesliga and its various income streams.

OVERVIEW OF THE CHAPTER

This chapter starts off with a brief introduction to German football and an outline of the historical milestones. The first case study describes the World Cup 2006, one of the most important events in the recent history of German football. Then the German football market and its main stakeholders are introduced, followed by a description of the structure of German football. The importance of the German national teams (men and women) for Germany as well as the international football world, will then be discussed. Subsequently, the Bundesliga will be described in terms of clubs, fans, players, income streams and expenditures. Finally, the second case study is dedicated to VfB Stuttgart, one of the most interesting German football clubs.

INTRODUCTION

Football is the national sport in Germany. In 2008, more than 33.1 million Germans (51 percent of all Germans over 14) were interested in football (DFL, 2008, page 52). On a European and global level, the German national teams (both men and women) are highly successful. In addition, the German Bundesliga is one of the top professional football leagues in the world. The German football market is therefore an important submarket of the international football business.

THE HISTORY OF GERMAN FOOTBALL

The history of German football officially began with the establishment of the German Football Association (Deutscher Fußball Bund—DFB) in 1900. During the 1930s and 1940s, football was misused by the Nazi regime as a tool to promote their ludicrous paradigm. The DFB played an inglorious role and it took them 60 years to account for their Nazi past. The victory in the World Cup of 1954 in Hungary was the first German landmark in the history of football and was simultaneously a signal of awakening for a whole nation that was scarred by World War II. Empacher (2001) notes that the "Wunder von Bern" (miracle of Berne, as it was called) enabled millions of Germans to regain their national pride, which was lost in the war. In 1963, the top league in German football (the Bundesliga) was established and soon became the "love baby" of the German people. The first season of the newly established Bundesliga started with 16 teams from all over Germany and experienced an attendance rush, with Cologne being the first German Champions. In the 1970s a bribery scandal damaged the image of Germany's top football league. More than 50 players and ten clubs were embroiled in this scandal, where players took money from other clubs in order to lose games. Some of the protagonists were initially punished with a lifelong ban from football but they were later pardoned. In 1974, Germany not only hosted the World Cup but emerged as world champions. The following years of international football were dominated by the German squad and the German sense of self-esteem was widely based upon the success of the national team. In the 1980s, privately owned television stations were introduced in Germany, which led to more competition in the market for broadcasting rights and therefore higher income streams for football clubs. The 1990s were once again a successful decade for the German national team, which won the World Cup in Italy in

1990 and the European Championship in England six years later. The introduction of pay-per-view (PPV) television led to a further rise in revenues from broadcasting rights. Nowadays, professional football clubs in Germany can be compared with medium-sized companies in terms of annual turnover and number of staff. The Bundesliga itself is one of the most important football leagues in the world but it is the success of the German national team which has been the prime driver of football in Germany. The latest milestone in Germany's football history, the World Cup 2006, is described in Case Study 18.1.

CASE STUDY 18.1: The FIFA World Cup 2006 in Germany

In 2006, "the best World Cup ever," according to the world governing body FIFA (*The Guardian, 2006*), took place in Germany. Indeed, the 18th FIFA World Cup broke every record in number of participating nations, number of spectators and total media consumption. Thirty-two teams were competing in 64 games in front of 3.2 million live spectators and a cumulative TV audience of 26.29 billion viewers in 214 countries. Another 18 million people attended the official Fan Fests that were created in every one of the 12 host cities. These public viewing events contributed significantly to the success of the World Cup as they provided a good opportunity for fans from all over the world to experience the world's most important football competition without attending the games. The World Cup changed Germany's public image because the vast majority of football tourists experienced Germany as a hospitable and friendly country. Indeed, Germany and its people tried everything to fulfil the official World Cup motto - 'A time to make friends'. The peaceful and happy way of celebrating led not only to a different perception outside Germany but also inside the country. A lot of Germans experienced a new sense of national identity. For the first time in more than 60 years, it didn't feel wrong to show some kind of genuine patriotism. Indeed, it seemed that Germany reinvented itself. Of course, the performance and playing style of the German team reinforced this process. A new generation of national heroes (including Sebastian Schweinsteiger and Lukas Podolski) was born at the World Cup 2006 when the German national team (with former international Jürgen Klinsmann as manager) fascinated a whole nation with refreshing football. In economic terms, the World Cup resulted in positive effects as well, creating €2 billion in additional revenues for the German retail industry and €100 million additional tax income for the German government. All in all, the World Cup 2006 changed Germany in a very positive way and can therefore be seen as a small revolution.

Source: Bühler, 2006a; Fifa.com

THE GERMAN FOOTBALL MARKET AND THE MAIN MARKET PLAYERS

The German football market is a complex system of various interrelated stakeholders with different interests and motives. The most important market players will be briefly described below.

Governing Bodies

German football is firstly under the jurisdiction of the world governing body FIFA and the European governing body UEFA. The German Football Association, DFB, regulates the game on a general level, whereas the Deutsche Fußball Liga GmbH (DFL) acts as the governing body for the Bundesliga (1st and 2nd division).

Clubs

In 2007, the DFB (2007) had 25,869 registered football clubs, with 175,926 teams taking part in numerous football leagues across Germany. Thirty-six football teams play in the first and second division of men's professional football; twelve teams compete in the women's professional league.

Sponsors

Football has established itself as an ideal marketing instrument for companies in the German market. The Bundesliga therefore generates an extremely high level of income from sponsorship as will be shown in detail later in this chapter. Amongst the most significant football sponsors are German-based companies such as Adidas, Deutsche Telekom and Mercedes-Benz.

Media

The German media landscape is complex, sophisticated and determined by competitive pressure. Hundreds of daily newspapers want to attract as many recipients as possible, and football is therefore an important source of stories and coverage. Nearly every newspaper in Germany, on a local, regional or national level, extensively covers football from different perspectives and with different styles. Tabloids such as the *BILD-Zeitung* cover football in a more sensational way, whereas serious papers such as the *Süddeutsche Zeitung* (SZ) or the *Frankfurter Allgemeine Zeitung* (FAZ) try to comment on football in a more intellectual style. Furthermore, sports magazines such as the *Kicker, Sport-Bild* and *11 Freunde* focus mainly on football. In addition to the print media, there are around 20 free-to-air channels (such as *ARD, ZDF* or *DSF*) covering football to some extent. The only pay-TV station in Germany, *Premiere*, offers its subscribers live games of the Bundesliga and other international top leagues.

Players

Some of the most famous German football players are Uwe Seeler, Franz Beckenbauer, Lothar Matthäus, Jürgen Klinsmann and Oliver Kahn, who collectively represent nearly five decades of German football. Regarding female football, players such as three times World Cup player Birgit Prinz or goalkeeper Nadine Angerer have become famous within and outside Germany.

Agencies

A number of various agencies focusing on marketing rights and broadcasting rights have entered and developed the German football market in the last few years. One of the most important sports rights agencies is Sportsfive (based in Hamburg) who hold the marketing rights of many German professional football clubs. In addition, sports research consultancies such as IFM (based in Karlsruhe) and Sport+Markt (based in Cologne) advise football clubs and sponsors on a national and international level.

Key Figures

Although the governing bodies regulate the game and the competitions, German football is said by some to be unofficially ruled by a handful of key figures. Probably the most influential figure in German football is Franz Beckenbauer (famously called "The Kaiser") because of his wide national and international influence as a player, manager and official. Other former German internationals such as Uli Hoeness (commercial manager of Bayern Munich), Oliver Bierhoff (commercial manager of the German national team), Klaus Allofs (commercial manager of Werder Bremen) and Günther Netzer (TV pundit) all influence the German football market as well as public opinion.

THE STRUCTURE OF GERMAN FOOTBALL

In total, 36 professional clubs play in two professional leagues, which are run by the Deutsche Fussball Liga GmbH. The German Football Association (DFB) is responsible for all levels of German football, from the top leagues to the bottom leagues of amateur football. The leagues are linked by the exchange of teams, which are relegated from the upper league and promoted from the lower leagues. The German Bundesliga was run by the DFB until 2000, when the Ligaverband (Association of the League) was founded. The Ligaveband, which consists of the 36 members of the First and Second

Bundesliga, adopted the responsibility for professional football under the broader context of the DFB. The various tasks and specific arrangements are settled in a so-called Grundlagenvertrag (foundation agreement) between the Ligaverband and the DFB. Both institutions are also linked by mutual appointments to various committees. The day-to-day business of the Ligaverband is carried out by the Deutsche Fussball Liga GmbH (DFL) which is organised as a limited company. Figure 18.1 illustrates the structure of German football.

The German National Teams

Grünitz and von Arndt (2002) claim that no other team influences the attitude towards football in German society more deeply than the national team. Indeed, the German identity has been shaped significantly by the performance of its national team which in turn represents "typical" German characteristics like devotedness and an irrepressible desire to win. The notion that German football always seemed to be unattractive but very effective led the English international Gary Lineker to seriously conclude, "Football is a simple game; 22 men chase a ball for 90 minutes, and at the end the Germans always win." The playing style of the German team changed when Jürgen Klinsmann took over in 2004 in order to prepare the team for the World Cup two years later. He introduced a new system and made the style of playing more attractive. Although the team

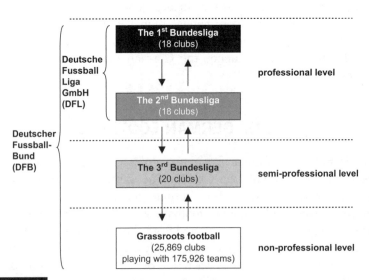

FIGURE 18.1 *The structure of German football.*

ended up in third place in the World Cup 2006, they won a lot of sympathy in Germany itself as well as respect from other footballing nations for their more attractive style of play. However, the changes affected were not only on the pitch, but also off the pitch. The former German international Oliver Bierhoff became the team commercial manager and thus the primary point of contact for sponsors. The sponsor pool of the DFB consists of a number of renowned companies such as Mercedes-Benz (the main sponsor), Adidas (the kit supplier), Coca-Cola and Deutsche Telekom (premium partners), as well as Lufthansa and McDonald's (partners) who pay millions of Euros in order to be associated with the German national team (DFB, 2009).

Although the female national team is traditionally overshadowed by the men's team, it has begun to raise awareness and to create its own profile after winning the World Championship two times in a row. As a consequence, the main players such as Birgit Prinz and Nadine Angerer are in the limelight of public attention and are therefore used as testimonials for companies in advertisements.

The German Bundesliga

The German Bundesliga is one of the top professional football leagues in Europe with an annual turnover of €1.45 billion in 2007 (DFL, 2008, page 168). Furthermore, it is considered to be one of the most business-like football leagues in the world. For example, the German licensing model is widely recognised as a beneficial model and acted as a prototype for the UEFA licensing scheme, which defines the minimum quality of standards in five main criteria categories: sporting, infrastructure, personnel and administration, legal and financial (Bühler, 2005). The strict regulations set by the DFL have led to financial stability in Germany's professional football. As a result, all 18 Bundesliga clubs were reporting profits in the 2006/2007 season (DFL, 2008, page 173).

Clubs of the German Bundesliga

In terms of image, each Bundesliga club has its own profile and reputation. Bayern Munich, for example, is considered by many to be a very arrogant club due to its huge sporting success and allegedly patronising attitude towards smaller clubs. Schalke 04 and Borussia Dortmund have a working class image because of their roots and their ability to attract huge fan bases from amongst the working classes of the historically industrial regions in which they are based. Clubs such as Leverkusen or Wolfsburg, in turn, find it difficult to fill their rather small stadia but do not have any financial problems in view of the fact that both are backed (and partly owned) by large German companies (Bayer and Volkswagen respectively). Hamburg is the only German club that has never been relegated from the Bundesliga. Stuttgart and Bremen are respected for their serious and sound management as well as their ability to develop young players. Figure 18.2 provides an overview of clubs playing in the Bundesliga in the 2008–2009 season.

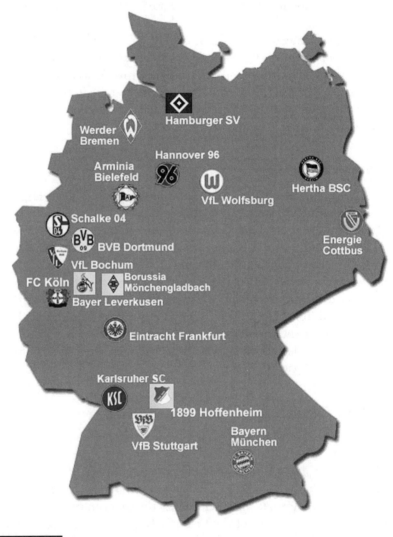

FIGURE 18.2 *Clubs of the German Bundesliga (season 2008–2009).*

Fans

Bayern München is not only the most successful but also the most popular football club in Germany. A recent study revealed that around 10.2 million German fans support the club that holds the record for winning the most number of Bundesliga championships (Sport+Markt, 2007a). Bremen (3.7 million fans), Dortmund (3 million), Hamburg (2.9 million), and Schalke (2.7 million) follow by a wide margin. A very interesting phenomenon is the relationship between Schalke and Dortmund supporters, which is characterised by cordial dislike and even hatred. Other rivalries exist between supporters of Karlsruhe and Stuttgart, and Bremen and Hamburg. On the other hand, there are quite a few friendly associations between competing fans such as Bayern and Bochum fans, and Schalke and Nürnberg fans.

Players

In the 2007–2008 season, a total of 503 players were playing in the German Bundesliga, 47 percent of them from other countries (DFL, 2008, page 154). The Bundesliga has been attracting more international star players such as Frank Ribéry (France), Luca Toni (Italy), and Diego (Brasil). However, German clubs have a huge competitive disadvantage in comparison to other leagues in view of the fact that the payroll taxes are very high in Germany (up to 45 percent of the total income). On the other hand, German clubs are known for paying the wages correctly and without delays that makes them reliable and therefore attractive for players.

INCOME STREAMS

German football clubs generate most significant revenues from five sources: media rights, match day income, sponsorship, merchandising and transfer receipts.

Media Rights

The biggest income stream is generated by the sales of broadcasting rights. Just over 33 percent of all revenues in 2006/2007 (DFL, 2008, page 166) could be attributed to income from television, radio and other media. (This includes all income from the Bundesliga, German FA Cup, and international match broadcasting and media rights). Television deals are arranged between the broadcasters and the league (i.e., the DFL), which then distributes the revenues among all league members. The centralised sale of broadcasting rights favours the smaller clubs and therefore secures some level of competitive balance within the league. However, the top clubs could make considerably more money if they were allowed to sell their rights individually. This is a controversial issue whenever it comes to new negotiations and leads to fierce disputes between bigger and smaller clubs. The DFL, (2008, page 184), however, has been able to increase the broadcasting revenues directly from Bundesliga and Bundesliga 2 significantly over the last 20 years (from €9.2 million in 1988 to €122.7 million in 1998 to approximately €433 million in 2008). In December 2008 the DFL announced a deal to broadcast live Bundesliga games over the 2009–2013 period with the Premiere pay-TV company for €412 million a year, slightly more than it was currently receiving for these rights (*Sport business International*, 2008).

Matchday Income

On average in 2006/2007, Bundesliga clubs made around 21 percent (i.e., €17.2 million) of their total turnover from ticket sales. The Bundesliga recorded the highest attendance record in European football with a total of 11.5 million spectators (that is 37,644 spectators per game) in 2007 (DFL, 2008, pages 67, 150 & 153). More than half of all tickets sold are season tickets, which is important as it ensures that the clubs generate significant revenues before the first kick-off of the new season. One reason for the attendance record is the fact that ticket prices are relatively low in comparison to other European top leagues. On average, fans have to pay less than €19 for a single ticket. The match day income differs between clubs, of course. Dortmund, for example, makes significantly more money from ticket sales than Bielefeld because of the differing stadium capacity (82,000 vs. 22,000). However, only one Bundesliga club (Schalke 04) owns its arena, while the other stadia are in the possession of companies, regional governments or the respective city which leads to lower match day income in view of rental payments and reduced revenues from catering.

Sponsorship Income

Around 25 percent of total income can be accounted by revenues generated by sponsorship deals. In 2007, more than 300 companies paid around €357 million in order to be associated with the 18 Bundesliga clubs (DFL, 2008, page 168). On average, each club made €5.3 million from shirt sponsorship alone, which is the highest amount in European football. Again, the sponsorship fees differ significantly between the individual clubs (Sport+Markt, 2007b), as the top five clubs made €24.6 million each from sponsorship, whereas the last five clubs collectively made "only" €14.8 million from the sales of sponsorship rights. In terms of shirts sponsorship, Energie Cottbus generates around €1.2 million only, whereas Bayern München earns up to €20 million each season from its main sponsor Deutsche Telekom. Revenues from sponsorship are likely to increase in the near future because German football clubs are considered to be effective marketing tools for companies who wish to raise awareness and improve their image on the German market (Bühler, 2006b).

Merchandising

In 2007, Bundesliga clubs generated around €108.5 million from the sales of merchandising and half of all merchandising revenues can be accounted from the sales of replica shirts. The unequal distribution of revenues is also evident in this field. The top five clubs account for two thirds of all merchandising revenues with Bayern Munich (€30 million) and Schalke 04 (€10 million) leading by far (Rohlmann, 2008). The German clubs will increase their merchandising revenues in the near future if they are able to break into new markets and improve their online shops.

Expenditures

The total income spent on players' salaries in 2006/2007 was €530 million and total expenditure on transfer fees was €164.5 million (DFL, 2008, pages 69–70). The wages/turnover ratio, a key performance indicator, is the lowest and therefore the most effective one in all the European top leagues at 39.3 percent (in comparison to 63 percent in the English Premier League and 64 percent in the Spanish Primera División) in 2005/2006. The restricted spending policy contributes to the financial soundness of German clubs on the one hand; on the other hand, however, German clubs find it increasingly difficult to compete with top European clubs in international cup competitions because top players go where they can earn the most.

CASE STUDY 18.2: VfB Stuttgart—a modern football club with a long history

VfB Stuttgart is a prime example of a top German football club which incorporates tradition as well as modern structure and management approaches. Established in 1893 as *Verein für Bewegungsspiele* (literally "club for moving games") in the capital of Swabia (a South German region), the club soon became known as 'the VfB' in and around Stuttgart. In 1950, the club won its first German Championship and in 1963 it was one of the sixteen founding members of the German Bundesliga. The recent history, however, seems to be most interesting. At the beginning of the new millennium, VfB Stuttgart was facing the threat of financial administration with debts of more than €20 million. The club had only 3,000 members and the first team was performing poorly. Seven years later, the club won the German Championship for the fifth time, had more than 40,000 members and recorded a financial profit. The successful turnaround was due to many reasons and coincidences. The financial difficulties left the club with no option but to sell expensive players and rebuild the team by relying on home developed talents such as Kevin Kuranyi, Timo Hildebrand, and Alexander Hleb. Although the VfB had (and still has) one of the most successful youth programmes in German football, the introduction of young players was a highly risky strategy – but one which paid off well. In 2003, the team surprisingly finished as Bundesliga runners-up and therefore qualified for the Champions League. The focus on youth development not only improved the image of the club (the team became popular as the "the young and wild" across Germany) but also led to significant financial revenues. In the meantime, Erwin Staudt was appointed as the first full-time president of the club. The former boss of IBM Germany introduced many business and management innovations to the club. For example, a modified version of the Balanced Scorecard (BSC) was installed in order to control risks, calculate key figures and make strategic decisions (Jordan, 2008). Furthermore, a sophisticated Customer Relationship Management (CRM) programme was introduced in order to manage and maintain relationships with various customer groups such as fans, spectators and sponsors (Wehrle, 2008). In addition, an in-house marketing company (the "VfB Stuttgart Marketing GmbH") was founded in order to take care of the club's marketing and communication rights. All these steps led to a further professionalisation of the whole club. In 2009, VfB Stuttgart is seen as a modern and financially sound club with a good reputation both on a national and international level. As a consequence, the club made it into the top 20 ranking of Europe's most valuable football clubs with a brand equity of €288 million in 2007 (BBDO Consulting, 2007). These developments culminated in the club winning the German Bundesliga Championship in 2007 with the youngest VfB team ever. Again, the widely respected youth programme of the club proved to be successful in view of the fact that fresh talents such as Mario Gomez, Semi Kedhira, and Serdar Tasci emerged as key players. Although the club struggled in the following season with an early exit in the Champions League and few convincing games in the Bundesliga, the prospects for success on and off the pitch seem to be promising. The club is run professionally by Erwin Staudt and his staff, the youth programme is able to produce one talent after the other and famous business partners such as Puma and Porsche engage themselves in long-term partnerships with the VfB. Mercedes-Benz, as one of the exclusive partners of the club, contributed around €20 million for the refurbishment of the Stuttgart stadium which will be turned into a football-only arena. In addition, all marketing rights belong to the club itself, which means that they can sell them on their own without having to pay brokerage fees to third parties. Another factor for the future success lies in the history of the club. The red chest ring on white jerseys with the popular VfB crest is a unique feature in professional European football and therefore a valuable tool for national and international brand recognition. All in all, the club seems to have the potential to become one of the most important football clubs in Germany and Europe (DFL, 2008, page 122).

CONCLUSIONS

Germany is one of the most successful football nations in the world. The German national teams (both men and women) have won many trophies and titles, German key figures such as Franz Beckenbauer and Jürgen Klinsmann have a huge influence in international football and the Bundesliga is considered to be one of the most successful European leagues. The financial soundness and spending discipline of Bundesliga clubs is well known and should act as an example in international football. However, German football clubs have to cope with relatively high income taxes and relatively low media revenues due to a very complicated TV market (with a lot of free-to-air channels and only one pay TV station). In addition, German clubs refuse to accept foreign investors and industrial tycoons as owners who might use football clubs as their private plaything. This in turn leads to a competitive disadvantage in comparison to other top leagues that are able to attract more international top players as they pay higher wages. As a consequence, the recent performance of German clubs in international competitions is not as good as it used to be. The Bundesliga, however, is still an attractive product which casts a spell over millions of football fans each season. The stadia continue to fill to near full capacity, the sponsorship market increases from season to season and the financial soundness of German clubs might turn into a competitive advantage in the forthcoming years. In addition, the German national teams will still play an important role in the international competitions in the future. All in all, the future of German football looks promising.

DISCUSSION QUESTIONS

1. Which events would you consider to be the most important milestones in German football?
2. Would you agree with the statement that the German national team is more important for German football fans than the Bundesliga?
3. What are the most important income streams for German Bundesliga clubs?
4. Where do you see the competitive advantages and disadvantages of German football in comparison to other countries?

GUIDED READING

The annual report of the DFL (e.g., the *Bundesliga Report 2008*) provides a detailed overview of the German Bundesliga each season. The report highlights the key developments in the Bundesliga and describes in detail the various income streams for the league and the individual clubs.

REFERENCES

BBDO Consulting. (2007). *Top 25 ranking of Europe's most valuable football clubs*. BBDO Consulting.

Bühler, A. W. (2005). *Fans und Fanverhalten im Profifußball: Ein Vergleich zwischen England und Deutschland*. In G. Schewe, & P. Rohlmann (Eds.), *Sportmarketing* (pp. 221–236). Verlag Hofmann.

Bühler, A. (2006a). Point of Emotion: The Fan Fests at the FIFA World Cup 2006. *Sport Marketing Europe*, Issue 2, p. 8–13.

Bühler, A. W. (2006b). *Professional Football Sponsorship in the English Premier League and the German Bundesliga*. Unpublished dissertation.

Deutscher Fussball Bund (DFB) (2009). *www.dfb.de*. Retrieved on July 13, 2009, from http://www.dfb.de/index.php?id=500665

Deutscher Fussball Bund (DFB) (27th March, 2007). *Close to 6.5 million members*. Deutscher Fussball Bund. Retrieved on July 13, 2009, from http://www.dfb.de/index.php?id=500016&tx_dfbnews_pi1[showUid]=10685&tx_dfbnews_pi1[sword]=175,926 &tx_dfbnews_pi4[cat]=117

DFL (2008). *Bundesliga Report 2008*. Deutsche Fußball Liga GmbH. Retrieved on July 13, 2009, from http://www.bundesliga.de/media/native/dfl/dfl_bundesliga_report_2008_eng.pdf

Empacher, S. (2001). Die Entwicklung vom Volkssport zu profitorientierten Einheiten: Dargestellt am Beispiel des Fussballs. In A. Hermanns, & F. Riedmüller (Eds.), *Management-Handbuch Sportmarketing* (pp. 201–215). Verlag Vahlen.

Fifa.com. TV Data. *Fifa.com*. Retrieved on July 26, 2009, from http://www.fifa.com/aboutfifa/marketing/factsfigures/tvdata.html

Grünitz, M., & von Arndt, M. (2002). *Der Fußball-Crash*. RRS.

Guardian (28th June, 2006). Blatter: this is the best World Cup ever. *Guardian*. Retrieved on July 13, 2009, from http://www.guardian.co.uk/football/2006/jun/28/worldcup2006.sport26

Jordan, C. (2008). Controlling im Sport. In G. Nufer, & A. Bühler (Eds.), *Management und Marketing im Sport*. Berlin: Eric Schmidt.

Rohlmann, P. (2008). *10. Fanartikel-Barometer der Fußball-Bundesliga*. PR Marketing.

Sport+Markt (2007a). *Football Top 20 2007/08*. Sport+Markt AG.

Sport+Markt (2007b). *Jersey Report 2007/08*. Sport+Markt AG.

Sportbusiness International (1st December, 2008). Premiere secures Bundesliga rights. *Sportsbusiness.com* Retrieved on July 13, 2009, from http://www.sportbusiness.com/news/168376/premiere-secures-bundesliga-rights

Wehrle, A. (2008). *Die ganzheitliche Sicht auf den Kunden—CRM beim VfB Stuttgart 1893 e.V.* Presentation at the ISPO Sport Sponsorship Conference 2008 in Munich.

RECOMMENDED WEBSITES (AVAILABLE IN ENGLISH)

Deutscher Fußball Bund (DFB)
www.dfb.de
Deutsche Fußball Liga (DFL)
www.dfl.de
FC Bayern München
www.fcbayern.de
VfB Stuttgart
www.vfb.de

PART 3

Managing Football in Emerging Markets

CHAPTER 19

Australia

Dave Arthur
Southern Cross University

Greg Downes
Southern Cross University

Objectives

Upon completion of this chapter the reader should be able to:

- Understand the growth, development, and emergence of football in Australia, and recognise some of the problems faced by football in Australia.

- Appreciate the impact of the Crawford Report as a seminal moment in Australian football and its value as a change agent.

- Have knowledge of the various levels of football in Australia.

- Appreciate the future challenges faced by football in Australia as it seeks to establish itself as a world force on and off the field.

OVERVIEW OF THE CHAPTER

Much has been written recently on the emergence of Australia as a successful football nation—one that competes on the international stage—and a true member of the world game. The euphoria of the days which immediately followed the memorable penalty shootout on November 16, 2005, that resulted in the Socceroos qualifying for the 2006 FIFA World Cup for the first time since 1974 had, for many, finally erased a long history of political infighting, rumour mongering, alleged illegalities and gross mismanagement that had denied the emergence of Australia as a true football nation for many years. As Fink (2007, page XIV) pointed out, the importance was monumental: "We'd done it. We'd finally made it to the FIFA World Cup, the biggest sporting event on earth, after 32 excruciating years. Nineteen seventy-four was a long time ago. It was another *time.*" Australia's participation in the World Cup in Germany in 2006, the creation of the A League in 2005–2006 and the entry into the Asian Football Confederation (AFC) all promise a brighter future for the game. In addition, the rapid rise of the women's game and the concurrent successes of the Matildas on the world stage add to the positioning of Australia as an emerging nation in the game.

A BRIEF HISTORY

The game of football in Australia has a long and tumultuous history, one which can be traced as far back as the 1880s. High levels of immigration at that time led to a huge increase in the U.K.-born population, where association football was establishing itself with the support of the working class. It was due to the British influence that the game began to develop formally in Australia.

The period leading up to the beginning of the First World War resulted in a significant surge of popularity in the game. As a result, every state within Australia had established a soccer competition by the early years of the new century and by 1906, there were 100 clubs registered in New South Wales alone (Thompson, 2006). Due to the increased popularity and the growing level of contact between the states, moves were made to form an effective national body. In 1912, the Commonwealth Football Association (CFA) was formed and is recognised as the first national football representative body of any code within Australia. In 1921, the CFA changed its name to the Australian Soccer Association (ASA), basing its headquarters in Sydney.

During this period, the game suffered its first significant political turmoil. A meeting of the ASA in 1914 decided to dispense with the system of representative district teams that had been introduced in 1903 in favour of a return to a league based on club representation. The supporters were mainly the British immigrants who were keen on returning administration of the game to a system which they were used to, as they did not agree with the Australians. This decision was subsequently rescinded and the dispute resulted in the breakaway Metropolitan Soccer League (MSL). The ASA finally dropped the district system in 1916 and reconciled with the new league in 1919. However, this dispute was merely a taste of things to come, as it highlighted and made public the tension that existed between the local and immigrant camps and provided a stark example of the future problems the game would face on its road to recognition and emergence.

The 20 years between the two world wars heralded the introduction of international football with the birth of the Australian national team in 1922. During this period, Australia welcomed visits from New Zealand (1923), China (1923, 1927), Canada (1924), a professional English team (1925), Czechoslovakia (1927), India (1938), and Palestine (1939). It is interesting to note that Australia did in fact tour the Dutch East Indies in 1928 and 1931, which represented Australia's first excursion into Asia. This was a precursor to the great change which was to occur in 2006, some seventy years later, with Australia's entry to the Asian Football Confederation (AFC).

The period prior to World War II represented "a domestic Revolution" in the game, once again on the back of a huge increase in immigration. This time, however, it was not British based; the majority of immigrants came from continental Europe and this resulted in a huge impact on the development of the game in Australia in the years to come. As Thompson (2006, page 52) related, the "inherited amateur Anglophile culture of the local district associations weakened and was swept away." Ethnically based football clubs began to form around the country as the new migrants sought to reinvent passionate pastimes from their homelands. For example, Juventus was formed in Melbourne due to the large numbers of Italian immigrants and the left over Italian teams of the prewar era, whilst others included the Yugoslavian team JUST and a Macedonian club. These clubs went from strength to strength and challenged the established local clubs for supremacy.

By the mid-1950s, ethnic teams were the dominant forces in all states of Australia except New South Wales (NSW). This was due to the administration of the time which prevented ethnic teams from reaching the senior division by placing insurmountable hurdles in their way. This caused great unhappiness and inevitably led to further disruption and to what was known as the 'soccer war'. In 1956, the formation of the Federation of NSW Soccer Clubs (which represented those teams which felt unsupported and vilified by the ASA) heralded a split from the ASA. This split resulted in the formation of two separate competitions beginning in 1957 and dragged the game down into ongoing disputes over money, transfer fees, property, grounds, players, and representative tours for several years to come. The so-called war reached its lowest point when FIFA decided to ban Australia from international competition until the ASA had settled the ongoing administrative problems facing the game at that time. Unfortunately, it wasn't until 1959 that they finally resolved to grant the Federation control of the game in NSW. FIFA subsequently lifted the ban in 1963 after disputes concerning transfer fees had been finally ratified.

On the international front, Australia won its first international tournament by defeating South Korea in the Saigon tournament in 1968. This win also saw the birth of the nickname 'Socceroos'. The term, penned by News Limited journalist Tony Horstead, was adopted by the players and the fans and has remained ever since. Australia had first applied to join the Asian Football Confederation (AFC) in 1964 but was denied and in response, they formed the Oceania Football Federation together with New Zealand in 1966. Australia's success on the international stage took a major leap forward when the Socceroos qualified for their first appearance at the FIFA World Cup in 1974, held in Germany. Although the team did not progress further than the group stage, the Socceroos had performed remarkably against world ranked teams and had promoted Australia as a country capable of performing on the world stage. Alas, this success was not to be the impetus that many thought would reignite the growth of the game on the domestic front and the future development of the Socceroos.

The Australian Soccer Federation (ASF) launched the first national league (NSL) containing 14 teams in 1976. The league was supposed to form the basis of a strong domestic competition and designed to facilitate the development of the international team. According to many, including Fink (2007), Solly (2004) and Thompson (2006), there were a variety of reasons why this did not in fact occur. The continued ineptness of the administration began to take its toll, and increasing costs and a decline in match attendance across the board as well as many ad hoc changes made to the game also had a detrimental effect on the game's potential for growth. The cause was hardly helped by the Socceroo's continual failure to qualify for the FIFA World Cup.

Alleged misconduct within the soccer fraternity, this time over the misappropriation of transfer fees, resulted in an inquiry. The *Stewart Report* (named after the judge who headed up the investigation) was published by a committee of the Australian Parliament in 1995, and was highly critical of management practices within Australian soccer.

The findings caused much distress, argument and counterargument but for the most part, the recommendations were largely ignored. The consequence of ignoring the recommendations was far reaching, as the domestic competition continued its inexorable decline and drew its last breath in 2003–2004. The Socceroos continued to fail in their quest to qualify for the FIFA World Cup—although some of this can be ascribed to a tortuous qualifying schedule that saw them eventually play the fifth placed South American qualifier in a home and away playoff. The game was continually caught in the glare of poor publicity related to financial and other mismanagement (see for example the transcripts of the *ABC* show the 7.30 Report–2002). Finally, the federal government was forced to intervene and in September 2002,

David Crawford, Chairman of multinational companies such as Fosters Group Ltd and BHP Billiton Ltd, and who had previously undertaken a similar role for Australian Rules football (AFL), was appointed to undertake a complete review of the effectiveness and efficiency of the way soccer in Australia was structured, governed and managed, under the auspices of the Australian Sports Commission and at the behest of the Federal Minister for the Arts & Sport, Rod Kemp. In contrast to previous reviews, Crawford's findings were thus backed by the Federal Government and the outcome became the major turning point for the game in Australia's long soccer history.

THE CRAWFORD REPORT

The national game had reached its lowest point, and had no financial security, no future direction, a losing national team and a total lack of ability at the board level to make the necessary changes required to move the game forward. Soccer Australia (SA) had no input into the development of the terms of reference for the Crawford enquiry; however, the board did provide a commitment that they would enact all the recommendations provided by the review. It should also be noted that the Australian Sports Commission (ASC) had stated that all funding would be cut if Soccer Australia did not cooperate. Although the SA board had agreed to abide by the decision to implement such an enquiry, they were obstructive in assisting its process and had little input into developing a blueprint for the future development of the game they purported to represent.

The Crawford committee held a total of 74 meetings nationwide, and received a total of 230 written submissions from parties interested in the future of the game. At the time of writing his final report, David Crawford was said to have been amazed that out of the 230 written submissions received, not one had anything positive to say about Soccer Australia. His final report (Crawford, 2003) was submitted in April 2003 and included 53 wide reaching recommendations. The Crawford Report (see Case Study 19.1) recognised that a complete change to the way soccer had been managed in Australia was the only answer to the woes of the game. As a result, the report recommended that constitutional change was imperative, including the immediate replacement of the current board with an interim board. Although this was only one of the many recommendations, it heralded the major directional change which was required to move the game forward in Australia. The new board was hand-picked and included the appointment of Westfield (the major international shopping centre development company) chairman Frank Lowy as chairman, with the assistance of other well-known Australian businessmen.

These appointments and the outcome of the enquiry were widely accepted and supported by almost everyone except the standing board members of Soccer Australia who were in total disagreement with the outcomes. Following many months of negotiation, funding cuts, threats and legal challenges, the sitting board reluctantly transferred the future of soccer to the new board on July 19, 2003. The future of soccer in Australia was finally secured. As Frank Lowy (*Goal.com*, 2008) opined at the November 2008 Football Federation Australia (FFA) annual general meeting, "Importantly, everything we do is now within a national strategic framework to advance the game in a uniform way across Australia."

CASE STUDY 19.1: The Crawford Report

As alluded to in the previous paragraphs, by 2002 Soccer Australia and soccer in Australia were in disarray. Prior to the formation of the Crawford Review, there were many incidents that highlighted this:

- The failure of the Socceroos to qualify for the World Cup and Confederations Cup (largely due to poor finances and a consequent inability to utilise European based players).

- An investigation by the Australian Broadcasting Corporation's *Four Corners* programme that uncovered conflicts of interest and wholesale mismanagement at board level in Soccer Australia.

- Constant in-fighting between political factions and concentration of voting and legislative powers in a relative minority of people perpetuating bad governance.

- Resistance to co-operation with government enquiries (Crawford and others).

In terms of governance, the membership of Soccer Australia was comprised of 12 state and territory-based associations, the Australian Soccer Referees Association, and the 12 Australian clubs participating in the National Soccer League (NSL). The total number of votes cast at general meetings was 61, 16 of which were allocated to the NSL clubs.

However, as only whole number votes could be cast and there was only 12 Australian clubs in the NSL competition at the time, the total number of votes exercised by the NSL was 12. The number of votes allocated to each state and territory varied. For example, Soccer Canberra had more registered players than Soccer Tasmania, but exercised 3 votes against Tasmania's 5. A number of junior or amateur associations with large registration numbers exercised 1 vote, compared with other state bodies with fewer registration numbers or financial contributions that might have exercised 4 or more votes.

The Review Committee found the following major issues resulted from this structure:

- Poor governance and management practices within the sport.

- Inappropriate conduct by directors including micromanaging day-to-day business at the expense of their broader strategic responsibilities.

- In-fighting between Soccer Australia and state federations, resulting in a poor working relationship.

- Lack of integration and mutual trust between Soccer Australia and its constituent bodies.

- Lack of strategic decision making, poor financial management, and lack of accountability within the sport.

- State- and territory-based associations competing against one another.
- Failure to translate the enthusiasm for junior soccer to senior soccer.
- Slow response by Soccer Australia in addressing the interests of referees, women in the sport and indoor soccer.
- Need for separate responsibility for the NSL.

The Review Committee also cited very strong positives available to the administration of soccer in Australia, including the following:

- A very strong participation base, particularly at junior levels.
- Programmes for developing talented athletes, including state- and territory-based national training centres and the Australian Institute of Sport.
- The large number of elite players of international quality.
- Strong growth in female participation.
- Passionate supporters.

The Committee concluded that the current structure of soccer in Australia was ineffective, did not work, and needed to change. The Committee also took the view that it was fundamental for Soccer Australia to have a truly independent board that had the responsibility to develop policies and strategies for the future of the sport. The management structure should also then address the key result areas of community soccer (game development and game operations), high-performance soccer, and corporate operations (commercial, financial, and administration). It was recommended that board members be independent of special interest groups and, through strict adherence to appropriate governance principles, be free of any conflict of interest of a financial, personal or representational nature. Finally, the Committee recommended that the NSL operate as a separate entity under license to Soccer Australia.

Recommendations

More than 50 recommendations were eventually put forward by the Review Committee, including the following:

- Streamline membership structures and arrangements with state bodies concerning membership fees.
- Replace Memorandum and Articles of Association with a new Constitution.
- Establish similar documents and a Memorandum of Understanding with state bodies concerning obligations and *key objectives*.
- Soccer Australia to be governed by a board of no more than six independent directors.
- CEO to attend board meetings, but to hold no formal voting powers.
- Four-year terms for directors to be established, with additional term limits strictly enforced.
- Change to voting structure at annual general meetings, including an even spread of votes amongst state bodies and additional votes allocated to large member bodies.
- Duty statements and conflict of interest protocols to be developed for board members.
- Soccer Australia to establish the National Soccer League (NSL) as a separate entity through a licensing arrangement.

Outcomes

Despite the initial attempts to spoil the reform process, the majority of recommendations made by the Independent Review Committee have been implemented by the National and State Associations. In particular, resistance to reforms at the National level were largely dealt with swiftly by the threat by the Australian Sports Commission to withhold funding to Soccer Australia, which it relied so heavily on.

Restructuring of the governance structures led to a more democratic approach and, in more substantial terms, has led to the resignation of the Soccer Australia board and their replacement with a board led by Frank Lowy.

The Lowy led board has completely overhauled the organisation. Now called Football Federation Australia (FFA), it has achieved financial stability to this end. It has also gained the confidence of the business community, having acquired several high profile sponsors. The re-launched domestic competition (the Hyundai A-League) can be seen as a byproduct of the change initiated by the Independent Soccer Review Committee's report. The National men's team, the Socceroos, after qualifying for the World Cup in 2006 and reaching the last 16, continues to perform well on the International stage and Australia's keynote players, in both genders, fill major roles in clubs in competitions throughout Europe, Asia and the United States.

Source: Hills, 2007; Crawford, 2003.

THE A- LEAGUE

One of the immediate actions of the new board was to commission an independent report into the way the National Soccer League (NSL) had previously been run. This particular review (Australian Soccer Association Limited, 2003), titled 'The Report of the NSL Task Force' clearly identified and recommended a new way forward for top level football in Australia. In the place of the NSL, the Australian Soccer Association, which (subsequently) became Football Federation Australia (FFA), announced plans for a new national, ten-team, professional competition to start in 2005. The competition was based on the one-city, one-club franchise system used in North America.

The main reasons for such a format were to concentrate player talent, and more importantly, to break the connection between clubs and specific ethnic groups, which was common under the NSL. The taskforce plan called for privately owned franchises to represent the large conurbations of Sydney, Melbourne, Brisbane, Perth, Adelaide, Newcastle, and New Zealand, with the eighth and final club to be selected from remaining expressions of interest. The selection of teams, with the Central Coast becoming the eighth area represented, was announced on November 1, 2004. The announcement directly resulted in the end of 'top flight' football for most of the 13 NSL teams, with only three former clubs making the transformation into the new league: Adelaide United, Newcastle Jets (formerly Newcastle United), and Perth.

The FFA scheduled the inaugural season to begin in August 2005, budgeting for an annual turnover of AUD50 million and average crowds of 10,000. A naming rights sponsorship was negotiated with the Hyundai Motor Company Australia for AUD10 million over four years and as a result, the inaugural Hyundai A-League season was launched.

The A-League has experienced four full seasons up to and including the 2008/2009 season, and based on the FFA's original objectives the league has proven successful with average crowds above expectations (with an average attendance of 11,627 in its inaugural season) and large attendance figures for the various finals series. A salary cap is currently in operation with various allowances made for "marquee" players in each club. The season is comprised of a home and away series with the leader of the competition declared the minor premier. Immediately following this a knock-out series is undertaken with the grand final winner declared the major premier (full details can be accessed from the official A-League website: *www.a-league.com.au*).

The A- League is set to expand in the 2009–2010 season with the inclusion of two new franchises from Queensland: Gold Coast United FC and North Queensland FC. Discussions are also underway for the possible inclusion of more teams in the future. Areas being considered include Wollongong, Tasmania, a second Melbourne team, Western Sydney and Canberra.

NATIONAL YOUTH LEAGUE

On the 5th March, 2008, it was announced that a national youth league would also be set up in conjunction with the A-League. This new competition was instigated in order to continue to develop young Australian talent that would eventually play in the A-League as well as for the Socceroos. The National Youth League is comprised of seven teams, each linked to the corresponding club in the A-League (further details on the National Youth League can be accessed from the A-League site: *www.a-league.com.au*).

THE WOMEN'S GAME

The rapid growth and rise in popularity of women's football globally and more latterly in Australia clearly supports the notion that Australia is a true emerging nation in the international arena of football (see Williams, 2007, for a more detailed review of the programme of Australian women's football). As with the history of the male game in Australia, the inherent problems within the domestic code and its ongoing upheavals did little to promote the women's game with the Australian sporting public. As a result, women's football suffered frequent periods of instability and a general failure to grow both as a participant and spectator sport. In addition, football in Australia grew up in the shadow of the sporting giants of the rugby codes of league and union, cricket and the Australian Football League (AFL). Indeed, it was not until 1979 that the Australian Football Association (AFA) recognised the first international "A" game played by their women's team. It is sobering to report that by that date, they had already played a total of 169 games and travelled to five of the six FIFA regional confederations.

In 1990, the Australian women's team (known colloquially as the Matildas, taken from the song Waltzing Matilda) joined with Fiji and Papua New Guinea to form the Oceania Women's Football Association. This lasted until 1991 when the FIFA-affiliated Oceania Football Confederation (OFC) created a stand alone women's committee.

By 1995, Australia had qualified to represent the OFC in the FIFA Women's World Cup in Sweden and went on to qualify for the World Cup in the USA in 1999. Great hopes were then held for a successful campaign in the 2000 Olympic Games, which were held in Sydney. Unfortunately, the previous momentum was not able to carry either the women's or men's teams at these Games. After their poor performance at Sydney 2000 the Matildas went on to win the Oceania Cup and subsequently qualified for the FIFA World Cup in 2003.

The lack of depth in the number of female players in comparison with the men's game and the overall position of football in Australian sporting culture have made it very difficult for the women's game to develop and grow. This development was further hindered by a complete lack of resources allocated to the development of women's football over the years 1969 to 1995. This situation indirectly led some members of the women's team to pose for an infamous nude calendar. The Matildas—A New Fashion in Football, was released in 1999 in an attempt to raise both the profile of the sport and much needed funds to support the national team. The release polarised opinions and sparked a major debate as to why women's sport (and indeed many minority sports) have to undertake such promotions merely to stay in existence (*Sydney Morning Herald*, 2006).

In a similar manner to the men's game, Football Federation Australia's (FFA) entry into the AFC in 2006 provided the Matildas with greater opportunities to compete on the international stage and a new pathway for qualification to the final stages of the FIFA women's World Cup. In their inaugural foray into the AFC Asian Women's Cup, the Matildas recorded a closely fought runner-up place to China. Despite the difficulties and lack of resources, the Matildas again qualified for the FIFA Women's World Cup in China in 2007. They defeated Ghana 4–1, followed by a 1–1 draw against Norway. A last-minute goal from Captain Cheryl Salisbury provided a draw against Canada 2–2 in the last group match. This win enabled the team to advance to the knockout stage of the tournament for the first time in history.

The Matildas came up against Brazil in their elimination match, losing the game 3–2 to end their 2007 World Cup run. Their run was a great achievement and placed Australia on the international map. It is particularly significant in light of the fact that no national league was operating in Australia at the time, but that has not always been the case. A women's National Soccer League (WNSL) began with six clubs in 1996 and continued in that form until 2004, but with the reorganisation of the sport generally around this time the women's game was not immune from changes.

The W-League (presently known as the Westfield W-League) is the current top level women's league in Australia. The new competition was established in 2008 and is composed of eight teams, including seven of the male A- League clubs, and one team based in Canberra. Its inaugural season commenced in October 2008. FFA Chief Executive Officer Ben Buckley observed that (*theage.com.au*, 2008), the establishment of a women's national league "completes the pathway for women in football, and creates an opportunity for the best players in the country to perform on a national stage."

The popularity of the women's game over recent years, coupled with the success of the Matildas, has greatly assisted the recognition of the women's game in Australia. Football Federation Australia indicates that during 2008, grassroots participation continued to increase with almost 100,000 girls and women playing football in formal competition, with even more playing informally. Buckley stated that women's football is an important priority for FFA, having enjoyed an average annual growth rate in participation of 6.3 percent over the previous five years. As a result of this growth and success, Football Federation Australia (FFA) was named as National Association of the Year at the annual Asian Football Confederation (AFC) Women's Awards in November 2008 (Downes, 2007).

INTERNATIONAL AND GLOBAL DEVELOPMENT

The history of Australia as a football nation on the international stage has been a fairly chequered one. However, recent successes highlighted by qual- ification for the 2006 FIFA World Cup in Germany and the Matildas various World Cup achievements have greatly improved Australia's global standing and ranking in the world game. The men's side was ranked 16th in the FIFA world rankings in June 2009, and the women's side was at number 14 (*FIFA.com*, 2009).

Some of this success can be attributed to Australia's entry into the AFC in 2006 and the subsequent successes made by the Socceroos, Matildas and under-age teams. In addition, the success of A-League clubs in the

AFC Club Championship has provided Australia with a sound basis for ongoing development on the international stage (see the Adelaide City Case Study). Australia has traditionally struggled to achieve internationally with the Australian national men's team only qualifying twice for the FIFA World Cup tournaments, with a round one achievement in 1974 and a solid second round performance in 2006, with both tournaments taking place in Germany. In lesser international competitions, the Australian men's teams did achieve four Oceania Nations Cup winner trophies (1980, 1996, 2000, and 2004) and a runner-up position in the 1997 Confederations Cup. The men's team also reached the quarter finals of the Asian Cup in 2007. Australian men's teams have participated in the Olympic Games in Melbourne 1956, Seoul 1988, Barcelona 1992, Atlanta 1996, Sydney 2000, Athens 2004, and China 2008. The Australian national women's team, on the other hand, has achieved a number of international appearances over a much shorter international time frame. The Matildas have qualified for all of the FIFA Women's World Cup tournaments, apart from the inaugural event which was held in China in 1991. Although the team had qualified for the World Cups held in 1995, 1999, and 2003 the Matildas had never progressed beyond the first round until the success of a quarter final appearance in China in 2007. The Matildas were crowned OFC Women's champions in 1995, 1998, and 2003 with runner up positions in 1983, 1986, and 1991. Olympic qualification however has not been as prolific with appearances only in 2000 and 2004. The move into Asia has provided the Matildas with greater opportunities and has resulted in achieving a runner-up position in the AFC Women's Asian Cup in 2006 and a fourth position in 2008.

CASE STUDY 19.2: Adelaide United FC

Adelaide United Football Club was founded in 2003, and is the only team from the state of South Australia which participates in the Australian A-League competition. They were announced as one of eight foundation teams to compete in the first season of the league, and are, along with Perth Glory and the Newcastle Jets, one of only three teams to survive from the National Soccer League's final season, which finished in 2004. Adelaide are one of the most successful clubs playing in the A-League, becoming minor premiers in the inaugural 2005–2006 season and reaching the Grand Final in 2006–2007. (The minor premiership is awarded to the top side in the A-League after the regular 'home and away' season. The top sides then play off in a series of knock out games to determine the major premiership).

The AFC Champions League is the premier Asian club football competition hosted by the Asian Football Confederation (AFC). In normal circumstances, 32 top clubs from 14 Asian countries, along with the defending champions, compete in the tournament. In its current format, the tournament has been running since 2002–2003. The 2007 draw also saw clubs from the A-League competition participate.

Adelaide is the only A-League club to compete in the AFC Champions League more than once, making them the most successful Australian club in Asia. They were selected, along with Sydney FC, as the first Australian representatives to play in the 2007 AFC Champions League. They finished third in their Champion's League group. They played in the 2008 AFC Champions League after finishing runner-up in the 2006–2007 A-League season to Melbourne Victory.

After a victory against Pohang 2–0 in Korea, a 0-0 draw against Changchun from China in their second game, another win against Bình Du'o'ng 2–1 in Vietnam, and a follow up 4–1 victory in the return leg, Adelaide defeated Pohang 1–0 to set up a deciding away tie against Changchun to determine the Group winner. In Changchun, Adelaide withstood considerable pressure to achieve an historic 0–0 draw, thus becoming the first Australian team ever to progress to the knockout stage of the AFC Champions League.

They consequently became the first Australian team to progress to the semifinals of the competition with a 1–0 win against J- League and Emperor's Cup champions Kashima Antlers. In the first leg of the semi-final, Adelaide won 3–0 against Uzbekistan's FC Bunyodkor. The match was attended by 16,998 fans (498 over capacity) at their home ground Hindmarsh Stadium. Although Adelaide lost the second leg, it went through to the final 3–1 on aggregate. Adelaide therefore became the first A-League club to reach the final of the competition. In the two-legged final, they took on Japanese team, Gamba Osaka. Unfortunately, Adelaide lost heavily over the two legs, with a 3–0 loss at Osaka and a 2–0 loss in Adelaide.

Although unsuccessful in the final, the result ensured that they progressed to the 2008 FIFA Club World Cup as the highest placed, non-Japanese team. They are the first Australian club to participate in this competition.

Source: www.adelaideunited.com

CHALLENGES

Football in Australia has overcome significant challenges to grow to its current levels. Poor administration and marketing were manifest throughout its development, but these issues appear to have been overcome. The ethnicity issues so commonplace in the 1970s and 1980s have been almost totally eradicated and hooliganism, whilst seen in Australia, was never at the levels experienced elsewhere. However, this is not to say there are no challenges to overcome in the future.

Player Drain

One of the greatest challenges is due to the fact that much of Australia's footballing talent is currently overseas plying their trade with rich European clubs in the very best leagues in the world. This so called "feet drain" has been found in many nations; however, the effect in Australia has been especially hard particularly prior to the establishment of the A League. Local competitions could not compete with, and will continue to struggle against, the cash rich competitions of Europe and players will naturally go where they can earn greater sums of money. This necessarily weakens local competitions and also leads to the next challenge.

International Player Release

Hand in hand with "feet drain" is the unwillingness of European clubs to release players for international duty. Lateral thinking on behalf of the FFA has seen friendly international matches involving the Socceroos being staged at neutral venues and training camps held in Europe. In both cases, travel times are cut dramatically and more players are released and therefore able to attend. However, there is still a general reluctance to release players although once again, this is not limited to Australian sides. This phenomenon inevitably impacts negatively on the competitiveness of the Australian national team.

Competition with Other Codes

The establishment of the A-League as an Australian summer sport ensured that direct competition with the iconic football codes of Australia was avoided. However, football is still ostensibly a winter sport when it comes to mass participation. It therefore competes for the hearts and minds of young Australians with more traditional sports such as rugby league (in the eastern states), Australian Rules (largely in Victoria, Western Australia, and Queensland) and to a lesser extent, rugby union.

CONCLUSIONS

The emergence of football in Australia has been shown to be tumultuous and full of intrigue and incidence. Without the support of the Federal Government, the code may well have floundered and remained at pre-Crawford Report levels. However, the future of the sport as a significant player in Australia, and indeed globally, looks assured. As recently as December 2008, Football Federation Australia reaffirmed its intention to bid for the FIFA World Cup in 2018 (*www.australia2018-2022.com.au*). This in turn has been bolstered by further Federal Government support via significant financial support in excess of AUD 40 million.

DISCUSSION QUESTIONS

1. Do you think the current structure of football in Australia would have been achieved without the intervention in the form of the *Crawford Report*?

2. Have other emerging or established football nations undertaken similar reviews to the *Crawford Report* and if so, what have the outcomes been? Have other sports attempted such undertakings?

3. Australia is considering bidding for the FIFA World Cup in 2018. What are the major hurdles to be overcome if this were to take place? Think locally, regionally and globally.

4. The women's game in Australia is relatively young. Given your reading of other chapters within this book, what lessons can be gleaned from other nations as the game in Australia develops and grows?

5. Gaze into your crystal ball, and use your knowledge of football and other sports within Australia and globally. How do you think the men's game in Australia will look in ten years time? The women's game? How will they be different?

GUIDED READING

For an in-depth and objective view of Australian football, *Shoot Out: Passion and Politics of Soccer's Fight for Survival in Australia* by Ross Solly is an informative read. Trevor Thompson's *One Fantastic Goal* is another valuable read that charts the rise of both domestic and international football in Australia.

REFERENCES

ABC (23rd April, 2002). Soccer Australia in financial trouble. *Australian Broadcasting Corporation*. Retrieved on July 12, 2009, from http://www.abc.net.au/7.30/content/2002/s538593.htm

adelaideunited.com.au. Retrieved on December 4, 2008, from http://www.adelaideunited.com.au/default.aspx?s=home

A.league.com.au. Retrieved on July 12, 2009, from http://www.a-league.com.au/default.aspx?s=history

Australia2018-2022.com.au. Retrieved on July 13, 2009, from http://www.australia2018-2022.com.au/

Australian Soccer Association Limited. (December, 2003). *Report of the NSL Task Force into the structure of a new National Soccer League competition.* Australian Soccer Association Limited. Retrieved on July 13, 2009, from http://fulltext.ausport.gov.au/fulltext/2003/soccer/Task_Force.pdf

Crawford, D. (April, 2003). *Review of the Independent Soccer Review Committee: into the Structure, Governance & Management of Soccer in Australia.* Australian Sports Commission. Retrieved on July 13, 2009, from http://fulltext.ausport.gov.au/fulltext/2003/soccerinquiry/reportfull.pdf

Downes, G. (2007). Returning to its Roots: *The future of women's football in the Asian Football Confederation (AFC).* Unpublished thesis. Gold Coast: Southern Cross University.

FIFA.com (June, 2009). *FIFA.com.* Retrieved on July 13, 2009, from http://www.fifa.com/worldfootball/ranking/lastranking/gender=m/fullranking.html#confederation=0&rank=183 and http://www.fifa.com/worldfootball/ranking/lastranking/gender=f/fullranking.html

Fink, J. (2007). *15 Days in June: How Australia became a Football Nation.* Australia: Hardie Grant Books.

Goal.com (27th November, 2008). 2018 World Cup A Priority For Australia. *Goal.com.* Retrieved on July 13, 2009, from http://www.goal.com/en/news/808/australia/2008/11/27/984269/2018-world-cup-a-priority-for-australia

Hills, J. (2008). *Performance Management for Sport.* Unpublished thesis. Gold Coast: Southern Cross University.

Murray, B., & Hay, R. (2006). *The World Game Downunder.* Melbourne, Australia: Australian Society for Sports History Inc. Studies, No. 19.

Solly, R. (2004). *Shoot Out. The Passion and the Politics of Soccer's Fight for Survival in Australia.* Australia Ltd: John Wiley and Sons.

Stewart, Hon. D.G. (10th January, 1995). *Report.* Published by the Senate Environment, Recreation, Communications and the Arts References Committee. Parliament House, Canberra.

Sydney Morning Herald (11th March, 2006). Notorious nude athletes. *Smh.com.au.* Retrieved on July 13, 2009, from http://www.smh.com.au/news/sport/notorious-nude-athletes/2006/03/10/1141701690155.html

theage.com.au. (28th July, 2008). W-League a boost for women's soccer. *theage.com.au* Retrieved on July 13, 2009, from http://www.theage.com.au/news/soccer/wleague-a-boost-for-womens-soccer/2008/07/28/1217097129758.html

Thompson, T. (2006). *One Fantastic Goal. A complete history of football in Australia.* Sydney Australia: Australian Broadcasting Corporation Books.

Williams, J. (2007). *A Beautiful Game. International Perspectives on Women's Football.* New York: Berg. Oxford.

RECOMMENDED WEBSITES

For a nonacademic view of the battle between Australian sporting codes see
www.convictcreations.com–football–battlestats.html
Official site of the A-League
www.a-league.com.au
Official site of Football Federation Australia (FFA)
www.footballaustralia.com.au
The official site of the W-League
www.a-league.com.au–default.aspx?s=wleague

CHAPTER 20

North America

Frank Pons, and André Richelieu
Université Laval

Objectives

Upon completion of this chapter, the reader should be able to:

- Comprehend the history of football in North America and how it impacts its current state and future development, in both Canada and the United States.

- Identify the marketing actions Major League Soccer (MLS) teams initiate in order to attract and keep fans, build their brand, and lay down the foundations for their long-term survival.

- Reflect on the marketing actions initiated by Major League Soccer teams and compare them with what some European football teams might undertake.

- Analyse the leverage branding could give a sport team in order to grow in a relatively hostile and extremely competitive environment, in the sport industry and even beyond.

- Define the cultural challenges a sport team organisation could face in building its brand.

OVERVIEW OF THE CHAPTER

In this chapter, we first look at the history of football in North America, followed by the marketing actions Major League Soccer teams initiate in order to attract and keep fans, build their brand and lay down the foundations for their long term survival. Even though professional football in the US and Canada has not been able to reach the status of the major professional leagues (American football [NFL], baseball [MLB], basketball [NBA], ice hockey

[NHL]), the organisational structure of the MLS provides a strong foundation to secure the survival and development of the League in the coming years. Indeed, professional football teams in the United States and Canada have shown a high level of marketing consciousness with corresponding strategies designed to conquer the complicated and difficult markets in which they operate. In this regard, there is a strong consensus among the four teams considered in this study (Chivas United States, Colorado Rapids, Real Salt Lake and Toronto FC) to widely support the importance of branding. However, despite this consensus, brand identity development and positioning through a unique selling proposition are not equally understood and implemented. This being said, most MLS teams undertake very similar implementation tactics. These marketing actions are the trademarks of this League and contribute to the economic viability and growth of the MLS.

First, fan experience on game day is considered as one of the key components of an MLS team at the gate. Fans come for more than a football game and they need to experience something unique. One of the biggest contributors to the success of fan experience is the stadium itself. In recent years, virtually all MLS teams have abandoned big impersonal stadia for new facilities with luxury boxes and a limited capacity (18,000–25,000 seats) in order to boost atmosphere at local games and play in full stadia. Second is the predominance of grassroots marketing programmes in which football is brought to the local community by team players and officials. This has taken town hall meeting formats, soccer camps for kids or year-long soccer academies to develop the love of football, skills and future players. Third, the consistent search and development of international partnerships with well-established European and South American teams is another trademark of marketing and business actions adopted by most MLS teams. Through these links, teams hope to quickly enhance the credibility of their football status, but also to offer local fans exciting friendly games and leverage both brands in a competitive domestic market.

At the end, the reader shall see that in order to be successful on and off the field, MLS teams have adopted solid business models to change stereotypical issues often blamed for the lack of popular success that football experiences in the United States and Canada. They position themselves as credible alternatives to other team sports and could be a source of inspiration for football teams around the world that lack this business edge and eagerness that characterises them.

INTRODUCTION

Combining football and North America in the same sentence does not come naturally. At least not when we refer to the "real" football the entire world has embraced—except for North America. "Soccer" was originally customised to fit the tastes of local sports fans during the North American Soccer League (NASL) in the 1970s but was perceived as unfit to suit the commercial needs of North American television. More recently it has been seen simply as a Saturday morning kids' game and has been hampered by the weak or catastrophic performances of the American and Canadian national teams in international competition. Football in North America at first looks like the adventures of the Last of the Mohicans: a lost cause in what FIFA considers the last frontier (Richelieu, 2006).

These could all be reasons to despise the state of football in North America and nurture long-time stereotypes about the state of the "beautiful game" in a part of the world where heroes sound more like Sidney Crosby (NHL hockey), Brett Favre (NFL American football), Kevin Garnett (NBA Basketball), and Derek Jeter (Major League baseball). But perhaps we need a new way to look at football in North America and get rid of all these stereotypes that only add to our cynicism about the general state of the world. As we shall see, despite or maybe because of all the adversity football has faced and is still experiencing in North America, the game is entering a new era—at least from a marketing standpoint.

Indeed, the level of sophistication of marketing strategies, the overall business orientation and the tenacity and innovativeness of professional football teams in the United States, and even in Canada, could serve as an important benchmark for teams throughout the world whose current survival is based solely on winning seasons or local support. North American professional football teams compete in one of the toughest sport business environments on the planet. Professional football teams face tremendous competition from other major sports and entertainment offers; they continuously fight for media exposure and sponsorships and, unlike European teams, they are confronted by a quasi-nonexistent loyal fan base. For these teams, marketing cannot be an afterthought: it is critical to their survival (Pons, 2006).

In this chapter, we shall first examine the history of football in North America. This shall set the stage for an examination of the current marketing actions Major League Soccer teams initiate in order to attract and keep fans, build their brand and lay down the foundations for their long term survival. We shall end this chapter with a recap and a look toward the future.

THE EVOLUTION OF FOOTBALL IN NORTH AMERICA

Canada and the United States

The history of football in North America can be traced back to the late 1800s. For instance, the first recorded game was played in Toronto, Canada in 1876, and from that point on, various football associations spread across the country and organised play took root. However, it was only in 1907 that the closest thing to a national championship was created, with the "People's Shield" (Canadian Soccer Association, 2008). In 1946, the North American Professional Soccer League was launched with teams from Canada and the United States.[1] However, the League lasted for only two years. In 1961, the Eastern Canada Professional Soccer League was created, with teams from Toronto (two), Montreal and Hamilton and this League lasted until 1966 (Richelieu, 2006).

The NASL

In 1967, two coast-to-coast professional leagues were formed in the United States: the National Professional Soccer League (NPSL) and the United Soccer Association (USA). In 1968, the North American Soccer League (NASL) was created following the merger of the NPSL and the USA. From the beginning, the NASL was facing huge challenges, as it was trying to sell a sport that was almost unknown, or at least neither understood nor appreciated by Americans. To resolve this issue, the NASL decided to focus on its offering and to alter its product through the "Americanisation" of the rules in an attempt to make the game more exciting for the average North American sports fan. These changes included a countdown clock, a 35-yard offside line, and a shootout to decide matches that ended in a draw. Furthermore, the NASL focused on attracting star international players who were at or near the end of their career: Carlos Alberto, Banks, Beckenbauer, Best, Bettega, Cruyff, Eusebio, Krol, Neeskens, Pelé, and so on. As a short-term result, these actions attracted more fans and provided role models for talented "local" players (Rick Davis, Gerry Gray, Tino Lettieri, Branko Segota, Igor Vrablic, etc.). Once the League started growing, new franchises were awarded quickly and it reached twenty-four teams in only a few years (Pons, 2006).

However, this apparent success hid structural issues that would later set the stage for the League's failure. In fact, this overexpansion brought in owners who did not have a common vision or the knowledge of football or sports marketing. It also resulted in the talent level being spread too thin. In addition, several teams in small markets lost huge amounts of money in paying aging stars in an effort to match the success of the New York Cosmos

---

[1] It should be noted that most professional sport leagues in North America combine Canadian and American teams. Very seldom do we see an exclusive Canadian or American professional league, aside from the Canadian Football League (CFL) and the National Football League (NFL), in American football for instance.

and on rental of football stadia that were far too big for the crowds the teams were able to attract. The average attendance of the League never even reached 15,000 spectators, even though some games sporadically attracted huge crowds.

As a result, the NASL suspended its operations in 1984. From 1984 to 1992, the Major Indoor Soccer League (MISL) was the only First Division football league operating in the United States. After the MISL folded in 1992 and was replaced by second-tier leagues (the Continental Indoor Soccer League, for example), there was no major First Division league in the United States until the start of Major League Soccer in 1996 (Pons, 2006).

The First World Cup Effect: The Launch of the MLS

The MLS started as a condition for the staging of the World Cup 1994 in the United States. The US Soccer Federation (USSF) had to fulfil the FIFA requirement to establish a "Division 1" professional football league to host this event. Therefore, MLS was launched in 1996, with ten teams divided among the Eastern and Western conferences.

The League has been through expansions and contractions. In 2008, there were 14 teams, spread evenly between the Eastern Conference (Chicago, Columbus, DC United, Kansas City, New England, New York, and Toronto FC) and the Western Conference (Chivas USA, Colorado, FC Dallas, Houston, Los Angeles, Real Salt Lake, and San Jose) (MLS, 2008).

Unlike the NASL, the structural decisions regarding the MLS were always made with the overall survival and prosperity of the league in mind. Specifically, the latest expansions were business decisions aimed at tapping into markets with great potential, such as (1) the Hispanic community, with the Mexican affiliation for Chivas USA; (2) the fast-growing youth market in Salt Lake City for Real Salt Lake; and (3) the vibrant multicultural economic capital of Canada, Toronto, for the Toronto FC.

In addition to the lack of a promotion/relegation system, which is consistent with every other major sport in the United States and Canada, the MLS is a "single-entity" organisation. In this framework, the league (rather than individual teams) contracts directly with the players in an effort to control spending and labour costs, share revenue, promote parity and maximise exposure. This organisational model dictates a strong central power that sets practical rules to ensure the League viability and development (Robinson, 2005).

For instance, the full roster for each MLS team is limited to 18 players, plus a maximum of 10 roster-protected (reserve) players. MLS teams are allowed a maximum of 4 senior (over the age of 25) international players on their active roster, as well as 3 youth international players (under the age of 25). These quotas allow prominent names in European football (such as Beckham and Stoichkov) to spend a few years in the MLS, but the rule also prevents the League from being seen as a "retirement" league for European players, as used to be the case with the NASL. In addition, since several MLS players have signed with wealthier teams in Europe following their time at MLS teams, MLS now appears as an opportunity to develop young American players, such as Carlos Bocanegra and DaMarcus Beasley. Most of the players in the League are from the United States and Canada, ensuring an outlet for a growing number of young athletes finishing their college years in the National Collegiate Athletic Association (NCAA). Even though professional football in the United States has not been able to reach the status of the major professional leagues around the world, the organisational structure of the MLS provides a strong foundation to secure the survival and development of the League in the coming years.

The Second World Cup Effect: The Rise and Fall of the Women's Professional League

Football became the fastest growing participant sport in the United States in 2002, mainly because of its popularity among young girls. In fact, female football players were estimated to reach 9 million in early 2002, and more than 90 percent of these players were under 18 years of age (*SGMA*, 2002). The 1999 Women's World Cup, organised by the United States, was a turning point. This event was a huge success, drawing more than 660,000 spectators overall and 413,000 for Team U.S. games. The United States and the entire world came to understand the great potential of women's football at this level.

The 1999 Women's World Cup final, in particular, elevated U.S. players as icons for the whole country. Attempting to build on the players' popularity, the 20 U.S. players sought out the investors, markets and players necessary to form the first USSF-sanctioned, Division 1, professional women's football league (Southall et al., 2005). Similar to the MLS, the Women's United Soccer Association (WUSA) was structured as a single entity formed from eight teams. However, the WUSA was organised in a way that gave a tremendous power to the players. In fact, the 20 founding players received an equity stake in the League and a representative on the Board of Directors (Southall et al., 2005).

Sponsors and investors rushed to support the League, hoping to tap into the female audience, which is traditionally difficult to reach through major league sports. Using inspiring athletes such as Mia Hamm, the League and sponsors empowered the players, and as a result the League was positioned as a trendy "first-class" product compared to other major U.S. sports. However, by emphasising the athletes first, it was difficult for the League to build its own identity and brand, as more importance was placed on personal stories than on the competition. This early positioning was a gamble, and significantly different from the conservative approach used by MLS.

The WUSA played for three full seasons, but failed to attract viewers and sponsors or draw the type of crowds experienced during the Women's World Cup. In fact, the WUSA was never able to achieve the level of attendance experienced by the only other US women's professional sports league, the Women's National Basketball Association (WNBA). Plagued by huge operating expenses, the League suspended its operations in September 2003. There is much conjecture suggesting that the unique business form of the WUSA (especially the central role of players) is what in large measure led to its suspension of operations (Pons, 2006). Undoubtedly, there is a market for professional women's football in the United States, but what is needed is a business approach capable of attracting consumers who are not the usual sport entertainment consumers (i.e., women and children), thereby establishing a viable niche for the survival and development of a professional women's football league (King, 2005).

Canada: No World Cup Effect

Contrary to the United States, Canada did not benefit from its participation in the World Cup in 1986. The Canadian Soccer League (CSL) took up the baton of the NASL in 1987, expanding to eleven teams coast to coast before folding in 1992. Up until 2007, three Canadian teams were part of the United Soccer League (USL), a second-tier North American soccer league: the Montreal Impact, the Toronto Lynx and the Vancouver Whitecaps. Toronto joined the MLS in 2007 under the name "Toronto FC," with the other two Canadian teams aiming to follow suit by 2010, according to plans by Soccer Canada (Richelieu, 2006). However, it might take longer to happen, as the next scheduled expansion teams in the MLS are Seattle (2009) and Philadelphia (2010) (MLS, 2008).

Team Canada qualified for the 1986 World Cup in Mexico, losing all three games—to France, Hungary, and the Soviet Union—without scoring a single goal. Team Canada was more prolific in 2000, when it won the CONCACAF Gold Cup, beating Colombia 2–0 in the finals. But Canada still has not qualified for a World Cup since 1986. Moreover, although it was ranked ninth by FIFA (2008), the women's team was eliminated in the first round of the FIFA World Cup in China, in 2007.

There are two key factors that have prevented the stability and long-term growth of football in Canada: the lack of infrastructure and the absence of quality ownership with financial strength. These were both underlined in a study conducted by KPMG in 2000 on the future of professional football in Canada (KPMG, 2000). First, the lack of infrastructure (playing facilities and a good calibre league) prevents the emergence of a nucleus of quality players that will continue to play beyond university at the highest level and feed the national team. This is especially critical in the case of Canada, which faces a relatively limited pool of players and lengthy, harsh winter weather. Furthermore, we should not overlook the relative scarcity of coaches and referees, who are essential actors in the player development programme, especially since there are more and more soccer players in Canada. According to Kevan Pipe (Richelieu & Lopez, 2008), former Chief Operating Officer of Soccer Canada, the federation forecasts there will be 1.2 million registered players by 2010. Second, the absence of quality ownership is another limiting factor, and Pipe underlines that "what we have failed to do up until now is to convince entrepreneurs to bet on the development of soccer, compared to what happened in the United States."

Indeed, the fact that local football is not considered major league calibre makes investors worry about the return on investment they might achieve. Additionally, the decline of professional clubs in Canada, first with the NASL and then with the Canadian Soccer League, has definitely damaged the performance of the men's national team at the world level. As a result, companies are even less inclined to support football in Canada. However, with Toronto FC in the MLS, two new football-specific stadia (BMO Field in Toronto and Saputo Stadium in Montreal), and grassroots programmes having appeared across the nation, there is a ray of hope for the future (Richelieu, 2006).

CASE STUDY 20.1: Managing the growth of football in North America? Lessons from the MLS

Even though the rigorous organisational structure and careful growth of the MLS have greatly contributed to the survival and development of professional football in North America, teams still face major challenges to market themselves, establish their brands and achieve the status traditionally reserved to the four major professional sports in North America (American football, baseball, basketball and ice hockey). In a study on the brand construction of major professional sport teams, Richelieu and Pons (2006) have identified key attributes of successful brands. These attributes are not yet part of the ethos of MLS teams and represent the key challenges that these teams face. They are presented hereafter.

A winning tradition and an intense rivalry between teams in the same league or division are often mentioned as common traits of successful sport brands. However in 2009, the MLS was only 13 years old, so this very young history does not allow any team to have established a strong tradition, much less a dynasty. Moreover the previous failures and disappearance of other professional football leagues (NASL and WUSA) contribute to create a climate of suspicion around the potential sport and economic success of the MLS.

In addition to the cultural distance between football and traditional North American sports, the lack of TV exposure of the MLS has slowed down the growth of popularity of football among American people. Typically, successful sports teams benefit from a strongly established fan base. These fans who support their team economically through tickets and merchandising, locally or not, add value to the team through their sense of belonging and the sport culture they help to develop. Advertisers and TV programmes have well understood that sport is a way to reach a vast and diverse audience and they invest huge amounts of money in securing TV rights and developing partnerships with well established sport brands. In the case of the MLS, the lack of TV rights has not allowed the league to grow economically

and attract sponsors and has also hindered its ability to penetrate further into its potential markets. This never-ending cycle of low TV exposure, limited popular success back to no TV rights represents a critical challenge for the league and its teams. The possibility to break this cycle lies in the fans that professional football tends to attract (immigrants, young families, women and teenagers). These segments are becoming increasingly attractive for advertisers and the lack of exposure previously may soon become an opportunity to grow for the MLS as marketers want to reach these targets.

Despite these challenges, professional football teams in the United States have shown a high level of marketing consciousness with corresponding strategies designed to conquer the complicated and difficult markets in which they operate. In this section, we present the approaches used by several MLS teams as potential benchmarks for other professional football leagues. These findings are all results of an empirical research project implemented over 2005–2008 (Richelieu and Pons, 2008). The methodology used to gather data was qualitative. It was based on in-depth case analyses with four MLS teams and utilized primary and secondary data. Primary data was based on in-depth interviews with vice-presidents, marketing directors, and general

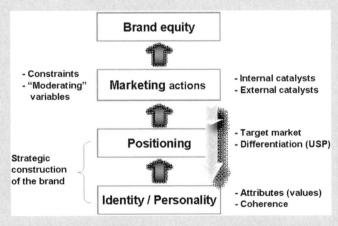

FIGURE 20.1 *The brand construction model.*
Sources: Kashani, 1995; Richelieu, 2004, 2008.

managers of the four football teams studied, using semi-structured questionnaires with open-ended questions. One to three representatives were interviewed for each team, depending on the expertise and availability of the respondents (Miles and Huberman, 2003; Pellemans, 1999). The validity was ensured through the use of several sources of information and the comparisons made between cases (Patton, 1980; Perrien et al., 1986). In order to structure the presentation of the strategic elements adopted by the four teams considered, we used the brand construction model presented in Figure 20.1 (Kashani, 1995; Richelieu, 2004, 2008).

The premise of this model is based on the fact that branding decisions are central to the development of a successful marketing strategy. Previous research has suggested that some professional teams do not see branding as an important component of their strategy and often struggle to thrive in their respective market (Pons and Richelieu, 2004). By contrast there is a strong consensus among the four teams considered in this study to widely support the importance of branding as suggested in the following quotes:

- "In a start-up environment like we've got here, you have to build up a brand and decide what you're going to be, and what you're going to stand for. It is critical!" (Real Salt Lake).

- "I think it's particularly important for us [to have a brand strategy]. If we want to be in the experiential marketing business, we can yield the right value regardless of whether or not we win or lose. But we need to unwind what has been done for years, develop a new brand strategy and stick to it, and invest in it. It's organic, it doesn't quit." (Colorado Rapids).

- "Our brand is what makes us stand out. It is our identity and it is why people come to games." (Chivas USA).

- "We need to get our brand out, and help it grow to generate other revenues. It should help passing on the tradition of football from one generation to another." (Toronto FC).

Despite this consensus, the initial steps in the model (brand identity development and positioning through a unique selling proposition) are not equally understood and implemented. For instance, the Colorado Rapids have clearly defined what they stand for and how they want to position themselves on this axis on a consistent basis. Their implementation is flawless and they have set long term goals to reach their branding objectives:

- "Our brand identity consists in bringing the 'world's game' to Colorado. ...You know, we've got three slogans, which are 'Experience the world's game' ... sometimes we change it up, it's 'Play the world's game' if we're doing something for our soccer camps, or 'Live the world's game,' 'Watch the world's game' if it's on TV, whenever we can we're pushing our stuff, our identity. So it all kind of fits back into that brand identity." (Colorado Rapids).

The Toronto FC is another example of a team with a clear brand identity. This identity is based on eight values (National, Aspirational, Traditional, Diverse, Exciting, Credible, Family, Fun) that are embraced within and outside the organisation. However, the uniqueness of this selling proposition may be questioned as these values could also apply to other sport competitors in the city (Toronto Maple Leafs or Toronto Blue Jays) or any other sport teams in North America. A clear brand identity is not enough; it also has to stand out and make you unique if you want to succeed:

- "The TFC brand is about fan experience. Our identity is articulated around eight values that we want to transmit to fans." (Toronto FC).

The case of Chivas USA is particularly interesting as the importance of branding issues is clearly accepted by team management. However, the latter seems to have difficulty focusing on a precise identity as suggested in the following quotes. Therefore, it struggles to position itself clearly on the market and this blurry positioning on a hyperfragmented market prevents the team from reaching its most interesting segments:

- "Where does our strategy stand now as far as our brand is concerned? It's simple. We're still very much going to concentrate on our Spanish and Mexican heritage. We can never forget our Spanish heritage. There is always going to be a majority of Mexican players on our team. At the same time, like I've said it earlier, we will not be here in 5 years if we can't emulate anybody else. We have to be as open as possible." (Chivas USA).

■ "We're the best soccer team in Los Angeles but you just don't know it yet. And that's been a struggle on different fronts. We're trying collectively, as a front office, to change perceptions of the team. Because there have been some ill perceptions. There have been customers that don't feel welcome at our games, mostly Anglo consumers. Mainly because they feel it's a very Mexican brand and this is just for Mexicans. That's kind of where we're leaning too: making this brand relevant to just about any consumer wanting to listen." (Chivas USA).

Despite differences in the strategic construction of their respective brand, most MLS teams share very similar implementation tactics. These marketing actions are the trademarks of this League and contribute to the economic viability and growth of the MLS.

Fan experience on game day is considered as one of the key components of an MLS team at the gate. Fans come for more than a football game and they need to experience something unique. One of the biggest contributors to the success of fan experience is the stadium itself. In recent years, virtually all MLS teams have abandoned big impersonal stadia for new facilities with luxury boxes and a limited capacity (18,000–25,000 seats) in order to boost atmosphere at local games and play in full stadia. The importance of this phenomenon in building fan experience is best described by the following quotes:

■ "On game day, BMO Field becomes the brand. There are tailgate parties before the game. Socialising becomes important. … Fans sing in the stadium. A soccer specific stadium with a smaller capacity helps create the atmosphere." (Toronto FC).

■ "We have probably one of the most beautiful stadiums on the West coast. It has 25,000 seats. Great stadium, it's modelled after some European stadiums. Our game-based strategy goes hand in hand with our branding. We want to provide a unique atmosphere unlike any other sport atmosphere. We have a beautiful facility. We have a large interactive area on one of our concourses where we put all of our media partners strategically in the pre-game atmosphere. In fact, what we've done is we've created a recreation of Guadalajara with a hall of fame for our partners. We have a beauty stage where we have talent every game. We raffle things off, the marketing team has a big prize wheel, people come and spin it. The Chivas girls are always a big part of our pre-game atmosphere. Our mascot is pretty funny, he's generally on the field, he's on the concourses shaking hands, taking photos, signing stuff for kids." (Chivas USA).

The second noticeable marketing action among MLS teams is the predominance of grassroots marketing programmes in which football is brought to the local community by team players and officials. This proximity between the team and individuals or groups in the public banks on the liberal and accessible nature of football, compared to other sports. This action is widely implemented in the league, as suggested by the following quotes:

■ "We now have two full-time academies: a little one about 70 miles from here in the city of Bell Gardens, it's a partnership with the city. We were very privileged enough to have this opportunity to create a complex. It's called John Anson Ford Park. Plus, there's a number of licensed academies across the United States." (Chivas USA).

■ "Players, we use them for everything. They're doing clinics, they're doing radio appearances, they even go to birthday parties." (Colorado Rapids).

■ "We target the soccer community through the state associations for both youth and adults, through various means. We go to their annual banquets, we go to Field Club Saturdays, we have them down on the field every game. Somebody is receiving something, so we get to the soccer community." (Real Salt Lake).

Finally, the consistent search and development for international partnership with well established European and South American teams is another trademark of marketing and business actions adopted by most MLS teams. Through these links, teams hope to quickly enhance the credibility of their football status but also offer local fans exciting friendly games and leverage both brands on a competitive domestic market. The following quotes highlight the importance of these international partnerships for teams in our study:

■ "I think Arsenal is our European partner, Pachuca is our Mexican partner but I think their brands are so strong that we are not a threat but rather an open door to the U.S. market for them and a way to build legitimacy in the US for us and to reinforce our "world's game brand identity"." (Colorado Rapids).

■ "This brand, Chivas USA, is obviously a variation of Chivas Guadalajara. We're never gonna be Chivas Guadalajara, and we never promised we would. We would need one hundred years and only Mexican players. And that's not gonna happen here. But thanks to our name, we do have a built-in fan base. We have a large awareness of who the team is. I think we're still trying to corral them into being true Chivas USA fans. So, in a sense, I think it hinders us because the expectations are very high. In another sense, I think it helps us a lot because we have a built-in audience. We have a partner in Guadalajara who can very often make us relevant by just mentioning us." (Chivas USA).

CONCLUSIONS

Perhaps Americans and Canadians will never be able to compete at the same level as Europeans in the arena of football and it's entirely possible that North Americans will never develop the same level of respect for football that is experienced in Europe. There is little doubt that football will continue to be an important participant sport for young kids and that football parents will continue to play an important role in the evolution of football in North America. However, based on our interviews with managers from MLS teams, we have now come to realise that none of this precludes the development of professional football in North America.

In fact, in order to be successful on and off the field, MLS teams have adopted solid business models to change stereotypical issues often blamed for the lack of popular success of football in the United States and Canada. Through the strategy described earlier and consistency, patience and grassroots techniques, they position themselves as credible alternatives to other team sports and could be sources of inspiration for football teams around the world that lack this business edge and eagerness that characterizes them.

DISCUSSION QUESTIONS

1. What are the structural elements of the MLS that favour/ help individual teams to develop their marketing strategies? Provide examples.

2. How would you describe the MLS fans? How homogeneous is this market? Investigate how individual teams try to reach each of their individual segments.

3. In addition to grassroots marketing programmes, soccer-dedicated stadia and international partnerships, discuss other marketing actions that may differentiate the MLS teams from other professional soccer teams in the world.

4. How would you compare the strategic construction of the brand in MLS compared to other sport brands in the US or other football teams in the rest of the world?

GUIDED READING

Sport Marketing (2007) by Sam Fullerton provides a very comprehensive overview of the sports marketing environment using a strong international focus. *The Business of Sports* (2004) by George Foster, Stephen Greyser and Bill Walsh is an advanced book on sport business presenting detailed cases about strategic decisions in this area. It should provide readers with an advanced and applied understanding of strategic decisions within the sport business arena.

REFERENCES

Canadian Soccer Association. Canadasoccer.com (2008). Retrieved in January, 2008, from http://www.canadasoccer.com/eng/about/index.asp.

FIFA (2008). *www.fifa.com*. Retrieved in January, 2008, from http://fr.fifa.com/worldfootball/ranking/lastranking/gender=m/fullranking.html.

Fullerton, S. (2006). *Sport Marketting*. McGraw-Hill.

Foster, S., Geyser, S., & Walsh, S. (2006). *Business of Sports: Cases on Strategy & Management*. Thomson Learning.

Kashani, K. (1995). Comment cre'er une marque puissante?. *Les Echos*. Retrieved in February, 2003, from www.lesechos.fr.

King, B. (2005). What's up with women's sports? *Sports Business Journal*. April 25, 18.

KPMG (2000). *Business Plan for a Canadian Professional League. A review of key findings*. Ottawa: KPMG.

Miles, M., & Huberman, A. (2003). *Analyse des données qualitatives*. Paris: Éditions De Boeck Université.

MLS (2008). *www.mlsnet.com*. Retrieved in May, 2008, from http://www.mlsnet.com.

Patton, M. (1980). *Qualitative Evaluation Methods*. London: Sage.

Pellemans, P. (1999). *Recherche qualitative en marketing: Perspective psycho-scopique*. Bruxelles: De Boeck Université.

Perrien, J., Chéron, E. J., & Zins, M. (1986). *Recherche en marketing: Méthodes et décisions*. Boucherville: Gaëtan Morin éditeur.

Pons, F. (2006). Marketing of professional soccer in the US: Some lessons to be learned. In M. Desbordes (Ed.), *Marketing and Football: An International Perspective*. (pp. 395–432). Oxford: Elsevier.

Pons, F., & Richelieu, A. (2004). Marketing stratégique du sport: Le cas d'une franchise de la Ligue Nationale de Hockey. *Revue Française de Gestion, 30*(150), 161–175.

Richelieu, A. (May, 2008). Creating and branding sport products. In S. Chadwick (Ed.), *Sport Marketing*. London: Henry Stewart Talks. Chapter 3. http://www.hstalks.com/main/browse_talk_info.php?talk_id=727&series_id=260.

Richelieu, A. (2006). The beginning of a new beginning? How to expand soccer in Canada – A look at the federation and one club. In M. Desbordes (Ed.), *Marketing and Football: An International Perspective*. (pp. 433–464) Oxford: Elsevier.

Richelieu, A., & Lopez, S. (2008). How and when is a sponsor's image beneficial to the sponsoree? The importance of a perfect match. *Journal of Sponsorship, 1*(3), 225–233.

Richelieu, A., & Pons, F. (2006). Toronto Maple Leafs vs. Football Club Barcelona: How two legendary sports teams built their brand equity. *International Journal of Sports Marketing & Sponsorship, 7*(3), pp. 231–250.

Richelieu, A., & Pons, F. (2008). Building and managing professional football team brands: Cases from Major League Soccer (MLS). Conference organized for the Euro 2008 Football Championship, *Challenges facing football in the 21st century*. Bern: Switzerland. May 2008.

Robinson, M. (2005). Interview with Don Garber, MLS Commissioner. *Sport Marketing Quarterly, 14*(2), 69–70.

SGMA International (2002). Youth reigns supreme in the world's sport. Retrieved in February, 2006, from http://www.sgma.com/press/2002/press1023217230-10882.html.

Southall, R. M., Nagel, S. M., & LeGrande, D. J. (2005). Build it and they will come? The WUSA: A collision of exchange theory and strategic philanthropy. *Sport Marketing Quarterly, 14*(3), 159–167.

RECOMMENDED WEBSITES

Chadwick, S. [Ed.] (2008). Sport Marketing. London: Henry Stewart Talks.

http://www.hstalks.com/main/browse_talks.php?father_id=260

The Hospitality, Leisure, Sport & Tourism Network (2008).

http://www.heacademy.ac.uk/hlst/

The National Soccer Hall of Fame of the United States (2008). The North American Soccer League.

http://www.soccerhall.org/NASL_Info.htm

The Warsaw Sport Marketing Center (2008).

http://www.warsawcenter.com/index2.htm

CHAPTER 21

China

Li Jingbo
Sun Yat-Sen University

Ruqi Zhou
Guangdong University of Foreign Studies

Adrian Pritchard
Coventry University

Objectives

Upon completion of this chapter the reader should be able to:

- Describe the development of Chinese football.
- Evaluate the current situation of the Chinese Super League (CSL).
- Explain the activities of European clubs in China.
- Consider the likelihood of success of entrants into this market.
- Outline the challenges faced by women's football in China.

CONTENTS

OVERVIEW OF THE CHAPTER

We begin this chapter with the history of football in China and why FIFA considers China the creator of modern football. We then discuss football's development in the twentieth century and the political situation that impacted it. Then we examine the participants, their role in the sport, and the league structure. This chapter includes a table that summarizes the teams in the CSL. The problems and challenges that face the league and international football, although not unique to China, are also discussed.

This chapter also examines why European clubs are interested in football in China. The activities of European clubs in China are categorized into six areas: tours, sponsorship, players, merchandise, commercial and management support, and media. We will look briefly at women's football in China and its relative success to date on the field. The chapter concludes by considering the futures of the three different segments of the men's game: the domestic league, the international team, and the activities of overseas teams in China. A case study examines the alliance between Sheffield United and Chengdu Blades.

THE HISTORY OF FOOTBALL IN CHINA

Evidence has shown that a type of football was played in Linzhi in 475 BC. The game was known as Cuju or Taju. *Cu* and *Ta* both mean "kick," and *Ju* is a kind of ball made of leather and filled with soft padding. Cuju or Taju literally means "kick the ball with one's foot." The game was played all over the country on a rectangular, walled pitch with a *juyu* (goal) with six holes at each end. The ball was made of eight pieces of leather and filled with hair, but later the ball was filled with gas, and a goal replaced the holes. The game was refereed. As the sport evolved, both men and women participated. The pace of development, however, slowed down during the Ming Dynasty (1368–1644) when the emperor banned the game and it eventually disappeared altogether.

China was acknowledged as the birthplace of football in 2004 by FIFA president Joseph S. Blatter, who said the organization concurred with the findings of the Chinese Football Association (CFA), which officially concluded that football originated in Linzi, Shandong province (*People's Daily Online*, 2004).

MODERN FOOTBALL

The game that is played today was introduced to China by the British. The first documented match in Shanghai in 1879 saw the Shanghai Athletic Club play The Engineers, and in 1887 the Shanghai Football Club was formed, with the first league being created in the city in 1907. Although initially dominated by British expatriates, other nationalities soon joined in.

The post–World War II period saw a rebirth of football under the auspices of the Shanghai Athletic Association. In January 1946, a new league got underway that consisted of Chinese, European, and one Jewish team, although it was not long before the non-Chinese broke away and formed their own league. Following the Communist revolution in 1949, there was a mass exodus of players. All forms of sport, including football, were placed under the auspices of the All-China Athletic Federation.

The Football Federation was reformed in 1951, and the initial League Championship was played. The majority of the clubs were army garrisons, and in many cases, teams represented regions rather than towns. From 1953 onwards, leading players were sent to the newly founded Sports Institutes, and a national team played mostly other Communist countries. In 1958, China withdrew from FIFA over the acceptance of Taiwan, but international matches continued (237 between 1958 and 1961), including tournaments with other Communist countries and touring teams from Africa.

DEVELOPMENTS SINCE THE CULTURAL REVOLUTION

In the mid-1960s, all competitive sports were banned, and the ban remained in place until the Cultural Revolution ended in 1972. China entered the Asian Games in 1974 and in 1976 was admitted to the Asian Football Conference (AFC). In 1977, Beijing held its first international football invitational tournament and welcomed a number of international guest teams, including the New York Cosmos from the United States and West Bromwich Albion from England. In 1980, China was once again fully accepted by FIFA and was immediately involved in the World Cup, Olympics, and Asian Cup qualifying matches. During this period, the national team was perceived as being far more important than the domestic clubs.

In 1988, a Chinese national football team entered the Olympics, and in 1990, Beijing held the 11th Asian Games Football Competition. The highlight for Chinese football came in 2002 with their qualification for the World Cup. The popularity of the sport is borne out by the fact that in 2007 there were over 1,000 clubs and 2.2 million players in China (Rollins and Rollins, 2007).

ADMINISTRATION AND LEAGUE STRUCTURE

The CFA was founded in 1924, with the current body being established in 1949. The year 1994 was considered a critical one in the sport, as the Chinese Professional Soccer League (CPSL) was established under the supervision of the CFA's Professional League Committee. This nationwide league was then divided into Divisions 1 and 2. Division 1 was subdivided into the Marlboro Chinese Professional Soccer Jia League Series A and Championship Series 1B, and Division 2 was divided regionally.

The CSL started in May 2004, replacing the former Jia A, with the Jia B being renamed as the new Jia A League. Twelve clubs took part in the first CSL, and the number increased to 14 for 2005 and 16 for 2006. Sichuan Guancheng, however, withdrew before the start of the season. In 2007, 15 clubs existed, with the merger of the two Shanghai clubs, Shenhua and United. In 2008, the number reached 16 following the promotion of Chengdu Blades and Guangzhou Pharmaceutical and the relegation of Xiamen Lanshi. In addition to the league competitions, there are two cup competitions. The CSL has a number of objectives, including promoting high-quality competition, financial probity, professional management, and youth development.

THE CLUBS

As we have just seen, most of the clubs do not have a very long history, (details of the CSL clubs in 2007 can be seen in Table 21.1), but they do have a very large catchment areas. Since the start of the CSL, numerous name changes and stadium moves have taken place—for example, Shaanxi relocated from Shanghai to Xian in 2005, a distance of nearly 1,000 kilometres. Shanghai Shenhua spent 2007 on the other side of the city while their usual home was updated for the Women's World Cup (*Shanghaiist*, 2008), which has made it difficult to build up supporter loyalty.

The CSL in its inaugural season had an average attendance of about 11,000, the lowest in the top tier in ten years coupled with a big drop in television viewing figures from the previous year (*People's Daily Online*, 2005a). The consensus is that the CSL is struggling to capture the imagination of the Chinese sporting public *(People's Daily Online*, 2007).

The CSL is broadcast live on local television, as is German, Italian, and Spanish football, so the viewer has many choices. The English Premiership was shown on local, free-to-air television (it is still shown videotaped), but the rights for the three seasons starting in 2007–2008 were sold to WinTV, which broadcast it on a pay-per-view basis. It is estimated that only about 20,000 customers paid the annual fee of about £40 (Bristow, 2007).

LEAGUE SPONSORSHIP

The CSL has struggled to keep a sponsor. Siemens paid 85 million yuan when the league debuted in 2004, but they withdrew after a season, and there was no sponsor in 2005. Internet phone maker iPhox was the sponsor in 2006, and it was followed in 2007 by the Shenzhen brewer Kingway,

Table 21.1	Super League 2007				
Position	Club	Year Founded	Stadium Capacity (in Thousands)	Share Capital (RMB Millions)	Non-Chinese Sponsors
1	Changchun Yatai	1996	38		
2	Shandong Luneng Tai	1988	45	66	Nike
3	Beijing Guoan	1992	60	45	Nike, Hyundai, Samsung, Red Bull
4	Shanghai Shenhua	1993	35	50	Umbro
5	Tianjin Kangshifu	1998	40	30	Kappa
6	Dalian Shide	1983	60	50	Adidas Dupont
7	Wuhan Guanggu	1994	30		
8	Qingdao Zhongneng	1993	62	50	Kappa
9	Changsha Ginde	1994	50	50	Kappa
10	Liaoning F.C	1995	33	50	Nike
11	Zhejiang Lvcheng	1998	60		
12	Shaanxi Baorong Chamba	1995	80	50	Nike
13	Shenzhen Kingway	1994	33	50	Nike
14	Henan Jianye	1994	29		
15	Xiamen Lanshi	1996	30		

Table compiled from www.sinosoc.com. *(In April 2008, £1 was approximately 14 RMB.)*

which paid 36 million yuan but announced early in 2008 that it would not renew the contract when it expired (*China Daily*, 2008). In 2008, the wine brand Jinliufu was the sponsor (*Shanghaiist*, 2008).

PROBLEMS AND CHALLENGES FACING THE INDUSTRY

The past few years have presented many challenges. Fraud has been an issue with the "black whistle" scandal that broke in 2001, exposing the bribing of referees and match fixing. This is believed to be the main cause of the decline in attendance. Violent football fans have also been a problem, although not one that is exclusive to China.

Another problem is player standards. Compared to other sports such as table tennis and badminton, football skill has not kept pace. Performances have not improved since 2002, and this has led to public criticism. The government has conducted much research to investigate the factors that hinder development, and the results indicate three main factors that contribute to this problem.

1. *The management system.* There are too many government departments managing the sport. Many clubs are supported by state-owned enterprises and enjoy preferential treatment. The clubs that are operated by private enterprises complain of not enjoying the same level of support. Also, many feel there are not adequate sports-related regulations to deal with these problems.

2. *Inadequate investment in public football, especially in early youth.* The facilities available for public games are insufficient, and as a result, fewer and fewer people participate in the sport. This makes it difficult to find and develop good youth players.

3. *Lack of support from young players' schools, teachers, and parents.* The examination-oriented educational system means many Chinese students' study load is very heavy. They are restricted from playing football at school despite the availability of pitches. After school, homework requirements leave little time to play, and pitches outside of school are difficult to find. It is generally accepted that in most sports, a lack of concentration on development in early youth is likely to restrict future competitiveness.

EUROPEAN CLUBS' ACTIVITIES

Desbordes (2007) points out that the reasons for interest in this market are that European and North American sports markets are at saturation levels, whereas South East Asian markets (particularly China) have the following advantages:

- Emergent, with high potential for commercial development.
- Highly populated.
- Increasing levels of purchasing power.
- Passionate about football.
- Consumers of merchandise and media.

As clubs look to the Far East to increase their revenues, China presents a potentially large opportunity because of its size (1.4 billion people), but it is also one with many difficulties. Readers who wish to examine the problems of doing business in China are referred to the texts in the Guided Reading section.

Clubs in the top divisions of the English, Italian, Spanish, and German leagues are among those who are increasingly looking to develop support and income here. A number of different approaches have been taken, and these are outlined following.

Tours

Many clubs have travelled to China during their off-season to increase their worldwide support. Real Madrid toured in the summer of 2003 and 2005, but the club received criticism during the second tour in Beijing. The ground was only half full, and a Chinese Internet survey revealed that over 90 percent of fans thought that the sole aim of the tour was to make money; 62 percent said they would not support Real if they came again. According to reports, the tour earned at least $4 million (*People's Daily Online*, 2005b). Manchester United toured Asia in the summer of 2007, playing in Japan, Korea, Macau, and China, but, again, the tour was criticized, as some believed it to be a purely money-making venture for the club and their sponsors. The game against Guangzhou in South China was played in front of a half-full stadium (Boyle, 2007). The scope for tours is also somewhat restricted by the European league calendar and a ten-hour flight each way.

Sponsorship

This can be viewed from two perspectives: European clubs want to generate income, and Chinese companies want to promote themselves. Keijan, a communications company, sponsored Everton from 2002 to 2004 to build awareness of its mobile phone brand in China, but it did not sell it in Europe. As part of the deal and following his appearances in the World Cup, the Chinese player Li Tie signed for Everton. The opportunities are not just for the top clubs, as demonstrated by the sponsorship deal between Desun and Sheffield United (see Case Study 21.1). The increasing number of Chinese corporations with global aspirations may see growth in this area.

Players

A number of clubs, particularly in England, have signed Chinese or other Asian players. Cynics argue that this has nothing to do with playing ability but is simply an attempt to increase interest and gain supporters in China. The most successful Chinese player in the Premiership has been Sun Jihal, who has played over 100 games for Manchester City; Li Tie appeared for Everton 34 times in two seasons. Zheng Zhi was a regular player for

Charlton Athletic in 2007/2008 but Dong Fangzhou has only appeared in one league game for Manchester United in three years at the club.

Merchandise

Figures on the sale of sport merchandise are difficult to find, but most European clubs are unlikely to have large sales in China because of its high cost to local consumers and the amount of piracy in the country. There are claims that English national and club shirts are the most popular (*Footballshirtculture.com*, 2007), but this research did not consider the authenticity of these claims.

Commercial and Managerial Support

A number of clubs have been active in this area. Real Madrid signed a deal to provide commercial and managerial support to Beijing Guoan, and Glasgow Rangers has a coaching and management contract with Shenzhen. Charlton Athletic offered support to Shandong Luneng (Zheng Zhi's previous club) in 2008, which involves devising a model for its youth academy as well as touring the region for the next three years. The offer was in exchange for the opportunity for Charlton to have the first refusal on the signature of players (*FIFA.com*, 2008a). At a lower level, the latest development has seen the AFC working with Chelsea to set up ten city leagues in the country (*FIFA.com*, 2008b).

Media Activities

Besides exposure through league games, other attempts have been made to increase media coverage. A number of clubs including Manchester United have set up websites in Mandarin, and some of these sites offer pay-per-view content.

Chelsea, which is trying to replace Manchester United as the most widely supported club in China, has joined forces with Guangdong TV Sports Channel to launch a *Soccer Super Star* television series that will be shown in the province in 2008, with the winners being trained at Chelsea's Academy (*FIFA.com*, 2008b).

WOMEN'S FOOTBALL

As mentioned previously, the original game of Cuju was played by women. However, the popularity of foot binding led to the game falling into decline. In spite of this, China was the first Asian country to introduce the modern game from abroad. In 1991, Guangzhou held the first World Female Football Championship, and in 2007, the FIFA Women's World Cup was held in

China. This event saw 80 percent of the tickets sold in advance and average attendances of 25,000 to 30,000 (*FIFA.com*, 2007).

Since the 1990s, the Chinese women's team has been far more competitive internationally than the men's, qualifying for most tournaments and generally being among the strongest teams. They lost to the United States in the 1999 Women's World Cup final, finished fourth in 1995, and reached the quarter finals in 2007.

Unfortunately, the women's game has encountered many problems, as sponsorship for a league has proved difficult to find and the number of women playing has decreased. The sport is not played much in schools because table tennis and swimming are the preferred choices, and parental consent is often difficult to obtain. The lack of money in the sport makes it difficult for players to make a living from it, and the specialist football schools that exist are not renowned for providing a good education or alternative career for their students (*China.org.cn*, 2007).

CASE STUDY 21.1: Chengdu Blades and Sheffield United—Cutting Edge or Blunt Edge Alliance?

Sheffield United acquired a controlling stake in Chengdu Five Bull Football Club in 2006, becoming the first foreign club to take over a Chinese team. They had a 90 percent stake in the team, and they renamed it Chengdu Blades. United's nickname is the Blades, reflecting the steel industry of its location. The club has subsequently formed alliances with Ferencvaros (Hungary), Central Coast Mariners (Australia), and Royal White Star (Belgium), and they were in discussions with São Paulo (Brazil).

The origins of the deal date from 2000, when Tony Xu, an agent, helped Sheffield negotiate a sponsorship deal with the Chinese company Desun for £200,000, spread over two years. During the course of negotiations, Kevin McCabe, chairman of Sheffield United, visited China for the first time. He thought there might be opportunities for the club in football, property, and leisure, since the holding company that owns the club has interests in all three areas. Property was initially purchased in Shenzhen as part of a joint venture with a Chinese partner, and an offer was accepted to run the Hainan Soccer Academy, even though Hainan is over 1,000 kilometres from Chengdu.

Chengdu, with 10 million residents, is the capital of Southwest China's Sichuan Province, which has a population of nearly 90 million. It is one of the fastest-developing areas within China and was declared a "pilot reform zone" in July 2007 with the aim of developing it and nearby Chongqing into China's fourth largest economic area. There were no clubs west of the city in the Chinese Super League in 2007 and none within the province itself.

McCabe pointed out that the takeover presented the club with a huge potential fan base for both clubs. They intended to improve Chengdu's off-field performance through sponsorship, increased attendance, and merchandise sales. They also intended to establish a leisure/football shop in the stadium, as well as a Blades bar in the city.

Sheffield also looked forward to Chinese TV stations buying the telecast rights to their matches in China, especially after signing national defender Zhang Yaokun on loan from the Chinese Super League club Dalian Shide. Zhang joined Hao Haidong as the second Chinese player at the club, and Li Tie was signed for the 2006–2007 season. However, by the end of the 2008–2009 season, a Chinese player had yet to appear in a league game for the club.

Chengdu Blades were promoted to the CSL for the 2008–2009 season, and their penultimate game attracted over 30,000 fans. One of their stars, Wang Song, has become the first player from the club to be called up to the national team. Sheffield were promoted to the Premiership for the 2006–2007 season but relegated after only one season. They are currently in the Championship trying to regain their Premiership status. Their relegation means a big loss in revenue, although for two years their finances were enhanced by "parachute payments" from the Premiership to help cover these losses. Most clubs who failed to regain their Premiership status in this period have had to make austere financial cutbacks.

Question

1. What are the football- and nonfootball-related benefits to Sheffield United of taking over Chengdu Five Bull?

2. What are the benefits of the alliance to the Chengdu Five Bull football club?

3. If Premier League status is not regained and financial cutbacks must be made, what arguments can be made for Sheffield United staying in China?

Source: People's Daily Online, 2006; Rollins & Rollins, 2007.

CONCLUSIONS

Chinese men's football still provokes an interesting debate. There are a number of issues that make its future direction unclear, and these can be understood by looking at three segments of the market: the international team, league football, and overseas football. In terms of the first two segments, many problems arise: the national team is now ranked about eightieth in the FIFA rankings and will struggle to qualify for the 2010 World Cup. Rumours regularly surface about bidding for the World Cup, and at the time of writing, automatically qualifying as a host nation probably represents the best chance of qualification. The staging of the Olympics in Beijing may increase domestic interest, although the better players do not play in a tournament that is regarded as important in most countries.

Attendances have been falling at CSL games for a number of years since the peak early in the millennium, but 2007 saw an increase that may signal a reverse to the trend. The problems discussed in this chapter may also lead to falling interest as people take more interest in sports where the Chinese perform well both as a team and individually. Their most well-known and probably most popular sportsman is Yao Ming, who plays in the National Basketball Association (NBA) competition in the United

States for Houston Rockets, and it is believed that his success has done much to popularize basketball in China.

The third segment, overseas football, may continue to increase in interest and at the expense of Chinese league football and the international team. A view generally held in the media is that there is more interest in overseas football, partially due to its quality or fashionability, or perhaps a combination of both. However, falling interest in domestic football may also lead to a loss of interest in overseas football.

The competition between the CSL and overseas leagues, and particularly the Premiership, is likely to increase. In 2008, the Premiership touted the idea of playing some games abroad, with Beijing as a potential venue, although this idea was swiftly rebuffed by FIFA and opposed by the Asian Football Conference (AFC). It was not the first example of conflict between Asian administrators and European clubs, as Manchester United had previously had to withdraw from a planned match in Malaysia in 2007 as it clashed with the Asian Cup (*Bangkok Post*, 2008).

The activities of European teams in China are likely to continue in the short term. The quality of available information and difficulty of verification make it hard to determine just how popular European football is in China. Continued economic growth means wealthier consumers, but there will surely come a point when European clubs start to evaluate these activities in both football and commercial terms. Some Chinese players have to date been successful in the European leagues, but the clubs have been far more successful in African alliances, particularly in West Africa.

One final point to consider is investment in one of the European teams by Chinese investors. The Thai entrepreneur and politician Thaskin Shinawatra bought Manchester City (but has since sold the club) and adopted a number of tactical measures to generate interest in the club in Thailand, including signing Thai players and organizing a tour of the country. Will a Chinese entrepreneur follow suit?

DISCUSSION QUESTIONS

1. The former French president Charles de Gaulle once described the country of Brazil as a "country of great potential, and always will be." Why should his words serve as a warning to football clubs trying to do business in China?
2. How do European clubs try to make money in China?
3. How can Chinese women's football attract more sponsorship?

GUIDED READING

Sinosoc.com The website provides a good background about the development of the sport, particularly during the twentieth century. It also serves as a good introduction to the clubs and provides results and league tables. The official FIFA website *www.FIFA.com* is updated regularly and gives an account of the latest developments in the country. It is particularly useful for finding out about the latest activities of European clubs.

The following commercial report has been written on the sport in China: *Football in China.* (2003). N. Eaves, N. Empson, and D. Fletcher., SportBusiness Group/FMMInternational. It describes in some detail the football market in China prior to 2003. The report was updated in 2005.

Fan Hong and J. A. Mangan consider the progress of the women's game in China in *Will the "Iron Roses" Bloom Forever? Women's Football in China: Changes and Challenges in Soccer, Women, and Sexual Liberation.* (2003).

Though not directly concerned with football, *The China Dream* by Joe Studwell (2005) and *The Writing on the Wall: China and the West in the 21st Century* by Will Hutton (2008) both discuss at length the problems of doing business in China. Studwell describes the role of the then British deputy prime minister Michael Heseltine in getting England to play China in Beijing in 1996.

REFERENCES

Bangkok Post. (14th February, 2008). Asian Chief Opposes Overseas Round. *Bangkok Post*.

Boyle, P. (September, 2007). Great Exploitations. *That's PRD*. Retrieved on March 28, 2008, from *http://www.thatsprd.com/index.php?option=com_content &task=view&id=845&Itemid=37*.

Bristow, M. (2007). Pay-TV Turns Off China Football Fans. *BBC News*. Retrieved on March 11, 2009, from *http://news.bbc.co.uk/1/hi/world/asia-pacific/ 7136677.stm*.

China Daily. (11th January, 2008). Kingway's Super League Sponsorship Goes Flat. *China Daily*.

China.org.cn (2007). Fewer and fewer Chinese girls play football. Retrieved on the March 28, 2008, from *http://www.china.org.cn/english/news/230727.htm*.

Desbordes, M. (Ed.) (2007). *Marketing & Football. An International Perspective*. Oxford: Butterworth Heinemann.

Eaves, N., Empson, N., & Fletcher, D. (2003). *Football in China*. Sport Business Group/FMMInternational. Retrieved on March 28, 2008 from *http://www. fmminternational.com/news/2005/index.html*.

FIFA.com. (2008a). Global Alliances Boost Charlton. *FIFA.com*. Retrieved on June 11, 2009, from *http://www.fifa.com/worldfootball/clubfootball/news/newsid=701462.html*.

FIFA.com. (2008b). Chelsea in Search for Chinese Superstar. *FIFA.com*. Retrieved on June 11, 2009, from *http://www.fifa.com/worldfootball/clubfootball/news/newsid=703199.html*.

FIFA.com. (2007). Women's Football More Popular Than Ever. *FIFA.com*. Retrieved on June 11, 2009, from *http://www.fifa.com/tournaments/archive/womensworldcup/china2007/news/newsid=590140.html*.

Footballshirtculture.com. (2007). England Football Shirts Number One in China. *Footballshirtculture.com*. Retrieved on March 28, 2008, from *http://www.footballshirtculture.com/index.php?option=com_content&task=view&id=416*.

Hong, F. & Mangan, J. A. (2003). Will the 'Iron Roses' Bloom Forever? Women's Football. In Fan Hong., & J. A. Mangan, (Eds.), *China: Changes and Challenges in Soccer, Women, and Sexual Liberation*. Routledge.

Hutton, W. (2008). *The Writing on the Wall: China and the West in the 21st Century*. Abacus.

People's Daily Online (31st October, 2007). China Super League lacks spectators. *People's Daily Online*. Retrieved on July 27, 2009, from *http://english.people.com.cn/90001/90779/90871/6293798.html*.

People's Daily Online (13th January, 2006). Sheffield United take over Chengdu football club. *People's Daily Online*. Retrieved on the 12th August, 2009, from *http://english.peopledaily.com.cn/200601/13/eng20060113_235136.html*.

People's Daily Online (2005a). Chinese Super League Attendance Hits Record Low in 2005. *Peopledaily.com*. Retrieved on March 31, 2008, from *http://english.peopledaily.com.cn/200502/27/eng20050227_174841.html*.

People's Daily Online (2005b). Real Madrid Win Money But Lose Loyalty. *Peopledaily.com*. Retrieved on March 31, 2008, from *http://english.peopledaily.com.cn/200507/25/eng20050725_198059.html*.

People's Daily Online (2004). FIFA Boss Hails China as Football Birthplace. *Peopledaily.com*. Retrieved on January 5, 2008, from *http://english.peopledaily.com.cn/200407/16/eng20040716_149849.html*.

Rollins, G., & Rollins, J. (2007). *Sky Sports Football Year Book 2007–2008*. London: Headline.

Shanghaiist. (2008). Return to Spiritual Home as Shenhua Kick Off 2008 Season. Retrieved on March 31, 2008, from *Shanghaist.com*.*http://shanghaiist.com/2008/03/28/return_to_spiri.php*.

Sinosoc.com. www.sinsoc.com.

Studwell, J. (2005). *The China Dream: The Elusive Quest for the Greatest Untapped Market on Earth*. London: Profile Books.

RECOMMENDED WEBSITES

A Chinese football website
www.sinosoc.com
A Chinese football website
http://sports.163.com *
A Chinese football website
http://sports.qq.com *
A football website which covers Chinese football
www.bigsoccer.com
FIFA's website
www.FIFA.com
Manchester United's website
http://www.Manunited.com.cn/ *

---

* In Mandarin

CHAPTER 22

South Africa

Urmilla Bob
University of Kwazulu-Natal

Scarlett Cornelissen
Stellenbosch University

Kamilla Swart
Cape Peninsula University of Technology

Objectives

Upon completion of this chapter the reader should be able to:

- Understand the nature of football development in South Africa across key historical periods.

- Grasp the issues and challenges relating to attempts to transform football in the era following the end of apartheid.

- Place South Africa's emergence as one of Africa's football powers in relation to wider developments on the continent.

- Detail the key contemporary challenges facing the management of football in South Africa.

- Provide assessments of the prospects and constraints for the future of football development in the country.

CONTENTS

OVERVIEW OF THE CHAPTER

This chapter reviews the history of football development in South Africa, commencing with the game's early origins during the era of colonialism. An outline of the game's development during the twentieth century is provided, in which its key phases of formalisation, professionalisation and commercialisation are discussed. Apartheid planning and legislation became major influences on the development and support for the game during this time. The second part of the chapter outlines the current administrative structures for amateur and professional football in the country. The most important issues and challenges which frame football's development and status in South Africa and within the wider African continent are discussed.

INTRODUCTION

With more than two million active players and more than 54 percent of the national population following football, this sport is the most popular and widely practised sport in South Africa, ranking in levels of participation and active support far above other major sports such as rugby, cricket or athletics (Department of Sport and Recreation, 2006; Makgabo, 2006, page 2). Like those sports, football's commercialisation has also been significant, although—in contrast to rugby in South Africa, for instance—it is only recently that this commercialisation has been more pronounced. Despite football's prominent place in organised South African sport and its highly popular appeal, little is known about the origins of the game in the country, nor of the circumstances by which it systematically developed into one of the most important sports—and an area of political contestation—during a key phase of South Africa's history. Indeed, the significance of football in South Africa extends beyond the social appeal of the game, and relates to the way in which its development was closely interwoven with aspects of racial polarisation and ideology that characterised twentieth-century South Africa. The main phases of football's diffusion and development therefore, i.e. its formalisation, organisational structuring, professionalisation and commercial development, were closely aligned to major structural processes underway in South Africa at the time. Colonialism, industrialisation, urbanisation and later, apartheid planning, became the major forces by which football's development was shaped.

All of these factors set South Africa apart from most other countries in Africa where, although colonial in origin (see, for instance, Darby, 2000), football development has not been affected to the same extent by major politicostructural forces. Indeed, the period of apartheid provided the formative conditions under which South African football took on a very idiosyncratic guise. Although isolated from international competition and played on the basis of racial separation, the game expanded and was well formalised. The end of apartheid enabled the game to flourish and allowed the incipient processes of commercialisation to exploit new opportunities for expansion.

South Africa's professional league is the most successful in sub-Saharan Africa, in part because it draws from domestic corporate support which is not present in many other parts of the African continent. This has raised the allure of the country's professional league for many players based in more impoverished and haphazardly organised leagues and the migration of footballers into South Africa from other African countries has become more pronounced (Cornelissen and Solberg, 2007). Together, aggressive commercialisation, a highly successful professional league and better infrastructural and financial resources place South Africa in a strong position vis-à-vis other African countries. South Africa's impending hosting of the 2010 FIFA World Cup™ will carry benefits and costs for the country. If anything, however, the hosting of the tournament marks the country's full reintegration into international football after a lengthy period of isolation in the twentieth century.

FOOTBALL'S DEVELOPMENT IN SOUTH AFRICA

While there is some dispute over when football first emerged as a game in South Africa, it is widely accepted that its introduction came by way of European—and specifically British—colonial contact in the latter part of the nineteenth century. Soldiers, traders, and missionaries were early exporters of the game (Holt, 1989). At times this entailed informal play with colonial subjects that resembled football, but for the most part football's early introduction took the form of games among Europeans themselves. Therefore, while football matches were being played by whites on a more formal basis in specific parts of colonial South Africa from about the 1870s onward, references to football among South Africa's black populations date from much later (Couzens, 1983). It seems clear, however, that by the start of the twentieth century, football was becoming more popular and actively participated in by black men. Impetuses for this development stemmed from events such as the Anglo-Boer War (1899–1902), which led to the immigration of greater numbers of British soldiers who helped to popularise the game among the indigenous populations. The discovery of minerals, the subsequent development of a mining economy, and the impacts of this on urbanisation patterns, framed the uptake and organisation of football during the early part of the twentieth century. Mines and mining towns drew young black labour, and in an effort to appease restless energy and provide opportunities for 'moralised leisure time', mining companies started to support the founding of football associations for mineworkers (Couzens, 1983, page 205).

Broad football organisation outside of these structures was more limited. However, by the late 1920s, more football associations were formed through the support of city municipalities. One of the first examples is the Johannesburg Bantu Football Association (JBFA), which was set up in 1929 (Thabe, 1983, page 5). The JBFA was emblematic of the strong racial division that historically characterised the participation and support of football in South Africa. Not only did rugby become more popular among white people during the corresponding period (Morrell, 1996)—and consequently sealed the racial division between the two sports which continues in South Africa to the present day—but football associations were also formed to represent Indian and Coloured clubs separate from black clubs.[1] The advent of apartheid reinforced football's racially separate development throughout the second half of the twentieth century. This was mainly as a result of contingent apartheid legislation which sought to prevent all aspects of racial mixing, and included, inter alia, restrictions on the movement and settlement of black people. On the other hand, sport provided an avenue for popular and political mobilisation against apartheid during this time, and the movement for nonracialism found its counterparts also in football. In 1951, a broad alignment of theretofore racially separate national associations founded the first non-racial football organisation, the South African Soccer Federation (SASF), which represented most black, Coloured and Indian footballers in the country. The SASF became embroiled in a bitter and lengthy battle with the white Football Association of South Africa (FASA), which enjoyed membership of the Fédération Internationale de Football Association (FIFA). The SASF demanded the inclusion of nonwhite players in FASA's competitions and also placed pressure on FIFA to suspend FASA's membership on the grounds of the latter's policy of racial separation. In 1961, FIFA yielded to sustained international pressure and suspended FASA. A year earlier, the Confédération de Africaine de Football (CAF) had already expelled South Africa from its organisation.

These actions constituted the first part of an extended campaign of international sanctions against apartheid South Africa and marked the beginning of the country's isolation from international sport from which it was to emerge only 30 years later. This period of isolation had a fundamental impact on football's further development in the country, of which racial division, even within the country's supposed non-racial sport organisations,

---

[1] Racial terminology in South Africa reflects early colonial categorisation which became institutionalised during the apartheid era when, by law, four racial groups were coexisting. These were whites, blacks (or Africans), Indians and Coloureds, a broad amalgam of mixed-race descendants of European, Khoisan, African, and Southeast Asian settler and slave communities. These terms persist in official and everyday usage in postapartheid South Africa.

was a persistent feature. This was also the period, however, of systematic professionalisation and eventual commercialisation of the game. The shift from amateurism to professionalism was incremental, starting with the founding of the first professional league, the (black) South African Soccer League, in 1961. Fledgling at first, the new league quickly became successful. Its popularity, and success, was perceived as a potential destabilising force by the minority white government, which used (in part) municipal laws to prevent league games from taking place (Alegi, 2004). By 1966, the South African Soccer League was stifled. Fresh attempts at establishing black professional leagues persisted during the 1970s and 1980s. Some of South Africa's most successful black football club owners, many of whom were entrepreneurs in their own right, led the efforts toward professionalisation. Support from some of the country's largest corporations resulted in the game's gradual commercialisation. It was in this context that some of the country's major clubs such as Kaizer Chiefs and Orlando Pirates became highly prominent. The commercialisation and professionalisation of football in South Africa, however, coincided with the escalating intensity of popular resistance against the apartheid regime, often violent in nature, and the country's increased isolation. Within the ranks of the black football bodies, intense battles were often waged on how far to forge the link between sport and politics (Booth, 1998). By the beginning of the 1990s, far-reaching political changes were being effected in South Africa, yet ideological polarisation still marked black football's governing bodies. Attempts were made to unify all the different football organisations and in 1991, the new nonracial governing body, the South African Football Association (SAFA) was founded.

CONTEMPORARY FOOTBALL ORGANISATION IN SOUTH AFRICA

SAFA became the apex of a progressively better organised and commercially more successful football order, although, as detailed below, many factors of constraint affect the financial and governance vitality of the game in South Africa. Football's current administration is determined by a division between amateur and professional sport. At the amateur level, SAFA, which is affiliated to FIFA, has the primary role of overseeing and enforcing adherence to FIFA regulations. The national body consists of 52 regional members drawn from eight of the country's nine provinces, and six associate members. It presides over amateur competitions organised in three leagues (see Figure 22.1).

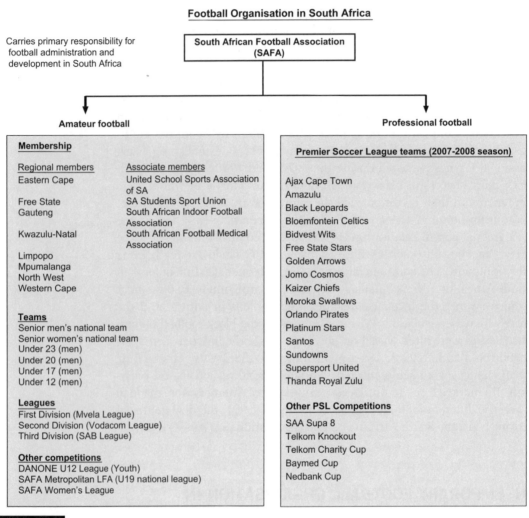

Football Organisation in South Africa

Carries primary responsibility for football administration and development in South Africa

South African Football Association (SAFA)

Amateur football

Professional football

Membership

Regional members
Eastern Cape

Free State
Gauteng

Kwazulu-Natal

Limpopo
Mpumalanga
North West
Western Cape

Associate members
United School Sports Association of SA
SA Students Sport Union
South African Indoor Football Association
South African Football Medical Association

Teams
Senior men's national team
Senior women's national team
Under 23 (men)
Under 20 (men)
Under 17 (men)
Under 12 (men)

Leagues
First Division (Mvela League)
Second Division (Vodacom League)
Third Division (SAB League)

Other competitions
DANONE U12 League (Youth)
SAFA Metropolitan LFA (U19 national league)
SAFA Women's League

Premier Soccer League teams (2007-2008 season)

Ajax Cape Town
Amazulu
Black Leopards
Bloemfontein Celtics
Bidvest Wits
Free State Stars
Golden Arrows
Jomo Cosmos
Kaizer Chiefs
Moroka Swallows
Orlando Pirates
Platinum Stars
Santos
Sundowns
Supersport United
Thanda Royal Zulu

Other PSL Competitions

SAA Supa 8
Telkom Knockout
Telkom Charity Cup
Baymed Cup
Nedbank Cup

FIGURE 22.1 *Football organisation in South Africa.*
Sources: SAFA, PSL.

Professional football is overseen by the Premier Soccer League (PSL), which was established in 1996. This league is made up of 16 clubs (Figure 22.1). Most of these clubs function as franchises by which they can be sold or even relocated, in much the same way as American sport teams. Statutorily, SAFA holds regulatory oversight over the Premier Soccer League, which is meant to operate autonomously. However, overlapping membership by individuals means that independence is not always maintained, as some of the PSL's prominent club owners serve as executive members of SAFA (Kunene, 2006).

ISSUES AND CHALLENGES FOR FOOTBALL IN SOUTH AFRICA TODAY

The Legacy of Apartheid

The apartheid legacy discussed earlier remains an overarching challenge facing South African football. This is particularly prevalent in relation to the organisation and management of football in the country. Alegi (2007) suggests that preparations for the 2010 World Cup illustrate how South Africa's engagement with global capitalism is not mitigating apartheid's legacies of racism, widespread material poverty, and extreme poverty. Indeed, some more critical observers have contended that current World Cup strategies undermine, rather than foster, grassroots football (Ebrahim, 2006).

Concentration of Support and Funding

The huge popularity of football in South Africa has attracted significant financial investments. In June 2007, the PSL signed a R1.6-billion broadcast deal with SuperSport International. In August 2007, South African Breweries (SAB) and Absa Bank announced a joint sponsorship of more than R500-million over five years for the national team, Bafana Bafana, and the PSL respectively. In February 2008, Nedbank announced that it would be putting up R20-million in prize money for the Nedbank Cup knockout competition as part of a five-year, R400-million sponsorship. And in August 2008, cellular giant MTN committed R400million over five years to sponsor the Top 8 knockout tournament. These deals combined were reputed to make South Africa's Premier Soccer League the seventh biggest earner of sponsorship revenue among football leagues worldwide (*South Africa Info*, 2007). However, support for professional football differs throughout the country, as the hub of South African football is Gauteng, South Africa's economic centre. The headquarters of the South African Football Association, the PSL and the 2010 Local Organising Committee are all located in Gauteng. As noted by Alegi (2007, page 316):

> *In sporting terms, the cultural, economic, and administrative centre of domestic football is located in Gauteng province … the home base of Kaizer Chiefs, and Orlando Pirates, the most popular and successful clubs in the country, as well as other important sides like Mamelodi Sundowns, Supersport, Jomo Cosmos, and Moroka Swallows.*

Table 22.1 illustrates the support base for the five most popular PSL teams. The dominance of the two major teams, Kaizer Chiefs and Orlando Pirates, who altogether capture more than three-quarters of national support,

Table 22.1	Support Bases of Five Top PSL Teams		
Team	**Shirt Sponsor**	**Supporters**	**Percent of all supporters**
Kaizer Chiefs	Vodacom	5,342,000	47
Orlando Pirates	Vodacom	3,339,000	29
Mamelodi Sundowns	TBA, previously MTN	920,000	8
Ajax Cape Town	MTN	420,000	4
Bloemfontein Celtics	Vodacom	303,000	3

Source: *Financial Mail, 2008.*

is clear. Kunene (2006, page 375) aptly describes the situation that characterises the PSL (even today):

> *The Premier League itself increasingly became an unequal battlefield where the half dozen or so leading clubs claimed most of the trophies, most of the better players, and most of the money, enviously tailed by the majority of the teams whose great fear was the dramatic loss of gate revenues and loss of sponsorships which would follow upon relegation back to the old Football League (today relegated to the First Division League).*

The massive investments that have marked football since the end of apartheid have tended to be concentrated in the PSL with very little support directed at First and Second Division clubs, and almost no support for grassroots club development (Alegi, 2004; Kunene, 2006). This reinforces many of the inequalities that so marked the apartheid era and reflects the challenges posed to wider processes of transformation in South Africa, where inequalities have become persistent features of the South African landscape despite attempts to increase and level the playing field.

Corporate Sponsorship and Broadcasting Rights

Corporate involvement and sponsorship of South African clubs has increased significantly over the years, with some of South Africa's largest corporations (such as Absa, Adidas, Castle Lager, Vodacom, SAA, Netcare 911, Coca Cola, Southern Sun, Sasol, First National Bank, Metropolitan, Avis, and Daimler) becoming key players in the marketing and promotion of South African football. However, this has not been without controversy. First, corporate sponsorship of rugby and cricket still tends to carry greater financial value than for football (Shandu, 2008), reflecting the favouritism (and to some degree corporate prejudice) which those two sports have historically enjoyed vis-à-vis football. Second, sponsorship has tended to be skewed toward the national team, Bafana Bafana, and specific football clubs such as Kaizer Chiefs and Orlando Pirates, which have become successful brands with which corporations have sought to associate themselves. In general, the PSL clubs draw most of the financial sponsorships.

The hosting of the 2010 World Cup has stimulated new corporate interest in professional football. As was mentioned earlier, in 2007, the PSL sold its television rights to the private cable and satellite provider Multi-Choice Supersport for more than R1 billion (approximately US$160 million) over five years. This represented a tripling of the PSL's television revenues from its previous television coverage agreement with the state-run South African Broadcasting Corporation (SABC) (Enslin-Payne, 2007). However, while the change in provider is a massive financial boost to PSL revenues, a significant proportion of South Africa's population will not be able to view matches live since they are unable to afford cable television. SABC is a public broadcaster and considerably more South Africans, especially from the poorer segments of society, have access to SABC channels. This issue raised several popular debates and underscores the centrality that is given to profits and finance over people (especially the average football supporter) in South Africa.

Another disconcerting trend is the focus of big business on lucrative, profit-making teams. According to Kunene (2006), this is an outcome of the trend towards commercialisation and the game's growing attraction for large-scale capital. Kunene (2006) cites the examples of African Rainbow Minerals magnate, Patrice Motsepe, who finances Mamelodi Sundowns (see Case Study 22.1), and M-Net's support of Pretoria City (which became Supersport United) in 1994 (when the television corporation was accused of not sufficiently supporting local football). Supersport United subsequently became a PSL team and emerged victorious as PSL champions in the 2008 season.

CASE STUDY 22.1: Private business involvement in football: The case of Mamelodi Sundowns

Mamelodi Sundowns Football Club originated from Marabastad, a cosmopolitan area northwest of the Pretoria Central Business District (CBD). The club was originally formed in the early 1960s by a group of youngsters, including Frank Motsepe, Roy Fischer, Ingle Singh, and Bernard Hartze, and became an official football club in 1970. For five years, Sundowns battled to gain promotion and during that period the management resolved to disband the club. However, they were approached by the late Boy Mafa who bought the franchise for R2000.00, a transaction facilitated by the lawyer Dikgang Moseneke. This resulted in the club's relocation to Mamelodi in the early 1980s. In 1988, the ownership of the club fell into the hands of Standard Bank, which repossessed the club from Mr. Zola Mahobe. The club was then bought by successful businessman Abe Krok, and the powerful Tsichlas family.

Patrice Motsepe is a passionate football lover and in 2003, he bought 51 percent shares in the club. In 2004, he took total control of the club by buying the remaining shares and thus became the sole owner and shareholder of the club. He is a leading South African mining entrepreneur whose company, Africa Rainbow Minerals, has interests in gold, ferrous metals, base metals, and platinum. He won South Africa's Best Entrepreneur Award in 2002, and in 2004 he was voted 39th in the Top 100 Great South Africans. In 2008, he was 503rd richest person in the world, according to the Forbes World Billionaires List. He is also a big contributor to the social development of South Africa, sponsoring some disadvantaged NGOs and school journeys aimed at discovering the future starts of South Africa football.

Adapted from:

Patrice Motsepe *http://www.blackentrepreneurprofile. com/profile-full/archive/2004/october/article/patrice- motsepe/*

Mamelodi Sundowns *http://www.sundownsfc.com/default. asp?id=10937&des=content*

Despite the presence and support of large capital in the PSL, and in spite of a strong reputation on the African continent, South Africa still experiences difficulty in grooming and retaining the most talented players. The possibility to play in some of the larger and more lucrative European leagues is a powerful incentive for many South African footballers. This has had important effects on domestic football, leading to some significant talent erosion that can partly explain the poor performances by the national team in recent years. This indicates that South Africa is following a pattern of football talent export which many African countries have exhibited for years (Darby et al., 2007). The PSL, and even some of South Africa's lower divisions, are nonetheless attractive to many players based elsewhere in the continent, who are drawn by the prospects of higher salaries, international coverage of the PSL's competitions and the possibility to display their talents to wider audiences, and the relative political stability of South Africa (Cornelissen and Solberg, 2007). Although still incipient, football migration to South Africa has evolved into a distinct segment of labour movement from the rest of sub-Saharan Africa, with attendant consequences for the game. South African football has undoubtedly benefited from talent injection from elsewhere, but this has often come at the expense of football development in other African countries. In addition, many migrant footballers are generally less secure in their contracts than their South African counterparts, being paid lower salaries or experiencing other forms of discrimination.

FOOTBALL GOVERNANCE

SAFA has been plagued with several controversies in recent years regarding the use of funds. Some of the most noteworthy illustrations include Mr. Irvin Khoza (vice-president of SAFA and PSL Chairman) awarding himself and his executive R50 million as commission for securing an Absa bank sponsorship of R500 million (Mantambo, December 4, 2007). Farouk Abrahams, (2007) a prominent sports journalist and commentator, summed up popular reactions to this when he wrote:

> *Millions and millions of Rands pumped into the South African Football Association and the Premier Soccer League with more and more going to the fat cats of the beautiful game, and still only the odd murmur from the powers that be about improved development structures all the way down to the grassroots level.*

Kunene (2006) notes that although SAFA has received generous sponsorships from large private corporations and parastatals, it has produced only a handful of professional players and coaches. Alegi (2007) further states that SAFA does not have a national training centre, has done little to build or develop playing grounds in townships and rural areas, and has generally ignored the plight of football in most South African schools. In recent years, SAFA has come under closer scrutiny for financial mismanagement. Observers have attributed this, and the organisation's lack of strategic planning, as primary causes for the body's failed development programmes.

Bafana Bafana's Performance and Coaching Woes

The recent poor performance of Bafana Bafana coupled with SAFA's inability to provide coaching stability for the national team (despite massive investments of funds) are symptomatic of the management problems that have plagued South African football. Bafana Bafana was ranked 17th in Africa and 70th in the world in January 2009 (*FIFA.com*, 2009). In the past five years Bafana Bafana had numerous coaches, ranging from national to internationally renowned individuals. After South Africa secured the rights to host the 2010 FIFA World Cup, given Bafana Bafana's spiralling downward performance, FIFA itself stepped in to boost their performance by financially supporting the employment of a top international coach, Carlos Parreira, to coach the national team. However, Parreira then resigned citing personal problems (*Citizen*, 2008) and Joel Santana (another international coach) took on the position. Abrahams (2008a) claims that FIFA has called for a semblance of structure and class in a national South African team that has never made it past the first round of the World Cup tournament. Linked to the coaching crisis are the frequent controversies surrounding the inclusion of certain players in the team and the perceived reluctance of specific players who evade national calls to play, such as Benni McCarthy. However, Abrahams (2008a) correctly contextualises this incessant problem as being related to the lack of talented South African players currently available. According to him (Abrahams, 2008b, page 74):

> *Zany politics, power struggles and a lack of accountability for the destruction of the once mighty football structures in South Africa have had a damning effect on the beautiful game. And more so on the development side of the game which as matters currently stand is a complete and utter shambles across the country.*

FOOTBALL DEVELOPMENT EFFORTS

SAFA has an overall responsibility for the game's administration, including the development of amateur and women's football as well as player development. SAFA's official manifesto, according to Kunene (2006), indicates that the organisation is committed to promoting and facilitating the development of football through a sustained and integrated approach to all aspects of the game, including player development programmes at all levels (including grassroots levels); providing regional and national competitions; coaching; talent identification; a soccer school of excellence; and training camps and competition schedules for national squads. In terms of football development, the authors of this chapter found it extremely difficult to identify sustained and wide ranging (in terms of geographical spread and targeting groups across the social spectrum including those from historically disadvantaged communities and women) programmes managed and implemented by SAFA. Abrahams (2008b, page 74) asserts that the development of grassroots football in South Africa is often left to companies to set up mass coaching clinics which usually entail "a once-off one-day event with all the fanfare and food and a couple of cheap T-shirts to ensure a measure of exposure in return for the expense".

Ebrahim (2006) warns that professional sport globally is a rapidly growing multibillion-dollar industry that undermines the development of sport in underprivileged and economically poor communities, with South Africa no exception. Football training and development at grassroots levels is ad hoc, concentrated in specific locations, of relatively short duration and there are very few resources invested to promote football on an extensive basis. Although not widespread and at a level that it should be, there are several examples of football development programmes. However, these generally target specific areas and face severe resource challenges. Additionally, although a key objective of SAFA, most development programmes are not spearheaded by SAFA. An example is the 2007 new high school league that took place in Mitchell's Plan township in Cape Town (Alegi, 2007). However, Alegi raises concerns as to whether this initiative will be sustained since it remains uncertain whether the football establishment will provide administrative support as well as operational and capital funds. Alegi (2007) also shows how Ajax Cape Town and Santos (both PSL teams) have developed and implemented successful programmes to train young players. Case Study 22.2 illustrates Ajax Cape Town's developmental approach. PSL team development programmes are often done in collaboration with international teams and these programmes have produced players that have joined PSL teams, while some have even been recruited by international professional football teams.

CASE STUDY 22.2: Ajax Cape Town's youth development programme

Ajax Cape Town's youth development programme is widely publicised as key to their success and their partnership with Ajax Amsterdam ensures that their youth coaches and senior technical team are constantly updated with the latest developments in the coaching world. Ajax recruits players from regularly run youth football trials. Their training programmes are based on targeting several youth age groups, starting from the U11's to U20's. These teams play abroad in several prestigious European competitions and have achieved notable successes. For example, in 2008, the U13's won the Mondial Pupilles de Plomelin (France). Ajax CEO John Comitis said:

This is a great achievement for the club and the players. They have achieved the impossible against the top U13 teams from across the football world. What makes this win more significant is that there are a number of new players in the team as well as a new coach. All the accolades must go to the Ajax Youth Academy, the coaches and the players.

The U11's finished second in the International APK Youth E-Tournament (Netherlands).

The training programmes have produced players of high quality who are sought after by the top local and international clubs, for example Benni McCarthy (via SevenStars, Ajax Amsterdam, FC Porto, and Blackburn Rovers), Steven Pienaar (Ajax Amsterdam, Borussia Dortmund and Everton), Stanton Lewis (Ajax Amsterdam), Thembinkosi "Terror" Fanteni (Macabbi Haifa), and Daylon Claasen (Ajax Amsterdam). Their success is also recognised by requests from European clubs for players to attend trials at their clubs—for example, Nathan Paulse (Sweden), Bryce Moon (Greece), Brett Evans (Norway), Russel Mwafulirwa (Sweden), and Eyong Enoh (France) have all been called upon to attend trials abroad.

Adapted from Ajax Cape Town website: *http://www.ajaxct.co.za/index.php?option=com_ content&task=view&id=251&Itemid=2.*

In a broader sense, the postapartheid government's decision to remove sport (and physical education more generally) from public school curricula has had significant consequences for general sport development. School sport is no longer receiving public funding for infrastructural development or the advance of human resources such as sport teacher training. For football, this has tended to exacerbate some of the historically derived inequalities that existed previously. Possibly the only national initiative that is driving football in South African schools across the spectrum is the United Schools Sports Association of South Africa's (USSASA) national school tournament. Kunene (2006) highlights that two of the past winners were sponsored to represent South Africa in international school competitions and several notable national players such as Doctor Khumalo, Benedict Vilakazi and Matthew Booth were first spotted and signed up by professional clubs while playing in these school sport competitions. Importantly, while affiliated to SAFA, USSASA's initiative has no links to the national body. In fact, Kunene (2006, page 381) asserts that SAFA runs a national talent scouting exercise (*Wonke Wonke* project), "as part of its Vision 2010, which is headed by its national youth team coaches but with little or no organic connection to USSASA." This is a typical example of the lack of coordination and integration of football initiatives in South Africa. Abrahams (2008b) comments that South African football is crying out for development programmes to allow it to take the game to the next level, but it needs to be more structured than it is currently. As football's custodian, SAFA has not adequately lobbied the national government for the greater allocation of resources for football development in public schools. Given sport's generally accepted potential to foster civic bonds (Vanden Auweele et al., 2006), this is an important oversight.

WOMEN'S FOOTBALL

As elsewhere in the world, women's football has been the historic stepchild of national football (Pelak, 2005). While some attempts have been made more recently to strengthen women's football, SAFA has remained reluctant to provide financial assistance to the sport—a factor that certainly does not bode well for its future development (Alegi, 2007). Despite the lack of support from SAFA, sponsors and media broadcasters, Banyana Banyana (the nickname for the national women's team) has consistently performed well in international competitions; their performances have indeed overshadowed that of the national men's team. The reasons for this may relate to a strong sense of commitment and dedication and effective management. Currently, there are in excess of 50,000 female players in South Africa. A new national league has recently been established, and the national team is rated among the best in Africa (Saavedra, 2003). While FIFA rhetorically supports the development and advancement of women's football, Alegi (2007) argues that this has not translated into practice on the ground. Indeed, the majority of

SAFA's limited efforts to develop football are devoted to the men's game (Kunene, 2006).

OPPORTUNITIES AND CHALLENGES IN RELATION TO THE 2010 FIFA WORLD CUP

South Africa's hosting of the 2010 FIFA World Cup has placed the game of football at the centre stage of several debates and discussions, including the aspect of football development and management in South Africa as well as Africa more generally. Alegi (2007) asserts that as South Africa prepares to host the 2010 FIFA World Cup, public and scholarly discourses have largely overlooked the consequences of interactions between global sport, professional leagues, and grassroots football. Much of the discussions pertaining to the benefits of hosting the 2010 FIFA World Cup relate to positive economic and developmental impacts (including infrastructural improvement and expansion); positive image building of South Africa and Africa internationally; impetus for promoting national and African pride; and developing football in South Africa and throughout the continent.

Previous bid processes suggest that there is little football unity on the African continent and that the antagonism other countries have towards South Africa persists. Kunene (2006) asserts that the local game's weaknesses are also illustrated by South African football's less than happy relations with the rest of Africa. He attributes these tensions to the politics of football in Africa (especially South Africa's recent success as the first country in Africa to host the FIFA World Cup in Africa in 2010), the dirty business of competitive football, resentment toward South Africa's financial muscle in the game of football, and the perception of South Africa's voluntary (as opposed to forced during apartheid) isolation in African football, often choosing to play teams from other parts of the world when preparing for tournaments.

IMPLICATIONS FOR MANAGEMENT

The issues raised in the previous section allude to the range of challenges facing football in South Africa. The institutional structures currently in place to manage football in South Africa need to be revisited. Alegi (2007) states that the recent structural changes in the reorganisation of SAFA have increased the number of administrative regions from 25 to the current 52. These changes were intended to facilitate coordination by SAFA officials with newly established municipal authorities. The increase in administrative regions has expanded the size of the football bureaucracy and added more service delivery responsibilities to already overburdened municipal governments (Alegi, 2007). It is imperative that SAFA develops effective strategies and structures to manage the different aspects of football in South Africa. This should include developing football at school levels, investing in football infrastructure in historically disadvantaged locations such as townships and rural areas, and developing professional players and coaches as well as retaining their services. The creation of a national training centre with regional subcentres, the support of women's football, the implementation of local amateur leagues to provide opportunities for young players, and the leveraging of financial support for local clubs are all vitally important. These activities require significant and sustained resources to ensure their effectiveness and viability. It is the responsibility of SAFA to have a National Football Policy that identifies priority areas, defines activities, leverages the necessary resources, and articulates a clear and workable implementation strategy.

It is imperative that football managers at all levels consider the potential impacts of a football strategy that focuses on mega-events (such as the 2010 FIFA World Cup) and on football development in marginalised communities. Alegi (2007) highlights the need to critically assess whether the development of lavish new stadia such as the Green Point stadium for the 2010 FIFA World Cup will have a positive impact on poor communities. Will the majority of South African citizens have access to these facilities? Will these facilities enhance football development in South Africa? The infrastructural legacy can best be sustained and leveraged to promote broader development outcomes if the event and football in South Africa is better managed. It is important to note that legacy benefits do not just occur but need to be identified as clear outcomes, planned and implemented. This implies the appropriate investment of human and financial resources. It is imperative that a football strategy is developed that looks beyond 2010 and addresses the numerous challenges identified in this paper.

In this regard, Alegi's (2007, page 328) warning regarding the possible outcomes of the impacts of the 2010 FIFA World Cup given current trends is apt:

> *Unless radical changes take place over the next 20 months, the 2010 World Cup in South Africa will bring out some important contradictions tied to mega-event development. Government investment in infrastructure could benefit the PSL by raising attendance, enhancing spectator comfort and safety, and improving administration and marketing. But these subsidies would hardly curb the game's spiral of decline in historically disadvantaged urban townships, schools, and*

rural communities. That the 2010 World Cup may result in greater inequality between elite professional clubs and grassroots teams mirrors recent macroeconomic trends in South Africa.

CONCLUSIONS

In spite of many historical constraints, football has seen significant development in South Africa, rising to a current status where the country showcases some of the best organised amateur and professional leagues in sub-Saharan Africa. The commercialisation of the game has occurred at a more intense pace in recent years, with some both positive and negative implications for the game. On a broader level, South African football occupies a position of paradox: the country certainly enjoys prominence in African football, but this is mainly due to the commercial success of its professional league. The country does not hold the same status—or legitimacy—as far as the management of football on the continent is concerned. Indeed, continental football diplomacy has become more difficult to negotiate for South Africa's football authorities, with the country often perceived as arrogant and overly dominant by its African counterparts. Poor performances by the men's national team in recent major international competitions have also served to taint the country's football image beyond Africa. If managed properly, South Africa's hosting of the 2010 World Cup can address many of these broader factors. SAFA's inability to successfully and meaningfully develop grassroots football (including lobbying for the integration and reinclusion of sport in public schools), the chronic lack of support for amateur clubs and women's football, and incidences of the mismanagement of funds and political turmoil all point to the problems which South Africa still faces in relation to the management and development of football. In this regard, the greater value of the 2010 tournament lies in the ability to improve some of the internal management deficiencies to which South African football has been subject in recent years.

DISCUSSION QUESTIONS

1. Outline the conditions under which football emerged as a major sport in South Africa, and detail the key historical phases to the game's development. How does the historical context of football development relate to the current position and nature of football in South Africa?
2. What are the key challenges facing the management of football in South Africa?

3. The hosting of the 2010 FIFA World Cup is viewed as a unique opportunity to enhance the international profile of the country and act as a catalyst for economic development. Critically examine the impacts and challenges associated with South Africa hosting the 2010 FIFA World Cup.

GUIDED READING

Football's popularity in South Africa has not found reflection in academic or popular publications on aspects such as the history, dynamics or organisation of the game. Alegi's (2004) text provides a very good overview of the cultural importance of football among South Africa's black communities, tracing the history of the game's development throughout the nineteenth and early part of the twentieth century. Raath (2002) provides a popular account of football's developmental phases. Commentary on the contemporary issues affecting football appears in Ebrahim (2006) and Kunene (2006). Armstrong and Guilanotti (2004) and Darby (2000) contextualise football politics in the wider African context.

REFERENCES

Abrahams, F. (2008a). Picking up the pieces *The Cup* 9: 8–12.

Abrahams, F. (2008b). Developing the game *The Cup* 9: 72–75.

Abrahams, F. (28th September, 2007). How much of the R500 will reach those at grassroots level? *Cape Times*. Retrieved on July 9, 2009, from http://www.capetimes.co.za/index.php?fArticleId=4054994.

Ajaxct.co.za. (2009). We will not stand in their way. Retrieved on July 9, 2009, from http://www.ajaxct.co.za/index.php?option=com_content&task=view&id=251&Itemid=2

Alegi, P. (2007). The political economy of mega-stadiums and the underdevelopment of grassroots football in South Africa. *Politikon, 34*(3), 315–331.

Alegi, P. (2004). *Laduma! Soccer, politics and society in South Africa.* Pietermaritzburg: University of KwaZulu-Natal Press.

Armstrong, G., & Guilanotti, R. (Eds.), (2004). *Football in Africa: Conflict, Conciliation and Community.* Basingstoke and New York: Palgrave Macmillan.

Black Entrepreneur Profile: Patrice Motsepe. Retrieved on July 9, 2009, from http://www.blackentrepreneurprofile.com/profile-full/archive/2004/october/article/patrice-motsepe/

Booth, D. (1998). *The Race Game: Sport and Politics in South Africa.* London: Frank Cass.

Citizen (21st April, 2008). South African football coach Parreira resigns. *The Citizen*. Retrieved on July 28, 2009, from http://www.citizen.co.za/index/article.aspx?pDesc=63270,1,22.

Cornelissen, S., & Solberg, E. (2007). Sport mobility and circuits of power: the dynamics of football migration in Africa and the 2010 World Cup. *Politikon: South African Journal of Political Studies, 34*(3), 295–314.

Couzens, T. (1983). An introduction to the history of football in South Africa. In B. Bozzoli (Ed.), *Town and Countryside in the Transvaal*. Johannesburg: Ravan Press.

Darby, P. (2000). Soccer, colonial doctrine and indigenous resistance: mapping the political persona of FIFA's African constituency. *Culture, Sport, Society, 3*(1), 61–87.

Darby, P., Akindes, G., & Kirwin, M. (2007). African Football Labour Migration to Europe and the Role of Football Academies. *Journal of Sport & Social Issues, 31*(2), 143–161.

Department of Sport & Recreation (2006). *Your Sport*. Third Quarter. www.srsa.gov.za

Ebrahim, Y. (2006). Comments in the future of South African sport. In C. Thomas (Ed.), *Sport and Liberation in South Africa Alice*. University of Fort Hare Press.

Enslin-Payne, S. (18th June, 2007). PSL scores on move to sell broadcast rights to SuperSport. *Business Report*. Retrieved on July 9, 2009, from http://www.busrep.co.za/index.php?fSectionId=553&fArticleId=3888815

FIFA.com (January, 2009). FIFA/Coca Cola World Ranking. Retrieved on July 9, 2009, from http://www.fifa.com/worldfootball/ranking/lastranking/gender=m/fullranking.html

Financial Mail (8th April, 2008). Sport sponsorship a growing market in South Africa. *Financial Mail*.

Holt, R. (1989). *Sport and the British: A Modern History*. Oxford: Clarendon Press.

Kunene, M. (2006). Winning the cup but losing the plot? The troubled state of South African soccer. In S. Buhlungu, J. Daniel, R. Southall, & J. Lutchman (Eds.), *State of the Nation: South Africa 2005–2006*. Cape Town: HSRC Press.

Makgabo, T. (2006). The 2010 FIFA World Cup: A development opportunity for South Africa. *Discourse, 34*(2), 3–5.

Mamelodi Sundowns. *www.sundownsfc.com*. Retrieved on July 9, 2009, from http://www.sundownsfc.com/club.aspx

Mantambo, L. (4th December, 2007). Christmas bonuses for SAFA officials, *Daily Dispatch*. Retrieved on July 28, 2009, from http://www.dispatch.co.za/2007/12/04/Sport/aalead.html

Morrell, R. (1996). Forging a ruling race: rugby and white masculinity in colonial Natal, c. 1870–1910. In J. Nauright, & T. J. H. Chandler (Eds.), *Making Men: Rugby and Masculine Identity* (pp. 91–120).

Pelak, C. F. (2005). Negotiating gender/ race/ class constraints in the new South Africa: A case study of women's soccer. *International Review for the Sociology of Sport, 40*(1), 53–70.

PSL. www.psl.co.uk

Raath, P. (2002). *Soccer through the years 1862–2002. The First Official History of South African Soccer*. Cape Town: Juta.

Saavedra, M. (2003). Football Feminine – development of the African Game: Senegal, Nigeria and South Africa. *Soccer and Society, 4*(2/3), 225–253.

SAFA. *www.safa.net.*

Shandu, K. (2008). The business of soccer and television – what's in it? *Journal of Marketing*. February/March: 36–37.

SouthAfrica.Info (March, 2009). Retrieved on July 9, 2009, from http://www.southafrica.info/about/sport/soccer.htm

Thabe, G. (1983). *It's A Goal! 50 Years of Sweat, Tears and Drama in Black Soccer*. Johannesburg: Skotaville Publishers.

Vanden Auweele, Y., Malcolm, C., & Meulders, B. (Eds.), (2006). *Sport & Development*. Leuven: Lanno Campus.

RECOMMENDED WEBSITES

Confederation of African Football
www.cafonline.com

FIFA Website
www.fifa.com

For information on the 2010 World Cup:
www.project2010.co.za
www.sa2010.gov.za

Kaizer Chiefs (biggest football brand in South Africa)
http://www.kaizerchiefs.com/

Kick Off
http://www.kickoff.com/

PSL Preview Soccer League (PSL)
http://www.psl.co.za/

SAFA Website
http://safootball.co.za/safa.htm

Soccer Laduma
http://www.soccerladuma.co.za/index.php?node=21

SouthAfrica.Info: Gateway to the Nation
http://www.southafrica.info/about/sport/soccer.htm

PART 4

Managing Football in Established Markets

CHAPTER 23

The Netherlands and Belgium

Trudo DeJonghe
Lessius University College, Antwerp

Sjef van Hoof
NHTV Breda University of Applied Sciences

Wim Lagae
Lessius University College, Antwerp

Jos Verschueren
Vrije Universiteit Brussel

Objectives

Upon completion of this chapter the reader should be able to:

- Understand the specific context of the Netherlands and Belgium as average-sized football markets.
- Understand the meaning of the Bosman Rule and the developments in media rights for professional football in the low countries.
- Understand the effect of an open labour market in a closed product market on clubs in smaller product markets.
- Understand the necessity of changes in structure and format of the leagues.
- Understand why the decline of the Belgium league since the 1980s has led to a position below the level of the Netherlands.
- Understand the definition of a "stepping stone" league.
- Understanding the differences in revenue sources between these leagues and the Big 5.

CONTENTS

OVERVIEW OF THE CHAPTER

Football in the low countries was, as in many other countries, introduced by British immigrants. Due to the proximity to England and early industrialisation, Belgium and the Netherlands adopted the game of football. Both countries share a lot of commonalities in football: the origin of the game was similar and they both stuck to the amateur principle of the game. Both countries also had their greatest success in the early 1970s and, as small product markets, have decided to learn how to adapt their professional game into a viable international business. In this chapter, we start with a short overview of the origin and history of football in both countries. Then we discuss the league structure and different governing bodies. We continue with an overview of the emergence of professionalism in both countries and the sporting successes of clubs from both countries in the 1970s and 1980s. The league format is examined and followed by an overview of the main data concerning football revenues in Belgium and the Netherlands. The migration, tax, and association law structure in both countries are used to indicate the main differences in policies dealing with foreign players. Finally, we explore the significance of the major shocks in the football environment: the Bosman rule and the multiplication of media revenues, and what these mean for the present and future position of Belgian and Dutch football.

THE ORIGIN AND EVOLUTION OF FOOTBALL IN THE LOW COUNTRIES

The first signs of football in Belgium can be traced to the 1860s, when an Irish student introduced it at the Roman Catholic "Abbey School" in Melle, near Gent, and some other schools in Bruges and Brussels. The first football, cricket and athletics clubs were formed in the 1880s by British employees in the harbour city of Antwerp, engineers in the industrial city of Liége and by the cosmopolitan "leisure class" in Brussels, Gent and Bruges. FCC Antwerp, founded in 1880, was the first official club in Belgium and became one of the founding fathers of the Royal Belgian Football Association. The Belgian league started in 1894 and became fully organised when the multisport association *Union Belge des Sociétés des Sports Athlétique* (UBSSA) was founded in 1895. In 1912, the football division became independent and developed into the *Union Belge des Sociétés de Football Associations* (UBSFA). One year later, the organisation also adopted a Dutch name and became also known as the

Koninklijke Belgische Voetbalbond (KBVB), currently known as the Royal Belgian Football Association (KBVB).

In the Netherlands, football was introduced in Enschede by English cotton labourers in 1865, however, as in many other countries, it was the cosmopolitan leisure class students from elite colleges who were the early adapters of the game and founders of the first multi-sport clubs (football, cricket and athletics). The first club was founded in 1879 in Haarlem, and the *Nederlandschen Voetbal—en Athletischen Bond* was established in 1889. The founding clubs were located in western cities such as Haarlem, Amsterdam, Den Haag, Rotterdam and Delft. In 1895, the football division separated themselves from this federation and formed the *Nederlandse Voetbal Bond* (NVB), now known as the Royal Dutch Football Association (KNVB) (Cohen, 1996; Colin and Mulder, 1996; Van Bottenburg, 2004; Dejonghe, 2006; Dejonghe, 2007a).

Belgium and the Netherlands were able to maintain amateurism in the game of football for a long time. Due to these strict amateur rules and the increasing professionalisation of the game in other countries, more and more players went abroad to play in professional leagues. The victory of an illegally paid professional Dutch team helped usher in an acceptance of professionalised football in 1954. However, it took Belgium until 1974 before the KBVB accepted the creation of the "Prof Liga" (Pro League, named LVP). Before formal professionalisation of the game, black money and employment with the sponsor or chairman of the club were the most common ways of providing remuneration to players (Colin, 1995; KNVB National Archives; Dejonghe, 2006).

LEAGUE STRUCTURES AND GOVERNING BODIES

The Netherlands

In 1954–1955, following the introduction of professional football in the Netherlands, a playoff was held between the winners of four regional leagues to determine the first official Dutch Football Champion. In 1956, the Eredivisie (First Division) was established together with the "Eerste Divisie" (Second Division) and two third divisions. In 1966, these two divisions merged into one second division, which ceased to exist in 1971 when the Council of Professional Football decided to reduce the number of teams from 51 to 38. In addition to a reduction of teams, the KNVB established a closed division system, consisting of an Ere (Premier) and First Division (Second Division). Today, the Dutch Professional Football League still has 38 teams; however, some teams located in or near a major conurbation disappeared and were in most cases substituted by teams located in centres with a higher market potential (Van Dam, 2000; Dejonghe et al., 2006).[1]

After the bigger teams in the League (Feyenoord, Ajax, and PSV) questioned the division of broadcasting rights income between the KNVB and its clubs, the clubs founded a public limited liability company on July 1, 1997, called the Eredivisie NV. They considered the voting of amateur clubs a drawback in their determination for a strategy for broadcasting rights and marketing development. The main tasks of the Eredivisie NV included marketing broadcasting rights and optimising sponsorship for the league as a whole by setting rules for television broadcasts. Due to high organisational cost, the clubs founded the Eredivisie CV in 2004 (Exempt Limited Partnership). The Eredivisie CV is, at the executive level, responsible for the marketing of broadcasting rights, and division of the broadcasting rights income and sponsorship deals at the league level. The board of supervisors of the Eredivisie NV controls the policy of the Eredivisie CV. Decisions are made with at least a two third majority stake of the 18 member clubs. After the launch of the Eredivisie CV, the tax authorities began taxing the individual clubs instead of the league as a whole.

Berdowski and colleagues (1997) conducted a strategic sector survey in Dutch professional football and concluded that an important shortcoming of the Dutch system was the fact that there is no relegation between the second division (today mostly semi-professional teams) and the six so-called "third divisions" (which are officially amateur leagues). At the bottom of the second division there are some clubs with small budgets that depend on a share in the broadcasting rights but due to the lack of relegation threat, they have no incentive to move up from the bottom positions in the league. In 2004, the KNVB divided the professional teams into four categories in order to examine their policies. The division was as follows: The top three clubs (Ajax, PSV, and Feyenoord); 10 ambitious teams playing in the Eredivisie; 10 dynamic teams (in the Eredivisie and the top of First Division); and the rest being stable teams with limited ambitions in the First Division. In their new policy plan, the KNVB mentioned that an international competition structure such as a Bene league (a league consisting of clubs from Belgium and the Netherlands) would allow Dutch clubs to be more competitive at a European level. However, UEFA did not permit them to create the Bene league and

---

[1] FC Amsterdam (1982), SC Amersfoort (1983), Schiedam VV (1991) and FC Vlaardingen '74 (1981) (both in the agglomeration of Rotterdam) and FC Wageningen (bankruptcy) disappeared and were replaced by RBC Roosendaal (1983), RKC Waalwijk (1984), FC Emmen (1985), Top Oss (1991), Apeldoorn VVOG (2003), and FC Omniworld Almere (2005)

Table 23.1		Playoff Systems in the Dutch League 2005–2006 to 2007–2008 and 2008–2009 to ?	
2005–2006 to 2007–2008		**2008–09 to ?**	
Champions	CL	Champion and runner-up	1 CL +1 qual CL
2–5 Playoffs	1 qualification CL 2 UEFA Cup places	3–5	3 UEFA Cup places
6–9 Playoffs	Winner against loser 2–5 for 1 UEFA Cup place	6–9 Playoffs	1 UEFA Cup place
10–13 Playoffs	1 Intertoto		
16–17 + 8 teams First Division Playoffs	2 places Eredivisie	16–17 +8 teams First Division Playoffs	2 places in the Eredivisie
18	Relegated, champion First Division promoted	18	Relegated, champion First Division promoted

Source: www.knvb.nl; *Van de Fiert, 2008.*

therefore, the KNVB started to look at modifications in order to make the football league more attractive. The KNVB introduced a system of playoffs at the end of the 2005–2006 season where teams competed for a place in the Champions League (CL) prequalification and two UEFA Cup spots. The total attendances in the regular competition rose from 4.96 million in 2004–2005 to over 5.14 million in 2005–2006 and to 5.52 million in 2006–2007. Despite the enlargement of stadia, a considerable amount of the growth can be attributed to the new, more attractive league structure. The 20 matches in the playoffs attracted an additional attendance of 290,000 in 2005–2006 and 318,500 in 2006–2007. However, the system was not without its flaws: the second-place team in the Eredivisie could be left without gaining admittance to Champions League football at the end of the season, as happened in May 2008. The second team in the league, Ajax, lost in the playoff against the fourth team, FC Twente. The Eredivisie and KNVB accepted the numerous complaints about this system and in the 2008–2009 season the playoffs for the clubs in second through fifth place were abolished (see Table 23.1).

The playoff system which sees bottom teams in the Eredivisie playoff against the top teams in the First Division is well-established. A proposed reform is that the First Division would be downsized to 16 teams after some potential mergers, relegations or eliminations.[2] The newly formed top divisions in the amateur league would have a chance to be promoted to the First Division and teams could, but would not be obliged, be promoted (Van de Fiert, 2008).

Because the top amateur clubs are spread around six leagues at present (three playing on Sunday, three on Saturday—initially because of religious reasons), the playing standard on average is not as high as it could be if there was a third division. Negotiations in 2009 between the KNVB and the amateur clubs resulted in the creation of two "top classes", or third divisions, commencing 2010/2011, consisting of 16 teams each. The respective divisional champions have the right, but are not obligated, to be promoted to the second division. The team that ends at the bottom of the second divison (The First Division) will be relegated.

BELGIUM

The Belgian League's pyramid structure is open and consists of a First Division (formed in 1995) called the Jupiler League (named after the league sponsor Jupiler, Belgium's leading beer brand), a Second Division, two Third Divisions, four Fourth Divisions and regional divisions divided on a provincial basis. The only barrier is the necessity to obtain a "Second Division" licence to be promoted from the third to the second division and a "First Division" licence to be promoted to the First Division. The teams from the First Division are members of the LPV, otherwise known as the Profliga. The Profliga negotiates the collective broadcasting rights for the Jupiler League; formulates the division of income from the broadcasting rights; decides changes in the league structure; creates the fixture list for the season; centralises the ticketing for match days; and negotiates sponsorship contracts with the league sponsor (Jupiler). In the Profliga, every decision must have a two thirds majority to pass, which means 12 out of 18 teams must be in agreement. Once this step is taken, major decisions (such as a change in league format) need a 81 percent majority in the Annual General Meeting of the KBVB. The First Division only has a "blocking minority" of 19.85 percent of the votes in that meeting. In other words, the democratic structure of Profliga and the KBVB makes the Belgian football structure

---

[2] The teams in the Dutch First Division received between 2005–2006 and 2007–2008 every year €11.5 million from the total of €69.9 million of the media rights generated by the sale of broadcasting rights for the top two divisions. Jan Rekers, director of PSV called some of the teams at the bottom of the First division "subsidizing junkies" because these media rights are for them the main revenue sources (Bouwes, 2008).

Table 23.2	New League Format in Belgium		
2008–2009		**2009–2010 to ?**	
1–2	Qualification CL	1–6	Post-season competition round robin. Clubs keep 50% of points of regular competition 2 places CL 1 Europa Cup
3	Qualification UEFA Cup	7–14	Round Robin in two groups from 7–14 with winner playing 4th place for Europa Cup place
15–16	Postseason round robin with 2 teams Second Division (2nd & 3rd) for 1 place in the First Division	15	Postseason round robin with 3 teams Second Division for 1 place in the 1st Division
17–18	Relegation Champion Second Division promoted	16	Relegation Champion Second Division promoted

static. The amateur clubs and the smaller professional clubs are rejecting the modernisation and adaptation of Belgian football to a new economic environment. Dejonghe (2006, page 4) defines the decision structure of the FA sometimes as *"the dictatorship of democracy."*

Since 1977, the Belgian First Division has been comprised of 18 teams. To begin with at the end of the season, two teams were relegated to the Second Division and replaced by the champion of the Second Division and the winner of a post-season competition between four clubs. In 2005–2006 and 2006–2007, the system changed and only the team in last place in the First Division was automatically relegated. The team in 17th place and three teams of the Second Division played for the remaining spot in the Jupiler League. However, in the 2007–2008 season, they returned to the previous system.

In September 2007, the Profliga decided that a new league format had to be created. This was due to a rapid decline in the performance of the Belgian top clubs in European competitions, the forthcoming negotiations for a new broadcasting contract and the threat of some top clubs to sell their broadcasting right individually. Hypercube, a consulting company that also reformed the Dutch League, was asked to analyse the different proposals and recommend a new format that could be approved by all members of the Profliga.[3] The new format (see Table 23.2) consisting of 16 teams was

---

[3] Some formats were deemed to offer greater potential value from an economic point of view but a reduction to 10, 12 or 14 teams would never be approved by a two thirds majority.

accepted in March 2008 by the Profliga, and in May 2008 by the Annual General Meeting of the KBVB and will be implemented in 2009–2010.[4] The season 2008–2009 will be a transition towards it.[5]

THE "DECLINE" IN PERFORMANCE AND REVENUES

There appears to be a quite universal agreement on one determinant for success in football: the budget of a club. Empirical research indicates that there is positive relation between budget and team performance.[6] The concept of cumulative causation by Myrdal may be used to analyse which factors contribute to rising budgets and therefore success. Although Myrdal developed this theory in order to explain the different development paths that regions and countries may follow, Dejonghe (2004a) applied the model successfully to the football business (see Figure 23.1). Cumulative causation reveals the unfolding of a series of indicators that are interlinked. On the supply side, this is the quality of the service (playing level, attractiveness of the game, uncertainty about the outcome, quality of the accommodation). On the demand side (of the football consumer), changes in the supply side may influence match-day income, revenue from merchandising, sponsorship and media rights. This influence is reciprocal: changes on the demand side influence the supply side and vice versa.

The number of customers available in the market area is one of the triggers for the cumulative causation process. Market size and market potential became a central topic in modern football in the 1990s and revenue sources changed from what Andreff and Staudohar (2002) called the Spectator-Subsidies-Sponsors-Local(SSSL)-model toward the more global Media-Corporations-Merchandising-Markets (MCCM)-model. The rising impact of television and media companies and the emerging interest

---

[4] The teams of the Second Division voted against the new competition format because they wanted to be assured of two promoted teams instead of one and wanted more money from the broadcasting rights. They wanted €4–5 million (20 percent) for all the teams together. The Profliga proposed to pay up to €1.5 million.

[5] The Second Division has 13.24 percent of the votes in the General Meeting. This is not enough to block the proposal of the new league format that was discussed in June 2008.

[6] Van Der Werff and Verlaan (1994); Szymanski (1999); Szymanski and Kuypers (1999); Dobson and Goddard (1998, 2001); Forrest and Simmons (2002); Hall et al. (2002); Dejonghe (2004b, 2006, 2007b).

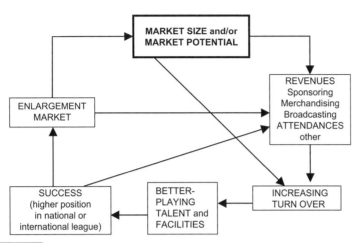

FIGURE 23.1 *Cumulative causation in modern football (based on Dejonghe, 2004a).*

of multinational corporations in professional football gave rise to a professional management approach. This transformation occurred almost at the same moment as the Bosman case. The Bosman ruling abolished the existing transfer system and liberated the professional footballers from their peculiar status as employees not entitled to sell their labour to the highest bidder once their contract of employment came to an end. The result was a drastic change in the labour market. Before Bosman, the clubs had monopsony power and kept player wages low. After Bosman, the power switched over to the players. The combination of this change coupled with the win maximisation objectives of the clubs and the exploding broadcasting rights in the United Kingdom, Spain, Italy, and Germany (and to a lesser degree France) resulted in very high salaries. These changes in the economic environment led to an exodus of talent out of smaller markets such as Belgium and the Netherlands (Dejonghe and Vandeweghe, 2006). Another short-term effect of losing transfer revenues was the lack of money to replace the lost players. Belgian and Dutch teams play in small national leagues which are closed product markets, but have attracted players due to an open international market. The financial risks taken in the last decade to keep up with the rising salaries of professional footballers has caused financial problems in both countries.

The most successful period of football in Belgium and the Netherlands took place in the 1970s and 1980s when the SSSL-model still dominated. In Figure 23.2, it is evident that the Netherlands had their best period in the 1970s, began to show a decline in the early 1980s, a recovery in the late

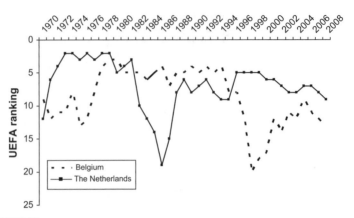

FIGURE 23.2   *The evolution of the UEFA ranking of the Netherlands and Belgium (1970–2008).* Source: Kassies–www.xs4all.nl–~kassiesa–bert–uefa.

1980s, and a gradual decline since 1995.[7] Belgium had its greatest successes from the late 1970s until 1994.[8]

Until 1984, clubs in Belgium were funded mainly through gate receipts, commercial receipts from bars, direct subsidies provided by national or local governments, or indirect subsidies (free use of municipal stadia, availability of civil servants to work in football-related activities, beneficial social security and tax laws). Typically for Belgium, there was also a lot of "black money" invested by local businessmen who were seeking to evade taxes. In 1984, a district attorney, Guy Bellemans, investigated the business of professional football clubs. The evidence uncovered in the Bellemans Raid proved that Belgium football was infested with tax evasion money. Until 1984, Belgium had been a financial paradise for foreign players from the likes of Holland, Denmark, and Poland. Nowadays the migration pattern of football players between the Netherlands and Belgium shows a flow in the opposite direction

---

[7] Ajax Amsterdam won the European Champions Cup 3 times (1970–1971 to 1972–1973) and the Champions League in 1994–1995. They lost the final of the CL in 1995–1996. They were also the losing finalist in the European Cup Winners Cup in 1987–1988 and won the UEFA Cup in 1991–1992. Feyenoord Rotterdam won the Champions Cup in 1969–1970 and the UEFA Cup in 1973–1974 and 2001–2002. PSV Eindhoven won the Champions Cup in 1987–1988 and won the UEFA Cup in 1977–1978. FC Twente (1974–1975) and AZ Alkmaar (1980–1981) were losing finalists in the UEFA Cup.

[8] RSC Anderlecht won the Cup Winners Cup in 1975–1976 and 1977–1978 and the UEFA Cup in 1982–1983. They lost the final of the Cup Winners Cup in 1976–1977 and 1989–1990 and the final of the UEFA Cup in 1983–1984. Club Brugge KV lost the final of the Champions Cup in 1977–1978 and the UEFA Cup in 1975–1976. KV Mechelen won the Cup Winners Cup in 1987–1988. Standard Liège (1981–1982) and RFC Antwerp (1992–1993) lost in the final of the Cup Winners Cup.

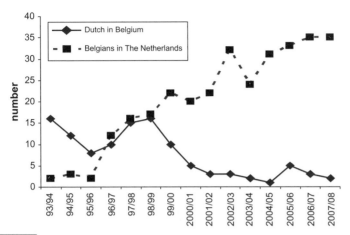

FIGURE 23.3 *The evolution of the number of Belgian players in the Dutch Eredivisie and Dutch players in the Belgian First Division (1993–1994 to 2007–2008). Source: Dejonghe, 2007b, page 277.*

and follows from the declining economic strength of both leagues. In other words, the higher wages in the Dutch league combined with limitation on the number of non-EU players (see later) can be seen as the main incentive (Figure 23.3).

THE REVENUES AND THEIR SOURCES

Total Revenues

Belgium and the Netherlands are two average-sized product markets in the European football business. The determining impact of turnover and wages towards success resulted in a decline in performance in a European context of the major teams in these leagues. The total turnover of the Belgian league rose from €107 million in 1999–2000 to €173 million in 2007–2008. In the Netherlands, the total turnover of the Eredivisie increased from €339 million in 2003–2004 to €388.5 million in 2007–2008. RSC Anderlecht (€35 million), ClubBrugge KV (€20 million), KRC Genk (€17.6 million) and Standard Liège (€16 million) in Belgium and PSV Eindhoven (€88 million),[9] Ajax Amsterdam (€65 million), Feyenoord Rotterdam (€38.6 million) and AZ Alkmaar (€28 million) are the teams with the highest budgets in their leagues but these sums, when compared with teams from the Big 5, are too small to be competitive in today's globalised market.

---

[9] PSV had the advantage of being the only Dutch team in the CL in 2006/2007 & 2007/2008. The €19.4 million in the Dutch CL market pool went entirely to PSV.

Table 23.3	The Main Revenue Sources of the Dutch and Belgian Top-Tier (in € m)	
Revenue Sources	Dutch Eredivisie (2007–2008)	Belgian First Division (2006–2007)
Matchday	124.9	46.1
Domestic Broadcasting	68.2	34.6
Sponsorship	146.5	61.2
Champions League	23.9	–
Merchandising*	25	11.6
Total	388.5	153.3

* VVV, Excelsior and Roda JC did not provide any information about merchandising but we assumed €0.5 m as the sum of these three (compared with other teams from the same level).
Source: *Dutch Eredivisie Sponsor Magazine, 2007; Voetbal International, June, 2008; Bouwes, 2008; Belgian First Division; Dejonghe, 2006; KBVB, 2008.*

The main revenue sources in today's football industry are ticketing, media, sponsorship, hospitality suites or boxes, the transfer of players, multifunctional stadia, merchandising, subsidies from government, and, in some cases, stock market investment or a rich investor. The Dutch League has (beside the Big 5) the next-highest "known" revenues of any top-tier domestic league in Europe.[10] In Belgium and the Netherlands, sponsorship and match day income are higher than broadcasting revenues (see Table 23.3).

Broadcasting Rights

Whereas increases in the value of broadcasting rights in the Big Five football countries (England, Spain, Italy, Germany, and France) have been a significant factor in driving the spectacular growth of overall revenues in these markets (Deloitte, 2008, pages 11–21), the issue of broadcasting rights has caused some divisiveness between clubs in the Low Countries. The broadcasting rights in 2005–2006 brought the winner of the Dutch League, PSV, an income of €6.4 million.[11] The collectively sold broadcasting rights are divided partly through a system of solidarity and partly through a merit fee.

However, there have been previous attempts to increase income from the collective sale of broadcasting rights. In 1996, the KNVB initiated a consortium with Philips, Telegraaf Media Group, Nuon, KPN, Endemol Entertainment and

[10] "Known" indicates in this case that for some leagues in Europe the real figures are not very clear. What is the total turnover in Russia, Ukraine, or Turkey, for example?

[11] Comparison: Bayern Munich earned €16.5 million, Chelsea €44 million, and Barcelona €95.1 million in the same season.

ING Bank. The idea was to launch a television channel (Sport 7) on different cable television networks which would become a pay channel after an temporary introduction period. Cable companies fought against charging their clients for Sport 7 and coverage was dropped only two months after the introduction. On December 8, 1996, the channel disappeared and the broadcasting rights were returned to the state television network NOS. The broadcasting rights paid for by Canal+ and NOS rose in value from €36 million to €43.3m between 1997–1998 and 2004–2005 (Van Westerloo, 2004). In 2004, media entrepreneur John De Mol tried to use the broadcasting rights to establish a new television station. In an agreement with MTV Networks Benelux, he launched Talpa on August 13, 2005, with the help of the €35 million a year broadcasting rights income he had previously obtained for re-selling the highlights of the Eredivisie football matches. However, De Mol was unable to make the television channel successful and resold the broadcasting rights to RTL in the 2007 season (Van Asch, 2007). In 2004, the rights for live matches were sold for €30 million a year to Tele 2-Versatel, which wanted to roll out its Triple Play offer (Internet, phone and television) based on an introductory offer for football fans. Penetration, however, was so low that the company decided to sell sublicences to CanalDigitaal, Sport1 (cable) and Digitenne (a subsidiary of their competitor KPN) after just one year of operations. In the beginning of 2008, there were about 300,000 subscribers to live matches in the Netherlands who paid €6.95 per month.

After the dissolution of Talpa, the 2008 media market for football in the Netherlands was not as promising as it had been in the four years previous. The cable company Zesko offered approximately €45 million for highlights and live matches, but the bid was refused. The Eredivisie chose to sell the broadcasting rights for the highlights to the state television company and start their own television channel for direct transmissions for subscribers and pay-per-view in August 2008. The NOS agreed to pay €21 million a year, €14 million a year less than Talpa in the previous period. Pay-per-view and subscribers to live television are anticipated to fill the income gap and make the exploitation of the broadcasting rights more profitable. However, the fact that the Netherlands is one of the only countries in Europe where income from broadcasting rights has dropped has led to turmoil among the top teams. AZ Alkmaar and Ajax have subsequently investigated the possibility of selling their media rights individually.

The broadcasting rights in Belgium were worth €15 million a year in the period 1997–1998 to 2004–2005, and at the time there was only one channel interested in their purchase. The negotiations for broadcasting rights for the 2005–2006 to 2007–2008 seasons took place between two competitors, Belgacom–VRT and Telenet–VTM. The change from a monopolistic market to an oligopolistic market resulted in an increase in the price of the broadcasting rights. The pay channel Belgacom (live) and the government channels VRT and RTBF (highlights and commentaries) paid €36 million a season. Belgacom was a new player in the "pay-per-view" market and the number of subscribers was below their expectations (although the high penetration of cable television and access to foreign leagues may be to blame). The amount of money from the collective sale of broadcasting rights that a club receives depends on recent and historical (last 5 years) performance (merit fee), solidarity and facility fees for live broadcasting. RSC Anderlecht got an average of €3.4 million (less than 10 percent of club turnover), FC Dender received €0.85 million (25 percent of club turnover). The relative importance of the broadcasting revenues is negatively correlated with the total turnover. In recent negotiations for the new broadcasting rights contract, some of the major teams wanted a bigger share of the total revenues. The negotiations for 2008–2009 to 2010–2011 started with a €44.7 million bid by Belgacom and VRT–RTBF, but the Profliga wanted €50 million, so the first bid was rejected.

Matchday Revenues

Another main source of revenue for many clubs is matchday receipts. One of the main reasons for the increasing average attendances in most leagues is the transformation of football following the recommendations in the 1989 *Taylor Report* (1990). This report, promulgated in England, transformed the game in England from a sport plagued by hooliganism and decaying stadia infrastructure to a more genteel family sport played in modern, all-seater stadia. This transformation began in England but was soon adopted by Dutch stakeholders. Stadia were renovated or new state-of-the-art stadia were built and new sport consumers began to take an interest in the game and watch the entertainment in these arenas (Dejonghe, et al., 2008). The social upgrading of football combined with modern football arenas and the professionalisation of management resulted in an increase in attendances. Many of the old stadia are, as Van Dam (1998, page 28) calls it, "Locally Unwanted Land Use." The new (in some cases, multifunctional) stadiums in the Netherlands are generally relocated near main traffic roads so that the journey time to attend games decreases. These stadia have become landmarks in their own right and are used as a branding platform for potential sponsors. Since 1994, almost all the stadia of clubs in the Eredivisie have been rebuilt or renovated to increase the market potential of the clubs. In a majority of cases, the new stadia have sold out and caused considerable increases in average attendance rates. As a whole, the average attendance rose from less than 8,000 in 1990–1991 to 18,500 in 2007–2008 (see Figure 23.4). Some examples are Ajax Amsterdam, which relocated from De Meer with a capacity of 29,500 to the 51,236 seats in the

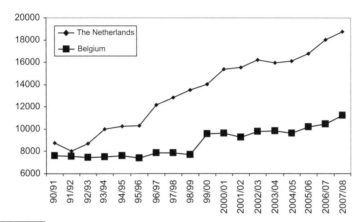

FIGURE 23.4 *The average attendances in the Dutch and Belgium leagues (1990-1991 to 2007–2008).*
Source: The Netherlands: european-football-statistics.co.uk–www.european-football-statistics.co.uk-attn.htm; *Voetbal International (2004–2008). Belgium: Dejonghe (2006); Voetbal Magazine (2002–2008).*

Amsterdam Arena. Consequently, the average attendance increased from 22,000 in 1994–1995 to 49,100 in 2007–2008 Additionally, FC Groningen and AZ Alkmaar moved last season to their new grounds with capacities of 19,740 and 17,000, respectively, and garnered an attendance increase from 12,000 to 19,350 and from 8,400 to 16,400 (Dejonghe, 2007b).

In Belgium, all stadia were built before 1990, and only two stadia— Club Brugge KV/SV Brugge and KRC Genk—have been built since 1975. The recent increase in the average attendances is purely due to the sociological transformation of football and the increasing professionalisation of the management and not due to modernisation of the arenas. In 1998–1999, the average match attendance was only 7,730 and increased to 11,251 in 2007–2008, which indicates an increase of 1.07 million visitors a year. By examining club data, it is evident that most of these additional supporters can be attributed to the major teams. Club Brugge KV attracted an average per game of 12,284 fans in 1998–1999 and an average of 26,375 in 2007–2008. RSC Anderlecht had an average of 24,846; Standard Liège had an average of 25,082 and KRC Genk had an average of 23,075. These teams, and recently some smaller teams such as KAA Gent, GB Antwerpen and KV Mechelen, have noticed capacity restraints and play the majority of their home games in a sold out stadium. At some of the major teams such as RSC Anderlecht, Standard Liège and Club Brugge KV, the number of season ticket holders has reached nearly the entire capacity of their grounds and the demand for business seats and boxes is larger than the supply. The result is that major stakeholders (clubs, local governments, lobby groups of potential organising cities of World Cup 2018), and in some cases private investors, are making plans for building new football stadia in Belgium. The first arena with a capacity of 20,000 will be built in Ghent and plans and studies are being made for Bruges (40,000), Brussels (40,000–50,000), Liège (40,000–50,000), Mechelen (20,000), Antwerp (20,000–40,000), and Waregem (15,000). The novelty effect combined with the withdrawal of capacity constraints could potentially result in increasing attendances and revenues to sustain a league average of 15,000.

In the Netherlands, a second wave of modifications and enlargements is in its planning phase. Feyenoord Stadium PLC wants to build a 75,000 capacity replacement for the Kuip stadium to be ready in 2016. The municipality of Amsterdam is investigating the possibility of building a new stadium between Amsterdam and Almere with an 80,000–90,000 capacity to continue to attract events like the Champions League final. In the summer of 2008, FC Twente will double its capacity from 13,500 to 27,000. SC Heerenveen would like to expand from the present 26,400 capacity to somewhere between 40,000 and 45,000 in order to be able to host games for the 2018 World Cup.

The Champions League

The Champions League (CL) is an important source of revenues for the major teams in both leagues. CL revenue also increases the differences between the Big 5 countries and the next tier of European football markets. The introduction of the market pool in 1999–2000 which favoured clubs in the Big 5 TV markets, diverted money to the major leagues. In the period 1992–1999, Dutch teams earned €44.43 million and Belgian teams €9.87 million in the CL. The market pool was introduced as a method to divide 50 percent of the CL revenues received. During the 2006–2007 season teams from the Netherlands received €19.4 million from this market pool, the sixth highest amount in the pool and Belgium received €4.81 million, the eleventh highest amount. Since the introduction of the CL market pool, the Netherlands has received €226.54 million and Belgium only €68.14 million. The Big 5 received an amount between €418.1 million (France) and €671.4 million (Italy). So clearly teams from the Big 5 benefit much more significantly from the CL than participating clubs from Holland & Belgium.

Nevertheless, for the teams in Belgium and the Netherlands, the CL revenues are still an important revenue source that can ensure their dominance in their national leagues. The total amount that teams in both countries have received can be seen in Table 23.4.

In the case of PSV Eindhoven, the CL revenues represented about 30 percent of their turnover in recent years. The result is that PSV has

Table 23.4	The Team Revenues from the CL in Belgium and the Netherlands (1992–2007) € M		
The Netherlands	**1992–1999**	**1999–2000 to 2007–2008**	**Total**
PSV Eindhoven	8.98	135.43	144.41
Ajax Amsterdam	31.77	52.95	84.72
Feyenoord Rotterdam	3.68	25.46	29.14
SC Heerenveen		7.62	7.62
Willem II Tilburg		5.08	5.08
Belgium			
RSC Anderlecht	5.36	44.14	49.50
Club Brugge KV	2.65	17.61	20.26
KRC Genk	—	6.39	6.39
KSK Lierse	1.86	—	1.86

Source: *Dejonghe (2006);Vandeweghe (2007);* Kassies–www.xs4all.nl–~kassiesa–bert–uefa–data–method3–match2008.html.

dominated the Dutch league since the introduction of the market pool and were Dutch champions in seven of the last 10 years. The elimination of Ajax in the preliminary phases of the CL in any season also benefitted PSV financially. Instead of a 55–45 split of the CL market pool all the revenue went to PSV in these seasons.

The CL revenues reinforce the existing competitive imbalance in the Belgian and Dutch leagues. The top teams become big fishes in two small ponds. In the long term, they dominate their respective national leagues, but in a European context their role is small (apart from PSV in the recent years). The fear of a marginal position in Europe led to an initiative called the Atlantic League in 2001 (Dejonghe, 2004b). The initiative was launched by former PSV president Harry van Raai and was supported by 11 clubs: the Dutch clubs Ajax Amsterdam, Feyenoord and PSV Eindhoven; the Belgian teams RSC Anderlecht and Club Brugge KV; Benfica and Sporting Lisbon from Portugal; Scottish teams Celtic and Rangers; and the Danish teams Brondby and FC Copenhagen. The clubs planned to make one common league with promotion and relegation. After the prohibition of the Euroleague by UEFA in September 2001 van Raai said, "UEFA protects its own interests by creating a platform favouring the four major markets. Top European soccer will exist only in four major markets unless drastic steps are taken to reshape league structures in small markets" (*Sportbusiness International* 2001).

The Commercial Revenues

Data concerning commercial revenues of the Belgian League are not available. However, the kind of commercial partners that Belgian clubs form relationships with are the same as in other European leagues. RSC Anderlecht with Fortis and Club Brugge KV with Dexia, have two major banks as their main sponsors whereas Standard Liège and KRC Genk are sponsored by telecom companies: Base (part of KPN) and Euphony. The industries of other team's main sponsors in 2007–2008 were banking–finance–insurance (4), travel–leisure (1), food (1), communication (1), and construction–real estate (6). In the Netherlands, the total amount of sponsorship in 2006/2007 was estimated to be approximately €146.45 million (*Sponsor Magazine*, 2007). Shirt sponsorship represented €35.74 million of the total, with the main sponsors coming from finance–insurance companies (€19.24 million) and electronics (€7.75 million). Ajax (ABN AMRO Bank) and Feyenoord (Fortis) both presently have a bank as their main sponsor, whilst the main sponsor of PSV Eindhoven is currently Philips (the club has its origin in the factory team for the Philips corporation with which it is still closely associated).

The collective selling of the "brand" name of the top leagues is a another modest source of revenues. Inbev paid €1.3 million to rename the Belgium First Division the Jupiler (a beer brand) League whilst in the Netherlands, the sponsor Loterij paid €5 million, but the league kept the name Eredivisie (Van den Wall Bake Consult, 2007).

CASE STUDY 23.1: Ajax: A Sleeping European Giant?

Michel Platini said in an interview with the Dutch daily *Volkskrant* (November 24, 2007): "I do not like it if an Ajax player is transferred to Juventus at the age of 15. Young players should be transferred at 21 or 22 and afterwards they can leave. That is what I want to achieve." Partly due to the fact that talented players can transfer at an early age, Ajax faced a dry spell in the first years of the third millennium. A commission of former players and board members made an analysis of the policy of the club in the last years entitled "The Road to Performance". The report was very negative about the new organisational structure of the club: in 1998, Ajax had founded a public limited liability company and floated on the Amsterdam Stock-Exchange where 73.3 percent of the shares remained in the hands of the club itself and the other 26.7 percent of the shares were sold to private persons and investors such as Aviva, Delta Lloyd, and Citigroup. The British insurance company Aviva sold its shares in 2003 to Adri Strating, former owner of a stock trading house.

In 1995, Ajax won the Champions League for the fourth time. The Amsterdam Arena was one of the most modern stadia in the world and the youth academy of the Amsterdam team attracted trainers from everywhere in the world to watch the famous Ajax training system. But the Bosman rule was a big blow for the club and following its implementation, several good players transferred almost for free (Davids, Bogarde, Kluivert, Reiziger). In order to remain competitive, the club issued shares to acquire capital to invest in a new team. Ajax wanted to have a structural position within the 16 best teams of Europe and win the Dutch title every second year. Majority stakes in affiliates in Belgium (GBAntwerp), South Africa (Ajax Cape Town) and Ghana (Ashanti) were purchased in order to bring new talent to the club. But 15 years later, the performance of the Amsterdam team has been below expectations. The share issue brought approximately €53 million to invest in the continuation of the club's position in the European football landscape, but they have only won two Dutch titles since 1998. Furthermore, elimination in European competitions by teams like FC Copenhagen, Lausanne Sports, Dinamo Zagreb, and Slavia Prague have contributed to the dry spell. In 2003, Ajax finished their affiliation with GBAntwerp and Ashanti (incurring a loss of €15.6 million). Ajax is still involved with Ajax Capetown where it has lost €3.9 million from its involvement. The equity value of Ajax dropped from €109.9 million in 1999 to €57.9 million in 2007.

The Coronel Commission concluded that the club had developed too far in its commercial aspirations and too far out of its roots as a football club with the characteristics of a family. "The director should be someone with a football heart instead of a salesman. The club should be withdrawn from the stock exchange and get back its family feeling. It should get back to an association instead of a limited liability company." One of the recommendations was to withdraw Ajax from the stock market, which could potentially cost €30 to €40 million to achieve.

Despite the weak track record in the last decade, the club's image in the Netherlands is still high. New sponsor Aegon ("We are a global company with a local name that wants to sponsor a local club with a global name") has paid an estimated €12 million a year for a seven year sponsorship contract beginning in August 2008. Additionally, Adidas will pay €100 million for a 10-year contract as sponsor of the club, bringing the club (at least in terms of sponsorship revenue) to a position amongst the 16 top performers in Europe. BBDO Consult estimated that the brand Ajax has a value of €368 million (fourteenth place in Europe).

Sources: *Lagae & Dejonghe, 2009.*

THE GOVERNMENT AS STAKEHOLDER OR "SPONSOR" OF PROFESSIONAL FOOTBALL

Income Taxes and Social Security

Government involvement (local, regional and national) is important for professional clubs in Belgium and the Netherlands. Governments build and subsidise facilities and apply tax laws and social security laws for the benefit of professional athletes.

For professional athletes in Belgium, the contribution to social security is calculated on the fixed minimum wage (13.07 percent on €1,832.49 for players during 2007–2008) instead of the real wages. Dejonghe & Vandeweghe (2006) estimated that these reductions in contribution are a kind of subsidy of around €30 million and pension rules in Belgium are generous towards professional athletes. Normally, an average person can receive pension payments at the age of 60–65 and pay 16.5 percent in income taxes (otherwise 33 percent). Professional athletes have the same possibility when they reach the age of 35. The Belgian League attracts a lot of foreign players. And clubs from England and the Netherlands, where the immigration laws on non-EU players are stricter, have cooperated with some Belgian teams. Some examples include Manchester United with RFC Antwerp, Blackburn Rovers with Cercle Brugge, Portsmouth with SV Zulte-Waregem, Ajax with GBAntwerp, Feyenoord with VC Westerlo, and Arsenal with SK Beveren. The reason is that the minimum wage of non-EU players is only €65,400 a year and there is no limitation on the number of players or a quality requirement. Another reason for the high number of foreign players in the Belgian League was a tax exception that was created for basketball, football and volleyball by a politician that was chairman of one of the major basketball teams in Belgium. On May 15, 2002, the government decided that foreign players living in France, Germany, Greece, or the United States only had to pay 18 percent in income taxes for four years instead of a maximum of 50 percent. The only condition besides living in one of those countries was that the players stayed less than 10 months a year in Belgium.[12] The result was an invasion of average foreign players because they were less expensive than more talented Belgian players. Teams such as RAEC Mons, EXC Moeskroen, and RSC Charleroi played with almost 11 foreigners, most of them French, and the youth development programmes of Belgian clubs were neglected (Dejonghe, 2007b). The discrimination in Belgium against home national athletes and the poor performances of the national team resulted in proposals in the Belgian Parliament to refer the system but it took until January 1, 2008, before the system changed. The new tax law indicates the following:

- Professional athletes older than 26 pay 33 percent income taxes instead of the 50 percent that other taxpayers have to pay for every euro they earn above €31,700 a year.
- Between their 16th and 25th years, professional athletes pay only 16.5 percent income taxes on their first €16,272 a year
- Eighty percent of the income taxes paid by the clubs to the government can be recuperated if that money is spent on youth development or wages of players younger than 23.

The main goal of the new tax law was the elimination of the discrimination against Belgian players and to encourage youth development programmes. The first part was successful, but the last addendum could lead to a massive import of young foreign players. Belgium could become a destination for young foreign players from all over the world, confirming its position as a "breeding" or stepping stone league. An example of this may be seen in the club SK Beveren. The club was almost bankrupt, until Jean-Marc Guillou "saved" the club. He used the Belgian system as a way to expose his talented players from his development centre in the Ivory Coast to the European style of play. Those players earned the minimum wage for

---

[12] This tax rule was created in the first place for athletes or artists which came for a short period to Belgium (tennis players, cyclists, pop groups, etc.). Some teams used it also for their Belgian players. A lot of the players of KRC Genk lived "officially" just across the border in the German city of Aachen.

non-EU players and Guillou received a percentage of the transfer money that was earned by the club. Players such as Yaya Toure (FC Barcelona) and Arsene Né (Metallursk Donetsk) are two examples of players that used the Belgian league as a stepping stone for higher income leagues.

In the Netherlands, player wages rose substantially after the foundation of the professional labour union VVCS in 1961. As players in the 1960s were paying a very elevated Dutch income tax rate of 72 percent, the advisor of Feyenoord player Willem van Hanegem started looking for a tax holiday. In 1961, the Dutch Ministry of Finance accepted the spread of income of football players over the years immediately after their retirement thus reducing their tax liability. In 1972 a football players' pension fund was established which in 2008 had around 2,300 participants and an investment portfolio of €560 million. Payment to the pension fund is compulsory and it is possible to invest up to 50 percent of gross income tax-free to acquire payments in the years after the player's career is over (Jongbloed Fiscaal Juristen, 2009). Players are allowed to withdraw payments out of the pension fund immediately after they cease playing professionally and 90 percent of the money invested can be used as a bridge to a second career. Ten percent of the money will remain in the fund until the age of 65 (Ernst and Young, 2006). Foreign players in the Netherlands can use the so-called "ex-pat" facility, which means that the first 30 percent of income is not taxed. In order to qualify for the tax holiday on the first 30 percent of income a player should meet one of the following criteria (Ministerie van Financiën, 2006):

1. The player played in the last two years in at least 50 percent of the A international matches of the national team of his country (top 30 FIFA or top 15 UEFA countries).

2. The player has been selected in the last two years for at least two or three of the A international matches of the national team of his country (top 30 FIFA or top 15 UEFA countries).

3. The player played in the last two years in at least two or three of the matches in the highest division of a FIFA top 30 or a UEFA top 15 country.

4. The player played in the last two years in at least eight matches in the Champions League or UEFA Cup (excluding the Intertoto Cup).

5. During his contract, the player earned at least 150 percent of the average gross income of a player in the Eredivisie. (In 2008–2009, the gross annual wage required to meet this rule was €405,000.)

The KNVB decided that there should be no limitation on non-EU players, playing in the Netherlands, but they had to create an added value for the league. This implies that if these players were better than those from the Netherlands or other EU countries, their yearly wages also have to be higher than the average wage paid in the Eredivisie. The minimum wage for non-EU players older than 20 years has to be 150 percent of the average wage and 75 percent for players younger than 20. This means that non-EU players have to earn at least €405,000 or €202,500 a year for players younger than 20 (FBO, 2008). This implies that most of the foreign players in the league should be from inside the EU, but the discrepancies with the turnover of the Big 5 means that the Dutch League is also a "stepping stone" league for non-EU players, although a step closer to the Big Five than the Belgian League. In the Spanish media (*El Universal, Marca*), PSV Eindhoven is nicknamed "El Trampolin" because of the number of strikers (Romario, Ronaldo, Kezman, van Nistelrooy, Farfan) that have catapulted into the Big 5 after having played in the Dutch League.

Financial Support by Governments

Most of the stadia in Belgium were built before World War II and are sometimes owned by the local municipality. Bruges and Genk are home to the two newest stadiums. Jan Breydel Stadium, home of ClubBrugge KV and Cercle Brugge, was built in 1975 and renovated for Euro 2000. The city of Bruges financed the majority of the project and both teams pay rent to the city. KRC Genk's stadium was built on the location of the former coal mines in Genk and financed by reconversion funds. In November 2007, Belgium and the Netherlands decided to submit a bid for the World Cup 2018. Belgium's problem, however, is that all the necessary stadia to qualify for consideration must still be built. In order to finance these facilities, different governments have already decided to give some financial support to potential World Cup venues, but also to smaller stadia for the other teams in the First Division. Another recently developed system is a private public cooperation between companies, clubs and (local) government to build multi-functional stadiums. The first example of this state-of-the-art facility is the new KAA Gent Stadium, as of August 2008. In 2008, the Minister of Finance submitted a tax shelter proposal in order to raise funds to encourage future spending on these stadia. A tax shelter is a system where private companies can pledge their financial support to a sport project. Their support can be brought in as a cost for 150 percent of the investment in their accounts.

The decisions of the 1995 Bosman case resulted in some structural changes in Dutch football and many Dutch clubs were mismanaged, leading to financial difficulties. In 2003, 30 out of the 36 licences necessary to compete in the top two divisions of the Dutch football leagues were initially rejected (Oldenboom, 2004). In order to satisfy all the conditions and avoid the loss of their licence, many local authorities ended up trying to financially support their local team. That financial support conflicted with European law and soon the European Commission wanted to know about financial relations between teams and local governments (KPMG, 2003). The local governments attempted to avoid the directives of the EU and Article 87[13] of the European Treaty through sponsoring multifunctional facilities instead of the teams (KPMG-BEA, 2003). The KPMG report concluded that between 1992 and 2002, local governments spent about €306.3 million to support their professional football club. The most common financing was through facilities (€243.3 million). Local governments argued that financing these facilities would enhance the image of the city, create potential consumer spill over (offices, pubs, shops, etc.) and create more jobs. In some cases, the local government acquired the stadium to rent out to the club, such as the city of Breda which bought the NAC grounds for €12 million; and Nijmegen, who paid €15.7 million for the NEC stadium. The city of Groningen also invested €15 million in the new ground of FC Groningen. Yet even in 2008, some of the clubs still have major debts. The total debt of ADO Den Haag was estimated at €14–€15 million (on a turnover of €10.8 million) and the debt of Vitesse Arnhem rose to €27 million (with a turnover of €14.2 million). In 2003, FC Utrecht faced a debt of €40 million and nearly went bankrupt. At that point, the local municipality extended a soft loan of €25 million to enable a property developer to buy the stadium, and the company then received permission to develop apartments in the surroundings of the stadium (Dejonghe, 2007b).

PROFESSIONAL WOMEN'S FOOTBALL IN THE NETHERLANDS

In 2007, the KNVB decided to create an Eredivisie for women. Kickoff was on 29th August, 2007, between six teams (ADO Den Haag, AZ Alkmaar, SC Heerenveen, FCTwente, FC Utrecht, and Willem II), while Roda JC and Feyenoord confirmed their interest in participating in the 2008–2009 season. All teams play two home and two away matches against each other on Thursday

---

[13] Under Article 87 of the EC Treaty (ex Article 92) part 1 it states that, save as otherwise provided in this Treaty, any aid granted by a Member State or through State resources in any form whatsoever which distorts or threatens to distort competition by favouring certain undertakings or the production of certain goods shall, insofar as it affects trade between Member States, be incompatible with the common market. (http://ec.europa.eu/competition/legislation/treaties/ec/art87_en.html)

evenings, and the KNVB aspires to eventually have 12 teams competing. Highlights are broadcast on television. One of the sponsors of the Eredivisie is also the main sponsor of the women's Eredivisie and the director of the Eredivisie is also a board member of the women's league. Before the beginning of the season there had been confusion about the division of the top players. In order to stimulate competitive balance, the KNVB ordered some players to play for other teams and paid subsidies in order to make the teams competitive. FC Twente would have had eight players who were internationalists, so they were required to transfer two players to SC Heerenveen and Willem II Tilburg. Players play as amateurs and starting season costs were to be financed by the league (€555,000 by the KNVB) and the participating professional clubs (€519,000 altogether). Matches attracted between 500 and 1,500 spectators in the first two months and only FC Twente charged entrance fees. Television ratings were low in the first season: about 34,000 viewers (a 1.6 percent market share).

CONCLUSIONS

The Low Countries were some of the first countries to begin playing football in Europe. Due to favourable circumstances (available flat playing fields, English-style boarding schools, easy adoption of the sports culture), both countries managed to develop their football system progressively.

Due to the fact that amateurism was, for a long time, considered to be the only way for football to be viable, the development of the game lost momentum, performance in international matches was weak and the best players moved abroad. The adoption of the SSSL system led to a relatively more favourable position in the 1960s. Stadia were made easily accessible and a football culture started to emerge. The successes in the early 1970s (the Netherlands) and in the later 1970s (Belgium) caused a process of cumulative causation: a reinforcing tendency that led to primacy and dominance of a few clubs in the Netherlands (Ajax, PSV and Feyenoord) and Belgium (Club Brugge, RSC Anderlecht).

The revenue from Champions League fixtures disturbs the competitive balance in both countries, which has led to discussions and questions about the league structure. In the Netherlands, a playoff system has been introduced to create more excitement and uncertainty of outcome in the league. However, this questions the legitimacy of the best-ranked clubs having the greatest access to Europe. In 2001, PSV director Harry van Raaij wanted to launch the Atlantic or Euro League, a supranational league that would enable top teams from smaller countries to compete in the broadcasting rights battle. It could be that the first supranational league might start in the Netherlands and Belgium and might bring additional revenue to the top teams.

Due to its favourable conditions for non-EU players Belgium has been used as a stepping stone by international players, managers and clubs in order to develop foreign players for a chance to play in one of the Big 5 leagues. The Netherlands has seen an exodus of younger national players and a replacement with foreigners from around the world.

In the new millennium, the professional football system in the Low Countries faces new challenges. Both leagues have major disadvantages in the new economic environment with an open labour market in a closed product market. Due to the increase in the importance of broadcasting rights to club budgets, clubs from both nations have a competitive disadvantage against clubs from the Big 5 and clubs from emerging football markets like Russia, Turkey and Poland. New innovations and sources of income are needed to keep the clubs competitive at European level in order to avoid a downswing. Recent positive developments include the popularity of the game in both countries, a high match attendance, and the willingness of state authorities to cooperate in improvements to stadia.

DISCUSSION QUESTIONS

1. Explain the impact of the Bosman rule on average-sized leagues such as the Netherlands and Belgium.
2. Find examples of foreign-born players that used Belgium and the Netherlands as a stepping stone.
3. Compare the dynamics of the top positions in the Belgian and Dutch leagues with those in Germany and England. Is there a difference, and if so, why?
4. What would be the effect of a so-called Euroleague on Belgium and the Netherlands?
5. What is the effect of an open labour market in a closed product market for Belgian, Dutch, and the other leagues in the EU?
6. What kind of advice would you give to the minor leagues?

GUIDED READING

The article by Dejonghe & Vandeweghe (2006) reviewing Belgian football in the *Journal of Sports Economics* (Vol. 7,1, 105–113) provides a useful overview of the recent development of Belgian football. *Sport et Strategie* magazine is a useful source of business information on Dutch football, as is *Voetbal* magazine and *Voetbal International* magazine. The Dutch Football Association is a useful source for background data on Dutch football (www.knvb.nl) as is the website of the Belgian Football Association for Belgian football (http://www.footbel.be/).

REFERENCES

Andreff, W., & Staudohar, P. (2002). European and US sports business models. In C. Barros, M. Ibrahimo, & S. Szymanski (Eds.), *Transatlantic sport: the comparative economics of North American and European Sports* (pp. 23–49). Northampton: Edward Elgar.

Berdowski, P., Van den Hoek, M., & Nanninga, H. (1997). *Strategisch bedrijfstakonderzoek Betaald Voetbal*. Rotterdam: KWW Krekel van der Woerd Wouterse bv.

Bouwes, E. (2008). De topklasse: KNVB op zoek naar extra laag in voetbalpiramide. *Sport & Strategie*, Jaargang 2, Editie 1, 20–21.

Cohen, B. (1996). *De geschiedenis van het voetbal*. Amsterdam: Arch Publishing.

Colin, F. (1995). *Eeuwige amateurs, Antwerpen*. Icarus: Standaard Uitgeverij.

Colin, F., & Mulder, L. (1996). *De Gouden voetbalgids*. Antwerpen: Standaard Uitgeverij.

Dejonghe, T. (2007a). *Sport in de wereld: ontstaan, verspreiding en evolutie*. Gent: Academia Press.

Dejonghe, T. (2007b). *Sport en economie: een aftrap*. Nieuwegein: Arko Sports Media.

Dejonghe, T. (May, 2006). *The evolution of Belgian football over the last decades*. Nyon: UEFA–IASE Seminar on The economic impact of the UEFA Champions League on national football economies.

Dejonghe, T. (2004a). Restructuring the Belgian professional football league: a location-allocation solution. *Tijdschrift voor economische en sociale geografie*, 95,1, p. 73–88.

Dejonghe, T. (2004b). *Sport en economie: een noodzaak tot symbiose*. Nieuwegein: Arko Sports Media.

Dejonghe, T., & Vandeweghe, H. (2006). Belgian football. *Journal of Sports Economics, Vol 7, 1*, 105–113.

Dejonghe, T., Lagae, W., Verschueren, J., & Vanclooster, B. (2008). Voetbalstadion sponsoring in de lage landen: naar een doorbraak? In Van Tilborgh & Duyck (Eds.). *Marketingjaarboek 2008*. Kalmthout: Pimms NV. 43–55.

Deloitte, (2008). *Annual Review of Football Finance*. Manchester: Deloitte.

Dobson, S., & Goddard, J. (1998). Performance and revenue in professional league football: evidence from Granger causality tests. *Applied Economics, 30*, 1641–1651.

Dobson, S., & Goddard, J. (2001). *The economics of football*. Cambridge: Cambridge University Press.

Ernst & Young (2006). *Europese aanpak pensioenopbouw profvoetballers*. www.ey.nl

European Commission. Competition Directorate. Retrieved on July 15, 2009, from http://ec.europa.eu/competition/legislation/treaties/ec/art87_en.html

European-football-statistics.co.uk. Retrieved on July 16, 2009, from http://www.european-football-statistics.co.uk/index1.htm

FBO(Federatie van Betaalde Voetbal organisaties) (2008). *Inkomensciterium Voor Het Seizoen 2008/09 Vastgeseld.* Retrieved on August 3, 2009 from http://www.fbo.nl/#inkomenscriterium%2008-09

Forrest, D., & Simmons, R. (2002). Team salaries and playing success in sports: a comparative perspective. *Sportökonomie 4* 221–236.

Hall, S., Szymanski, S., & Zimbalist, A. (2002). Testing causility between team performance and payroll: the cases of Major League Baseball and English soccer. *Journal of Sports Economics, 3, 2,* 149–168.

Jongbloed Fiscaal Juristen (2009). *Belastingvrij inkomen voor Sporters uit buitenland.* Retrieved on July 16, 2009, from http://www.jongbloed-fiscaaljuristen.nl/databank/artiesten_en_fiscus–belastingvrij_inkomen_wk_voetbal_2006/.

Kassies, B. *UEFA European Cup Football: Results and Qualification.* Retrieved on July 16, 2009, from http://www.xs4all.nl/~kassiesa/bert/uefa/.

KBVB (2008). *Data loges, business seats, season ticketholder 2006–07.* Brussel: KBVB.

KNVB.nl. *www.knvb.nl*

KNVB National Archives. Retrieved on July 15, 2009, from http://www.nationaalarchief.nl/knvb/inleiding/inleid106.htm

Lagae, W. & Dejonghe, T. (2009). Een Vergelijking Tussen De Merchandisinginkomsten In Het Professioneel Voetbal Europese Topclubs Versus De Pionier Ajaz En Challenger PSV. In Van Tilborgh & Duyck (Eds.) *Marketingjaarboek 2009.* Kalmthout: Pimms NV. 186–197.

Ministerie van Financiën (2006). *Mededeling over het criterium specifieke deskundigheid bij profvoetballers.* Retrieved on May 25, 2008, from http://www.minfin.nl–binaries–minfin–assets–pdf–dossiers–belastingplannen–belastingen-internationaal–internationale-fiscale-berichten–ifb06-003.pdf.

KPMG–BEA (2003). *De gemeente als twaalfde man.* Ministerie van Binnenlandse Zaken.

Oldenboom E. (2004). *Betaald voetbal in Nederland: aanzet tot een toekomstverkenning.* Amsterdam: Meerwaarde.

Sponsor Magazine (2007). Sponsoroverzicht betaald voetbal. Number 5, September, 2007, 14–15.

Sportbusiness International (26th November, 2001). UEFA must reshape leagues, says PSV chief. *Sportbusiness.com.* Retrieved on July 16, 2009, from http://www.sportbusiness.com/news/142618/uefa-must-reshape-leagues-says-psv-chief.

Szymanski, S. (1999). The market for soccer players in England after Bosman: winners and losers. In C. Jeanrenaud, & S. Késenne (Eds.). *Competition policy in professional sports: Europe after the Bosman case* (pp. 133–160). Neuchatel: Standaard Ed Ltd.

Szymanski, S., & Kuypers. (1999). *Winners and losers, the business strategy of football*. London: Penguin Books.

Inquiry by the Rt Hon Lord Justice Taylor (1990). *The Hillsborough Stadium Disaster: Final Report*. Cm962. HMSO.

Van Asch, J. (2007). *De TV-Rechten In Het Vovetbal EenVergelijkende Studie Tussen De Europese Competities*. Unpubished Master's Dissertation. Lessius University College, Antwerp.

Van Bottenburg, M. (2004). *Verborgen competitie: over de uiteenlopende populariteit van sporten*. Nieuwegein: Arko Sports Media.

Van Dam, F. (1998). Nieuwe voetbalstadions in Nederland, van Lulu tot hype. *Geografie*, 7(2), 28–33.

Van Dam, F. (2000). Refurbishment, redevelopment or relocation? The changing form and location of football stadiums in The Netherlands. *AREA, vol. 32*(2), 133–144.

Van De Fiert, W. (15th May, 2008). *Nederlandse hervormingen*. E-mail correspondence with Hypercube consulting.

Van den Wall Bake Consult (August–September, 2007). *Nieuwsbrief*. 152–153.

Van Der Werff, R., & Verlaan, K. (1994). *Professioneel voetbal in Europa: Een economisch-geografische analyse*. Thesis Geografie, Utrecht Universiteit, Utrecht.

Vandeweghe, H. (2007). Meer geld op het kampioenenbal dan ooit: Champions League halen steeds belangrijker. *Sport & Strategie*, Jaargang 1, Editie 2, 22–23.

Van Westerloo, E. (2004). *We hoeven er niet aan te verdienen: de geschiedenis van de miljoenendans om de uitzendrechten van voetbalwedstrijden*. Nieuwegein: Arko Sports Media.

Voetbal magazine – http://www.fc-voetbalmagazine.nl/html/standaard/nl-NL/pages/default/Home.html

Voetbal International – http://www.vi.nl/Home.htm

RECOMMENDED WEBSITES

The Belgian Football Association:
http://www.footbel.be
The Dutch Football Association:
www.knvb.nl
Sport & Strategie magazine:
http://www.sportenstrategie.nl/
Voetbal International magazine:
http://www.vi.nl/Home.htm
Voetbal magazine:
http://www.fc-voetbalmagazine.nl/html/standaard/nl-NL/pages/default/Home.html

CHAPTER 24

Mexico

Liz Crolley
University of Liverpool

Rogelio Roa
DreaMatch Solutions

Objectives

Upon completion of this chapter the reader should be able to:

- Have developed an understanding of the key issues and challenges facing the Mexican football industry.
- Understand the structure and organisation of domestic football in Mexico.
- Carry out a situation analysis of the Mexican football industry.
- Evaluate specific case studies within the broader context of the football industry in Mexico.

CONTENTS

OVERVIEW OF THE CHAPTER

This chapter begins by briefly introducing the historical background to the Mexican football industry. The main body of the chapter outlines the current issues, developments and challenges involved in the Mexican football business today. A detailed situation analysis of the environment in which Mexican football operates helps to identify the current issues, strengths and weaknesses of the business and its commercial structures. Features examined include the demand for football, the quality of the "product," domestic structures and organisation, patterns of ownership and control, marketing and sponsorship, and infrastructure and stadia development. A general overview of the revenue streams indicates that Mexican football enjoys a relatively unusual balance between the different revenues streams of broadcasting monies, matchday revenues, player transfers and commercial revenues. All these factors are then brought together within the framework of a SWOT analysis. The chapter includes two case studies that help to illustrate challenges particular to Mexican football within its cultural context: the transfer system and the "gentleman's agreement," and the relationship between TV and Mexican football.

INTRODUCTION

Mexico can be considered a well-established football nation. Football has a deeply-rooted history in Mexico and is firmly engrained as the main national sport among Mexico's population. Football was introduced into Mexico at the end of the nineteenth century by groups of Englishmen who were attracted to the country by the mining trade, and according to the Mexican Football Federation (the FMF), it was the workers of the Real de Monte de Pachuca company who formed the first football team in Mexico in 1900 (although it was already being played in other communities). The first Championship was held in 1902 but at this time teams were still made up largely of Englishmen. It wasn't until Club América incorporated Mexican players that the sport was taken seriously by the indigenous population. It then developed rapidly (Angelotti Pasteur, 2005). The first Mexican national team played in 1923, and its participation in the 1928 Olympic Games marked its entry into international competitions. Meanwhile, the Mexican Football Federation (FMF) was founded on 23 August 1927 and became affiliated to FIFA in 1929. Since then the FMF has been the organisation responsible for all aspects of the organisation and promotion of football in Mexico. Unlike football in emerging markets, where the professionalization of football is only recently established, or yet to be introduced at all, Mexican football officially entered its era of professionalism in 1943 and has since then existed as an industry. The main aims of this chapter are to provide an insight into the way in which this industry operates, highlighting the main issues and challenges of the Mexican football industry.

THE MEXICAN FOOTBALL INDUSTRY: KEY ISSUES, DEVELOPMENTS AND CHALLENGES

Mexico has a population of about 110 million people and is the 12th largest economy in the world (*CIA World Factbook*, 2008). Today, the Mexican football industry is estimated to be worth $370 million (*Expansión*, 2007).

It differs in some significant ways from other South American countries. First, unlike in most South American countries, football in Mexico only really obtained national dominance when its hosting of the World Cup finals in 1970 coincided with the advent of commercial television. Hence, the connections between football and TV are more firmly cemented than in other countries. We will see how this relationship is reinforced even further when we examine the patterns of ownership of football clubs and current broadcasting deals. Second, clubs do not usually operate as social clubs as they do in many other South American countries (Miller and Crolley, 2007) but instead are owned by large companies or organisations. This ensures that commercial interests in football are influential and a paramount consideration throughout the game. Third, this commercial model of football provides an important distinction between Mexican and most other football businesses in South American countries. Some of the principal features of the Mexican football industry have been analysed below under the following headings: demand for football; quality of "product"; structure and organisation; ownership and control; revenues; marketing and sponsorship; infrastructure and stadia development.

Demand for the "Product": The Popularity of Football

Football is the number one sport in Mexico and therefore holds a strong position. Mexican football enjoys a broad and loyal fanbase. According to Consulta Mitofsky (2008), some 61 percent of Mexicans claim to like football; this is a significantly higher percentage than any other sport. There are an estimated 31.5 million fans in Mexico (*Expansión*, 2007). In commercial terms, demand, then, for the product is high and the potential market is large. Football is popular at both domestic and national team levels. A study carried out by market researchers Serta de México concluded that while six out of ten people claim to support a particular football club, seven out of ten people support the national team (Consulta Mitofsky, 2008). Attendances are stable; around 3.8 million people watch football on a regular basis. Chivas de Guadalajara enjoyed the highest cumulative attendances for the 2006–2007 Closing season with 1.32 million (there are two championships each year — an Opening and a Closing season). They were followed closely by Pumas with 1.3 million and by América with 1.2 million. Tigres and Cruz Azul were next with 1 million and 0.9 million, respectively. However, stadium utilization figures were not as high as some clubs would have liked, with few games selling out completely. A rise in crowd violence in recent years and economic instability has also led to some concerns that fans will be dissuaded from attending live matches.

Other reasons might lie in the nature of the competition/leagues in which clubs participate. So despite the popularity of football, it is a challenge to fill stadia on matchdays.

Quality of the Football "Product"

Good-quality products help maintain business success. Though the demand for football is not like any other product (Beech and Chadwick, 2007, pages 8–13) the quality of football is important in Mexico. The high wages offered to players mean that relatively few Mexicans leave their country to play abroad (though a recent rise since the 2006 World Cup means that there are currently some 14 Mexican players in Europe), and Mexico is a favourite destination for players who do not go to one of the European "Big Five" leagues. Patterns of player transfers in Mexico differ from other South American countries: as well as retaining its finest players Mexican football imports players from the rest of South America (Miller, 2007). The quality of football is therefore high. Another ingredient deemed essential for success among Mexican consumers of sport is competitive balance, and an annual "draft" system ensures that a level of competitive balance is maintained (see Case Study 24.2). The current TV involvement in football also helps to maintain high competitive balance. TV companies are involved in the seeding of teams into groups to play league fixtures. Their involvement means that no group will consist entirely of unattractive clubs. Evidence of the success of maintaining competitive balance is not hard to find: since the introduction of the current system of holding two championships per year began in 1996, some 11 teams have shared the 23 championships. The "big four" clubs have shared just 5 of the last 20 championships, while relatively "small" clubs such as Pachuca, Toluca, Santos or Nexaca have enjoyed recent successes. So, mechanisms are in place to ensure that the quality of football and competitions are high, and that competitive balance is sustained.

Domestic Structure and Organisation of Professional Football in Mexico

A major determinant in the quality of professional football is the way in which it is organised and structured. In Mexico, national professional leagues are large and a lot of games are played. Currently, the FMF consists of four professional divisions: *Primera División Profesional, Primera A, Segunda, Tercera*. Each division is organised differently: The *Primera División Profesional* (or Premier League) has 18 teams, divided into three groups; the *Primera A* (First Division) has 27 teams divided into 3 groups; the *Segunda* (Second Division) has 70 clubs, who play in six regionalised groups; and the

Tercera (Third Division) has 173 divided into 14 groups. There are some 6,300 registered (professional) players and over 4,200 matches are played each year (FMF, 2008).

The league structure is not simple. In the Premier League, teams are seeded and put into three groups. Each year teams participate in two championships: *Apertura* (Opening) and *Clausura* (Closing). There is no overall annual champion. In all, some 344 matches are played each year. Unlike models in European football, winning the League is not a simple process. The winners and best two runners-up of the three groups enter a playoff (*liguilla*) competition. Neither is relegation a simple process. The team with the lowest ratio of points per game over the last three years (or last six championships) can be relegated. It is confusing, but not entirely out of synch with other leagues in Latin American countries. To further complicate matters not all teams are eligible for promotion to the Premier League. Many of the First Division clubs are in effect "feeder" clubs for Premier League clubs and cannot be promoted, and others do not comply with certain regulations which are necessary to play in the Premier League (a total of 12 in 2008–2009 Opening were ineligible for promotion). If an ineligible team wins the First Division, the first eligible team participates in a two-legged playoff with the team relegated from the Premier League to determine who plays in which division the following season. Fans (and therefore TV companies, sponsors and advertisers) like the excitement of the playoffs and this format has been so successful commercially for the Mexican football industry, that the model has been adapted in other countries such as Colombia and Chile. However, there are many "meaningless" matches and the fact that the stadia have not been filled recently has led some to suggest alternative structures to the league format: for example, Pachuca president, Jesús Martínez, appeared to support the notion of replacing the *liguilla* with two groups of four teams, the winners of each playing a final to decide who wins the league (*AzCentral*, 2008). Others have talked about abandoning the Opening and Closing competitions in favour of a year-long championship, along the European model, to give greater balance and integrity to the competition and remove what some see as an unfair seeding system decided upon by the TV companies to maximize ratings. So at the very heart of the current league structure lies the commercial interests of the TV companies, and this reflects the balance of power within Mexican football.

Mexican domestic clubs also participate in other competitions at various times of the year, and often for overtly commercial reasons. Two Mexican clubs participate in the Copa Sudamerica; three in the Copa Libertadores; eight in the Interliga played in the United States; and four in the CONCACAF Championships. Unusually, Mexican clubs take part in both CONCACAF and CONMEBOL tournaments. Four Mexican teams also compete in the Superliga against four U.S. teams, for a prize of $1 million. This "friendly" tournament is organised during the pre-season for commercial purposes by Soccer United Marketing (SUM) in order to exploit interest in football in the United States and to enhance rivalries between U.S. and Mexican football clubs. Clearly, the football calendar is complex and cluttered. Added to this are the many displays of the Mexican national team.

The Mexican Football Federation (*Federación Mexicana de Fútbol*, or FMF) forms part of CONCACAF (*Confederación Norte Centroamérica y Cáribe de Fútbol*), one of FIFA's six confederations. The FMF is also responsible for the Mexican national team. The Mexican national team plays on average 17 games per year, and can play up to 25 in one season (FMF, 2008). The Mexican national team plays lots of "friendlies," and there is great interest and support across the country. The national team is a strong force in its confederation. It enters the qualification phase for the 2010 FIFA World Cup in its customary position as favourite in the confederation. The national team has missed only 5 out of the 18 World Cup tournaments. Mexico's average FIFA World Ranking since records began is 11th (FIFA, 2008), but debates rage within Mexico as to why its team does not achieve more at the international level. Although its infrastructure, history and tradition are strong, compared to Brazil or Argentina, Mexico has not enjoyed comparable success at an international level.

All clubs and the national team are represented by the Mexican FA, and all in theory have a say in the running of football. Unsurprisingly, though, the balance of power is heavily weighted in favour of the big clubs (FMF, 2008). When we consider the fact that many clubs are owned by large companies, it becomes clear that corporate involvement in football is strong at the highest level. The management of the Mexican football industry is not, therefore, a simple assignment, and the autonomy of the FMF to work for the good of the game might be compromised.

Ownership and Control of Football

Owners of football clubs are currently huge investors who are prepared to subsidise football clubs with large amounts of money. Mexican football enjoys enormous amounts of investment from the game's main stakeholders. Some of the biggest industries in Mexico support Mexican football. Most Premier League clubs are owned by big TV companies, breweries,

Table 24.1	Owners of Football Clubs in the Mexican Premier League	
Club	**Owner**	**Industry**
América	Televisa	Broadcasting
Nexaca	Televisa	Broadcasting
San Luis	Televisa	Broadcasting
Morelia	TV Azteca	Broadcasting
Monterrey	FEMSA	Brewery
Santos Laguna	Grupo Modelo	Brewery
Toluca	Grupo Modelo	Brewery
Chivas Guadalajara	Omnilife	Food and drink
Tuzos Pachuca	Grupo Pachuca	Various
Tigres	Cemex	Industrial manufacturing
Cruz Azul	Cementos Cruz Azul	Industrial manufacturing
Atlas	Grupo Bernat	Various
Atlante	Grupo Pegaso	Technology
Jaguares Chiapas	Farmacias del Ahorro	Pharmaceuticals
Indios Juarez	Grupo Juarez	Various
Pumas UNAM	Mexican University	Education
Tecos UAG	Mexican University	Education
Puebla	Grupo Bernat	Various

telecommunication companies, pharmaceutical companies, etc. as seen in Table 24.1. However, the heavy subsidies by large companies mean that in times of economic crisis, there is a risk of big businesses pulling out of their commitment to football.

Television companies are heavily involved in the ownership structure and control of Mexican football. Contrary to FIFA regulations, one company owns three clubs in the top division: Televisa owns América, Nexaca, and San Luis. Only one football club is a sporting club: Atlas, who is owned by its members. The relationship between football and television lies of the heart of the Mexican football business (see Case Study 24.1).

Despite the involvement of some of the largest and most successful companies in Mexico, football clubs are renowned for being poorly managed. A lack of transparency in many areas of the governance of football, including its financial reporting, the dubious role of agents, and no one to oversee the authority of the FMF, has led to accusations of corruption from many commentators. It is argued that a "cleaner" image would actually increase the value of sponsorships, improve marketing potential and attract broader support (*Expansión*, 2005).

Revenue Streams

It is a healthy feature of Mexican football that it does not over-rely on a single source of revenue. Unlike football clubs in most other Latin American countries, Mexican football clubs do not depend on player transfers to survive. Again, in contrast to many other football industries, both in established markets and in the Americas, sponsorship is the main revenue stream with 26 to 30 percent of the annual income from this commercial source. Also in good shape are the revenues from gate receipts (25 percent) and player transfers (23 percent). It can be argued that the figure relating to player transfers is maintained at an artificial level because of the particular practices in place in the Mexican football industry (see Case Study 24.2). Media rights bring in just 15 percent of revenues.

Unlike some contemporary industries in the "established" European markets, Mexican football is not heavily dependent on broadcasting revenues. Just 15 percent of clubs' revenues come directly from broadcasting—compared to an average of 40 percent for the "big five" European leagues (Deloitte, 2007b). Given the role of the TV companies in football, it is probable that this indicates an undervaluation of the broadcasting rights. However, the clubs do benefit indirectly from their enormous exposure on free-to-air TV through healthy sponsorship and advertising deals. Though the actual amounts that clubs receive for their TV deals are confidential, estimates suggest that the bigger clubs earn several million dollars more per annum than small clubs.

Of the 37 percent of revenues from commercial sources, sponsorship accounts for at least 26 percent. The relatively high levels of sponsorship in Mexican football (certainly compared to other Latin American countries) appear to support the argument that football benefits from its (largely) free-to-air TV deals indirectly. Some 26 to 30 percent of club revenues come from sponsorship, much of this from kit sponsors. According to Deloitte (2007a, page 23) most clubs in the Mexican Premier League receive at least $750,000 to $1 million for sponsors' names to appear on the front of their shirts, and a further $400,000 to $800,000 for advertising on their backs. In Mexico it is not uncommon to see commercial advertising appear all

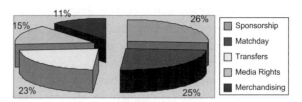

FIGURE 24.1 *Revenue Breakdown of the Mexican Football Industry 2007*
Source: Expansión, 2007

over the kit (shirt front, back, sleeves, shorts). On average a club kit will display the names of seven sponsors: all have at least 2, and Pachuca as many as 12. In all, each club earns between about $1.8 million and $2.5 million through kit sponsorship.

The national team earns an estimated $220 million from its official sponsors (Coca Cola, Banamex, Movistar, Adidas, Toyota, and Corona). Adidas began a new sponsorship deal with the Mexican national team in January 2007. Though again figures are confidential, reports suggest an eight-year deal, rumoured to be worth $80 million.

So revenues from sponsorship are in good shape. As most football is broadcast on free-to-air TV channels, it ensures good ratings and potential sponsors might expect high levels of exposure. Economic instability (either global or national) will impact not only directly (through attendances and commercial revenues) but also indirectly through a possible reduction in the value of sponsorship.

Marketing and Brand Development

Although traditional sponsorship forms a major element of the marketing/commercial departments of football clubs, the marketing of football in a way that is now familiar in established markets is still in its infancy in Mexican football. There are pockets of innovation, led by forward-thinking entrepreneurs and sports marketing agencies and there exists evidence of the application of marketing strategies to the football industry in order to increase commercial revenues. Such strategies include the development of brand identity, product extensions and basic segmentation of the market.

The development of brand identity is underway. The "big four" clubs in Mexico have ready-made identities which can be developed (further) into brands. Pumas, Chivas, América, and Cruz Azul have distinctive identities and represent different values, which brings potential for strong football brands: América symbolises capitalist competition and perhaps for this reason, though one of the most popular clubs in Mexico, they are also top of the "most hated" league; Chivas de Guadalajara, the only "national" team to be based outside Mexico City, pride themselves on being *puros mexicanos*, and this identity is reflected in their recruitment of players and the ideal of national autonomy (Magazine, 2007); Cruz Azul represents working class values; and Pumas, representing the National Autonomous University of Mexico (UNAM), follow the philosophy of youth. So these four "national" teams have strong identities that can be easily transformed into marketable brands. There is also some development of individual players as "brands". Pepsi recognised the potential power of individual endorsements when they signed a sponsorship deal with

Rafa Márquez, for example. Such is the brand reach of football/players and their social position as role models that this platform of sponsorship is increasingly popular (*Expansión*, 2005). Gol Marketing specializes in building brands around players and has worked with Sergio Santana (Pachuca), Aarón Padilla (América) and Héctor Castro (Monterrey). A few players have their own websites with the aim, they claim, to facilitate communication with fans, especially those based in the United States.

In terms of product extensions, most clubs have a line of merchandise available to fans, though the range, availability, and accessibility of this merchandise varies widely between clubs. While some club merchandise is limited to scarves and shirts, fans of Chivas de Guadalajara—guided by the commercially astute mind of owner, Jorge Vergara—are able buy a wide range of branded products, such as toothbrushes or their very own "Chiva-Cola'" in their club colours. Chivas has recently focused on brand development and extension. As well as the development of merchandise and over 300 licensed products, they have established official academy franchises across Mexico, with almost 200 schools carrying the Chivas brand. In addition, and most importantly, Chivas have begun to capitalize on the popularity of (Mexican) football in the United States. Chivas have bought a franchise in the United States, Chivas USA, who play in the American Football League, the MLS (Major League Soccer). Hence, they are able to capitalize on the huge interest in football of the Latino market. Chivas USA offers new opportunities for Mexican/U.S. border advertising, targeting the Hispanic population in the United States.

Pachuca has also worked hard in recent years to pioneer a brand and distinct positioning within the Mexican football industry. They have built a university to enhance the study of sport sciences and students can study alongside their football training. Pachuca's involvement in the local community has also been exceptional within Mexican football. Alongside these initiatives, they have integrated imaginative marketing and media campaigns to enhance their market position and increase awareness of their brand, though some might question their attempts to target a national market while they still have to work to establish themselves within their local region. They have made good progress with marketing initiatives via a TV channel, official programmes, price promotions, and tickets for local schools. Pachuca president, Jesús Martínez Patiño, is acknowledged as being a leading light in the advancement of marketing communications in Mexican football.

These are not the only clubs to be actively developing marketing strategies: Clubs such as Tigres, Monterrey, América, and Cruz Azul have attractive membership schemes with cross-promotions with sponsors who, following the pattern emerging in Europe, are beginning to grow their relationship into one of partners.

The national team is one of the most recognised Mexican brands abroad and one with positive associations domestically: Some 93 percent of Mexicans believe the image of the Mexican national team is excellent, fair, or good (Castañeda Ramírez, 2006). The FMF, who are responsible for the Mexican team's commercial rights, claimed that Mexico's commercial rights are worth over $100 million (*Expansión*, 2005). They outsourced the selling of these rights to Warner Bros. who are responsible for maximizing the value of the national team's commercial rights.

The development of marketing strategies in Mexican football has, therefore, begun. There has been an attempt to gather information about the Mexican football fanbase and to carry out basic segmentation. Consulta Mitofsky (2008) has analysed the extent of football support and estimated the percentages of fans who support Premier League teams. According to Consulta Mitofsky (2008), six out of ten Mexicans claimed to like football. Some 23 percent of these claim to support Chivas of Guadalajara, followed closely by Club América with 22 percent. Cruz Azul claimed 14 percent of the nationwide fanbase and Pumas de UNAM enjoyed 10 percent of fans. Then three percent for Zorros del Atlas. So some 69 percent of football aficionados support one of just four teams. The report begins to carry out basic segmentation strategies. It gives a breakdown of fans based on gender and age. Club América, for example, has a younger fanbase than others while Chivas enjoys stronger support from the over 50s. Data of this type can be exploited in the future as Customer Relationship Management (CRM) systems are introduced.

Looking forward, there are opportunities for Mexican football to consolidate its position. New interest in strengthening the football industry by professionals with experience in other sectors can only serve to boost the professionalization and organisation of Mexican football and it will not be long before football attempts to apply CRM (Customer Relationship Management) techniques to strengthen its relations with its fanbase. While the development of websites and their exploitation as a revenue stream are still in their infancy (some clubs do not even have an official website), in the future, we might expect technological developments to enable clubs to benefit from increased internet access, mobile technology, etc. in order to facilitate communication with fans in a cost-effective way.

Infrastructure and Stadia Development

The infrastructure of Mexican football is being redeveloped and modernized sometimes alongside other rebranding strategies. Three new stadia are currently being developed (Chivas, Santos and Indios) and other clubs are redeveloping existing stadia: Cruz Azul, Monterrey, and Tigres. Plans for the Estadio Chivas in Guadalajara, currently under construction, are ambitious and the aim is to accommodate not only football fans watching matches in comfortable surroundings, but also to extend the match-going experience so that people eat and socialize within the stadium before and after the match. Amenities will include restaurants, a children's crèche, and a cinema on the site to make use of the facilities on non matchdays. Club Santos Laguna is also committed to carrying out a grand plan to build a new stadium within a much larger commercial complex, the Territorio Santos Modelo. The Estadio Corona, named after its sponsors, will not just provide comfortable seating for 28,000 fans (or 20,000 at pop concerts) but will also accommodate a gym, hotel, restaurants, conference and banqueting suites, and space for community activities. As well as diversifying revenues streams for the club, it is expected that the venture will lead to a closer relationship between the club and its local community. The current lack of social/community schemes at most football clubs in Mexico means that ground redevelopment provides an opportunity to reinforce its position within its locality. These stadium plans suggest a model of stadium utilization that is moving towards the European model: increased commercialization and more opportunities for fans to spend time—and money—in and around the stadium to maximize the use of the stadium as an asset as well as reinforce the brand (Estadio Chivas, 2008). It is also hoped that a cleaner, secure, more modern milieu will help ensure that fans can watch football in a safe, violence-free environment, thus attracting more fans.

SWOT ANALYSIS

It is important to understand the environment in which Mexican football operates, as it differs in several fundamental ways from European markets. Environmental analyses are one of the best ways of identifying the strengths and weaknesses of an industry. There are many techniques employed by businesses, and in particular by marketers, in order to assess the strength of a company's position in the market (Kitchen, 2007). We can draw together some of the main points covered in this chapter via a situation analysis, or SWOT, analysis (Table 24.2). The strengths, weaknesses, opportunities and threats within Mexican football will vary according to the nature of the football organisation (club, FA, commercial partner, TV company, and so on). However, a SWOT analysis is a useful

Table 24.2	SWOT Analysis of the Mexican Football Industry

Strengths	Weaknesses
Strength of fanbase at domestic and international levels Owners of football clubs are currently huge investors Strong infrastructure and recent stadia development Quality of football is high Long history and tradition of some clubs The distinctive identities of the "big four" clubs (Pumas, Chivas, América, and Cruz Azul) Strength of sponsorship Maintenance of good competitive balance Popularity in the United States	Lack of transparency in governance: corruption; no one to oversee the authority of the FMF Power of TV companies and the duopoly of TV Azteca and Televisión Complicated league structure and the high number of "meaningless" matches Lack of club-based social/community schemes Risk of big businesses pulling out of football

Opportunities	Threats
Interest in football in the United States and development of franchises in the U.S. market A relatively healthy national economy Possibility that new TV companies will break the Mexican football duopoly Technological developments New interest in strengthening football by professionals with experience in other industries	Strengthening global governance and increasing interference by FIFA in Mexican domestic football. Economic instability (either global or national) Introduction of foreign ownership Rise in hooliganism Uncertainty of future TV rights Rise in other leisure activities

tool with which to examine Mexican football as it can help to identify the internal and external forces which can shape the success of the Mexican football industry. Internal forces (strengths and weaknesses) lie within the control of the football industry and cover such issues as business culture, image, organizational structure, personnel, financial resources, contracts, brand awareness and efficiency. External forces (opportunities and threats) impact on the football industry but lie beyond its direct control (Parker, 2007). Factors such as the economic environment, social changes, competitors, the regulatory framework and technological advances might be included as external forces.

CASE STUDY 24.1: TV and Football in Mexico

The Mexican football industry is dominated by two major TV networks: Televisa, which has been the great power behind Mexican football for decades, and TV Azteca, now the second major force. These two companies dominate Mexican TV: Televisa owns four of the national networks and TV Azteca two (*SportBusiness International*, 2008). Between them they control almost all of the television advertising in Mexico. Televisa also owns the country's largest cable operator, Cablevisión, as well as the satellite operator, Sky Mexico. This power of television companies in Mexican football lies partly in the historical relationship between football and TV in Mexico and partly in the ownership structures of football clubs themselves; Televisa owns America, Nexaca and San Luis, and TV Azteca owns Morelia.

There exists a strong duopoly in the football market between these two media giants and there is currently no room for entry into the market for keen competitors such as Telemundo, Fox, ESPN, or Univisión. TV rights are sold individually by clubs in Mexico and there are no 'collective' deals. However, Televisa owns the rights to broadcast the home games of ten of the eighteen clubs in the Mexican Premier League and TV Azteca own the rights to broadcast home matches of the other eight clubs. On top of this Televisa and TV Azteca share the rights to broadcast the games of the Mexican national team. So, the duopoly is in a firm position in Mexican football. About seven league matches are broadcast each week on free-to-air TV. Another two are broadcast by Sky on pay-per-view (Sky is also run by Televisa). It is common for the Mexico matches to be shown live on more than one channel, thus increasing market share. Football in Mexico is still broadcast primarily on free-to-air, terrestrial TV. No more than six percent of the population of Mexico subscribes to TV (cable or satellite). The market is generally not considered as ready yet for subscription TV (Rosique, 2008). Clubs are happy to remain broadcast on free-to-air TV as it maximizes their exposure. The high accessibility of watching football on TV means that advertisers are content and sponsorship revenues are high. Sponsorship and advertising provide an important revenue stream for Mexican football clubs. The relationship between football and TV is one of a close partnership.

Furthermore, given the huge importance of football to the TV companies, they themselves are committed to advertising the football "product" and making it appear as attractive as possible in order to maximize viewing figures. It is not unusual to see glamorous, scantily-clad dancing girls swinging their hips while singing about how Mexico is going to win the World Cup! Apart from the political ramifications of breaking the duopoly between TV Azteca and Televisa, any move to Pay TV would jeopardize a club's relationship with commercial partners and risk losing a key revenue stream.

The power of the "Big Two" TV companies cannot be underestimated. They are involved in the running of the game at the highest level and can influence the seeding of clubs, for example, to form leagues. They have been known to flex their muscles on the rare occasion when their duopoly has appeared under threat. As is common when a duopoly exists (indeed as it did in the English Football League before the advent of the Premier League in 1992 with regard to the BBC and ITV), some clubs complain that their TV rights are undervalued and there have been rumblings of discontent, as well as a few attempts to negotiate with other broadcasting companies. In September 2007, Puebla Football Club attempted to break the duopoly and broker a deal with Fox Sport, who offered a substantial amount of money for a new deal. While the dispute was taking place (and Puebla owner, Ricardo Hernaine, agreed a deal with Fox Sports to broadcast a 'friendly' match against Atlético de Madrid) Televisa and TV Azteca refused to cover any news from Puebla. Puebla received no coverage at all on the main TV channels for a period of two weeks. So, eventually, despite the greater monetary offer from Fox Sport, Puebla could not afford to be alienated from mainstream TV and signed again with TV Azteca.

Not all football clubs, however, have been treated this way. Chivas de Guadalajara were recently in dispute with Televisa over the value of their TV rights (*El Economista*, 2008). They believed their rights had been severely undervalued by the TV company and were set to launch their own TV channel, Chivas TV (or Chivas Channel). The idea was to sell the content and matches to the highest bidder, unless a much improved deal with Televisa could be negotiated. The

President of Chivas, Jorge Vergara, was asking for a five-year deal worth over $175 million for the club's TV rights. They eventually agreed a new deal worth considerably more than their previous one. The most important club side in Mexico is not treated the same as Puebla!

What are the chances that new TV companies might break the Mexican football duopoly? Though many believe it is unlikely that this monopoly will be broken easily, if it were it could push up the value of media rights for some clubs. It would undoubtedly lead to a period of uncertainty for future TV rights: new deals (such as that recently negotiated by Chivas de Guadalajara) that might maximize the value of TV rights for some clubs could destabilize the current status quo and ultimately lead to a greater imbalance in the distribution of TV revenues, thus reducing the competitive balance of the league.

Questions

1. What are the advantages and disadvantages to the Mexican football industry of maintaining the current status quo regarding the relationship between football and TV companies?

2. What would be the consequences to the Mexican football industry of a club, such as Chivas, breaking the TV duopoly and signing a deal with a competing TV company?

CASE STUDY 24.2: Player Transfers and ''The Gentlemen's Agreement''

The Bosman ruling in Europe in 1995 changed the face of football transfers across the globe. In Mexico the clubs' owners argued that it would destabilize the financial position of their clubs and threaten the survival of some. Though the Bosman ruling applied to Mexico the Mexican FA were given three years' grace to comply with the new transfer rules. The three years drifted by without FIFA taking action to ensure that Mexico adhered to the new transfer system. Apparently, FIFA requested formally in 2001 that the Mexican FA adhere to FIFA regulations concerning player transfers, but this has been ignored so far. Eventually, the owners of the eighteen Premier League clubs agreed their own *pacto de caballeros* ("gentlemen's agreement"), established in 2003. This agreement determines that once a Mexican player's contract is ended, his club should still be consulted in any subsequent transfer and is entitled to a transfer fee, contrary to FIFA regulations (which determine that a player who is out of contract is free to sign for any club without any transfer fee being involved). This agreement—known also as "federal rights"—applies to Mexican players only. The "gentleman's agreement" is that no Mexican club will buy a Mexican player who is out of contract without negotiating a transfer fee with his former club. A player might be free to sign for any club outside Mexico, but cannot negotiate his own transfer within Mexico.

Even if the player goes overseas, on his return his new club would need the approval of his previous Mexican club. For example, Cruz Azul player, Aaron Galindo, was found guilty of drug-taking in the Confederations Cup in 2005 and was banned from playing football for a year. The club honoured his contract during the ban but at the end of the ban, as his contract was coming to an end, Galindo wanted to leave Cruz Azul. He left Mexico to play for Spanish club Hercules de Alicante in 2005. Cruz Azul believed their faith in the player had been betrayed and according to the "gentleman's agreement" he would not have been able to sign for any other club within Mexico. Since then, Mexican players who are out of contract are haggled over at the

"Mexican draft"—in effect a two-day annual transfer window in which most of the local player trading takes place. So Mexico ignores the usual transfer windows—prescribed by FIFA—and prefers a "draft" system organised by the FMF, whereby any transfers are negotiated by the owners of the 18 clubs in the top division over a two- or three-day period, usually in a warm, idyllic setting on the coast. This draft system, known colloquially as "the leg market," has been in place since 1990 and continues today despite FIFA's disapproval. The players are often not even consulted in the transfer process. Those who benefit are agents, the TV companies and even managers as talk of corruption is widespread (Huerta, 2008).

There is now a Players' Union, established in 2002 to protect players' rights. However, it falls under the auspices of the FMF so is unlikely to enjoy any real independence or bring real player power to Mexico, at least in the short term. It is, however, possible that FIFA may choose to intervene in the politics of football in Mexico, and this would bring a serious threat to the status quo of the Mexican football industry. If FIFA were to flex its muscles and insist that Mexico abandon its draft system and gentleman's agreement, there could be severe financial implications for Mexican football.

Question

1. What would be the financial implications to the Mexican football business if FIFA were to interfere in the transfer system in Mexico?

CONCLUSIONS

In this chapter the key issues which influence the commercial success of the Mexican football industry have been identified and the main challenges which determine its future direction have been indicated. It is important to contextualize the football business within its specific historical and cultural context, and in Mexico's case the exceptional role of the TV industry in the popularization of the sport led to a continued commercial relationship between football and TV. This chapter has highlighted ways in which this is reflected in the patterns of ownership and control within the governance of the game and in the structures and organisation of professional leagues.

It is apparent that the commercially astute structures and organisation of professional football attempt to maximize competitive balance. The demand for football and the quality of the product are currently high, but there are also signals that suggest that football should not be complacent and needs to work hard to maintain competitive balance and integrity, particularly in the current economic climate. The subject of integrity is particularly pertinent given the lack of transparency in governance and financial reporting. Ways in which Mexican football is addressing challenges have been analysed, with commercial developments at club level taking place—though embryonic in some cases—in terms of marketing, brand development, increased merchandising and stadia development. Looking forward, we might predict greater sophistication in marketing strategies, especially those relying on technology such as the Internet or mobile telephony, as skilled personnel attempt to professionalise the commercial aspects of the sport.

Finally, a situation analysis (or SWOT) has been used to draw together many of these ideas and to demonstrate how a situation analysis of a football industry can be undertaken. The information provided within this chapter will have provided the tools with which to analyse specific case studies such as those presented on the transfer system and the relationship between football and TV.

DISCUSSION QUESTIONS

1. Outline the current structure of domestic leagues in Mexico and discuss the potential merits and disadvantages both from a club's perspective and from the perspective of the TV companies of changing to a "European style" season in which each team plays each other twice and three teams are relegated from the Premier League to the first division.

2. Discuss the main challenges faced by the Mexican football industry and suggest ways in which they can be overcome.

3. Discuss the potential impact on the Mexican football industry of developments in technology.

GUIDED READING

There are very few resources on the Mexican football industry available in English. The best way to keep up-to-date with developments is via the (online) media: ESPN's Spanish language sports website *espndeportes.com* and *Expansión* generally provide well-researched articles on current developments in the Mexican football industry, although some knowledge of Spanish is an advantage if you want the more in-depth articles. On the academic front, Beech and Chadwick's *The Marketing of Sport* (2007) provides an excellent collection of articles on a range of issues relevant to the study of sports marketing. Of particular relevance to this chapter is Kitchen's contribution on 'Understanding the Sports Marketing Environment' (Chapter 4), which provides a useful overview of the main tools used by sports marketers to obtain information with which to analyse a particular sports marketing environment. As well as the SWOT analysis, Kitchen explains the ETOP and PESTLE techniques of "environmental scanning" (p. 80). Parker (2004) also provides a good introduction to using SWOT analysis in sports industries. Deloitte's *Latin American Football Money League, 2006–07* is also worth exploring and provides a useful comparison between the revenue streams of football clubs in the main Latin American football markets: Argentina, Brazil, Chile, Ecuador, Mexico, Uruguay.

ACKNOWLEDGMENTS

The authors would like to thank our colleague, Antonio Rosique, for his valuable advice on some of the background information provided in this chapter. We are also indebted to Efrén Cervantes Mendoza, MBA (Football Industries, University of Liverpool) candidate, for imparting his broad knowledge on the Mexican football business and in particular his research on the development of technology in football. However, all judgements and interpretation of information remain those of the authors.

REFERENCES

Angelotti Pasteur, G. (2005). La dinámicá del fútbol en México. Retrieved in August, 2008, from *Efdeportes.com: Revista Digital*, Año 10, No. 82. http://www.efdeportes.com/efd82/pachuca.htm.

AzCentral (11th April, 2008). Proponen cambiar format de Liguilla. *AzCentral*. Retrieved in June, 2009, from http://www.azcentral.com/lavoz/deportes/articles/041108revisan-CR.html

Beech, J., & Chadwick, S. (eds.) (2007). *The Marketing of Sport*. Harlow: Prentice Hall.

Beech, J., & Chadwick, S. (2004). *The Business of Sport Management*. London: Prentice Hall.

Castañeda Ramírez, A. (2006). Fútbol e investigación de mercados. *Asociación Mexicana de Agencias de Investigación de Mercado y Opinión Pública*. AMAI. Retrieved in August, 2008, from http://www.amai.org/pdfs/revista-amai/AMAI-14_art5.pdf.

CIA World Factbook (2008). *Mexico*. Retrieved in September, 2008, from https://www.cia.gov/library/publications/the-world-factbook/geos/mx.html.

Consulta Mitofsky (1st February, 2008). Fútbol en México: January 2008. *Sport Factory*. Retrieved in August, 2008, from http://www.dreamatchsolutions.com/pdfs/Sport-Factory-Febrero.pdf.

Deloitte (2007a). *Latin American Football Money League, 2006–07*. Deloitte. Retrieved in July, 2008, from http://www.deloitte.com/dtt/cda/doc/content/mx%28es-mx%29Football07_versionFINAL_191207.pdf.

Deloitte (2007b). *Annual Review of Football Finance*. Manchester: Deloitte.

El Economista (5th September, 2008). Chivas TV, una opción para el Guadalajara. *El Economista*. Retrieved in September 6, 2008, from http://economista.com.mx/articulos/2008-01-23-53963.

Estadio Chivas (2008). *Estadio Chivas Sitio Oficial*. Retrieved on September, 2008, from http://www.estadiochivas.com.mx/ventajas.php.

Expansión (2007). Football in Mexico: The sole monopoly in the world that loses money. August, pages 89–90. http://www.cnnexpansion.com/expansion

Expansión (2005). http://www.cnnexpansion.com/expansion

Federación Mexicana de Fútbol (FMF) (2008). Retrieved in August, 2008, from http://www.femexfut.org.mx/portalv2/(t1xcz13wf3plin3jlaatla55)/default.aspx?s=135).

FIFA (2008) *Mexico*. Retrieved in August, 2008, from http://www.fifa.com/associations/association=mex/ranking/gender=m/index.html.

Huerta, H. (2008). Investigación Especial: Amor a la Camiseta, Parte 1 *ESPN*. Retrieved in August, 2008, from http://sports.espn.go.com/broadband/video/videopage?videoId=3368144&categoryId=3269261&n8pe6c=1&brand=deportes, 24 April 2008.

Kitchen, P. (2007). Understanding the Sport Market Environment. In J. Beech, & S. Chadwick (Eds.), *The Marketing of Sport* (pp. 61–82). Harlow: Prentice Hall.

Magazine, R. (2007). Football Fandom and Identity in Mexico: the Case of the Pumas Football Club and Youthful Romanticism. In R. Miller, & L. Crolley (Eds.), *Football in the Americas: Fútbol, Futebol, Soccer*. London: Institute for the Study of the Americas.

Miller, R. (2007). Introduction: Studying Football in the Americas. In R. Miller, & L. Crolley (Eds.), *Football in the Americas: Fútbol, Futebol, Soccer* (pp. 1–36). London: Institute for the Study of the Americas.

Miller, R., & Crolley, L. (2007). *Football in the Americas: Fútbol, Futebol, Soccer*. London: Institute for the Study of the Americas.

Parker, C. (2004). Strategy and Environmental Analysis in Sport. In J. Beech, & S. Chadwick (Eds.), *The Business of Sport Management*. Harlow: Prentice Hall.

Rosique (Axteca TV) (2008). Personal communication with the authors, August 2008.

SportBusiness International. (2008). World Football League and TV Rights: SportBusiness Report. *SportBusiness International*. Retrieved in August, 2008, from http://www.sportbusiness.com/reports/160422/world-football-leagues-and-tv-rights

RECOMMENDED WEBSITES

CNN Spanish language news website
http://www.cnnexpansion.com/expansion
ESPN Spanish language sports news website
http://espndeportes.com

The Mexican Football Federation website
http://www.femexfut.org.mx
Mediotiempo's Spanish language sports news website
http://mediotiempo.com
Mediotiempo's Spanish language sports news messageboard
http://sportfactory.mediotiempo.com

CHAPTER 25

South Korea

Chong Kim
Hanyang University

Objectives

Upon completion of this chapter the reader should be able to:

- Understand the unique characteristics of football in Korea, how it is organised, and its revenue streams.
- Highlight the size of football industry in Korea.
- Determine the future prospects for football in Korea over the next 20 years.

CONTENTS

OVERVIEW OF THE CHAPTER

This chapter provides a general introduction to the football industry in Korea, focusing on the Korea Football Association and the professional league (K-League). The unique characteristics and scale of the Korean football industry will be described through their history, status, structure, profitability and operating system. Finally, the chapter provides an outlook for the future of Korea's football industry.

INTRODUCTION

Football was first introduced into Korea in 1882 (the 19th year of the reign of King Kojong) by the crew of the British battleship *Flying Horse,* which made a call at Port Incheon. A look at an ancient historical document called "The

History of Three Kingdoms," however, reveals that Koreans in ancient times had a ball game called "Chuk-guk," which was very similar in form to contemporary football. As such, football is one of the oldest and most celebrated sports in Korea. As a sport that can be enjoyed without special equipment, football became instantly popular among the general public at that time. Moreover, the highly competitive and strongly physical nature of the game struck a chord with the Korean people (*kfa.or.kr*).

The Korea Football Association (KFA) is the governing body for all football-related activities in Korea. The KFA was established on September 19, 1933. Disbanded by the Japanese colonial authorities, it made a fresh start in September 4, 1948 soon after the country achieved liberation in 1945. In the same year, the KFA became a member of FIFA with the official acronym of KTA, followed by its membership of the AFC (Asian Football Confederation) in 1954 (*kfa.or.kr*).

ORGANIZATION OF THE KOREA FOOTBALL ASSOCIATION (KFA)

A special feature of the structure of the KFA is that it has the Korea Professional Football League (K-League) under its wing. Although financially independent, the KFA still holds a significant influence on key decision-making matters related to the K-League (Figure 25.1).

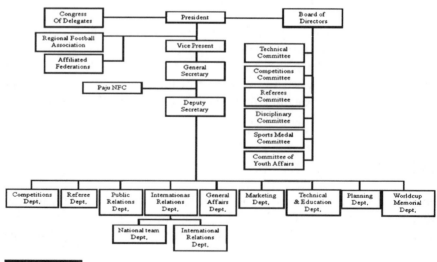

FIGURE 25.1 *Organization of KFA.*

THE REVENUE OF THE KOREA FOOTBALL ASSOCIATION

The KFA's income can be divided into two types: public sources including government subsidies and donations, and business-related income including TV rights fees, gate receipts, advertising, leasing, sponsorship, and so on. In 2008, the KFA's financial independence from public funds had reached 74.7 percent, which is high compared to that of other South Korean sports associations which is typically about 10 to 20 percent. This demonstrates the popularity of football in Korea (Table 25.1).

FIFA WORLD CUP AND KOREAN FOOTBALL

A description of the Korean football landscape would be incomplete without mention of its World Cup performances. Korea has set the Asian record for the most World Cup appearances by qualifying for the World Cup Finals a total of seven times and also achieving the most consecutive World Cup appearances in Asia (six times), from the 1986 Mexico World Cup to the 2006 German World Cup. Most of all, Korea caught the world by surprise by reaching the semifinals at the 2002 World Cup, which was hosted simultaneously by South Korea and Japan (*kfa.or.kr*).

Through the 2002 World Cup, Korea reaped a considerable profit, provoking an impressive jump of 0.74 percent in the country's economic growth. The effect of hosting the World Cup was multifaceted: first, the

Table 25.1	The Revenue of Korea Football Association (Cost Unit: million USD)	
	2007	**2008**
Government subsidy	10.6	13
Broadcasting rights	3	7.4
Gate receipt (A-match)	4.4	7.5
Advertising	0.7	2.7
Sponsorship Revenue	22	14.9
Leasing	0.9	0.3
Donation	2.2	2.5
Others	2.8	3.1
Total	46.6	51.4

Source: *KFA Official Homepage* (www.kfa.or.kr).

increase in investment and consumption; second, numerous intangible benefits, such as increased awareness of the benefits of new leadership such as that demonstrated by the national team head-coach, the Dutchman Gus Hiddink; and third, consolidation of citizens' national spirit ("We can do it") and confidence. In conclusion, the 2002 World Cup served as an opportunity for Korean football to make a leap both in size and in quality. Along with this growth, the construction of infrastructure and an expanded fan base has made the future of football in Korea a bright one.

WOMEN'S FOOTBALL IN KOREA

While the men's national team has been at the top of Asia for quite some time, women's football in Korea has a relatively short history. It was in the early 1990s when women's club teams were first founded and the total number of teams currently includes: 26 elementary school clubs, 19 middle school clubs, 18 high school clubs, 6 university clubs, and 5 semiprofessional clubs. Thanks to continued efforts and investment, the standard of women's football in Korea has grown rapidly and the women's national teams at various age levels have reached the top class in the Asian region (*kfa.or.kr*).

AMATEUR FOOTBALL IN KOREA

Amateur football is the backbone of Korean football. With a view to encouraging young footballers to focus on school work while playing, the KFA is putting great efforts into activating the regional league system for junior players. The KFA is planning to combine various existing tournaments organised at the elementary school, middle and high school levels by 2010 and replace them with regional leagues, where the top teams of the leagues play against one another to determine the champion (*kfa.or.kr*).

FOOTBALL CLUBS AND PLAYERS IN KOREA

The number of football clubs and football players can be a proxy for the size of the football industry within the country. In the case of Korea, players are trained and nurtured through an elite sports system. Given this background, one can legitimately argue that the 14 football clubs belonging to

Table 25.2	Team Registry Status 2008					
	Elementary School	Middle School	High School	College/ University	K2	Total
Men's	245	168	120	69	N/A	602
Women's	26	19	18	6	4	73

* K2: The League of Women's Amateur Clubs

	K-League	N-League	Under-12	Under-15	Under-18	Over-19	Total
Clubs	14	11	80	17	42	61	225

Source: *KFA Official Homepage (www.kfa.or.kr)*.

the K-League is significant by comparison with the size of its second league or the amateur leagues. Since the 2002 World Cup finals, the KFA has set up numerous youth clubs to strengthen the grass roots structure for the sport, but compared to the strong and large size of the K-League, the grass roots structure is still relatively weak (Tables 25.2 and 25.3).

THE INTRODUCTION OF THE K-LEAGUE

Asia's first professional league, the Korea Professional Football League (now called the "K-League") was launched in 1983 under the name "Super League," with two professional clubs and three amateur clubs.

Table 25.3	Player Registry Status 2008					
	Elementary School	Middle School	High School	College/ University	K2	Total
Men's	6,607	6,019	4,387	2,045	N/A	19,058
Women's	524	401	392	149	100	1,566

* K2: The League of Women's Amateur Clubs

	K-League	N-League	Under-12	Under-15	Under-18	Over-19	Total
Clubs	543	327	1,835	322	991	1,742	5,760

Source: *KFA Official Homepage (www.kfa.or.kr)*.

Encouraging the spread of professional football leagues to its neighboring countries, the Super League in Korea contributed tremendously to the development of football in Asia. It also provided a firm stepping stone for the Korean national football team to compete effectively in international competitions. Having made remarkable progress for the past quarter-century since its inception, the K-League now has 14 official member clubs (*k-leaguei.co.kr*).

Comprised of professional clubs and amateur clubs in the early years, the K-League reinvented itself as an entirely professional league in 1987, by grouping five full professional clubs (Daewoo, Pohang, Yukong, Hyundai and LG). Buoyed by the national team's consecutive World Cup appearances and the growing popularity of football, the K-League assigned each member club a home base, allowing them to use the names of their home cities in their club designations. It was only in 1998 the term *K-League* became commonly used among the Korean people (*k-leaguei.co.kr*).

ORGANIZATION OF THE K-LEAGUE

At the time of writing, the K-League did not operate on the basis of a promotion-relegation system, as in English football. Hence, the second league (N-League) and the third league (K3-League) operate independently of the K-League (Figure 25.2).

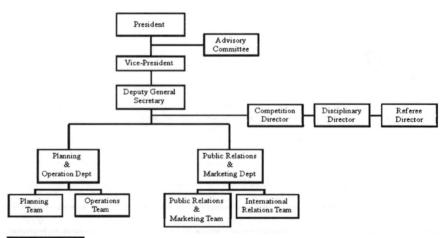

FIGURE 25.2 *Organisation of the K-League.*

Table 25.4	The Status of the K-League Clubs			
	Franchised City	**Owner**	**Foundation**	**Years of Championships**
Jeju United FC	Jeju	SK	1983	89
Pohang Steelers	Pohang	Posco	1984	86, 88, 92, 07
Busan I'Park	Busan	Hyundai	1984	84, 87, 91, 97
FC Seoul	Seoul	GS	1984	85, 90, 00
Ulsan Hyundai Horang-i	Ulsan	Hyundai	1984	96, 05
Seongnam Ilhwa Chunma	Seongnam	Ilhwa	1989	93, 94, 95, 01, 02, 03, 06
Chunnam Dragons	Gwangyang	Posco	1994	
Chonbuk Hyundai Motors	Chunju	Hyundai Motors	1995	
Suwon Samsung Bluewings	Suwon	Samsung	1996	98, 99, 04
Daejeon Citizen	Daejeon	Citizen club	1997	
Daegu FC	Daegu	Citizen club	2003	
Gwangju Sangmu Phoenix	Gwangju	Military	2003	
Incheon United	Incheon	Citizen club	2004	
Gyeongnam FC	Chang won	Citizen club	2006	

Source: *Yoo (2004).*

THE K-LEAGUE FOOTBALL CLUB

Of the 14 K-League clubs, four are publicly owned (citizen clubs) and nine are corporate clubs. The nine corporate clubs effectively serve as marketing tools to promote corporate brands. The reason why there are so many corporate clubs is because during the early stages of the Korean football league, companies came under direct political pressure to participate in the league. However, one of the most striking features of the K-League is that it contains a military football club Gwangju Sangmu Phoenix. This can be seen as a special concession to Korean male athletes who must fulfill two years of obligatory military duty when they turn 20 years of age (Table 25.4).

THE REVENUE FOR THE K-LEAGUE

The major source of income for the K-League comes from TV rights, title sponsorship, other types of sponsorships, licensing, and so on. Such income is primarily used to finance the operations of the K-League, with the remaining sum given out equally to the 14 clubs regardless of their performance.

REVENUE FOR CLUBS

Club income sources can be mainly divided into three types: K-League subsidies, including TV rights and official sponsorship; owners' grants; and ticket sales. As just indicated, the revenue structure as it stands today is relatively simple, and total revenue size is relatively small. About 60 percent of club revenue is derived from the owners' grants, which also includes an advertising fee from the owners' companies. Between 60 and 70 percent of club revenue is paid out through the salaries of the players, while marketing expenses are negligible. This can be attributed to the fact that clubs opted for a focus on optimising the number of games won rather than increasing profits (Tables 25.5 and 25.6).

K-LEAGUE CLUBS' USE OF STADIA

Ten new stadia were constructed right before the 2002 World Cup finals and have become important assets for football in Korea. These stadia will decide the future of the Korean football industry. However, one factor influencing the professional football clubs' profitability is the stadium rental fee paid out to the Korean local government authorities that own these football facilities.

Currently, only two professional teams have their own stadia and use them exclusively for football: Pohang Steelers and Chunnam Dragons. This makes it very difficult for the professional clubs to conduct marketing activities using the stadia and to create diverse channels through which they can generate additional revenue (Table 25.7).

Table 25.5	Revenue Source of K-League Clubs (Based on Data from 10 Clubs in 2006)
Contents	**Rates (percent)**
Advertising revenues:	24.7
Sponsorship	3.9
Licensing	1.2
K-League subsidy	2.6
Ticket sales	3.5
Player trading fee/Player lease fee	11.6
Owners' grants	33.9
Others	18.6
Total	100.0

Source: *K-League (2007), Vision Project K.*

Table 25.6	Expenditure of K-League Clubs (Based on Data from 10 Clubs in 2006)
Contents	**Rates (percent)**
Salaries of staffs and players	65.2
Marketing promotion	2.2
Training	2.0
Stadium rental	2.8
Road trip expenses	1.5
Administrative overhead	11.4
General operational expenses	14.8
Total	100.0

Source: *K-League (2007), Vision Project K.*

Table 25.7	K-League Clubs' Use of Stadia		
Team	**City**	**Stadium**	**Capacity**
Jeju United FC	Jeju	Jeju World Cup Stadium	42,256
Pohang Steelers	Pohang	Pohang football stadium	18,960
Busan I'Park	Busan	Busan Asiad Stadium	53,926
FC Seoul	Seoul	Seoul World Cup Stadium	64,728
Ulsan Hyundai Horang-i	Ulsan	Ulsan Munsu Stadium	43,606
Seongnam Ilhwa Chunma	Seongnam	Tancheon Sports Complex	16,000
Chunnam Dragons	Gwangyang	Gwangyang football stadium	13,496
Chonbuk Hyundai Motors	Jeonju	Jeonju World Cup Stadium	42,477
Suwon Samsung Bluewings	Suwon	Suwon Big Bird Stadium	43,138
Daejeon Citizen	Daejeon	Daegu World Cup Stadium	65,857
Daegu FC	Daegu	Daejeon World Cup Stadium	40,782
Gwangju Sangmu Phoenix	Gwangju	Gwangju World Cup Stadium	43,121
Incheon United	Incheon	Incheon Munhak Stadium	50,256
Gyeongnam FC	Chang won	Changwon Civil Stadium	27,085

Source: *Yoo (2004).*

CHANGE IN THE NUMBER OF FOOTBALL SPECTATORS IN THE PAST

The K-League kicked off in 1983, quickly achieving an average number of 20,000 spectators per game. However, this number dwindled to a half of that figure in the following year. The stagnation continued throughout most of the early 1990s, which was aggravated by an International Monetary Fund crisis in the middle of the 1990s in Korea. However, the number of spectators started to pick up again in 1998 with the emergence of young star players. The biggest "leap-forward" happened in 2002, as the Korean national team advanced to the semifinals of the World Cup causing a football fever among the public. It was then that football began being recognised as an industry (Yoo, 2004). However, people paid an unusually strong amount of attention to professional football right after the World Cup finals, indicating that the public attention level for professional teams fluctuates depending upon the relative success or failure of the national team. Considering Korean people's sentiments (it might be argued that they have a strong tendency toward being nationalistic), the Korean national team remains consistently popular whilst the popularity of the professional club teams ebbs and flows over time (see Table 25.8).

LEVEL OF COMPETITION IN THE K-LEAGUE

The competition structure in the K-League has been relatively stable over the past 26 years, although it has evolved and continues to do so. The continuous changing and upgrading of the K-League's structure can be interpreted as a sign of growth, but it also serves as a probable cause for the restricted growth in popularity of the league. The conclusion to the competition as of 2008 is a series of playoffs amongst six finalists.

ROSTER SYSTEM OF THE K-LEAGUE

Currently the K-League selects players largely through a draft system, which is very unusual for football throughout the world. The reason behind opting for the draft system is to make the skill levels at each of the clubs as even as possible, thus making professional football as competitive as possible (see Table 25.9).

Table 25.8	Change in the Number of Football Spectators in the Past/K-League				
Year	Game	No. of Team	Total Attendance	Average Attendance	Appendix
1983	40	5(2)	838,956	20,974	Record (Average)
1984	114	8(2)	1,051,446	9,223	
1985	84	8(2)	452,972	5,393	
1986	102	6	344,028	3,373	
1987	78	5	341,330	4,376	
1988	60	5	360,650	6,011	
1989	120	6	778,000	6,483	
1990	90	6	527,850	5,865	
1991	121	6	1,480,127	12,232	
1992	123	6	1,353,573	11,005	
1993	105	6	851,190	8,107	
1994	126	7	893,217	7,089	
1995	144	8	1,516,514	10,531	
1996	182	9	1,911,347	10,502	
1997	180	10	1,218,836	6,771	
1998	185	10	2,179,288	11,780	
1999	191	10	2,752,953	14,413	Record (Total)
2000	190	10	1,909,839	10,052	
2001	181	10	2,306,861	12,745	
2002	181	10	2,651,901	14,651	
2003	265	12	2,448,868	9,241	
2004	240	13	2,429,422	10,123	
2005	240	13	2,873,351	11,972	
2006	275	14	2,448,128	8,806	

Source: *K-League Official Homepage* (www.k-leaguei.com).

CONCLUSIONS

The K-League currently has ambitious plans to develop into a world-class professional league by, for example, introducing the promotion-relegation system in the National League (second division). The K-League anticipates, over the next twenty years, achieving 10 million spectators, and a tenfold increase in current revenues, garnered by strengthening the role of the K-League, integrating the marketing rights, establishing a win-win relationship between local governorates and football clubs and gradually changing the business models of each club. The 20-year stretch targets of the Vision Project K are shown in Table 25.10.

Table 25.9	Regulation of Players' Management
	Contents
Contract fee	Contract fee is not paid to those players who are signing for the first time as a professional or free agent players, or to players who are extending a contract period with the same team.
	For foreign players, the contract fee as well as performance bonus (linked to numbers of participating matches and number of scored goals etc.) can be paid.
Preferred appointment	Annually about 4 players from the clubs can be preferentially appointed from outside the draft.
Draft	**1.** The order of appointment can be decided by lot.
	2. The required contracting period for rookies is 1 or 3 years.
Salary cap	None
The period to win free agency	1 to 3 years.
	(For those players who have made their first contract as professionals before 2005, they must have participated in more than 50 percent of matches in a year for 1–3 years to earn a free agency right.)
Restrictions on the numbers of players in one team	None
Restrictions on the number of foreign players.	Up to three players in one team. Up to three players in one match

Source: *K-League (2007), Vision Project K.*

The K-League is currently making active efforts to raise the profile of Korean professional football by promoting exchanges with the professional leagues in China and Japan. Korean professional football showcased its sporting strength when the K-League Champions, Seongnam Ilhwa, Suwon Samsung and Ulsan Hyundai, won the A3 Tournament and the three-nation

| Table 25.10 | The 20-Year Stretch Targets of the Vision Project K |

	Number of Spectators (millions)	Number of Football Clubs	Average Salary ($ million)	Total Revenue of the League (Excluding Subsidy) ($ million)	Total Expenditure of the League ($ million)	Profit/Deficit ($ million)
2007	2.5	14 Clubs	0.95	46.7	187.7	−141
2027	11	36 Clubs (K1/K2)	1.5–2.6 (K-1)	420	370	+50 (min.)

Source: *K-League (2007), Vision Project K.*

professional league tournaments involving China, Japan and Korea, three times in a row from 2004 to 2006 (k-leaguei.co.kr). The A3 tournament was conceived in 2003 after Korea, Japan, and China agreed on the necessity of creating a common platform to promote football and to cultivate players' skills in the region. Since then, they have gone beyond their original intention to strengthen their reciprocal interaction by forming an inter-country competition, and they are pressing forward with plans that aspire to make it as successful as the European Champions League. Korea and the K-League stand at the centre of this long-term project.

CASE STUDY 25.1: South Korea and its relationship with European Football

It is clear that there is a strong passion for European football in South Korea. In July 2007, a friendly match between F.C. Seoul and Manchester United F.C., part of an Asian promotional tour by United, was attended by 65,000 people. During the Peace Cup Final in 2007 held in Seoul, the final between Bolton Wanderers and Olympique Lyonnais attracted 56,218 spectators. Yet, the average attendance at F.C. Seoul home games in 2006 was only 21,642 and an average of only 11,972 people attended each match in the K-League.

The German Bundesliga was the first televised European football league in South Korea in the mid-1970s. Now European football matches are broadcast live by several sports channels in South Korea. There are four sports channels, namely KBS N Sports, MBC ESPN, SBS Sports, and Xports. Apart from Xports, each channel broadcasts live coverage of matches from various European leagues, through exclusive contracts each broadcaster has with European leagues. MBC ESPN televises English Premier League, English FA Cup, German Bundesliga, UEFA Champions League, and the UEFA Cup. KBS N Sports has rights to telecast Italian Serie A and Spanish Premera Liga, but French Le Championnat and Dutch Eredivigie are broadcast by SBS Sports.

Each of the channels broadcasts live European football with two to six matches on every weekend and one or two mid week. These sports channels are able to be viewed through cable or satellite television.

Source: Thanks to June Kyu Choi (Choi, 2007) for providing some of the information contained in this case study.

Questions

1. Do you think South Korean people's interest in European football is a hindrance to domestic football or a stimulant that will help it grow?

2. In the light of your answer to question 1, what challenges do you think football administrators in South Korea face in ensuring the successful development of football in the country?

3. In the light of your answers to questions 1 and 2, what measures would you propose to the South Korean football authorities in order that professional and amateur football develops and prospers, while the national team continues to grow in stature?

DISCUSSION QUESTIONS

1. Compared to other countries, what are the unique characteristics of Korean football and the K-League?
2. What problems do you think the Korean football industry has?
3. What might be an effective strategy to develop the football industry in Korea?
4. What are the advantages and disadvantages of the three Asian nations Korea, China, and Japan operating an integrated league?
5. Assess the prospects for the future development of Asian football?

GUIDED READING

The reader is directed to the official websites of both the Korean Football Association, and the K-League. Both provide an overview of South Korean football, as well as in-depth data about the nature, structure and organization of South Korean Football. Readers will also find it helpful to look at the chapter written by Chang: "Sponsorship, Marketing and Professional Football: The Case of South Korea" in the book edited by Desbordes (2007).

REFERENCES

Chang, D.-R. (2007). Sponsorship, Marketing and Professional Football: The Case of South Korea. In Michel Desbordes (Ed.), *Marketing and Football: An International Perspective*. Oxford, UK: Butterworth Heinemann.

Choi, J. (2007). *Motivational Factors and Team Identification of European Football Fans in South Korea*. Unpublished MSc Dissertation; Birkbeck College, University of London.

kfa.or.kr. Korean Football Association. *www.kfr.or.kr*

K-League. (2007). *Vision Project K*. Seoul, South Korea: K-League.

k-leaguei.com. k-leaguei. *www.k-leaguei.com*

Yoo, Eui-Dong (2004). *How to use professional sports to promote regional economy*. Seoul, South Korea: Korea Institute of Sport Science.

RECOMMENDED WEBSITES

Korean Football Association
www.kfa.or.kr
Korean K-League
www.k-leaguei.comK-League

Glossary

Administration   In Chapter 8, the word *Administration* is used in a specific legal way. A club entering Administration is placing itself in the hands of a court-appointed Administrator in order to achieve protection from its creditors. The Administrator is tasked with taking over the running of the club with a view to placing it on a firmer financial footing and ultimately rescuing it. In this situation, the company may not be wound up without the court's permission. The state of Administration thus offers both hope and protection to the insolvent club. The appointment of an Administrator may be initiated by either the club or one or more of its creditors. A common outcome of Administration with a football club is the sale of the club to new owners.

Agent   A person who plays the role of middleman in the context of a deal between commercial partners. In football, agents mainly work on players' transfers from one club to another.

Alliance   An agreement between two or more clubs to work together, usually from different countries.

Alternative Investment Market (AIM)   A market regulated by the London Stock Exchange (LSE). However, the regulatory requirements are not as strict or expensive as on the main stock exchange (the LSE).

Ambush marketing   An entity or organization that is not actually a financial sponsor attempts to give the impression that it is in fact a sponsor, thereby gaining a financial advantage by the perceived association with the individual, team, or event.

Apartheid   Apartheid was the political system that existed in South Africa from 1948 to 1994. This system, based on a racist ideology of racially separate development, identified four major racial groups (whites, blacks, coloureds and Indians) and took the form of institutionalised racist discrimination and oppression against the non-white population in which they were denied the full citizenship accorded to the white population. This institutionalised racist discrimination applied equally in the field of sport. Apartheid is defined as a criminal system in international law, and whilst the system existed South Africa was the subject of an international campaign of trade and other, including sporting, sanctions which meant that the country was not allowed to participate in almost all international sporting competitions. The apartheid system was finally brought to an end in 1994 when, in South Africa's first ever free elections, the African National Congress political party, which had led the opposition to apartheid within South Africa, achieved a majority in the election and formed the country's first democratically elected government. Its leader, the Nobel Peace Prize winner and former political prisoner Nelson Mandela, became the country's president with a new constitution affording equal citizenship to all.

Atmospherics   The ambience of the shop, encompassing visual, aural, olfactory, tactile, physical, and human (staff) attributes designed to provide an overall sense of the shop.

Benefactor   A benefactor is an individual who provides large amounts of funding to a club. While this funding is normally in the form of "soft debt" from the club's perspective, this may change over time.

Black whistle   A scandal involving the bribery of Chinese referees.

Bosman ruling   A legal decision by the European Court of Justice in 1995. The ruling deemed illegal both the payment of transfer fees for players who were out of contract and so-called "quota systems," whereby only a limited number of foreign EU players were allowed to play in a national league club match.

Brand equity   Brand equity is the value, both tangible and intangible, that a brand adds to a product or service. According to the literature, it encompasses, from a consumer-based perspective: brand awareness, brand associations, perceived quality, and brand loyalty.

Brand identity   The brand identity is a unique set of associations that an organisation aspires to create or maintain. These associations represent what the brand should stand for and imply a potential promise to customers. The brand identity refers to the strategic goal intended for the brand by the organisation.

Branding   Branding is a strategy through which an organization articulates a clear vision of its identity (or personality) with a set of specific brand attributes (or values), and defines a unique positioning in the market. Branding allows an organization to differentiate themselves from the competition and, consequently, to bond with their customers in order to create loyalty.

Bridgehead   A person who binds together two networks that are largely separated one from the other. In the football industry, this person, often an agent, maintains a strategic advantage to manage players' transfers.

British Olympic Association   The independent voice for British Olympic Sport, liaising with the various Olympic bodies and the focus for "Team GB."

Broadcasting rights   The rights to broadcast football matches in various forms: live; highlights; clips etc. In English football these rights belong to the appropriate league, which negotiates with the broadcasting company, and then distributes the proceeds among the clubs of the league.

Bundesliga   The first division of the German footall league.

Civil law   The body of private law in common law jurisdictions. Typically this deals with areas of law such as contract and tort between individuals, with penalties designed to compensate those who have been wronged by an act.

Comarketing (cooperative marketing)   The process by which two or more entities, private or public, one of which is strictly identifiable as being part of a sports organization, cooperate to develop planned, organized, controlled marketing activities in order to achieve marketing objectives, which may be common or specific but mutually compatible, through the satisfaction of the customers.

Combined code   A requirement for companies listed on the London Stock Exchange (LSE) to either comply or explain noncompliance with the principles and provisions of the Code. It was introduced in 1998, taking into account the recommendations and the principles of good corporate governance from previous reports on corporate governance and revised in 2003 and 2006.

Commercial sports partner   Companies interested in cooperating with sport organization for sponsorship and commercial reasons.

Commercialisation   A phase in the evolution of a sport as business in which the professionalised sport and its organisations form business relationships with organisations outside the sport, such as sponsors, broadcasters, endorsers etc.

Consolidation   Process through which the size of firms in a particular economic sector of the economy expands. This occurs through vertical (mergers) or horizontal (joint ventures) integration.

Consumer sports market   People interested in buying sports experiences for personal reasons.

Corporate naming   In recent decades, to help take the burden of the massive expense of building and maintaining a stadium, many American sports teams have sold the rights to the name of the facility. This trend, which began in the 1970s but accelerated greatly in the 1990s, has led to sponsors' names being affixed to both established stadia and new ones. In some cases, the corporate name replaces (with varying degrees of success) the name by which the venue has been known for many years—for example, Toronto's Rogers Centre, previously known as SkyDome. But many of the more recently-built baseball parks, such as Milwaukee's Miller Park, have never been known by a non-corporate name. The sponsorship phenomenon has since spread worldwide. There remain a few municipally owned stadia, which are often known by a name that is significant to their area (for example, Minneapolis' Hubert H. Humphrey Metrodome). In recent years, some government-owned stadia have also been subject to naming-rights agreements, with some or all of the revenue often going to the team(s) that play there.

Corporate social responsibility   CSR refers to the involvement by private businesses in social or charitable programmes for the benefit of the wider community.

Costs   All cash flows out of the club.

Criminal law   Body of law within a given jurisdiction, enforceable by the State, with penalties designed primarily to punish the offender.

Cuju   An ancient Chinese game accepted by FIFA as providing the origins for football.

Customer Relationship Management (CRM)   CRM refers to techniques within a business plan which involve attracting, maintaining and strengthening relations with customers.

Director of Football   A person appointed at the level of the Board of Directors of a club to oversee the commercial aspects of and arrangements for player transfers.

Distribution channels   The routes along which products (and their ownership) travel from production to consumption.

Dominant paradigm   The most frequently cited model way of thinking.

Experiential marketing   Experiential marketing attempts to connect consumers with brands in personally relevant and memorable ways. It presents an experience that people choose to attend to and participate in after identifying the relevance of a brand or product to their needs.

Fit and proper test   The "fit and proper" person test is to prevent an individual from becoming a director or owner of a football club if he or she does not meet the necessary criteria, notably if they previously have a criminal conviction.

Football club   Originally, football clubs were entirely membership organisations, where members paid an annual subscription to fund operations, and day-to-day decisions were made by a club committee who could be voted out at an annual general meeting. In some countries, this system is still preserved for the larger clubs (e.g., Barcelona and Real Madrid in Spain, and most of the German clubs), but elsewhere clubs have become limited liability companies with shareholders. While in the United Kingdom this has enabled clubs to operate almost like any other business, in other countries rules have been specially devised to limit the commercial freedom of sporting limited companies (e.g., in France and Spain).

Football league   A format for competition among football clubs. The organisation of leagues typically involves some centralised functions (e.g., scheduling) which require someone to take responsibility. In professional leagues, these operations can be quite diverse and complex (e.g., disciplinary procedures or the negotiation of broadcast rights). In these cases, a league body is usually created to take decisions. The league may be owned by the clubs themselves or owned by the governing body or may be created as an independent entity.

Governance   Governance refers to the rules and institutions surrounding the organisation of an activity. Any social activity requires a means of coordination among individuals and groups to avoid conflict and ensure that the benefits of cooperation are realised. Governance systems work best with the consent of the governed, and this usually requires that all interests be represented and valued. When governance breaks down, groups that feel their interests are not being represented tend to seek out organisational independence.

Governing body   An organisation created to provide services to its members, to agree rules and administrative procedure for ensuring the observance of rules, and on the imposition of penalties when the rules are broken. Governing bodies may be created from below—that is, by agreement among founder members (as in the case of the FA)—or from above above—that is, by government fiat (as in the case of China or in the former Communist regimes of Eastern Europe). The operations of a governing body in sport, as in the broader political system, always involves a balance of competing interests, whose influence is usually determined by their relative economic and political power.

Grassroots football   Football played and organised outside of professional structures.

Grassroots marketing   Grassroots marketing consists in delivering important organisational messages to key audiences where they live, work, and play. It intends to develop strong and meaningful relationships, as well as increasing loyalty and brand awareness among the main target audiences of the organisation. An important aspect is the "word-of-mouth" phenomenon, which provides additional marketing value, as the organisation becomes part of regular conversations.

Holding company   A company that owns several others, normally set up for this purpose.

Human Resource Management (HRM)   Essentially a business-oriented philosophy designed to obtain value from employees, who are viewed as assets, which increases competitive advantage in the marketplace.

Industrial and Provident Society (IPS)   A mutual, not-for-profit organisation without share capital. An IPS is often used by cooperatives, social enterprises, and mutual investment companies. It remains democratic through the one member, one vote status, with additional features including the explicit commitment to community benefit and the use of profits to improve services or facilities.

Intermediary   An organisation or business, such as a wholesaler, that provides support functions in linking distribution activities.

Inventory or stock   Unsold products.

Licence to operate   Support and interest from an organisation's publics that allows the organisation to exist and function.

Limited company   A company in which the liability of the members and shareholders is limited to the amount that they have invested.

Logistics mix   The activities of inventory, storage facilities, communications, unitisation, and packaging, and transport, which require management to meet cost and service demands.

Logistics service provider   An organisation that provides logistics management activities to other organisations.

London Stock Exchange (LSE)   A market where shares in public listed companies (PLCs) are traded. The LSE is the main stock exchange in the United Kingdom.

Merchandise   Goods bought and sold in a business. Team merchandise can include shirts with the team and sponsor's logo and any other item that can be "branded" with the name of the sponsor to create brand familiarity and recognition and ultimately increase financial gain for the sponsor.

Merchandising   Goods sold to its fans by a club that bear the club's logo and, where appropriate, the logo of a club sponsor. The most common example is a replica kit.

Merchandising   Merchandising refers to the methods, practices, and operations conducted to promote and sustain certain categories of commercial activity, regional, national, and international. It is the practice in which the brand or image from one product or service is used to sell another. The list of products in the football business includes but is not limited to flags and banners, scarves and caps, training gear, jerseys and fleeces, footballs, videos and DVDs, blankets and pillows, watches, lamps, tables, clocks and signs, and so on.

Mutually beneficial relationship   A two-way relationship that gives participants an equal share, something that is at the heart of public relations.

Naming rights   Rights granted to an individual or corporate identity to name a building, facility, or event in exchange for some financial consideration. Traditionally, naming rights have long been associated with institutions such as universities, hospitals, even schools, where the financial contribution secures the right to have the donor's name ascribed to the facility.

Occupancy   The extent to which the full capacity of a stadium is utilised.

OFEX   A regulated share market formed in 1995 to provide a facility for share trading for unlisted companies. It became the PLUS market in 2006.

Outsourcing   The use of logistics service providers to provide some or all of the required logistics mix activities.

Parachute payment   A special payment made by the English Premiership to relegated clubs. The payment softens the financial blow of losing Premiership status. At present it is paid for the two years after a club is relegated in the event they are not promoted at the first attempt.

Platforms of sponsorship   Different types or levels of sponsorship are known as platforms. Examples of platforms include sponsorship of clubs, leagues, events, tournaments, individual player endorsements, or stadium naming rights.

Player draft   A strategy for trying to ensure the preservation of competitive balance in a sports league; entails a central, coordinating authority allocating players to different teams across a league so that talent is equitably distributed; designed to ensure that no one team can acquire a significant proportion of the best, most-talented players.

Players' representation business   The various activities related to the management of football players' professional careers, from negotiation of contracts to personal brand building.

PLC   A Public limited company.

PLUS market   Formerly the OFEX, the PLUS market is a London-based stock exchange for small companies. PLUS is a "recognised investment exchange" that is regulated by the Financial Services Authority, which ensures that it is a competitive stock exchange.

Professional football   Professional football means football where the players are paid. Professional footballers are paid out of the revenue generated by the sale of tickets, merchandising and broadcasting rights. Professional football inevitably requires that football is organised along commercial lines, be it in leagues, clubs or governing bodies (which organise commercial competitions such as the World Cup). Professional football therefore inevitably gives rise to a conflict between commercial and noncommercial goals.

Publics   This generic word is used exclusively in public relations to mean all those groups and/or individuals with whom an organisation wishes to engage in a relationship.

Quiniela   The state-run betting system in Spain, similar to the football pools in the United Kingdom.

Relational capital   Set of social relations that an actor can mobilise to reach an objective, such as, in the agents' case, the placement of a player in a club.

Retailing   The sale of products, normally individually or in small quantities, to a final consumer.

Revenues   All cash flows into the club. Most of these arise from the fans of the club, either directly in the form of tickets and merchandising or indirectly in the form of broadcasting rights.

Season tickets holders   A season ticket is a ticket that grants privileges over a defined period of time. In sport, a season ticket is a ticket that grants the holder access to all regular-season home games for one season without additional charges.

Segmentation   A tool used by businesses, especially marketers, to break up their market into groups or segments with similar characteristics, often so that they can be targeted by marketing campaigns in a meaningful way. Segmentation might take place according to socio-demographic variables such as age, sex, marital status, or according to lifestyle factors, such as club supported, and so forth.

Specificity   A European Commission concept relating to sport, holding that there are specific characteristics of sport which require specific attention in the framing of laws. These include gender issues, competitive balance, restrictions on the number of participants, the organisation of sport around national associations and pyramid league structures.

Sponsorship   An important marketing tool utilised by corporations. They obtain a commercial advantage by gaining rights or association with a particular individual, team, or event. It can be seen as a reciprocal arrangement, where those being sponsored receive funding (for ongoing team costs such as development costs), resources (such as the team kit), or services (training facilities, support services, etc.) and the sponsoring corporation receives the financial benefit from its strong visual imprint on the team or individual.

Sport marketing   Sport marketing is a form of marketing in which brands use mainstream or alternative sports and the figures associated with these sports to connect with both a broad and targeted group of consumers. Examples of sport marketing include athlete endorsements, event marketing, sponsorship, as well as the strategic construction of sport team brands, and so on.

Sport mega-events   Major international sport competitions which involve elite participants, and which draw high volumes of media coverage, corporate sponsorships and attention. The FIFA World Cup and the Olympic Games are the two prime events on the mega-event calendar.

Sportscape   The summation of elements, both tangible and intangible, derived from the "servicescape" concept, which represent the surrounds of a service experience in a sporting stadia context.

Stock market/stock exchange   A market in which shares in companies are bought and sold and prices vary due to supply and demand. The three main markets in the United Kingdom are the LSE, the AIM, and the PLUS.

Supply chain   The organisations involved in the production and distribution of products and services.

Supporters trust   A supporter trust is an independent, not-for-profit democratic organisation that seeks to influence the governance of a football club through improved supporter representation, and also develop stronger links among a club, a community, and a supporter base.

SWOT analysis   A situation tool used by organisations to identify the (internal) strengths and weaknesses and (external) opportunities and threats with the goal of planning a strategy.

Unique selling proposition (USP)   The factor or consideration presented by a seller as the reason that one product or service is different from and better than that of the competition. In other words, it is the unique product (or service) benefit that the competition cannot claim.

Usage   The extent to which sports stadia are used for multipurpose activity other than simply staging events, such as the wider provision of leisure and retail activities.

Vision   The highest and broadest level of business objective is the vision of the club. This is a statement of broad aspiration, as it deals with where the club hopes to be in the future.

Word of mouth communications   Any form of, usually, marketing communications that is conducted by people talking to each other and passing on information about, for example, a product, service, or company.

Index